A HISTORY OF THE BAPTISTS

A History
of the Baptists

(Revised)

by

ROBERT G. TORBET

With a Foreword by
Kenneth Scott Latourette

VALLEY FORGE
THE JUDSON PRESS
CHICAGO   LOS ANGELES

A HISTORY OF THE BAPTISTS

Copyright, 1950, 1963, by The Judson Press

FIFTH PRINTING, 1963

LIBRARY OF CONGRESS CATALOGUE CARD NO. 63-8225

PRINTED IN THE U.S.A.

To the Memory
of
Benjamin T. Livingston, D.D.
(1869-1948)

FOREWORD

THE story of the Baptists is eminently worth telling. In one way
or another it has been written many times. However, a great
need exists for a fresh account which will take advantage of
what has been done earlier, and which will give a comprehensive view
of the entire course of Baptist history and bring it down to date. So
varied and so rich is the record of the Baptists that to reproduce it
in its entirety would require many volumes and would entail several
lifetimes of research in the pertinent printed and manuscript books,
reports, periodicals, diaries, and letters. However, the main outline
can be compassed in one volume.

This Professor Torbet has done. What he has here given us
represents years of reading and patient research. Nowhere else
is there to be found in so nearly inclusive and up-to-date fashion
a summary of the people who bear the name of Baptist. Obviously he has not been able to cover all the material, printed and
in manuscript, which bears upon his story. To demand that he
should do so would be to require more than is humanly possible.
In his bibliography and footnotes he has carefully indicated the books
and other material from which he has drawn his information. This
is of great advantage, for it tells the informed reader the sources
upon which the author has depended. Moreover, for the student who
wishes to pursue detailed studies, a guide is provided to a beginning
for further investigation.

Professor Torbet writes as a Baptist, and as one to whom the
Baptist heritage is very precious. However, he has endeavored not
to allow his deeply held convictions to distort his view of what
actually happened. His book is not intended as a defense of Baptists or as an argument for them. He has tried to portray them as

they really have been and are. He has also sought to place them in their setting in the history of mankind in general and of the Christian Church in particular.

Yet in this very striving for objectivity lies the best case for the Baptists. They need no defense. Their record speaks for itself. That record is far from perfect. Indeed, no achievement in which we human beings share is free from defect. Every faithful account of Baptists has pages which we must view with sorrow and regret. Yet we who are its beneficiaries have reason for profound gratitude for the Baptist heritage. That gratitude is for noble spirits, many of them far from perfect, but all of them among those who are "being saved." Most of them were humble in the sight of the world and usually found no place in enduring human memory. Nevertheless they were great souls who dreamed and built better than they knew. It has been a special privilege given to the Baptists, more than to any other body of Christians of comparable size, to preach the gospel to the poor. For the most part the poor leave no written traces of their lives. The historian is often baffled when he seeks to reconstruct what they have said and done. For this reason no history of the Baptists can ever be complete. Yet none of His children are forgotten in the sight of God. It is to Him that our gratitude for our spiritual ancestors is primarily due, for it is His Holy Spirit who has been working in them and through them.

KENNETH SCOTT LATOURETTE

Yale University

CONTENTS

APPENDICES

PREFACE

THIS is a history of the people called Baptists. Its purpose is to set forth once again a story which has been told in various forms many times, but which requires retelling and fresh interpretation for twentieth-century readers.

The Baptists are convinced that their teaching is based upon the New Testament. It is not surprising then to find both in the past and in the present, people of various religious designations who resemble the Baptists. Yet those to whom the name is applied have a definite history. This volume is an attempt to tell their story. As will be seen from the table of contents, this book is not intended to give an account of all the bodies which resemble the Baptists. It begins with a brief summary of the views held by the people called Baptists. It then provides a brief survey of those spiritual ancestors from whom the Baptists are immediately descended. While British and European Baptists have not been neglected, the main story concerns Baptists in the United States, both northern and southern. Others are mentioned, but the limitation of space, the interest of readers, and the dearth of materials for some groups of Baptists have dictated the course adopted.

It should be said that the author has tried sincerely to be objective in his task, but being a convinced Baptist, his convictions may at times be evident. This may be seen especially in Chapter One concerning Baptist principles.

This work is based chiefly upon printed materials, including what the historian calls sources (i.e., the proceedings of societies, local associations, and conventions) and the secondary literature in the field, both ecclesiastical and secular.

While every effort has been made to safeguard accuracy in the presentation of factual data, the author is very conscious of the possibility of error. Corrections, therefore, will be welcomed in the interest of eliminating errors in later editions.

An expression of appreciation is due those who have given assistance in the preparation of this history. First to be mentioned are the host of historians of the past whose earnest endeavor to gather, preserve, and interpret Baptist records has placed us all under obligation to them. The author is also deeply indebted to the counsel of contemporary historians: Dr. Kenneth Scott Latourette, D. Willis James Professor of Missions and Oriental History in Yale University; Dr. John W. Brush, Professor of Church History in Andover Newton Theological School; Dr. Richard D. Pierce, Professor of History in Emerson College, Boston, and Curator of the Backus Historical Collection and Instructor in Church History at Andover Newton Theological School; Dr. William W. Barnes, Professor of Church History in Southwestern Baptist Theological Seminary, Fort Worth, Texas, and his associate, Dr. Robert A. Baker; and Dr. R. E. E. Harkness, Professor of the History of Christianity in Crozer Theological Seminary, Chester, Pennsylvania. A word of thanks is due also to the staffs of the following libraries and societies for special courtesies and assistance in research: the Library of the American Baptist Historical Society, Chester, Pennsylvania; the Library of Andover Newton Theological School; the Andover-Harvard Library; Harvard University Library; the Library of the Boston Athenaeum; the New York Public Library; the Library of the Eastern Baptist Theological Seminary; the American Baptist Foreign Mission Society and the American Baptist Home Mission Society in New York City; and the American Baptist Publication Society in Philadelphia. Last to be mentioned, but not the least in helpfulness, is James H. Christian, for two years my fellow in Church History and now a member of the faculty of Western Baptist Theological Seminary, Portland, Oregon.

This volume is dedicated to the late Benjamin T. Livingston, D.D., in recognition of his leadership among Baptists and of his warm friendship and constant encouragement to the author who was once his student and later his colleague and close friend on the faculty of the Eastern Baptist Theological Seminary.

ROBERT G. TORBET

PREFACE TO THE NEW REVISED EDITION

SINCE publication of this volume in 1950, minor revisions were made in 1952 and again in 1955. A more extensive revision has been needed, however, in view of the number of developments which have occurred both in historical research and in the history of Baptists during the past dozen years. The author is indebted therefore to the Reverend Frank T. Hoadley, Book Editor of The Judson Press, for his encouragement and assistance in the preparation of this new edition.

The changes include: (1) a new chapter 1 which condenses the former chapters 1 and 2 and seeks to define Baptists within the context of the issues which brought them into existence; (2) a new chapter tracing developments of Baptist life since 1950; (3) a re-titling of the chapter on smaller Baptist bodies, formerly "Free to Differ," and an enlargement of the introduction to it; (4) some minor revisions throughout the book which reflect new developments in scholarly research; (5) a complete revision of the appendices; and (6) an enlargement of the bibliography to include nearly seventy new titles.

While the author is entirely responsible for any failings or omissions that may occur in this revision, he is deeply indebted to a number of persons for any of its success. He is especially grateful to Dr. Norman H. Maring, professor of church history at Eastern Baptist Theological Seminary, Philadelphia, Pa., for valuable criticism of new chapters. He is also appreciative of helpful counsel provided by the following church historians: Dr. John W. Brush of Andover Newton Theological School, Newton Centre, Mass.; Dr. Pope A. Duncan of Southeastern Baptist Theological Seminary, Wake Forest, N.C.; Dr. Robert T. Handy of Union Theological Seminary, New York, N.Y.; Dr. Winthrop S. Hudson of Colgate Rochester Divinity School, Rochester, N.Y.; Dr. James D. Mosteller of Northern Baptist Theological Seminary, Chicago, Ill.; Dr. W. Morgan Patterson of Southern Baptist Theological Seminary, Louisville, Ky.; and Dr. Richard D. Pierce, Lecturer in Church History at Andover Newton and Dean and Professor of History and Religion at Emerson College, Boston, Mass.

R.G.T.

PART ONE: BAPTIST BEGINNINGS

CHAPTER ONE

AN APPROACH TO BAPTIST HISTORY

T HE people called Baptists have their roots within what may be called, for want of a more precise term, the Free Church movement, which found variant expression throughout the history of Christianity. Although the term cannot be defined strictly, it is useful to describe the effort of Christians of varying theological beliefs and ecclesiastical backgrounds to restore the New Testament emphasis upon a Spirit-filled community of faith. In essence, the Free Church ideal stressed the necessity of a person-to-person confrontation with God, and so placed only secondary emphasis upon liturgy, formalism, organization, and creedalism in its hardened form. The Baptists belonged, in this respect, to what Ernst Troeltsch has called the "sect-type" of Christianity. In contrast is the "church-type" with its emphasis upon institutionalism and with an ecclesiastical authority vested in a priestly ministry that is entrusted with the sacraments of grace. Accordingly, Baptists historically have stressed the necessity of a Christian experience for church membership, the subordination of organization to a secondary position, a democratic expression of church life, a single standard of Christian living which is radical in its ethical demands, and the principle of voluntarism in church support as opposed to state support.[1]

---

[1] Ernst E. Troeltsch, *The Social Teaching of the Christian Churches,* transl. Olive Wyon, 2 volumes (London, 1931), Vol. II, 694 ff.; Alfred C. Underwood, *A History of the English Baptists* (London, 1947), 16-20. The classification "Free Church movement" is used here in a general sense to encompass those churches which are opposed to the "territorial church" concept, which stress in essence the "gathered church" point of view, and which usually are congregational in polity and more fluid in patterns of church life than the more formal churches. It is readily admitted that certain denominational groups partake of characteristics of both groups. Some may tend more toward one of these poles at one time and place, then toward the other in a different situation. For example, the Congregationalists of Massachusetts Bay Colony were in some respects very much in the Free Church tradition, but were not so with respect to relations between church and state. Or, the Methodists, with the authority given to bishops in the United States, partake of a tradition which is strongly institutional, but they are very much of the Free Church type in other respects.

Owing to the fact that there has been some confusion among Baptists concerning their origin, it seems best to preface a consideration of this problem with a brief survey of the more important theories which have been advanced within the past two hundred years.

Theories Concerning the Origin of Baptists

One of the oldest and most generally accepted theories until recent times may be called for our convenience the *successionist* theory. According to this opinion, Baptists have been in existence ever since the days of John the Baptist's ministry along the Jordan River. While there are various statements concerning the exact origin of Baptists, either with John the Baptist, or with our Lord's public ministry, or at the Day of Pentecost, the chief emphasis of those who thus trace Baptist history from primitive Christianity is upon the concept of what may be called an apostolic succession of Baptist churches. Among the Baptist historians who have held this view are the following: (1) Thomas Crosby, the English author of four volumes entitled, *The History of the English Baptists,* written between 1738 and 1740.[2] (2) G. H. Orchard, an English Baptist minister, who in 1855 wrote *A Concise History of Foreign Baptists.*[3] (3) J. M. Cramp, professor in Acadia College in Nova Scotia who in 1868 wrote a *Baptist History: from the Foundations of the Christian Church to the Close of the Eighteenth Century.*[4] (4) William Cathcart, editor of *The Baptist Encyclopedia,* published in 1881.[5] (5) John T. Christian, professor in the Baptist Bible Institute (now Seminary) at New Orleans, Lousiana, who wrote a two-volume work in 1922.[6]

There have been various theories of succession by which a chain of authority from Christ to the present can be ascertained. Among these are the following: (1) apostolic succession, by which is meant a chain of ordination; (2) baptismal succession, a chain of baptism by those properly baptized; (3) church succession, a chain of local

---

[2] Thomas Crosby, *The History of the English Baptists from the Reformation to the Beginning of the Reign of King George I* (London, 1738-40), I, lvii-lxi and II, 2. He traces Baptist principles back to John the Baptist.

[3] G. H. Orchard, *A Concise History of Foreign Baptists* (Nashville, 1855), 2.

[4] J. M. Cramp, *Baptist History from the Foundation of the Christian Church* (Philadelphia, 1868), 15.

[5] William Cathcart, ed., *The Baptist Encyclopedia* (Philadelphia, 1881), (one vol. edition), 74.

[6] John T. Christian, *A History of the Baptists* (Nashville, 1922), 2 vols., I, 5-6.

churches bearing the true marks of the church; (4) a succession of principles which are evident in individuals or groups who have held essentially the Baptist witness. We have listed several Baptist historians who have claimed that a perpetuity of Baptists can be proved explicitly. Their efforts were based upon *a priori* reasoning, without consideration of a critical, scientific methodology. Their approach, according to W. Morgan Patterson, church historian, was apologetic and polemical at a time when Baptists were engaged in a developing sectarian rivalry with the Methodists, the Presbyterians, and, in particular, the Disciples of Christ. The successionists saw an example of communions claiming historical precedence among the apologists of the Roman Catholic Church, the Church of England, and the Eastern Orthodox Churches. Accordingly, they borrowed the principle and the method, and gave to a sensitive denomination without a long and rich historical heritage a reason for pride by carrying their history back to the first century.[7]

The *Anabaptist spiritual kinship* theory is held by those who trace a spiritual relationship of Baptists through the long line of Anabaptist sects, such as German, Dutch, and Swiss Anabaptists, the Waldensians and Petrobrusians, the Henricians, the Novatians, and the Donatists. While many of its adherents admit the difficulty of establishing any historical connection between these groups, they find a satisfaction in the succession of regenerated baptized believers which may be traced through such minority groups during the centuries following the defection from New Testament Christianity. The following Baptist historians are among those who entertained this view: (1) David Benedict, who in 1848 wrote "that the peculiar sentiments of that portion of Christian professors, now called baptists, have always lived, and been maintained among the different sects and parties which have been constantly seceding from the Greek, the Roman, and other great bodies, which may properly be denominated."[8] (2) Richard B. Cook, of the late nineteenth century, who held that there is a spiritual kinship between Baptists and Anabaptist sects.[9] (3) Thomas

[7] W. Morgan Patterson, "A Critique of the Successionist Concept in Baptist Historiography." A Th.D. dissertation, New Orleans Baptist Theological Seminary, 1956. A typescript, vi, 126 pp.

[8] David Benedict, *A General History of the Baptist Denomination in America and Other Parts of the World* (New York, 1848), 1.

[9] Richard B. Cook, *The Story of the Baptists in All Ages and Countries* (Baltimore, 1884), chap. 6.

Armitage, whose familiar and voluminous work has been in circulation since 1887.[10] (4) Albert H. Newman, who reflects this view in his story of the Anabaptists, written in 1897.[11] (5) Walter Rauschenbusch, of Rochester Baptist Theological Seminary (now Colgate-Rochester Divinity School) at Rochester, New York. Writing in the early years of the present century, his interest in democracy and the social gospel may have influenced his willingness to identify Baptists with the socially radical Anabaptists.[12]

According to the *English Separatist descent* theory, Baptists originated with certain English Separatists who were congregational in polity and who had come to consider believers' baptism alone as valid according to the Scriptures. This position has been held in various forms by several Baptist historians of recent years. One variety of the theory is that the origin of Baptists should be dated from 1641, when immersion was renewed in England by a few English Separatists who came out of the Jacob Church at Southwark, London, having become convinced that the biblical practice was dipping under water. William H. Whitsitt, while professor at the Southern Baptist Theological Seminary in Louisville, Kentucky, set forth this view, amid much controversy, in a book published in 1896, entitled *A Question in Baptist History: Whether the Anabaptists in England Practiced Immersion before the Year 1641?* The late Professor Augustus H. Strong of Rochester Baptist Theological Seminary concurred with Whitsitt in a historical address delivered in 1904. In it he traced Baptist origins to the 1640's, when Particular or Calvinistic Baptists of London and General or Arminian Baptists (a short time later) began to practice immersion as the true mode of baptism.[13]

John H. Shakespeare, noted British clergyman and Evangelical Free Church leader in England, at the turn of the century, set forth another form of this theory. He argued that the Particular Baptists represent the unbroken Baptist witness. He eliminated the succession through the old General Baptist churches which had begun with

---

[10] Thomas Armitage, *A History of the Baptists; Traced by Their Vital Principles and Practices, from the Time of Our Lord and Saviour Jesus Christ to the Year 1889* (New York, 1889), 2-12.

[11] Albert H. Newman, *A History of Anti-pedobaptism* (Philadelphia, 1897), chaps. 2-3.

[12] Based upon the testimony of some of his former students.

[13] Augustus H. Strong, *Miscellanies,* (Philadelphia, 1912), I, 3-4.

Helwys' congregation at Spitalfield outside of London about 1612. He did so because those churches, for the most part, had become Unitarian, and had maintained no intercourse with the main body of Baptists since 1770, when the General Baptist New Connexion was organized out of the General Assembly of General Baptists in protest against the theological trend. The General Baptist New Connexion body amalgamated with the Particular Baptists in 1891, hence linking the original General Baptists with the Particular Baptists whose origin occurred a few years later. Thus, he regarded the Calvinistic Baptists as the real forefathers of the modern denomination.[14]

Henry C. Vedder, well-known church historian at Crozer Theological Seminary in Chester, Pennsylvania, from 1894 to 1927, came to the conclusion that "after 1610 we have an unbroken succession of Baptist churches, established by indubitable documentary evidence," and that "from about the year 1641, at the latest, Baptist doctrine and practice have been the same in all essential features that they are today."[15] Such a conclusion is apparently the most plausible one for several reasons: (1) It does not violate principles of historical accuracy, as do those views which assume a definite continuity between earlier sects and modern Baptists. (2) Baptists have not shared with Anabaptists the latter's aversion to oath-taking and holding public office. Neither have they adopted the Anabaptists' doctrine of pacifism, or their theological views concerning the incarnation, soul sleeping, and the necessity of observing an apostolic succession in the administration of baptism.

Baptists and the Reformation Heritage

Although the English Separatist descent theory seems reasonably adequate to describe the origin of Baptists, this theory must be seen in the larger context of the continental Reformation and its effects upon English reformers. It has been contended quite plausibly by Ernest A. Payne, British Baptist church historian, that the Anabaptists were in all likelihood an influence in England which affected both Congregational and Baptist development. Thus we are obliged to consider the influence of Anabaptist spiritualism upon early Baptists as well as the influence of the Puritan Separatists and non-Separatists

[14] John H. Shakespeare, *Baptist and Congregational Pioneers* (London, 1905), 179-80.
[15] Henry C. Vedder, *A Short History of the Baptists* (Philadelphia, 1907), 201.

with their more churchmanlike Calvinism. To this end the remaining pages of this chapter are devoted; to the thesis that the faith and life of Baptists cannot be separated from that of other reform groups of the sixteenth century.[16]

Baptists shared with Lutherans, Zwinglians, and Calvinists their protest against the totalitarianism of the papacy and their zeal to recover the spirituality of the church. Theologically they were Calvinists; the General (or general atonement) Baptists adhering to the Arminian modification of Calvinism, and the Particular (or limited atonement) Baptists standing within the covenant theology expressed in the Westminster Standards. Both groups emerged from English Puritanism which sought in congregational polity a means of maintaining the purity of a gospel church. The General Baptists, as we shall see, were originally English Separatists or Puritans who broke entirely with the Church of England, which they regarded as a false church, perverted by error. Their sectarian spirit and point of view was carried over into their Baptist church life. The Particular Baptists arose out of non-Separatist Independency a few years later. Like the Separatists, the non-Separatists were congregational in polity, but they were more ecumenical in spirit. They were not willing to renounce the Church of England as being entirely corrupt. Moreover, they sought to maintain some bond of unity between themselves and Christians of other communions. This spirit was carried over into their church life, a fact which is documented by a reading of their confessional statements concerning the nature of the church. Among these Baptists were those who were willing to admit to membership in their churches, without rebaptism, Christians of other communions. They were advocates of open membership as opposed to the closed membership embraced by the more sectarian Baptists.[17]

The relationship between the early English Baptists and the Continental Anabaptists (or Mennonites) has been described by Ernest A. Payne, British church historian, as "an intricate and

[16] Ernest A. Payne, "Who Were the Baptists?" *Baptist Quarterly* (London), Vol. 16, No. 8 (Oct., 1956), 339-42; cf. an article by Winthrop S. Hudson on the same question in the previous issue of *Baptist Quarterly* which in effect rejects Payne's thesis. See also Payne, *The Anabaptists of the 16th Century and Their Influence in the Modern World* (London, 1949), 18-21; and Payne, *The Fellowship of Believers.* Enlarged edition (London, 1952), 15-19.

[17] Winthrop S. Hudson, ed., *Baptist Concepts of the Church* (Philadelphia, 1959), 12-13.

thorny historical problem." It is his considered judgment that the Mennonite influence was responsible in part for the first Baptist witness.[18] Certainly the Anabaptist-Mennonite movement of the sixteenth century was so significant and vital in developing the Free Church point of view that its influence upon early English Baptists must not be overlooked.

The Anabaptists arose in Switzerland among the followers of Ulrich Zwingli. When, however, their leader, Conrad Grebel (c. 1490-1526) of Zurich, urged Zwingli to abolish the state church system in the interest of a church of converted believers free from civil authority, they were repulsed and eventually persecuted. A similar plight befell the German Anabaptists, whose leader, Balthasar Hubmaier (1481-1528), was burned at the stake as a heretic after three years of notable leadership. His most significant contribution was a plea for religious toleration, entitled "Concerning Heretics and Those Who Burn Them."

The false claims made by Thomas Münzer (1490-1525), a socialist and leader in the Peasants' War of 1525, and the horrors of the Münster Rebellion ten years later under the leadership of Melchior Hofmann and Jan Matthys, combined to bring the Anabaptists into complete disrepute.[19] The extravagant cruelty and wanton destruction of the visionaries who sought to establish the millennial kingdom in the Catholic city of Münster made an indelible impression upon Europeans. The successful suppression of the Rebellion was the signal for nearly all of Europe to intensify the persecution of Anabaptists on the grounds that they, like the fanatics of Münster, were a potential menace to law and order. It is said that "Philip of Hesse was the only prince in Western Europe who still ventured to discriminate between wild fanatics and those who quietly opposed infant baptism and sought by purely spiritual means to restore Christianity to its primitive position."[20] Had other leaders manifested the same fair-mindedness and distinguished between the few who taught resistance against government by the sword and the majority who taught acquiescence to the magistrate in civil matters, the terrible slaughter of

[18] Ernest A. Payne, *The Fellowship of Believers*, 16-17.

[19] For detailed account, see Albert H. Newman, *A History of Anti-pedobaptism* (Philadelphia, 1897), chaps. 7, 21, 22; and E. Belfort Bax, *Rise and Fall of the Anabaptists* (London, 1903), chaps. 5-9.

[20] Newman, *op. cit.,* 291.

Anabaptists might not today remain such a dark blot upon the history of Protestants and Roman Catholics alike.

After 1535 the Anabaptist testimony survived against great odds because it was not dependent upon organization for the continuance of its teachings and because it found in Menno Simons (c. 1496-1561), a converted priest in West Friesland, an able leader and wise counselor. From 1536, when he openly renounced Roman Catholicism, he devoted his life to the Anabaptists first in West Friesland, then in East Friesland, and later in Cologne and Wismar. Taking advantage of the tolerant spirit of some of the political leaders, Menno sought to organize his followers under a discipline whereby they might grow in their Christian witness without antagonizing the state.

During Menno Simons' leadership of the Anabaptists, they sought to rid themselves of that epithet, not only because they resented its implications of rebaptizing, but also because of the stigma attached to it since the Münster Rebellion. They preferred to be called simply brethren, but came to be known as Mennonites, after their leader.

In time, three distinct branches developed, differing principally in matters of discipline: the Waterlanders who were mild, the Friesians who were moderate though somewhat more strict, and the Flemish who were severely strict. They suffered greatly from persecution, and between 1531 and 1597 comprised three-fourths of the two thousand martyrs in the Netherlands. Yet their numbers increased because they were willing to endure persecution quietly and because they followed a simple way of life, distinguished by a faithful adherence to pacifism, non-interference with government, and pietism. Moreover, they benefited by the policy of toleration practiced by the Prince of Orange after 1579 when the Netherlands were freed from Spanish control.[21]

Extensive studies within recent years by Mennonite and non-Mennonite scholars alike have led to a fuller and more accurate appreciation of the contribution of the Anabaptist-Mennonite tradition to the Protestant understanding of the church. Franklin H. Littell, church historian of Methodist background, describes the Anabaptist-Mennonite position as "integral Christianity," as opposed to traditional

[21] John C. Wenger, *Glimpses of Mennonite History and Doctrine* (Scottdale, Pa., 1947), 83.

orthodoxy.[22] They sought, he explained, a restitution of the True Church instead of a "culture religion" in which the church was so aligned with the state and secular values that its true nature was distorted. The Anabaptist-Mennonite testimony regarded discipleship in terms of Christian community. To them the church was the People of God, a corporate community which possessed the Holy Spirit. They restored the laity to its proper function and importance and gave substance to the Reformers' teaching concerning the priesthood of all believers.

This integral Christianity of the classical Free Church style was shared, according to Littell, by John Robinson, the English Puritan Separatist. It set forth the viewpoint that:

the True Church was a visible and disciplined Community, and not spiritualized in the Lutheran style as "the invisible church." It was a covenantal community.[23]

The essential matter for the church was neither a specific type of ecclesiastical structure or order, nor a particular creedal formulation, but rather a devotion of mind and heart to respond obediently to the will of God. The essence of the church was daily witnessing, unfeigned love, and a willingness to share Christ's suffering for a broken humanity.

There is little doubt that these ideas were abroad in England during the sixteenth century. Not only had Lutheran and Calvinistic teaching spread from the Continent, but Anabaptist ideas as well. They were a part of the heritage of the Reformation which influenced the English Separatists from whom the early English Baptists emerged.

Anabaptists in England

There are conflicting opinions concerning the number of Anabaptists to be found in England prior to 1550. Burrage indicates that "the Calendars of State Papers plainly record (that) a few isolated Anabaptists had been found in England, but they seem to have been chiefly, or only, foreigners, and these were soon banished from the country or burned to death." In addition, according to him, there is no evidence of Anabaptist writings by Englishmen or continentals in

[22] Franklin H. Littell, *The Free Church* (Boston, 1957).
[23] *Ibid.*, 38.

England prior to that date. There were, however, two or three books printed criticising the advocates of such views; hence their teachings were known. Even up to the last quarter of the century, the number of foreign Anabaptist immigrants was not large. Burrage concludes that the teachings of the Anabaptists, which never appealed strongly to the English mind in the sixteenth century because of the too recent association of the name with the Münster rebellion, had practically no influence on English separatism before 1612.[24]

On the other hand, according to relatively recent students of Mennonite history, it appears that Anabaptist teaching was to be found in England quite early in the sixteenth century. Large numbers of this sect came in 1528 and the years that followed until 1573, when it was estimated that some fifty thousand were in the country. Economic conditions encouraged the influx since there was a ready market for steady labor. They congregated in towns such as London, Norwich, Dover, Sandwich, Canterbury, Colchester, and Hastings. The earlier Anabaptist refugees were disciples of Melchior Hofmann's fanatical teaching, while the later ones were Mennonites who had repudiated such radicalism.[25]

In 1530 an assembly of bishops and other theologians, convened by Archbishop Warham at the command of Henry VIII, condemned an Anabaptist book entitled *The Sum of Scripture.* In 1535, when that monarch became Supreme Head of the Church of England, two edicts were issued against Anabaptists and Sacramentaries. And in 1538 efforts were made to expel from the country those holding Anabaptist views. In 1549, during the reign of Henry's son, Edward VI, Bishop Latimer's sermons contained warnings against this "sect of hereticks." He accused them of being anarchistic, which was a typical charge of the times.[26]

The problem of determining the true picture is complicated by the fact that the people of that day used the name "Anabaptist" to describe many different groups of radicals. A case in point concerns

[24] Champlin Burrage, *The Early English Dissenters in the Light of Recent Research, 1550-1641,* 2 volumes (Cambridge, 1912), I, 41-2, 55-61, 64, 68.

[25] Bax, *The Rise and Fall of the Anabaptists,* 332 ff., provides a detailed account. See also Dosker, *The Dutch Anabaptists,* 45-6. Dosker feels that Vedder is not justified in assuming that the decline of persecution on the Continent caused the number of Anabaptists in England to dwindle till they disappeared. "Too many traces of them are left in the non-conformist life of England to accept this theory."

[26] Bax, *op. cit.,* 337.

a group of so-called English Anabaptists, known as the Family of Love. They were present in the country during the reign of Queen Elizabeth, who came to the throne in 1558. This sect had its origin on the continent with Henry Nicholas (Niklaes), a native of Münster, who migrated to Amsterdam in 1530 to establish his business as a mercer. While having no connection with the Münster Kingdom, he reputedly heard in 1540 a call to become a prophet. Six years later he wrote a little book, still to be found in the Mennonite library at Amsterdam, entitled *Of the Spiritual Land of Promise, Of the Heavenly Jerusalem, and the Holy People*. In this work he advocated and defended "spiritual marriage," somewhat akin to Mormon teaching in nineteenth-century America. He also taught that nothing is unclean in the body. On the continent, "naked-runners," as they were called, appeared in many cities. These "naked-runners," who reputedly were Anabaptist fanatics, seem to have been Nicholas' disciples. The sect, as transplanted to England, was known as Familists and gained an unsavory reputation for immorality, much as did the Mormons in America three centuries later.[27]

Nicholas is known to us through the writing of his biographer and disciple, Tobias. According to the latter, Nicholas may have traveled to England. The mystical language used by the biographer does not make his destination clear. At any rate, the ablest apostle of Nicholas' teaching in England was Christopher Vitell, a Southwark joiner, who translated many of Nicholas' writings from the Dutch into English. Toward the close of the sixteenth century and in the first part of the seventeenth, several tracts appeared attacking and defending the doctrines of H. N., as Nicholas was known. Bax, an able historian of the Anabaptist movement, admits that the historical connection between the Family of Love and Anabaptists generally, and Ranters, Quakers, John Bunyan, and modern Baptists in particular is obscure. Yet, there is strong similarity in emphasis upon the Holy Spirit, the pious life, and the doctrine of nonresistance. Bax sees in John Bunyan's *Pilgrim's Progress* a striking parallel to Tobias' book, *Mirabilia opera Dei: Certaine wonderfulle Works of God which happened to H. N. even from his youth*. He thinks it prob-

[27] Dosker, *op. cit.*, 52-8.

able that Bunyan must have previously read the writings of Tobias.[28]

It appears that Edmond Jessop about 1620, after he had become an Anabaptist, nearly fell in with the Familists. He knew of them, therefore, from experience, when he wrote his account of their views and described them as extremely mystical and not typical of traditional Christian teaching concerning Christ and redemption. They regarded their Family of Love as the perfect church, of which all other churches were but shadows and types.[29] We may safely conclude that this sect cannot rightly be regarded as a branch of the Anabaptists. The fact that many have so looked upon it is evidence of the confusion which is attendant upon the use of the name "Anabaptist."

The Barrowists, as they are known, were followers of Henry Barrowe. When he became a martyr to the cause of Puritan separatism in 1593, they migrated to Campen, Holland, under the leadership of his more fortunate contemporary, Francis Johnson. There the influence of Dutch Anabaptist views upon some of them became manifest in the congregation, and resulted in the formation of the earliest group of English Anabaptists of whom there is *certain* knowledge. This is not surprising since Barrowists generally were Catabaptists, though not Anabaptists; that is, they opposed infant baptism when it was, in their opinion, improperly administered in the Church of England, preferring to let infants go unbaptized until they could be baptized by a true preacher of the gospel. It was but another step for the more consistent students of biblical practice to forsake infant baptism altogether and resort solely to believers' baptism. Those who did this were excommunicated by Johnson's church for their views. Thus Burrage infers that this English "Anabaptist movement occurred at Campen about 1594 through Dutch Mennonites, and may have led to the removal of Johnson's congregation from Campen to Naarden soon after." In fact, there is evidence of one, an Englishman, who baptized himself about this time. Hence, John Smyth, the reputed father of English Baptists, about whom more will be told in the next chapter,

[28] Bax, *op. cit.*, 338-65, 368-83. A copy of Tobias' book (possibly translated by C. Viret, London, 1550) is in the Houghton Library, Harvard University, Cambridge, Mass., a reading of which causes this writer to concur with Bax's opinion.

[29] Edmond Jessop, *A Discovery of the Errors of the English Anabaptists* (London, 1623), cited by Burrage, *Early English Dissenters,* 1, 212-4.

was surely not the first English Christian to become a se-Baptist.[30]

Like other separatist sects, the Anabaptists were harassed and persecuted out of England by the Tudor monarchs. Near the close of the seventeenth century, when the Stuarts pursued much the same policy toward them, many of them sought refuge in the Netherlands. Among the paedobaptist refugees was the Gainsborough congregation led by John Smyth in 1606 or 1607, from which was destined to emerge later the first strictly English Baptist church.

With respect to the relationship between Anabaptists and Baptists, it is safe to say that the latter are the spiritual descendants of *some* of the former. No historical continuity between the two groups can be proved. Moreover, not all Anabaptists can be claimed as spiritual forebears of Baptists, owing to the variance of their teachings. In fact, such a relationship can be traced only to those Anabaptists who taught believers' baptism, regenerate church membership, and the supremacy of the Scriptures. The admirable tradition of civil and religious liberty for which so many of them gave their lives has been kept alive by the people we know as Baptists. However, the refusal of the latter to follow the Mennonites' principles of pacifism, nonparticipation in government, and unwillingness to take oaths provides a marked distinction between the two groups.

Baptists and the Free Church Principle

Baptists can be understood best by seeing them as a part of the expression of the Free Church movement in Christianity. While evident from time to time in the centuries prior to the Protestant Reformation, the movement became most articulate in the sixteenth century in the Anabaptist-Mennonite tradition of the Continent and in the Puritan Separatist and Non-Separatist tradition of England. Both sought to restore the purity of the church by freeing it from the dominance of secular influences in the social order.

The Free Church understanding of the church's nature did not preclude authority. To be sure, this authority was not in terms of external political or ecclesiastical pressures, but of the inner leading of God within the community of faith. The congregations claimed

[30] Burrage, *op. cit.*, I, 126-7, 222-4. On the se-Baptist, he cites as witness an English author, Henoch Clapham, *Antidoton: (or) A Soveraigne Remedie Against Schisme and Heresie . . .*, 1600.

to be governed by the Holy Spirit as He led them to understand the mind of Christ, the rightful head of the church. They sought, therefore, means by which they could arrive at a consensus as to the will of God. Through congregational Bible study, discussion, prayer, and decision, the congregation explored matters concerning their understanding of faith, morals, ethics, church organization, mission, and education. Basic to their discussion, and not subject to debate, was the *fact* of faith. Thus the principle of consensus by which the congregational meeting ordered its common life became the legacy of Anabaptists and English Separatists to Protestantism. In this principle was laid the foundations for the pattern of voluntarism in church life in the nineteenth century.[31]

The Free Churches made their most direct contribution to the individual citizen by upholding liberty of conscience. Their position held that a church is truly free when it can assemble individuals who have the right to exercise their personal beliefs. They also held that a church has a right and duty "to be in its situation representative in the fullest sense of the Church Universal."[32] In other words, a church must be free, as a community of biblical faith, to be governed by the Spirit of God not by political or cultural influences.

From this brief analysis of the Free Church tradition to which Baptists belong, it should be clear that Free Churchmen did not ascribe to the principle of unbridled individualism. Instead, they insisted on a disciplined church; one disciplined from within, not by external coercion. They had a vision of the True Church as a gathered fellowship of believers, bound together in a covenantal relationship to God to witness fearlessly to their faith wherever they might be. To them, "the Church which had achieved worldly status by political and social acculturation was a 'fallen' Church."[33] Freedom, then, meant not license in doctrine or personal living but "the *freedom to participate* in the discussions by which discipline was arrived at democratically."[34]

Early Baptists, as they emerged as a group in history, were characterized by emphases which distinguished them from other Protestants. Although they regretted at times the need to be a

[31] *Ibid.*
[32] *Ibid.*, 49.
[33] *Ibid.*, 85.
[34] *Ibid.*, 114.

separate denomination, they were deeply convinced that there were some things to which they must be faithful in their witness. In particular, they pointed to the idea of the gathered church, with its attempt to maintain a regenerate membership by practicing believer's baptism and discipline. In this, they were in sympathy with the Anabaptists' thinking about the church. Their view of the church was developed by seventeenth century Baptists like John Smyth, Thomas Helwys, and John Bunyan, and influenced by the Congregationalist, John Owen, whose writings on the church were read widely by Baptists of that period. They also held to a view of congregational church order which involved all members in the total life of the believing community, and stressed the importance of the church-power of the congregation. It was their conviction that God had entrusted the authority to proclaim the gospel not to a clerical class, but to the whole community of faith.

These early Baptists emphasized the need for a wider fellowship of the congregations through membership in what were called associations. This was based not only upon expediency but upon a conviction that such connectionalism was essential to express the church universal, a position clearly indicated in their early confessional statements.[35] Their protection of the autonomy of each congregation with respect to its inner life was intended not to stress independency from other congregations nor to disavow the reality of the larger church, but to recognize the Lordship of Christ over each congregation rightly organized and invested with the powers of a gospel church.

The stress which Baptists have placed upon the need for freedom to obey God has been one of their most significant contributions. To uphold this principle many gave their lives, and for its observance they, as a group, were often disavowed by other Christians and deprived of privileges in the state.

In most of these matters, which will be understood best as the story of the Baptists unfolds, they represented a distinctly minority viewpoint concerning the nature of the visible church. It was this witness which distinguished them from most Protestants. To be sure, it was shared with Congregationalists (Separatist and non-Separatist Puritans), but the Baptists were still left in the minority. In fact,

[35] William L. Lumpkin, *Baptist Confessions of Faith* (Philadelphia, 1959), 143-334; see the sections of the various Confessions of early English Baptists on the Church.

they were distinguished from Congregationalists largely in the matter of their refusal to baptize infants and in their insistence upon the separation of church and state.

The identity of Baptists needs to be understood within the context of the principal issue which gave rise to their origin as a distinct group of Christians. That issue was whether or not it is possible to have a visible church of visible saints, a truly regenerate church membership. The affirmative position of Baptists on this question identifies them in a general sense with what we have called the Free Church movement, and yet distinguishes them in some respects from such Free Church groups as the Congregationalists.

It is to be hoped that the story of the Baptists which follows will serve to identify them as an important segment of the Body of Christ. Their history should clarify the reason for their rise and explain the variant strands of tradition along which their church life has developed. It will also call to mind those basic issues which produced the Baptist witness, and will enable the reader to determine what relevancy it has for the present and the future.

CHAPTER TWO

BAPTIST BEGINNINGS AMID PERSECUTION

THE history of English Baptists begins in Holland with a religious refugee, John Smyth, who has been claimed by some as the "founder of the modern Baptist churches," because he adopted believers' baptism and formulated to a marked degree Baptist principles in his historic Confession.[1] It is necessary to correct certain mistaken traditions about Smyth, if an accurate picture of the man is to be obtained. He was not the John Smyth who matriculated at Christ's College between 1571 and 1575-6. Nor was he the separatist Smyth who was imprisoned at the Marshalsea for nine months in 1592. Finally, he was never vicar of Gainsborough, "the living there being held successively by John Jackson, Jerome Phillips, and Henry Clifford, from 1566 to 1610."[2]

We do know, however, that Smyth was educated for the Church of England at Cambridge, and that at Christ's College he had been a pupil of Francis Johnson, who had matriculated in 1579 and was destined to become a prominent Separatist leader. Smyth himself must have enrolled about the year 1586. He received the Master of Arts degree in 1593. From this data one may conjecture his birth to have been sometime around 1570. Historical certainty is reached, however, with his election as lecturer or preacher of the city of Lincoln on September 27, 1600, by a vote of eight to seven. On August 1, 1602, the Council, according to the records, settled on him the stipend of forty pounds a year plus house rent for life, but annulled it on October 13, when he was abruptly deposed from office for having "approved himself a factious man in this city by personal preaching, and that untruly against divers men of good place."[3] We may gather

[1] John H. Shakespeare, *Baptist and Congregational Pioneers*, 125-6. See also W. T. Whitley, *The Works of John Smyth*. 2 vols. (Cambridge, 1915).
[2] *Ibid.*, 128.
[3] *Ibid.*, 129, based on the *Minutes* of the Lincoln Corporation; see also Champlin Burrage, *The Early English Dissenters in the Light of Recent Research (1550-1641)*, 2 volumes (Cambridge, 1912), I, 227-9.

that he was indiscreet in his criticisms and in the setting forth of his ideas, which rapidly were becoming nonconformist.

After the termination of his lectureship, he published in 1603 and 1605 two little volumes of discourses preached by himself at Lincoln. By the latter date he was at his home town of Gainsborough on Trent, not yet a Separatist, but passing through a troubled state of mind relative to the church. In that town was a Congregational church which had been organized as early as 1602. By 1606 the congregation divided for convenience into two parts, one group worshiping under the leadership of Richard Clyfton at Scrooby Manor House. This became the famous Pilgrim Church led by John Robinson, William Bradford, and William Brewster, which was destined to be transplanted eventually in the New World. The other group remained at Gainsborough; Smyth joined it and almost at once became its minister.

Because of persecution from a government hostile to nonconformists, the two congregations sought refuge in Holland, a country which, since 1595, had welcomed groups of separatists who realized their helplessness in England after the execution in 1593 of their leaders, Barrowe, Greenwood, and Penry. The Gainsborough branch was the first to leave England, probably late in 1607. Led by Smyth and Thomas Helwys, a fair-sized company of separatists from the surrounding countryside of Yorkshire, Lincolnshire, and Nottinghamshire established themselves in Amsterdam. The Scrooby Manor Church, composed chiefly of natives of Norfolk, Suffolk, Essex, London, and Kent, and led by John Robinson, after much difficulty arrived in 1608 at the same destination. At first the congregation may have joined the Congregational church established in 1597 by Francis Johnson, and have remained with it until the end of April, 1609, when Robinson with most of his original members removed to Leyden. It appears that the undemocratic procedures of Johnson had invoked much criticism and discontent. The Leyden church ultimately emigrated to America, settling Plymouth Colony in 1620.

Smyth's congregation of some eighty persons seems to have had a separate existence in Amsterdam, for in a tract entitled, *The Differences of the Churches of the Separation* (1608), Smyth described his congregation as "the second English Church at Amsterdam."[4] In fact, the aforementioned tract was written to explain why his congregation had given up the possibility of fellowship with Johnson's Ancient Church, as it was known. His reasons did not include the matter of baptism, for he had not yet rejected infant baptism. His chief reason for separation was that he felt that a minister should not preach with any manuscript before him, not even a translation of the Scriptures, lest the Holy Spirit should be hampered. He justified his position by the fact that Jesus at Nazareth closed the sacred scroll before he began to preach.[5] His individualism and literalism were carrying him beyond the views of most nonconformists.

Late in 1608 or early in 1609 Smyth, undoubtedly under the influence of the Waterlander Mennonites, became an Anabaptist. He had come to the decision "that infants ought not to be baptized, because (1) there is neither precept nor example in the New Testament of any infants that were baptized by John or Christ's disciples, and (2) Christ commanded to make disciples by teaching them and then to baptize them.[6] Not yet, however, theologically prepared to turn to the Mennonites, he baptized himself by affusion, then Helwys, and the rest of his congregation who so desired, a total of about forty persons. He was not unique in this respect, for he was neither the first nor the only English se-Baptist.[7]

Since they worshiped in a block of buildings belonging to a Mennonite merchant, the ever-searching and impressionable Smyth came increasingly under Mennonite influence. Indeed, it was not long before he reached the conclusion that private baptism was an error and that the Amsterdam Mennonites constituted a true church and had a true baptism. Thereupon, he told his congregation that he had

---

[4] Shakespeare, *Baptist and Congregational Pioneers,* 137. A letter written by Helwys on September 26, 1608, describing the differences between the two congregations, provides no indication that Smyth's party ever joined Johnson's church; see Burrage, *op. cit.,* I, 32, 235-6, II, 167-8.

[5] Luke 4:20.

[6] Whitsitt gives the date as October, 1608. See William H. Whitsitt, *A Question in Baptist History* (Louisville, 1896), 55-8. Burrage places the date as late in 1608 or early in 1609; see *Early English Dissenters,* I, 237. Shakespeare gives March, 1609, possibly because Smyth finished a tract against infant baptism, *The Character of the Beast,* on March 24, 1609; see *Baptist and Congregational Pioneers,* 140.

[7] See Burrage's reference to Henoch Clapham in footnote 29 of chap. II. Burrage also points out that in all probability the Anabaptists of Johnson's congregation, whom that church had excommunicated for their views, were also unsuitable theologically to Smyth.

acted hastily in baptizing himself and them.[8] Accordingly, about February, 1610, the majority of his group united with him in presenting a petition to the Mennonites, writing it in Latin, since they found the Dutch language difficult for precise expression. They confessed their error in baptizing themselves and requested membership in the Mennonite church. By March the remaining eight or ten, of whom the male members were Thomas Helwys, William Piggott, Thomas Seamer, and John Murton, parted company with Smyth. Helwys accused Smyth of having sinned against the Holy Spirit in doubting the validity of his own baptism, especially since he was willing to recognize ordination when privately given. Helwys' group, sensing the differences between Mennonite and Baptist views more than Smyth did, excommunicated Smyth and his followers and drew up a Confession of Faith to present to the Mennonites so that they might not be confused with those of Smyth's congregation who had applied for membership. Some time in 1611 or early 1612, Helwys' little group returned to England.

Either because of their knowledge of the quarrels in the Ancient Church of Johnson, or because of Smyth's repeated change of views, or because of a letter written in English and sent to the Mennonites by Helwys and Murton along with their Confession of Faith urging them not to receive Smyth, the Mennonites were wary of admitting his congregation to membership without careful examination. Hence a doctrinal statement was requested. In all, four such documents were prepared during the negotiations. The first consisted of twenty articles written in Latin by Smyth; the second was a translation of a Dutch confession written by Lubbert Gerrits and Hans de Ries, Mennonite elders, and signed by Smyth and forty-three others; the third, composed of nineteen articles, had been drawn up by Helwys and his company; and the fourth was a confession of one hundred propositions embodied in *The Last book of John Smyth called the Retraction of his errors.* The first and third comprise the earliest English Baptist creeds.

Although Smyth was anxious for union with the Mennonites, he did not press the matter when he saw controversy arise. He was destined not to receive the long delayed reply, for he died at the end of August, 1612, a victim of consumption. He was buried in the

[8] Whitsitt gives the date as January or February, 1609.

Nieuwekerke at Amsterdam on September 1, 1612. With the exception of a few who had died or fallen away, the remainder of his followers were admitted into Mennonite membership on January 20, 1615.

It should be observed that in the confessions presented by Smyth and by Helwys, no mention was made of immersion; in fact, there is no difference of view indicated from the Mennonite practice of baptism by affusion. The actual points of difference between Helwys' group and the Mennonites concerned other matters, as will be shown.

The Rise of English General Baptists

The organization of General Baptist churches (that is, those holding the Arminian view of a general or unlimited atonement) on English soil dates from 1611 or early in 1612, when Thomas Helwys and his handful of followers returned to London. They had returned to the country from which they had fled persecution a few years before with one purpose in mind—to propagate their faith. Thus, the Baptist witness was preserved and perpetuated by no more than ten courageous folk. They were fortunate in their leader, however, for he was a man of good background and training, being a country gentleman who had been educated at London in law. The congregation seems to have met surreptitiously at Spitalfield, just outside of London's walls. This was the first Baptist church on English soil for whose origin there is historical proof.[9] It was Arminian or General Baptist in doctrine and affusionist in mode of baptism.

In a series of four books written between 1611 and 1612, three in Holland and the fourth in England, Helwys set forth his beliefs, which went beyond Smyth's in several respects. In fact, on points of difference he did not hesitate to attack the main religious groups of his day. He found fault with Calvinists for their rigid predestinarian doctrine. On the other hand, he criticized Mennonites for their overemphasis upon human free will, insisting that only Adam, before his fall, enjoyed complete freedom of choice, whereas all others, since the fall, have been increasingly dependent upon Christ. He also took issue with their insistence upon apostolic succession of the *true*

[9] Churches at Hill Cliffe, Eythorne, Coggeshall, Braintree, Farrington Road, Crowle, and Epworth have been claimed by some to have originated in the sixteenth century, but there is little more than tradition to substantiate their claim; cf. Whitley, *History of British Baptists,* 49-50.

church. In addition, he controverted their teaching that Christians should not participate in civil government. He had a grievance against Puritan preachers who, to avoid a break with the Anglican Church over uniformity, sought nonparochial posts as private chaplains or city preachers, in which positions they might be free from administering those rites which they regarded as unbiblical. Finally, he attacked the hierarchy of the Anglican and Roman Catholic Communions alike for robbing men of their freedom in Christ.

Helwys expanded Smyth's plea for liberty of conscience, setting forth in his fourth book, *A Short Declaration of the Mistery of Iniquity,* the first claim for freedom of worship to be published in the English language:

> Let the King judge, is it not most equal that men should choose their religion themselves, seeing they only must stand themselves before the judgment seat of God to answer for themselves. . . . (We) profess and teach that in all earthly things the king's power is to be submitted unto; and in heavenly or spiritual things, if the king or any in authority under him shall exercise their power against any they are not to resist by any way or means, although it were in their power, but rather to submit their lives as Christ and his disciples did, and yet keep their consciences to God.

An even stronger word, written in the inscription to this book (1612), brought him imprisonment in Newgate Prison by order of the irate monarch, James I:

> The King is a mortall man and not God, therefore hath no power over y immortall soules of his subjects to make lawes and ordinances for them and to set spiritual Lords over them.[10]

That the pastor of the Spitalfield Church was not the only spokesman for religious liberty is evident from the fact that Leonard Busher, allegedly a member of this church, and described as "a poor man labouring for his daily bread, yet with some measure of learning, issued in 1614 a tractate entitled, *Religious Peace or a plea for liberty of conscience,* in which, anticipating Milton's *Areopagitica,* he argued that it should be 'lawful for any person or persons, yea Jews and Papists, to write, dispute, confer, and reason, print and publish any

[10] W. T. Whitley, *A History of British Baptists,* 33-4; a reproduction of Thomas Helwys, *A Short Declaration of the Mistery of Iniquity* (London, 1612), is in the New York Public Library.

matter touching religion.' " In addition, Busher championed adult baptism by immersion, nearly thirty years before the Calvinistic or Particular Baptists of England adopted it as the correct mode.[11]

After Helwys' imprisonment, little was heard of him except that he died sometime prior to 1616.[12] The leadership of the Spitalfield Church was taken over by John Murton, a furrier who had been wedded to a farmer's daughter. Hence the little congregation enjoyed the pastoral care of two men of very different social backgrounds and training. Murton, like his predecessor, was an author of books defending the new Baptist position on theology and polity. He wrote two: *Objections Answered ... That no man ought to be persecuted for his religion, so he testifie his allegiance by the Oath, appointed by Law* (1615), and *A Description of what God hath Predestined concerning Man,* the first edition of a work later known as *Truth's Champion ...* (1620). Apparently, such writings aroused the concern of paedo-baptists, for in the early 1620's several tracts appeared against Ana-baptists by such eminent Independents as Edmond Jessop, Henry Ainsworth, and John Robinson.

It appears from several letters preserved in the Mennonite Ar-chives at Amsterdam that before May, 1624, sixteen persons, includ-ing one Elias Tookey, who apparently became their leader, had been excommunicated by Murton's congregation. This group formed a church and sought union with the Waterlander Mennonites so that they might have an ordained ministry. After a lengthy correspond-ence with Hans de Ries at Amsterdam, the request of the English congregation was denied, not so much because of difference in doc-trine as because they desired permission to take the oath of allegiance, which the government required. This seems to have been a major

[11] Shakespeare, *Baptist and Congregational Pioneers,* 148; cf. Burrage, *Early English Dissenters,* I, 276-8. Burrage says that Busher was an English Anabaptist who wrote this tract in Holland, not in London, "as has generally been supposed." He differs, however, with W. T. Whitley's theory that he was a Dutchman, on the grounds of his superior use of English; cf. Whitley, "Leonard Busher, Dutchman," *Transactions of the Baptist Historical Society,* Vol. I, No. 2 (April, 1909), 107-13. Burrage adds that his name, as spelled at Delft in 1642, is English. Shakespeare assumes that Busher was a member of Helwys' church. This is a matter of conjecture, although it is assumed that he was a citizen of London who was in exile from his native land for some time; cf. Introductory Notice to Busher's *Religions Peace: or A Plea for Liberty of Conscience* in Hanserd Knollys Society, *Tracts on Liberty of Conscience* (London, 1846).

[12] Cf. Burrage, *Early English Dissenters,* I, 256: "Helwys was certainly not living in 1616, for in that year Geoffrey Helwys, who was probably Thomas Helwys' brother, speaks in his will of Thomas Helwys as no longer being alive (*Dictionary of National Biography*)."

issue with the Mennonites in determining their relationship to English Baptists. To the Baptists it was a vital matter for the preservation of their own personal safety in the country. After Murton's death about 1625 or 1626, his church also requested union with the Waterlanders. On November 25, 1626, they too were refused on account of their views on the administration of the sacraments, on oath-taking, and on holding government positions. The total number of Baptists in England at the time was at least one hundred and fifty in five congregations at London, Lincoln, Sarum, Coventry, and Tiverton.[13]

In 1630 there were six such congregations, which were again in correspondence with the Waterlander Mennonite Church at Amsterdam, seeking fellowship with them and recognition as a London group. Lack of pastoral leadership may have been a strong motivating factor in this effort. The Mennonites, however, refused to join in any formal union, although they welcomed friendly relations with the English Baptists. To the present day, Dutch Mennonites and English Baptists do not consider themselves as belonging to the same communion, and the issues of difference remain practically the same.[14] By 1644 there were forty-seven General Baptist churches, Arminian in theology, evangelistic in purpose, and dedicated to religious liberty, even at the price of severe persecution at the hands of Archbishop Laud in the reign of Charles I.

The Rise of English Particular Baptists

Particular Baptists had no connection with continental Anabaptists. Instead, they represented a further step in the movement of English Independency (Congregationalism) towards its logical conclusion in believer's baptism. The origin of Particular Baptist churches in England may be dated from about 1638. Their antecedents are to be

[13] *Ibid.*, I, 257-73.

[14] Whitley, *op. cit.*, 53-6. Ernest A. Payne takes exception to Whitley's viewpoint in an article, "Contacts Between Mennonites and Baptists," *Foundations*, Vol. 4, No. 1 (Jan., 1961), 39-55. He cites the following evidence for concluding that Mennonites influenced John Smyth and the General Baptists who returned to England: (1) Smyth showed a growing agreement with the Mennonites on theological matters; (2) the General Baptists bore certain resemblances to Mennonite congregations in general church polity (use of the "ban" as an instrument of discipline, refusal to recognize marriage outside of the community, observance of the rite of foot-washing); (3) correspondence between General Baptists and the Mennonites in Amsterdam, 1630-31; (4) Benjamin Evans drew on material in the Mennonite archives for his history of *Early English Baptists;* and (5) The London Missionary Society received financial support from Mennonites, 1821-47.

found in a non-Separatist or Independent congregation which had been organized in 1616 at Southwark, London, by Henry Jacob, who had emerged from Puritanism after six years as a refugee in Leyden under the influence of John Robinson. For six years (1616-1622), Jacob was pastor of this church, which came to be known as the "Jacob Church." According to the Jessey Records, which provide a great deal of scattered information concerning this church, Jacob resigned to move to Virginia, where he died in 1624.[15] The names of several prominent members of the congregation are enshrined therein. John Lathrop, who was made Jacob's successor in 1625, was imprisoned in 1632; upon his release in 1634, he with thirty members of the congregation fled to New England to escape further persecution by Archbishop Laud. Those who remained in England were led by two pastors. The humorously named member of Cromwell's "Nominated" Parliament of 1653, Praise-God Barebone (Barbon), the leather-seller, was chosen pastor of half of the Jacob Church which met in his great house, "The Lock and Key," in Fleet Street. This arrangement was by mutual consent in 1640 with Jessey who cared for the other half. It is probable that Barebone did not become a Baptist until much later, for in 1642 he published a defence of paedobaptism. Yet his name is listed with a Declaration of Baptists issued in 1654 and signed by twenty-two "as of the church that walked with Mr. Barebone." In the summer of 1637, Henry Jessey, a Cambridge graduate, succeeded Lathrop as pastor; in time, he accepted believer's baptism and was baptized by Hanserd Knollys, himself a Cambridge graduate and an Independent. Knollys had migrated to New England in 1638, only to find as much persecution there as in England. Returning to London in 1641, he eventually accepted Baptist principles and was ordained in 1645 to serve a Baptist congregation in London.[16] William Kiffin

[15] The Gould Manuscript, which is preserved at Regent's Park College, Oxford, contains the *Jessey Memoranda* (which contains the history to 1640 of the Independent Puritan Congregation organized by Henry Jacob at London in 1616) and the *Kiffin Manuscript* (which traces the history of the first English Particular Baptist congregation, which resulted from two withdrawals from the Jacob's Church in 1633 and 1638). According to Burrage, they are generally trustworthy and a careful transcription from Benjamin Stinton's lost "Repository." See Burrage, *op. cit.*, I, 312-35; for selected documents from the Gould MS, see II, 292-308. On Barebone, see *Dictionary of National Biography*, Vol. I, 1071-3 and Burrage, *op. cit.*, II, 302.

[16] Isaac Backus, *A History of New England with Particular Reference to the Denomination of Christians Called Baptists* (Newton, Mass., 1871), Vol. I, 82-3. This history was first written in three volumes between 1777 and 1796.

was a wealthy merchant and faithful preacher, who eventually became a strict communionist Baptist and a member of Spilsbury's congregation which had separated itself from the Jacob Church in 1638.

Divisions within the Jacob congregation began to occur as early as 1633 when some members of the church received a friendly dismissal to form a new body. They differed as to the administrator of baptism, holding "that baptism by the parish clergyman was invalid," not because it was infant baptism, but because it was received in the Church of England. Obviously, this was not strictly a Baptist group. This company, with some paedobaptists, organized a church apparently under the leadership of Samuel Eaton. In 1638 others were added, including William Kiffin. In that same year, a further dismissal was granted by the Jacob Church, of which Jessey was now pastor, to some who differed as to who should be baptized, holding that according to the Scriptures only regenerated believers should receive the ordinance. These united with John Spilsbury, who seems in the meantime to have become pastor of Eaton's mixed church. This became the first Calvinistic Baptist church, often called Particular Baptist owing to its doctrine of a limited atonement.[17]

According to Burrage's corrected reading of the Kiffin Manuscript, "during 1640 Richard Blunt and certain other members of Spilsbury's and perhaps a few of Jessey's church, became convinced that baptism by sprinkling or pouring, whether administered to believers or adults, or to infants, was not the form of baptism employed in the time of the apostles, but that true baptism 'ought to be by diping the Body into the Water, resembling Burial & riseing again.' "[18] Since immersion had been practically discontinued in the Church of England by 1600, Blunt, who understood the Dutch language, was sent to the Rhynsburgers or Collegiants, a minority group of Mennonites at Rhynsburg in the Netherlands, who practiced immersion. The Kiffin Manuscript does not say that John Batte(n), an elder there, immersed him, as has been generally understood, but only that he received him kindly and gave him letters for the church at London. It is altogether likely that Blunt was not immersed by the

---

[17] The origin of the Particular Baptists has been dated erroneously 1633, owing to Crosby's incorrect version of an extract from the Kiffin MS. See Shakespeare, *Baptist and Congregational Pioneers*, 180-3. For text of the Kiffin MS., see Burrage, *Early English Dissenters*, II, 302-5.

[18] Burrage, *op. cit.*, I, 370.

Rhynsburgers, but only given instructions concerning the administration of immersion to take home with him. Hence, the record reads that "Mr. Blunt Baptized Mr. Blacklock that was a Teacher amongst them, and Mr. Blunt being Baptized, he and Mr. Blacklock Baptized the rest of their friends that were so minded, & many being added to them they increased much. . . ." Thus, it appears that Blunt baptized Blacklock, their leader, who then baptized him, and the two together baptized the rest. This is the more logical view, for it would be no more reasonable to suppose that Calvinists would have accepted baptism of Arminian Collegiants than that Smyth would have done so thirty years before. By January, 1642, there were fifty-three members in two congregations, one under Blunt, the other under Blacklock. By 1644, the number of churches had increased to seven.[19]

In that year to clarify their stand on the proper mode of baptism, fifteen Particular Baptist ministers, including Spilsbury, Kiffin, and Knollys, incorporated a definition of baptism by immersion in a Confession of fifty articles of faith to which they affixed their signatures. Seven Particular Baptist churches adopted this London Confession, as it was called, which expressed Calvinistic theology, stipulated baptism by immersion, and advocated religious liberty. With the consequent revival of immersion, the Baptists took another step away from their Anabaptist forebears.

The Origin of Baptist Associations

Whitley bears witness to the fact that "from the beginning Baptists were not 'Independents'; they always sought for fellowship between the different churches, and they were very successful in arranging for permanent organization."[20] Their purpose was framed by a desire to have fellowship between local churches and to carry on evangelistic work. As early as 1624, five General Baptist churches took joint action to repudiate the characteristic Mennonite views regarding oaths, magistracy, and military service. While General Baptists did not seek any outward organization with Particular Baptists, each group of churches organized informal meetings of those of their number, which they called "associations." In this enterprise, General Baptists took the lead.

---

[19] *Ibid.*, II, 302-4 (the so-called Kiffin MS), also I, 330-5.
[20] Whitley, *History of British Baptists*, 53.

The pattern of the more formal associational organization, as it was worked out, was provided by a military expedient with which Baptists had become familiar during the Civil Wars (1642-49) between King and Parliament. During that first winter, counties were organized into "associations" for defense purposes. This plan was adapted to the raising of money and troops from the counties. Then Cromwell's New-Model Army, thus organized, brought into being a council for political action and protection of communities against plunder, to which each regiment sent representatives. In 1653 that part of the Army which was disbanded in Ireland, and which was largely composed of Baptists, transferred this plan to church organization as they sought to maintain fellowship between their lonely congregations in a strange country by correspondence and the frequent meeting of delegates. These Irish Associations sought contact with Welsh, Scotch, and English Baptists who were attempting a similar type of interchurch communication.

The specific nature of the associational organization differed with the two bodies of Baptists. Particular Baptists were satisfied for a time, with a loose organization for exchange of correspondence and more or less regular meetings of representatives of the member churches in a practicable area. General Baptists, on the other hand, took more kindly to associational organization of a more centralized character, and emphasized uniting all churches into one annual assembly which should be national in scope.

From the records of early associational meetings, it is possible to arrange in chronological order the first several occasions of interchurch relations among Baptists in England.[21] (1) The joint action of five or six General Baptist churches between 1624 and 1630 to seek union with the Waterlander Mennonites. (2) The adoption of a Confession of Faith by seven Particular Baptist churches in 1644. (3) The meeting in 1650 of three Welsh churches for concerted action. (4) The meeting in 1651 of thirty General Baptist churches of the midland counties, who sent two messengers each for a territory of one hundred miles by twenty-four miles, thereby setting a pattern for future General Baptist associational organizations. (5) Berkshire churches organized with a formal constitution on October

[21] W. T. Whitley, ed., *Minutes of the General Assembly of the General Baptist Churches in England, with Kindred Records:* 1654-1728, 1731-1811 in two volumes (London, 1909-10), Vol. I; see also, Whitley, *History of British Baptists,* 86-93.

8, 1652. (6) Churches in the western countries are known to have sent representatives to a meeting at Wells in 1653. The records imply that this was not the first of such gatherings. (7) By 1655 the title "Association" was well recognized among Baptists. (8) In 1660 a General Assembly, or annual meeting, of the churches of all Associations of General Baptists in England was organized in London. From these early beginnings of interchurch relations was eventually to develop a denominational consciousness.

Early Confessions of Faith and Their Use[22]

Of the numerous creedal statements formulated by English Baptists prior to 1689 when the Act of Toleration was passed by Parliament, the more prominent are the following: (1) The Confession of John Smyth drawn up probably in 1609. (2) The Confession of Thomas Helwys written in 1611. (3) The first Particular Baptist Confession of Faith, known as the First London Confession, drawn up in 1644 by seven churches to distinguish the Particular Baptists from Anabaptists and General Baptists. (4) The first General Baptist Confession of Faith, published in 1651 by thirty congregations in Leicestershire, Lincolnshire, and adjoining counties to set forth their views. (5) The Somerset Confession published in 1656 by sixteen churches of Particular Baptists in the Somerset Association to show their agreement with the London churches and to bear a witness for the Lord. (6) The Confession of General Baptists which was signed in 1660 by representatives of some twenty thousand throughout the Kingdom who were anxious to persuade Charles II, upon his restoration to England, that they were law-abiding citizens, rather than anarchistic Anabaptists as had been charged. (7) The Second London Confession of Particular Baptists which was written in 1677 primarily to show their agreement with the Westminster Confession of the Presbyterians in practically all points but baptism. It was signed by representatives of one hundred and seven churches from England and Wales, meeting in London. (8) The Orthodox Creed drawn up by General Baptists in 1678 "to unite and confirm all true Protestants against the errors and heresies of Rome." The Confession manifested a tendency to modify Arminian doctrine in the

[22] For a study of this topic, see Donald N. Thompson, *The History of Baptist Confessions of Faith: 1610-1800*, a B.D. thesis in the Library of the Eastern Baptist Theological Seminary (1945).

direction of Calvinism, perhaps to facilitate a united witness of all Baptists in carrying out their anti-Catholic mission.

The uses of Baptist confessions of faith have been both numerous and varied. They may be summarized as follows: (1) to maintain purity of doctrine; (2) to clarify and validate the Baptist position; (3) to serve as a guide to the General Assembly or local association in counselling churches; (4) to serve as a basis for fellowship within local churches, associations, or a General Assembly; (5) to discipline churches and members. This last mentioned use of confessions should not be interpreted as identifying them with formal creeds which have been used to assure and often to enforce conformity to the authorized interpretation of Scripture with reference to doctrine or polity by a state church. Although Baptist churches have had the power to discipline, they have refrained from inflicting bodily punishment or material penalty by the civil government upon those with whom they dealt. Instead, they have on occasion withdrawn fellowship from those whose doctrine might prove harmful to the accepted teaching of the churches in the Baptist fellowship. In this way, Baptists have sought to protect the individual's freedom of religious belief and practice before God, while at the same time safeguarding the doctrinal purity of the churches.

The Baptist Struggle for Liberty in England

Not until the Commonwealth Period (1640-1660) did Baptists find themselves in a position to labor effectively in behalf of religious liberty. Both the General and the Particular Baptist bodies had grown more numerous, and among them were several persons of influence and property. In Oliver Cromwell, Puritan and Revolutionist, they felt that they had found one who favored the cause of the Independents. Thus it was that "almost to a man they were supporters of the Parliamentary cause, which was the cause of liberty, religious as well as civil. Large numbers of Baptists took service in the armies of Parliament, some of whom rose to a high rank, and were much trusted by the Lord Protector, Cromwell."[23] Whitley points out that the zeal of Baptists in Cromwell's New-Model Army indicated sharply their difference from Mennonites who were pacifists. The

[23] Vedder, *A Short History of the Baptists*, 219; this view is supported by Samuel R. Gardiner, *History of the Great Civil War, 1642-1649* (London, 1886), I, 314, 365-6; cf. Adam Taylor. *The History of English General Baptists*, 2 volumes (London, 1818), I, 121.

most popular drill books for cavalry and infantry were written by Baptists. Yet in the camps Baptist officers, schooled in the science of war, frequently did the preaching in place of the clergy. To them, the Civil War was a struggle for political and religious liberty which justified the use of arms as well as the singing of psalms.[24]

In their struggle for religious liberty, they found a foe in Presbyterians who desired "presbyterial" in place of "episcopal" uniformity. Westminster divines rebuked the Long Parliament for allowing Baptists to increase. Indeed, Presbyterians were restrained from inducing that body to repress Baptists only by their need of uniting all anti-Anglican forces in order to defeat the Royalists. As it turned out, Presbyterians and Independents enjoyed many more privileges than Baptists during the Long Parliament.

An example may be cited from the account of John Denne, who after his reception in 1643 into the Baptist church which met in Bell Alley, Coleman Street, London, was encouraged by the congregation to go into Bedfordshire and Cambridgeshire to preach. He was instrumental in establishing several churches, including those at Warboys and Fenstanton in Lincolnshire. Although the times were more favorable since the Long Parliament had destroyed the Court of High Commission and the Star Chamber, he met with persecution at Cambridge, for Baptists did not enjoy there the freedom accorded to Presbyterians and Independents. In 1644 he was imprisoned and taken in custody to London. Some time after his release, he determined to aid the cause of freedom from tyranny by serving in Cromwell's Army. While in that service, he was involved in a mutiny of democratic "levellers" within the army who were discontented with the slowness of Parliament to establish a true republic. This uprising, which occurred in May, 1649, was suppressed vigorously by Cromwell at Burford on May 14, for he was unwilling to jeopardize his cause by allowing radicalism to get out of hand. Denne was imprisoned, along with others, for his part in the event, but released through the intercession of members of the General's own family. For a time thereafter he dropped out of sight, possibly unhappy over the Protectorate which Cromwell established, as were many other Baptists. The same love of liberty was manifested by a contemporary, Henry Denne, who wrote in 1659 a tract entitled, *The*

[24] Whitley, *History of British Baptists*, 73-5.

Quaker No Papist, in which he pleaded for toleration of Quakers and Roman Catholics by the government.[25]

To the Baptists, who comprised so large a part of Cromwell's army, particularly after the death of the king on January 30, 1649, has been attributed the credit for preventing the Presbyterians from establishing their own state church. This the army had accomplished by purging Parliament in 1648 of those who were not in accord with the ideals of a free church as well as a free state. The resulting "Rump" Parliament was soon prorogued, however, and in its place there was established a Protectorate under an "Instrument of Government" drawn up by the army council just prior to Charles' execution.

Baptists were active also in government positions. Vavasor Powell, a Welsh Baptist living in London, was appointed one of several commissioners sent out into the country by Parliament for the conservation of religion. His task was to propagate religion in Wales, an assignment which he undertook with energy and zeal. Praise-God Barebone, a pastor in London, likely of Baptist views, was prominent in the Rump Parliament of 1653. Three other Baptists, John Tombes of Salisbury, Daniel Dyke, a joint elder with Kiffin at the Devonshire Square church, London, and Henry Jessey, also a London clergyman, were members of the Board of Examiners, or "Tryers," which Cromwell as Lord Protector had set up to settle creedal disputes, examine ministers of immoral or doutbful character, and fill vacancies with thoroughly orthodox men. Acceptance of such an office would appear today to violate the Baptist principle of separation of church and state. Indeed, it appears that the Baptists of that day generally had no sympathy with the "Tryers." In London, in 1654, a company of 143 members of ten churches, including those led by Jessey and Barebone, signed a protest against the "Tryers," which was, to them, another High Commission Court, and a threat to religious liberty.

The discontent of the republican-minded Baptists in the army and out of it was voiced against Cromwell's Instrument of Government by which he hoped to rule England as Protector. Vavasor Powell and several other ministers, from their pulpits, boldly chal-

[25] *Records of the Churches of Christ, Gathered at Fenstanton, Warboys, and Hexham, 1644-1720.* (Hanserd Knollys Society publication, London, 1854), Introductory Notice, vii-xvii, xx.

lenged his right to such pretensions of power. Major-general Thomas Harrison, an Independent who was to become a Baptist in 1657, said that he could not support it. The criticism became general as republican Baptists and Independents alike felt bitterness at what they regarded "as treachery on Cromwell's part, a step back from following scripture towards monarchy and arbitrary power."[26] Their behavior was a source of discomfiture to a man who at heart did not relish a dictatorship and who was sympathetic with many of the principles for which they stood; yet their impatience with his policies was embarrassing and dangerous to his leadership. Accordingly he dismissed Baptists, in particular, from public employment and from the army. Major-general Harrison "was cashiered and sent home to live under surveillance"; other Baptist officers—Allen, Alured, Joyce, Ludlow, Okey, Overton, Wigan, and Wildman—received similar treatment. The Baptist historian, Crosby, refers to the disbanding of an entire regiment in the Earl of Essex's army, because "the Colonel entertained and gave countenance to *Separatists* and some *Anabaptists*."[27]

As Cromwell's power expanded, many extremists regarded it as a threat to the cause of freedom. There came into prominence a radical group known as Fifth Monarchy Men, led by General Thomas Harrison and Thomas Venner.[28] These were radicals who expected an imminent physical return of Christ to establish the "Rule of the Saints." While some Baptists held chiliastic ideas of establishing Daniel's Fifth Kingdom by force and thereby ushering in the reign of Christ, not all of them shared these aspirations. On the contrary, many hastened to disavow any connection with the movement, for they remembered the stigma which the Münster Rebellion had brought upon the Anabaptists. Especially was this true of the General Baptists, whose General Assembly in 1654 had repudiated the program. Particular Baptists, who had been more susceptible to the propaganda, were divided on the issue. Such leaders as William

---

[26] Whitley, ed., *Minutes of the General Assembly of the General Baptist Churches in England, 1654-1728, 1731-1811*, 2 volumes (London, 1909-1910), I, 1; B. Evans, *The Early English Baptists*, 2 volumes (London, 1864), II, 175-206.

[27] Thomas Crosby, *The History of the English Baptists*, II, 4-5; *Minutes of the General Assembly of General Baptists*, I, 2.

[28] Louise F. Brown, *The Political Activities of the Baptists and Fifth Monarchy Men in England During the Interregnum*. (Washington, 1912.) This provides the best source on this subject.

Kiffin, John Spilsbury, Samuel Richardson, and Thomas Collier, however, were uncompromisingly opposed to Fifth Monarchism. The position taken by Kiffin is not surprising, for this Baptist minister in London was also a wealthy merchant who was a favorite at court because of his liberality in providing occasional loans to the monarch. While Cromwell was Lord Protector, Kiffin was always careful to protect himself against the malicious accusations of envious enemies who claimed that he spoke seditiously of the government.[29]

When the armed uprising of Thomas Venner in 1661, aimed at overthrowing Charles II who had just returned from exile in France, ended unsuccessfully, the Fifth Monarchy movement collapsed. The association of some Baptists with it, however, tended to discredit the Baptist witness, for in the public mind, Baptists were associated with violence and anarchy. Naturally, Baptist leaders lost no time in seeking to correct the unfortunate impressions made upon the government and public alike. "On the very day of the royal proclamation (i.e., January 10, 1661), forbidding the assembling for worship of 'anabaptists, quakers, and other sectaries,' the London baptists presented to the king 'An Humble Apology,' with their names and those of other leading baptists appended to it, protesting against their supposed participation in Venner's rebellion."[30] William Kiffin and Denne led the representatives who presented this apology, which sought to persuade the monarch that the rebels were chiefly paedobaptists. At the same time, paedobaptist Independents and Quakers were also addressing apologies to the Crown and the public. Six days later (January 16, 1661), the Baptists of Lincolnshire presented their "Second Humble Address." In February they offered another plea; but the appeals were useless, for while the king promised protection, all too many local officials were hostile. Hanserd Knollys and many others were imprisoned in the capital. Vavasor Powell's home there was entered forcibly, and he, with others, was seized and kept prisoner for nine weeks. During the eighteen weeks between Venner's insurrection and the king's coronation, about four hundred were crowded into Newgate Prison alone, while other city pri-

---

[29] *Minutes of the General Assembly of General Baptists*, I, 1-5. See also Winthrop S. Hudson, "Variation among the Early Baptists," *The Chronicle*, Vol. IX, No. 2 (April, 1946), 70, 74; Joseph Ivimey, *History of the English Baptists, 1760-1820*, 4 volumes (London, 1811-1830), III, 318, Ivimey, *Life of Kiffin*, 54.

[30] *Records of the Churches of Christ, Gathered at Fenstanton . . .* , xxi.

sons were likewise filled. At the coronation, a general pardon was proclaimed, but in May, persecution was revived when a bill was introduced in Parliament for the prompt suppression of Baptists and Quakers.[31]

The unhappy accounts of the treatment of Baptists in various counties away from London indicates that public prejudice rather than royal disfavor was their strongest obstacle to security. In fact, the public frame of mind in the wake of the unfortunate insurrection was not averse to the launching of a government policy which would restore total conformity to the Establishment. Within just a few years a series of measures was passed by Parliament to this end. One was the Corporation Act (1661) which excluded nonconformists from public office; another was the Act of Uniformity (1662) which forced them out of the schools and the Church. These were followed by the Conventicle Act (1664) which declared the Elizabethan Act of the same name to be in force for three years, thereby prohibiting nonconformists from absenting themselves from the Established Church services without penalty and from conducting their own worship. Indeed, this Act, carried over from Elizabeth's reign, had been utilized four years earlier (in 1660) when John Bunyan was imprisoned for preaching without a license and for failing to attend the services of the Anglican Church. For twelve years Bunyan remained in Bedford jail, the symbol of Baptist resistance to religious oppression.

Another case in point, less familiar to be sure, is that of a company of sabbatarian General Baptists who held their assemblies for public worship on Saturday. This congregation met in London at Bull-stake-alley, Whitechapel, under the leadership of John James. On October 19, 1661, James was removed forcibly from his pulpit by a justice of the peace and constable, and charged with treason for having called Jesus Christ King of England, Scotland, and Ireland. In spite of proof in court that four witnesses had been coerced to testify falsely against him, he was convicted and hung, drawn, and quartered on November 26. The thirty members of his congregation were taken in groups to a justice of the peace to take the oath of

---

[31] *Tracts on Liberty of Conscience, 1614-1661* (Hanserd Knollys Society, London, 1846), 315-8; Crosby, *op. cit.*, II, 91-4.

allegiance; as many as refused were committed to Newgate Prison.[32]

The issue was clear: from the point of view of the Established Church, all Baptist preachers were unordained laymen, while Baptists insisted that every Christian is bound to witness and is divinely licensed to preach. From the point of view of the government, Baptists were looked upon as anarchists. While the Conventicle Act was not uniformly enforced, most Baptists suffered its restrictions without open protest, enduring persecution and frequently the loss of their church property. In 1665 the Five Mile Act was passed. This added to their plight by forbidding nonconforming clergy to teach school or to conduct religious services within five miles of any town. Hundreds of Baptists, Quakers, and other dissenters were imprisoned for violating these legislative bulwarks of Anglican supremacy.[33]

On March 15, 1672, a Declaration of Indulgence was passed to favor Catholics and Dissenters. It was but a temporary breathing spell, planned to win support for the unpopular monarch whose sympathies really were with the Catholics. While the privileges granted by the Declaration stopped discontent among dissenters temporarily, fears were aroused that the Catholics again would come into prominence. To offset this danger to Protestantism, Parliament enacted the Test Act of 1673 by which every officer of the Crown was required to renounce the doctrine of transubstantiation and to receive the Lord's Supper at his parish house. The pro-Catholic king was obliged to agree to this legislation, for otherwise the Commons would not have voted more money for his military undertakings. By this test, Baptists, along with Catholics and other nonconformists, were precluded from naval, military, civil, and municipal services. Most of them had to turn to farming or commerce for their livelihood.

In the reign of James II (1685-1688), brother of Charles II who died in 1685, a lull in persecution occurred, for the new monarch, in order to frustrate the Anglicans and assist his fellow Catholics (for he was openly of that faith) issued a Declaration of Indulgence in 1687 for Catholics and nonconformists alike. This order

---

[32] Adam Taylor, *The History of the English General Baptists*, 2 volumes (London, 1818), I, 256-9.

[33] Crosby, *History of the English Baptists*, II, 94-209; see also *The Records of a Church of Christ Meeting in Broadmead, Bristol, 1640-1687* (Hanserd Knollys Society, London, 1847), 104-7 for persecution of this church as an example.

suspended all laws against dissenters, permitted them to worship in public, and dispensed with tests for public office. Most Baptists accepted the benefits without giving thanks to James, whose motives and illegal procedures they knew all too well. Those few who did respond to the appeals of agents of the Crown for expressions of gratitude which might be interpreted as demonstrations of public support of the monarch, forfeited their popularity with their fellow Baptists.[34] Meanwhile, Anglican churchmen saw the need of currying favor with dissenters in those Corporations where the voters at the polls were displacing Anglicans and electing dissenters in their place. Hence, they urged Parliament to pass an Act of Toleration for Protestants only, which would be better than a royal declaration. Actually, they desired to win the favor of the nonconformists without permitting the Roman Catholics to benefit by the legislation. The result was that for Protestant dissenters the general persecution practically ended. The scattered occurrences of persecution which continued into the eighteenth century showed, however, that complete victory had not yet been won.

It had been an era of severe testing, yet Baptist growth had not been retarded seriously. Among General Baptists, new churches had been planted and old ones were flourishing both in Lincolnshire and the adjacent counties under the able leadership of the revered Thomas Grantham and of younger ministers. In Cambridge and Huntingdon, John Denne and his associates continued an active ministry. In Buckinghamshire and Northampton, the story was virtually the same. At London, congregations had increased in number and size and were served by able ministers. Kent was a center of Baptist activities. In the southern counties, there were here and there General Baptist churches. Indeed, the era of the Peaceful Revolution, as it has been called, was the apex of prosperity among these people. It is estimated that between the Restoration in 1660 and the Revolution in 1688, their numbers increased from approximately twenty to thirty thousand. While accurate figures for Particular Baptists are not easily accessible, the generalization can be made that they too were making steady advances in London, as well as in the surrounding

<hr>

[34] Taylor, *History of English General Baptists*, I, 304-5.

counties, and also in many of the farther northern parts of England.[35]

With the voluntary exile of the unpopular James II in 1688, and the advent of those constitutional monarchs, William and Mary of Orange, Parliament early in 1689 passed the Act of Toleration which favored nonconformists although it did not grant full religious liberty. The law required the taking of certain oaths or, if one scrupled against oath-taking, he was obliged to make a declaration of faith in the Trinity and to acknowledge the inspiration of the Scriptures. Baptist ministers were expressly exempted from subscribing to that part of the articles of the Church of England which taught infant baptism.[36] Places of public worship for dissenters might be open if certified to the bishop or to quarter sessions court. Preachers did not need a license to preach as had been true under Charles. The universities and professions, however, were still closed to dissenters, and the ecclesiastical courts were allowed full authority to enforce payment to the state church of tithes and other parochial dues. Actually, only a degree of religious freedom had been won. But strangely enough, this victory, partial though it was, seems to have exhausted the Baptists, for it was followed by a period of spiritual decline, particularly amongst the General Baptists.

In Retrospect

It may be noted that Baptist roots lay within the Puritan Separatist movement. There were four groups of Baptists in England during the seventeenth century: the General Baptists with their Arminian emphasis in theology, the Particular Baptists who upheld a strict Calvinism, the Seventh Day Baptists who were recruited largely from the disappointed Fifth Monarchy men, and a cross section of General and Particular Baptists who fraternized with the Independents (Congregationalist paedobaptists) and held to a higher social life and culture.

This latter group was Baptist by conviction, but not sectarian in point of view; it may be regarded as the forerunner of a more liberal, ecumenical strain among Baptists. These seventeenth-century Bap-

[35] Taylor, *op. cit.*, I, 300-2; David Douglas, *History of the Baptist Churches in the North of England from 1648 to 1845* (London, 1846), chaps. 1-2; W. T. Whitley, *The Baptists of London, 1612-1928* (London, 1928), 97 ff.

[36] Daniel Neal, *The History of the Puritans,* 4 volumes (London, 1732-1738), IV, Act of Toleration, article IX, Appendix No. 1, p. 630.

tists were not pietists; they held no aversion to involvement in the social order. Indeed, they were quickly drawn, as we have seen, into the political and constitutional struggle between King and Parliament, inspired by their passion for liberty and their claim for religious toleration. Most of them were of moderate economic circumstances, living in the country districts.[37]

English Baptists of the seventeenth century were clear on what makes a true church. They regarded the church as a gathered community of redeemed men and women who had covenanted to walk together under the discipline of the Word of God and, with a properly appointed leadership, to proclaim the gospel and observe regularly the ordinances. Believer's baptism became the symbol of their identification with the risen Christ through the experience of individual conversion. There were two traditions regarding the church which were held by Baptists. One was the Smyth-Knollys tradition which stressed the importance of believer's baptism as a public testimony to the experience of repentance and faith. The other was the tradition of Jessey, Hardcastle, and Bunyan which held an open-membership view of the church, stressing the importance of public testimony of repentance and faith, and obedience to the church covenant, but not requiring rebaptism of those who came from other Christian communions. The first group regarded infant baptism as a threat to personal commitment, the central emphasis of the Christian faith. The second group refused to break fellowship with paedobaptists through a reluctance to unchurch other Christians. Baptism was for both groups a visible word, as preaching was an audible word. The Lord's Supper was generally observed each Lord's Day, with a preparation service conducted on a preceding weekday, as was the custom of the Mennonites.

The churches remained self-governing as congregations gathered by Christ and sustained by the Holy Spirit. It was believed that Christ had endowed the local congregation with authority in all matters of church life and order. The ministers were selected from the witnessing community of believers on the basis of their special gifts, and were ordained to preach, administer the ordinances, exercise discipline, and dispense pastoral care. The ministry was in most

[37] Robert C. Walton, *The Gathered Community* (London, 1944), 68-73. Many of the insights in this section are derived from this excellent book.

instances unpaid and non-professional. It was locally conceived, each minister being ordained or commissioned by his own congregation. By the eighteenth century there was to develop a wider conception of the ministry, to include evangelists without a settled church. Those who held this wider view linked it with their support of associations and sought to express this broader fellowship in the ordination service. This service included the congregation's act of recognizing the call, a response by the one being ordained, and an act of the laying-on-of-hands by other ministers. Ordination enabled the minister to act with church approval. Thus did the churches safeguard their ministry of the Word and the ordinances.

These early English Baptists felt the need of denominational solidarity, and traveled great distances to attend associational meetings. Instinctively, they drew from their Puritan background a healthy regard for the larger concept of the church from which the local congregations drew inspiration and mutual benefit.

There were marked differences between General and Particular Baptists. In many respects, General Baptists were closer to the continental Mennonites and the English Quakers in their stress upon the subjectivity of the inner response to the Spirit, in their distrust of human learning, and in their extemporaneity in worship. John Smyth was in some respects the English precursor to George Fox. Moreover, the Quaker leader reported that many of his followers were drawn from Baptist communities. General Baptists were more radical than Particular Baptists. They based their faith and practice on the six principles drawn from Hebrews 6:1-2. They stressed the laying-on-of-hands at baptism, and observed three distinctive ordinances: foot-washing, the love-feast, and anointing with oil. Moreover, they were unwilling to sing hymns in worship. While they laid more stress than did Particular Baptists on uniting all of their congregations in one General Assembly, the latter were careful to limit the authority of their regional associations. The reluctance of the Particular Baptists to form any kind of national organization reflected the stress on local autonomy which they inherited from English Separatism.

The Particular Baptists were closer to Congregationalists and Presbyterians in their stress upon the covenant basis of church order. During the Commonwealth era they drew their converts from a higher social level than did the General Baptists, a trend which continued during the Restoration period.[38]

Such were the beginnings of English Baptists. In spite of persecution, they made significant contributions to their own day and to future generations. They were among those Christians who had discovered the individual in religion. They took the church seriously, building gathered communities of faith upon personal commitment, symbolized by believer's baptism. They, like their Puritan Separatist forebears, sought to realize the ideal of a pure church without forsaking their involvement in the social order. They upheld more valiantly than many the principle of religious liberty, not as a political expedient, but as a cardinal conviction that true religion must be voluntary to be valid.

[38] Horton Davies, *Worship and Theology in England from Watts and Wesley to Maurice, 1690-1850* (Princeton, 1961), 123-39; C. E. Whiting, *Studies in English Puritanism from the Restoration to the Revolution, 1660-1688* (New York, 1931), 83-93.

PART TWO: BRITISH AND EUROPEAN BAPTISTS

CHAPTER THREE

REACTIONS TO TOLERATION: 1689-1800

IN view of the varied backgrounds from which seventeenth-century English Baptists had come, it is not surprising to discover among them a degree of instability as they reacted to the trends and influences of the times. This was as true in the formative years of the seventeenth century as in the era of development in the eighteenth century. Many of them had traversed a long spiritual pilgrimage from the ecclesiastical uniformity of Anglicanism to the free and simple polity of Baptist church life. Others had emerged from Presbyterianism or Congregationalism, with which they had fewer differences, to be sure, yet from which they had separated themselves because they had become convinced that the Bible taught that the church is composed only of those who have had a personal experience of regeneration prior to baptism. In both cases, they had manifested a degree of individualism in spiritual life not allowed in those communions. Because they relied upon their experience with Christ and their private interpretation of the Scriptures as the basis for the formulation of their confessional statements, they safeguarded themselves from a static dogmatism without weakening the significant function of a vital theology. This resulted quite naturally, however, in a measure of creedal diversity which divided Baptists into two major segments, Arminian and Calvinistic, depending upon the system of theology with which they found themselves in sympathy. There were still others who did not align themselves with either system.

The seventeenth century had closed with a significant victory for English nonconformists. The Act of Toleration, as we have seen, had afforded a measure of religious freedom hitherto not enjoyed by any of the reform sects. For Baptists, with their evangelistic zeal, this should have resulted in a marked degree of expansion. Actually, while they experienced a measure of progress, there was no quickening of evangelism to match the new opportunities.

A preview of developments after 1689 indicates the susceptibility of Baptists to the varied and often adverse currents which had been set in motion by the Protestant Reformation. The theological preoccupations of that era were producing extremist reactions which took varying forms. Arianism, a denial of the full deity of Jesus Christ, appeared among the more rationalistic; hyper-Calvinism with its extreme emphasis upon divine predetermination of man's eternal destiny, appeared among those of the reformed faith.

These influences caused the Baptists to react rather disappointingly to their opportunity for growth and expansion. A condition of apostasy laid hold upon the General Baptists, whereas hyper-Calvinism plagued those of the Particular group. Not until the Wesleyan Movement made its influence felt upon certain of their leaders in the second half of the eighteenth century did they make any marked progress in missionary outlook and activity. To some extent the period was for Baptists one of adjustment to a changing *milieu*, even as it was for other religious groups. The newly won constitutional privileges, the advent of the industrial revolution, the influence of theological controversy and the growing need for organization as society adapted itself to an increasingly complex mode of life undoubtedly affected dissenters generally. They needed to consolidate the gains which had been won, and they needed to achieve new victories, if they were to assure their continuance in English religious life. Certainly this was true among Baptists, whose genius for liberty had contributed so large a part to the winning of religious toleration in England. Indeed, this very strength was a significant factor in carrying them through the stress of theological conflict and the considerable measure of fragmentation which occurred in the eighteenth century. The period, happily, closed more auspiciously than it had commenced; it witnessed the initial undertakings of a well-developed missionary movement.

The Theological Trends

The main theological divisions among Baptists in the seventeenth and eighteenth centuries concerned chiefly the extent to which they applied the atonement to sinners. The General Baptists taught that Christ had died for all, and followed quite generally an Arminian doctrine. There was among them, however, some confusion with respect to the trinitarian concept of God. This was due to the influence of Arian thought which was then being felt also by Anglicans and Presbyterians. In spite of their professed committment to the proposition that all men are capable of receiving the gospel upon their own free choice, they were lacking in evangelistic zeal. This was in all probability the result of their preoccupation with theological speculation and church organization.[1] By 1750 they had adopted quite generally a form of unitarian teaching that explained deity as one person in three manifestations, rather than three persons in one God. This defection from orthodoxy eventuated in the withdrawal of the conservative party in 1770 to organize the New Connection General Baptists.

The Particular Baptists taught that the atonement was limited to the elect; this was in conformity with their Calvinistic theology. To some extent there developed among them an extreme form of Calvinism which blighted their evangelistic vigor. The extremists became antinomian; they overemphasized the biblical injunction that Christians "are not under law, but under grace," to the exclusion of the idea that sin in their lives was a menace to their salvation. The effect of Arianism was felt slightly in some of the churches. Calvinism claimed the great majority of Particular Baptist churches throughout England; London and Bristol being the chief centers of their strength. Indeed, it is notable that there was a tendency, particularly in London, for General Baptists to adopt Calvinism, as was the case of four ministers, including Benjamin Keach. This was a trend which the six General Baptist churches of that city found difficult to change.[2]

The extent of doctrinal variation among English Baptists may be illustrated by a classification of the ministers of London in 1731, which was as follows: seven antinomian or hyper-Calvinist, seven Calvinist, six Arminian, three Unitarian, and two Seventh-day.[3]

The Trends in Polity

Among General Baptists centralization was the characteristic of church organization. Their desire for strong central government

[1] Whitley, *History of the British Baptists*, 213-4.
[2] Whitley, *The Baptists of London*, 67-8; *Minutes of the General Assembly of General Baptists*, I, xix.
[3] Whitley, *The Baptists of London*, 51.

is reflected in the number of associations formed and eventually amalgamated for joint endeavor. This was dictated in part by the necessity of stemming the drift toward Calvinism noted above. A General Assembly had been organized some time after 1650. The proceedings of that body are contained in two volumes covering the years 1654-1728 and 1731-1811 respectively. While its origin is veiled in some obscurity, it is known that in 1651 thirty congregations of General Baptists met in the Midlands to publish a confession entitled "The Faith and Practice of Thirty Congregations," by which they intended to publicize Baptist views for the benefit of the Long Parliament, which was then revising the Anglican Thirty-nine Articles. In March, 1660, a second preliminary step to national organization was taken when, soon after the return of Charles II, a meeting was held in London "of certain Elders, Deacons, and Brethren, of a representative character" to agree upon and publish "A Brief Confession or Declaration of Faith" in twenty-five articles. Four months later a copy was presented by two messengers to the king. Three years thereafter, it was reviewed by another Assembly of their churches and ratified.

The third step was stimulated by the appearance in 1677 of a revision of the Westminster Confession of the Presbyterian Church, which was prepared by a Particular Baptist minister named Collins as an answer to the Arian teachings of Matthew Caffin, a General Baptist clergyman of the church at Horsham in Sussex. While Caffin's influence was felt primarily in his own county and Kent, the General Baptist churches in Hertfordshire, Bedfordshire, Buckingham, and Oxford sent their representatives, fifty-four in all, to a meeting in the same year where there was drafted what they chose to call "An Orthodox Creed." The moderately Calvinistic cast of this lengthy confession indicates a trend on the part of the more conservative General Baptists toward that theological point of view. In fact, four ministers, in the succeeding years, left the General Baptists to become Particular Baptists. They were Richard Allen (*circa* 1679), Benjamin Keach (1688), Mark Key and Shad Thames (1689).

Even in Kent where Caffin's influence for Arianism was strong, there were local ruptures over his teaching. It was not long before the entire General Baptist denomination was torn by the controversy.

While it is difficult to determine at what specific time General Baptists developed an organizational life along denominational lines, it is fairly safe to assume that such was the case at the time of these theological difficulties. Several meetings had been held prior to 1686. They were in the form of a General Assembly of messengers from local associations in Staffordshire, Lincolnshire, Northamptonshire, Leicestershire, Buckinghamshire of the Midlands, some in Essex and Kent in the southeast, as well as others from the west and north. After 1686, as it became increasingly safe for such gatherings, regular meetings were held. It was not long, however, before the General Assembly was faced with the knotty question of whether unity or orthodoxy was to be preferred. The majority favored the preservation of unity and sought to find it by taking refuge in the words of Scripture as a doctrinal basis. To this end they secured acceptance of the six principles which they believed were set forth in Hebrews 6:1-2, namely: repentance, faith, baptism, laying on of hands, resurrection of the dead, and eternal judgment. This creedal formula offered by the moderates, although in the direct words of Scripture, actually by-passed the issue by providing no statement on the particular point of controversy, the deity of Christ, which the unitarians among the General Baptists denied. Those who adopted this confession were frequently called "Six Principle" Baptists.

The conciliatory value of this confession was not widely recognized, however; for the churches in the Midlands, which had opposed Caffin's teachings consistently for twenty years, withdrew in 1696 from the General Assembly, which they accused of tolerating heresy. They formed a "General Association," of which the Whites-alley church in London was a member. It refused to countenance communion with heretics. Nevertheless the desire for denominational unity was strongly present and in 1704 a reunion was effected on the basis of a book and a new confession. The book was written by a member of the General Assembly and was entitled *A Vindication of the Ancient General Assembly*. The confession of six articles, which carefully set forth the deity of Christ, was drawn up and approved along with the sentiments of the book by both the General Assembly and the General Association. These became the basis for an agreement which every representative to the General Assembly was required to sign before he could sit as a member. This led to another rupture in the Assembly, when the friends of Caffin withdrew in 1708.

The Kent Association was typical of those Baptists who were not agreeable to a creedal test as a means of dealing with the problem of heresy. They preferred to adhere only to the Six Principles and the Declaration of 1660, upon which there was a possibility of unity, since neither statement dealt particularly with the Arian heresy. The General Assembly, meeting in 1709, refused to require signatures as in 1704; instead, it affirmed general agreement with the Six Principles and the Declaration of 1663. "Thus," as Whitley observes, "the question of freedom of conscience became entangled with the question of contending for the truth; and there was much bewilderment for awhile. Nearly half of the General Baptists refused to face the new question raised, and took their stand on the past." Having failed to face frankly a doctrinal issue, the influence of General Baptists declined. The General Assembly maintained a semblance of unity, but the orthodox men of the Midlands and Lincolnshire viewed it with misgivings. The attention of the General Assembly was fixed on the past and not on the needs of the present.[4] Moreover, the virility of its witness was lost to the extent to which its members were unable to agree on the doctrine of the person of Christ.

Among General Baptists there was a stricter control over the churches than among Particular Baptists. A reading of the proceedings of the General Assembly indicates the extent and variety of influence which that body exerted over churches and individuals alike. For example, a careful watch was kept over the young people. In order to maintain their identity and witness as Baptists, they required their young folks to be married within the Baptist communion on pain of suspension for violation of the rule. Thus the Associational and Assembly meetings "became great opportunities for matchmaking." Such practices as cock-fighting, dancing, and gambling were denounced by the General Assembly. Immorality and the slave trade were consistently looked upon as grievous sins. A Puritan standard of Christian conduct prevailed among Baptists generally and dis-

---

[4] *Minutes of the General Assembly of the General Baptist Churches in England . . .*, I, xxii-xxiii; for records of the "General Association" and the General Assembly sessions, see 43, 45-8, 87-90, 101-6; Whitley, *History of British Baptists*, 173-4.

cipline was strict.[5] In a very real sense, General Baptists had developed in their organizational life a denominational consciousness which was felt by all of its members. Indeed, it has been observed that their church order, to some degree, was more presbyterian than congregational in character.[6]

This was in contrast to the Particular Baptists who were reluctant to organize, fearing the loss of their local autonomy and freedom of conscience. However, they "were never independent in their attitude to other churches of similar outlook;"[7] they felt the need of closer association, particularly in the metropolitan areas. Thus they were led by the London churches to call a convention to create a loose type of union. "Invitations to the convention of 1689 were issued to churches which sympathized with the confession of 1677 [a Baptist revision of the Westminster Confession], which was reprinted for the purpose; and the convention 'owned' it, commending it to outsiders as a fair expression of their views. But no one proposed to erect it into a standard."[8] Their unwillingness to attribute final authority to a confessional statement is indicated further by the policy of many associations and local churches to formulate their own creedal expressions. For example, the Western Association issued another confession in 1691; moreover, Keach's church in London issued its own doctrinal statement in 1697, a practice which was common among local congregations. However, the Particular Baptists were definite about their theological position, whereas the General Baptists evaded basic issues by preferring to repeat the Confession of 1660 with slight revisions which often failed to cover new issues of controversy.[9] It is quite clear that Baptists did not object to writing and using creedal statements, but they did refrain from lifting them to the authoritarian standing of the Holy Scriptures for purposes of maintaining theological uniformity. They relied instead upon the Holy Spirit to guide willing readers of the Bible to a common understanding of divine truth.

[5] Whitley, *op. cit.*, 173; for practices mentioned, see index to *Minutes of General Assembly of General Baptists Churches . . .*; see also W. T. Whitley, ed., *The Church Books of Ford or Cuddington and Amersham in the County of Bucks.*

[6] Ashley J. Klaiber, *The Story of the Suffolk Baptists* (London, 1931), 108.

[7] *Ibid.*, 108.

[8] Whitley, *History of British Baptists*, 181; the parenthetical statement is inserted by the writer.

[9] Whitley, *History of British Baptists*, 181-2.

In 1689 a General Assembly of Particular Baptists was organized. This meeting, and those which followed periodically, possessed several distinctive characteristics. (1) Close membership was practiced; thus only churches of baptized believers were admitted. (2) Open communion was permitted, leaving each church to decide for itself whether visitors of non-Baptist fellowships should be allowed to partake of the Lord's Supper. (3) At its first session, the Assembly upheld the Lord's Day for worship in preference to the Seventh Day. (4) The Assembly aimed to have an educated as well as an ordained ministry. (This is noteworthy, for most Baptists were poor and uneducated. Hanserd Knollys, who had once been an Anglican clergyman, was the exception in academic preparation. A man like Benjamin Keach was a fair type of their leaders, one who was "earnest, self-educated, intensely evangelical and orthodox, [his] outlook narrowed to the denomination, and almost to the congregation," but wielding great influence within those limits.[10]) (5) Its growth was rapid, there being one hundred and seven churches in attendance at the General Assembly of 1692.[11] (6) In later years hyper-Calvinism caused some trouble, particularly in the London Association where Dr. John Gill was its ablest exponent through his treatise, *The Body of Divinity,* published in 1769. In time the Association condemned this Antinomian perversion of Calvinistic doctrine.

After 1692 the General Assembly met annually in two regional meetings: one in the west at Bristol during the Easter season; the other in the east at London at Whitsuntide. To maintain a sense of unity each meeting sent two messengers to the other. The assembly and associational meetings among Particular Baptists were congregational in type, with a minimum of centralization.

The Prelude to Revival

From the enactment of toleration until after the middle of the eighteenth century, English Baptists were more devoted to consolidation and organization than to evangelism. The struggle for complete religious liberty was as yet unfinished. Theological tensions, which had occupied so much attention following the Protestant

[10] *Ibid.,* 177-8.
[11] Thomas Crosby, *The History of the English Baptists,* III, 271.

Reformation, undoubtedly were reflected in the preoccupation with doctrine on the part of both General and Particular Baptists. In addition, the churches failed to adapt themselves to the new demands of a country undergoing an industrial revolution which was producing population shifts that offered new opportunities for successful evangelism.

Within their own ranks there was not a united witness. The General Baptists, as we have seen, found difficulty in preventing loss of numbers due to the aggressive teaching of Calvinistic Baptist ministers. In 1700 the General Association, which had been organized in 1696 to combat the Unitarian heresy in the General Assembly, voted to silence such Calvinists as might seek to disturb the peace of congregations by propagandizing. In that year Joseph Stennett, minister of the church at Paul's-alley, London, was dismissed for preaching such doctrines and encouraging schism in the church in White's-alley.[12] Thereafter, Stennett became prominent among Particular Baptists.

In the early years of the century, Baptists were still preoccupied with the winning of religious liberty. Joseph Stennett and John Piggott, both General Baptists (although Stennett became a Particular Baptist in 1700), had been the foremost ministers representing Baptist views before the government in the late 1600's. They served as members of the Committee of the Three Denominations of Protestant Dissenting Ministers. This was a joint agency of Presbyterians, Independents, and Baptists, both General and Particular. On the accession to the throne of George I, following the death of Queen Anne, the Committee prepared an address of congratulation to the monarch, which set forth an expression of loyalty to the throne and also to the principles for which they stood, especially religious liberty. This Committee gave rise in later years to the Deputies for Defending the Civil Rights of Dissenters.[18]

Another interest occupying the attention of Baptists was the problem of maintaining a ministerial leadership. The Particular Baptists were the first to take action respecting it. In June, 1717, they

[12] *Minutes of the General Assembly of General Baptists,* I, 65 (provides records of the General Association organized in 1696, meeting in White's-alley church in London); Taylor, *History of English General Baptists,* I, 331-2.

[18] Joseph Ivimey, *History of English Baptists,* III, 24-5, 110-5, 198.

established the "London Fund" to assist needy ministers and to educate young men for the ministry. Benjamin Stinton, son-in-law of
Benjamin Keach and Keach's successor in the pastorate of the Horsley Down church in Southwark near London, argued against restricting it to the Particular Baptists. He felt that such a course would
cause confusion since many Baptists did not go under either name.
Although his view did not prevail, he became a member of the Society.
By August, the sum of eight hundred and seventy-four pounds was in
hand. Thomas Hollis, a wealthy merchant, was a manager and generous contributor; upon his death, he left a legacy of eleven hundred
pounds. His father and a brother also gave assistance. In the first
year four hundred and nineteen pounds were distributed. This sum
provided financial assistance to ninety ministers in England and ten
in Wales. Several students were given grants to attend Bristol Academy, which, since 1679, had been the principal training school of
Baptists. Out of this Society, the London Education Society was to
be formed in 1752. In July, 1725, a General Baptist Fund was instituted, which distributed annually about two hundred pounds.[14]

The role which the clergymen played in the churches is illustrated
by a review of the functions of the Society of Ministers of the Baptist
Particular Persuasion, organized on January 20, 1724, at the Glouces-
tershire Coffee-house in London. The twelve members met regularly,
gave advice to churches in difficulties, received applications from
rural ministers who desired assistance from the Baptist Fund, sanc-
tioned and recommended the repair of rural meeting-houses, funds
for which were to be collected in London, watched over the purity
and orthodoxy of each other, received new ministers, supplied destitute churches, and preached at ordinations.[15] It appears that this
Society performed many of the functions now delegated to a state
convention secretary. In the metropolis it was the only point of contact between the churches, for associational life had not developed
there as early as in the provinces.[16] Apparently the need for fellowship was not felt as strongly in the city as in the county areas.

The number of Baptists in the country at the mid-century was
not indicative of marked growth. John Collett Ryland, youthful pastor

[14] *Ibid.*, III, 150-9, 183-4, 208.

[15] Ivimey, *History of English Baptists,* III, 179.

[16] Whitley, *The Baptists of London,* 59.

at Warwick in the Midlands, in 1753 gathered statistics for the Particular Baptists. He estimated there were nearly five thousand members in one hundred and twenty-one churches; nine in London, twenty-four east and south of London, eighteen in the west, twenty in South Wales, and fifty in northern England. The average number of members per church was forty. Ivimey, who wrote in 1823, calculated that even if one allowed one-third deficiency in the numbers given and two-thirds more for hearers who were not members, there could not have been twenty thousand persons attending the Particular Baptist churches in England and Wales. He went on to observe that the General Baptists at that time "were but few in number, and their congregations small and languishing," and that, "there is no reason to doubt that our churches [i.e., Particular Baptist] were far more prosperous and numerous at the Revolution in 1688, than at this period, sixty-five years afterwards; so that prosperity had indeed slain more than the sword."[17]

It is noteworthy that the first half of the eighteenth century had been devoted more to consolidation and organization than to evangelism.[18] This was typical of English dissenters generally. Their preoccupation with theological problems, chiefly Christological and ethical, together with the development of a censorious spirit, did not produce a warm evangelistic ministry. The spiritual awakening so desperately needed by the country came, not from dissenters, but from Anglicans like Whitefield and the Wesleys, beginning about 1738.

General Baptists, those most likely to benefit from the inspiration of John Wesley's evangelistic zeal owing to the common theological point of view, were barely affected by the revival. Moreover, the influence of the Countess of Huntingdon, an ardent promoter of the Wesleyan movement in Leicestershire, did not arouse the rather large group of Baptists in that county. Their organization was kept intact, to be sure, but the earlier practice of sending forth paid itinerant evangelists had been virtually abandoned. Local ministers were sometimes selected for evangelistic work without being relieved of local

[17] Ivimey, *op. cit.*, III, 279; cf. Whitley, *History of British Baptists,* 224, who estimates that there were 5,410 Particular Baptists, 104 pastors, and 65 General Baptist pastors, with a total of about 10,000 members of Baptist churches generally, exclusive of hearers.

[18] For the analysis that follows, the writer is indebted mainly to Whitley, *History of British Baptists,* 211-7; A. C. Underwood, *A History of the English Baptists* (London, 1947), 116-48.

duties. In general, "they raised up no evangelist, and they discouraged those who offered."[19] Since most of the ministers were farmers, as the spiritual glow dimmed, less and less time was devoted to the churches, which were shrinking in size. Accordingly a spiritual decline in numbers and influence took hold of General Baptists, a condition which may be attributed to several factors. First, old methods of conducting associational and assembly meetings were being retained. These meetings consisted of a rather set pattern: the reading of a paper with discussion and the conducting of matters of business without much opportunity for inspiration. Hymn singing was frowned upon as a worldly innovation; long sessions were devoted at times to debates on doctrine or discipline; in general, the gatherings lacked warmth and enthusiasm. Second, the spread of Arian teaching robbed the churches of theological vigor. Third, they had ceased to be evangelistic, thereby becoming ingrown and sterile.

Particular Baptists likewise manifested a religious decline, but for different reasons. In the first place, they gave more attention to consolidation and organization than to a forward looking outreach and expansion. It was for them an era of church building. In London so many schemes were being promoted that pastors and laymen alike grew weary of the continuous begging for money, a task which fell to the ministers when funds were to be raised. The erection of city churches was costly in other respects than money, for a loss of members often resulted from the circumscribing of the minister's duties to the locality where the church edifice was situated. As his duties became concentrated upon a limited parish surrounding the new edifice, the parishioners on the outskirts of the city were left without pastoral care and found it difficult to attend preaching services because of the distance. Pastors ceased to be "circuit-riders" who ministered to many outlying communities. In the second place, an abstractly doctrinal type of preaching did not inspire a vibrant sense of responsibility to witness to others. This was especially true of the hyper-Calvinists, who represented an antimissionary force in the ranks and were a source of theological conflict. In the third place, a censorious spirit arose to plague the brethren in the persons of self-appointed critics who appeared on the scene. An extreme example of this tendency is to be found in Anne Dutton of Northampton, who

[19] *Ibid.*, 216.

was, while in London after her marriage, very vocal as a member of Curriers' Hall church early in the century. During her ten years in the city, her husband died and she eventually married a man who in 1732 became pastor of the Great Gransden church in Wellingborough, Northamptonshire. There, with her own funds, she erected a meeting-house for the congregation and "aspired to be the Countess of Huntingdon of the denomination." For a period of thirty years she wrote pamphlets in which she set forth her spiritual biography, presumably as an example to others, while also criticising the teachings of such evangelists as Wesley and Whitefield.[20]

The influence of Wesley was not at once felt among the Particular Baptists, largely because his Arminian views were not acceptable to their ministers. For example, Dr. Gill, of London, the leading hyper-Calvinist among them, was a vigorous opponent of Wesley's tenets.[21] Yet Whitefield, though a Calvinist, was no more agreeable to many because of his evangelistic zeal. Truly, a theological hypnotism had dulled that sense of responsibility to witness which had been typical of earlier Baptists.

Signs of Revival

The second half of the eighteenth century was marked among Baptists by an awakening to new zeal and missionary activity. In a large measure this was due to the influence of the Wesleyan movement. It is possible to trace a direct influence of Wesley's preachers upon General Baptists. In November, 1755, out of a group of Methodists in Leicestershire, who were witnessing at Barton-in-the-Beans in spite of constant persecution by the populace, nearly seventy persons adopted believer's baptism under the leadership of Joseph Donisthorpe and William Kendrick. Donisthorpe baptized Kendrick, who then baptized him; then together they baptized the rest. By 1760 five Baptist churches had been formed at Barton, Melbourn, Kegworth, Loughborough, and Kirby-Woodhouse. Ten years later there were nearly nine hundred and fifty members in six churches with ten ordained pastors serving in the four counties of Leicester, Warwick, Derby, and Nottingham.[22]

[20] Whitley, *History of British Baptists*, 214-5.
[21] Ivimey, *History of English Baptists*, III, 290.
[22] Adam Taylor, *A History of the English General Baptists*, 2 volumes (London, 1818), II, 55. Based on periodical literature and association records.

These Baptists in the Midlands were characterized by zeal for evangelism and by attention to the building of church edifices for the growing congregations. Their preachers were laboring men with families to support. As an example of their zeal, Samuel Deacon, the pastor at Barton-in-the-Beans, frequently traveled from twenty to forty miles on foot each Lord's Day to preach two or three times. Regardless of the text chosen, the sermons dealt chiefly with the themes of sin and of salvation through faith in Christ. In many respects these preachers imitated the Methodists, for they required a probation period of six months for new members, furnished members in good standing with a ticket every six months, and collected a monthly subscription to the church treasury. Weekly meetings were held for prayer and exhortation.[23]

Farther north in the vicinity of Halifax in the West Riding district of Yorkshire, five Methodist converts, Dan Taylor, John Slater, John Parker, William Crossley, and a woman whose name is unknown, became Baptists as the result of their study of the Scriptures. When they requested administration of the ordinance at the hands of the Particular Baptists in their vicinity, they were refused because of their views on the unlimited extent of the atonement. The Particular Baptist clergymen referred them to a General Baptist minister at Gamston, who baptized them in 1763. Taylor then joined the Lincolnshire Association, with which Gamston was connected; it being the nearest General Baptist fellowship. After Taylor's ordination in the autumn of 1763, he organized the first General Baptist church in Yorkshire at Wadsworth. This congregation soon erected a meeting-house on a steep proclivity of rock, from which it was named "Birchcliff." It adopted the practice of holding experience meetings, a practice soon copied by other General Baptist churches throughout Yorkshire, thus indicating the influence of Methodism upon them. By 1770, the membership of the Birchcliff church numbered sixty-nine.[24]

Taylor found the Lincolnshire Association cold and spiritually apostate.[25] As early as the 1730's, doctrinal disputes had troubled its

[23] *Ibid.*, 65-8.
[24] *Ibid.*, 77, 79.
[25] The following account of the formation of the New Connection is based largely on Taylor, *op. cit.*, 108-218.

fellowship. Just prior to 1770, two unsuccessful attempts had been made by the more orthodox to establish some standard of faith. The older members either denied the old doctrines or explained them in a manner which seemed, to Dan Taylor and his friend, William Thompson, pastor at Boston in the Association, to detract from their dignity. Here was an instance in which the older communicants were departing from the traditional interpretation of the faith, although they maintained strict standards of life and a strong insistence upon a regularly called ministry. It was largely the younger group, whose conversion had been a product of the revival led by Taylor and his friends, which supported orthodoxy. Within the Association the decline in spiritual life did not attract replacements to the ministry. Hence, as the older clergymen died, some of the churches became extinct. In 1766 the meeting-house at Lincoln, which had been the leading center of General Baptists for seventy years, was turned over to the Particular Baptists upon their agreement to keep it in repair.

As a means of reviving the Association, Taylor tried to get the conservative Baptists of Leicestershire to join the Lincolnshire Association, a proposal which was turned down because of heresy in that body. In 1769 tensions ran so high in the Association and in the General Assembly that many decided to withdraw. Taylor's great zeal and driving force had brought the leaders of Leicester under his spell. Accordingly, he and Thompson, with Francis Smith of Melbourn, Grimley of Loughborough, and several other ministers, met with a delegation of Leicestershire churches at Lincoln at Michaelmas, 1769. It was decided to hold the first association of the orthodox churches at London in June, 1770. Several ministers and their churches in the Lincolnshire Association did not participate in the schism, although they agreed doctrinally with the seceders, for they feared the consequences of division. The desire to maintain organizational unity at all costs was strong among General Baptists.

The organizational meeting of the seceders was held at the meeting-house in Church Lane, Whitechapel, London, on June 6, 1770. It was attended by eight ministers of the midland counties and by ten from the counties where General Baptists were prominent, including London. Their first act was to send a deputation to the General Assembly which was meeting in the city at the same time. Having thus expressed their farewells, they settled down to establishing what they called "The New Connection of General Baptists formed in 1770; with a design to revive Experimental Religion or Primitive Christianity in Faith and Practice." Usually they were styled "Free-Grace" or "New Connection" General Baptists, in order to differentiate them from the Old Connection churches. At their initial meeting they adopted a confessional statement of six articles, the signing of which became a prerequisite for ministers in its membership. In addition, each clergyman was required to give an account of his religious experience at the next assembly meeting so that all might be satisfied as to the reality of his conversion. The only church in Lincolnshire which permanently united in this organization at this meeting was Thompson's at Boston.

At the second meeting, May 22-24, 1771, also held at London, four other churches of Lincolnshire were added to the "New Connection." Some efforts were made to effect a union with the old group, but without success, for the Lincolnshire churches could not subscribe fully to the creedal statement. The "New Connection" was divided into two associations: the northern, composed of churches in the Midlands, Yorkshire, and Lincolnshire; the southern, composed of churches in London, Kent, Essex, and Surrey. The two associations exchanged representatives.

It is significant that in 1775 the creedal test for membership was removed; the statement of experience, however, was still required. In 1777 a plan was adopted for the reception of new member churches. This plan required each applicant church to submit to all member churches in the "New Connection" fellowship a statement of its religious sentiments, its thoughts on who were worthy of baptism and church fellowship, plus a statement from the minister concerning his spiritual experience. If the churches then voted that they could hold communion with such a people as a church of Christ, the applicant church was admitted. Between 1777 and 1785 the dwindling Lincolnshire Association sought reunion, but it was unwilling to give up its membership in the General Assembly and to forsake such practices as laying on of hands, abstaining from the eating of blood, and the prohibition upon the singing of hymns.

The "New Connection" maintained friendly relations with other groups of Baptists, but without a full realization of how to make its influence felt to the greatest extent. For example, it entered into union with the General Assembly of old General Baptists in 1786, preferring to be known simply as the Leicester Association. It sent to meetings of the Assembly only one or two messengers, instead of the fifty to which it was entitled. This type of relationship continued for about seventeen years. A more significant influence might have been exerted had the "New Connection" sent its full quota of representatives and urged that some meetings of the Assembly be held in Leicestershire.[26]

Upon the cessation of Taylor's personal leadership in 1786 when he removed to London, the northern districts began to lose ground. Progress, however, was maintained in the Midland counties and Lincolnshire. In 1793 it was widely decided that the annual meetings should rotate over a period of eight years among six counties and London. Thus the metropolis did not come to dominate it as it had the old General Assembly. Two years later a change occurred in the nature of the "New Connection." Prior to that time it had been considered a conference of all the officers of the churches; now it was restricted to delegates elected specifically to represent the congregations at the meetings. The next year, plans were begun to find a method of training young men for the ministry. By 1797 a fund for that purpose was created; and in January of the following year, an academy was opened at Mile End, near London, under the superintendence of Dan Taylor. About the same time, Taylor began to edit a monthly periodical called, *The General Baptist Magazine*. In December, 1800, when the third volume had been completed, the effort was discontinued for want of funds.[27] The "New Connection" was particularly well adapted to function in an era of change marked by industrialization and urban development, for it was not handicapped by old traditions and a lack of zeal.

The Wesleyan movement also had a salutary effect upon Particular Baptists. It resulted in a revived associational life among them, which was accompanied by a modification in doctrinal emphasis. For example, by 1770 the spiritual declension which had characterized Baptist churches in the north of England in the counties of Northumberland, Durham, Cumberland, and Lancashire, was replaced by a general condition of revival. This was largely the work of Charles

---

[26] Whitley, *History of British Baptists*, 221.

[27] Paragraph is based on Taylor, *History of the English General Baptists*, II, 328-33.

Whitfield, pastor at Hamsterley in his native Durham. This Whitfield (who is not to be confused with George Whitefield, the evangelist) had been born in 1748 and converted to Methodism as a lad at Newcastle in Northumberland, where he was serving an apprenticeship. By 1770 his views had undergone a transition from Arminian Methodism to a moderately Calvinistic Baptist position. He united with the Baptist church at Tuthill-stairs, and in June of 1771 he began a pastorate of fifty years at Hamsterley. The low incomes of Baptist ministers is illustrated by the fact that at the close of fifteen years of service there, his salary was still so small that he was obliged to supplement it by teaching school. Yet his influence among Baptists was wide throughout the Northern Association, in London, and over the country generally. He was active in the home and foreign mission undertakings that began to occupy the attention of Particular Baptists near the close of the century.[28]

A similar story might be told concerning the Yorkshire and Lancashire Association of seventeen Baptist churches, organized under the leadership of John Fawcett in 1787 for the purpose of reviving associational life in that area. Essentially, it was the product of a vigorous spiritual life which permeated the whole district through the influence of George Whitefield and John Wesley. A second factor in the growth of the churches was the movement of workmen into the area as a result of the development of the textile industry due to new inventions in spinning and weaving machinery which utilized water power and, later, steam. Fawcett saw the opportunity for evangelism and worked for a strong associational life which would strengthen the churches.[29]

In London a new era for Particular Baptists opened in 1770. They had just been reinforced by Abraham Booth, a moderate Calvinist who had been converted from the teachings of the General Baptists; by John Rippon from the west, who succeeded Dr. Gill at Goat Street church; and by John MacGowan at Devonshire Square church —all energetically evangelistic. Down to 1796, one new church was founded every two years, all of them in the newer districts of the city. The older churches in the downtown area were hyper-Calvinistic

[28] David Douglas, *History of the Baptist Churches in the North of England* (London, 1846), 199-267.

[29] C. E. Shipley, ed., *Baptists in Yorkshire, Lancashire, Cheshire, and Cumberland* (London, 1912, 2nd edition), 273-6; Whitley, *History of British Baptists*, 227.

with no challenging appeal. Between the churches in the metropolis there was little fellowship, possibly because of theological friction and the absence of that sense of needing one another's help felt by churches in the country areas.

The cause of ministerial education also received impetus from the revived enthusiasm of the Particular Baptists. The Bristol Education Society was founded in 1770 to aid the Baptist Academy in Bristol. It was the result of fifty years of planning which had gone on ever since a writing-master of that city, Edward Terrill, had left funds to assist students for the ministry. On the whole, however, educational progress among Baptists was slow, owing to a generally low level of cultural appreciation among them. The general pattern of schools was of a private type, owned and conducted by ministers. The Bristol Academy did not reach college status; it remained a training school for ministerial recruits. The great impetus to Baptist education was to come in the nineteenth century.

It was not until 1781, sixteen years after American Baptists had established Rhode Island College, that plans for a Baptist college in England were formulated by Robert Robinson, a clergyman at Cambridge. His purpose was to provide college training for the sons of gentlemen who did not wish their sons to become Anglicans, as happened all too frequently when young men were sent to the universities. A change in Robinson's theological views, which caused him to depart ultimately from the traditional Calvinistic position, may have hindered the actualization of his plans. His criticism of the practice then in vogue of restricting the use of the Education Fund to Particular Baptists likely was prompted by the difficulties encountered when hyper-Calvinists and more moderate Calvinists tried to agree as to who was a deserving recipient of the aid available.[30]

It was becoming increasingly obvious that Calvinistic Baptists were undergoing some doctrinal modification. The hyper-Calvinists of Yorkshire, Wales, and London were being replaced in leadership by the more aggressive moderates who were imbued with evangelistic purpose. Influences contributing to this change were the Wesleyan movement and the "New Connection" movement among General Baptists. The change was notably evident in the Northamptonshire Association, and in the Midlands generally, where the influence of Andrew

[30] Ivimey, *A History of the English Baptists*, IV, 46-8, 50-3.

Fuller, an able exponent of moderate Calvinism, was felt widely. He was the pastor of the Baptist church at Kettering in Northamptonshire from 1782 to 1815. As a scholarly man of deep devotion and marked literary gifts, he was well fitted to restate Calvin's teaching in terms of the individual's responsibility to witness to the gospel. Indeed, his missionary zeal and sound judgment constituted the chief cause for the awakening of Baptist missionary impulse among Particular Baptists. To him also belongs the credit for doing much to break down the antimissionary spirit of hyper-Calvinists. It was he who gave William Carey, the youthful prophet of missions, encouragement and recognition of his talents. While others were staying away from Carey's preaching because they thought they sensed Arminianism in his message, Fuller was moved by deep emotion and gave to the young man the support that paved the way for the establishing of the first Baptist foreign missionary society.

The Awakening of Missionary Interest

William Carey (1761-1834) was the heart and soul of the initial missionary enterprise of the Baptists. It might not be too much to say that, in the early days, he was the movement. In many respects he was a child of his age, influenced by the momentous trends of the Era of Romanticism in which he lived. Politically, he was a republican who suffered no disillusionment when the French Revolution spent itself in an orgy of terror and bloodshed. He was an abolitionist and an ardent defender of human rights in all respects. As a pastor in Leicestershire, he actively aided the dissenters in their fight against the Test and Corporation Acts. Religiously, he was influenced greatly by William Law's book, *The Serious Call.* He avoided, however, the extremes of pietism, resolving always to go into a deeper study of the Bible, relying more upon the written revelation than upon mystical intuitions to guide him. He was fortunately located in the Northamptonshire Association in which were such unusual leaders as the elder Hall, the Rylands, Sutcliff, and Andrew Fuller. Here also the rigid Calvinism of Particular Baptists was yielding to moderation. The influence of Wesley's evangelistic zeal was not a little responsible for this change.

At the early age of seventeen, Carey, who had been brought up in an Anglican home, was introduced to the prayer meeting and preaching services of nonconformists by John Warr, a shoemaker's apprentice. Carey himself was a journeyman cobbler at Piddington. Soon after his conversion he became a lay preacher. Upon hearing in his twenty-first or twenty-second year a sermon in defense of infant baptism, he undertook a study of the point in the Scriptures. The result was a decision to be baptized as a believer. This was done on October 5, 1783, in the River Nen by Dr. John Ryland, pastor of the Baptist church at Northampton. Later, Carey moved to Moulton where he opened a school and became pastor of the Baptist church there. In August, 1787, he was ordained by Sutcliff's church at Olney, with Ryland and Fuller participating in the service.

During his pastorate, he followed a rigid system of study, working in the classics on Mondays; in science, history, and composition on Tuesdays; in the Hebrew Bible and Greek New Testament on other days in preparation for midweek and Sunday expositions. Thus he laid the foundation for his great missionary work. As a cobbler of shoes and as a preacher of the gospel, there burned within him with ever-increasing intensity the flame of evangelism. He saw in the Great Commission a challenge to win the heathen to Christ. With a growing boldness, he overcame his natural shyness and pleaded with his fellow ministers to support a foreign mission enterprise.

In 1791, at the Easter gathering of the Northampton Association meeting at Clipstone, the missionary challenge was presented to English Baptists through sermons preached by Sutcliff, Fuller, and Carey, the latter pleading for action without delay. But those in attendance only advised the speedy publication of a pamphlet on missions which Carey then had in preparation. They desired that the response of the churches should be gauged before any action was proposed. A month later, at Carey's induction to the pastorate of the Leicester church, he read that portion of his study which he had completed by that date, entitled *The Enquiry into the Obligations of Christians to Use Means for the Conversion of the Heathen.* He called attention to the tragic fact that of the world's population of seven hundred and thirty-one millions, more than a fifth were Moslem, and more than half were of other pagan religions, making a total of seven-tenths without any profession of Christianity. "If baptism concerns us," he pleaded, "world missions must no less"—else why baptize? The program which he presented was straightforward and simple: pray, plan, pay.

Then came what has been called the "Deathless Sermon," preached by Carey at the Association Meeting held at Nottingham on May 30, 1792. The text was Isaiah 54:2-3; the theme was "Expect great things from God; attempt great things for God." As he preached on that Wednesday morning, a profound impression was made upon his hearers. But at the business session the next day, when a plan of action was proposed, many cautioned delay. Finally, Carey turned to Fuller, who was sitting beside him, and gripping his arm, cried, "Is there nothing again going to be done, sir?" The urgency of his words won Andrew Fuller to speak for his cause, and Fuller's prestige in turn won others whom "the hare-brained enthusiast," as Carey was called, could not win. Before the meeting adjourned at noon, a resolution presented by Fuller was adopted, which read as follows: "Resolved, that a plan be prepared against the next Ministers' Meeting at Kettering, for forming a Baptist Society for propagating the Gospel among the Heathens." Thus, upon the initiative of those two men the whole missionary movement had hung that day as by a thread. Had Fuller not acted at that moment in response to the plea of Carey, the missionary cause might have been delayed a hundred years. As it was, the fledgling movement was to become a significant part of a rapidly changing world.

On October 2, 1792, at the Ministers' Meeting held in a widow's home at Kettering, Carey challenged the fourteen men[31] present to "see what Moravians are daring, and some of them British like ourselves, and many only artisans and poor! Can't we Baptists at least attempt *something* in fealty to the same Lord?" The challenge was accepted and a resolution passed which brought into being the long awaited missionary society:

Humbly desirous of making an effort for the propagation of the Gospel amongst the Heathen, according to the recommendations of Carey's *Enquiry,* we unanimously resolve to act in Society together for this purpose; and, as in the divided state of Christendom each denomination, by exerting itself separately, seems likeliest to accomplish the great end, we name this the Particular Baptist Society for the Propagation of the Gospel amongst the Heathen.[32]

The ministers present then pledged from their own pockets the sum of thirteen pounds, two shillings, six pence, plus one pound

[31] S. Pearce Carey, *William Carey* (Philadelphia, 1923), 90. Several were young men; Fuller was 38 years of age; Pearce, 26; Ryland, 39; and Sutcliff, 40.

[32] *Ibid.,* 91.

proceeds which had come in that day from the sale of Carey's *Enquiry* in Kettering. The money was placed in a snuffbox, which thereupon became the first depository of missionary funds of the newly organized society. At a later meeting, Andrew Fuller was elected secretary, and Reynold Hogg of Thrapstone, who was absent from the initial meeting, was made treasurer.

At the fourth meeting of the Society, held on January 9, 1793, Carey presented John Thomas, a British surgeon who had served in Bengal and who desired to return as their representative. In spite of his own eagerness to be the Society's first missionary, Carey recommended that Thomas be the first appointee because of his value as an experienced doctor. When Thomas addressed the members present, he told them that it was possible for a missionary to support himself to a large extent. This aroused Carey's hopes at once, whereupon he volunteered to go with Thomas on that basis. The two men, filled with emotion, embraced and from that moment were one in the cause of foreign missions.

The Society's cause was promoted effectively in different parts of the kingdom as Pearce and Fuller preached eloquently and procured funds for its support. So marked was the interest in behalf of missions that three societies for developing itinerant and village preaching in untouched areas of Britain were organized, one at Braintree in Essex in 1796, a second at London in 1797, and a third at Hamsterley in Durham known as the "Northern Evangelical Society." The London Society sent preachers to Cornwall, northern Somerset, Devon, and Shropshire in southwestern England, with scarcely any opposition from antimission forces. Beneficial effects were felt almost at once in the Baptist churches, for in a span of five years revivals tripled the membership of some congregations. Meeting-houses were enlarged and new ones erected.[33] Without doubt, a new era of Baptist progress was dawning. Within a comparatively brief period, as we shall see in the next chapter, home mission societies, Sunday school work, Bible publication, new schools, as well as foreign missions, were claiming the enthusiastic attention of Baptists who not long before had been quite indifferent to the spread of their witness.

[33] Ivimey, *A History of the English Baptists*, IV, 68-75; Douglas, *History of the Baptist Churches in the North of England*, 241.

CHAPTER FOUR

DENOMINATIONAL EXPANSION

FOR England, the nineteenth century opened with a titanic struggle for survival against the aggressive ambitions of Napoleon, who dreamed of world conquest in the tradition of all dictators. However, when the Congress of Vienna had met in 1815 to settle a questionable peace of Europe, Britain returned to her customary policy of virtual isolation from continental politics. Thus, her people had time which they could devote to the pursuits of industry, culture, and religion. In general, it was a century of progress and relative peace, interrupted only intermittently by the rumblings of economic strife and political discontent at home and throughout the far-flung Empire. Romance and realism commingled in British life, and under Queen Victoria it wove a strange pattern of imperialism and reform idealism. To many, England and her queen personified bourgeois respectability and conservative Christian standards. It was a Protestant England in which dissenters were attaining an increasing freedom of expression. Indeed, it was a missionary-minded England which carried to the ends of the seven seas English culture and the Christian gospel.

In such a setting, the Baptists quite naturally found greater opportunity than in any previous era of their history. The Carey Missionary Movement was continued with enthusiasm. Through the influence of the New Connection movement among General Baptists, there eventually emerged an evangelical Baptist doctrine which was moderately Calvinistic, thereby making possible the union of General and Particular Baptists before the close of the century. In the social reforms of the times, Baptists played a role which did them credit. It was likewise an era of outstanding pulpiteers and unprecedented growth in numbers.

From the vantage point of the present, it is possible to see developing in the nineteenth century a denominational life whose roots lay in the earlier period. During the eighteenth century Baptists had been creating a sort of co-operative life, in spite of the fact that at the time, the various experiments were all too frequently unrelated to one another. Several societies which provided financial assistance to ministers and churches, education societies which established schools, and missionary agencies had come to life among both Particular and General Baptists. Fraternal relations between the churches in the form of associations and conferences of ministers and laymen continued to provide the people with valuable experience in working together, so necessary to the larger work of the nineteenth century. Indeed, their church life provided also a training school for the democratic processes which were coming gradually within the reach of the common man.

Although the headquarters of most of the societies were to be found in London, it is not to be supposed that the metropolis afforded the chief impetus for co-operative church life.[1] On the contrary there was less co-operative activity among the London Baptists than among the Baptists in the provinces. The greatest stimulus and support to a denominational life came from the midlands and the northern counties where the Methodist evangelical revival was arousing Baptists to face the challenge of the increased population which had been attracted to those areas by the growth of the textile industries during the industrial revolution.[2]

The closing years of the eighteenth century, it will be recalled, had witnessed the rise in Northamptonshire of a foreign missionary enterprise, to which moderate Particular Baptists responded. It was not long before the enthusiasm reacted favorably upon General Baptists as well. A complementary feature of the evangelistic zeal was the emergence of home missionary agencies, sponsored chiefly by the associations and local churches. These agencies undertook work in areas hitherto untouched by the Baptists. A combination of these interests —the foreign missionary interest and the home missionary interest— provided the basis for the denominational expansion that culminated in the union of Particular and New Connection General Baptists in 1891. Indeed, it was the missionary concern which was destined to triumph over differences in doctrine and polity in the interest of a closer co-operative life among British Baptists.

[1] W. T. Whitley, *The Baptists of London* (London, 1928), 38-40, 45-60.

[2] C. E. Shipley, *Baptists in Yorkshire, Lancashire, Cheshire, and Cumberland*, chap. 11.

The Expansion at Home

Baptists met the criticism "that there were plenty of heathen to be converted at home"—a criticism which was leveled frequently against the Baptist Missionary Society, which had begun its foreign work in 1793—by undertaking a variety of home missionary methods. The initial type of home mission work took the form of itinerant preaching tours conducted by individual ministers in the northern counties. For example, William Steadman, who later became the first president of the Northern Education Society (now Rawdon College), and the students at Bristol Academy engaged in several such tours. Out of the inspiration of such itinerancy, the Particular Baptists developed a second method which was embodied in the creation in London in 1797 of the Society for the Encouragement and Support of Itinerant Preaching, a name which was later changed to the Home Mission Society. By 1835 it was employing one hundred full-time missionaries. In 1879 this agency's work was taken over by the Baptist Union of Great Britain and Ireland, which had been established in 1813 to promote home missions.

In northwest England, a region which affords an illustration of the spontaneous rise of the society type of work, such able ministers as Steadman, John Fawcett, and Robert Hall gave leadership to the organization in 1809 of a Northern Itinerant Society to match the home missionary endeavors of the Methodists and New Connection Baptists. By 1810 the New Connection Association of General Baptists initiated in London an "Itinerant Fund" to send ministers to needy fields where older General Baptist churches had fallen into decay, particularly in Lincolnshire.[3]

It appears, however, that the larger work was accomplished by the Particular Baptists' Itinerant Society, which was undertaking to awaken the churches of Yorkshire, especially at Sheffield, Liverpool, Burslem, and York, and to establish new ones.[4] So many preachers were registering under the provision of the Act of Toleration that Lord Sidmouth sought to limit the privilege of registration on the pretext that the militia was being depleted on account of the growing

[3] H. Wheeler Robinson, *The Life and Faith of the Baptists* (London, 1946), 121; Adam Taylor, *History of the English General Baptists* (London, 1818), II, 457-8.

[4] The following account is based on Shipley, *Baptists in Yorkshire, Lancashire, Cheshire, and Cumberland*, Part II, chapters 16-24.

number of men gaining exemption from military service as clergy-men. At London in 1811, Baptists rallied in a successful effort to defeat Lord Sidmouth's attempt. In the meantime, the pace of missionary work in northwest England was too fast for some churches of the hyper-Calvinist type. They were not given to an aggressively evangelistic ministry, but depended rather upon the frequent help of visiting preachers. When continuance of this aid was denied to them by the moderates, they withdrew in 1835. By 1838 the Yorkshire Association, which was composed of sixty-six churches and nearly six thousand members, felt that it had become too unwieldly for effective service, and so divided into the Lancashire and Cheshire Association and the Yorkshire Association, the latter carrying the original name. By 1851 fifteen new churches had been added to the Lancashire and Cheshire Association by reason of the home mission enterprise. It is significant that this Association, being close to Scotland, cultivated friendly relations with the Baptist Union of Scotland, which had been organized in 1844. During the fifties, some churches left the Association as a protest against a modification of Calvinism which they saw in their sister churches; these represented the more reactionary element among Particular Baptists.

From 1860 to 1876 half of Lancashire suffered from a cotton famine caused by the American Civil War (1861-1865). That war had cut off the supply of raw cotton; but in spite of their economic plight, Baptist mill workers favored the abolition cause and new churches sprang into existence. This growth was accompanied by the rise of new organizations, although some new churches kept aloof from associational connections. The East Lancashire Union was organized in 1863; Manchester College was established in 1872 for the primary purpose of training ministers; and the Cheshire Union was formed in 1880. It is evident, therefore, both from these activities and from the associational statistics, that Particular Baptists were growing in numbers and influence.

The New Connection Baptists made little progress in the northern hill country, which was strongly Calvinistic. In the midland plains, however, they were strong. Unlike the Particular Baptists, the New Connection Baptists, following the Methodist pattern, had but one Association, which was national rather than local. It was composed of district conferences which met quarterly or semiannually as subordinate divisions. The central body was evangelical; but although it had broken with the General Assembly of General Baptists over unitarianism in 1803, it was not so exclusive as were the Particular Baptists. Just as the evangelistic note which Andrew Fuller had put in his Calvinism had done much to break down the exclusiveness of the Particular Baptists, so the rise in the eighties of Dr. John Clifford, a strongly evangelical General Baptist, became a factor favorable to a union of General and Particular Baptists. Accordingly, the Lancashire and Cheshire Association eventually became willing to welcome the New Connection into its fellowship in a merger in 1891, thus swelling its ranks to 142 churches with 21,123 members. Only a few Scotch or Strict Calvinist churches in Lancashire, Cheshire, and Cumberland remained outside of the fellowship. By this time the earlier objection to large associations was a thing of the past. The Association, though larger than ever before, was kept a unit although organized in five districts, each with its own moderator and full-time secretary, an innovation which set an example for other associations in later years. Home missionary work was not neglected, for early in the 1900's churches were established at summer seashore resorts in North Wales. Liverpool, Manchester, and the Burnley District continued to maintain an increasing predominance in northwest England.

Home missionary work was carried on also in the area of London by two associations. In the immediate vicinity of the great metropolis, the London Baptist Association was formed in 1865. In 1871 a number of churches which did not feel able to join it established the Metropolitan Association of Strict Baptist Churches. Although typically predestinarian and strict communionist, they were not averse to preaching the gospel to all who would hear. They established a Loan Fund in 1871 to assist struggling congregations and to found new churches within a radius of twenty-five miles of St. Paul's Cathedral. Lay preachers, Sunday schools, and printed materials were utilized in this work. The results may be judged from the fact that about four baptisms occurred annually for every one hundred church members. This enterprise represented an effort of London Baptists to meet the urban problem in religious work. In 1890 the New Connection General Baptists united with the London Baptist Association, thereby strengthening their impact upon the metropolitan area.

This move was typical of the trend toward union taking place also in the northern counties.

The other association was concerned with those town and country areas in the counties around London which were connected with the city by railway lines. It was known in the seventies as the Berks and West London Association. As churches in other counties such as Surrey and Middlesex were included, its name was changed in 1890 to the Home Counties Association. By that date seven hundred baptisms were reported within one year by fifty-six churches whose combined membership numbered twelve thousand persons. The work of the Association has been extended since then to include the Bourne (now Holborn), West Bourne, the Chilterns, Essex, and Herts.[5]

The accounts just related illustrate several significant points. First, the pattern of home mission expansion included itinerant evangelists, spontaneously organized societies which frequently did the work associations might have done,[6] and more recently the assumption by the associations of leadership in the task of establishing new churches. Second, the Baptists of the Northwest gave leadership to the task of evangelism. This work, in large part, was led by William Steadman and his students who revived nearly defunct churches in industrial and city areas. In this effort, evangelism was aided and steadied by education.[7] Third, evangelism provided the basis for the denominational solidarity which had been attained to a marked degree by 1891, when Particular and New Connection Baptists merged in the Baptist Union. Doctrinally, the two bodies had been drawn together on the common ground of evangelism. Organizationally, the older associations had continued side by side with the new societies which had sprung up in the fresh flush of missionary enthusiasm to carry on a work which the older organizations had not then assumed. Once doctrinal unity was attained, organizational solidarity became a reality so far as it could be achieved within a polity which was designed to safeguard the prerogatives and autonomy of the local church. This was no small accomplishment, in view of the Baptists' characteristic emphasis upon individualism.

[5] Whitley, *The Baptists of London*, 80-5.
[6] Whitley, *A History of British Baptists* (London, 1923), 266.
[7] *Ibid.*, 250, 269.

Baptist Developments in Wales, Scotland, and Ireland

The Baptist witness, almost from the beginning, was not restricted to England. Not long after the first Baptist congregation was established in the vicinity of London, a small Baptist church was formed, according to reports, in Wales, at Olchon, about 1633. While the records, if there were any, have been lost, the name of the minister remains. He was Howell Vaughan.[8] During the era of the civil wars in England (1640-1649), two young nonconformist clergymen of the Church of England, Walter Craddock and Vavasor Powell, preached in that area. Powell, a Welshman of Radnorshire, left Wales for London at the outbreak of the Civil War. In 1646 he returned upon an invitation to continue his evangelistic work. He was converted to Baptist views in 1655. Since Craddock did not agree with him on baptism, the evangelistic efforts of the two men were destined to produce a mixed communion of paedobaptists and Baptists in the churches which were established as the result of their ministry.

There were no Welsh Baptist churches, properly speaking, with the possible exception of that at Olchon, until 1649, when a church was established at Ilston, near Swansea in Glamorganshire. Its existence is known best through the writings of Isaac Backus of New England. The pastor, John Myles, had left Wales in 1661 in order to escape persecution and had brought the church record book to the New World. While Vaughan at Olchon had shared with him a conviction that a Baptist church should not include paedobaptists, Myles is the first whose stand was well known throughout Wales.

In 1650 three churches, Hay (including the Olchon congregation), Llansfan, and Ilston, formed the Baptist Association in Wales. Within three years, two other churches were added, Caermarthen and Abergavenny. During the period of the Commonwealth (1649-1653) there were nearly thirty Baptist ministers in Wales, many of whom lived long enough to suffer from the persecution that was resumed upon the restoration of Stuart rule over England in 1660. Vavasor Powell, known as the "Whitefield of Wales," established some twenty churches prior to his death in 1670. These, however,

[8] Joshua Thomas, *A History of the Baptist Association in Wales from 1650-1790* (London, 1795). Much of the survey that follows is based upon this source.

were of mixed membership and practiced open communion. It was not long thereafter that the Welsh Baptists abandoned this policy, preferring to restrict their services and membership to those holding Baptist views.

From 1660 to 1688, at least eleven ministers bore the hardships of persecution.[9] When toleration was won in 1689, the Particular Baptists at London invited their Welsh brethren to send messengers to a general meeting held on September 3. The ministers who attended were William Jones and Griffith Howell of Pembrokeshire, William Prichard and Christopher Price of Monmouthshire, and Lewis Thomas and Francis Giles of Swanzey. The famous London Confession of Particular Baptists was adopted jointly by the English and Welsh attendants in order to acquaint King Charles II with their views. In 1695 the first meeting-house was erected by a Welsh congregation.

Welsh Baptists, by and large, were Calvinists; and from as early as 1689, they had practiced the laying on of hands on the newly baptized believers. But changes were not long in making their appearance. By 1737 the necessity of continuing this custom was questioned at the Newcastle meeting of the Association. In the following year, the churches gathered at Hengold complained in their Association circular letter of the spread of Arminianism throughout the country. The subject of the laying on of hands was debated again in 1764; some were very zealous for it; others were more moderate.[10]

Near the close of the eighteenth century, Baptists were increasing in Wales. In 1788, as new churches were added to the Association, the advantage of creating more than one such body was discussed. Accordingly, two years later, the Association was divided into three associations: the Northern Association composed of nine churches, the Eastern and Western Associations in South Wales composed of nineteen and eighteen churches respectively. Plans were made also for all three to meet, through deputies, in a General Assembly.[11] By 1867, all Welsh associations were united in the Baptist Union of Wales. Theologically, they were still Calvinists.

[9] *Ibid.*, 20.
[10] *Ibid.*, 48, 50, 59-60.
[11] *Ibid.*, 70, 72, 74.

Their greatest preacher in the nineteenth century was the noted evangelist, Christmas Evans (1766-1838), who travelled extensively through Wales during a ministry of half a century. Periods of spiritual refreshing were frequent throughout the century. By 1900 there were eight hundred and thirty-five churches in the country, including Monmouthshire, with a membership of more than one hundred and six thousand. By that time Baptists, Congregationalists, and Calvinistic Methodists comprised the majority of the population.[12]

Baptists in Scotland date from the Commonwealth Period when Cromwell's troops, many of whom were Baptists, were in the country. Although Baptists were tolerated by the government, the Presbyterians, who represented the ecclesiastical majority, looked upon them with disfavor.[13]

The identity of the earliest Baptist church in Scotland has not been determined with certainty. According to Vedder, an American historian, it was a congregation which met under the leadership of Sir William Sinclair on his estate at Keiss in 1750. Sinclair had been immersed in England and then had returned to preach in his native land. The British church historians, Yuille and Whitley, however, consider the first church to have been the Bristo-place church in Edinburgh, which was organized in 1765 by the Reverend Robert Carmichael. He originally had been a member of the Church of Scotland, then became a Glasite, that is, a follower of John Glas and his son-in-law, Robert Sandeman, Congregationalists, who sought to restore what they regarded as correct New Testament church administration by a plural rather than single eldership. It appears that Carmichael became a Baptist as the result of an agreement which he made with a fellow Congregational minister, Archibald McLean, to investigate the scriptural foundation for the subject of baptism.[14] McLean was the first to become convinced of the biblical validity of believers' baptism by immersion. Carmichael, however, was more hesitant to change his views; in the meantime, he had accepted a pastorate in Edinburgh. It was there that he finally resolved to seek believers' baptism. Since he knew of no

[12] *The Baptist Handbook for 1900* (London, 1900).

[13] G. Yuille, ed., *A History of Baptists in Scotland* (Glasgow, 1926), 25.

[14] The following account is based on an article by Robert B. Hannen (then a Scottish Baptist minister and editor), "The 'Scotch Baptist' Churches: An Episode in Scottish Baptist History," *The Chronicle*, Vol. VII, No. 4 (Oct., 1944).

Baptist minister in Scotland who could administer the ordinance, he invited the hyper-Calvinist, Dr. John Gill, of London, to come to Edinburgh for the purpose. Gill, to avoid the trip, recommended that Carmichael contact David Fernie, a Baptist clergyman in the North of England. Apparently this was unsatisfactory to the new convert, for instead he went himself to London to be baptized by Dr. Gill in 1765, an event which caused some stir and debate in the metropolis. It is significant that this contact between Scotch and English Baptists should center in a mutual acceptance of hyper-Calvinism. The sturdy Calvinism of the Scotch Reformation was responsible.

On his return trip to Edinburgh, Carmichael baptized five Baptists at Leith, where many baptisms had occurred during the Commonwealth Period, a fact unknown to Carmichael at the time. The first meeting place of the little congregation was the Magdalene Chapel in Edinburgh, which was leased by a physician member of the group, Dr. Robert Walker. Thus, in the very building in which the First General Assembly of the Reformed Church of Scotland had met under John Knox's leadership in 1560, the Scottish Baptists began a new kind of witness. Within a comparatively short time, a congregation developed in Dundee, which Carmichael went to supervise, leaving his flock to the direction of Dr. Walker and McLean, a man recently come to Edinburgh to manage a printing establishment. When another group came into existence at Glasgow, it was McLean who baptized them. From that time on, under the guidance of the Edinburgh church, centers of the Baptist witness developed throughout the country on the average of two a year during the first twenty-years of the nineteenth century. Indeed, "the movement spread to England and Wales and formed a considerable part of the Baptist strength of those days."[15]

The Scotch Baptist churches were characterized by a strict Calvinistic doctrine, a literal interpretation of the Scriptures, a "plurality of pastors" to administer a local church, a sternly Puritan view of morals and amusements, the practice with discretion of the kiss of charity and of foot washing, and the abstaining from "eating blood and things strangled." The Lord's Supper and love feasts were observed weekly to promote fellowship; in this the principle of close communion was followed.

[15] *Ibid.,* 170.

Yet all was not harmonious, for not all of the churches were willing to abide by the insistence of the Edinburgh church "that the Lord's Supper could not be celebrated unless there was a pastor present to officiate." Another source of contention was the rise of churches of the "English" type of polity. The introduction of English influence had come principally from Baptists in the North of England who commonly engaged only one pastor for a congregation and who paid him a salary. They also practiced open communion. It was this latter type of church which advanced in Scotland. They naturally attracted a larger membership because they did not restrict their fellowship to Baptists. They also appealed to a more cultured class and maintained an association with Baptists in England. Meanwhile, the more narrow and intolerant "Scotch" churches accomplished little. They lingered on for a long period of years as a protest against change. But their day was in the past. Their contribution had been to introduce to Scotland, without help from England, the doctrine of believer's baptism by immersion and to prepare the way for a more permanent development of the Baptist witness by churches under English influence.[16]

To the Haldane brothers, Scotch Baptists are greatly indebted. The evangelistic zeal which won for them the epithet, "the Wesley and Whitefield of Scotland," was a major factor in the spread of the Baptist cause in Scotland. Robert (1764-1842) and James (1768-1851) were trained navy men of financial means, whose religious interests prompted them to devote their later years and fortune to the ministry. Robert provided the funds while James was the evangelist. Having left the Church of Scotland to enter the Congregational ministry, they devoted themselves to evangelism, organizing in 1798 a Society for Propagating the Gospel at Home, principally in the Highlands.[17]

In 1808 they rejected infant baptism and became Baptists. James Haldane, during his ministry, was instrumental in founding thirty-eight churches, nearly one-third of the total number in Scotland at the time; this he accomplished with the aid of the Baptist Home Mission Society for Scotland, which was organized in 1816.[18]

[16] *Ibid.*, 181.
[17] Yuille, *History of Baptists in Scotland*, 55-6, 75.
[18] Vedder, *Short History of Baptists*, 274.

In 1856 an association of Baptist churches was established. It continued in existence until 1869, when the Baptist Union of Scotland took its place. Thereafter, progress was steady. Theologically, this Union was Calvinistic. In polity the "Scotch" churches of the Union maintained their customary plurality of elders over each church, whereas the "English" churches had one pastor over each church. While the Union held no jurisdiction over the churches, it might "suspend the membership of any Church for a stated period, or withdraw from its fellowship *sine die,* should such a course be necessary." It also served as an arbiter in matters of dispute and in questions of polity, whenever requested by the churches. That policy has continued to the present.[19]

Baptist beginnings in Ireland date from the occupation of the island by Cromwell's Army in 1649, and possibly even earlier. It is certain that a goodly number of Baptists in the Army and a few ministers who had come with them provided the nucleus for about eleven churches which were organized between 1652 and 1654. By the latter date, there were approximately one hundred and twenty members in the church at Dublin, including Governor-general Fleetwood, Cromwell's son-in-law, and Colonel Jones, one of the commissioners. When the first pastor, Thomas Patient, was appointed an evangelist-at-large toward the close of 1654, he was succeeded by Christopher Blackwood, who had accompanied Fleetwood to Ireland two years before. The extent of Baptist influence in the country is indicated by complaints issued by Dr. Harrison, an Independent clergyman of Christ Church, Dublin, till 1665 and then of Cook Street Church until his death in 1668. He mentioned that at least twelve Baptists were governors of cities and towns, about sixty-four were officers of varying rank in the Army, two were preachers to the Army, and twenty-three were officers in the civil list. Their strength was such that when Cromwell declared himself Lord Protector of the Commonwealth, Fleetwood and other Baptists in the Irish Council were induced only with difficulty to proclaim him. Cromwell tried unsuccessfully to allay their indignation by sending his son, Henry, to Ireland. While Fleetwood was continued in office as lord deputy, he soon after was recalled and left Dublin in September, 1655. During the later part of the protectorate, the Presby-

[19] Yuille, *op. cit.,* 88.

terians gradually recovered their influence, but the Independents did not thrive.[20]

The early Baptists, then, were mainly Cromwellians and Englishmen, most of whom returned to England when the Commonwealth was overthrown. They failed to leave any permanent impress on the native population. As a consequence, the churches established in Ireland grew gradually weaker until the nineteenth century, when the great Haldane revival swept over the North of Ireland. Churches organized on Scotch Baptist principles were founded at Tubbermore, Coleraine, and in other small places. Perhaps its greatest result was the winning to Baptist convictions of the scholarly Alexander Carson (1776-1844). He had been born of Scotch Presbyterian parents who had settled in Tyrone County. At twenty-two he was ordained to the Presbyterian ministry. Six years later, in 1804, he became a Baptist at considerable financial sacrifice to himself, for there was no Baptist society in the country to support him. For some years he preached in barns and in the open air, winning converts gradually. By 1814, a meeting-house was erected for his use at Tubbermore, where he labored for thirty years, building a congregation which grew to five hundred members. Having been educated at the University of Glasgow as a young man, he had a background and proficiency in the Greek New Testament which enabled him to produce a scholarly work on baptism, in which he replied to objections that had been raised against anti-paedobaptist teaching.

The main source of encouragement to Baptist work in Ireland came from the English, although it was not until the nineteenth century that they undertook the task of strengthening the feeble churches there. Andrew Fuller, secretary of the Baptist Missionary Society, became impressed with the need for home mission work in Scotland and Ireland as he traveled about collecting funds for the foreign mission enterprise. In 1813 the Society appointed John Saffery of Salisbury and George Barclay of Kilwinning to visit Ireland. Saffery reported the predominance of Roman Catholicism in the country and the presence of Sandeman's type of polity among the Protestants in the North. Only five of the eleven churches which

[20] Joseph Belcher *et al., The Baptist Irish Society: Its Origin, History, and Prospects* . . ., lix-lxvii. Dr. Harrison's figures are based on the Thurloe State Papers, Vol. IV, 91, cited on p. lxi.

had been founded one hundred and fifty years before were still in existence.

This report led almost at once to the formation of the Baptist Irish Society. On December 6, 1813, "The Baptist Society for propagating the gospel in Ireland" was organized by eight persons meeting at the Eagle Street meeting-house of Particular Baptists in London. Its purpose was "to employ itinerants in Ireland, to establish schools, and to distribute bibles and tracts, either gratuitously or at reduced prices."[21] The Society was to be managed by a secretary, a treasurer, and a committee of twenty-seven governors who should work with a corresponding committee of Baptists in Ireland. The latter was organized in Dublin on May 28, 1814. Joseph Ivimey, pastor of the Eagle Street Church in London, became the first secretary. He received the hearty support of Andrew Fuller and other leading Baptists.

The Society functioned largely through itinerant evangelists and schools. The latter were set up for the primary purpose of teaching children and adults to read the Scriptures. In the sixteenth annual report of the Society, twenty evening schools for adults are mentioned. "The greatest number of children at any one time in the Society's schools, somewhat exceeded ten thousand."[22] Instruction was kept nonsectarian in character. After 1833 the numbers attending the schools began to diminish, owing to a loss of financial support from many individuals who had given generously at first, and due also to the support which was then being given to the new national public schools.

By the close of the nineteenth century, Irish Baptist churches numbered thirty-one, with a total membership of 2,696. The first half of the twentieth century witnessed an increase in the number of churches to sixty-three, and in the membership to 4,058.[23]

Foreign Missionary Advance

The evangelistic impulse which had stimulated Baptist growth within the British Isles had stemmed, as we have seen, from the

[21] Joseph Ivimey, *A History of English Baptists*, IV, 167.

[22] Belcher *et al.*, *op. cit.*, 49.

[23] Vedder, *op. cit.*, 276; *The Watchman-Examiner*, Vol. 34, No. 37 (Sept. 12, 1946), p. 934.

desire of William Carey, Andrew Fuller, and their Calvinistic associates to win the heathen to Christ. While the Baptist Missionary Society's promotion of the foreign missionary enterprise had been largely responsible for the spread of the home mission activities just surveyed, it should not be supposed that its support of foreign missions had been neglected. Lancashire Baptists, for example, contributed one-tenth of the income of the Baptist Missionary Society in 1800.[24] To be sure, the principal backing of the movement came from the moderate Calvinists, particularly those in Northamptonshire, rather than from the hyper-Calvinists who did not engage in missionary work until 1861, and then independently. Moreover, the New Connection General Baptists did not support the Baptist Missionary Society either, but established the General Baptist Missionary Society in 1816.

In spite of obstacles, the initial undertaking of the Carey movement was progressing in India. In twenty years from the founding of the Baptist Missionary Society, Carey and his associates had published tracts in twenty languages and portions of the Scriptures in eighteen. More than seven hundred converts had been baptized, twelve of whom had volunteered for Christian missionary service. The splendid service of Carey at Serampore as linguist and translator of the Scriptures and of Thomas as surgeon was received with enthusiasm by English Baptists, but not by the East India Company whose members feared that the coming of Christianity to their fields of lucrative commerce might uproot slavery and rob them of their rich profits. While the British government at Calcutta was not critical, it apparently followed the dictates of the East India Company, and refused permission to two English Baptist missionaries, Chater and Robinson, to land. Robinson moved on to Java. Adoniram Judson and his wife, who had been sent out by the Congregational Mission Board in America, but who became convinced of the rightness of Baptist views on the sea voyage, were obliged to move on to Burma, where Felix Carey had prepared the ground.

In 1807 the Society was obliged to defend its work in the face of hostile criticism from British residents in India who had returned to England. Through its secretary, Andrew Fuller, a reply was drafted on June 9, which explained that William Carey and John

[24] Shipley, *Baptists in Yorkshire, Lancashire, Cheshire, and Cumberland*, Part II, 299.

Thomas had gone to Bengal with no thought of interfering with the trade of the East India Company, but only to preach to the natives, to open schools for free instruction, to distribute religious tracts, and to translate, print, and circulate the Scriptures. It was also pointed out that no evil consequences had arisen in Bengal from twenty years of preaching. On the contrary, Fuller pointed out that the presentation of the gospel had lessened the influence of the native idolatry which had hampered and endangered the British government because it did not teach native employees to be honest and affectionate toward their white rulers. The Society sought permission for its nine missionaries to itinerate and establish additional missionary stations in the country.[25]

As news of the unwelcome reception accorded to missionaries in India became generally known, public opinion was aroused. When the charter of the East India Company was to be renewed in 1813, with the inclusion of a provision that a bishop and three archdeacons should be appointed for India, Baptists took the opportunity to issue a strong plea for legal protection of their mission property and for liberty to send their missionaries to India in the company's ships. Through the *Baptist Magazine* and circular letters, Baptist pressure upon Parliament was created. A petition which contained, according to Fuller's estimate, well over fifty-one thousand names, was presented to both houses of Parliament in behalf of the same facilities and protection which were granted to other denominations. A deputation, headed by Fuller, visited Lord Liverpool, the prime minister, on May 20. Members of the committee also visited many noblemen and leading members of the House of Commons. Their efforts were rewarded by Parliament's adoption of a resolution in behalf of free exercise of the Christian missionary's provision for the improvement of India. When, a short time later, the Reverend William Yates, a Baptist missionary, was refused a license to proceed to India, the Board of Control ordered the Directors of the East India Company to issue it.[26] This first test case was a victory for Baptists and all other dissenters as well.

In that same year, a catastrophe resulted in increased support for the missionary cause. A fire in Serampore, which destroyed the

[25] Ivimey, *A History of the English Baptists*, IV, 94-107.
[26] *Ibid.*, 134-57.

printing press and much of the work done by the missionaries, called forth such general sympathy in England that the Baptist Missionary Society gained the support of British Baptists generally. Throughout England, over ten thousand pounds were subscribed to replace the printing press and make good the general damage. Although Baptists in Suffolk failed to contribute to the wide-spread support of the emergency effort, it was only because they were absorbed in support of their own pastors and in liquidating debts on newly erected chapels. Within a few years they established in support of the Mission auxiliary societies in the churches, so as to ensure regular contributions to the Baptist Missionary Society. This was an innovation in fund raising in the county, for the usual method was to take a collection on the occasion of a visit by a missionary.[27]

On May 7, 1815, Andrew Fuller died; he was succeeded as secretary of the Society by the Reverend John Ryland of Bristol. With the passing of the old leadership, for Sutcliff had died less than a year earlier, changes began to occur in policy making. The newcomers had less courage with which to face the challenge of the missionaries who sought to lead out into a larger and more far-reaching work of establishing colleges in India. It had been Carey's policy to concentrate upon the preparation of an indigenous ministry and church in that country. He realized the futility of attempting to convert its teeming millions by means of a few foreign missionaries sent out and supported by British Baptists. For this reason, he established a training college at Serampore as the center of a group of schools. From this focal point, with its printing press, he translated and distributed the Scriptures to outlying regions. It was also the plan of these pioneer missionaries to concentrate first on creating centers of missionary activity in urban centers like Calcutta, on the theory that from such points travelers would carry the gospel to the rural areas. Their recommendations were not closely heeded. Instead, Serampore was permitted to become for missionary purposes a mere country station. However, work was carried on bravely by the missionaries and converts in that city, in Calcutta, and in other towns, but not on the scale envisioned by the missionaries.

In 1812 the Baptist Missionary Society had become interested also in taking the gospel to Ceylon and, in 1814, as far west as

[27] Ashley J. Klaiber, *The Story of the Suffolk Baptists* (London, 1931), 185-6.

Jamaica. The latter was a flourishing tropical colony with a large Negro population where since 1784 there had been some Baptist teaching. The opposition of the Jamaica planters was keen, for they saw in Christianity a threat to their slave trade. Although England had abolished the nefarious practice in the dominions by Acts of Parliament in 1807 and 1811 and had advised the legislatures of Jamaica and other self-governing colonies to do the same, the planters had refused to comply. Instead, they treated the slaves even more cruelly than before. The result was an insurrection of slaves in Jamaica near the end of 1831, in spite of all efforts of the missionaries to maintain order. Because they sympathized with the slaves, the missionaries also were arrested and mistreated, and mission property was destroyed. Such was the background of the crusade of William Knibb, a Baptist missionary there, who returned to England the next year to arouse the nation to a consciousness of the dire conditions in that island colony. Motivated principally by his testimony and by public feeling, Parliament passed a Bill in 1833 which ended slavery by a plan of apprenticeship for five years, during which period the former slaves would work as apprentices and then be completely free. In this way, the planters were to be reimbursed for their loss. In time, schools were built on the island under Baptist direction, and a Jamaica Baptist Association was formed, which grew to a membership of more than thirty thousand self-supporting members. Calabar College, however, was maintained by English Baptist funds.[28] The type of missionary enterprise begun on Jamaica was opened in the Bahamas and other islands to the north, as well as in Cape Colony in South Africa.

During this period, Carey's older version of the Bible had been replaced in Bengal by a new translation made by William Yates, in which the Greek word *baptizo* was translated by a word meaning "immerse" in the Bengalese language. This choice was in keeping with "the habitual method of ceremonial purifying" in vogue in that country, which was immersion. The paedobaptist missionaries, however, objected on the grounds that it encouraged a sectarian view of baptism. It became necessary, therefore, to present the issue to the British and Foreign Bible Society. This interdenominational agency

[28] H. Wheeler Robinson, *The Life and Faith of the Baptists* (London, 1946, revised), 115-6, 133-4.

had been organized in England in 1804 with a Baptist minister, Joseph Hughes, as its first secretary. When the Society decided by a considerable majority that it could give no financial aid to the printing of versions which translated rather than transliterated so controversial a word as *baptizo,* Baptists were incensed. They promptly established the Bible Translation Society in 1840 with a view to carrying on their own Bible translation and publication work.

A similar trend occurred in America about this time, where Baptists withdrew from the American Bible Society for the same reason. After some years of producing private denominational versions under great financial difficulty, Baptists returned to their former participation in interdenominational co-operation. In 1881-1885 they assisted in the preparation of the Anglo-American Revised Version, and in 1905, in the publication of the American Standard Version. In the intervening period, however, Yates' version in the Bengalese had found much favor with non-Baptists as well as with Baptists. It followed that the Baptist Bible Translation Society continued its important task of revising and translating the Scriptures into Hindu, Urdu, Sanskrit, and Cingalese, even providing explanatory notes as a helpful innovation.[29]

In the years that followed, the foreign mission enterprise continued to expand in several directions. In 1845 the Society's missionary, Alfred Saker, established the first Baptist mission station in Africa. It was on the west coast in the territory known as the Cameroons. Later, a work was planned for the newly discovered Congo River region far to the south. When the Cameroon territory was transferred in 1884 from British control to German rule, the Baptist Missionary Society turned the field over to German missionaries. However, the Congo mission stations, which extended a thousand miles up the river, remained in English hands. There British and American Baptists have shared in the work of evangelism.[30]

In 1856 the Baptist Missionary Society introduced an innovation in its work among the women of India; this was in recognition of the social customs of that country, which sheltered Indian women from contact with men outside of their families. The Society began

[29] Whitley, *A History of British Baptists,* 315-6.
[30] Robinson, *op. cit.,* 116-7.

the practice of appointing women missionaries to work among those of their own sex. The following year a tragic mutiny of the Bengal army at Delhi resulted in the destruction of the Baptist mission there. It was not an unmixed evil, however, for the courageous role of General Havelock, who led the rescue army and who was a well-known Baptist, won further prestige in that country for the Baptists.

Missionary work was begun in China in 1870, when Timothy Richard arrived in Shantung. Between 1876 and 1878 he played a prominent role in famine relief, which afforded him an opportunity to extend the missionary undertaking inland as far as Shansi. He was also active in producing Christian literature for use in China, serving after 1891 as a leader in the Christian Literature Society in that country. In 1900 the permanence of the enterprise was threatened by the antiforeign outbreak known as the Boxer Rebellion, which took the lives of scores of missionaries, including eight of the Baptist Missionary Society. Out of the tragedy, however, arose the Shansi University, established in 1901 by the Chinese Government from the indemnity imposed upon that province by the foreign powers. It will be recalled that the United States, in particular, had returned the indemnity payment for lives lost and for property damaged, with the stipulation that it should be used as a fund for the establishment of educational opportunities for Chinese youth. Timothy Richard became Chancellor of the University, another indication of the close relationship which existed between evangelism and education in the missionary enterprise.[31]

In 1891 when the New Connection General Baptists united with the Particular Baptists in the Baptist Union of Great Britain and Ireland, the mission stations of the former group, which had been established in Orissa, India, since 1816, were transferred to the supervision of the Baptist Missionary Society. At the present time this Society is working in Bengal, Bihar, Orissa, Ceylon, and North India. In these areas the educational emphasis is strong. Medical missions, the translation and circulation of the Scriptures, and preaching have been important missionary methods utilized by British Baptists.

General support of foreign missions has not been evenly distri-

[31] *Ibid.*, 117-8.

buted throughout Britain. However, in spite of the impact of two world wars since 1914, the income of the Baptist Missionary Society has been remarkably maintained, the greater support coming from London where the Baptist strength is relatively stronger. In the northern counties, contributions to the Baptist Missionary Society had decreased steadily from one-tenth of that agency's income in 1800 to one-thirteenth in 1913. Yorkshire, Lancashire, Cheshire, and Cumberland together gave less than half as much as London alone. An increasingly larger proportion of their giving went to home missions.[32] On the other hand, Suffolk Baptists in the forties and fifties of the last century steadily increased their contributions. As early as 1834, they had begun to send missionary volunteers to the field. By 1906 the annual contributions of their churches for the first time totaled five hundred pounds. By 1920, after some decline, owing to the effects of World War I, the amount had doubled. In 1946 seven missionaries from Suffolk were serving on foreign fields. This is all the more notable when one recalls that in 1861 the Strict or Particular Baptists in Suffolk withdrew their support from the Baptist Missionary Society on theological grounds and established their own Strict Baptist Mission with work around Madras in southern India. This mission, formed in London at the Eagle Street church, held to the principle that each home church should be represented directly in the conduct of the Mission, in opposition to "Society" control of the missionary enterprise on the field as followed by most Baptists. It appears that complete accord could not be reached among the Strict Baptists, for in 1897, a second agency was established, known as the South India Strict Baptist Mission. Hence, there were two claims upon Suffolk Baptists in addition to that of the older Baptist Missionary Society. In 1929, however, the two Strict Baptist Mission societies joined forces to strengthen their financial position.[33] What was true in Suffolk was true also in other parts of England where there was keen interest in the points at issue, whether theological, as between strict and moderate Calvinism, or organizational, as between local church control of mission stations and society control.

In their missionary enterprise, British Baptists have been

---

[32] Shipley, *Baptists in Yorkshire, Lancashire, Cheshire, and Cumberland*, Part II, 299.
[33] Klaiber, *The Story of the Suffolk Baptists*, 186-96.

pioneers among Protestants. Their example stimulated the formation of missionary societies by other denominations of the nonconformist type. Even among the Anglicans, their influence became a stimulus to more vigorous efforts. It is worthy of note that a Baptist minister, Joseph Hughes, should have been a participant in the organization of the Religious Tract Society in 1799 and of the British and Foreign Bible Society in 1804, and the first secretary of both.

Trend Toward Denominational Union

Early in the nineteenth century, British Baptists gave indication of a serious desire for denominational union, principally in the interest of more effective missionary advance. In 1811 the *Baptist Magazine,* the Calvinists' periodical established two years before, expressed a desire "to see such a Union prevail in our Denomination as shall most effectively combine all our efforts in the cause of Truth and Righteousness at home, and give ten-fold vigour to our exertions on behalf of the heathen abroad."[34] This trend was in line with commercial developments which were giving rise to partnerships and large companies for the more adequate financing of large enterprises. Baptists had been learning also the costliness of divided effort; consequently, as evangelistic fervor balanced theological preoccupation, they were, with few exceptions, neither averse to creating societies of their own in this period nor to participating in interdenominational organizations for missionary endeavor. An early example of the latter type of co-operation is to be found in the Protestant Union, which was established in 1798 to provide a fund for the relief of aged ministers. John Rippon, a prominent Baptist clergyman of London, was one of its charter members. A year later a second nonsectarian enterprise was introduced when some London clergymen formed the Religious Tract Society, previously mentioned. Joseph Hughes, Baptist minister at Battersea, became its first secretary. Although the New Connection and Particular Baptists organized separate societies in 1810 and 1840 respectively to prepare tracts on denominational teachings, Baptists contributed their fair share to this enterprise. When, in 1804, at the suggestion of Hughes, a new interdenominational venture emerged from the Religious Tract Society,

[34] *Baptist Magazine* (London), 1811; cited in Whitley, *A History of British Baptists.* 263. For more detailed account of this trend, see pp. 263-78.

organized for the translation and printing of the Bible, Baptists participated. It was known as the British and Foreign Bible Society, a joint project of Episcopalians, dissenters, and some foreigners in London. Hughes, a Baptist, was also the first secretary of this organization.

The creation of new denominational agencies for the home missionary enterprise under the leadership of the western associations has been traced in a previous section. Suffice it to note here that the period witnessed the organization of education societies, which were actually schools for the purpose of training ministers. An account of them is given hereafter. As further indication of a growing sense of denominational responsibility, an Aged and Infirm Baptist Ministers' Society was established in 1816. This Society, brought into being by the western associations, disbursed within the century nearly thirty-four thousand pounds.[35] Other districts undertook similar projects; by 1874 most of these societies were merged in a Union Annuity Fund.

To promote the varied interests of Baptist groups, an increasing number of periodicals were brought into existence. Among the most important were the *Baptist Register,* edited by Rippon from 1790 to 1803; *Periodical Accounts,* published by the Baptist Missionary Society beginning in 1794; and the New Connection's *General Baptist Magazine,* which was issued from 1797 until 1891 when it was merged with the Particular *Baptist Magazine,* which had been in existence since 1809. After 1830, when Baptists were manifesting a renewed interest in evangelism and political and social reform, a host of new periodicals appeared, among which were the old General Baptists' *General Baptist Advocate,* the *Christian Observer,* the *Revivalist,* the *Gospel Herald,* the *Family Magazine,* the *Gospel Standard,* the *Christian Review,* and the *Messenger.*

The hymnal first came into use among Particular Baptists in Benjamin Keach's church at Horsley Down, Southwark, in 1691, then later among the New Connection General Baptists. The collection of Ash and Evans, which had been used by Particular Baptists since 1769, and that of Taylor and Deacon used by the New Connection since 1772, were superseded by newer collections near the close of the century. One, in 1787, was Rippon's hymnal of 588 hymns

---

[35] Whitley, *op. cit.,* 270.

to be used in addition to Watts by Particular Baptists; the others were three revisions of the New Connection Hymnal made by Samuel and John Deacon between 1784 and 1830. The hymnal was an important means of indoctrinating congregations; therefore it is not surprising that a variety of privately prepared books were in use among the churches in addition to the more important ones mentioned.

These varied indications of a slowly developing denominational solidarity during the first four decades of the nineteenth century reveal the influence of several factors, foremost of which was the missionary task, which could be performed best through co-operation. A second influence was that of polity, particularly upon New Connection General Baptists and to some extent upon Particular Baptists in the northern counties. In many respects, a satisfactory solution for extension work in unchurched areas was found in an adaptation of a plan used by Methodists. It called for a stationary leadership attached to the settled churches which superintended the home base, while co-operating with a movable group of itinerant evangelists supported from a general fund.[36] A third influence was the tempering of theological differences. By 1802 the old General Assembly of General Baptists had lost the support of the New Connection group. The latter had withdrawn in protest against the acceptance of a London minister, William Vidler, who entertained unitarian-universalist views and practiced open membership. From that time on, the General Baptist Assembly became a negligible factor in Baptist life, except for a brief period of revival after 1858 under the leadership of John Clifford.[37]

After 1803 the Assembly complained that no correspondence was being received from General Baptists in America. Even Welsh General Baptists were neglecting active contacts. From these indications, it appears that the Assembly's policy of countenancing unitarianism and open membership had cost it heavily in support. This was particularly true in the face of the strong missionary program being conducted by New Connection and Particular Baptists. It

[36] David Douglas, *History of the Baptist Churches in the North of England*, 307-8; Shipley, *Baptists in Yorkshire, Lancashire, Cheshire, and Cumberland*, Part I, 316-7; Part II, 157-8.
[37] *Proceedings of the General Assembly of General Baptists*, II, 243-57, 260-93; cf. Whitley, *The Baptists of London*, 71-73.

must also be noted that the New Connection lost in 1802 an opportunity to save the Assembly from drifting under Unitarian influence by failing to use its full voting strength. When the Assembly had polled each member church for an individual expression of approval or disapproval of admitting the Parliament Court church of which Vidler was pastor, only eighteen of the forty-one New Connection churches replied to the query. Had they all voted, they might have altered the decision of the Assembly.[38]

The Victorian Era (1837-1901) provided a remarkable stimulus to Baptist progress towards denominational solidarity.[39] Life in Great Britain was undergoing significant changes. The population more than doubled. The Industrial Revolution reached a new peak of production and prosperity for the nation, and there was an accompanying restlessness among those classes not fully represented in Parliament. A wave of political and social reforms followed upon the passage of the great Reform Bill of 1832, which had extended fairer representation to the middle class without granting an equal privilege to the lower classes. At the same time, a strong feeling of national pride was felt not only in England, but also in Scotland, Wales, and Ireland. As British influence and power were extended to the far corners of the newly widened empire, greater protection and prestige were tendered to the missionary enterprises of British subjects. Moreover, the commercial pattern of incorporating in companies and societies was being adapted to religious needs, even among Baptists whose polity had kept centralized control at a minimum. Actually, the autonomy of the local church was not seriously affected by the development of societies and national bodies to carry on a co-operative effort which could not have been achieved otherwise. In addition, as the religious restrictions were lessened, Baptists took a more active part in civic and national life.

As early as the 1830's there had begun a long struggle to relieve dissenters from paying "church rates" for the support of the Establishment. It ended in 1868 when Gladstone's government passed a bill which relieved them of that obligation. In 1836 a plan was adopted whereby marriages might be performed legally by a dissent-

[38] *Proceedings of the General Assembly of General Baptists*, II, footnote by the editor, W. T. Whitley, pp. 250-1.
[39] For details, see Whitley, *A History of British Baptists*, chap. 8.

ing minister, if done in the presence of a civil registrar in a place duly registered for the purpose. A sentiment against state-churchism was expressed in Scotland in 1843, when a Free Church was established by those who had seceded from the Established Presbyterian Church of Scotland. The following year witnessed the advent of a British Anti-State-Church Association. Interestingly enough, this movement opposed education as well as an established church, because government proposals in the bills for factory legislation provided exceptional powers for the clergy. An Act passed in 1844 permitted dissenters the right to hold title to church property, if they had occupied it for a period of twenty-five years without hindrance, and if there were no provisions to the contrary in the trust. However, it was not until the twentieth century that congregations which had relied upon leases for obtaining the use of land on which to build their meeting-houses were enabled to acquire ownership. By a Burials Act of 1852, dissenters for the first time were allowed an unconsecrated share of the town cemetery in which to bury their dead. But not until 1880 were they allowed to conduct funerals in consecrated burial grounds. Between 1868 and 1880 further barriers were removed, making it possible for dissenters to attend the universities, to obtain commissions in the army and navy, and even to hold civil posts in the government service.

During the first generation of Victoria's long reign, England provided the center of gravity for British Baptists; nevertheless there were fewer Baptists in the country in proportion to the population than in Wales, and less leadership than in Scotland. Within England itself during this period, the leadership was not from London, but from the counties or provinces, as they are often called. This was due for the most part to the fact that London Baptists were strongly conservative. They held on to old methods and suffered from inertia and want of solidarity, while their provincial brethren were actively evangelistic and progressive. In addition, the London Baptists had accepted the viewpoint of dissenters generally that the chief task of nonconformists was to maintain their independence. The metropolis did not foster a spirit of unity, and they were not strong enough to overcome the influence of a large urban center.[40]

[40] Whitley, *A History of British Baptists*, 302-5; Whitley, *The Baptists of London*, 63; Klaiber, *The Story of the Suffolk Baptists*, 127-34.

Then, too, theological tensions arose again in the 1840's to preclude any possibility of unity. In 1845 the New London Strict Association was organized. It was indicative of the displeasure of the more conservative Calvinists with the moderates. Among Suffolk Baptists the same tensions were abroad, resulting in 1848 in the formation of the New Suffolk and Norfolk Association of Strict Baptists in protest against the non-creedal and open communion Suffolk Baptist Union which had been organized only two years before. For a time, London and Suffolk Strict Baptists entertained plans for establishing a national body, but they came to nought. The influence of this controversy, which centered in London, was felt especially among the Baptists of the north in the fifties. Some churches left the Lancashire and Cheshire Associations in protest against sister churches which allegedly were on the "down-grade" from strict Calvinism and close communion. The controversy reflected liberal-conservative tensions which continued throughout the century.

But among the Baptists of the provinces also, there were signs of inadequacy. At a time when great population shifts were flooding the counties north and west of London with migrants seeking employment in the mills and factories which had sprung up as a part of the Industrial Revolution, Baptists generally had failed to keep touch with the urban laboring classes. This was not so true in Lancashire and West Riding (Yorkshire), where the spinners and weavers were influenced by their ministry. In the second place, they had failed to grapple adequately with the urban movement that gave rise to the multiplication of new industrial and commercial centers. Lack of funds for church buildings frequently hindered their effectiveness. In the towns their progress likewise was poor. In Northamptonshire, where Baptists were relatively strong, only six new town churches were added between 1837 and 1900 despite greatly increased population. The situation was typical of other areas throughout the country.[41]

Organizationally, the picture was brighter. Associational life was becoming stronger, and a few new schools were being established on a modest scale. At the same time, Calvinistic Baptists were being crystallized into three groups: strict Calvinists, who held to the Confession of 1677, close communionists, and the majority group who followed the evangelistic emphasis of Fuller and Hall.

[41] Whitley, *A History of British Baptists,* 303-4.

Robert Hall (1764-1831) was one of the most eloquent pulpiteers and best known Baptist preachers of the nineteenth century.
His entire life was a battle against ill health, and this produced in him
an extreme sensitivity to discouragement. As a precocious child Hall
studied the theological works of Jonathan Edwards, the Calvinist
divine of the American Colonies, and wrote essays of his own before
he was ten years of age. At fifteen, after his initial training at North-
hampton, he entered Bristol College to prepare for the ministry; and
after three years of study there, he went to King's College, Aberdeen,
where he stayed from 1781 to 1785. His rich background in the
classics and philosophy served him in good stead in the pastorate to
which he was called. From 1785 to 1791 he served as assistant to Dr.
Caleb Evans, then pastor of Broadmead Church, Bristol. His sermons
attracted prominent citizens of the town, including some Episcopalian
clergymen. In 1791 he accepted a call to the Baptist church in Cambridge, where he acquired the reputation of being both scholarly and
eloquent in his preaching. After fifteen years at this university center,
he served nearly twenty years in Leicester, and then returned to
Bristol in 1825 where he preached until his death on February 21,
1831. His life was the more courageous and remarkable because, due
to his ailment, he had endured pain from childhood.

Hall's preparation of sermons was thorough. Although he sel-
dom wrote them in entirety, he studied his notes carefully and then
preached with considerable freedom and eloquence. Doctrinally, he
was a moderate Calvinist. He taught open communion and was willing to tolerate in his membership unbaptized persons as evidence of
his belief in Christian liberty, a policy which brought him under severe
criticism from a large number of Baptists in his own day. He attracted much attention by his *Apology for the Freedom of the Press.*
This statement, which was true to Baptist tradition, was written in
1793, at a time when Pitt's government had become quite reactionary
toward the cause of liberalism in consequence of the anxiety aroused
by the radical turn which the French Revolution had taken in the
"reign of terror."

New Connection Baptists were not hindered in their progress
by theological differences. During this period they established three
new conferences in Methodist style: for Warwick, Derby, and Che-
shire-Lancashire—all under the one national association. Leicester-

shire, rather than London, was maintained as the seat of their educational work. In foreign missions they were represented principally in Orissa, India. The trend among Baptists of the old General Assembly was not so auspicious. Indeed, that body had become little more than a group of Unitarians, chiefly of Kent and Sussex, while other ancient General Baptist churches, not affiliated with it, united with the New Connection.

In London the lethargy of Particular Baptists was shaken by the influx of immigrants from the provinces who brought fresh ideas and new methods. Among these was a lad from Essex, Charles Haddon Spurgeon, who was destined to become a distinguished preacher within a comparatively short time. Under the stimulus of fresh leadership and faced with the problem of dying churches among the older city congregations, the Baptist Union, which had been organized in the old Southwark church during the pastorate of Dr. Rippon in 1813, took the occasion of its jubilee celebration in 1863 to re-examine its status. Accordingly, a strong call was sounded in behalf of evangelism and of consolidating the work of strong associations, the inspiration of whose individual achievements all too frequently had been lost to one another for lack of a vital unifying agency. The revitalized Union included 1,245 churches belonging to various associations and some which were unaffiliated. The total membership was 134,000, with 158,000 pupils in Sunday schools. It was a notable year; for by its close, ten new churches had been formed, thirty-one new chapels had been built, fifteen ministers from Baptist colleges had been settled in pastorates, and 9,300 baptisms had occurred. The tide had turned.[42]

In a very real sense, the period of "watching and passing resolutions" was past. The Union began to be "a real factor in denominational life." By holding two meetings yearly, one in London and one in the provinces, wholesome contacts were established which led to better understanding and co-operation. Under the leadership of its secretaries, the Union sponsored church extension work through the Home Missionary Society, formed in 1865 by a merger of the English and Irish societies which had been established earlier for the same task in their respective areas. It also undertook a national Annuity Fund for aged ministers. This fund was patterned after similar funds in operation in Scotland and Wales.

[42] Whitley, *A History of British Baptists*, 314.

Baptists in the northern counties maintained a close relationship with the Union, although their support was not won to any effective degree until after the stirring reforms of 1832. It appears that they then saw in this national co-operation benefits hitherto unperceived. In 1840 the Lancashire Association expressed formal approval of the objectives of the Union and requested every member church to contribute to its support. Two years later the Association united with Yorkshire Baptists in endorsing a resolution prepared by the Union in demand of Anglican disestablishment "as the best preservative of Protestantism." In the years that followed, the Lancashire, Cheshire, and Yorkshire Associations contributed leadership and financial backing to the Union.[43] Another important factor in the success of the Baptist Union was the role of outstanding clergymen such as Spurgeon, Maclaren, and Clifford.

Perhaps the most widely known preacher of the age was Charles Haddon Spurgeon (1834-1892), a man whose unusual gifts of pulpit delivery, administrative talent, and literary skill have left a heritage of sermons and commentaries of great value. He was born on June 19, 1834, at Kelvedon, in Essex County, but spent several years of his early life at his grandfather's home at Stambourne. Since his grandfather was pastor of an Independent church, he was reared in the paedobaptist tradition. At fifteen he served as assistant in a school at Newmarket which was conducted by a Baptist, thus bringing him his initial contact with that denomination. The impressions received there must have been lasting, for not long after his conversion in a Primitive Methodist Chapel in Colchester on January 6, 1850, he became a Baptist, with the reluctant consent of his family, on May 3, 1850.

A year later he moved to Cambridge where he continued to teach as an assistant master, attending St. Andrew's Street Baptist Church of which Robert Hall and Robert Robinson had been pastors. He preached in the mission chapels of this church, and finally was called to be pastor of the one at Waterbeach, which he served from 1852 to 1853, when he was invited, at the age of nineteen, to the ancient church at Southwark, London. This church had been made famous by the ministry of Benjamin Keach, Dr. Gill, and Dr. Rippon. At

[43] Shipley, ed., *Baptists in Yorkshire, Lancashire, Cheshire, and Cumberland*, Part II, 287-93.

once, the much depleted congregation began to grow in numbers. A larger building was needed and the Metropolitan Tabernacle was built in 1861, to seat over fifty-five hundred persons. To this great congregation Spurgeon devoted his life. The extent of his influence, however, was not confined to the church. He wrote voluminously; edited a monthly magazine known as the *Sword and Trowel,* which he began in 1865; founded an orphanage for boys at Stockwell, London, in 1867, and one for girls at the same place in 1880; organized and directed a pastors' college in 1856, which is known as Spurgeon's College in London; and operated a Colportage Association and Book Fund for ministers.

Theologically, Spurgeon was a moderate Calvinist. As a staunch conservative, he withdrew from the Baptist Union in 1887, because it included in its membership some who held liberal doctrinal views. This action precipitated what came to be known as the Down Grade controversy, so-called to indicate the direction which conservative Baptists believed orthodoxy was taking. Actually, the new theological currents abroad in the Baptist Union reflected the necessity for the re-evaluation which Darwinian evolutionists and critics of the Bible were forcing upon church leaders in all denominations. Leading Baptist clergymen like John Clifford, then president of the Union, and Alexander Maclaren had rejected the doctrine of the inerrancy of the Scriptures while one outstanding Baptist minister, Samuel Cox, openly taught universal restoration of all sinners to salvation. The Union, under Clifford's guidance, sought to preserve both unity and freedom of thought, and accordingly refused to accede to Spurgeon's demand for adopting a specific creed in place of its Declaration of Faith. The controversy was symptomatic of the intellectual unrest of the times and of the growing conflict emerging within Protestantism between advocates of traditional biblicism and a restatement of Christian theology.[44]

Although Spurgeon remained staunchly conservative, he main-

[44] It is interesting to note that the Baptist Union of Great Britain and Ireland adopted in 1888 "a declaration of principles commonly believed by the Churches of the Union," which set forth briefly the main tenets of orthodoxy; a statement was appended, however, to indicate that brethren had been working cordially in the Union who, "while reverently bowing to the authority of Holy Scriptures . . . have not held the common interpretation of these words of our Lord." Cited in *The Chronicle,* Vol. VII, No. 3 (July, 1944), 136-7, from J. C. Carlile, *C. H. Spurgeon, An Interpretive Biography,* 253 ff.; Alfred C. Underwood, *A History of the English Baptists,* 229-33.

tained the practice of open communion which had been established by his church in 1838. His preaching was vitalized by the use of heart-warming truths and homely illustrations drawn from everyday life. To his church were attracted the humble and the great of society; they came to see what manner of man he was and to hear the eloquence of his message. Politically, he was a Liberal and a staunch friend of Gladstone, though not uncritical of the prime minister's advocacy of Home Rule for Ireland. Gladstone, in turn, was an admirer of Spurgeon and exchanged occasional correspondence with him.[45]

Spurgeon's greatness lay in his inherent goodness. Adulated all of his life, he remained humble and deeply sincere. Potentially wealthy through the vast sale of his publications, he died in modest circumstances, having given a fortune to the evangelistic, educational, and social agencies which he had created. His chief appeal was to the common people whom he loved and understood and who responded to the rare combination of common sense and Christian idealism which they found in him. His influence is still felt through the evangelistic ministry of the youth trained in his college and through the continued distribution of his writings. To those Baptists who are in sympathy with the combination of Calvinistic theology, Puritan morality, and evangelistic fervor which they discover in him, Spurgeon has become something of an ideal.

A contemporary of Spurgeon, though born a few years earlier and in Scotland, was Alexander Maclaren (1825-1910), the son of the pastor of the Scotch Baptist Church in Glasgow, the city of his birth. After his father moved to Australia, Alexander attended the Hope Street Baptist Church where he was baptized on May 7, 1840. He was educated in London, at Stepney College and at London University, where he excelled in the Greek and Hebrew Scriptures. He began his ministry at Portland Chapel in Southampton where he made a reputation for himself as being original in his thinking and manner. Not wearing clerical attire and treating scriptural themes in a distinctive style, it took him several years to live down the suspicion of heterodoxy which many entertained toward him. Nevertheless his ministry thrived, and in 1858 he was called to Man-

[45] H. S. Curr, "Spurgeon and Gladstone," *The Chronicle*, Vol. VI, No. 3 (July, 1943), 109-18, an article from the Quarterly of the British Baptist Historical Society, based on Spurgeon's *Autobiography* and Morley's *Life of Gladstone* in two volumes.

chester where he preached to great throngs. His sermons, published on both sides of the Atlantic, have served as models of eloquence and devotion. In 1878 Edinburgh University conferred upon him the degree of Doctor of Divinity in recognition of his outstanding attainments as a pulpiteer and expositor. He died on May 5, 1910.

By 1891 full union of Particular and General Baptists was attained when the Lancashire and Cheshire Association expressed willingness to welcome the New Connection into its membership. Significantly, Dr. John Clifford, a General Baptist, was in the chair at Burnley when the merger was effected. The membership of the Association was swelled thereby to 142 churches with 21,123 members. Only a few Baptist churches in the northern counties still remained outside of the fellowship; they were either Scotch or Strict Particular Baptists. This large association functioned through five districts, each with its own moderator and a full-time paid secretary, a practice which was copied by other associations.[46] As a result of the merger, "associations were rearranged, and some of the corporate spirit of the New Connection came over to the Baptist Union."[47] The move was consonant with the spirit of the times; for in 1892 a Free Church Congress assembled, being representative of the major nonconformist bodies in the country. Out of its deliberations developed the National Council of Evangelical Free Churches in England, which included Baptists, Congregationalists, Methodists, and Presbyterians, united to protect their common interests within a country where state-churchism prevailed. Indeed, by this time even the Anglicans were more friendly to dissenters. The spirit of tolerance was spreading.

Indicative of the Baptist leadership in the Free Church movement was John Clifford (1836-1923), a man of varied gifts and broad vision. He was born in Sawley, Derbyshire, on October 16, 1836. He studied at Midland Baptist College at Leicester, at the University College in London, and at the Royal School of Mines where he pursued graduate studies. Clifford gave to Baptist leadership a scholarly and forceful pen which served well not only the cause of the denomination, but also the whole cause of nonconformity. Always an ardent

[46] Shipley, ed., *Baptists in Yorkshire, Lancashire, Cheshire, and Cumberland,* Part II, 237-44.

[47] Whitley, *A History of British Baptists,* 327.

believer in nonsectarianism in public school education and in the co-operation of Free Evangelical Churches for their mutual benefit, he wrote politically on these matters. From 1870 to 1883 he edited the *General Baptist Magazine*. His leadership was pronounced among Baptists and non-Baptists alike. For fifty-seven years he was pastor of the Praed Street and Westbourne Park Church in London (1858-1915). From 1898 to 1899 he served as president of the National Council of Evangelical Free Churches in England. Between 1905 and 1911 he was president of the Baptist World Alliance, which he had helped to found in the aforementioned year. In many respects he had an ecumenical outlook without any sacrifice of his Baptist principles. Universities in England and America honored him with degrees of distinction. Dr. Clifford died, after a long and full life, on November 20, 1923.

As one reflects upon these developments, one should avoid the conclusion that the attainment of a large measure of denominational solidarity was the solution to the problems faced by British Baptists. On the contrary, it should be noted that in 1900 the spirit of the times was, in all probability, less friendly to evangelism than it had been in 1837; for there had developed a materialistic outlook and a preoccupation with a variety of interests which rivaled the voice of the evangelist and the clergyman. It is significant that the evangelistic meetings conducted by visiting American revivalists, including Dwight L. Moody, Reuben A. Torrey, and William E. Biederwolf, did not result in an increase in converts and churches in proportion to the population growth. While revivalism, to be sure, was more suited to large areas of the American scene with its free frontier culture, the lack of marked results in England has been attributed by an English Baptist historian to secular interests which were competing with the Christian gospel.[48]

Social Contributions

To measure the social attitudes and contributions of Baptists is not easy, because their relatively decentralized organization makes it difficult to trace the actions of Baptist groups. Then, too, it is not easy to determine when Baptists are acting as *Baptists* on social issues. The average man's social views and political behavior often

[48] Cf. Whitley, *A History of British Baptists*, 322-3.

are as much the product of economic, social, and political considerations as of religious convictions. Nevertheless, Baptists have had in
their membership a high percentage of the common people, and their
influence should not be overlooked. Even a limited survey of Baptist
influence upon social reform has its value, for it shows the impact of
the religious factor in the struggle of the lower classes to improve
their lot.

It will be recalled that parliamentary reform was an important
issue in nineteenth-century England, particularly in the second and
third decades, when the middle class sought to gain representation
in the House of Commons. The shift in population due to industrial
changes caused Englishmen in the northern counties to find themselves with inadequate representation, while nearly empty boroughs
in the South retained a full quota of seats in the House of Commons.
It is not surprising that Yorkshiremen should then share in the enthusiasm for reform. Indeed, in this respect, the Baptists of that county
evinced a striking change of attitude toward participation in political
affairs. A historian of the Yorkshire Association summarized their
concern in the following statement:

In the early days of the Association little interest was taken in political
questions. Very few of the members of our Churches had a vote, and as Mr.
Upton says, they seemed quite satisfied with the wise and benignant legislation
which gave them the Toleration Act. . . . But as we approach the year 1830,
the Pastors and Messengers show quite another disposition. Either politics had
invaded the Church, or the Church was girding herself, as she ought, to take
her share in politics. Frequent resolutions appear, intended to strengthen the
hands of Lord John Russell and his colleagues in their religious disabilities, and
chiefly in the Repeal of the Test and Corporation Acts, the results of which
have been perhaps more favorable to our denomination in Yorkshire and Lancashire than in any other part of England.[49]

There is little doubt that economic and political interests had
become very strong to arouse Baptists to support officially moves for
reform in the face of their usual unwillingness to participate as a
church unit in state affairs. In fact, among Baptist leaders generally,
a more or less active participation in the movement was evident. Such
Baptists as Robert Hall, Joseph Ivimey, and Francis Cox were active
dissenters who entered into an alliance with Whigs in the struggle
to reform Parliament between 1815 and 1830. Indeed, in the later
year, the May and June issues of the *Baptist Magazine* carried full

[49] Shipley, ed., *Baptists in Yorkshire, Lancashire, Cheshire, and Cumberland*, 300-1.

details of dissenters' activities. Moreover, churches were asked to send petitions to Parliament in behalf of the Reform Bill and other measures.[50]

Although the passing of the great Reform Bill of 1832 redistributed seats in the House of Commons in favor of the middle class, the Act proved of little benefit to the working classes who had supported the measure in hopes of bettering their lot. However, without the right to vote and the privilege of representation, their anticipation was not realized. As a result, the poorer classes organized what came to be known as the "Chartist Movement." They set forth a charter of rights that made such demands as annual parliaments, salaries for members of Parliament which would enable a working man to hold that office, and full manhood suffrage. Since the rank and file of Baptists were of the common people, it is understandable that their sympathies were with the Chartists and with the Free Tradists who advocated abolishing tariffs on cereals so as to lower the price of bread. One writer has concluded that:

> From the beginning the sympathies of English Baptists were with the Trade Unionists. . . . When the Anglican Church and all the other non-conformist bodies turned against the Chartists, with their demands for such reforms as universal suffrage, vote by ballot and abolition of property qualifications for membership in the House of Commons, many Baptist leaders such as Cooper, O'Neil, and Vince, espoused their cause, urged their claims and sent delegates to their Convention.[51]

An issue of equal importance to reformers in the same period was the abolition of the slave trade. In this struggle, Baptists took a lively interest. In the late eighteenth century various organizations expressed their sympathy with the abolitionist cause and proffered aid. From 1787 to 1791 the Western Association and the Midland Association sent money to the abolitionists in London for use in their fight to abolish the slave trade.[52] In 1787 the General Assembly of General Baptists participated in the widespread agitation for abolition which was then pressing Parliament for action.[53] Joseph Ivimey, a prominent Baptist clergyman, served on the Agency

[50] Raymond G. Cowherd, *Protestant Dissenters in English Politics:* 1815 to 1834 (Philadelphia, 1942), 61-9, 87.

[51] Austen K. deBlois, "Social Rights and Baptist History," *The Christian Review*, March and June issues, 1936. For petition of Yorkshire Association in behalf of Corn Laws repeal, see *Baptists of Yorkshire, Lancashire, Cheshire, and Cumberland*, Part I, 304.

[52] Ivimey, *History of English Baptists: 1760-1820* (London, 1830), 63.

[53] *Minutes of General Assembly*, II, 194, 196.

Committee of the Anti-Slavery Society. This was the inner circle of an interdenominational organization.[54] Thus, in 1830 the slavery issue had much to do with the revival of Baptist interest in public life. The Baptist Union actually sent delegates to the American Baptists to win their support, but Southerners in the Triennial Convention of American Baptists ruled their petition out of order.[55]

As early as 1811 Parliament had acted to abolish the slave trade, but slaveowners in those colonies which, like Jamaica, enjoyed self-government were reluctant to do the same. As we have seen, the Jamaican planters sought to restrict missionaries and actually mistreated them when a slave rebellion occurred in 1831, although the missionaries had taken no part in encouraging it. As a result, William Knibb, a Baptist missionary on the island, became thoroughly aroused in behalf of the maltreated Negro population. In the summer of 1832 he returned to England to awaken public sentiment to the seriousness of the situation there. Parliamentary committees listened to his testimony. By 1838, pressed on by an incensed public opinion, Parliament passed an Act to reimburse the planters for the slaves who were to be set free.[56]

The continuation of slavery in America caused English Baptists much concern, especially the participation of many American Baptists in the traffic. As early as December 31, 1833, the "Board of Baptist Ministers in and near London" sent a lengthy appeal to the Triennial Convention's headquarters in Boston (mistaking this foreign mission agency for a denominational body with supervision in America), urging it to abolish slavery in the States as the British were doing in Jamaica. American Baptists replied with cautionary explanations of state rights and of the need to suppress any question which would cause agitation and possible disunion. In the spring of 1835 the Reverend F. A. Cox, chairman of the London Board of Baptist ministers, and the Reverend J. Hoby were appointed by the Baptist Union of England to promote the cause of emancipation in the churches in the United States. Upon their return to England, the Baptist Union sent a resolution to American Baptists condemning their alliance with slavery. During the next few years, English Baptist Associations passed numerous resolutions

[54] Cowherd, *Protestant Dissenters in English Politics*, 74.
[55] Whitley, *History of British Baptists*, 277.
[56] John H. Hinton, *Memoir of William Knibb, Missionary to Jamaica*, chs. 10-12.

condemning slavery, some declining "any fraternal union" with their American brethren who approved slavery. For example, the Yorkshire Association, in 1841, declared that it refused to maintain communion with any Christian who was either a slaveholder or an advocate of slaveholding. Obviously, the sentiments of the resolution were directed across the Atlantic.

When the Civil War (1861-1865) brought emancipation to the slaves in the United States, the Yorkshire Baptists were jubilant and at once commended the claims of the National Freedmen's Aid Society to the generosity of the churches. The same attitude was manifested by the Lancashire and Cheshire Association in spite of the fact that many of its members were millworkers dependent for their livelihood upon a steady supply of American cotton which was cut off during the American conflict.[57]

Baptists were also concerned about another type of human need, namely, unhealthy and improper prison conditions. In John Howard, Baptists had a spokesman whose studies of prison conditions throughout Europe and Britain aroused a reform-minded public to the need for prison improvement. In 1774 a Parliament committee heard his report. The result was the passage of two bills which improved England's prison facilities considerably.[58]

Until the late eighteenth century, Baptists were somewhat slow to realize the importance of education. A few of their ministers, to be sure, taught promising youths in private boarding schools of the type maintained by Hanserd Knollys in London, John Fawcett near Hebden Bridge, and Dan Taylor at Birchcliff; but little was done by way of developing a parochial system. Under the impetus of the Evangelical Revival, a new type of school was hit upon, a school held on Sunday when children were not obliged to be at their places of employment. Thus, in 1780, the Sunday school movement got under way as a means of teaching boys and girls who worked all during the week to read and write, and to know

[57] Robert A. Baker, *Relations Between Northern and Southern Baptists*, 43-46; H. Wheeler Robinson *et al.*, *The Baptists of Yorkshire*, 301; Shipley, ed., *Baptists in Yorkshire, Lancashire, Cheshire and Cumberland*, Part I, 301; Part II, 194.

[58] See John Stoughton, *Howard, the Philanthropist and His Friends*, and William E. H. Lecky, *History of England in the Eighteenth Century*, Vols. 3 and 7. Howard, a Congregationalist, worshiped for many years in the Little Wild Street Baptist Church in London, of which Dr. Samuel Stennett was pastor; cf. Underwood, *A History of the English Baptists*, 148, and Cathcart, *The Baptist Encyclopedia*, 548-49.

the Bible. The origin of the plan is attributed to Robert Raikes, proprietor and editor of the *Gloucester Journal,* who established a reading and catechism school for "ignorant and depraved children" in his own town. The experiment worked so well that it was continued and even begun in other communities. On Sundays, the children's free day, they were marched to church for their only instruction of the week.

In 1785 William Fox, a deacon of the Prescott Street Baptist Church in London, proposed to his friends a plan to have a Sunday School Society for the sponsoring of Sunday schools. The idea stemmed from a practice in which he had engaged for several years as Lord of the Manor of Clopton near Bourton-on-the-water. His custom was to conduct a free day school for the children of the parish. Before the second meeting of his friends was held to consider his proposal, Fox heard of Raikes' Sunday schools in the neighborhood of Gloucester. Much impressed, he adopted the plan at once and proposed it to his fellows. On September 5, a Sunday School Society was established at the Paul's Head Tavern on Cateaton Street, with considerable patronage. An innovation in its organization was that the administrative committee should be composed of an equal number of Anglicans and dissenters. A principle was adopted that only the Bible should be used as the principal studybook, even to the exclusion of all catechisms. For several years, the Society supported schools in various parts of the country, paying for teachers, for spelling books, Bibles and Testaments. However, when the expense became too great, voluntary teachers were relied upon to conduct the schools. At first, employers and those of the Tory school of thought forbade Sunday schools to teach writing; the reading of the Bible they could scarcely forbid. Their reason was prompted by fear that poor youths would be unwilling to work with their hands and to submit to the rule of a privileged class.[59] The Baptists were not deterred in their purpose, however, and William Brodie Gurney, a layman who served as stenographer in the House of Lords, began his long career of public service by founding the Sunday School Union in 1803, which more than ever united the workers in the various denominations in a great educational enterprise.

[59] Ivimey, *A History of the English Baptists,* IV, 83-4; Whitley, *History of British Baptists,* 261.

In 1814 an interesting educational experiment for poor Irish children in the St. Giles section of London was begun at the suggestion of a Baptist minister. He hired rooms in Baynbrigg Street, and employed an Irish schoolmaster to teach the children on Sundays. Soon Protestants of all denominations were supporting what came to be called "St. Giles Catholic School," where children of Roman Catholic parents were taught evenings and on Sundays. The only textbooks used were the Bible, without note or comment, and a spelling book. The children were free to attend whatever church their parents preferred. A Society was organized to promote the project. Among its officers were noblemen and members of Parliament. Three other schools were founded on the same principle for children of Roman Catholic parentage in the Borough, Whitechapel and Westminster areas of the metropolis. In addition, relief was provided for needy parents when necessary.[60] The broad humanitarian principle on which this enterprise was conducted by church people in these communities indicates a development of the practical expression of Christian service within the spirit of religious tolerance which transcended even Protestant-Catholic differences.

When the National government began in 1833 to issue an annual grant of twenty thousand pounds to religious bodies to build new schools, Baptists viewed it for what it was—a concession to win support of nonconformists. They refrained from applying for their share on the grounds that to receive such state assistance as a sectarian body would violate their commitment to the principle of separation of church and state.[61] Their prophecy that schools receiving such grants would be subject to government inspection was fulfilled in 1839 when a Government Board was established for the purpose. In the face of this threat to the independency of church schools, a Baptist educational conference was held in 1844 at the instigation of George Foster of Sabden in the Lancashire and Cheshire Association. The churches were called upon to establish day schools under distinctly denominational auspices and to refuse government aid which would place education under government control or hinder the use of school premises for preaching stations.

[60] Ivimey, *op. cit.*, 171-4.

[61] In this account, the Association of Lancashire and Chesire is used as being generally typical of Baptist reaction in England; see Shipley, ed., *Baptists in Yorkshire, Lancashire, Cheshire, and Cumberland*, Part II, 193-4, 200-3, 208-9; cf. Whitley, *op. cit.*, 289.

For this project, a committee of the Association was appointed to collect subscriptions and to supervise its establishment.

In the fifties the churches not only maintained numerous Sunday and day schools in addition to the private schools run by clergymen, but contemplated the enlargement of Horton Academy (now Rawdon College), which had been founded in 1804. The program was defeated, however, by opposition to such ambitious educational plans from strict Calvinists and by lack of sufficient funds. When the public conscience became stirred against child labor in the rapidly multiplying mills of the period, legislation was enacted in 1862 requiring that children be given time for schooling. The growing sentiment in favor of every child going to school caused the churches to be faced with a new challenge. But when Forster's Education Bill was proposed in 1870, providing for the establishing of public elementary and secondary schools under sectarian supervision, Baptists adopted at once a negative position. They favored public education only so long as it should be nonsectarian. To be sure, they themselves had not set up their own parochial schools to help meet the need, but their failure to do so was only partly due to an insufficient concern on their part for general education. It was due also to a lack of funds and to a too ready reliance upon the Sunday schools to provide basic instruction for their children. Many other dissenters likewise had failed to respond to the voluntary principle of public education under church auspices.

By the Forster Act, grammar schools and public secondary schools were opened to dissenters; even Cambridge and Oxford were made available to them for higher education, except in divinity. For training in theology, dissenters were accepted by the Universities of Wales and Manchester. Quite naturally, Baptist students, like other dissenters, took advantage of these new privileges, and so slipped out from under the influence of their own denomination.

While the State reorganized old endowed schools and opened them to dissenters with some safeguards against proselytizing, Baptists, like most other nonconformists, failed to do more than oppose Anglican domination. When they might have been constructive by creating a system of elementary and secondary schools under their own guidance and supervision, they had lost their opportunity. Yet many, like the Yorkshire Association, felt that "the education of the people was not within the province of Government."[62] Such a conflict of interests can only be explained when the Baptists' fear of any infringement upon religion by the state or by a state church is understood. In addition, it must be observed that the strong emphasis in their polity upon independency cost Baptists heavily in their educational program, for only with strong denominational machinery run in democratic fashion could the task have been accomplished.

At the turn of the twentieth century, Baptists and other independents, led by Dr. John Clifford, engaged in a Passive Resistance Movement, which was an effort on the part of the evangelical free churches to protest effectively against the Education Bill of 1902. By it Balfour's Conservative Government sought to abolish the old school boards and local control of elementary and secondary education by bringing all such schools under borough and county governments. The voluntary schools were also brought under the Government's supervision so far as educational methods were concerned. While they were allowed to maintain their own buildings, the cost of education was to be paid from the local tax rates. Thus, while each denominational voluntary school could give religious instruction at the beginning or end of the class day as before, so that parents might withdraw their children if they so desired, all schools —Anglican, Catholic, and Dissenter—were to be supported by public funds. Such an arrangement, Dr. Clifford felt, would give the Anglicans undue control over the educational system and possibly might increase the number of Catholic schools, which were thereby eligible for state support.[63]

The Passive Resistance Movement really began in Birmingham where Dr. Dale, a Liberal member of the Birmingham School Board, and four associates refused to honor the power of the Board to pay the fees of poor children at the denominational schools in the town. Dr. Clifford made the "We-will-not-submit" campaign nationwide. As president of the National Council of Evangelical Free Churches in England, his influence was great in encouraging resistance to the payment of the tax rate on the grounds that it was a violation of religious liberty to use public funds for sectarian educa-

[62] H. Wheeler Robinson *et al., The Baptists of Yorkshire,* 304-5.
[63] Charles T. Bateman, *John Clifford: Free Church Leader and Preacher* (London, 1904), 252, 284-5.

tion. At first, many were jailed or had their property sold for payments. But the Liberals won in 1906, when a new bill provided that schools supported by public taxes should be managed by the state and could maintain no religious tests for teachers.

It may be said that the English Baptists' chief accomplishments in the field of education have been in the training of ministers and in the safeguarding of the public schools against sectarianism. Beyond these worthy attainments, their achievements have not been great. Of their theological colleges, the more important are the following: Bristol College, founded as an Academy in 1680; Midland College, in Nottingham, founded by the London New Connection Baptists in 1797; Rawdon College, near Leeds in Yorkshire, founded as Horton Academy in 1804 by the Northern Baptist Education Society; Stepney (1810), which was moved to London in 1855, renamed Regent's Park College some time later, and then relocated under that name in Oxford in 1928; Spurgeon's College, in London, founded in 1856; Manchester's strict communionist college established in 1866; Cardiff, in Wales, founded in 1897; and Bangor College, also in Wales, established in 1862. In Scotland, there is the Baptist Theological College of Scotland in Glasgow. The Irish Baptists have a similar type of institution in Dublin. The attendance in these institutions is not large, but each has sent forth a steady stream of ministers of the gospel.

The major factor responsible for the converting of the early academies or boarding schools for ministerial candidates into theological colleges was the inspiration and example afforded by American Baptists, who established the Rhode Island College in 1764. It is significant that this institution, which was founded with the financial assistance of English Baptists, was intended from the first to provide a general college training as well as ministerial preparation. Since associations, controlled by older ministers, who themselves were often destitute of education and without vision for higher learning, were not eager to encourage the cause, education societies were developed, independent of associational control, but reliant upon the churches for support. It is indicative of the rise in educational and cultural appreciation among British Baptists that there has developed this group of educational institutions in a country where Baptists are not very numerous or wealthy.

Perhaps a significant contribution of English Baptists, as indeed of all Baptists, is their emphasis upon religious liberty. This was the chief reason why Baptists felt justified in joining with dissenters on numerous political issues. There were several who kept the torch of religious liberty burning during the nineteenth century. At Bristol Academy, Robert Hall, through the influence of his teacher, John Ryland, came to appreciate the significance of civil and religious freedom. Both men were Baptists. William Carey in Leicestershire had not hesitated to assist his fellow dissenters in their efforts to secure repeal of the Test and Corporation Acts. Indeed, the leadership among dissenters generally realized that only by a political alignment with the popular Whig Party could they hope to achieve religious liberty.[64]

On at least two occasions early in the century, Baptists sought out political assistance in order to safeguard their rights. The first was in 1807, when they sought Whig support to gain government protection for their missionaries in India, the story of which has been related already. The second was in 1809, when they attempted to defeat Lord Sidmouth's efforts to restrict the freedom of Protestant dissenting ministers in securing licenses to preach under provision of the Toleration Act. According to his plan, each minister would have been required to provide recommendations of six respectable housekeepers of the congregation to which he belonged, and he would have to have a congregation which would listen to him preach. Obviously, it was an attempt to prevent lay and itinerant preachers from securing licenses which would grant them the privileges accorded to ordained ministers. The general body of dissenting clergymen at once appointed a committee to watch the progress of Sidmouth's bill; Dan Taylor, leader of the New Connection General Baptists, was its chairman. It prepared resolutions declaring that the bill violated religious liberty and the right to gather peaceably for religious worship and public instruction. These resolutions were adopted by the Society of Deputies, an organization of ministers of various denominations who represented the interests of dissenters in the face of government action. When petitions against the bill arrived in London from congregations from far and wide, Lord Liverpool, the prime minister, and Dr. Sutton, the Archbishop

[64] Cowherd, *Protestant Dissenters in English Politics,* 61.

of Canterbury, advised that the bill be rejected. Accordingly, on July 23, 1812, a new Toleration Act was passed, repealing the Conventicle and Five Mile Acts and granting new privileges to dissenters. While the victory was largely the product of Wesleyan Methodists' efforts, Ivimey, the contemporary Baptist historian, states that Baptists took their part and were treated respectfully by other denominations.[65]

British Baptists Since 1900

It is important for an understanding of British Baptists to remember that their development has taken place within a state-church environment. For mutual benefits they had found it expedient to unite in 1893 with other nonconformists, such as Presbyterians, Methodists, and Congregationalists, in the National Free Church Council. Things that divided them were set aside for the greater interests that challenged them in the face of a national ecclesiastical uniformity. As borrowing took place on a large scale with respect to hymns, forms of worship, leadership, and scholarship, Baptists have experienced many perplexities in the maintaining of their own witness. Another trend to challenge their denominational emphasis is the decline of nonconformity in recent decades with the accompanying change of outlook of the Anglican Church in the direction of ecumenicity.[66]

In such a changing milieu, the Baptist Union of Great Britain and Ireland has maintained a steady leadership. Dr. John Howard Shakespeare, who was appointed secretary in 1898, shaped the authority and prestige of the Union over a period of twenty-six years. With headquarters in London, this organization represented the concerted efforts of twenty-seven Baptist Associations in the British Isles to give forth a united witness. Theoretically, the Union has been a voluntary association of churches, associations, colleges, and individuals who make contributions to its work; it has no legal authority to challenge the autonomy of the local church. Actually, it has become a strongly centralized organ of the entire Baptist community, maintaining the efficiency and responsibility which formerly

[65] Ivimey, *A History of English Baptists*, IV, 110-7.

[66] Ernest A. Payne, *The Fellowship of Believers: Baptist Thought and Practice Yesterday and Today* (London, 1944), pp. 76-90. A good account of the Baptist Union since 1900.

rested upon local churches or associations. In much the same trend as in America, the local units have lost a degree of initiative and responsibility in the face of this development.

During the First World War, the Union was responsible for the appointment of Baptist chaplains for the armed services. As a member of the National Council of the Evangelical Free Churches, it was the mouthpiece of all Baptists in their relation to other religious bodies. In 1898 its invested funds were £180,000. By 1926 they had mounted to £750,000; by 1944 the figure had reached £1,250,000. It has given increasing attention to ministerial pensions, the training of preachers, the establishing of an Order of Deaconesses, and the expression to the public of Baptist opinion.[67] The financial support of the Union comes from its member churches, associations, and from individual contributors. A local church has the privilege at any time, if it deems it right, to leave the fellowship of the organization. Nevertheless, as a British Baptist spokesman has put it, "it has been recognized that the sovereign authority of Christ may be seen and expressed within the ordered life of the whole Baptist community as well as in the local company of believers, and the latter voluntarily accepts certain limitations of and restrictions upon its authority as the price of wider fellowship and more effective service."[68]

The changes in the thinking of English Baptists are indicative of what has been happening to nonconformists generally. While London Baptists, for example, still regard adherence to Calvinism as highly important, the majority of Baptists pay little attention to questions of dogmatic theology, preferring to give their interest to the practical and moral implications of Christianity. Experiments have been tried in the uniting of Baptists and paedobaptists in one church, with equal rights. These experiments have not been very successful, for out of thirty-five such churches established in London, only thirteen survived in 1928. Of that number, three returned to a thoroughly Baptist constituency, two became Congregationalist, leaving only eight as union congregations. Yet, throughout the Baptist fellowship in Britain, there are persons who do not attach major importance to believers' baptism by immersion as a requisite to membership.[69]

[67] Payne, *The Fellowship of Believers*, pp. 78-9.
[68] *Ibid.*, p. 81.
[69] W. T. Whitley, *The Baptists of London: 1612-1928* (London, 1928), pp. 27, 29; Payne, *op. cit.*, p. 84.

The invitation of the Anglican bishops, in 1920, to all Christian people to consider the subject of church union—an appeal issued by the Lambeth Conference—brought the Baptists as well as all other nonconformists face to face with the imperative of restating their position with reference to the church and the ministry. The Baptists did not set forth their own reply to the appeal until after the National Council of the Free Churches of England had reported on their conversations with the Anglican bishops concerning the details of the proposal for church union. When the conversations were suspended and statements were issued by each body, the Baptist Union, in annual assembly on May 4, 1926, issued a document which set forth its position. The statement defined the catholic church "as the holy society of believers in our Lord Jesus Christ . . . to be found wherever companies of believers unite as Churches on the ground of a confession of personal faith." The document then went on to explain that "the headship and sole authority of our Lord in His Church excludes any such relations with the State as may impair its liberty."

Having expressed their views concerning the church, the Baptists made it clear that they could not give the ancient creeds of the Christian community equal value with the Sacred Scriptures. They insisted that they could administer the ordinance of baptism only to those who make a personal confession of repentance and faith. "In our judgment," they explained, "the baptism of infants incapable of offering a personal confession of faith subverts the conception of the Church as the fellowship of believers." They differed also with respect to their conception of the ministry, which they considered not to be a priesthood, but "a gift of the Spirit to the Church, and is an office involving both the inward call of God and the commission of the Church." On such grounds, then, the Baptists declined courteously to admit the possibility of church union, although they expressed willingness to engage in "a federation of equal and autonomous Churches in which the several parts of the Church of Christ would co-operate in bringing before men the will and the claims of our Lord."[70]

In the following year, 1927, the World Conference on Faith and Order was held at Lausanne, Switzerland, at which time represent-

[70] Quotations from the Baptist Reply to the Lambeth Appeal are cited from the document in Payne, *The Fellowship of Believers*, pp. 102-5.

atives of the various communions participating discussed the nature of the church and its ministry. This prompted the Baptist Union, meeting at Liverpool, in 1930, to make its position clear once again. "We cannot agree," they said, "that the ministry, as commonly understood, is essential to the existence of a true Christian Church, though we believe a ministry is necessary for its highest effectiveness. We think of the function of the ministry in terms of leadership rather than of government and discipline.[71] In such terms they maintained their traditional refusal to admit the validity of the statement, "no bishop, no Church."

It is significant that in 1939, only two years after the historic meeting in Oxford and Edinburgh of most of the great communions of Christendom (except the Roman Catholic Church) the world was plunged into a devastating war. Except for the Southern Baptist Convention, which sent only observers, American and British Baptists were participants in these great ecumenical conferences. The Christian church was drawing together, but not so the nations of the world. International hostilities soon engulfed the energies of the British people. During the "blitz" of Nazi bombers in 1940-41, the church life of the British Isles was seriously disrupted. Children were evacuated from the cities, thus interrupting Sunday schools; evening preaching services were omitted because of blackouts; destruction of churches often necessitated union meetings of Evangelical congregations.

Yet in the midst of wartime preoccupations, English Baptists undertook the celebration of the one hundred and fiftieth anniversary of their Baptist Missionary Society, which had been organized in 1792 at Kettering, England, under the compulsion of William Carey's missionary zeal. The celebrations were officially launched in London during the Spring Assembly of the Union, when the Reverend B. Grey Griffith, the retiring Home Secretary, succeeded to the presidency of the Baptist Union. Thereupon the Campaign to raise additional funds for the missionary enterprise was carried to the churches, and special meetings were held by the various Associations in the late spring and summer. The response of the churches in evacuated, bombed and other war-scarred areas, was both enthusiastic and sacrificial. Sunday schools also helped. Baptist women formed teams of speakers to visit women's gatherings. The smallest church in Wales,

<hr>

[71] *Ibid.*, p. 33.

with two members, sent £5 2s. 6d. Indeed, Welsh Baptists contributed a total of £28,324. Scotland contributed £13,413. The British mission fields each made their gifts, India sending £961; Ceylon, £862; the Congo, £1,047; and the West Indies, £50. By the close of the drive on December 31, 1943, the total of £157,677 had been received, with the promise of more to follow. However, there were other than financial returns. Spiritually, the churches were inspired and invigorated, and 257 young people volunteered for foreign missionary service. In addition, the good will manifested by other religious organizations, including the Anglican clergy, reflected the added prestige which British Baptists have come to enjoy in recent years.[72]

Baptists of Britain faced an almost overwhelming task following World War II. Of the four thousand churches which had been destroyed or damaged during the war, 740 were Baptist. Of these, sixty were completely demolished and 680 repairable. Although the Government planned to reimburse congregations so that they could erect simple buildings for worship, it was necessary for the congregations to purchase all interior equipment themselves. Many were the adjustments which had to be made. Churches whose membership had been scattered by wartime conditions had the problem of reuniting their members. Congregations which had grown accustomed to union services had to resume the support of an independent ministry. The disrupted organizational life was restored to normal only slowly. The most pressing concern which confronted all of the denominations was how to overcome the spiritual inertia and war-weariness which had accompanied the general letdown and disappointment over postwar problems.[73]

Baptists met their responsibilities courageously. Through the Baptist Union, a Reconstruction Campaign was launched in the churches for the purpose of raising six hundred thousand dollars, of which four hundred thousand was to be used at home and two hundred thousand for Baptist reconstruction on the continent of Europe. It was planned that German Baptists should share largely in this assistance. Social concerns at home also occupied the churches. In Birmingham and Norwich homes for the aged were opened; in the latter case, as a joint project of Free churches. As a result of the

[72] Baptist Missionary Society, *Ter-Jubilee Celebrations, 1942-4,* pp. 9-19.
[73] William B. Lipphard, "Hope and Disillusionment in Postwar England," *Missions,* Vol. 37, No. 8 (Oct., 1946), pp. 460-6.

postwar desire for greater unity in religion as in politics, the question of church unity again emerged. Conversations were begun relative to the uniting of the Baptists and the Churches of Christ, or Disciples, as they are called in America. Union on a larger scale was proposed by Dr. Geoffrey Fisher, the Archbishop of Canterbury and chairman of the British Council of Churches, which was the British section of the World Council of Churches. He called upon the Free churches to take episcopacy into their systems. The Baptists, determined to maintain their distinctive witness and loth to break their tradition of aloofness from paedobaptist connections, made a reply which did not go beyond the courteous appointment of a committee of the Baptist Union to assist the National Council of Free Churches in making a study of the Archbishop's appeal.[74]

The missionary outreach of British Baptists has been maintained steadily since the days of Carey through the Baptist Missionary Society which worked in three countries of Southeast Asia, two in Africa, and three in the Western hemisphere. In 1959 a total of 189 missionaries and 1,084 national workers served the work in India, Pakistan, and Ceylon, where the Society operated 688 churches, 240 schools, and seven medical units. In the Congo Republic and Angola, 158 missionaries and 2,236 national workers served 1,430 churches, 1,094 schools, and 28 medical units. In Jamaica, Trinidad, and Brazil, 14 missionaries and 62 national workers served 278 churches and 77 schools. On all of the fields there was a combined Baptist community of 107,963.[75]

At home Baptists have experienced a decline in membership common to all denominations in Britain. The churches once closely allied with the Liberal Party in government have suffered loss of prestige as this party has disintegrated in the face of war and postwar pressures. Baptists in the British Isles in 1960 numbered 321,000. Over 75,000 of these were not affiliated with the Baptist Union of Great Britain and Ireland. Churches in England and to some extent in Wales have supported the ecumenical movement, but the Baptist Union of Scotland and the Baptist Union in Ireland have withdrawn from the World Council of Churches. About one-half of the churches

[74] *Ibid.*, 466; Gilbert Laws, "British Letter," *The Watchman-Examiner*, Vol. 35, No. 2, pp. 36-7. Dr. Laws formerly was pastor of St. Mary's Baptist Church in Norwich, England.

[75] *The Baptist World*, Vol. 8, No. 2 (Feb., 1961), 7.

in 1960 were pastorless. Lay preachers and paid deaconesses were recruited for vacant pulpits. Open membership has been widely practiced except in some areas of Wales and the North of England where there is a strong sectarian feeling in spite of financial problems and a shortage of ministers. Since the war more than one hundred new churches have been established as the product of a new emphasis on evangelism.[76] Perhaps the outstanding Christian statesman among English Baptists is Ernest A. Payne, general secretary of the Baptist Union of Great Britain and Ireland, and a member of the executive committee of the World Council of Churches. He typifies the readiness of the Union to preserve the best of the Baptist heritage within the context of an ecumenical witness.

[76] Leonard Gittings, "British Baptists Look to the Future," *Crusader*, Vol. 15, No. 8 (Sept., 1960), 4-6.

CHAPTER FIVE

BRITISH DOMINION BAPTISTS

A CROSS the plains of Canada there stretches a chain of Baptist churches. Their congregations, some large, most of them small, have grown in spite of many handicaps. Prejudice on the part of those who have not understood the principles for which these churches stand has been a serious obstacle. Because of this prejudice, there are but few Baptists in Quebec, where the population is largely French Catholic. The broad expanse of the country with its populace scattered over wide areas has taxed the decentralized type of Baptist polity. Where planning and supervision have been necessary, there has been the problem of maintaining a balance between local autonomy and a denominational co-operation adequate for the task. Yet the present status of Baptists, although numbering little more than four per cent of the total population of the country, is sufficiently strong to indicate that many of the difficulties are being overcome.[1]

The Maritime Provinces

The rise of Baptist work in Canada occurred quite naturally in the Maritime Provinces, which lie to the north of New England. From this area, beginning in the late eighteenth century, Baptist influence spread westward. It appears that the earliest Baptist churches were the product of colonists' efforts, rather than of the efforts of missionaries to spread the gospel. This was true also of beginnings among the Anglicans, Congregationalists, Presbyterians, and Methodists. A direct relationship may be traced to New England emigrants who about the middle of the eighteenth century were escaping persecution for their religious convictions. Some were "New Light" Congregationalists, others were Baptists—all of them products of the Great Awakening. They shared belief in the necessity for

[1] J. L. Gilmour, "The Baptists of Canada," a chapter in Adam Shortt and Arthur G. Doughty, editors, *Canada and Its Provinces*, Vol. XI, 347. Statistics are based on a report contained in the *Encyclopedia Britannica* (1947 edition), Vol. IV, 694-5.

the conversion of adults, in the primacy of the Bible and preaching, and in a congregational type of church government.[2]

Both groups labored in the Maritime Provinces, as may be typified by the Reverend Ebenezer Moulton, a Baptist immigrant from Massachusetts, and Henry Alline, a "New Light" Congregationalist, who never became a Baptist, but who paved the way for Baptist work. Prior to 1760 Moulton lived in Brimfield, Massachusetts, where he combined business with preaching in order to make a living. But the depression which accompanied and followed the Seven Years War (1756-1763) prompted him to escape from straitened financial conditions by migrating to Nova Scotia. He settled at Chebogue, Yarmouth County, becoming almost at once a Justice of the Peace. He preached in several private homes, won converts, and organized a Baptist church at Horton in 1763. About the same time, a Baptist congregation which had emigrated from Swansea, Massachusetts, under the leadership of its pastor, the Reverend Nathan Mason, arrived at Sackville, at the head of the Bay of Fundy. Most of the company, however, became dissatisfied with the country and returned to New England in 1771, leaving only a few to maintain the Baptist witness there. Almost at once, the Horton church lost its pastor, for Moulton returned to Brimfield. While a few converts remained to constitute the nucleus of a more permanent organization to be established in 1778, the little church, for all practical purposes, lost its identity. Nevertheless, the seed was sown by these two New England clergymen and by others who followed.

Typical of the "New Light" Congregational preachers was Henry Alline, whose family had migrated from Newport, Rhode Island, to Falmouth, Nova Scotia, in 1760. Very early, the youth felt the stirrings of religious conviction, but he did not become a Christian until he was twenty-seven years of age. His emphasis upon conversion was not congenial to many of his fellow Congregationalists or to the Anglicans and Scotch Presbyterians. However, this did not deter him from traveling tirelessly through the province from 1776 to 1783, preaching a moderate Calvinism and winning converts, many of whom became either Congregationalists or Baptists. While

[2] George E. Levy, *The Baptists of the Maritime Provinces, 1753-1946* (Saint John, N. B., 1946), 3, 10. This study has been relied upon to an appreciable degree for the survey of Maritime Baptists that follows.

the view of the latter on baptism was relatively unimportant to him, he willingly helped to establish the Baptist church at Horton (now known as Wolfville) on October 29, 1778. Several of its members were of that group who had been baptized fifteen years before by Moulton. His preaching and defense of religious liberty, which was akin to that of the Baptists, paved the way for an influx of shepherd-less Congregational churches into Baptist ranks when the ideals of the American Revolution made state-church Congregationalism in Massachusetts unpopular.[3]

After the Treaty of 1783, which recognized American Independence, thousands of Loyalists poured in from the States, doubling the population of Nova Scotia in less than two years. The strong Tory views of the majority strengthened the Established (Anglican) Church; some, however, were dissenters. The hitherto friendly relations between Protestant denominations began to deteriorate. Politically, there was a restiveness which led to the separation of New Brunswick from Nova Scotia, creating out of New Brunswick a new province under Tory control. Needless to say, the Baptists opposed the "Tory clique" and the strongly entrenched Anglican Church. They saw clearly that the advantages they had gained during the previous years were to be offset by unfriendly forces.

The Horton church fulfilled an important role as "mother" of new congregations, twenty in all within the first hundred years of her history. It started out as a close communion church, but within two years opened not only communion but also membership to non-Baptists. This became a practice characteristic of most of the early Baptist churches in the provinces. A notable exception was the church organized at Halifax in 1795. Baptist teaching exerted a strong influence in spite of the open membership policy, as is indicated by the fact that several "New Light" preachers, and in some cases their congregations, became Baptists.[4]

It soon became apparent that the fruits of such progress could be preserved only by an association of the churches which might give

---

[3] *Ibid.,* 30-5.

[4] Among these were Thomas H. Chapman at Lower Granville Baptist Church, an associate of Henry Alline; Theodore Seth Harding, of Congregational background and Methodist conversion, at Horton church; John Burton, of the Church of England, pastor at Halifax; Edward Manning, a New Light Congregationalist, at Cornwallis; Harris Harding, of similar background, at Yarmouth. See *Ibid.,* 45-54.

direction and inspiration to the work and serve as a check upon individual laxness in doctrinal and moral standards. This was needed, for discord was being produced by an emphasis upon hyper-Calvinism on the one hand and by insistence upon the validity of prophecy and special revelation to certain individuals on the other. For these various reasons, then, New Light Baptist and Congregational churches met in 1798 at Cornwallis, Nova Scotia, to organize "The Baptist and Congregational Association." A year later, owing to the predominance of Baptists in the meeting which was held from June 23 to 24, the word "Congregational" was dropped and rules were adopted to provide for a strictly Baptist fellowship to be known as the Nova Scotia Baptist Association. This was the first step in organizational development among Canadian Baptists. From the outset the association served as an agency to carry on home missions. This practice was in contrast to that of American Baptists, who conducted their missionary activities through especially constituted societies rather than through the associations. The Baptists of Canada have retained to the present time the associational method of administering the missionary program.

At first, some churches kept aloof from the Association, for it included in its fellowship churches that had received into their memberships unimmersed New Light Congregationalists. After 1809, when the Association adopted the policy of close communion and Calvinistic doctrine, some churches withdrew for a time, but later returned. In every respect this organization, in conducting its own affairs, recognized the independence of the local church. The body was unique, however, in that it assumed the function of examining and ordaining candidates for the ministry. Baptists usually have regarded the latter as a prerogative of the local churches. In 1827 the right of ordaining was restored to the individual churches. In 1821, at the request of the New Brunswick churches, the Association was divided into two separate bodies, one for Nova Scotia and the other for New Brunswick; but fraternal relations between the two were maintained.

Free Baptist work had begun with the Barrington church some time before 1795. It was Arminian in theology and it practiced open communion. In 1834 an association was organized. Three years later it took into membership the "Christians" under the leadership of Elder Norton, a group which held views similar to those of the Baptists. Symbolic of the union was the name adopted by the new body, the "Free Christian Baptist Conference." Its polity was more centralized than that of the Regular or Calvinistic Baptists.

The initial impulse for a missionary interest among Regular Baptists came in 1814 when Edward Manning, pastor of the Cornwallis church, wrote into the Nova Scotia Baptist Association's circular letter of that year an appeal for support of foreign missions. It was an effort to parallel the contributions of Baptists of the British Isles during the preceding two years. The next day an offering was taken for the cause, and each year thereafter a contribution was sent to the British and Foreign Bible Society to support foreign mission work. At the same time, two home missionaries were appointed to labor in the vicinity of Chester. In 1815 the Association constituted itself a missionary society and sent additional workers to the territory east of Halifax. It is noteworthy that this pattern developed contemporaneously with the rise of the Baptists' Triennial Convention in the United States, yet it differed from the American pattern. In the States, mission societies were created as agencies separate from the associations. This was done to protect the local churches from losing their autonomy to the association. Even the Triennial Convention was a missionary agency which had no ecclesiastical control over the churches.

After the division of the Association in 1821, each body assumed responsibility for mission work in its own area, the Nova Scotia Association caring for Prince Edward Island. In 1826 the New Brunswick Association, which had constituted itself a separate mission society, set up the first Home Mission Board of Baptists in Canada. While growth during this period was significant, the number of ministers was not large, there being "in New Brunswick only fifteen ministers for twenty-eight churches, with a membership of 1,347, and in Nova Scotia seventeen ministers for twenty-nine churches and a membership of 1,711."[5]

The influence of New England Baptists was felt steadily in the first century of Baptist development in the Maritime Provinces. Exchanges of delegates and visitors between the churches in the two territories quite naturally resulted in mutual helpfulness and inter-

[5] Levy, *The Baptists of the Maritime Provinces*, 95.

change of ideas. This was particularly true in the establishment of educational institutions, the stimulating center of which was the Granville Street Baptist Church. This church had been organized in Halifax in 1827 by a group of Anglicans who had become Baptists. It was a congregation of cultured people, among whom were Dr. E. A. Crawley, a lawyer who became pastor of the church and later the head of Acadia College, and the Honorable J. W. Johnstone, who eventually occupied the significant post of prime minister of Nova Scotia, and later that of Lieutenant-governor of the Province. Largely through the efforts of the men of this church, the Nova Scotia Baptist Education Society was organized in 1828. Its first task was to establish Horton Academy in 1829 at Wolfville for the principal purpose of training candidates for the ministry. New England Baptists and the Newton Theological Institution in Massachusetts, in particular, assisted in the organization of both the church and the school.

While plans were developed to expand the Academy into a seminary or college, they did not materialize at once for two reasons. New Brunswick Baptists were anxious to set up their own seminary at Fredericton. In addition, a provincial university was organized at Halifax under the control of the Nova Scotia Assembly. This school, which came to be known as Dalhousie University, was to be nonsectarian and was to be supported jointly by various denominations including Baptists. Therefore, when the application of Dr. Crawley, pastor of the Granville Street Church, for a teaching position was rejected on the grounds that he was a Baptist, a general call was revived for a Baptist college at Wolfville. Because religious tests kept Baptists out of the Anglican colleges, many young men were forced to leave the country for an education. Maritime Baptists were desirous of putting an end to these conditions. Accordingly, Acadia College came into being at Wolfville, and like Horton Academy, which also was situated there, it imposed no "denominational restrictions on professors or students."[6] After the opening of the college in 1839 there was a delay of two years before a charter was obtained, owing to difficulties with the Legislative Assembly and Council. In 1844 a Department of Theology was added with the aid of a gift of one hundred pounds from the Baptist Missionary

[6] *Ibid.*, 118. For detailed account, see pp. 109-23.

Society of England. Dr. Crawley was the first head of the college, although not president in name. When he returned to the pastorate of the Granville Street Church in 1847, John Pryor succeeded him and was made the first president of the college. By 1850 the school had won the hearty support of Maritime Baptists, in evidence of which the Maritime Baptist Convention, which had been organized four years earlier, assumed responsibility for the institution. In 1851 Dr. J. M. Cramp of Montreal succeeded to the presidency.

Meanwhile, New Brunswick Baptists, although under a severe financial strain, had erected a seminary building at Fredericton in 1836. Not until 1840 were they able to secure a grant from the Provincial Legislature; then the sum of five hundred pounds was voted to relieve their situation. The school had opened as a co-educational institution, the first of its kind in all Canada. When schools for girls were opened in the city under other auspices, this department was closed in 1843. While the seminary continued to operate, financial difficulties mounted; for Baptists had not yet developed either the ability or sufficient interest to support educational institutions adequately.

In the meantime, New Brunswick Baptists were inaugurating a missionary program. In 1826 a home mission board was appointed, but it did not function effectively until 1832. The decade of the thirties opened auspiciously for work among the Indians and for the founding of new churches. Under the prevailing frontier conditions, the Association faced the problem of protecting the small, scattered churches from "non-Baptist itinerant preachers and perennial trouble-makers." Its only recourse was to recommend to the congregations that ministers should not be received in their pulpits who were not in good standing with some Calvinistic Baptist church or association.

Not until 1837 were the churches able to enter upon a definite foreign mission program. Because the enterprise was too great for a single association, the Baptists of the Maritime Provinces united in 1838 in the support of foreign missions. By 1845 the first missionary, Richard Burpee, a young preacher of New Brunswick, sailed with his wife for Burma, only to be forced to return five years later because of ill health. For several years, the work seems to have lapsed, but it was resumed in 1870.

By the early 1840's, it had become apparent that a measure of co-ordination was being attained in denominational activities. Several factors had been contributing to this trend. Over a period of years, periodicals had been published, providing a means of interchange of ideas and of the development of a denominational consciousness. The earliest had been the *Missionary Magazine*, a monthly organ for Nova Scotia and New Brunswick, begun in 1828. In 1839 it was superseded by a weekly, the *Christian Messenger*. Ten years later the New Brunswick Baptists founded the *Christian Visitor*, which in 1884 united with the *Christian Messenger* under the title of the *Messenger and Visitor*. Another factor contributing to the spirit of union was the existence of several organizations which claimed the support of Maritime Baptists. In 1840 the Nova Scotia and New Brunswick Sunday School Union was formed by a merger of two earlier organizations. In addition, there were temperance societies, a fund for infirm ministers, three educational institutions, and agencies for home and foreign missions.

It is not surprising then that the Reverend Charles Tupper, pastor first in Amherst, Nova Scotia, then in St. John, New Brunswick, received support in his leadership in the uniting of the Associations of New Brunswick and of Nova Scotia and Prince Edward Island in the Baptist Convention of Nova Scotia, New Brunswick, and Prince Edward Island in September, 1846. Its primary task of attaining a closer co-ordination of the work of the separate associations and their societies was attempted through the functions of five Convention Boards set up within the following two years to supervise the educational, the home and foreign missionary, and the general administrative affairs of the Convention. The first president of the Convention was Theodore Seth Harding, a prominent pastor in New Brunswick and Prince Edward Island. He possessed outstanding gifts as an evangelist.

By 1870 the Convention embraced six separate associations, the New Brunswick Association having divided in 1848, and the Baptist Association of Nova Scotia having separated two years later into three associations (Central, Western, and Eastern); Prince Edward Island constituted the sixth. The number of accessions to the ranks of the ministry had increased appreciably, one hundred and thirty-two having been ordained between 1850 and 1870. There were now

303 churches having a total membership of 27,981 with seventy-three ordained ministers in New Brunswick, eighty-six in Nova Scotia, and nine in Prince Edward Island.[7] In 1879, the rather cumbersome name of the Convention was shortened to "The Baptist Convention of the Maritime Provinces." Five years later, the African Association of seventeen Negro churches with about five hundred members was admitted on an equal basis with the other associations.

This move toward consolidation of Baptist efforts gave fresh impetus to the missionary enterprise. In 1863 Maritime Baptists began a move to establish a Canadian Baptist foreign mission field. Hitherto, they had been sending their missionaries to Burma to work under the aegis of the American Baptist Missionary Union. The first step was the incorporation in 1865 of their own Foreign Mission Board so that it might receive and hold property in its own name.

In the years that followed, the missionary advance continued. Out of the Woman's Mission Circles, which were formed as early as 1870 by Miss Maria Norris of Nova Scotia for the support of foreign missions, there developed the Woman's Baptist Missionary Union, organized at Moncton on August 14, 1884, and later known as "The Woman's Convention." This project of Maritime women originally was to assist the Foreign Mission Board, but within two years it had undertaken a responsibility in connection with home and western missions as well. By the end of the century, its efforts were joined with those of similar societies of the Free Baptists.

Encouraged by an increasing number of new missionary volunteers between 1865 and 1870 and assisted by the Woman's Mission Societies, the Board decided in 1875 to abandon its work in Burma and to cross the Bay of Bengal to a territory adjacent to the Telugu field occupied by Northern Baptists of the United States. In that area, Baptists of Ontario and Quebec were already working. This move stimulated an enthusiasm which resulted in a steady flow of personnel and money to India. By 1900 there were in that country, representing Maritime Baptists, "seven mission stations and eight churches with a membership of 415; twenty missionaries, and ninety-five native preachers, teachers, and Bible women."[8]

Further evidence of the salutary effects of consolidation was

[7] Levy, *The Baptists of the Maritime Provinces*, 185, 188.
[8] *Ibid.*, 205.

manifest in the introduction of a Free School System in Nova Scotia by 1864, largely through the efforts of Dr. Crawley and Dr. Tupper, the latter being the prime minister of the province at the time. Under the new system, a third Baptist, Theodore Harding Rand, a graduate of Acadia College, was appointed Superintendent of Education for the province. Five years later, he accepted a similar post in New Brunswick, which he held for thirteen years.[9]

The future of Fredericton Seminary became increasingly precarious; its debts accumulated until it became necessary in 1871 to close the school and sell the buildings. New Brunswick Baptists still felt, however, that a seminary was needed in the province; accordingly, they established a new school at Saint John in 1882, without affiliation with the Convention. Two years later the Free Baptists of New Brunswick, who had no school of their own, united with its supporters to form the Union Baptist Education Society. The school was renamed the Union Baptist Seminary; in 1888 it was moved to new quarters at St. Martin's. Although this joint enterprise failed in 1896—the institution went out of existence due to financial problems —the co-operative effort of Free and Regular Baptists was significant with respect to further union of the two bodies.

By 1894 New Brunswick Baptists were feeling dissatisfaction with the administration of the Convention's Home Mission Board; this dissatisfaction led to the establishment of their own Board. In the meantime, however, the home mission work of the Convention was broadened. Annual contributions were made as early as 1882 to western missionaries and to churches which were laboring with the European immigrant settlers on the western plains of Canada. Nearer home, eighty new churches were organized and one hundred and seventy-eight church edifices were erected between 1870 and 1900. In the same period the total increase in membership for the provinces was approximately 22,000, bringing the figure to 51,390 Baptists by the opening of the new century.[10]

In addition to the Regular or Calvinistic Baptists whose developments have been surveyed briefly, there is another group of Baptists, only briefly referred to heretofore. They are the Free Baptists, known also as Free Will or Free Christian Baptists. While they

[9] *Ibid.,* 181.
[10] *Ibid.,* 227-8.

stem back in spirit to the "New Light" revivalism of the Great Awakening, their actual origin as an organized body may be found in the Free Will Baptist movement which Benjamin Randall led against a resurgence of hyper-Calvinism in New England during the last two decades of the eighteenth century. Through removal of Free Will Baptists to Nova Scotia, such as Elder Asa McGray of Yarmouth, Maine, and the Reverend Joseph Norton of Swansville, Maine, in the early years of the ninetenth century, Free Baptist churches were organized. The first was established at Barrington in 1821 when an existing Calvinistic Baptist congregation became Arminian. In 1834 a conference of several churches was constituted under McGray's leadership. Union with the Free Christian Baptists, whose leader was Norton, was not effected until 1867. It appears that the chief distinction between the two groups of Free Baptists was that the latter emphasized freedom from the bondage of sin while the former used the word "free" only in the sense of freedom of the human will. At that time there were but twenty-nine churches in the merger, twenty-seven being Free Christian Baptists.[11]

While evangelists of the Free Will Baptist and Christian bodies in Maine planted the seed in New Brunswick, thereby hampering the progress of Calvinistic Baptists, their beginnings were small. In 1832, there were only six churches. These were organized into the Free Baptist Conference for New Brunswick. Out of deference to the Christian ministers from Maine, the new organization was called simply, the "New Brunswick Christian Conference," a fact which caused confusion and allowed those holding radical beliefs to enter on the ground that they also were "Christian." Consequently, the name was changed in 1847 to "Free Christian Baptist;" fifty-one years later, it was modified again to "The Free Baptist General Conference." Its early leaders were mainly Scotch and English immigrants; the most important being Ezekiel McLeod (1812-1867) of Upper Sussex, minister at Saint John and later at Fredericton. He founded *The Religious Intelligencer* in 1854, the official Free Baptist periodical.

The polity of Free Will Baptists differed in several respects from that of Regular Baptists. The district meetings sent repre-

[11] *Ibid.*, 241. For further details, see *Ibid.*, 235-64.

sentatives to the General Conference, yet the latter body had direct authority over the local churches in discipline and in the licensing and ordaining of ministers. Such authority would have been regarded as a menace to local autonomy by Regular Baptists. Its Arminian theology stood in sharp contrast to the Calvinism of the latter. Moreover, the Puritan standards of Free Baptists in some cases were more rigid than those practiced by Regular Baptists. They also entertained a strong aversion to a settled and paid ministry, and were not as sympathetic toward education as Regular Baptists. Both groups, however, were ardent promoters of Sunday schools, temperance, and Bible colportage work. Regular Baptists outnumbered Free Baptists. In 1847, for example, there were seventy-three churches, forty-eight ordained ministers, and approximately five thousand members in the New Brunswick Regular Baptist Association as over against forty churches, fourteen ordained elders, and two thousand members in the New Brunswick Free Baptist Conference.[12] In that year the New Brunswick and Nova Scotia Conferences entered into a partial union, regarding themselves as one denomination, although each organization remained intact.

In the years that followed, the Free Baptists enlarged their sphere of service by creating new agencies. In 1850 a Conference Fund was established to assist home missionaries in destitute areas. Five years later a Free Baptist Home Mission Board was organized by the New Brunswick Conference; this was succeeded in 1863, after several financially lean years, by a Home Mission Society, which worked under the direction of the Conference. Through its efforts, temporary assistance was given to pastorless churches. Missionaries were dependent chiefly upon this aid for their slender stipend, the Society supplementing what small sums they received from the churches out of offerings received at its annual meetings. The Nova Scotia Conference established two separate Home Mission Societies in the late 1860's, but financial difficulties prompted a merger in 1878. The new organization was known as the Nova Scotia Free Baptist Home Mission Society.

Foreign missions received rather sustained support during this period. Stimulated by the interest among American Free Will Baptists, the New Brunswick Free Baptists organized a Foreign Mis-

12 *Ibid.*, 246-50.

sionary Society in 1864 as an adjunct to the Free Will Baptist Foreign Missionary Society in the United States. Three years later the Nova Scotia Free Baptist Conference established its Society to work together with its New Brunswick counterpart as an auxiliary to the American agency. It was twenty years, however, before missionary volunteers were forthcoming. The first missionaries were sent to the field occupied by Free Baptists in the Balasore and Midnapore districts of Bengal. The effect of having immediate contact with foreign missions was very stimulating, one outcome being the organization in 1875 of a Women's Foreign Mission Society in each Conference, an action which was in keeping with a similar movement among Regular Baptists that had begun five years earlier.

Other agencies had come into existence in this period to widen the scope of service rendered by Free Baptists. The New Brunswick Conference established an Education Society in 1865, followed two years later by a similar organization for the Nova Scotia Conference. Although both societies worked closely together, financial support from the churches was meager, largely because "there was a general failure throughout both Conferences to realize the need for an educated ministry, and the importance of an educated laity."[13] However, after 1860 most candidates for the ministry had received some academic training prior to ordination. The fact that many of them were educated at Bates College at Lewiston, Maine, a school supported by Free Baptists of that state, resulted in a loss of ministers for Canadian churches since some who studied there accepted pastorates in the United States. To solve this problem, the Union Baptist Education Society was formed in 1884, followed by the establishment of St. Martin's Seminary for the training of a native Free Baptist leadership.

Sunday School Conventions were sponsored in New Brunswick after 1869 and in Nova Scotia after 1873. In 1894 local Young People's Societies were encouraged by a Young People's League formed in New Brunswick and a Young People's Union in Nova Scotia. By 1900, however, the wave of interest in this type of work had receded appreciably among both Free and Regular Baptists.

In both provinces social interests gave rise to Temperance

---

[13] Levy, *The Baptists of the Maritime Provinces*, 258.

Leagues, which stimulated the organization of local societies in the churches. In 1867 and 1878 respectively, Fund Societies were established in New Brunswick and Nova Scotia for the relief of aged ministers.

The general spirit of unity which had existed in both Conferences was disturbed by a debate over the doctrine of holiness. The controversy led to the formation of the "Primitive" and "Reformed" Free Baptists, both of which were critical of the older bodies. A happier condition was the growing desire for a union of Free and Regular Baptists, which in 1905-1906 culminated in the formation of the United Baptist Convention of the Maritime Provinces. Earlier efforts to achieve the merger had been frustrated chiefly by Free Baptists, owing to their close associations with their denomination in the United States and to their insistence upon Arminianism and open communion. The New Brunswick Baptists entered into the union on October 10, 1905, followed by the Nova Scotia Conference on September 3, 1906. The number of pastorless churches was reduced by a judicious regrouping of congregations. In addition, a larger constituency had been created from which their educational institutions could draw students. To some extent, the pooling of financial resources made possible more adequate remuneration for workers in mission churches, although even then the maximum salary for most of the workers was but five hundred dollars. Of the 580 churches within the Convention in 1910, 357 were self-supporting. The total membership was reported as 64,865.[14]

The unification of Baptist resources also strengthened the foreign mission work in India. "By 1910, out of a staff of thirty-eight Maritime Baptist missionaries in India, twenty-two had gone in the last ten years, and of these, eighteen since Union had been consummated in 1905." This remarkable growth was the product not only of the new co-operative effort, but also of the enthusiasm of Young People's groups and of the "Laymen's Missionary Movement," an organization of men who studied the missionary enterprise and contributed to its support. The merger in 1906 of 280 local women's societies into the United Baptist Women's Missionary Union also constituted a dominant influence.[15]

[14] *Ibid.*, 282-3.
[15] *Ibid.*, 285.

Ontario and Quebec

Baptist work in the province of Quebec has been small, owing to the strength of Roman Catholicism in its French population. Yet in the eastern townships—those which skirt the east bank of the St. Lawrence and are bounded on the south by Vermont and on the east by Maine—contacts with American Baptists have resulted in a few churches. A greater number of Baptists, however, are to be found in Ontario in the area of the Great Lakes.[16]

The earliest church is supposed to have been organized in 1776 on the Niagara Peninsula which borders Lake Erie on its north shore. The site was Clinton, later called Beamsville after Jacob Beam, a Baptist of prominence in the community. Its actual existence prior to 1796, however, cannot be proved. A second church was established by Reuben Crandall, who came from the United States in 1794 to Prince Edward County in Ontario. It was situated in Haldimand township in the adjoining county of Northumberland. A third congregation constituted itself in 1799 in the eastern townships of Quebec under the name of St. Armand Baptist Church, after the county in which it was located. It developed out of a work begun at Caldwell's Manor (now known as Freleighsburg in Missisquoi County) three years earlier under the leadership of William Marsh, a native of Vermont who had emigrated because of the loyalist sympathies of his father. He was a typical "farmer-minister," farming in the summer, making shoes in the winter, and preaching as he had opportunity. Not long after his ordination, he moved to Sutton Flats in the neighboring Brome County, and in 1798 the Hatley and Stanstead Baptist Church was organized. Although it is now extinct, it has been called "the foster-mother of the Association." The main contact of Baptists in the eastern townships was with those of Vermont, for they were cut off from their brethren in Montreal by the intervening French parishes. Accordingly, the few Canadian churches in this area for sometime had membership with the Danville Association in Vermont.

Eventually, other churches were established in the Province of Ontario; they were located at intervals along the shores of Lake

[16] Material for this section is based chiefly on J. L. Gilmour's chapter, "The Baptists in Canada," in Shortt and Doughty, editors, *Canada and Its Provinces*, Vol. XI.

Ontario and Lake Erie. The easternmost one was organized in 1803 at Harlem, in Leeds County, through the labors of Joseph Cornell, a missionary from the United States. West of the Niagara Peninsula, in Norfolk County, the Vittoria church was established at Charlottsville in 1804.

In the Ottawa Valley, which is formed by the course of the Ottawa River as it makes its way southeastward into the headwaters of the St. Lawrence, Baptist beginnings stemmed from a number of settlers from the Highlands of Scotland, who had established homes there as early as 1816. These people had been influenced by the evangelistic work of the Haldane brothers in Scotland. It was in 1819 that John Edwards, a convert under James Haldane, arrived in Canada. Within three years, he had settled at Clarence, a town on the river in Russell County, and there began to hold religious services. From this humble beginning, small congregations developed. Impressed with the need for additional workers, he visited Great Britain in 1829 at his own expense. Whiie in Scotland, he induced John Gilmour and William Fraser to move to Canada as missionaries. The following year found Gilmour settled at Montreal in Quebec, where shortly thereafter the first Baptist church of that city was organized. Fraser went to Breadbane. Gilmour's choice was strategic, for Montreal became an important link between the eastern townships and the Ottawa Valley. The result was the organization of the Ottawa Baptist Association in 1836, which included churches in eastern Ontario and Quebec.

In 1839 the Baptist Theological College at Montreal was established under the leadership of Dr. Benjamin Davies, a Hebrew scholar, who had come from England to fill that post. When he returned to his native land in 1843, he was succeeded in turn by Dr. R. A. Fyfe and Dr. J. M. Cramp. The school's future was not bright, however, and by 1849 its doors were closed and the property was sold to liquidate its indebtedness. The failure of this experiment in ministerial education was due partly to its great distance from the majority of churches and to suspicions entertained by western churches with respect to the institution's views on the question of open or close communion. In 1838 the *Canada Baptist Magazine and Missionary Register* came into existence; but its brave attempt as a Baptist periodical ceased in 1849. Its disappointing history and ultimate suspension may be attributed to the same reasons that caused the college to fail.

It is significant that each attempt at co-operative effort among the Baptists of these provinces met with a similar fate. As early as 1816 the churches of Niagara Peninsula and part of the Lake Erie District had organized the Clinton Conference, which in turn established the Upper Canada Domestic Missionary Society. Both were in existence only for a short time. In 1833 the Baptist Missionary Convention of Upper Canada was set up. It was composed of churches of the Eastern, Western, and Haldimand Associations in the Niagara Peninsula, of the Lake Erie district, Northumberland County, and of other parts of Central Upper Canada. Membership was open to all who paid one dollar or more a year. Its responsibility included oversight of missionary work, educational work, and the publication of a paper. Further union came in 1843 when Baptists of the two provinces were joined in the Canada Baptist Union. But this effort collapsed because of controversy between the open communionists of the east and the close communionists of the west. Accordingly, the latter group established in 1848 the Regular Baptist Union of Canada. It should be noted, however, that this division did not parallel in all respects the differences between the Regular and Free Baptists of the Maritime Provinces, for both groups were moderately Calvinistic.

Such frustration among the Baptists of these provinces prevented development of either a missionary society, a college, or a periodical until as late as the middle of the nineteenth century. To meet the obvious need for such agencies, a prominent Baptist layman, N. T. McCord, who held the political post of chamberlain of Toronto, asked for a conference to be held at Hamilton in October, 1851. Its outcome was the formation of the Regular Baptist Missionary Convention of Canada West (Ontario). This continued until the union of Baptists of the two provinces in 1888. The Convention was concerned chiefly with home missions, but it adjusted itself to such projects as education, the financing of the building of church edifices, foreign missions, and ministerial pensions. In 1864 the Superannuated Ministers' Society came into being with William McMaster, a generous Baptist layman, as its first president. Three years later the Church Edifice Society was organized under the presidency of Alexander Mackenzie, a member of Parliament from 1861 until his election in 1873 as prime minister of Canada for the Liberal Party. Up to 1866, contributions to foreign missions had been sent by individual churches to the American Baptist Missionary Union of Northern Baptists in the United States, but in that year steps were taken to establish a Canadian auxiliary, which led by 1874 to a missionary society independent of the American Baptists. Work then was begun among the Telugu tribes north of Madras; in 1897 a mission was opened in Bolivia, South America.

Further results of the co-operative effort established in 1851 became evident in the founding of a periodical, the *Christian Messenger,* in Brantford, Ontario, in 1854. Five years later, it was sold to Dr. Robert A. Fyfe, principal of the Literary Institute at Woodstock; its headquarters were moved to Toronto where it became known as the *Canadian Baptist.* Since 1882 it has been owned by the denomination, Dr. Fyfe having died in 1878.

Ontario Baptists also took the lead in establishing a Baptist theological seminary to be located centrally for all of Canada. "It was hoped that Acadia in the east, Woodstock College under the direction of the Baptists of Ontario, and a third college to be established for the Baptists of Western Canada, should all send their theological students to Toronto for graduate study."[17] . It appears that the project received its initial impulse from Dr. Fyfe, who had become principal of the Literary Institute at Woodstock upon its opening in 1860.[18] His institution was comprised of academic, business, and theological departments. Within six months' time, a fire destroyed its building and equipment. Since the Baptists did not regard it as being consistent with their principle of separation of church and state to accept for rebuilding funds raised by taxation, support was sought from private quarters.

Assistance came principally from William McMaster, who had become increasingly interested in the educational enterprise of his denomination. When, therefore, the plan for a seminary at Toronto was broached at a meeting of Baptists at Guelph in 1879, McMaster contributed funds for the erection of the first building. In 1881, Mc-

[17] Levy, *Baptists of the Maritime Provinces,* 211.

[18] J. L. Gilmour, "The Baptists in Canada," Shortt and Doughty, editors, *Canada and Its Provinces,* XI, 368.

Master Hall, as it was called, was opened at Toronto, to which the theological departments of Acadia and Woodstock were transferred by mutual agreement. The new institution became known as the Toronto Baptist College. In 1887 a charter was secured which provided it with university status. Woodstock College for boys and Moulton College, in Toronto, for girls became affiliated with the institution. The next year, the institution attained a degree of financial independence through the generosity of McMaster, whose name it received.

This ambitious attempt to centralize educational work in Central Canada met with only modest success. Very few students were attracted from the Maritime Provinces to the seminary at Toronto. The cost of travel was offered as a reason, although a fund was raised to pay the traveling expenses of students who would attend. The actual explanation was that those academy and college students who did not go directly into the pastorate without further preparation, continued to go to the United States for postgraduate training at Newton and Rochester seminaries in Massachusetts and New York respectively. After eight years of the experiment, Acadia College resumed theological instruction, and by 1892 it offered the degree of Bachelor of Theology. Yet even the presence of seminary facilities within Nova Scotia "did not prevent young men from going to the United States to pursue their theological studies."[19] Nevertheless, the original proposal for a central seminary in Toronto had not been a failure, for out of it developed McMaster University. In the late 1920's the institution was moved to the city of Hamilton where a larger site of land made possible the needed expansion. A school of theology is still an integral part of the university.

The general success of co-operation among western Baptists through the Regular Baptist Missionary Convention of Canada West prompted eastern Baptists to organize in 1858 the Canada Baptist Missionary Convention East for a similar purpose. As the communion question became less a source of contention between Baptists of the two sections, the two conventions found it possible to unite in their educational, foreign missionary, and ministerial relief projects. In 1881 a Baptist Union was formed, but as we have seen, it was short-lived.

[19] Levy, *op. cit.*, 212.

In 1888 the Ontario and Quebec Baptist Convention was formed. Two years later it undertook work among young people through a board responsible to the Convention. In 1907 a Sunday School Board was established. Home mission work was carried on in western Ontario among German immigrants, Negroes, and Indians. In addition, an enterprise among French Catholics has been under the direction of the Grande Ligne Mission with headquarters thirty-five miles south of Montreal. It began when Henrietta Feller, a French-Swiss immigrant, settled about six miles from St. Johns, on a road called *la grande ligne,* a name for a country road. In time, Baptists of Canada, of the United States, and of Great Britain were contributing to the undertaking. The project attracted the support of various other denominations until such time as they developed their own missions to the French. Baptist work among the French in the Maritime Provinces, in Ontario, and in the West is under the Grande Ligne Mission. Its policy has been to avoid offensive attacks upon Catholics and to be constructive in education and evangelism. By 1911 there were in the two provinces 53,723 Baptists, 511 churches, 111 missions, 304 ordained ministers, 23 unordained, and 100 in special service.[20]

Western Canada

Between the western edge of Ontario and the Pacific shore line there lie the three prairie provinces of Manitoba, Saskatchewan, and Alberta, and the coastal province of British Columbia. It appears that the earliest missionary work to be done in this territory was begun in British Columbia by a certain John Morton in 1862, but permanent activity was undertaken seven years later when the Ontario Convention sent two clergymen, the Reverend L. L. Davidson and T. Baldwin to visit the Northwest and report on prospects of missionary achievement there. In consequence of their report, the Reverend Alexander McDonald was sent out in 1873 to Fort Garry in southern Manitoba, now known as Winnipeg. A building was erected the following year, and by 1875 a church of ten members had been organized. Within six years the Red River Association of Baptist churches came into existence. In 1882 it merged with the Missionary Convention of Manitoba, which two years later

[20] J. L. Gilmour, *op. cit.,* 370.

was enlarged into the Baptist Convention of Manitoba and the Northwest Territories. In 1887 a superintendent of missions was appointed and the work was made known to Baptists of eastern Canada by means of committees and boards set up to disseminate information and to gather funds.

During the same period of time, three educational projects developed. Prairie College was opened at Rapid City in Manitoba in 1880; three years later it transferred its interest to Toronto Baptist College. Brandon College, also in Manitoba, came into existence in 1899 at Brandon; in time it was affiliated with McMaster University, which granted degrees to its students after examination. Okanagan College was opened in Summerland, British Columbia, in 1906, offering academy and junior college studies.

Accompanying these educational developments were other signs of denominational consciousness. Two periodicals were established: the *Northwest Baptist* in Winnipeg in 1885 and the *Western Baptist* at Vancouver in 1899. These were amalgamated as the *Western Outlook,* with headquarters in Winnipeg. The development of women's organizations for missions dates back to 1883. Work among Germans, Scandinavians, Ruthenians, and Indians was prosecuted vigorously by the Baptists of western Canada.

Signs of further unity became evident as the century drew to a close. The Baptist Convention of British Columbia was organized in 1897, the year in which Baptists of the United States ceased to give further financial assistance. In 1900 a general fraternal meeting of Canadian Baptists was held in Winnipeg and there was hope of organic union. After much deliberation, the Convention of Ontario and Quebec in 1907 decided not to join; but western Baptists set up within two years the Baptist Union of Western Canada with a more elaborate organization than was resorted to in the East, yet still safeguarding the autonomy of the local church. Baptists in the four western provinces had in 1911 a combined membership of 14,200 in 228 churches with 143 ministers, not including unordained workers.[21]

A government census taken in that year revealed that the Baptist position in Canada had improved considerably. Baptists stood fourth in strength among Protestant communions, the Pres-

[21] *Ibid.,* 375-6.

byterian Church being the largest, with over a million communicants and representing more than fifteen per cent of the population. Baptists throughout the country numbered less than two hundred thousand members, although it was estimated that over 382,000 were under Baptist influence as unbaptized church and Sunday school attendants.[22]

Although relatively small in size, their influence was not lost. Baptists, for example, aided appreciably the cause of the separation of church and state by their faithfulness to that principle. When in 1854 the Canadian Legislature alienated from sacred purposes the church property, which amounted to one-seventh of the land, it provided a permanent security for the existing clergy, but commuted a fund of one million dollars for permanent endowment of the Church, which monies were to be shared proportionately by the various religious bodies in the State. Baptists, however, refused to accept their share, although Roman Catholics and Presbyterians shared somewhat with the Anglicans in its distribution. This action, and the discussion which resulted, led ultimately to the separation of church and state in Canada.[23]

Canadian Baptists Since 1900

The evident trend in the direction of denominational solidarity which had been heralded by the organization of societies and conventions among Canadian Baptists in the latter years of the nineteenth century bore significant fruit. Between 1900 and 1908 several efforts were made to unite the three Conventions representing the Maritime Provinces, Ontario and Quebec, and the Western Provinces respectively.[24] At Ottawa, in November, 1908, success was thwarted by the declaration of the Baptist Convention of Ontario and Quebec that it was not yet ready for union. The only tangible result of more than ten years of such attempts occurred in 1912

[22] *Ibid.*, 299, 376; Gilmour sets the number of Baptists at 133,000 whereas Levy gives 171,332 for the Maritime Provinces alone; however, Levy admits that included in his figure are Baptists of other than the Convention membership. It should be noted that census reports of church memberships are not satisfactory where local churches must be relied upon to provide the government with a report of their membership. See Levy, *Baptists of the Maritime Provinces*, 297.

[23] Lewis N. Tucker, "The Anglican Church and Its Mission," a chapter in Shortt and Doughty, editors, *Canada and Its Provinces*, XI, 236-7.

[24] Levy, *Baptists of the Maritime Provinces*, 287-8.

when the Canadian Baptist Foreign Mission Board was established to provide nation-wide guidance to the missionary enterprise.

It is not surprising that Baptists should have been giving so much consideration to consolidation, for a similar concern was being felt by other church bodies.[25] In 1875 the Church of Scotland and the Free Church branches of Presbyterianism merged into the Presbyterian Church of Canada. The Methodists, who had been attempting union unsuccessfully since 1833, effected in 1883 a permanent merger of Methodist Episcopal, Primitive Methodist, and Bible Christian churches. In 1899 the Presbyterians and Methodists began to discuss a merger of their bodies. The Roman Catholic Church, in the same year, received an apostolic delegate for Canada, thus completing its hierarchy on a national basis. Undoubtedly, the trend was due in part to the new national spirit which had resulted from the confederation of the provinces into the Dominion of Canada in 1867. Among Protestants, at least, it had become apparent also that organic division was absurd when actual co-operation was already in practice among boards and societies engaged in educational and missionary work.

The First World War had an ill effect upon the churches; for they suffered from dislocation of membership, from a shortage of ministers owing to the number serving in the chaplaincy, and from a general lowering of spiritual standards and ideals. As a remedial measure taken even before the war came to its close, the United Convention of Regular and Free Baptists in the Maritime Provinces initiated in 1916 a Five Year Program. Although it fell short of the goals established, the results were gratifying. The financial income of the churches increased; nearly ten thousand accessions were made to the churches by baptism, and fifty young men were preparing for the ministry at Acadia University.[26]

Several factors contributed to make the years that followed a period of difficult adjustment for Baptists. Population shifts left hitherto well-filled churches without adequate support in funds or leadership. The Maritime Provinces felt most keenly the steady flow of migration to other parts of Canada and more particularly to the United States between 1910 and 1929, stimulated first by

[25] Shortt and Doughty, *op. cit.,* XI, 282-3, 307-11.
[26] Levy, *op. cit.,* 294-6.

wartime conditions and then by the postwar years of readjustment and halted only by the economic depression that struck in 1929. At the same time, immigration into the country was reduced. The effect on the churches was reflected by a decrease in membership within the convention between 1910 and 1935 from 64,868 to 59,565. A commensurate decline was noted among the ordained ministers. Their number decreased from 313 to 265. The number of Sunday schools dropped from 635 to 540, and the enrollment declined from 38,000 to 34,469. Only a slight gain in membership has been made since that time, while the rest of the picture looks darker.[27] This population shift was accompanied by an exodus from rural to urban areas which left many churches without adequate leadership, while all too frequently the city churches did not benefit from a transfer of membership, for many members were lost to the distractions of urban life.

Among some of the younger ministers, the press of economic and social problems prompted a strong acceptance of the "Social Gospel" emphasis then being advanced by several American theological seminaries, particularly at Rochester Theological Seminary, where Professor Walter Rauschenbusch gave leadership and direction to the task of applying the gospel to the economic order.[28] In line with this aim, a Social Service Board was established in the Convention in 1920 (successor to an earlier committee on social and moral reform), which united with Methodists, Presbyterians, and Anglicans in promoting aid to the underprivileged and exploited, in advocating liquor and gambling control, in combating race prejudice, and in working for religious liberty.[29]

In the thirties, the impending world conflict revived interest in the formation of a national Baptist union in Canada. To be sure, the steady practice of co-operation in home and foreign missions and in support of educational and reform efforts, reinforced the growing sentiment in favor of a united front against the forces that endangered Christianity. As early as 1931 an Inter-Conventions Committee of ten was formed, four representing the Baptists of the

---

[27] *Ibid.*, 297; "In 1945, there were 261 ordained ministers, 586 churches with a total membership of 62,704; 526 Sunday schools with an enrollment of 29,266." (Footnote, p 319; based on *The United Baptist Year Book*, 1945, p. 298.)

[28] For a fuller discussion, see Chapter Fifteen.

[29] Levy, *Baptists of the Maritime Provinces*, 299-301.

Maritimes, four those of Ontario and Quebec, and two the Baptist Union of Western Canada. It continued in existence until 1943 when it requested the three Conventions to select a joint committee to enact the final stages in creating a Canadian Baptist Union. The chairman of the new committee, appointed in October, 1943, was Professor Watson Kirkconnell of McMaster University. The constitution drafted by this committee was adopted after study by each of the three Conventions in 1944. On December 7 of that year, the organization meeting was held at the Germain Street Baptist Church in St. John, New Brunswick, at which time the Baptist Federation of Canada came into existence, with Dr. G. C. Warren of Wolfville, Nova Scotia, as its first president. It was to be what its name implied, a federation, which "was not intended to supplant the executive functions of the different Conventions, or to prejudice in any way the autonomy of the local church."[30]

The main body of Baptists in Canada had thus achieved a significant degree of national unity but not without the loss of churches. Those which had withdrawn over a period of years represented a conservative reaction to the more progressive approach of the Baptist Federation to the changing times. They had their counterpart in the fundamentalist segment of Baptists in the United States. In Canada they constituted in 1953 three main bodies. One was the Fellowship of Evangelical Baptist Churches in Canada, which was formed that year by the merging of two independent groups: the Union of Regular Baptist Churches of Ontario and Quebec founded in 1927, and the Fellowship of Independent Baptist Churches of Canada organized in 1933. The Union of Regular Baptist Churches constituted a body of seventy churches which, under the leadership of Dr. T. T. Shields of Toronto, had withdrawn from the Baptist Convention of Ontario and Quebec in protest against alleged modernism at McMaster University. The other two main bodies were of a similar type although smaller in size: the Convention of Regular Baptists of British Columbia, and the Prairie Regular Baptist Fellowship. All three organizations shared similar ideals and held to the inerrancy of the Bible and opposed any effort to interpret the Bible more broadly. They opposed open membership in Baptist churches and rejected any participation in the ecumenical movement. By 1961 the three fellowships, in the

[30] *Ibid.*, 314.

order mentioned, reported 268 churches, 52 churches, and 11 churches. Together, they comprised the Trans-Canada Fellowship of Evangelical Churches with a combined membership of more than 27,000 Baptists.[31]

The Baptist Federation, on the other hand, maintained membership in the Baptist World Alliance and the Canadian Council of Churches. It had not found agreement, however, on seeking admission to the World Council of Churches to the time of this writing. Baptists in 1960 had an even smaller place in Canada's national life than earlier. Their membership had increased only 63 per cent in the first half of the century as compared with a population increase of 160 per cent during the same period. Yet the only denominations increasing faster than the population growth were the Roman Catholic Church (with 43.3 per cent of the population) and the United Church of Canada (with 20.5 per cent). Baptists shared with other communions the problem of keeping pace with a mobile population. Moreover, they were confronted by the need to achieve greater internal unity and to gain a larger measure of public respect for their tradition if they were to increase in strength.[32]

Baptists in Australia and New Zealand

Baptist beginnings within the six states of Australia extend over a period of sixty-three years, from the establishing of the first Baptist meeting in Sydney, New South Wales, in 1831 to the forming of a church in Perth, Western Australia, in 1894. The initial work, which was undertaken at Sydney by the Reverend John McKaeg, expanded under the leadership of the Reverend John Saunders, who was sent out by the Baptist Missionary Society of England after McKaeg's resignation in 1834. The governor, upon request, granted a site of land on Bathurst Street, upon which the growing congregation erected a church. This Bathurst Street Baptist Church, which was incorporated formally on November 17, 1836, became the "mother of the Baptist work in Australia."[33] It was a

[31] Fellowship of Evangelical Baptist Churches in Canada, *Year Book* for 1961, cover page and p. 29.

[32] Watson Kirkconnell, "Seven Years of Federation" and "A Century of Canadian Baptist History," *The Maritime Baptist,* Vol. 54, No. 49 (Dec. 5, 1951), 3; Vol. 57, No. 3 (Jan. 20, 1954), 1-2.

[33] James Worboys, "Early Australian Baptist History," *The Chronicle.* Vol. VI. No. 3 (July, 1943), 104.

Regular Baptist congregation formed, however, on an open membership basis, a pattern followed by several Australian churches, owing to the presence of Congregationalists who were desirous of membership. But in 1840, when the need was no longer felt for mixed membership, close membership was adopted, although the practice of open communion was continued. On April 9, 1851, another church was established at Parramatta, which was for the most part the product of the efforts of William Hopkins Carey, a grandson of the veteran Baptist missionary, who had come out from England about 1850.

In point of time, however, the second Baptist church in Australia was founded by the Reverend Henry Dowling, a strict Baptist minister, who at the age of fifty-four arrived in Hobart, Tasmania, from England on December 2, 1834. Since young manhood, he had combined a business career with the preaching of the gospel. In response to the urging of his son and friends living in Tasmania, he had come to assist in the evangelizing of the penal settlements on that small island. Although Tasmania is located about two hundred miles to the south of the Australian mainland, it is included among the six states of the Australian Commonwealth. Baptists were rather late in establishing work there, having been preceded by the Anglicans, Methodists, Presbyterians, and Congregationalists between the settlement of the island in 1803 and 1830. A series of lakes, affording a vast system of hydroelectric power, was to give the small island industrial importance. Through the efforts of Dowling, two churches came into existence, one at Hobart on June 14, 1835, and the other at Launceston about one hundred and twenty miles away. Neither survived, however, for "like so many of the early Particular Baptist Churches in Australia, they lived to themselves and were continually being split over doctrinal matters."[34]

About forty years later, a resurgence of evangelistic zeal took hold of the Tasmanian Baptists. Mary Dowling, daughter of their first and only leader of note, married William Gibson, a successful grazier; together they brought out from Spurgeon's College in London a number of young men who initiated a campaign of evangelism. As need for churches and parsonages arose, the Gibsons

[34] H. G. Hackworthy, "The Tasmanian Baptists," *The Chronicle*, Vol. V, No. 1 (January, 1942), 25; Wesley J. Bligh, "Henry Dowling," *The Chronicle*, Vol. X, No. 4 (October, 1947), 172-9.

financed the erection of them and established ministers in them at their own cost. As a consequence, new strong churches came into existence at Hobart and Launceston, where their predecessors had become extinct. By 1897 the first missionaries were sent to Eastern Bengal, India. In spite of a continually changing ministry from the mainland and a migration of young people to the mainland, there has been amazing growth during the first half of the twentieth century. From "eleven churches or preaching stations with 305 members and a Sunday school enrolment of 483," the number has increased to "nineteen churches with eighteen preaching stations and a membership of 1,600 . . . and a Sunday school enrollment of the same number."[35]

The first Baptist services in Victoria were held at Melbourne by laymen in 1838, some of whom had come from Great Britain and some from Tasmania. The first to arrive was Thomas Napier, in 1836 or 1837; he made his home in Collins Street in "a wattle and daub dwelling, thatched with rushes . . . one of the most pretentious in the settlement."[36] He was a Scotch Baptist, and while having little ability to preach himself, he gave staunch support to early Baptist ministers in Melbourne. In 1838 two recent arrivals from Sydney, a cabinetmaker, Samuel Crook, and an estate agent, Robert Reeves, opened tent meetings. The preacher was a Scotch Baptist farmer, Peter Virtue, who lived a few miles north of the town. From this small beginning, a congregation was formed, composed chiefly of immigrants from the British Isles. In December, 1842, when the Reverend John Ham arrived in Melbourne from England, en route to Sydney, the Baptists persuaded him to stay as their minister for three months. At once they moved from a tent on Collins Street to Mechanics Institute (now the Atheneum Club), which they rented for services. When Ham decided to remain as permanent pastor, the congregation of fifteen persons constituted themselves a church on July 20, 1843. Within a year the membership had doubled. A church edifice was erected, therefore, to seat four hundred persons, the site being on land allotted by grant of the governor of the colony.

With the discovery of gold in 1851, the population began to in-

[35] Hackworthy, op. cit., 27.

[36] F. J. Wilkin, Baptists in Victoria: Our First Century, 1838-1938 (East Melbourne, 1939), 9. This provides a good source of information concerning organizational development.

crease. By 1860 it had risen from 76,000 to 540,000. Melbourne suddenly became important. Other churches were established, two within the city, one being a Particular Baptist Church, and seven in outlying communities. By 1858 the Collins Street Church found it necessary to erect a larger building to accommodate over a thousand persons. With the increase of churches, organizational life developed. The Baptist Association of Victoria, composed of ten churches, was established in 1858; its first action was to dispatch to the Baptist Missionary Society of England a request that ministers be sent to Victoria to meet the great need. Three came the next year. In 1862 a Home Mission agency came into being to establish and sustain Baptist churches and to facilitate the training of young men for the ministry. Three years later, an auxiliary of the English Baptist Missionary Society was formed; its main enterprise being support of work in Eastern Bengal. In 1891 a Baptist Theological College was organized with Dr. W. T. Whitley, of England, as Principal. It opened with four students, and met in the Collins Street Church. By 1912 permanent buildings had been acquired in North Melbourne. A second educational institution was founded at Kew in February, 1923, known as the Carey Baptist Grammar School; it had sixty-eight boys in attendance. Its purpose was to provide a Christian schooling for children of Baptists at a time when public education was becoming secularized.

The first Baptist church in South Australia dates its beginning from the arrival of Mr. and Mrs. W. Finlayson on February 14, 1837. They came as missionaries to the aborigines. In their home in Adelaide, they established a church of thirteen baptized believers. By September of the following year, services were commenced in a wooden building on park lands opposite Trinity Church, where the members met regularly until January, 1846, when a church building was completed for their use. It was known as the Hindley Street Baptist Church. Some dissension was caused in its membership because of its observance of close communion and close membership. Some time prior to 1843 an open membership church had been established, for in that year its congregation erected a building which came to be known as Ebenezer Chapel. This was the earliest church edifice erected by Baptists in South Australia. Other churches were formed in different centers in subsequent years.

The advance of Baptists in this region was not great, because the debate over church membership and minor points of theology had caused a neglect of evangelism. Unity was prevented by the differences which were inherent in the Scotch and English backgrounds represented in the churches—differences over open communion and open membership in particular. Harmony was further disrupted by the presence of Campbellites and Plymouth Brethren. Moreover, there was no leader strong enough to bring the divergent groups together.

In spite of these difficulties the South Australia Baptist Association was organized in 1863 by the Reverend James Hannay of Angaston, with the assistance of the Reverend Silas Mead, pastor of the Flinders Street Church in Adelaide. At the time, there were twenty-two or twenty-three Baptist churches in South Australia, with a combined membership of between 650 and 700.[37] After an initial period of controversy, a happy spirit of conciliation prevailed, and understanding and co-operative enterprise developed among the churches. The South Australia Missionary Society, which was organized in 1864, gave support to Baptist work in East Bengal. In 1868 the first periodical appeared, called *Truth and Progress.* Twenty-six years later, it was merged with *The Southern Baptist,* the new paper becoming the joint property of the Victorian and South Australian Associations. Dr. W. T. Whitley, principal of the Victoria Baptist College, was the first editor. In 1910 this magazine, in turn, was merged with *The Australian Baptist,* which was the joint property of the Baptist Unions in the Commonwealth. In 1923 a Book and Publication Department was organized for South Australia. In the same year, King's College was established at Kensington as the united project of the Congregational and Baptist Unions of South Australia.

By 1928, sixty years after the organization of the Association (known since 1926 as the Australian Baptist Union), the number of churches had risen to eighty-five with a total membership of more than five thousand and the number of ministers had reached fifty-seven. In addition to these were scores of Baptists who of necessity were worshiping in churches of other denominations, owing to their distance from any Baptist church. The growth of Baptist work in

---

[37] H. Estcourt Hughes, *Our First Hundred Years: the Baptist Church of South Australia* (Adelaide, 1937), 83.

South Australia would have been greater in these years had there not been a deep-rooted aversion to the circuit system, so successfully used by the Methodists in areas where the population was widely scattered. Then, too, there was the unfortunate, although often necessary, policy of sending untrained youth into home mission projects that demanded more mature leadership.[38]

In Queensland, the first Baptist church was the Wharf Street Chapel. It was opened in Moreton Bay on August 5, 1855, on an open membership basis in accordance with the pattern typical of Australian Baptists. Later, however, when the Congregationalists withdrew to form their own church, the basis was changed to close membership with open communion. Between 1860 and 1875, eight other churches were established along the southeast coast of the province. They were located in Ipswich, Fortitude Valley, Rockhampton, Brisbane, and Toowoomba.

A Baptist church did not come into existence in West Australia until October, 1894, when J. H. Cole, a lay preacher from Victoria, gave up his business to preach in Perth. From this beginning "a good measure of progress has been made." The outstanding churches are in Perth and Canberra, the capital city of Australia.[39]

The great Northern Territory, hitherto virtually untouched by Baptists, with its important port at Darwin, was the next objective for Baptist expansion following World War II. Since the close of the last century, the number of Baptists in Australia has increased from approximately 150 churches with a total membership of nearly 12,000 to 454 churches with a combined membership of 31,469.[40]

The strongest center of Australian Baptists is in Victoria where mining centers have attracted a population and developed a prominence not enjoyed by other states. In South Australia, where a variety of types of people are to be found, open membership has been the custom, and believer's baptism has been stipulated only for the pastor of a congregation. In Queensland, the semitropical climate does not attract European settlers; hence, only a score of churches have stability. The supply of ministers for Australian churches is sought from England, often through the assistance of the

[38] *Ibid.*, 234, 299-300.

[39] Worboys, *Early Australian Baptist History*, 108.

[40] Vedder, *Short History of Baptists*, 285; recent figures are based on report in *Year Book of the Northern Baptist Convention* for 1947, p. 677.

Baptist Missionary Society in London. In a very real sense, Baptist work, like Australian life itself, is yet in its "colonial" era; its prospects of expansion and development still lie in the future. Great distances, the scarcity of urban centers except along the seacoast, the opening of new mines causing population shifts, and the predominant agricultural interests of the country, make great demands upon energetic missionaries, while the more settled communities call urgently for resident pastors. The problems of a pioneer enterprise have not yet been fully solved, and Baptists are still a minority body.[41]

In New Zealand, the first Baptist church was formed in 1851 in the town of Nelson, a colonial outpost to which the Reverend Decimus Dolomore came from Sydney, Australia, with funds to erect a Baptist meeting house. From then on to the close of the century, progress was steady, but not spectacular. Always in the minority, Baptists were scattered throughout the settlements and overshadowed by other denominational groups. Yet, a century later, there were a total of ninety-four churches with a combined membership of 10,165. These are in the Baptist Union of New Zealand, which was formed in 1882.

In addition to the work among the white populace, evangelism has been carried among the native Maoris. With considerable zeal for their numbers, Baptists organized the New Zealand Baptist Missionary Society in 1885. Its field of operation has been East Bengal, where, since 1920, the missionaries have given leadership over to the Bengali Christians, who are organized in the East Bengal Baptist Union.

Baptist work in New Zealand has been maintained in spite of the antipathy to Free Churches which is characteristic of the New Zealand colonists, who have come from Anglican and Scotch Presbyterian backgrounds. The influence of Spurgeon College evangelists was felt strongly until 1924, when the Baptist College of New Zealand was organized. The period of greatest expansion has been since 1925.[42]

The spread of Baptist teaching to the dominions and colonies of the British Empire has given evidence of the evangelistic virility of its adherents. Moreover, it has been an indication of the adapt-

[41] Whitley, *History of British Baptists*, 341-6.

[42] Detailed information may be obtained from two manuscripts by E. P. Y. Simpson, "A History of the Baptists in New Zealand" (1950) and "A History of the New Zealand Baptist Missionary Society, 1885-1947" (1948).

ability of Baptist polity to communities widely differing in customs and tradition. A common missionary enterprise has drawn these scattered elements together. In 1960 Baptists of Australia only numbered 37,000, but they were supporting forty missionaries in Pakistan, Assam, and Fureedpore, India, and some thirty-five in New Guinea. Australian Baptists also maintained missions to the Aborigines, a primitive people in the northern part of their own continent. New Zealand Baptists, with a membership of 13,872, were conducting in the same period missionary work in India, South Africa, and Syria, as well as a mission to the Maoris in their own country.[43]

[43] *The Baptist World,* Vol. 9, No. 5 (May, 1962), 14-15.

CHAPTER SIX

THE BAPTIST WITNESS IN EUROPE

THE voice of freedom, so clearly expressed on the continent by the Anabaptists of the sixteenth century, was all but silenced by an era of persecution in which the radicals of the Reformation were suppressed by Roman Catholics and Protestant state churches alike. Only in Great Britain and in a few isolated areas of Europe was a witness to the principles of a regenerate church membership and of a free church kept alive. In the nineteenth century, the missionary zeal of British and American Baptists became an important factor in the reviving of the Baptist witness on the Continent.

The agencies through which this was effected were varied and numerous. Contacts with American or British dissenters have, in some cases, resulted in the conversion of Europeans who became Baptist leaders. Through the missionary projects of the American Baptist Publication Society, the American Baptist Missionary Union, and the English Baptist Societies, evangelistic centers were established and literature distributed in various countries. A third influence, seen in Russia, came through contacts with Mennonites. A fourth resulted from the missionary impulse of German Baptists who set out to evangelize the Scandinavian countries and Russia. In 1905 a fifth agency came into existence through the organization of an international fellowship of Baptists, known as the Baptist World Alliance. Its purpose was to unite Baptists throughout the world and thereby to create and express a Baptist world consciousness.

The initial meetings of the Baptist World Alliance were held in London, and an outstanding English Baptist, Dr. John Clifford, was elected its first president. Three years later, a congress of European Baptists was held in Berlin. In the years that followed, periodic meetings of the Baptist World Alliance were held: in Philadelphia in 1911; in Stockholm in 1923, the First World War having prevented the regular meeting scheduled for Berlin in 1916. Others were held in Toronto, 1928; Berlin, 1934; Atlanta, 1939, on

168

the eve of the Second World War; Copenhagen, 1947; Cleveland, 1950; London, 1955; and Rio de Janeiro, 1960. Through the promotion of regular contacts between Baptists of Europe, Australasia, Canada, and the United States, mutual understanding and world concern have been developed. These proved most helpful to the continuance of the Baptist witness in Europe in the tragic years prior to, during, and since the Second World War.

Baptists in France

It appears that the earliest kindling of the Baptist testimony on the European continent occurred in French Flanders. As early as 1810, in the village of Noumain, a farmer found a Bible hidden in the corner of his old house. He and his neighbors read it eagerly, and finally gathered together in 1819 to form a church. At that time they welcomed as their spiritual guide a young man, Henri Pyt, who had been converted under the influence of Robert Haldane, the Scotch evangelist. Pyt taught them Baptist principles during his eighteen-month stay with them. After his departure, some of his followers became colporters of the truths which they had learned.

At that critical period providential assistance came from abroad. Reverend Howard Malcolm, an American Baptist pastor who in 1831 had traveled in France for his health, became impressed with the evangelistic opportunities there. Accordingly, he persuaded the American Baptists to establish a mission in that country. Shortly thereafter, a brilliant young native of Marseilles, who had become a Baptist pastor in America, was appointed the first missionary. He was Casimir Rostan, a man of mature learning and evangelistic zeal. He sailed in October, 1832, with Irah Chase, professor at Newton Theological Institution and general director of the new venture. After thirteen months of successful labor amongst the intellectuals of Paris, Rostan, while attending the sick during an epidemic, was stricken with cholera. Upon his untimely death, a young graduate of Newton, the Reverend Isaac Wilmarth, who had been converted in Paris some years before, volunteered to take his place. During his five-year ministry there, he made contact with the Baptist followers of Pyt in the north of France. When he had to return to America because of failing health, Sheldon and Willard, two missionaries who had arrived in Paris in 1835, continued the mission. Upon Sheldon's departure from Paris in 1837, that station remained vacant, but Willard continued on with a school at Douai until 1856.

The early efforts of Baptists in France were hindered by persecution from the State. This ended, however, with the Revolution of 1848 when the Second Republic came into being and guaranteed religious toleration. Growth of the work thereafter was steady, though not spectacular. As early as 1851 the American missionaries thought it wise to develop regional organizations of churches as a means of spreading the Baptist witness to Belgium and Switzerland, both of which were French-speaking countries. Therefore, two groups of churches eventually were developed. One was the Federation of Baptist churches in the north of France, which was to labor there and in Brittany and Belgium. The other was the Federation of Franco-Swiss Baptist churches, to serve the great Catholic urban centers of France, the Southern Cevennes, the Pays de Monbeliard, and French Switzerland. In 1919 the two bodies were joined in a French Baptist Union. Work in Brittany had been begun near the middle of the nineteenth century by the Baptist Missionary Society of England.

At the opening of the twentieth century there were in France thirty Baptist churches with approximately twenty-five hundred members. While the number of churches had decreased to twenty-seven by 1908, ten had become self-supporting. Through a French Baptist Missionary Committee, these people were also supporting a missionary among the Moslems in Algeria and were conducting their own work in Belgium and Switzerland. In the homeland their assistance in the preparation of a new translation of the Bible into French won the respect of biblical scholars.[1]

The effects of the First World War were felt keenly in France. Buildings were destroyed; congregations disintegrated as members and pastors were called for service. Missionaries of European nationality were interned, while Americans returned to the United States. Yet the attendance at religious services increased, as did the spiritual fervor of the people. The Belgian mission, ever

[1] *Proceedings of the first European Baptist Congress,* 1908, p. 162; *Proceedings of the second Baptist World Congress,* 1911, pp. 44, 438. These citations will be referred to hereafter by the initials, E.B.C. and B.W.C.

small, was almost entirely disrupted. Before the war there had been forty-one Sunday schools with one thousand pupils, but due to the destruction of several buildings only twenty-two remained after the conflict, with facilities for only five hundred children.[2]

At the close of the war, dissension between some local churches and the French Baptist Union hindered to some extent the spread of the Baptist witness. It grew out of differences over the appropriation of funds for carrying on French-speaking work. Nevertheless, the Union continued to grow, with twenty churches in France and three in Belgium by 1923.[3]

French developments in Baptist missions to the end of the third decade of the twentieth century have been characterized by divisiveness and a tendency to rely overmuch upon assistance from abroad, in spite of a marked advance in self-support. The total membership included less than two thousand, and progress was slow.[4] By 1939 France once again was engulfed in war with all of its attendant miseries. During the occupation of the country by the German Nazis, little was known of the welfare of Baptists. But when France was liberated in 1945, a French Baptist leader was able to report that all Baptist churches were still in operation and that two new mission centers had been opened. By mid-century the French Baptist Federation, composed of seventeen churches in secondary towns, was seeking to establish congregations in large urban centers. Inability to achieve a strong degree of internal unity and self-support continued to weaken the Baptist witness in France.[5]

Baptists in Germany

The pioneer of German Baptist work was a native of Varel, in Oldenburg, Johann Gerhard Oncken (1800-1884). At the age of thirteen this Lutheran lad was taken to Scotland by a Scottish merchant whose interest in the boy had been aroused on one of his visits to Varel. During Oncken's nine years of service to his patron, he traveled extensively through Scotland, England, France, and Ger-

[2] *Annual of the Northern Baptist Convention*, 1915, pp. 516-8; 1916, pp. 447, 606-8. This citation will be referred to hereafter by initials, N.B.C. B.W.C., *Proceedings*, 1923, 1923, p. 146.

[3] N.B.C., *Annual*, 1923, pp. 603-4.

[4] J. H. Rushbrooke, *Some Chapters of European Baptist History*, p. 27.

[5] N.B.C., *Annual*, 1945, p. 202; *The Watchman-Examiner*, Vol. 38, No. 46 (Nov. 16, 1950), pp. 1104-6.

many. The most significant influences upon his life came from the Presbyterian environment of Scotland and later from an Independent family in London, where he lived for a time. In the latter's home he was led to conversion. At once he dedicated himself to evangelism, spending a large portion of his small earnings upon tracts which he distributed faithfully.

In 1823 he accepted appointment by the Continental Society as a missionary to Germany and settled down in Hamburg as a member of the English Reformed Church of that city. With the encouragement of his pastor, he began to preach to small groups in private homes. Soon his meetings were so well attended that they attracted the hostility of the local clergy. When forbidden to continue this service, he took to street-corner preaching despite the danger of being expelled from the city. In time, it became clear to him that his wisest course was to open a bookshop and become a citizen of the town. From this headquarters he distributed Bibles, circulated tracts, helped to establish Sunday schools, and continued his preaching ministry.

As early as 1829 his reading of the Scriptures led him to inquire of British Baptists concerning baptism. It was not until 1834, however, that he, his wife, and five others were baptized in the River Elbe on April 22 by Professor Sears, of Hamilton, a Baptist school in New York State (see p. 311). Sears had been traveling in Europe and had become acquainted with Oncken's desire for believer's baptism from a report made by a sea captain, Calvin Tubbs, to the headquarters of the American Baptist Triennial Convention in Boston.

Oncken's witness as a Baptist drew upon his head a greater storm of persecution than he had endured as an Independent. He was disowned by the missionary society under which he had served and by the Independents generally. The Triennial Convention in America thereupon appointed him as its agent in 1835. For a time a friendly chief of police in Hamburg protected the little Baptist church from destruction, but upon his replacement, the new prefect set upon a determined course to uproot the Baptist heresy. By this time, the congregation numbered nearly one hundred persons. Undaunted by imprisonment, fines, the dispersal of his meetings by the military, and the threat of ultimate confiscation of his property, Oncken refused to accommodate his persecutors by leaving the country. His cause was aided by petitions from England and the United States—petitions which caused the commercially sensitive Hamburg authorities to relax their prohibitions on private meetings. As the congregation continued to grow, it was delivered unexpectedly from persecution when a great fire left a third of the city's inhabitants homeless in May, 1842. The sacrificial service of Oncken and his congregation in behalf of the suffering citizens won the gratitude of the senate and prevented further acts of hostility.

By 1845 there were 380 Baptists in Hamburg, and two years later the first chapel was erected. A year later another chapel was opened in Berlin under the leadership of G. W. Lehmann, a friend of Oncken. At this time there were twenty-six churches with fifteen hundred members in such centers as Breslau, Stettin, Bremen, Elbing, Memel, Kassel, Marburg, Bitterfield, and Oldenburg. The chief advance was in East Prussia; the least in Mecklenburg, Saxony, and Bavaria. In all probability, the officials in the latter states reflected the more reactionary character of their religious life. There were three major hindrances to Baptist work, the first of which came from the long-standing German antipathy to Anabaptists, whom they associated with the hated Münster rebellion of an earlier period. The second was the resentment of the Lutheran clergy to Baptist growth among the common people. The third was a government policy of intolerance, encouraged by the clergy, by which Baptists suffered indignities and loss of property. With the Revolution of 1848, however, official toleration was granted.

In view of the more favorable circumstances, Oncken urged his followers to accelerate their missionary activity and to strengthen their organization. Assisted by funds from England and America, Lehmann and Oncken conducted preaching tours in Denmark, Lithuania, and Switzerland for the purpose of strengthening the existing churches and of establishing new centers of activity. By 1851 there were forty-one churches with a combined membership of 3,746 persons, 137 Sunday school teachers, and 1,035 pupils.[6] As early as 1849 four Associations of Baptists in Prussia, northwest Germany, south-central Germany, and Denmark had been united in a "Union of the Associated Churches of Baptized Christians in Germany and Denmark." Its pattern and purpose were much the same as that of the Triennial Convention in the United States, even to meeting every

[6] J. H. Rushbrooke, *The Baptist Movement in the Continent of Europe*, 21.

three years. Through its facilities, an active missionary program was carried on in neighboring countries.

Between 1850 and 1854 persecution of the Baptists was resumed. It was instigated chiefly by the clergy, who resented the opposition of Baptist people to infant baptism and to payment of the church tax. In many places, ministers of Baptist chapels were curbed in the administration of the ordinances and in the conduct of public worship. They were subjected to slights at funerals; assemblies were broken up by mobs, while the police tacitly withheld protection; many were imprisoned and treated as common criminals; and infants were snatched from their mothers to be carried off for baptism by the state church. Through the earnest overtures in their behalf by British and American state officials, as well as by Baptist constituencies in those countries, the attention of King Frederick William the Fourth was called to the plight of German Baptists. Persecution did not cease, however, until that monarch's illness brought Prince Wilhelm to the throne as Regent. The state church even then continued to be unfriendly.

Owing to their fear of an autocratic priesthood, German Baptists were not anxious to have a trained ministry; but Oncken finally persuaded them to establish a theological seminary at Hamburg in 1880. A publishing house was founded at Kassel and flourished under Dr. Philip Bickel's direction. The number of German Baptists increased from 11,275 in 1863 to 45,583 by 1913 in 213 churches. Their property was valued at nearly one million dollars.[7] Missions were conducted in Scandinavian countries, Holland, Poland, Switzerland, Russia, Hungary, Bulgaria, and in Africa. From the original leadership of Oncken, Julius Köbner, and Lehmann, a well-organized fellowship had been developed, but not without some difficulty with Oncken who was reluctant to surrender the authority which he had acquired through the years by virtue of his pioneer work. This weakness does not detract from the greatness of the man who, more than any other, has been responsible for the spread of the Baptist witness throughout Europe.

While World War I depleted the leadership of Baptist churches, their influence spread as booklets and tracts were published for the soldiers. The African work in the Cameroons suffered, and because

[7] *Ibid.*, 28-9.

of hostilities little relief from fellow Baptists abroad was available. With the end of the conflict, relief was given and relations between German Baptists and Baptists of America and Great Britain were restored. Between 1920 and 1922 there was an increase of four thousand members, bringing the total German Baptist membership to 53,900. A similar growth was reported for the Netherlands where in 1923 there were 2,833 members, a 10 per cent increase in two years.[8] By the close of the twenties, the number of Baptists in Germany had swelled to sixty thousand.[9] For the time being they enjoyed a larger degree of freedom than heretofore, but they were to be confronted with new problems in the years that followed.

With the infiltration of Nazism into German political life and its ultimate triumph in the rise of Hitler to power in 1933, the Baptists showed little concern. Their strong antipathy to involvement of the church in politics in any way, plus their recognition that the new regime did not hinder their work since they were not a state-church sect, caused them to be somewhat blinded to the real issues involved in the emergence of totalitarianism. In 1934 they entertained, without interference from the state, the fifth Baptist World Congress. Five years later, however, when the sixth Congress was held at Atlanta, Georgia, just a few weeks prior to the outbreak of the Second World War, German Baptists were warned of the dangers facing them. It was reported that a "complacent bourgeois mentality" was gripping many Baptists, and that German Baptists, in particular, were withdrawing from a frank facing of the burning questions of the day.[10] When war came, they shared in its terrible privations, misery, and destruction. Fully half of their 275 churches were destroyed or damaged beyond repair. In the eastern areas, they suffered a total loss of church buildings. The Baptist Theological Seminary at Hamburg was reduced to ruins. The publication office and printing plant at Kassel was destroyed completely. Yet Baptist congregations participated bravely in the overwhelming task of providing relief for refugees. In the Russian occupied zone, congregations were allowed to meet for worship, but the pastors were carefully watched by the secret police with respect to the content of their preaching. Since

[8] N.B.C., *Annual,* 1915, p. 519; B.W.C , *Proceedings,* 1923, p. 90.

[9] J. H. Rushbrooke, *Some Chapters of European Baptist History,* p. 19.

[10] An address delivered by Dr. William A. Mueller, B.W.C., *Proceedings,* 1939, p. 208.

very few Baptists had allied themselves with the National Socialist Party of the Hitler regime, they emerged from the war in a position to share with other evangelical Christians in the spiritual reconstruction of Germany. By 1950 a German Baptist Union was organized, composed of 559 churches, 406 ministers, and 100,219 members. The publication house at Kassel was rebuilt and seventy-five new congregations were established in centers which had no Baptist witness before the war.[11]

Scandinavian Baptists

With the conversion in America of two Swedish seamen, the seeds were planted for the development of Baptist work in Sweden. One was G. W. Schroeder, a sea captain, who joined the Baptist Mariners' Church in New York City in 1843. The other was F. O. Nilson, who did not become a Baptist at once, but who returned to his native country as a missionary to his fellow sailors. It was at Gothenburg, in 1845, that he came into contact with Schroeder. Under Schroeder's guidance Nilson accepted Baptist views, went to Hamburg, and was baptized by Oncken on August 1, 1847. Upon his return he was instrumental in establishing the first Baptist church in Sweden, in 1848, near Gothenburg. After his ordination at Hamburg, he became pastor of the Swedish church, only to meet with severe opposition from the authorities, who were bound to protect Lutheranism. Consequently, he was banished in July, 1851, whereupon he went to Copenhagen to serve as pastor of the Baptist church there until 1853. At that time he accepted the invitation of a band of twenty-four harassed Swedish Baptists to lead them to the United States. He remained in America until 1860, when the King annulled his banishment. He returned the next year to become pastor of a newly organized Baptist church in Gothenburg.

Another center of Baptist work was Stockholm, where a church had been organized on June 18, 1854, by two furriers, D. Forsell and P. F. Hejdenberg, the latter of whom had been ordained in Hamburg during the previous May. A year later he undertook evangelistic work, and Andreas Wiberg, a learned convert from the state church,

---

[11] William B. Lipphard, "Misery and Hunger in Post-war Germany," *Missions,* Vol. 37, No. 9 (Nov., 1946), p. 527; _____, "Unsolved Problems in Post-war Germany," *Ibid.,* Vol. 37, No. 10 (Dec., 1946), pp. 593-5; *The Baptist Times* (London), Vol. 99, No. 5110 (Feb. 19, 1953), pp. 1-2.

replaced him as leader of the growing congregation. Wiberg had the support of the American Baptist Publication Society, and so was enabled to engage four evangelists to assist him in establishing new churches, Sunday schools, and eventually a publishing enterprise.

In 1857 the first Conference of Swedish Baptists was held, and it was without disturbance from the authorities. Nineteen delegates from eight different provinces were present. When the second gathering occurred the following year, there were one hundred delegates present. The third Conference, which met at Stockholm in 1861, was significant for two reasons. It was reported that there were in the country 125 Baptist churches with a total of 4,930 members. When the Executive Committee was authorized to establish a school for training preachers, Bethel Seminary was founded in 1866. Financial aid came from both England and America. The American Baptist Missionary Union gave liberal support from 1866 until near the end of the century. In 1889 the Swedish Conference set up special committees for foreign missions, home missions, publication, and Sunday school work. Their members composed the Executive Committee which directed the affairs of the Union.

Persecution almost entirely subsided after the sixties, although legal restrictions remained on the books by which some intolerant clergymen sought, through the years that followed, to hinder Baptists' work. Usually, however, the higher courts failed to give approval to a rigid application of these laws. Indeed, in time, the presence of several Swedish Baptists in the National Parliament did much to secure legislation favorable to dissenters. Hence, by 1914, the country was open to Baptist evangelization. That the Baptists had not failed to take advantage of their opportunities is evident from the statistics of that year: 21 associations; 635 churches; 54,159 members; 377 ministers; 699 local preachers; 70 students for the ministry; 65,404 Sunday school members; 623 chapels. Total contributions in 1913 amounted to nearly $300,000, of which nearly $17,000 was spent for foreign missions.[12] Stations were maintained on the Aaland Islands in the Baltic and in Sweden where the American Baptist Foreign Mission Society was also at work; in addition, missionaries were supported at St. Petersburg, Russia, and in Esthonia.

Baptist beginnings in Norway date from the arrival of Frederik

[12] J. H. Rushbrooke, *The Baptist Movement in the Continent of Europe*, 66.

L. Rymker, a Danish sailor who had been converted and baptized in America. He settled at Prosgrund, near Skien, where a pietistic element in the Lutheran Church was becoming vocal in behalf of the necessity for conversion. The first Baptist church was organized on April 22, 1860, at Tolnaes, a farm near Skien, with seven members present. Another church was founded at Larvik in 1860, although it was destined not to survive for long. In 1862 a third church was formed at Kragerö. The lack of an educated leadership and of sufficient funds hindered the progress of Baptist work in Norway. Yet the number of congregations continued to increase until it was possible to organize, at Skien in 1872, a "Southern District Association"; and in 1877 a similar district association for the churches north of the polar circle, with Tromsö as a center. In the same year the Norwegian Baptist Conference was formed at Bergen, being composed of all of the churches in the country, which numbered fourteen, with 511 members and twelve ministers, but only two houses of worship—those at Tromsö and Bergen. English Baptists gave generous support to the struggling groups.[13]

Training ministers for their churches was a problem for Norwegian Baptists. If they sent them to the seminary at Stockholm, they returned using the Swedish language; if they sent them to the Danish-Norwegian Theological Seminary at the University of Chicago, they usually did not return to their native land at all. The result was that a Norwegian Baptist Theological Seminary was established at Christiana in 1910, with the American-trained Norwegian, O. J. Öie, as principal. The American Baptist Foreign Missionary Society joined with the English Baptists in assisting the Norwegian brethren in their mission work. The increase in membership between 1900 and 1910 was 29.75 per cent as over against a mere 6.75 per cent gain in the population of the country.[14] It was apparent that this minority sect, despite difficulties, was making progress.

The First World War did not ravage Scandinavian lands as it did the Continent; nevertheless Baptists in Norway and Sweden, like the populace generally, felt the effects of wartime restriction on trade. Some churches could not pay the salaries of their ministers. On the other hand, an increased attendance of members was charac-

13 *Ibid.*, 133.
14 Rushbrooke, *op. cit.*, 136.

teristic of the times, and plans were being laid to undertake missionary work in Africa in co-operation with the American Baptist Foreign Mission Society.[15] Baptists were growing in esteem in all ranks of society, and many of them filled positions of responsibility in local and state politics. By 1923 there were close to sixty thousand Baptists in Sweden in 680 churches. Yet it should be admitted that they represented only 1 per cent of the population. The majority of them were from the industrial, rural, and middle classes.[16] By 1930, however, these people of low incomes had become entirely self-supporting after seventy-five years of aid from abroad. Norwegian Baptists were not so fortunate, having only about five thousand adherents as compared with the sixty-two thousand in Sweden.[17] Baptists in Sweden have developed a flourishing publication society, and they have a missionary enterprise which includes several fields in different parts of the world.

During the Second World War, the Scandinavian countries did not fare so well as during the preceding world conflict. Norway was invaded and occupied by the Germans; Sweden, although remaining a neutral, found herself in the unenviable position of having to withstand the demands of the Nazi regime without incurring their actual hostility. Baptists sought to keep alive their work and to extend relief to fleeing refugees who made their way to Sweden, in particular. Since the war, the Swedish Baptist Union declined in membership, losing more members each year than it gained. In Norway the work developed slowly. By 1955 the Norwegian Baptist Union included 63 churches with 7,422 members.[18]

Baptists in Other Countries

Through the influence of German Baptists, such as Oncken and Köbner, eleven persons were baptized at Copenhagen in October, 1839, creating thereby the first Danish Baptist church. Its pastor was an engraver by the name of Mönster. This gallant leader, imprisoned at the hands of the police, was succeeded by his brother, who, in turn, met the same fate for baptizing new converts. In spite of petitions from American and British friends, persecution continued until

[15] N.B.C., *Annual*, 1915, p. 523; 1916, p. 612; 1917, pp. 826-7.
[16] B.W.C., *Proceedings*, 1923, p. 79.
[17] B.W.C., *Proceedings*, 1928, p. 74; N.B.C., *Annual*, 1930, p. 432.
[18] *Crusader*, Vol. 10, No. 5 (Oct., 1955), p. 7; Vol. 10, No. 6 (Nov., 1955), pp. 3 ff

nearly 1850 when a new constitution of the kingdom secured religious toleration. At that time there were but six Baptist churches with about four hundred members in addition to Mönster's church in Copenhagen, which had withdrawn from fellowship with the rest. For the next fifteen years, however, progress was evident. While Mormon influences hindered the work in Copenhagen, the number of churches increased to nine with a total membership of sixteen hundred. This was followed by a period of organization, which lasted until 1883.[19] To supply much needed leadership, Köbner returned in 1865 to his native Copenhagen to be pastor of the church there. He instituted the holding of annual conferences, which were characterized more by study of theology and polity than by actual conduct of business. Lack of funds and leadership, however, prevented any marked growth in numbers until 1883 when relations were established with the American Baptist Missionary Union, which gave assistance to the Danish Baptists. Many of their preachers were trained in the Danish-Norwegian Department of Morgan Park Seminary, near Chicago.

Between 1883 and 1899 there were about 3,500 baptisms; the total membership increased from about 2,200 to 3,906. Then the upward advance began to level off. Indeed, by 1915 the number of Baptists in the country did not exceed 4,226. Attention was being given to the development of leadership through the establishment in 1910 of a small training school for ministers in Copenhagen, and the development of young people's work and Sunday school teacher training.[20] When during the First World War the Lutheran state church became somewhat unsettled in its traditional views concerning baptism, the Lord's Supper, and the separation of church and state, the Baptists hastened to take advantage of the situation by having printed fifty-five thousand copies of a pamphlet on the identity and program of the Baptists. By 1928 the Baptists numbered six thousand. The Baptist witness has been borne faithfully by this minority group. In 1947, the Danish Baptists entertained the seventh Baptist World Congress at Copenhagen. By 1952 they had increased to 7,000 members and had attained from the government legal status as a "community of faith," an action which granted to them the right to

---

[19] Rushbrooke, *The Baptist Movement in the Continent of Europe*, 40.
[20] *Ibid.*, 42.

perform legal marriages and also to maintain their own records.[21]

Three factors favored the introduction of the Baptist witness to Russia in the late eighteenth century. One was the migration of a large host of Mennonite refugees from military service in Prussia. Upon the assurance of freedom from coercion given to them by the Empress Catherine II, they settled on farm land in southeastern Russia. About the same time a restlessness among the peasants, or serfs, issued in their emancipation soon after the Crimean War. Their organization in *mirs* or village communities provided fertile fields for Mennonite evangelism, so much so that town meetings frequently became preaching services. During the height of this spiritual awakening, the British and Foreign Bible Society secured permission from the Imperial Government to distribute the Scriptures among the peoples. In this work the Greek Orthodox clergy also concurred. In all probability they did not foresee the consequences of their action, for, in the 1860's and 1870's, groups of peasants who had become dissatisfied with the Orthodox Church began to forsake the services of that church and to turn to heart-warming Bible study groups that met in private homes. These periods of worship were called "Stunden," or "Hours." This Stundist movement, which developed in the Kherson province of the Ukraine under the influence of German Mennonite and Nazarene colonists, was one of two major sources from which Russian Baptists stemmed. One of these pietists who eventually became a leader of Baptists was Michael Ratushny.

A second source was the Molokans, a religious sect very much like the Quakers in teaching. Centered in Tiflis, capital of Georgia, they came under the influence of a German Baptist named Martin Kalweit about 1862. As a Baptist community was built up in time, Basil Pavlov, a gifted youth, was converted and became a fine preacher. Later, he and Ratushny met, and so the two movements of Caucasian Baptists were united eventually into the Russian Baptist Union (1884).

The most notable Baptist convert from the Molokans was Ivan Prokhanov, who became associated with a group of well-educated Baptists during his student days in St. Petersburg about 1888. He founded the first Russian Baptist periodical, *Beseda,* and in 1902 published a Russian Evangelical hymnbook. He did not wish, however,

[21] N.B.C., *Annual,* 1917, p. 826; B.W.C., *Proceedings,* 1923, p. 144; 1928, p. 73; *The Christian Century,* Vol. 70, No. 2 (Jan. 14, 1953), p. 60.

to work with the Russian Baptist Union, because he was unable to accept the rigid views which the Caucasian Baptists held. He also regarded the name "Baptist" as alien to his people. He preferred, instead, the name "Evangelical."

His was the smaller of the two groups in 1914 (with only 8,472 compared with 97,000 in the Russian Baptist Union), but it grew to more than 250,000 in eight years. Although Prokhanov was a recognized Baptist leader and had been elected vice-president of the Baptist World Alliance in 1911, his group differed from the Russian Baptist Union in interpreting Baptist principles. Moreover, they were mostly "the well-to-do peasants and Cossacks in the country and small shop-keepers and independent artisans in the towns."[22]

These Baptist groups encountered severe persecution from the Russian Government. Baptist leaders were exiled to Siberia and the Caucasus like common criminals. But this persecution, instead of stemming the growth of the Baptists, increased their numbers; for wherever they went, they won new converts. By 1905 the severity of the measures was relaxed. Sectarians were granted a semblance of liberty; the policy of exile was abandoned, and imprisonment was imposed only on those who sought to persuade anyone to leave the Orthodox Church.

During the First World War aggressive work by the churches was brought to a standstill, because most able-bodied men were called to the armed services. Many Russian Baptists, however, refused for conscience' sake to go to the front to fight, although they expressed willingness to do noncombatant work for the Army. In this, they reflected the influence of their contacts with Mennonite teaching. Twelve preachers were reported exiled in 1915 along with many other Protestant preachers who were regarded as dangerous to the Government. The Revolution of 1917, which overthrew the Czarist's regime, brought deliverance to all sectarians from the repression of the state church. As political and religious exiles were permitted to return home, Baptist leaders were restored to their churches.[23]

In many respects the new Soviet regime in Russia proved to be a boon to the Baptists. The new-found freedom made possible a fuller fruitage of their evangelistic labors than had been possible at any

[22] Serge Bolshakoff, *Russian Noncomformity* (Philadelphia, 1950), p. 120.
[23] N.B.C., *Annual,* 1915, p. 522; 1916, p. 611; 1917, p. 826.

time previously. Between 1914 and 1923 the number of Baptists increased from well over a hundred thousand to one million. Some even placed the figure at two million, while one government official expressed his belief that there were about three million Baptists in the country. In appraising this remarkable growth, Dr. Rushbrooke, the British Baptist leader, said: "It is safe to say, when comparison is made with the membership of the churches before the war, that in no country of the world has there been proportionately such an increase; but it is also certainly the case that for lack of resources and organization not all the fruit of widespread revival movements has been garnered in orderly churches."[24]

While the Government did not view Baptists as a political menace, it did set obstacles in the way of their work, particularly with children and young people, by forbidding organized religious education of children under eighteen years of age and by demanding the service of all able-bodied young citizens in the Army. By 1929 the Baptists, like other religious bodies in the country, were tasting the full bitterness of governmental suppression of religion. Because of Baptist evangelistic zeal in the cause of Christianity, the atheistic regime sought to stamp out Christian leadership by arresting hundreds of Baptists and other evangelical Christians. Pastors were disfranchised, deprived of food tickets, subjected to special taxation, forbidden to teach their children except at home, forbidden to circulate Bibles, and forbidden to hold services in their churches. In the years that followed, intervention from other governments failed to win any concessions for the harassed Christians within Russia.[25]

In the revised constitution of the Union of Socialist Soviet Republics, adopted in 1936, the Communists announced that religious freedom had been guaranteed to all of its citizens. Actually, however, it granted freedom of belief only; propagation of one's faith was still forbidden as hostile to the welfare of Marxian doctrine. During the critical days of the Second World War, some few concessions were made to win popular support of the military effort.

In 1942, both groups of Baptists (the Russian Union and Prokhanov's Union) made a joint appeal to Baptists throughout the world. They claimed to speak for four million followers. In 1944, they formed

[24] *Ibid.*, 1923, p. 595; Rushbrooke, *Some Chapters of European Baptist History*, p. 103.
[25] N.B.C., *Annual*, 1924, p. 501; 1930, pp. 397-8; B.W.C., *Proceedings*, 1928, p. 77; 1939, p. 44.

the Council of the United Baptists and the Evangelical Christians. In August, 1945, the Pentecostals were invited to join. The enlarged federation, known as the Council of the United Baptists, Evangelical Christians, and Pentecostal Churches and Groups in the U.S.S.R., functions like the British National Council of Free Churches.

There were, however, some 700,000 Russian Baptists who apparently did not join, for between 1941 and 1947 the membership of the United Baptists declined from one million to 300,000. Some persons have suggested that "these Baptists left the Government-sponsored organization and 'went underground,' objecting to the close relations between the new Council and the atheist government."[26]

Since 1950 some direct contacts have been made by western churchmen with Russian Christians. In 1951 a group of English Quakers reported that two church groups are recognized by the government: the Russian Orthodox Church and the Baptist Evangelical Union. An estimated 400,000 Baptists comprise the combined membership of 4,000 Baptist churches in the Soviet Union. About three million attenders are served by these churches. Religious education is not undertaken except through the worship services, since Sunday schools are discouraged. There is no salaried ministry. The function of the church is limited to the saving of souls and their preparation for the life hereafter. No attention is given to the social order. Most of the church buildings belong to the state, and the Baptists pay a modest ground rental and the cost of repairs. In some places small churches rent a room from a farmer or house-owner. The nearly half-million members constitute the vital core of what is believed to be a much larger company of believers. Many of the latter are under eighteen and therefore too young to receive baptism according to membership regulations. Others are on probation, awaiting admission to baptism. Still others are in areas where their number is not large enough for them to be registered as an organized church.[27]

Along the Baltic, the Swedish and German Baptists have spread their witness with the result that small groups of believers are to be found in most of the small countries bordering on that sea. In Finland, for example, two conferences of Baptists exist, one of Swedish-

---

[26] Bolshakoff, *Russian Noncomformity,* p. 122.

[27] *Baptist World Alliance Youth News* (1952), 16; *Crusader,* Vol. 11, No. 5 (May, 1956), 9; *Baptist Leader,* Vol. 18, No. 1 (April, 1956), 4.

speaking Finns and the other of Finns proper. The former has been the stronger, having been organized by the opening of the present century out of a group of churches, the earliest of which had been established at Jacobstad in 1869. By 1911 its constituency numbered twenty-nine churches with 1,992 members, twenty-one full-time pastors and forty part-time. In 1923 the membership was reported as 2,928, a modest increase.[28] The latter conference was organized in 1905; by 1917 it totaled twenty-five churches. A struggle within the country against Communists and the rise in their midst of a fanatical Pentecostal movement combined to cost this group an appreciable loss of members. Their lack of education and their emotional instability were a serious disadvantage to the permanent strengthening of their influence in a land in which persecution had been negligible. Financial assistance has come from Swedish and British Baptists respectively.[29] However, recent years of war have cut Finnish Baptists off from contact with this aid, resulting in hardship and suffering for them.

The Baptist witness in Esthonia, a Russian satellite along the Baltic, may be dated from 1884, when some Evangelicals, who for some time had been emphasizing the importance of conversion, became convinced of the significance of baptism as a "burial" with Christ. Accordingly, with the aid of the German pastor of a Baptist church in St. Petersburg, nine believers were immersed on February 11 at Hapsal. By 1896 an Esthonian Baptist Association was formed. In the years that followed, however, the severity of persecution from the Russian Government prevented appreciable growth and caused the churches to be scattered. In 1918 the little country became a republic with religious liberty. In 1920, American and British Baptists agreed to give financial assistance to Esthonian Baptists so that they might be able to maintain adequate leadership. Two years later, they established a seminary for preachers at Reval, the rector being the Reverend Adam Podin, an outstanding European Baptist leader. The Baptists' appeal in Esthonia has been very strong to a people, long under tyranny, who have discovered the privileges of democratic government. Their influence has been felt widely. Besides the seminary, they established in the twenties some elementary schools under Baptist management and planned for the future

[28] B.W.C., *Proceedings*, 1911, p. 42; 1923, p. 86.
[29] Rushbrooke, *Some Chapters of European Baptist History*, p. 34-5.

development of high schools. A Blue Cross Society was organized to win drunkards to Christ. They worked in behalf of full women's rights in their own churches and within the country in general. Podin's church established a mission among university students. Thus these five thousand Baptists were making a contribution to the life of their country. During the war years they endured great hardship, being persecuted, losing property, and suffering from starvation. Many fled to Sweden. Relief funds have been sent to their aid by the American Baptist Foreign Mission Society and by Esthonian Baptists in the United States.[30]

Latvian Baptists trace their beginnings from contacts with German Baptists made by Jakobsohn, a young ship's carpenter, who went from the port of Libau to Memel to find work. This was during the Crimean War, when his home port was blockaded by the British. In time, settlers from Memel came to Libau, many of them being Baptists. Thus was begun in 1860 a group who, at peril to their own safety from the authorities, made their way to Memel to receive baptism. In September, 1861, the first baptisms on Latvian soil were held secretly in the night; seventy-two believers were immersed. After severe persecution by the authorities, the Russian Government in 1879 granted a Baptist petition for toleration and recognized the independent religious status of Baptists in the Baltic States. Gradually the churches at Libau, Windau, and Sakkenhausen became independent of their earlier relation to the mother church at Memel. A Lettish Baptist Association was organized and the nucleus of a publication house was formed in the eighties under the leadership of John Alexander Frey, a man of unusual ability, training, and vision. He sent evangelists throughout the country and even into Russia and among the Letts who had colonized in Brazil. At the opening of the twentieth century, Lettish Baptists were supporting five Bible-women in India and one missionary in China.

The effects of the First World War were so devastating as almost to crush the splendid work which had been begun. To add to their plight, Baptists for a time in 1917 came under the persecution of Russian Communists. Frey and other leaders were exiled to Siberia. When the country attained in 1918 the status of a republic, the exiles returned and the work was renewed with the aid of the

[30] B.W.C., *Proceedings*, 1923, p. 21; N.B.C., *Year Book*, 1945, p. 202.

Northern Baptist Convention in the United States and of English and Canadian Baptists. A seminary was opened at Riga in 1922. Here also progress was hindered somewhat by the rise of a fanatical Pentecostal movement. At least sixteen Baptist churches were influenced by these teachings to stay out of the Latvian Baptist Union, which they regarded as an obstacle to the free working of the Holy Spirit. Under Pentecostal teaching there was a strong aversion to organized Christianity and an ecstatic anticipation of the Lord's return. As a matter of fact, the impact of Pentecostalism was a serious problem not only to Latvian Baptists, but also to Baptists in other countries of Europe. While the churches in the Latvian Union declined in number from eighty-four in 1921 to seventy-seven in 1929, the total membership increased from 8,099 to 10,000.[31]

At the outbreak of World War II there were about eleven thousand Baptists in Latvia. It is possible that the terrible toll of the years that followed have reduced that number. In 1940, when the German-Russian Pact gave the little republic to the Soviet Union, religious freedom became a thing of the past. One Latvian Baptist pastor reported that church buildings were confiscated and converted into dance halls, movie houses, and Red Army clubs. The ones not used for such purposes could be rented for church functions, but only at a prohibitive price. The seminary at Riga was closed, and the building was used as the headquarters of the Russian Secret Police. Several of the Baptist ministers were deported to Siberia; church organizations were suppressed; Bibles and songbooks were destroyed and in many cases property was confiscated. Many Baptists were victims of the mass executions, rapings, and plunderings to which the wartime populace was subjected. Consequently, when Latvia was "liberated" in 1944-45, many Baptists in Displaced Persons Camps in Germany were reluctant to return to their homeland, which was still under Soviet control.[32] The future, indeed, looked dark for Latvian Baptists, who already had suffered sorely under the privations of war.

In Lithuania, the number of Baptists is small, as it always has been since the first church was established in 1841 in Memel under the

[31] Rushbrooke, *Some Chapters of European Baptist History*, pp. 55-71; B.W.C., *Proceedings*, 1923, p. 86; 1928, p. 80.

[32] Lerrigo and Amidon, *All Kindreds and Tongues*, p. 257; Carlos Purgailis, "Latvian Baptists in Germany," *The Watchman-Examiner*, Vol. 34, No. 47 (Nov. 21, 1946), p. 1187.

guidance of Oncken, the German Baptist leader. This church, as we have seen, was influential in the beginnings of Lettish work. Another German-speaking church was founded in the capital city of Kowno in 1879. After the First World War, the work among Baptists centered in the activities of the Reverend T. Gerikas, who was supported by Northern Baptists in America, and by British Baptists, so that he might fulfill his long cherished desire to preach to his own people. He established a church at Siauliai and effected a union of Lithuanian. German, Lettish and Russian Baptists in the Republic in a "Co-operating Committee."

In 1923 the total number of Baptists in the country was under five hundred.[33] The progress of evangelization there has been slowed by many obstacles, among which are the poverty of these rural people, the varied language groups within the state, and the strong Catholic influence, that church having been favored by the Government in spite of the guarantee of religious liberty. The Second World War has created problems similar to those faced by the Lettish Baptists.

Baptist growth in Poland had its first impulse in the missionary labors of German Baptists in the mid-nineteenth century. The greater number of organized Polish Baptist churches, however, came into existence after the Edict of Toleration was issued by the Russian Czar in 1905. In 1911, despite a constant migration of Baptists to other lands, there were reportedly five thousand Baptists within the country. By 1923 this number had increased to 8,783, or one in every three thousand of the population. Five years later, according to the records, there were seven thousand German-speaking Baptists in the country and an equal number of Slavic Baptists. While freedom of conscience was guaranteed by the Polish Constitution in what was formerly Austrian Poland, the old Austrian law still prevailed which enabled the authorities, under pressure from Roman Catholic leaders, to jail Baptists for preaching, baptizing, or refusing to allow their children to receive Roman Catholic instruction in the public schools.[34] After the outbreak of war in September, 1939, the Baptists shared with their countrymen the terrible fate of being ravaged by the armies of friend and foe alike.

[33] Rushbrooke, *op cit.*, pp. 72-9; B.W.C., *Proceedings,* 1923, p. 87.
[34] B.W.C., *Proceedings,* 1911, p. 43; 1923, p. 54; 1928, pp. 78-9.

Baptists in the Balkans and Southern Europe

The Balkan states in southeastern Europe, composed of hetero-geneous language and racial groups, each with its own intense na-tional feelings, have rightly been called the "witches' cauldron" of the continent. Their peoples have been subjected to all of the tensions which usually exist between minority factions. In an increasing sense, this area has come under Russian domination, due to Slavic affinity and proximity as well as to economic interests. This influence repre-sents another threat to the Baptist witness which may be added to the ever-present Catholic opposition. While there have been Baptist churches in practically all of these little countries since the close of the nineteenth century, they have been weak and struggling, facing persecution everywhere except in Bulgaria, where a large measure of tolerance was shown until a communist regime opened an offensive against church leaders at the close of the forties.

Bulgarian Baptists have stemmed from Russian religious refugees who moved into the country in the eighties to escape perse-cution in their native land. The earliest churches were established at commercial centers such as Rustchuk, Lom, and Tchirpan, as well as at the capital, Sofia. There have never been more than a few hun-dred Baptists in the country.

In Rumania there were in 1915 only four German-speaking churches and one Russian-speaking congregation left of those which had been organized among immigrants during the late nineteenth century. Rumanian Baptist congregations began to thrive about 1910 when a German-American clergyman, the Reverend B. Schlipf, visited the country at the request of American Rumanian Baptists. He remained there and built so well that he aroused the antagonism of the civil and ecclesiastical authorities. Owing possibly to a success-ful work among thousands of Hungarians resident in Bucharest, the officials were persuaded that the Baptists were in the pay of Hungary and represented antinational, antimonarchial, antimilitary, and Bol-shevistic elements, opposed to the state. Without seriously examining the charges, the Government instituted severe measures against them which did not become less severe until the Rumanian Parliament passed a bill in 1928, giving almost full liberty to Baptists. By 1930 only local infractions of the law, incited by hostile Catholic priests, remained to harass the Baptists.[35] The executive committee of the Baptist World Alliance was influential in the winning of these concessions.

In that year there were 43,763 Baptists in the country, organized into a Rumanian Baptist Convention which had been formed seven years before. It was comprised of four language groups—Rumanian, Hungarian, German, and Russian—a fact which caused some internal dissension over leadership. Friction was caused also by a tendency of the Convention to dominate the local churches. However, under the guidance of Dr. Rushbrooke, the proposed constitution, which would have placed power in the hands of convention officials, was modified in 1929 to protect the autonomy of the local churches. Southern Baptists in the United States provided missionary leadership to train native preachers. Need for such assistance lessened in the early thirties. In 1936 Rumanian Baptists were strong enough to organize their own Foreign Mission Society, which sent a missionary to Yugoslavia. Home mission work was also in progress among the Gypsies in spite of vigorous persecution from the state church.[36]

As Fascism came to dominate the Government, a new era of persecution began in 1937. Officials, abetted by the Greek Orthodox Church, broke up meetings and forbade Baptist preachers to perform their functions. From December 15, 1938, until April 14, 1939, all Baptist churches in the nation were closed. Many members were imprisoned and whipped for refusing to worship in the state church. Ministers were forbidden to hold meetings, to perform weddings, or to hold burial services for their dead. Some relief was granted under pressure exerted upon the Government by the American Baptists and the Baptist World Alliance. Then came the disruption of war.

By 1944, however, the lot of Baptists in Rumania had improved. The King signed a decree on October 30 of that year which gave them the same legal status as was granted to the Moslems and Jews. The Rumanian Baptist Convention was able to meet one year later, for the first time since 1939. About fifteen hundred delegates and visitors gathered from all parts of the country in the city of Arad, which was the place from which the "holy war" had been launched against Baptists in 1942 by Dictator Antonescu and

---

[35] B.W.C., *Proceedings*, 1923, pp. 52-3; *Annual of the Southern Baptist Convention,* 1929 (hereafter indicated by the initials, S.B.C.), p. 255; 1930, p. 156.

[36] S.B.C., *Annual*, 1929, p. 256; 1934, p. 222; 1936, p. 200.

the Greek Orthodox bishops. To many, it was a hopeful sign for Baptists. Between 1927 and 1947 their numbers had grown from fifty thousand to two hundred thousand.[37]

Perhaps more than in any other European country, Baptists in Hungary enjoyed the greatest increase. They trace their history from the testimony of six Budapest artisans who had sought work during the Kossuth Rebellion in 1845 in Hamburg, Germany, where they were converted and baptized under Oncken's ministry. They returned to Hungary in 1849 and carried with them their new-found faith. Because of their associations with German Baptists, it is understandable that the relationship was very close. It was the more particularly centered in Heinrich Meyer, a German subject, who settled with his wife in Budapest in 1873 as an agent of the British and Foreign Bible Society. In the space of ten years he baptized 629 men and women, opened several Sunday schools, and set the stage for the next decade, during which more than thirty-eight hundred persons were baptized. With the assistance of the German Baptist Union, with which the Hungarian churches were affiliated, translations of the Scriptures were published and distributed widely in several languages.

Unfortunately for the greater good of the work, Meyer exercised dictatorial leadership, making little provision for the development of local pastors among the churches. Nor did he recognize the growing national feeling among the Magyars, who in time broke away from the German-speaking Baptists to form the Magyar Baptist Union. Tension between the two groups developed to the point where the matter was set before the Executive Committee of the Baptist World Alliance for arbitration. The inquiry which was made in 1907 resulted in the formation the next year of the Hungarian Baptist Union, which included Baptists of all national groups in the country. This serious threat to unity having been settled, the new Union made rapid progress in setting up a publication department and a Sunday school committee to guide in the establishing of new schools. Already there were fifty churches with 12,555 members and 229 Sunday schools. Fifteen years later, the

[37] *Ibid.*, 1937, p. 158; 1939, pp. 194, 259; 1945, p. 165. See also a letter from John R. Socaciu, president of the Rumanian Baptist Union until 1945, for recent statistics, *The Watchman-Examiner*, Vol. 35, No. 2 (Jan. 9, 1947), p. 41.

number had increased to 16,832.[38] As treaty arrangements cost Hungary the loss of territory and as immigrants moved out to other countries, the number of members fluctuated in the years that followed. With the aid of the Southern Baptist Convention in America, a seminary was maintained at Budapest. Two homes for the aged and an orphanage also were supported.

In the thirties, the denominational life was affected seriously by the political, economic, and religious status of the nation. Revival of Roman Catholicism in Europe added to the difficulties; indeed, the Catholics began to adopt some of the methods which the Baptists used to win converts. In the urban centers, the Communists pointed to the depressed economic conditions as propaganda in support of their cause. In general, the unpeaceful atmosphere of the Continent produced a prevailing sense of uncertainty which discouraged progress. Yet, much was accomplished and the increase in converts continued. Hungarian Baptists undertook foreign mission work through the Foreign Mission Board of the Southern Baptist Convention. Home mission work was carried on by the Baptist Union as aid was given to eight district associations. With Southern Baptist aid, a girls' training school was opened in the late thirties at Budapest.[39] The effects of war were felt in Hungary, as throughout the rest of the Balkan states, so that progress has been hindered for a time.

Soon after the creation of Yugoslavia as an independent state following the Versailles Conference, Southern Baptists undertook an extension of their missionary enterprise into that field. By 1930 there were 1,148 Baptists in contrast to six hundred in 1922. German Baptists, also desirous of working in Yugoslavia, and apparently unwilling to abide by the decision of the London Conference of Baptists in 1920 which directed the Southern Baptists to be responsible for work in Hungary, Rumania, and Yugoslavia, caused a schism in the Baptist Union in 1939. The basic issue was the resentfulness of Croatian Baptists at being placed under German leadership. It provided an example of the great need to adapt the missionary program to the national character of a country. The

[38] Rushbrooke, *The Baptist Movement in the Continent of Europe*, 99-112; *Proceedings of the First European Baptist Congress*, 1908, p. 115; B.W.C., *Proceedings*, 1923, p. 89.

[39] S.B.C., *Annual*, 1929, p. 230; 1931, p. 244; 1934, p. 223; 1935, p. 216; 1937, p. 226; 1941, p. 257.

political tensions have been too great in most European countries for this need to be overlooked. Among the Yugoslavs themselves there has been dissension also over an educated ministry, the majority opposing the new seminary at Belgrade on the grounds that educated leaders might influence government officials and cause trouble.

When, in 1941, Yugoslavia was partitioned among Germany, Bulgaria, Italy, and Hungary, the Baptist Union was shattered, for the small, scattered groups of believers were separated from one another. In Serbia, the Belgrade church continued during the years following, but many of its members left the city in search of food. In Croatia, where government recognition is given only to Roman Catholics and Mohammedans, Baptists sought union with their brethren of Germany, hoping thereby to gain protection from persecution. The few Baptist churches in the territory which passed to Hungary enjoyed freedom, since Baptists have been recognized in that country. Truly, the war has been a deterring factor in Baptist work in Yugoslavia.[40] The Baptists at present are not strong enough to withstand the pressures within that country.

In Spain, Baptists have been a small group ever since their beginnings there in the nineteenth century. The American Baptist Missionary Union undertook a mission in Madrid, headed by Dr. Knapp, around the middle of the century, but it failed to materialize into a permanent station. In 1879, Dr. E. Lund was sent out by the same body to work in the province of Catalonia, where he built a small and scattered, but continuing enterprise. In 1885 the Swedish Baptist Mission undertook missionary work in the province of Valencia, when C. A. Haglund, an earlier companion of Lund, began the establishing of little churches in the villages. By 1915 the number of Baptists in the province was 350.

In 1921 the Foreign Mission Board of the Southern Baptist Convention became responsible for the continuation of Baptist missions in Spain. The following year, a seminary was opened in Barcelona, but closed seven years later for want of students and funds. Thereupon the Board decided to limit its work to an evangelistic program in the country until an enthusiastic support of education could be aroused. In 1930 the Spanish Baptist Convention

[40] S.B.C., *Annual*, 1930, p. 155; 1939, p. 257; 1941, p. 259; 1942, pp. 185-6.

was organized in Barcelona. This was the first step in the development of a self-supporting constituency. During the Spanish Civil War (1936-1939), the Baptists were in sympathy with and fought for the Loyalist cause, supporting the republican government. During the hostilities, most of their church equipment was lost and one-fourth of the church members were killed or scattered. The degree of religious freedom varies in each of the three districts in which Baptist work is being carried on. In Madrid there is full freedom to preach; in Catalonia, only private worship at home is permitted; while in Valencia, pastoral visitation is possible, but meetings of any kind are forbidden. In this way, the Franco regime seeks to discourage dissenters.[41]

The story of the opening of Baptist missions in Italy is best told in connection with the work of the Foreign Mission Board of the Southern Baptist Convention, which has been one of three agencies bringing the Baptist witness to that country. The other two are the Baptist Missionary Society of London and the Mission to Spezia and the Levant. Thus, since 1863, the ancient seat of the Popes has been an object of Baptist evangelism. The results have never been written in large numbers. In 1905 there were only fourteen hundred Baptists united in a Baptist Union, with their own publication and theological school which is located in Rome. Since 1923, a unification of the work in Italy has been made more possible by the withdrawal of the London Baptist Missionary Society in favor of the Southern Baptist Convention.

Italian Baptists have faced several problems which have threatened their progress. One is Roman Catholic persecution; another is the constant emigration of their numbers to other countries; and still another is the lack of sufficient funds to erect adequate buildings and to provide expansion of the publication work. Yet, their successes have been sufficiently evident to cause Catholics to issue an edition of Bunyan's *Pilgrim's Progress* in 1930, and to imitate their methods of work. By the terms of the Concordat which was drawn up by Mussolini and signed by the Pope in 1929, religious discussion was permitted and non-Catholics were no longer required to receive religious instruction in the public schools. In 1933-1934

---

[41] Rushbrooke, *op. cit.*, pp. 137-40; B.W.C., *Proceedings,* 1923, p. 91; S.B.C., *Annual,* 1929, p. 258; 1938, p. 244; 1940, pp. 240-1, 1941, p. 260.

the Southern Baptists found it necessary to cut their appropriations to the Italian work. To add to the difficulties of the Italian
Baptists, the Government, under the influence of the Roman Catholic
Church, began to curtail their freedom to preach. This was true
especially after the invasion of Ethiopia which tended to create
a strong anti-Protestant feeling in the country. Nevertheless, the
conversions increased each year. The Baptist Union was given
greater responsibility in 1939 when the Southern Baptist Convention adopted a policy of merely assisting and guiding Italian Baptists, instead of supporting their churches. During the war years
they suffered the usual hardships of decreased income, hunger, loss
of members, and the ravages of fighting on their own soil. There
was a general pooling of resources; the stronger churches shared
with the weaker ones, so that the work might be continued.[42]

Toward a United Witness

Perhaps the most notable advance in Baptist work in Europe has
been the establishing of the European Baptist Federation in 1949 at
Zurich by official representatives of the 700,000 Baptists who are divided nearly evenly between Great Britain and the Continent. Many
factors had contributed to the creation of this Federation. One was a
common faith in the New Testament and a zeal to restore the purity
and simplicity of the primitive church. A second was the experience
which European Baptists had in two European Baptist Congresses
held in Berlin in 1908 and in Stockholm in 1913. There they discovered a common history and mutual problems and potential for the
future. This feeling was intensified within the larger fellowship of
the Baptist World Alliance, which had been organized in 1905. A
third factor was the need which they felt to promote a united fellowship, to co-ordinate their witness, and to stimulate and co-ordinate
their world mission outreach beyond Europe.

The Federation's first organization meeting was held in Hamburg, Germany, in 1951; the first general biennial session took place
in Copenhagen, Denmark, in the summer of 1952, with nearly five
hundred delegates present from more than a dozen countries and the
British Isles. Henry Cook of England was elected the first president.

[42] B.W.C., *Proceedings*, 1905, p. 6; 1923, p. 91; S.B.C., *Annual*, 1929, p. 232; 1930,
p. 228; 1933, p. 207; 1934, p. 219; 1936, p. 201; 1937, pp. 158, 226-8; 1938, p. 245;
1939, p. 261; 1942, pp. 181-2; 1943, p. 148.

It soon became apparent that the Federation offered a significant means for relating the Baptist Unions in the several countries of Europe. By 1961 there were 23 Unions of 21 countries in co-operation in the Federation. They represented a total membership of nearly 1,100,000 Baptists. Dr. Erik Ruden, an associate secretary of the Baptist World Alliance, was secretary of the Federation, thereby assuring a meaningful relationship between European Baptists and those in other lands.[43] A further unifying factor among European Baptists is the European Baptist Theological Seminary founded in 1950 by Southern Baptists at Ruschlikon, Zurich, in Switzerland. It has become a center of study not only for European Baptists but also for leaders and youth of other Baptist bodies within the Baptist World Alliance.

In summary, it may be said that while Baptists may be found in almost every country of Europe, they play an important numerical role only in England, Sweden, Germany, and possibly Russia. Their chief significance has been in religious rather than in social or political influence, a fact which is consistent with the traditional role of Baptists whose primary concern has been to gather converts into a regenerate church. The main impetus to Baptist growth on the Continent, which has been significant even in countries where their numbers are small, has come from three principal sources: the missionary zeal of German Baptists under Oncken's leadership; the extension of missionary support from British and American Baptists; and the earnest desire on the part of converts to share their new-found faith after Baptist churches have been organized in their respective countries.

In the relations between European Baptists and those of Great Britain and America, the principle of acknowledging the autonomy of national organizations has been observed by entrusting to the responsible Baptist Unions existing in most countries the handling and disbursing of funds given as financial assistance. In this way, any semblance of outside control has been avoided, and those who know best the needs in their own lands have been able to direct freely the use of much needed monies coming from abroad. Caution has been used also with respect to the oversight of the work

[43] *The Watchman-Examiner*, Vol. 38, No. 6 (Feb. 9, 1950), 145-47; *The Commission* (organ of Foreign Mission Board of the Southern Baptist Convention), Vol. 15, No. 9 (Oct., 1952), 265; *The Baptist World*, Vol. 8, No. 9 (Nov., 1961), 9.

conducted in the various countries of Europe. Southern Baptists have followed the policy of placing missionaries from America in strategic locations to develop an indigenous leadership. Baptists of the north have only one representative on the continent, a liaison officer between national Baptist leaders in Europe and the American Baptist Foreign Mission Society. This post was occupied by Dr. Walter O. Lewis until 1944, by Dr. Edwin A. Bell to 1960, and since then by Dr. Gordon R. Lahrson. An important area of cooperation between European and non-European Baptists has been developed through the years by the training of young people in Baptist schools in England and the United States in preparation for leadership in their own countries.

Outside of the United States, the Baptist witness has never been numerically strong when compared with that of other communions. Its effectiveness has been none the less significant. Wherever Baptists are to be found there has been kept alive a testimony to the validity of a regenerate church membership and a free church which refuses to be coerced by civil or religious institutions. European Baptists have shared with British and American Baptists in maintaining the worth and freedom of the individual before God in a free and democratic society. By their evangelistic zeal, this witness has been kept bright, often at the very peril of their lives. While it has not been primarily in the social sphere that these peoples have made their greatest contribution, the impact of their religious teaching has made itself felt indirectly upon the social and political ideals of many nations. Within that teaching has ever been the power to revitalize Christianity. When Europe all but destroyed Baptist principles in the sixteenth and seventeenth centuries, they found congenial soil in free America. Now that witness is being restored to the continent where it was first enunciated.

PART THREE: AMERICAN BAPTISTS

CHAPTER SEVEN

BEGINNINGS IN A NEW LAND

THE heritage and background of American Baptists is chiefly British. While it is true that in America the earliest advocates of strictly Baptist views stemmed from the little band that surrounded Roger Williams—whose expulsion from the Massachusetts Bay Colony because of his insistence upon the separation of church and state issued in the establishment of the Providence Plantation—the majority of early Baptists in the New World came from the British Isles, being English, Welsh, Scotch, and Irish. The origin of Middle Colony Baptists was certainly English, although their arrival was later than the Baptist beginnings in New England. One other source of Baptists was German—a small group of Dunkards, as they were called from their practice of immersing, settled in Pennsylvania.[1]

In the seventeenth century, the more courageous exponents of the Baptist witness set sail for America to escape the restrictions which had been placed upon their religious practice and faith in the Old World.[2]

Baptists in New England

Those Baptists who came to the Colonies were neither numerous nor unduly prominent. Undoubtedly, when making the long sea journey, they joined with Congregationalists and Anglicans. The earliest arrivals found their way to New England communities, possibly because they thought that the Puritans who had shared persecution with them in England would receive them gladly. There is little evidence of Baptist growth in the South during this early period. No doubt, the dominance there of the Anglican Church provided

---

[1] Much of the material in this chapter is drawn from the author's previous study, *A Social History of the Philadelphia Baptist Association, 1707-1940* (Philadelphia, 1944), chap. 1.

[2] For a somewhat similar view, see Thomas C. Hall, *The Religious Background of American Culture* (Boston, 1930), chap. 14.

no more congenial atmosphere than did the dominance of the Congregational Church in New England. Early Baptists in the Massachusetts Colony met with much opposition, especially because they refused to countenance the state church's control over them.

Roger Williams, for example, who came to Boston in 1631 to escape the persecution of Archbishop Laud, and who became teacher of the church at Salem, Massachusetts, was banished from the colony because of his views on the separation of church and state. In 1636 he founded Rhode Island Colony, with its famous guarantee of religious liberty. This guarantee was written into the royal charter obtained from Charles II in 1663. In 1639 some Baptists, newly arrived in Rhode Island and seeking refuge from religious oppression, influenced Williams to accept briefly their view of the church. He became convinced that their insistence upon adult conversion and a rejection of infant baptism provided the pattern for freeing the true church from its Jewish antecedents. He was rebaptized in March, 1639, by Ezekiel Holliman, who had been a member of his church at Salem, and participated in establishing the First Baptist Church of Providence. A few months later, however, he withdrew from the group, taking the position of a Seeker. Like the Seekers of England, Williams despaired of finding the true church on earth through the usual visible structures. Thomas Olney succeeded him as pastor of the little congregation. Williams' significance to Baptists is to be found in his courageous devotion to religious liberty and the creation of a climate in which their witness could be heard.[3]

In 1652 the Providence church split into two factions: an Arminian Six Principle group led by Wickendon, Brown, and Dexter; and a Calvinistic group, led by Olney, which rejected the doctrine of the laying on of hands as a requirement after baptism. Olney's group disbanded about 1720, while the main body continued as the First Baptist Church of Providence. In 1771 President Manning of Rhode Island College persuaded the majority of the congregation to adopt a Calvinistic Confession, which prompted the Arminians to secede. Although the First Baptist Church of Providence is regarded as the oldest Baptist Church in America, the claim has been contested by

[3] Perry G. E. Miller, *Roger Williams: His Contribution to the American Tradition* (Indianapolis, 1953), 156; cit. in H. Shelton Smith, Robert T. Handy, and Lefferts A. Loetscher, *American Christianity, 1607-1820* (New York, 1960), 145.

the church which was organized at Newport by one Dr. John Clarke.[4]

Clarke was another immigrant from England who was previously a Baptist or became one soon after his arrival. He is reported to have organized a church in Newport, Rhode Island, in 1638. The records, however, that clearly indicate its being a Baptist church only go back to about 1648.[5] Thus, it appears that the earliest Baptist churches in America were organized in Rhode Island, the First Baptist Church of Providence, established by Roger Williams, and the First Baptist Church of Newport, founded by Dr. John Clarke. The founders of both these churches were men of unusual distinction, Williams being the father of religious liberty in America and Dr. Clarke being an able partner by whose excellent service Rhode Island Colony obtained its charter in 1663.[6]

It seems that several persons were baptized by these men. Undoubtedly others of Baptist convictions came from various churches in England. The groups in New Hampshire, Massachusetts, Connecticut, and Rhode Island were small. With the exception of the colony last named, New England did not provide a congenial home for Baptists. On the contrary, Baptists were the victims of persecution. In the first place, they insisted upon believer's baptism and hence refused to baptize their infants, thus violating the requirements of the state church, which was paedobaptist and congregational in polity. In the second place, the Baptists insisted upon their right to worship in their own way and in their own churches; consequently, they resented the efforts of the state to curtail these rights. Finally, they insisted upon the separation of church and state, a principle which had its best illustration in the work of Roger Williams. *all of persecution*

Between 1642 and 1649 particularly, their refusal to baptize their infants caused them to be haled before the Salem Court. Thomas Painter of Hingham was whipped in 1644. Henry Dunster, first president of Harvard College, was compelled to resign his office in 1654, after twelve years of service, because he had accepted Baptist views and refused to remain silent on the subject of baptism. With

---

[4] S. Adlam, *Historical Facts versus Historical Fictions; The First Baptist Church in America: not founded by Roger Williams* (Memphis, Tenn., 1890); see also Isaac Backus, *A History of New England with Particular Reference . . . to the Baptists* (second edition with notes by David Weston), pp. 125-6.

[5] See note in Backus, *op. cit.*, I, 125; cf. Vedder, *Short History of Baptists*, p. 295.

[6] The petition of the town of Newport, R. I., carried by Clarke to Parliament in 1651, is in the possession of the Backus Historical Society, Newton Centre, Mass.

inordinate haste, the Overseers of the College accepted his resignation, which had been forced upon him by public pressure, while professing not to know the real reason for its presentation. When Dunster, in desperation for the care of his family during the winter months, appealed to the Overseers for permission to remain in the house which he himself had built as the president's home—at least for six months while he was settling his affairs—they refused his request. But this persecution was not all that he was to suffer; for in 1657 he faced two court trials for failing to present for baptism a daughter born on December 29, 1656. Shortly thereafter he removed to Scituate, where he died on February 27, 1659, only five years after his removal from Harvard College.[7] Dr. John Clarke, the founder of the Baptist church at Newport, was fined; and Obadiah Holmes, the man who was to be his successor, was imprisoned and whipped in Boston for having preached against infant baptism to some Baptists at Lynn, Massachusetts, in 1651.

Although persecuted, the Baptists increased in number. For example, John Myles, the founder of the first Baptist church in Wales, arrived in 1663 with a number of his members, hoping in this way to escape the effects of the Act of Uniformity at home. They organized a Baptist church at Rehoboth in that same year; four years later, it was moved to Swansea. In 1665 a church was founded in Boston in the home of Thomas Gould, who ten years before had refused to present his child for baptism, an incident which gave the authorities excuse for persecuting him as pastor of the new congregation.[8] Notwithstanding the opposition, a meeting-house was erected in 1678.

At Kittery on the Piscataqua River in the province of Maine, there developed another nucleus of Baptists amidst a similar type of persecution. The most gifted among them was William Screven, a

[7] See Chaplin, Jeremiah, *Life of Henry Dunster: First President of Harvard College* (Boston, 1872), chaps. 9-15.

[8] Two documents for the arrest of Baptists, presumably for failure to attend services of the state church, are in possession of the Backus Historical Society. One, an order for the commitment to jail of William Turner and John Farnum, who were sentenced by the General Court in Boston on April 29, 1668, is dated July 30, 1668. The other, dated October 20, 1668, is an order demanding the appearance of Thomas Gould, Edward Drinker, John George, William Turner, and Thomas Skinner before the General Court in Boston "to give an answer for your schismatic practise in sending yourselves from the communion of the Church of Christ here (as informed), notwithstanding the Court of Assistants in September last prohibiting you from persisting in such scandalous and sinful conduct . . ."

prosperous merchant of prominence. According to the provincial records,[9] he bought land at Kittery in November, 1673, having moved from Massachusetts where he first had appeared upon his arrival from England five years before. He married, on July 23, 1674, Bridget Cutts, daughter of a prominent Kittery planter who had died the previous month. His mother-in-law, Mary Hole Cutts, later married Captain Francis Champernowne, nephew of the first wife of Sir Ferdinando Gorges. Not only was he a man of some prominence, but one determined to safeguard his liberties. When Massachusetts Bay Colony purchased Maine, Screven joined, about 1679, with other residents of Kittery in forwarding to the king a petition requesting the Crown to establish direct rule over Maine, inasmuch as Massachusetts was suppressing religious liberty. In 1680 he signed the Shapleigh petition which embodied a similar plea.

It appears that he and his wife and Humphrey Churchwood, who later married Mary Cutts, his wife's sister, were baptized in the Baptist church at Boston on July 21, 1681. In all likelihood, Screven's action influenced several of his neighbors, for Backus, the eighteenth-century New England Baptist historian, refers to a small group of people in Kittery who had been baptized during the year 1681.[10] Anxious to organize a church with an ordained minister in charge, they sent their most gifted member, William Screven, to Boston, with a request that the Baptist church there license him. This was done on January 11, 1682. When the magistrate and the Congregational

[9] The following account is based on a revealing study of records made recently. See Robert E. Moody, editor, *Province and Court Records of Maine*, Vol. III (*Province of Maine Records, 1680-1692*), Portland, 1947, pp. xxxiv-xxxix. For records pertaining to William Screven, see index. The summary herein recorded may serve to correct what appears to be an erroneous view generally accepted that Screven was driven out of Maine by persecution in 1683, in which year he and his congregation are supposed to have migrated to South Carolina where they established the first Baptist church in that colony on the site of the present city of Charleston. This view is set forth in so recent a study as George W. Paschal, *History of North Carolina Baptists: 1663-1805* (Raleigh, 1930), p. 45, in which he traces the early Baptist beginnings in the Carolinas before their division into North and South Carolina. A more recently published study by Leah Townsend, *South Carolina Baptists: 1670-1805* (Florence, S. C., 1935), p. 5, however, corrects the error on the basis of an examination of A. S. Salley, Jr., *Warrants for Land in South Carolina, 1692-1711* (Columbia, Historical Commission, 1915), p. 137, and Henry S. Burrage, "Some added facts concerning Rev. William Screven," in collections and *Proceedings of the Maine Historical Society*, 1894, pp. 275-84, which bears out the fact that Screven was still in Kittery in January, 1696.

[10] Isaac Backus, *A History of New England with Particular Reference to the Denomination of Christians Called Baptists.* (Newton, Mass., 1871), I, p. 400. This history was first written in three volumes between 1777 and 1796.

minister at Kittery heard of this event, they began to spread slanders concerning the Baptists in Boston, and the magistrate, Captain Francis Hooke, began to summon Baptists before him, threatening them with fines and other penalties for attending Baptist meetings.

When Screven returned to Kittery, he was summoned, on March 13, before the justices and accused of offensive speeches "tending to blasphemy," presumably on the subject of baptism. Screven charged Hooke with prejudice, and when asked to give bond of one hundred pounds for his appearance at the next Court of Pleas, he refused. For this he was sent to jail. His case was heard by the Council, acting as a court, at York on the twelfth of April. The Council fined him ten pounds, forbade him to hold services in his home or elsewhere in Kittery, and ordered him to attend public worship according to the law. He paid four pounds of the fine, the rest being carried on the books. On June 28, he was brought before the Assembly "for non-observance of the decree of 12 April and, being unwilling to obey it, agreed to leave the province."[11]

But he did not leave; instead, on September 13 he wrote to the Boston church asking Elder Hull to come to Kittery to organize the Baptists there into a church. Accordingly, on September 25, 1682, the covenant was signed by ten men and several women. The meetings were carried on for less than a year, "probably at Screven's house, which was located on a point of land just west of the Cutt's mansion near Spruce Creek."[12] For this, he was haled before the Court of Sessions at Wells on October 9, 1683, which declared the sentence of April 12, 1682 "in full-force during the Court's pleasure." Although he was ordered to appear before the General Assembly in June, the records of that session contain no mention of the case.

Screven was still in Maine on September 29, 1685, when he is mentioned in the records as the guardian of Joseph Atwell. On July 22, 1685, he purchased twenty acres of land at Spruce Creek. On July 17, 1688, he witnessed a will. From 1691 to 1695 he appears repeatedly in the records; during this period he was deputy to the Massachusetts General Court, moderator of Kittery, and special commissioner. In November, 1693, he signed the oath of allegiance to

[11] Moody, ed., *Province and Court Records of Maine*, III; xxxv; cf. Backus, *op. cit.*, I, 400-4. The original court sentence and executive order of August 17, 1682, are in the Backus Historical Collection.

[12] Moody, *op. cit.*, xxxv-xxxvi; cf. Backus, *op. cit.*, I, 404-5.

King William and Queen Mary. The last official record of his appearance at Kittery was on June 28, 1695, when he witnessed a mortgage for Robert Cutts.[13]

Screven's first appearance in the records of South Carolina was on December 7, 1696, when he obtained a warrant for one thousand acres where Georgetown now stands. Instead, on January 23, 1698, he took 804 acres at the headwaters of the Cooper River, forty or more miles from Charleston. "Here he was surrounded by several of his Kittery relatives, the Wethericks, Elliotts, and Axalls.[14] From letters written from Dorchester, South Carolina, to Dorchester, Massachusetts, on February 21, 1698/99, and in September, 1702, by a nonconformist clergyman, the Reverend Joseph Lord, who had led his congregation from Massachusetts to South Carolina, we learn of Screven's presence and preaching in South Carolina. In 1708 he declined a call to the Baptist church in Boston. Two years later, he purchased lands at "Winyah" or "Winyan," later called Georgetown, where he died on October 10, 1713 in his eighty-fourth year.[15]

From this rather lengthy account, it would seem unlikely that persecution drove Screven from Kittery. The evidence indicates, to the contrary, that he remained and held an honorable position in public office. Since he lived in a port town and may have had shipping of his own, it is not improbable that he visited South Carolina, even taking some settlers there between 1684, the date claimed for the founding of the first Baptist church of Charleston, and December, 1696, when it is certain that he was located there.[16] But that he

---

[13] Moody, *op. cit.*, xxxvi; cited from *York Deeds*, IV, 68, 112, 132 and *Maine Wills* (1887), 107. A list of references to Screven in Maine records is in the *South Carolina Historical and Genealogical Magazine*, IX (1908), 230-1. Dating is according to the Old Calendar, in use prior to 1752.

[14] *Ibid.*, xxxvi.

[15] *Ibid.*, xxxvi-xxxviii; cited from Massachusetts Historical Society Collections, XLV, 305; Prince MSS, Massachusetts Historical Society; letter to Elias Callender, Charleston, August 6, 1708, in Library of the Andover-Newton Theological School; *South Carolina Historical and Genealogical Magazine*, IX (1908), 87.

[16] An early Charleston Association history relates that Baptists from Maine settled at Somerton on the Cooper River, a small distance from the present site of Charleston, where "they were formed into a Church under the care of Reverend William Screven." The narrative goes on to say that "Mr. Screven with his Church removed to Charleston about the year 1693." There he was pastor for many years and then went to Georgetown, where he died in 1713. See Wood Furman, *A History of the Charleston Association of Baptist Churches in the State of South Carolina* (Charleston, 1811), 5-6. It is not unlikely that Screven may have had some supervision over the small congregation prior to his settling in South Carolina permanently, especially if business trips took him south occasionally.

settled permanently in South Carolina before 1695 seems unlikely from the evidence. It is known definitely that he did not sell his lands in Kittery until 1704/05, and then through his son, Robert, who had his power of attorney.[17] There is no doubt that he met persecution courageously, but being a man of money and having influential friends, he seems to have fared better than some of his fellow Baptists. It is true that the eventual exodus of Baptists from Maine was responsible for the retarded development of Baptist work in that colony.

The persecution likely would have been more effective throughout New England but for the fact that the Baptists were organized in autonomous groups. As such, they could not be brought under control so easily as those under a central authority. Another factor in their favor was the American atmosphere of freedom, which was too strong to tolerate Puritan persecution indefinitely. Moreover, the pressure from English Congregationalists and other dissenters in England, who were shocked that Massachusetts Congregationalists should persecute minority sects, acted as another deterrent. Thus the courageous stand of the Baptists was fortified and maintained until the defeat of the Puritan Theocracy in 1691, when a new charter required the Puritan leaders to bring Massachusetts' law into conformity with the English Act of Toleration of 1689.

Nevertheless, the growth of Baptist churches in New England in this period was slow. In 1700 there were only ten small churches with not more than three hundred members.[18] The Puritan regime with its state church was hostile toward Baptists and Quakers in particular, because their emphasis upon individual liberty threatened the theocratic ideal of the Boston clergy. Such an attitude did not encourage immigrants of these sects to come to New England. For while Baptists, like other dissenters except Catholics, were freed from persecution, they were not exempt from taxation to support a state church.

Baptists in the Middle Colonies

It is not surprising, therefore, that the center of Baptist growth should have been in the Middle Colonies. In this section, midway

---

[17] Moody, *Province and Court Records of Maine,* III, xxxviii; cited from *York Deeds,* VII, 14-5, 24-5.

[18] Vedder, *A Short History of Baptists,* 302.

between New England and the South, there was a commingling of religious and cultural groups which made for a greater toleration than would have been possible otherwise. In this region the indications of intolerance toward Baptists were few, and were associated almost entirely with New Amsterdam when it was under Peter Stuyvesant's administration. Only for a short time were Baptists persecuted by the governor, and when complaints of such treatment reached the Dutch West India Company's headquarters in Holland, orders were issued to put an end to such molestation.

Since Pennsylvania and New Jersey offered religious liberty, the Philadelphia area provided the center for the most important and influential group of Baptist churches in the colonies by the early eighteenth century. It appears from such facts as are available that each of these churches was built around a core of a few men and women who had been Baptists before emigrating to the New World. There were others who had held Baptist beliefs for a long time, but who had not been able to identify themselves with Baptists for lack of such a church in their community. Most of these people were English. In Philadelphia and its immediate vicinity there were also Welsh Baptists and a few Irish, but the heritage and associations of American Baptists were primarily English.[19] A survey of the beginnings of these early churches in the Philadelphia area corroborates this view. It seems likely that too much attention has been focused upon Roger Williams and the Providence Plantation as the chief Baptist center in the colonies.

There were several reasons why Philadelphia and vicinity provided a favorable environment for the growth of Baptists in the American Colonies. The Quaker policy of religious toleration in Pennsylvania, coupled with a similar policy guaranteed by the proprietors of the Jerseys, contributed to the well-being of Baptists. Moreover, the absence of a state church in the Middle Colonies provided freedom from the kind of hindrances which they faced in the New England and Southern Colonies.

In 1684 Thomas Dungan, a native of Ireland, who had removed in his later years to Rhode Island, came with a group from the Baptist church of Newport in that colony to Cold Spring, Pennsylvania.

---

[19] This view is borne out in a study by Morgan Edwards, *Materials towards a History of the American Baptists* (Philadelphia, 1770 and 1792), Vols. I and II.

He had come to America to escape the hostility to Baptists under the reign of Charles II, only to find the same spirit of persecution in New England.[20] At this spring, about three miles north of Bristol in Bucks County, Dungan and his followers established a church which survived until about 1702. It is thought by some that the father of the celebrated physician, Dr. Benjamin Rush, was a member, for his remains lie in the burial ground of the church.[21] Thus the church that stemmed from Rhode Island died. It remained for a church made up of British immigrants to Philadelphia to continue in existence as the Old Pennepack Church. Now called the Lower Dublin Baptist Church, it is located near Pennepack Creek in Dublin township of Philadelphia County.

The Pennepack Church was founded in 1688 by Pastor Elias Keach, son of the well-known London Baptist minister, and twelve members, five of whom were Baptists from Radnorshire in Wales; another was a member of a Baptist congregation in Kilkenny, Ireland; and the rest were from England.[22] Elias Keach had come to Philadelphia from London in 1688, a young man of twenty who thought it sportive to garb himself as a clergyman. Because of the prestige of his father, the Reverend Benjamin Keach of London, he secured invitations to preach. At his first service, he suffered pangs of conscience and thereupon confessed his imposture. Through the kindly offices of the Reverend Thomas Dungan at Cold Springs, he was baptized. From then on he preached at Pennepack with unusual effect. Indeed he extended his parish to include a large circuit of congregations in Trenton, Chester, and other small towns in New Jersey and Pennsylvania. When the Pennepack Church was organized, these Baptists united with its membership. The entire membership was to gather together twice a year, in the spring and in the fall. But the distances were too great, and as the membership increased, daughter churches in New Jersey were organized at Middletown in 1688. Piscataway in 1689, and Cohansey in 1690; and at Philadelphia in 1698. The last named congregation was to be known as the First Baptist Church of that city.

[20] David Spencer, *The Early Baptists of Philadelphia* (Philadelphia, 1877), 19.
[21] A. D. Gillette, ed., *Minutes of the Philadelphia Baptist Association: 1707-1807* (Philadelphia, 1851), Preface, 3.
[22] Robert T. Tumbelston, *A History of "Old Pennepack,"* incorporated in the 250th Anniversary Program Booklet of the church (1938). The following narrative is based on this history and on David Spencer, *op. cit.,* 22-6.

The Pennepack Church was typical of the early colonial Baptist congregations. Meetings were held in the homes of its members, who numbered only forty-six by 1700. By 1707, however, a meeting-house was erected near the burial ground. The ground was the gift of Samuel Jones, who was later a pastor of the church. This modest building was only twenty-five feet square. In 1774 it was enlarged, and by 1805 was replaced by a colonial structure which still stands a few hundred yards from the present Lower Dublin Baptist Church at Bustleton, Philadelphia.

Although the First Church of Philadelphia had been organized in 1698, its members were connected with the Pennepack Church until 1746, when the former congregation found it necessary to become incorporated in order to make certain legacies operative.[23] The congregation had no building in its early years. Its members worshiped alternately with the Presbyterians in the Barbadoes store-house, situated at the northwest corner of Second and Chestnut Streets, until September, 1698, when, upon the insistence of the latter group, they were compelled to find other quarters. Accordingly, they moved to Anthony Morris' Brewhouse near the drawbridge, which was on the east side of Water Street near Dock Street. A little later they accepted the invitation of an almost extinct group of Quaker Baptists (former Quakers who retained their traditional dress and manners) to use their building, a frame structure located in La Grange Place, on Second Street above Market. This they continued to use until 1856, when they built a large edifice at Broad and Arch Streets where the United Gas Improvement Company's building now stands.

These two churches, Old Pennepack and the First Baptist of Philadelphia, were typical of the small congregations that were to form the Philadelphia Baptist Association in 1707. Life was comparatively simple in those early days; yet there were problems of faith and discipline which harassed these small groups, and it became clear to pastors and laymen alike that some kind of general meeting was necessary to deal with the questions which arose from time to time. As early as 1688 such a joint meeting of several churches occurred at Lower Dublin for the purpose of administering baptism, of ordaining ministers, and of providing inspirational preaching. The next

[23] J. C. Walker, "Historical Sketch of the Philadelphia Baptist Association" in the *Association Minutes* for 1907, p. 81. The account that follows is based on Walker, and on David Spencer, *Early Baptists of Philadelphia*, pp. 32-8.

occasion for a similar gathering was in March, 1689, at Philadelphia; the third at Burlington, New Jersey, the following summer. Thereafter, periodic meetings were held in Cohansey, Welsh Tract, and Middletown. This came to be known as a yearly meeting by the people of these towns, since it came to them annually, but it was called a quarterly meeting by the ministers who attended each one held during the year. In time, the nature of these gatherings became fixed in accordance with a decision made at the session held on July 27, 1707, when "the general meeting which had been held at Philadelphia from 1689, was transformed into 'an association of messengers authorized by their respective churches to meditate and execute designs of public good.' "[24]

In this manner, then, five small Baptist churches organized the Philadelphia Baptist Association. These churches were cosmopolitan in their origin. The Lower Dublin Church was composed of settlers from the British Isles. The Piscataway Church organized in 1689 in Middlesex County, New Jersey, was composed of a small company of refugees from persecution in Piscataway, New Hampshire. The Middletown Church in Monmouth County, New Jersey, was comprised mainly of the persecuted Baptists from New York and other colonies. The Welsh Tract Church in New Castle County, Pennsylvania, was organized in 1701 by a group of Welsh who would not fellowship with the Pennepack Church because that congregation did not require the laying on of hands upon newly baptized converts. In this decision, language barriers may have been an additional consideration.

The Philadelphia Association's plan of organization was not of American origin; it had its prototype in England and Wales, and like its sister organizations in Britain, was loose in structure and without power or authority to bind the churches composing it. The Association was regarded as both an advisory council in matters of local concern and an expression of the larger church through which the mind of Christ might become known.[25] It was therefore looked to for decision and guidance in matters both trivial and important.

A reading of the minutes from year to year indicates that the

[24] William W. Keen, *The Bi-Centennial Celebration of the Founding of First Baptist Church of the City of Philadelphia*, 461.
[25] Samuel Jones, *A Treatise of Church Discipline and a Directory* (Philadelphia, 1798), 37-8.

various churches relied upon the Association for advice and even for the settlement of disputes, At times, it acted in the capacity of a council for ordination.[26] To its discretion was left the disciplining of ministers. The Association was particularly careful to examine the credentials of itinerant preachers and to warn the churches of such as were impostors. In addition to queries concerning communion, baptism, church membership, ordination, the place of women in the church, and the propriety of using musical instruments in the service, there were presented for consideration questions pertaining to the relations of a member to Free Masonry, to other Protestant groups, to gambling, and to slavery. Usually, the matter was the subject for counsel and advice, but the decision was left to the discretion of the local church. In a very real sense this organization played an important part in helping Baptists to adjust themselves to changing conditions and new surroundings. "The Association was a guiding force in a fluid polity which tended to make relatively easy the necessary adjustment to changing circumstances."[27]

It should not be concluded, however, that the Philadelphia group had no defined powers. To the contrary, a statement of these powers was prepared by the Reverend Benjamin Griffith, pastor of the Montgomery Baptist Church of Bucks County, Pennsylvania, and signed by all of the delegates present at the annual meeting on September 19, 1749. It affirmed that the Association was not a "superior judicature" over the churches concerned, and that each church was autonomous. Nevertheless, the author made it quite clear that the Association had considerable power over its member churches in cases of defection from generally accepted doctrine or practice. It was allowed that such power might manifest itself in the exclusion of such a church from the fellowship of the Association.

To provide a basis for doctrinal agreement, the Association, in 1742 authorized publication of the London Confession of Particular Baptists of 1689 as its statement of faith. The Association's identification thereby with Calvinistic theology was destined to give direction to American Baptists theologically. This Confession was coupled with a treatise of church discipline prepared by two pastors, Benjamin

[26] J. G. Walker's "Historical Sketch" in the *Philadelphia Association Minutes for 1907*, 85.

[27] John P. Gates, "The Association as It Affected Baptist Polity in Colonial America," *The Chronicle*, Vol. VI, No. 1 (January, 1943), 31.

Griffith and Jenkin Jones. In 1749 the Association approved for publication an essay prepared by Griffith which defined "the power and duty of an Association of churches."[28]

As the Philadelphia Association, which was the first organization of American Baptists, grew in prestige and membership, this definition of relationship was necessary. However, its leadership did not go unchallenged. Some churches attacked the principle of associational organization unreservedly and withheld financial support from the Association. Possibly the objections were not based solely on matters of church polity, although some Philadelphia leaders like Morgan Edwards and Samuel Jones were anxious for a centralized organization of American Baptists headed up in the Philadelphia Association. It is quite likely that the General Baptists, who were predominant in New England, New York, and New Jersey, were disturbed by the fact that the Association in 1742 had adopted a Calvinistic doctrinal statement.[29]

During the first half century of its existence, the Association was comprised of congregations which were small, struggling, and separated by great distances. In 1757 it had a membership of twenty-five churches which were situated in the colonies of Pennsylvania, New Jersey, Connecticut, New York, Virginia, and Maryland. The statistics on membership were not recorded until 1762, when there were twenty-nine congregations with 4,018 members. The significance of the Association cannot be overemphasized, for without violating Baptist church autonomy it provided a source of guidance and unity at a critical period of organization in the denomination. In addition, it afforded a pattern of democratic polity which was destined to be well received in the liberty-loving colonies.

Baptists in the Southern Colonies

Prior to the Great Awakening, which began about 1726, the larger number of Baptists were in the North, there being only scattered congregations in Virginia and the Carolinas and possibly a

---

[28] Gillette, ed., *Minutes of the Philadelphia Baptist Association: 1707-1807*, 46, 60-3.

[29] *Ibid.*, 60-3. See also a letter of September 23, 1787, from the Southampton (Pa.) Baptist Church to the Philadelphia Baptist Association warning that ". . . should an Association forget her Bounds and assume a power to do the Business peculiar to the Churches of Christ, the Connection would be no longer desireable . . ." The McKesson Collection of Letters, 1755-1811, in the library of the American Baptist Historical Society, Chester, Pa.

sprinkling in Georgia after 1733. Some of these Baptists had come from England to escape persecution or to better their economic lot in the New World. Others had drifted south from New England for much the same reasons. The greater number of them settled down in rural communities, occupying for the most part a humble station in colonial life.

Virginia, from the first, had been inhospitable to dissenters. The Church of England had been established there as early as 1619, and severe penalties were provided for nonconformity. Indeed, passage of the Act of Toleration by Parliament in 1689 made little difference in the religious situation in that colony. It prompted the removal of only a few of the more severe restrictions against nonconformists. For another hundred years dissenters were harassed by clergy and magistrates alike. Inasmuch as the Act of Toleration legally protected their right to worship without interference, the charge usually brought against them by their enemies was that of disturbing the public peace.[30]

Virginia Baptists originated from three sources. The earliest to arrive, so it appears, were a number of General or Arminian Baptists who had come from England. They settled in Isle of Wight County, in the southeastern part of the colony, as early as 1700. Having brought no preacher with them, it was but natural that some years later they should appeal to their brethren in London to meet their need. In response, the London Baptists ordained Thomas White and Robert Nordin and sent them to America. Nordin alone survived the voyage. In 1714, soon after his arrival, he organized the Isle of Wight Baptists into a church at Burleigh, just across the James River from Jamestown. This is the present Mill Swamp Church in the Blackwater Association. Later, he established a church in Prince George County and held meetings there and in other places until his death on December 1, 1725. It appears that these early congregations became extinct soon after 1756.[31] This was due to divisions within the membership and to removals of many

[30] Lewis P. Little, *Imprisoned Preachers and Religious Liberty in Virginia* (Lynchburg, Va., 1938), 1-13.

[31] Material in the aforegoing paragraph is based on George W. Paschal, *History of North Carolina Baptists*, Vol. I (1663-1805), 125; cf. Richard Knight, *History of the General and Six-principle Baptists in England and America* (1827), 316 ff., and Robert B. Semple, *A History of the Rise and Progress of the Baptists in Virginia* (rev. edition), chap. 32.

farmers to North Carolina to escape the competition with slave labor which had become popular in Virginia after 1700.[32]

A second contingent was from Maryland; it moved into the northern part of Virginia between the years 1743 and 1756, three churches being founded in the counties of Berkeley and Loudoun and their vicinities. While some of these Baptists were Arminians, the Calvinists or Regular Baptists predominated in this area in later years, owing in all probability to their contacts with the Philadelphia Association.[33]

The third group was composed of New Englanders who settled in the back country about 1760. These were the product of the Great Awakening; they were known as New Light or Separate Baptists, converts of the Whitefield-Edwards revival. Their emotionalism and hostility to organization or authority other than that of the Holy Spirit, whose leading alone they felt obliged to obey, had made them unpopular with the authorities in New England who had insisted upon their conformity to the licensing features of the laws which tolerated dissenter sects. Their lot was not improved in Virginia, for as it turned out the Anglican Church persecuted them as severely as had the Congregationalists in New England.

The province of Carolina was constituted a proprietary colony by King Charles II in 1663, when he granted a charter to eight of his courtiers as Lords Proprietors. From the beginning, religious freedom was guaranteed to dissenters by Article Eighteen of the charter. This provision was made even more explicit in the second or revised charter of 1665. It is not surprising, then, that the colony attracted Quakers, Moravians, Lutherans, Methodists, and Baptists.

There is a strong tradition that the earliest Baptist settlers in the province of the Carolinas came to the vicinity of Charleston, South Carolina, about 1682-1683 from the Piscataqua region of Maine and from England.[34] A little company of Baptists from

---

[32] See Thomas J. Wertenbaker, *The Planters of Colonial Virginia* (Princeton, 1922) for complaints by Virginia authorities on loss of their people to North Carolina; see also *Colonial Records* I, 631, 646, 690, 692; cited in Paschal, *op. cit.*, 70.

[33] David Benedict, *A General History of the Baptist Denomination in America*, 643-6.

[34] Morgan Edwards, Manuscript History of the Baptists in South Carolina (ca. 1770-1772) is the basic source for Benedict, *op. cit.*, 701-2 and for Wood Furman, *A History of the Charleston Association of Baptist Churches in the State of South Carolina* (Charleston, 1811), 5-6. A statement made by Edwards that in North Carolina "there have been some Baptists since the settlement in 1695" led Benedict to suppose that there had been no

Kittery, Maine, reportedly settled at Somerton on the Cooper River, a short distance from the present site of Charleston, where "they were formed into a Church under the care of Reverend William Screven." The report continues that "Mr. Screven with his Church removed to Charleston about the year 1693," as a large number of the congregation were being drawn to the port town for commercial reasons.[35] As we have seen, Screven's permanent residence in South Carolina prior to 1696 cannot be established, owing to the recent discovery of evidence of his continuous activity at Kittery, Maine, between 1683 and 1695. It seems most plausible, as we have noted previously, that Screven may have led a company of his brethren to Somerton as early as 1683 and visited them from time to time while on business trips, providing occasional oversight of their affairs until he established permanent residence in the colony after 1695.[36]

There were Baptists among two other groups of colonists who arrived from England late in the seventeenth century. In 1682-1683 "a number of pious and respectable dissenters from Somersetshire," led by Humphrey Blake, the brother of the renowned Admiral Blake, settled along the Ashley and Cooper Rivers. Among these settlers were Lady Blake and her mother, Lady Axtell, who were staunch Baptists, and Joseph Blake, a nephew of the admiral and a trustee of Lord Berkeley, one of the Lords Proprietors of the province, who was "thoroughly sympathetic with Baptist principles." About 1683 "a colony of north Britons . . . mostly Baptists" came to Carolina under the patronage of Lord Cardross, settling on Port Royal Island. Since Lord Cardross was unable to sustain his claim to the territory, he returned to England, but the populace remained; they removed, however, to an island near the mouth of the Edisto River for protection from the Indians and Spaniards.[37] The Baptists of this company soon associated themselves as a branch of

Baptists in that colony prior to 1695, an erroneous opinion perpetuated by later historians. Actually, Edwards was in error in determining the date of settlement of the colony, which began shortly after issuance of the charter in 1663.

[35] Furman, *op. cit.*, 5; cf. A. H. Newman, *A History of the Baptist Churches in the United States* (New York, 1894), 221-4.

[36] See above, footnote 9. Townsend takes the view that the date 1683 for the founding of the Charleston Church is based erroneously upon the untenable assumption that Screven came to South Carolina in 1682 or 1683. See *South Carolina Baptists, 1670-1805*, 8-9.

[37] Newman, *op. cit.*, 222-4.

Screven's church. Their assembly became known in time as the Euhaw Church. The Ashley River Church was organized in 1736.

In 1737 several Welsh Baptists, from the Welsh Tract on the Delaware River to the south of Philadelphia, settled on the banks of the Pedee River. In January of the year following, this group constituted itself as the Welsh Neck Church, which became eventually the mother of all the churches in that region. Unlike the Charleston Church, which was strongly Calvinistic, this congregation seems to have shared Arminian views in its early years.

While there were doubtless some Baptists among the earliest settlers in North Carolina and others who shared their views of liberty of conscience, there is no contemporary record of their presence prior to June 12, 1714, when the Reverend John Urmstone, since 1710 a missionary of the Church of England's Society for the Propagation of the Gospel in Foreign Parts, complained that two of his vestrymen in the Chowan Precinct were "professed Anabaptists."[38] Since many references are to be found concerning the presence of dissenters in the colony, such as Quakers, Presbyterians, and Congregationalists, "it is hardly possible then that there was any regularly organized congregation of Baptists in the Province or any Baptist preacher before Paul Palmer," who did not arrive in North Carolina until 1720.[39]

Palmer, who is regarded as the founder of the first Baptist church in the colony, was a native of Maryland. He was baptized at the Welsh Tract Baptist Church in Delaware, was ordained in Connecticut, for a time was in New Jersey, then came to Maryland. There he preached in the home of Henry Sator, a Baptist layman who had come from England in 1709, and baptized nine persons, thereby laying the foundation for the organization in 1742 of the Chestnut Ridge Church, the first Baptist church in Maryland. The date of his arrival in North Carolina is not known. By 1720, according to the records, he was settled already in Perquimans Precinct in North Carolina where he had married the widow of Thomas Peterson, who had died in 1714, one of the most prominent and wealthy men in the province. It was not until 1726, however, that his preaching began to attract attention. During the following year, he estab-

[38] Colonial Records, II, 131; cited in Paschal, *History of North Carolina Baptists, 1663-1805*, 130-1.
[39] Paschal, *op. cit.*, 127-30.

lished the first Baptist church in North Carolina in Chowan Precinct in the vicinity of the present town of Cisco. It was composed of thirty-two members. Its first local pastor was the youthful Joseph Parker, who might be called a disciple of Palmer. It was not the older man's nature to settle down to a pastorate; his work was that of an itinerant evangelist. The church became extinct, apparently after Parker moved to Meherrin about 1730.[40]

The oldest Baptist church in North Carolina which is still in existence, therefore, is not in Chowan, but at Shiloh in Camden County. The earliest information concerning it is known from a petition filed with the court as required under the terms of the Toleration Act. It includes names of eight petitioners; among these names are those of William Burges, its first pastor, and Paul Palmer, who was the leader in its formation. The date on the document, although faded, has been made out to be September 5, 1729. This church sent out nine ministers from its congregation and developed six churches from its membership. In 1757 it became a Particular Baptist Church, having been Arminian until then.[41]

The leadership of Palmer in Baptist work was so notable as to astound Governor Everard, who wrote as a good churchman to the Bishop of London on October 12, 1729, that he "was powerless to prevent or withstand the great tide of religious enthusiasm which under the preaching of Palmer was sweeping over the Province."[42] The governor was impressed likewise with the low level of the ministry provided by the Church of England for his colony. Through Palmer's itinerant preaching, hundreds of converts were being won to Baptist churches, although it must be confessed that his Arminian views did not make him cautious about requiring of them "an experience of grace previous to their baptism, but (he) baptized all who believed in the doctrine of baptism by immersion, and requested baptism . . ."[43] The consequent ingathering of converted and unconverted represented a weakness in his ministry, only offset by his

---

[40] Paschal, *op. cit.*, 131-42, 160. The date of the Chowan church has been ascertained from an entry, dated September 27, 1729, in *The Diary of John Comer,* pastor at Newport, Rhode Island, at the time, stating that the church had written a letter to him reporting the date of its organization, etc.

[41] *Ibid.*, 143-8. The petition is printed on p. 144.

[42] Paschal, *History of North Carolina Baptists, 1663-1805*, 154-5.

[43] Burkitt and Read, *History of the Kehukee Association,* 28; cited in Paschal, *op. cit.*, 155-6.

untiring zeal and evangelistic passion which bore so much permanent fruit. The lack of pastors to train the converts was a serious handicap, for most of the converts had to depend for religious instruction upon the infrequent visits of Palmer to their communities.

It is significant that the earliest Baptist witness in North Carolina was carried by Arminians. Undoubtedly, their message on the frontier was more appealing than the heavier emphasis of the Calvinists upon the helplessness of the sinner and predestination. Yet, after the Great Awakening in the midcentury, most of the churches established by the General Baptists became at least moderately Calvinistic under the influence of the Separate Baptists. For the latter came fresh from the revivalistic preaching of such Calvinists as Jonathan Edwards and George Whitefield, and hence were in a frame of mind to combine evangelistic zeal with Calvinistic doctrine. This influence will be traced in the next chapter.

The development of Baptist work in Georgia did not manifest itself in the organization of churches until 1772, although there may have been individuals in the colony who shared Baptist views between 1733, the date of its settlement, and 1772. On the whole, Baptist growth throughout the colonies prior to the Great Awakening was slow. It was not until that revival of spiritual vigor in the colonies that Baptists began to show a marked increase in numbers and influence. It has been well said that the early colonial period of American Baptist history was characterized by faithful witnessing to the truth amidst much persecution, while the era to come was to be one of phenomenal growth and organization for missionary activity.[44]

[44] Vedder, *A Short History of Baptists*, 287.

CHAPTER EIGHT

EXPANSION AND STRUGGLE FOR FREEDOM

THE period from 1740 to 1840 was fraught with remarkable significance for the American people. During it, American liberty took root and flowered into civil and religious freedom. It was also an era of expansion westward. The times were characterized by a national development which involved multifarious problems. The new nation was passing through a period of infancy and adolescent growth with a corresponding enthusiasm and breadth of vision. Moreover, it was a period of spiritual growth through frequent revivals, particularly in the latter half of the eighteenth and early nineteenth centuries. The circumstances which made this an important era for Americans proved to be no less significant for Baptists. It was for them an epoch of struggle for religious liberty, for organization, and for wide missionary enterprise and growth.

An Era of Revivals

The Great Awakening actually began about 1726 with the preaching of two men in New Jersey—Frelinghuysen, the Dutch Reformed evangelist in the Raritan Valley, and Gilbert Tennent, a young Presbyterian who was ordained at New Brunswick in the fall of that year. In a short time, the movement thus begun received a fresh impetus from the ministry of the scholarly theologian of Northampton, Jonathan Edwards, which set in motion a wave of revivals that "spread from town to town through the whole Connecticut Valley until one hundred and fifty communities in Massachusetts and Connecticut were visited with scenes similar to those which took place at Northampton."[1] Between 1736 and 1737 John Wesley's work as a young Anglican missionary in Georgia laid the foundation for revival there, a fact which he was not to realize until later in his lifetime. It was George Whitefield, the popular English evangelist

[1] Wesley M. Gewehr, *The Great Awakening in Virginia, 1740-1790* (Durham, N. C., 1930), 5-6.

and Calvinist, a contemporary and friend of Wesley, who unified the work begun in those scattered earlier revivals. Whitefield, with a true ecumenical spirit, in 1739 preached with marked success in the middle and southern colonies, and in the fall of 1740 in New England.

The effects of the revivals were divergent in character. The preaching for conversion, which was typical of the Great Awakening, issued in a deep consciousness of sin with an accompanying anxiety for salvation, and these aroused thousands to have what came to be known as "experienced religion," in contrast to the rather perfunctory type of church membership which had resulted from such compromises as the "Half-Way Covenant." The emotional appeal of the evangelists reached the masses, most of whom hitherto had been indifferent to religion. Their reaction to a harrowing conviction of sin was manifested in unusual expressions of primitive emotions: weeping, wailing, the "holy laugh" which frequently accompanied the convert's ecstasy of joy, dancing, and the cruder forms of emotional excitement, such as barking like a dog, uncontrollable jerking or muscular spasms of the body, and falling to the ground in a dead faint. These phenomena tended to divide Christians into two camps: those who approved and encouraged such occurrences as evidences of the working of the Holy Spirit and those who strongly disapproved them.

Such difference of opinion as to the validity of methods used by the untutored disciples of the more sane preaching of Edwards and Whitefield was clearly evident among Congregationalists, Presbyterians, and Baptists. It became quite obvious that the more urban and conservatively cultured people did not favor the emotional excesses so freely created by the great stress which was placed by the revivalists upon sin and the need for an emotional upheaval type of conversion. The more rural and uneducated, on the other hand, just as strongly favored the warmth and zeal of the simple preachers who proclaimed the gospel of salvation from sin with homely illustrations and who preached in a loud and often monotonously hypnotic "holy tone" of more or less nasal quality accompanied by violent gestures. The uninhibited and emotional preaching of the revivalists appealed to their need for a heart-warming spiritual experience.

It is quite evident that one of the outstanding effects of the revivals was the increase of dissent among the regular churches and the furthering of schism and controversies. Separatist or Strict Congregational churches appeared in New England, so-called because they insisted upon an experience of regeneration for membership and separated themselves from any half-way measures. The Philadelphia Presbytery was torn by an "Old Side-New Side schism" which lasted from 1741 until 1758. The Old Side comprised those, particularly of Scottish background, who were rigid predestinarians and strongly opposed to any kind of emotional appeal to the individual. The New Side, led by the Tennents and the New Brunswick Presbytery, favored the revivalistic methods, although they did not reject their Calvinistic tradition. In like manner, the Baptists split into Regular and Separate churches.

The Separate Baptist movement had in it the fire and fervor of the Whitefield revival. Its earliest adherents were converted in New England, where there were frequent occurrences of entire Congregational churches and their ministers, who had separated from the established church and its Half-Way Covenant, becoming Baptists.[2] It was an easy step for Separate Congregationalists to safeguard a regenerate church membership by accepting believer's baptism.

Separate Baptists would not adhere to the Philadelphia Confession as did the Regular churches, but insisted that the Bible alone served as the platform of their beliefs. They were critical of the Regulars also for not being strict enough in requiring new church members to give clear evidence of a conversion experience. In manner of preaching, they were more zealous and noisy. Exhortation rather than exposition characterized their sermons. Their preachers were known and often derided for their mannerisms of voice and gestures, which were typical of the revivalism of the times. In the popular mind, Separate Baptists occupied a clearly defined social status which often was described by their critics as ignorant, poor, awkward, and even uncouth. Undoubtedly, they were of the less privileged class on the frontier and in the villages of rural areas; whereas, the Regular Baptists were comprised chiefly of the town people and those of better education. Separate Baptists were known

[2] Philip S. Evans, *History of Connecticut Baptist State Convention, 1823-1907* (Hartford, 1909), 10-11.

also as "New Lights," because of their emphasis upon the possibility of individual inspiration and enlightenment through the Holy Spirit. This view caused them to regard with suspicion any indication of associational authority over the local congregations. Their strongly personalized emphasis provided a strong religious sanction for their intense individualism in politics, a factor which was significant, particularly in Virginia, during the American Revolution.

A direct result of the Great Awakening among Baptists after 1740 was the stimulus it provided for evangelism. It was but natural that its first effects should have been felt in New England, where the influence of Edwards' preaching was so profound. The leading missionary spirit in Massachusetts was Hezekiah Smith, who had been reared in New Jersey, educated at Hopewell Academy, a school established by the Reverend Isaac Eaton of the Philadelphia Baptist Association, and at Princeton College. He began his ministry as an itinerant evangelist, traveling in the South. Upon his return, he became interested in the Philadelphia Association's plans to found a college in Rhode Island, and manifested his educational foresight by assisting in that enterprise. In 1766 he assumed the pastorate of the Baptist church in Haverhill, Massachusetts, and continued in that capacity for thirty-nine years. Between 1740 and 1790, eighty-six new churches were formed in the Massachusetts Commonwealth, an enterprise in which Smith was active. By the latter date, there was in Massachusetts a total of ninety-two churches, with a combined membership of six thousand and thirty-four.[3] Smith gave valuable leadership to New England Baptists. In 1767 he participated in the organization of the Warren Association at Warren, Rhode Island. During the American Revolution he served as a chaplain in the American Army. In 1802 he aided in the founding of the Massachusetts Baptist Missionary Society, which was the first state organization of its kind in the denomination.

In other areas of New England, revivals were conducted with beneficial effects upon Baptist growth. After 1728 revivals in Vermont were experienced frequently. Between 1792 and 1800 there was an unusual period of enlargement in most of the churches. The Shaftsbury Association, which had been organized in 1780 to include

[3] A. H. Newman, *A History of the Baptist Churches in the United States* (Philadelphia, 1898, revised edition), 271.

churches in Vermont, Massachusetts, and New York, increased in size from twenty-six churches with an aggregate membership of 1,754 in 1791 to forty-six churches with 4,100 members nine years later. The trend continued with periodical revivals until about 1840. In Connecticut, by 1800, there were approximately sixty churches with a combined membership of four thousand. From incomplete records it appears that there was a revival in at least one church each year between 1797 and 1831. These times of spiritual awakening tended to be like those of the Congregationalists, rather than like the less restrained camp meeting variety of the Methodists. Every effort was made to keep them subdued.[4]

In Maine, where restrictions on religious freedom in the seventeenth century had stifled the Baptist witness, there was no appreciable growth until the 1780's. Churches which had been established in Maine through the efforts of itinerant preachers like Hezekiah Smith of Massachusetts were connected with the New Hampshire Association, which was organized in 1785. By 1800 the membership of the Association had increased from about four hundred to over fourteen hundred, a growth due primarily to the revival emphasis. The trend continued with few interruptions until 1840.[5]

The Philadelphia Association seems to have felt the impetus of the Awakening and to have been stirred by it to evangelistic endeavors.[6] The city became a center for the dissemination of the gospel by the Baptists. As evidence of this, the Association voted, in 1755, to send two ministers, one from New Jersey and one from Pennsylvania, to visit North Carolina in the interests of evangelism. In 1766 a special fund was created to lend assistance to destitute churches in need of the help of itinerant evangelists. By 1771 the Association appointed, as its evangelist at large, the Reverend Morgan Edwards (1722-1795).

Edwards had been invited in 1761 to come from England to the pastorate of the First Baptist Church of Philadelphia, a position which he occupied until 1770. He was a man of versatility, being

[4] Stephen Wright, *History of the Shaftsbury Baptist Association from 1781 to 1853* (Troy, N. Y., 1853), 37; Evans, *op. cit.,* 11; Charles W. Keller, *The Second Great Awakening in Connecticut* (New Haven, 1942), 194-201.

[5] Henry S. Burrage, *History of Baptists in Maine* (Portland, Me., 1904), 78-9, 84-5, 157-8, 195.

[6] Some of the following material is drawn from the author's *A Social History of the Philadelphia Baptist Association: 1707-1940,* chap. 1.

both a capable leader for many years and a historian of some importance.[7] In temperament he was eccentric and choleric. During the Revolution he was one of the few Baptists to refuse aid to the patriot cause. As an educator he was largely responsible for proposing that the Philadelphia Association establish a college to prepare a better-trained ministry. He saw the importance of organization and urged that a national body be incorporated with the Philadelphia Association as its nucleus and head.[8] With all of his varied gifts, he was always evangelistic in spirit.

Another itinerant missionary for the Philadelphia Association was the Reverend John Gano (1727-1798). He was born and reared in Hopewell, New Jersey. As a young man, he was appointed by the Association to travel through the South on a preaching mission. On his return north, he became pastor of the first Baptist church established in New York City. Its congregation had been gathered by Mr. Jeremiah Dodge, a member of the first Calvinistic Baptist church in New York Colony, which had come into existence in Fishkill, Dutchess County, about 1740. By 1753 a sufficient number were meeting in two homes in the city, one of which was Dodge's, to make it worth while to become a branch of the church at Scotch Plains, New Jersey. They occupied this status until 1762 when they were strong enough to constitute a church of their own with Gano as pastor. With the exception of eight years of service as a chaplain during the American Revolution, he devoted twenty-six years to his pastorate there. Always he was a zealous preacher and a leader in the denomination. By 1780 there were ten Baptist churches in Dutchess County and its vicinity, all of which were members of the Philadelphia Association until they established their own Association in 1791.

Also within the membership of the Philadelphia Association were Baptists in Delaware and Maryland. In both states their number was small, probably not more than six churches with a total of 480 members in Delaware and twenty-five in Maryland with a combined membership of about 1,200 by the opening of the nineteenth century. The Maryland churches were scattered over

---

[7] He prepared *Materials towards a History of Baptists* in 4 volumes: Vol. I on Penna. Philadelphia, 1770); Vol. II on New Jersey (1792); Vols. III and IV on Rhode Island (1867), Delaware (1885). Materials for other states in MSS.

[8] Morgan Edwards, *Materials towards a History of Baptists,* I, 128.

the state and lacked cohesiveness; they were variously connected with Associations in Pennsylvania, Maryland, and Virginia. In general, their numbers were increasing about as rapidly as the Baptists in the Middle States, but their strength and aggressiveness were far behind that of the other Southern States. Compared with the Methodists of Maryland, the Baptist churches were not gaining ground very rapidly.[9] Had the Separate Baptists settled in these states on their migration from New England, the story might have been different. As it was, Virginia and the Carolinas were the recipients of their unflagging zeal.

Between 1743 and 1762 there were at least four churches founded by missionaries of the Philadelphia Association along the Atlantic Coast as far south as Charleston, South Carolina. For a time these churches were members of the Philadelphia body. Then in 1765 four of them were among the ten in Virginia that secured permission to withdraw from the Philadelphia Association to form the Ketockton Regular Baptist Association. The Regular Baptists had made good progress in northern Virginia, but it was the Separate Baptists who became the most numerous, covering the region south of the James River after 1770 with wave upon wave of revivals and dotting the countryside with Baptist churches in the face of severe persecution. After that year the popular reaction to the Separate Baptists became friendly, although the hostility of the Anglican Establishment and of the civil authorities which replaced it was more severe.[10]

The Separate Baptists had been led south from New England by a man of natural gifts and a profound sense of mission, Shubael Stearns, a native of Boston. In 1745 he associated himself with the New Light or Separate Congregationalists. Six years later he was immersed at Tolland, Connecticut, and became a Baptist. Feeling a distinct call to the Southland, he left New England in 1755, stopping for a time in Berkeley and Hampshire counties in Virginia; but failing to experience the success anticipated, he moved to North Carolina, settling on Sandy Creek in Guilford (now Randolph) County. There he erected a meeting-house and organized the Sandy

[9] David Benedict, *A General History of the Baptist Denomination in America* (New York, 1848), 630; Norman H. Maring, History of Maryland Baptists, 1742-1882, an unpublished doctoral dissertation (University of Maryland, 1948), 9, 25.

[10] Gewehr, *The Great Awakening in Virginia, 1740-1790*, 117.

Creek Church of which he remained pastor during the rest of his life. Although small of stature and limited in education, his native ability and sound judgment made him highly successful. His preaching, aided by a strong and musical voice, was deeply moving, producing in his hearers many of the emotional responses which were typical of the revivalism of the times.

The central and western counties of North Carolina were fertile soil for evangelism, with twenty to thirty thousand inhabitants in 1755, followed by a steady stream of settlers who were attracted by land grants and the state of freedom existing there. It was chiefly to the English settlers, rather than to the Scotch-Irish, Welsh, or Germans, that Stearns and his assistants ministered. From the Sandy Creek Church as a nucleus, forty-two churches were established in seventeen years. Also under his guiding hand, the Sandy Creek Association was organized in 1758. For twelve years the Separate Baptists of Virginia and the Carolinas were members of this Association.

Stearns was ably assisted by his brother-in-law, Daniel Marshall, and by Colonel Samuel Harriss, a Virginian of distinction who had been baptized by Marshall. Together, these three constituted the leadership of the Separate Baptists. Harriss ministered to his own countrymen in Virginia and later to settlers in Georgia. Marshall, a native of Connecticut and a Presbyterian missionary to the Mohawk Indians between 1753 and 1754, became a Baptist in 1754 at forty-eight years of age, while in Winchester, Virginia, to which he had moved after giving up his work among the Indians. He joined Stearns at Sandy Creek in 1755 and was ordained pastor of Abbott's Creek Church in 1756. An untiring evangelist, he preached throughout North Carolina and Virginia between 1755 and 1760, baptizing hundreds of converts; then at the age of fifty-five he went to South Carolina where he labored for ten years. The last years of his ministry were devoted to Georgia where he preached until his death in 1784, in his seventy-eighth year. There he carried on a faithful work among the small and struggling churches during the American Revolution. Deeply sympathetic with the patriots' cause, Marshall won from his contemporaries respect for the Baptists. When the war was over, the prestige of Baptists had grown because of their support of the patriot forces. Hence, Marshall's efforts had borne more than average fruitage in preserving a Baptist witness for the future.[11]

The softening influence of the periodic revivals was evident in the union of Regular and Separate Baptists in the eastern part of North Carolina in 1777 and in the western part after the Revolutionary War had ended. In Virginia the union was not affected until 1787.

Baptist beginnings in Kentucky may be traced to the exploration and settling of Boonesboro on the Kentucky River in Madison County between 1769 and 1775 by the Boone family. The entire settlement appears to have been Baptist. Regular and Separate Baptists planted churches in the new territory during the 1780's. At the close of 1785 there were eleven Regular Baptist churches and seven Separate churches, the latter being south of the Kentucky River. Revivals from 1785 on resulted in marked growth. When Kentucky was admitted to statehood in 1792, there were already fifty-five Baptist churches in three Associations, with a total membership of 3,331. Beginning in 1794 a tide of immigrants swept in from Pennsylvania, Virginia, and the Carolinas; yet without producing any appreciable increase proportionately in the number of Baptists. It was not until the Great Revival of 1800-1803, which was predominantly the work of the Presbyterian evangelist, James McGready of Logan County, that Baptists enjoyed a large ingathering. It came without the excessive emotionalism which accompanied the camp meetings utilized by both the Presbyterians and Methodists. A significant result was a union of Separate and Regular Baptists in 1801. Between 1810 and 1813 and again from 1837 to 1843, periods of revival bore added fruit. By 1840 there were fifty associations with 711 churches and an aggregate membership of 49,308 or one Baptist to every fifteen in the population.[12]

The impact of the revival which had begun among Baptists in 1800 in the Elkhorn Association in Kentucky was felt before long in the Sandy Creek Association in North Carolina. It is noteworthy

[11] The main sources of information for the Separate Baptists have been Gewehr, *op. cit.*, chap 5; George W. Paschal, *History of North Carolina Baptists, 1663-1805* (Raleigh, 1930), chaps 11-3; Leah Townsend, *South Carolina Baptists, 1670-1805*, chap. 4; George W. Purefoy, *History of Sandy Creek Baptist Association* (New York, 1859), chaps. 7, 9.

[12] J. H. Spencer, *A History of Kentucky Baptists from 1769 to 1885*, 2 vols. (Cincinnati, 1885), I, 102-11, 254, 279-80, 535-46, 567, 673.

that Baptists again did not share in the emotional excesses which accompanied the camp meetings of the Presbyterians and Methodists. Although urged to join with them, Baptists generally kept aloof from the union meetings, principally to avoid compromise of their cherished tenet of believer's baptism as a prerequisite for communion.[13] The Kehukee Association caught the flame when Lemuel Burkitt, a most influential minister in the state, reported to that body in 1801 concerning his visit to Kentucky during the previous weeks. His zeal for the revival is the more remarkable in that he and the Association were ardent Calvinists.

South Carolina Baptists, who had suffered from the ill effects of the war, also experienced an awakening about 1790. "Many of the older Baptist meetings were apparently reconstituted, new ones grew and flourished unrecorded, until with all the suddenness of revival, a teeming religious life is shown covering the back country after 1790, when the Bethel Association began to keep minutes of its meetings. . . . Separate tendencies still lingered, but regularization was so rapid as associations gathered in the groups that the names Separate and Regular disappeared and only Baptist remained."[14]

Illustrative of the notable growth in the back country is the record of Bethel (originally called Jameys Creek) Church, located on the ridge between Enoree and Tyger Rivers. In 1790 it had 116 members; thirteen years later, 390, an increase of more than three hundred per cent. The Bethel Association, with which this church united when the Association was organized in 1789, epitomized this era of revival. In 1789 it had sixteen churches with perhaps fewer than one thousand members; by 1800 there were fifty-two churches with over twenty-eight hundred members; and three years later, owing to the withdrawal of nine churches to organize the Saluda Association, the number of churches was reduced to thirty-three, yet the membership had been so augmented by conversions as to exceed the figure for 1800 by 828.[15]

In the Carolinas, the Charleston Association in South Carolina influenced theological thinking, changing it, as we have seen, from

---

[13] Paschal, *History of North Carolina Baptists, 1663-1805*, 538; Purefoy, *History of Sandy Creek Baptist Association*, 68.

[14] Townsend, *History of South Carolina Baptists, 1670-1805*, 181.

[15] *Ibid.*, 261, 267.

Arminian to Calvinistic doctrine. By 1794, for example, the last General Baptist church in North Carolina, that at Meherrin, became Calvinistic upon the death of its pastor, William Parker, a lifelong leader of General Baptists. With the exception of those who retained Arminian teaching under the name Freewill Baptists, the General Baptists as a distinctive body in North Carolina were no more.[16] The lengthy Philadelphia Confession (the London Particular Baptist Confession of 1689 printed by the Philadelphia Association in 1742) which had been accepted in 1767 by the Charleston Association, had more influence in the older coastal cities than in the back country churches. Yet it did color Baptist thought generally, for the covenants adopted by most churches reflected its spirit and expressed its point of view in briefer form.[17] Charleston also gave to Baptists their most prominent leader in the South at the time, Dr. Richard Furman, pastor of the first church and a man of unusual ability whose interest in education profited the entire denomination.

In Virginia the story is much the same. The revival among the Baptists, which as elsewhere was shared by Presbyterians and Methodists also, began about 1785 in the region of the James River. It reached its culmination in the years 1787-1789, affecting both the Regulars and Separates, particularly in the northeastern and north central counties. John Leland, whose field of labor embraced approximately twenty square miles and included parts of Orange, Culpeper, Spotsylvania, and Louisa Counties, baptized about four hundred people from October, 1787, until March, 1789. When the revival seemed to slacken in one neighborhood, it broke out in another. It differed from the revival among the Baptists in Kentucky and the Carolinas, for in Virginia it produced many of the physical and emotional manifestations felt by the Methodists. In the midst of the revival and undoubtedly influenced by it, a union of the Separates and Regulars was effected. The terms of agreement consisted of the acceptance of the Regular Baptist Confession of Faith with the understanding that it should not be a strictly binding document, and the use of a new name, "The United Baptist Churches of Christ in Virginia." The move was indicative of the triumph of a more tolerant spirit and of a feeling of denominational solidarity

---

[16] Paschal, *op. cit.*, 223.
[17] Townsend, *op. cit.*, 287.

which had been fostered partly by the ameliorating influence of the revivals, but also by the exigencies of the common struggle for religious liberty in which the Baptists of Virginia had been engaged.

With the increasing number of churches in various parts of the country, the natural tendency was to organize new associations after the pattern of the original organization at Philadelphia. The earliest to be formed were in the South, namely: Charleston Association in South Carolina (1751), Sandy Creek Association in North Carolina (1758), Ketockton Association in eastern Virginia (1765), Kehukee Association located in the eastern part of North Carolina (1769) and Strawberry Association in southern Virginia (1776). The New England associations came into being with the Warren Association in Rhode Island (1767), followed by the Stonington Association in Connecticut (1772), and the Shaftesbury Association in Vermont (1780). In the Middle Colonies the first new association to be organized was the Redstone Association in southwestern Pennsylvania (1776) followed by the New York Association (1791) and the Chemung Association which included churches in Northumberland County, Pa., and western New York (1796). By 1800 there were forty-eight associations in the country: thirty in the southern states, and eight beyond the Alleghenies—six in Kentucky alone.[18]

Although the Philadelphia Association became smaller as new associations were formed to include churches formerly within its membership, its influence increased as pastors and laymen who had been identified with its standards of faith and polity became a part of the newly organized bodies. For example, the Reverend John Gano, formerly of the Philadelphia Association, but later living in Kentucky, visited the recently organized Yadkins Association in the northwestern section of North Carolina in 1793 to prevail upon them to adopt more orderly methods of conducting their affairs. They had feared the loss of democratic control if they appointed a moderator. In time, Gano allayed their fears and helped them establish rules of order for their meetings.[19] The Philadelphia Baptists also exercised an influence over these later associations by encouraging an exchange of correspondence and annual reports. Other associa-

[18] Vedder, *A Short History of Baptists,* 318. For details on associations, see David Benedict, *General History of the Baptist Denomination* (New York, 1848), in which associations are arranged by states.

[19] Benedict, *op. cit.,* 696.

tions welcomed such contacts with the Philadelphia Association; a typical example was the Redstone Association in western Pennsylvania which requested such correspondence in 1803.[20]

That many Baptists, even in this early period, were not satisfied with local organizations in which the churches enjoyed so much autonomy as to nullify the value of association with sister churches, is clear from the attempts which were made, beginning in 1770, to create a broader type of affiliation. In that year, as has been indicated before, Morgan Edwards actually proposed a plan for a national union of Baptists "in one body politic, by having the Association of Philadelphia (the center) incorporated by charter, and by taking one delegate out of each Association into the corporation."[21]

While New England Baptists opposed such a "general church view," they seemingly took advantage of the proposal in the interests of their struggle for religious liberty when the Warren Association called for a "continental association" to meet in Virginia on October 17, 1776, for the purpose of finding means to obtain deliverance from the encroachments upon their liberty. While it cannot be ascertained, it is possible that this move was implemented and encouraged in part, at least, by the American Revolution. A survey of the Baptists' struggle for religious freedom in the Colonies indicates that New England Baptists in particular saw in the Revolution an opportune time to press for their cause, and that they anxiously sought the co-operation of all other Baptists.

It is even more clear that sectional organization was in its pristine stage, indicating the development of a desire for closer co-operation between churches in areas which were far removed from the Philadelphia center. In 1794 the Bethel Association of South Carolina invited the associations of the Southern States to form a general committee for the whole South. Then in 1802, as if to implement, in part at least, the earlier proposal of a national organization, the Philadelphia Association presented a plan for a committee of correspondence to be set up in Philadelphia to examine communications from the various associations and "to adjust the same as they may deem necessary."[22] The implication of these last words is not clear.

[20] James A. Davidson, "The Redstone Baptist Association of Western Pennsylvania," *The Chronicle*, Vol. V, No. 3 (July, 1942), p. 140.
[21] Morgan Edwards, *Materials towards a History of Baptists*, I, 128.
[22] *Philadelphia Association Minutes: 1707-1807*, p. 371.

However, the plan did go into effect simply as a means of caring for the correspondence between associations.

It is evident that influential Baptist leaders felt the need for some kind of national co-operation. Indeed, these early stirrings to create a denominational connectionalism were to be revived in 1814 when a national missionary convention was organized. The drive to bring this about was provided by the missionary movement of the early nineteenth century, which itself was one of the fruits of the Great Awakening and the subsequent revivals which in the preceding century had aroused the evangelistic zeal of most Protestant denominations. The stage was being set for the formation of missionary projects on a national scale and along international as well as denominational lines. Thus, while the story of associational growth to 1800 is not directly related to the influence of the Great Awakening upon Baptists, it was influenced indirectly by that movement in American religious life.

The Baptist Struggle for Religious Liberty

The great colonial awakenings in the revival of the mid-eighteenth century created an environment which was favorable to the increase of dissenters and to the growth of religious freedom.[23] As emphasis was placed upon individual responsibility to God, men responded; but none more than the Baptists whose tradition of freedom had been so marked in the Old World. Since the new charter granted to the Massachusetts Bay Colony in 1691 had guaranteed only religious toleration, and had not exempted Baptists from taxation for the support of the state church, they refused to pay on the principle that no man should be coerced to support another man's church. As a result, their property frequently was sold for tax costs, as at Ashfield, near Boston, where they suffered keenly.[24]

In 1728 an Exemption Act was passed by the General Court of Massachusetts which exempted Baptists and Quakers from payment of such taxes if they supported a parish of their own within five miles of their home. This act expired in 1733. After some difficulty it was

---

[23] Much of the material in this section is drawn from the author's *A Social History of the Philadelphia Baptist Association: 1707-1940*, chap. 2.

[24] Henry S. Burrage, *A History of the Baptists in New England*, 108 f. and Isaac Backus, *A History of New England Baptists*, II, 149 f.

renewed in 1747. But in 1753, the Court amended the law, making it illegal for any minister or church to issue exemption certificates without the testimony of three other "Anabaptist" churches in the neighboring provinces that the recipient was a good "Anabaptist."

Objecting to such a measure to gain exemption, the Baptists in New England subscribed money to carry their case against the Court's decision of 1753 to England. By 1757 the Exemption Law of 1747 had expired; whereupon a new law was passed which exempted only those Baptists whose names were on a particular list of those in good standing by July 20 of that year. The list had to be signed by three principal members of the Anabaptist church to which they belonged. Such a requirement was resented deeply by the Baptists, who refused to recognize the state's right to judge a man's religious standing.

In 1767 New England Baptists, some of whom until then had been members of the Philadelphia Association, organized the Warren Association at Warren, Rhode Island. One of the chief purposes of this move was to strengthen their fight for religious liberty.[25] Dr. Manning, president of Rhode Island College, his brother-in-law, the Reverend John Gano, from the Philadelphia Association, and the Reverend Isaac Backus, a prominent Baptist preacher in Massachusetts, were chiefly instrumental in its formation.[26] Later, Backus was engaged by the Warren Association as its agent to promote the cause of religious freedom. He was vigorous in his evangelistic work; between 1756 and 1767 he preached 2,412 sermons, and traveled almost fifteen thousand miles outside of his own parish in New England. As an historian and as a leader of his denomination, he appears again and again during the Baptists' struggle for complete religious liberty.[27]

By 1769 the Warren Association, having received many letters of complaint and grievance from Baptist churches which had been harassed by the exemption requirements, appointed a committee to draft petitions to the General Courts of Massachusetts and Connecticut for redress. Encouraged by moral support from Philadelphia Baptists, who frequently received appeals from their New England

[25] William W. Sweet, *Religion in Colonial America* (New York, 1942), 333.
[26] Edward F. Humphrey, *Nationalism and Religion in America: 1774-1789* (Boston, 1924), 326.
[27] Burrage, *op. cit.*, 96.

brethren for assistance, they stated in their "plan to collect grievances" that they were uniting with the Philadelphia Association to work out a remedy for their plight. In 1770 the Warren Association decided to send "to the British Court for help if it could not be obtained in America." When the General Court of Massachusetts opened, the Baptist Committee of Grievances addressed a petition to it.[28] The Reverend Hezekiah Smith was appointed as agent of the Baptists to sail to England in November. The Philadelphia Association directed the collection of funds from its member churches to help defray his expenses.[29]

A new exemption law was passed by the General Court in 1772, evidently under the pressure of Baptist action, which provided that Baptists might be exempt from paying the church tax if they furnished the authorities with certificates indicating their good standing as Baptists. This was not, however, to the satisfaction of the Baptists, for obedience to the law implied a recognition of man's right to determine the religious standing of his fellow men. So, in September of that year, the Warren Association appointed another Committee on Grievances with Mr. Backus as chairman, a position which he held for the next ten years. Backus wasted no time in acting; in 1774 he urged Samuel Adams to adopt a consistent policy of separation of church and state, pointing out that British taxation of American Colonies was no more unjust than Massachusetts' taxation of Baptists for support of a state church.[30]

In this same year, 1774, the Continental Congress was called to meet in Philadelphia on September 5. The Warren Association, therefore, taking advantage of this new effort in behalf of freedom, requested Backus to go to Philadelphia for the purpose of laying before its members their claims for religious liberty. Upon his arrival in October, he met with the Philadelphia Association which was then in session and which appointed a large committee to assist him in his mission. Through their efforts, a conference was arranged for the evening of October 14, with the delegates of Massachusetts to the Congress.[31] The purpose of this preliminary meeting was to secure

[28] *Minutes of Warren Association* for 1769 and 1770; quoted in Burrage, *op. cit.*, 108-9.

[29] *Minutes of Philadelphia Association: 1707-1807*, 114.

[30] Alvah Hovey, *A Memoir of the Life and Times of the Reverend Isaac Backus* (Boston, 1859), 196-7.

[31] Backus, *A History of New England Baptists*, II, 201.

an opportunity to present their grievances before the Continental Congress. At the conference were delegates from Massachusetts, New Jersey, and Pennsylvania.

President Manning of Rhode Island College read the memorial prepared by the Warren Association. It was not received with sympathy. Samuel Adams insinuated that the complaints had come from fanatical rather than *regular* Baptists. He referred to the New Light Baptists whom he held in disdain. Robert Treat Paine, also of Massachusetts, contended that there was nothing of conscience in the Baptists' complaints. To this accusation, Backus replied that it was absolutely a point of conscience with him, for he could not turn in the certificates that the authorities required in order to grant exemption without acknowledging "that power in man which . . . belongs only to God." Thomas Cushing admitted that this conviction "quite altered the case; for if it were a point of conscience, he had nothing to say."[32]

The four-hour conference ended with a promise on the part of the Massachusetts delegates that they would do what they could for the relief of the Baptists. John Adams, however, gave them a warning that they might as well expect a change in the solar system as to expect Massachusetts to give up her establishment. The outcome of the meeting was unsatisfactory, for it had not established the Baptists' cause as a "national political grievance."[33] It was necessary to carry the matter back to Massachusetts. But Backus was not easily discouraged, not even when the Baptists were defeated in their efforts to have religious freedom incorporated in the new Revolutionary Constitution of Massachusetts.

The cause was not entirely lost, however, for the Reverend Samuel Stillman, pastor of the First Baptist Church of Boston, was selected to deliver the election sermon on May 26, 1779. This may have been an effort to appease the New England Baptists, or it may have been evidence of respect for their stand and support in the Revolution. At any rate, he had the opportunity to present the Baptist principles of religious freedom before the Council and Representatives of the Commonwealth of Massachusetts Bay.[34]

---

[32] The account of the conference is based on Backus, *op. cit.*, 201-2.

[33] Humphrey, *Nationalism and Religion in America*, 330.

[34] *Ibid.*, 120.

In many respects, Baptist support of the patriot cause in the American Revolution was regarded by them as support of the cause of religious liberty. Backus outlined five reasons for their support of the war, and strongly emphasized among them was the fact that the worst treatment that had been accorded Baptists in America had come from the same principles that had caused the Revolution.[35] With the exception of the Dunkards or German Baptists, who like the Quakers and the Mennonites arrayed themselves against war, the Baptists with but few exceptions, had supported the revolutionary governments loyally. Their men had served in the Army, while their pastors had volunteered as chaplains.[36]

The Revolution was destructive to the churches, particularly in the occupied areas about New York and Philadelphia and some points in the South. For example, in New York City, the church of which the Reverend John Gano was pastor had only thirty-seven out of two hundred former members to greet him when he returned in 1784 from service as a chaplain in the Army. The meeting-house had been used by the British cavalry as a stable. It took two years to bring the membership back to its former size.[37] In Philadelphia also, the British occupation had retarded the progress of Baptist work. Churches in the path of marching armies, like the Great Valley Church of Welsh Baptists in Chester County, were ransacked and looted. For some years many of them had difficulty in preserving their existence. It was not until 1792 that there was evidence of any vigorous missionary enterprise.[38]

As the years dragged on, the preoccupation of the Baptists with the struggle for independence produced a gradual deterioration of their religious life. Political factions, the general spiritual decline of war-time, and the scattering of congregations brought despair to many of the churches. In the South, men like Daniel Marshall in Georgia did yeoman service by staying with their congregations in the difficult war years. When news arrived in Philadelphia concerning the military triumph of Washington at Yorktown on October 19, 1781,

[35] Backus, op. cit., II, 197-8.

[36] Wm. Cathcart, The Baptists and the American Revolution (Philadelphia, 1876).

[37] Vedder, A History of the Baptists in the Middle States (Philadelphia, 1898), 29-30.

[38] Based on the histories of these churches in Philadelphia Association Minutes for 1888, p. 59; 1883, 72; 1883, 55-7. See also Torbet, A Social History of the Philadelphia Association, 49-51.

with the ensuing surrender of the British Army, the Philadelphia Association was in session. On the following morning, which was the 24th, that body met to praise God for the victory. Such a spirit was characteristic of Baptists generally.

The success of the American Revolution and the liberal actions of the Virginia Assembly contributed to the ultimate attainment of religious liberty. In that colony, persecution of Baptists was generally restricted to the New Lights or Separates, who refused to conform to the provision of the Act of Toleration which required dissenting ministers to secure a license to preach in various localities. They saw no reason why they, who had received a mandate from the Holy Spirit to preach, should secure a license from men. Moreover, they did not hesitate to criticize the Episcopal clergy as being unspiritual, worldly in their practices, and more concerned with their salaries than with the service which they might render to God. To cause further distrust and dislike of these Separate Baptists, their growth was phenomenal and therefore alarming to the state church whose parishes were large geographically but not great in numbers. For these reasons, Baptists were subjected frequently to fines or imprisonment, usually on the grounds of "disturbance of the peace" or of having violated the restrictions placed upon itinerant preachers of the dissenting variety, whose only claim to ordination was from God.

Illustrative of the earlier form of popular violence to which Virginia Baptists were subjected is the case of Samuel Harriss. He was driven out of Culpeper County in 1765, upon preaching his first sermon there, by a mob armed with sticks, whips, and clubs. In Orange County he was pulled down from a platform by a ruffian and dragged about by the hair of the head, then by the leg, until rescued by a friend. In his own county of Pittsylvania, however, where he had gained some prominence, he preached without molestation. On more than one occasion, John Waller was beaten severely, as in 1771, in Caroline County, when the parson, his clerk, and the sheriff led an attack upon him. John Taylor, John Koontz, Lewis Lunsford, William Webber, James Ireland, David Barrow, John Pickett, Elijah Baker, and others suffered similarly. While they were in jail, mobs would try to do away with them, as in the case of the attempt to blow up the building in which Ireland was incarcerated in Culpeper in 1770. The public hostility was based principally on what was regarded as parental cruelty to children in that the Baptists refused to have their infants baptized, plus the customary prejudiced opinion that Baptists were social radicals.[39]

Beginning in 1768 Baptists in Virginia began to face legal prosecution by the authorities. This prosecution was stimulated largely by irate clergymen of the Established Church, who resented the barbed criticisms leveled at them by the Separate preachers and who envied the swift growth of the Baptist congregations. This type of treatment continued until the outbreak of the Revolution, during which period "about thirty-four ministers were imprisoned, some on several occasions. The first instance of actual imprisonment occurred on June 4, 1768, in Spotsylvania County, when John Waller, Lewis Craig, James Childs, James Reed, and William Mash were arrested as disturbers of the peace." When they refused to agree to cease preaching in return for release from jail, Craig was held for four weeks and the others for forty-three days.[40] The charge, it may be noted, was not for violation of a regulation regarding religion, but of a civil statute against disturbing the peace. While there is no evidence from Virginia court records that any Baptist preacher was whipped by sanction of legal authority, there is one case at least where a sheriff whipped a minister, John Waller, so severely that he carried the scars to his grave; but there is no proof that he was carrying out an order of the court.[41]

While the preachers were often recalcitrant and unwilling to secure licenses to preach—an attitude particularly characteristic of Separate Baptists—they had difficulty in securing them owing to the fact that county courts claimed to be without authority to grant licenses for preaching places, and the Colonial Court of Virginia placed the narrowest interpretation upon the Toleration Act. Then, too, the preacher, in order to get a license, had to have the certification of two magistrates that the signers of the petition were inhabitants of the locality. Owing to official prejudice and dislike, this was not easy to get. Even when petitions were put through, they were not always received with favor by local sheriffs.[42]

[39] Gewehr, *The Great Awakening in Virginia,* 119-21.

[40] *Ibid.,* 122.

[41] Lewis P. Little, *Imprisoned Preachers and Religious Liberty in Virginia* (Lynchburg, Va., 1938), 180-1.

[42] Gewehr, *The Great Awakening in Virginia,* 127.

The leading Baptist spokesman in behalf of religious freedom was John Leland of Culpeper County, a minister in whose church Thomas Jefferson is said to have worshiped on occasion and with whom Leland enjoyed friendship. He was a Jeffersonian Republican and later became a follower of Andrew Jackson. In a series of political essays, he set forth his views on government, which were to the effect that the republican form is the best preservative of the good of society, that all power is vested in and consequently derived from the people, and that laws made by legislatures which are inconsistent with the constitution are not binding. He also insisted that legislators have no right to alter that compact, and that a man is not obliged to surrender his conscience to the state. To Leland, that government is best which rules least, which is economical, which maintains a favorable balance of trade, which sponsors soil improvement, and which affords broad educational opportunities for its citizens.[43]

As early as 1758 the Baptists and Presbyterians joined forces in the common cause. Jointly, they sent petitions to the Virginia General Assembly, requesting that the Establishment be abolished and that dissenting clergymen be allowed the right to perform the marriage ceremony. To encourage their efforts, Thomas Jefferson in 1779 introduced in the Assembly a Bill for Religious Freedom. While it did not win adoption, it paved the way for future victory.

In 1788 the Baptists resorted to the device of organizing a General Committee to gain their objectives, a procedure which they justified because the issue was a religious one. By constant pressure effected singly and together with other sects, they won some concessions, including the right of their clergymen to perform marriage ceremonies. Finally, when Thomas Jefferson's Bill for Religious Freedom was passed by the Assembly in December, 1785, it was largely the product of the combined efforts of such persecuted sects as Baptists, Presbyterians, Catholics, and Quakers. With the sympathetic leadership of James Madison, Patrick Henry, and Thomas Jefferson, these same groups were instrumental in obtaining repeal of the Incorporation Act. Thus, in 1787, the Established Church was brought to an end in Virginia. When the glebe lands were sold in 1799,

43 *Ibid.,* 189-91.

thereby severing all financial ties between the Episcopal Church and the state, the work of the General Committee was completed.[44]

A similar story might be told concerning the struggle of Baptists in North Carolina, where between 1765 and 1771 they faced religious oppression under Governor Tryon. Both Baptists and Presbyterians resented the legal restrictions which rendered them incapable of performing the marriage ceremony, a privilege which was accorded their brethren in England without question under the Act of Toleration. A second issue between Baptists and the governor concerned the "Regulator" movement. This was an agitation, led by small farmers in the back country, to induce the government to put an end to unjust taxation and extortion on the part of sheriffs, registers of deeds, clerks of the courts, and judges. While much violence occurred in several western counties where money was scarce and taxes unduly burdensome, the agitators actually took up arms against the government only in Orange County. This conflict issued in what came to be known as the Battle of Alamance in May, 1771.

It is not without significance that when Tryon in 1768 called out troops to suppress the violence, he found the militia of Orange County unwilling to serve. Baptists were particularly numerous in that area. While their ministers urged them not to take up arms against the government—a plea strengthened by an action of the Sandy Creek Association in 1769, forbidding members to participate on pain of being disbarred from fellowship—Baptists were not forbidden to belong to the Regulator movement. It is altogether likely that many Baptists participated as individuals in the effort to gain redress of the grievances which they shared with their fellows. Moreover, they were Separates with a strong predilection for democratic procedure in politics as well as in church polity.

When the Battle of Alamance ended in the apparent defeat of the Regulators, a general exodus of back-country North Carolinians took place. Among them were great numbers of Baptists who moved on to the new frontiers in Tennessee, South Carolina, and Georgia, spreading as they went their principles and doctrine. Their victory over injustice, like that of their Virginia brethren, was to be won

---

[44] For a detailed study of the Virginia Baptists' struggle for religious liberty, see W. T. Thom, *Struggle for Religious Freedom in Virginia: The Baptists* (Baltimore, 1900); and Robert B. Semple, *A History of the Rise and Progress of the Baptists in Virginia* (Philadelphia, 1894).

ultimately with the triumph of the patriot cause in the American Revolution.[45]

The efforts put forth by Baptists in behalf of religious freedom, during and after the American Revolution, contributed greatly not only to the ultimate achievement of their goals, but also to their popularity. Indeed, the Revolution provided them with a unique opportunity. They had little to lose and much to gain. Like Congregationalists and Presbyterians, they were bound by no ties of loyalty to a state church in England. Their participation in the War of Independence was therefore a contribution to the cause of religious liberty.

The ultimate safeguard for complete liberty in America was the adoption of a Constitution which included no religious test clause and which plainly prevented the interference of the state in religion. That such a clause was written large in the famous "Bill of Rights," as the first ten amendments to the Federal Constitution are called, was due in no small part to the agitation of New England and Virginia Baptists. The latter petitioned President Washington personally that such a safeguard should be written into the Constitution. He replied with a promise that he would lend his support to such a move for religious liberty.[46] In New England, Isaac Backus maintained a strong leadership to the same end.[47] Even then, disestablishment did not come in Massachusetts until 1833 to mark the final triumph of a long struggle in behalf of religious freedom.

Missionary Enterprise and Expansion

The increase in the number of Baptist churches in the colonies between 1740 and 1776 was significant, for by the latter year there were 472 churches as over against approximately sixty at the time of the Great Awakening, a tenfold gain. By 1795 Backus estimated that there were a total of 1,152 churches scattered through sixteen states and territories.[48] The most marked growth, however, came in the

[45] Paschal, *History of North Carolina Baptists, 1663-1805*, 361-83, 462-9, 516-20.

[46] A. H. Newman, *A History of the Baptist Churches in the United States*, 372-4.

[47] Henry S. Burrage, *A History of the Baptists in New England* (Philadelphia, 1894), 121-7.

[48] Frederick L. Weis, *The Colonial Churches and the Colonial Clergy of the Middle and Southern Colonies, 1607-1776* (Lancaster, Mass., 1938), 18. Weis lists 41 churches throughout 1740, including Keithian, German, and Seventh Day Baptists. Backus lists 20 churches in New England in his *History of New England Baptists*, II, 391-401. Vedder, *Short History of Baptists*, 307, gives 47 churches for the same period.

postwar period, when the climate of opinion was more favorable to Baptist expansion. In the first place, religious liberty had been won with the very considerable aid of Baptists. Then, too, the Baptist congregational form of polity with no state-church connections was in harmony with prevailing democratic sentiments. Finally, their support of the patriot cause had won for the Baptists popularity among leaders and the masses alike.

Not only was the time favorable, but the Baptists had within themselves qualities and ideals which gave impetus to their progress. Their ministry, though frequently lacking in advanced formal training, was aggressively evangelistic; most of their ministers along the frontiers were unpaid and self-sacrificing men, and hence independent in the administration of their duties. Usually they were farmers or artisans during the week, and so shared with their congregations in the hardships of early American life. Baptist leaders held in common a vision of winning the West for Protestantism, and they actively participated in the westward movement. Entire congregations with their pastors frequently moved out into the little-known territories beyond the Alleghenies, and courageous missionaries broke trails side by side with the frontiersmen. In this enterprise they were stimulated by the good-natured rivalry of the Methodist circuit riders, whose crusading spirit was equally valiant with their own.

In many respects the time was ripe for the successful spread of religious groups which were democratic in spirit and which made their appeal to the common people, who understood the simple and somewhat emotional message that their preachers brought. Within American religious life, the old principle of a union of church and state had weakened in the face of the development of a voluntary system of church support. The democratic emphases of the Revolution upon individualism and toleration had loosened the ties of church and state, as we have seen. At the same time, there was a trend toward the organization of independent national churches. This was a reflection of the national consciousness of the young republic in the political sphere. It was also a natural result of the separation of church and state; for churches which were supported voluntarily needed some central organization for an efficient dispensing of funds, particularly in missionary enterprises. Another trend was the advent of co-operation between these new national churches. The decline of denominational friction was due possibly to two factors: a development of tolerance among Protestant denominations and a common fear of Catholicism. These, in the early nineteenth century, stimulated united efforts to claim the frontiers for Protestantism.

These changes occurred, moreover, in association with a new evangelical enthusiasm—a second Great Awakening.[49] From 1798 to 1820 a large number of local and state voluntary missionary societies were formed within the various denominations to work on the frontier. Heretofore, missionary work had been done haphazardly by the General Assembly, the Synod, the Classis, the Association, or the Conference of the respective denominations. The new frontier was the Mississippi Valley.

The first voluntary interdenominational missionary organization was the New York Missionary Society, formed on September 21, 1796, by a group of ministers and laymen of New York City to convert the Indians. Presbyterians, Associated Reformed, Reformed Dutch, and Baptists participated in the enterprise. At the request of the New York Baptist associations, a Baptist minister, the Reverend Elkanah Holmes, was appointed as an agent to the Tuscarora and Seneca Indians. He continued his work until a schism occurred between the Baptists and those who did not share their stand against infant baptism.

Soon all major Protestant churches were participating in missionary activities. The stronghold of American Presbyterianism in the eighteenth century was in the middle region along the Atlantic seaboard. When the General Assembly of that Church was instituted in Philadelphia in 1789, a permanent fund for missionaries was obtained through church contributions. In 1798 the Congregationalists established the Missionary Society of Connecticut. They, like the Presbyterians, worked among the Indians. The Presbyterians were trying to educate and civilize the Indians south of the Potomac, many of whom were willing to have schools established. The Congregationalists' work centered mainly in New England and the Ohio country. The Baptists and Methodists in the early nineteenth century were more active among the Negroes in the South.

It will be recalled that during the second half of the eighteenth

[49] Good surveys may be found in Goodykoontz, *Home Missions on the American Frontier* (Caldwell, Idaho, 1939); and Elsbree, *The Rise of the Missionary Spirit in America, 1790-1815* (Williamsport, Pa., 1928).

century, local missionary work was carried on by the associations. Indeed, the Philadelphia Association in 1771 had appointed an "evangelist at large" to preach in the South. The Shaftsbury Association of Vermont, which was organized in 1780, developed an extensive domestic missionary program, appointing its own committee in 1802 to handle funds, examine missionary candidates, and supervise the work of the missionaries. Through this means the Baptists had increased their number from less than ten thousand before the Revolution to over one hundred thousand by the close of the century. The very existence of the denomination was dependent upon the maintenance of the missionary spirit. It was also true that home missions gave expression to a growing denominational consciousness, because the associational method was in a sense a denominational program based upon the participation of the churches in a formal connection.[50]

A rival method was introduced in New England at the beginning of the nineteenth century when the Baptists formed missionary societies which were independent of the associations. In Massachusetts and Maine, missionary journals were launched. In 1802 the Massachusetts Domestic Missionary Society was organized. It was the outgrowth of the missionary activities of ministers and laymen in the Warren Association. In spite of the Baptist emphasis in some quarters upon "close communion," the policy of missionary organization in Massachusetts was "open door." That is, anyone could join the society, regardless of denominational affiliation, who was willing to pay at least one dollar a year. Of the twelve trustees, four might be non-Baptists. No doctrinal or other standard was set up for the workers. Undoubtedly the organizers of the society were anxious to avoid the development of ecclesiastical considerations in connection with missionary endeavor. They had suffered too much from denominational exclusiveness at the hands of the Establishment in Massachusetts only a century or more before. Accordingly, they were developing an agency which had no relationship to organized churches as far as representation was concerned. The basis for membership was determined solely by voluntary financial support of the tasks to be performed. The work of the Massachusetts Domestic Missionary

[50] Elsbree, *The Rise of the Missionary Spirit in America*, 76-7. Robert A. Baker sets forth the view of the rival methods of conducting home missions in his admirable study, *Relations between Northern and Southern Baptists* (Fort Worth, Texas, 1948), 10-4.

Society extended into Maine, lower Canada, western New York, Pennsylvania, Ohio, Illinois, and Missouri. Its main purpose was to evangelize the Indians and frontiersmen.

As new streams of migrants moved across the Alleghenies into the Ohio and Mississippi River valleys and even beyond into the Missouri country, Baptists of other states adopted this form of organization, with the result that the transition from the associational method of conducting home missions to the society method continued until the latter method had become permanently established. The Maine Baptist Missionary Society was organized in 1804. In the same year the Philadelphia Baptist Association led in organizing a society which supported a missionary in the eastern parts of Ohio. In the years that followed, new societies were formed almost annually in one or another of the states; for example, in New York in 1806 and 1807, in Connecticut in 1809, and in New Jersey in 1811. The triumph of the society method among Baptists was not strange. They were influenced by the example of English and European missionary societies. Moreover, other Protestant denominations in America had already adopted this method. Finally, American Baptists were extremely eager to avoid "the development of ecclesiastical bodies that might usurp the autonomy of the local churches. The fear of centralization was in the minds of many as they saw the associations, based immediately upon the churches in an ecclesiastical connectionalism, begin to increase in activity and authority. The formation of a missionary *society* by-passed this problem completely." [51]

The Baptist missionary movement, like those of other evangelical denominations, was somewhat dependent upon England for its impetus. This was natural, for the American States were economically dependent upon Europe up to 1812 and culturally dependent for a long period thereafter. Besides, interdenominational missionary cooperation began in England about the same time, if not a little earlier, than it did in America. It will be recalled that in 1795, three years after English Baptists organized a missionary society and sent William Carey to India, the London Missionary Society was organized by Independents, Presbyterians, and adherents of the Church of England. Before the end of the century the Established

[51] Baker, *Relations between Northern and Southern Baptists*, 13. For a full list of missionary societies formed, see Albert L. Vail, *The Morning Hour of American Baptist Missions* (Philadelphia, 1907), 116-45.

Church had launched the Church Missionary Society. Protestants in this country borrowed methods of organization and evangelism from their English brethren. The Philadelphia Baptists, for example, received frequent reports concerning the missionary endeavor of Carey in India and were zealous in their efforts to collect money to aid the English Baptists.[52]

Dr. William Staughton, a prominent Baptist clergyman of Philadelphia, affords a good example of this intimate relation with England. He was an Englishman by birth and education. In 1792 he was present at Kettering on the occasion of the formation of the English Particular Baptist Missionary Society. He was impressed greatly by the missionary spirit manifested at that time. Three years later he came to America, first to South Carolina, then to New Jersey, and finally to Philadelphia where he became pastor of the First Baptist Church. There, among Baptists of a similar Calvinistic theology, he advocated the East India Missionary Enterprises, and wrote a book entitled *The Baptist Mission in India*, in order to raise money for the support of the British missionaries. He carried on an extensive correspondence with Baptists in England and those who were missionaries in India.[53]

Other associations also manifested a lively missionary interest in Carey's work at Serampore by observing special seasons of prayer and by making generous contributions to its support. Baptists from Charleston to Boston and in the outlying regions gave two thousand five hundred dollars to that Mission in 1806, and shared in contributing a total of over eighteen thousand dollars, not denominationally designated, during the years 1806-1814. When in 1810 the American Board of Commissioners for Foreign Missions was established by the Congregationalists, Baptists contributed, prior to the organization of their own national society in 1814, three thousand dollars to aid in sending Rice and the Judsons to India. In the twenty-year period prior to 1814, American Baptists gave through

[52] *Philadelphia Association Minutes: 1707-1807*, pp. 360, 412, 423, 430. These are but sample references to indicate the nature of affiliation between American and British Baptists. See also *The Columbian Star and Christian Index*, Vol. I, for reports of London Missionary Society in a column, "The Missionary Record." This year, 1829, is but a sample.

[53] S. W. Lynd, editor, *Memoir of the Rev. William Staughton, D.D.* (Boston, 1834), chaps. 1-6.

the channels mentioned between seven and eight thousand dollars for foreign missions.[54]

In 1813 two events converged to direct Baptist missionary spirit toward a national organization. News had arrived of the dilemma of Adoniram Judson, the American missionary sent out by the Congregational Board. On his ocean voyage to India, he had accepted the Baptist view of immersion, through his own study of the Bible, which Luther Rice also adopted a short time later. As a result of their decision, the two men had sent their resignations to the Board in the United States. Judson went to Burma, hoping to establish missionary work there under Baptist auspices, while Rice returned to America to seek aid for the fledgling American Baptist Missions in the Far East. Fortunately for them, the missionary enthusiasm of American Baptists was ripe for such a challenge.

In spite of the economically depressed condition of the country following the War of 1812 and the hazards of travel on the high seas, the Baptists did not hesitate in the great undertaking. Even before the arrival of Rice, Boston Baptists organized "The Baptist Society for the Propagation of the Gospel in India and Other Foreign Parts." Thus they were prepared to accept Rice and the Judsons as their responsibility when the former arrived in September, 1813. Backed by Dr. Thomas Baldwin of the Second Baptist Church in Boston and the Reverend Lucius Bolles, pastor in Salem, Rice toured the Middle and Southern States. As a result, the local interest needed to create a national Baptist missionary organization was generated in such centers as Philadelphia, Charleston, and Savannah. The great debt of Baptists to Rice for his determinative influence upon the denomination deserves more attention than it has received.[55] He was only thirty-one years of age at the time, but his zeal and untiring energies did for the Baptist foreign missionary enterprise at home what Judson did for it abroad.

In May, 1814, a convention was called by mutual agreement of Baptist Associations throughout the country to meet in Philadelphia to create a national missionary society. That city was chosen because

[54] Vail, *The Morning Hour of American Baptist Missions*, 241, 244, 250-1.

[55] For a recent study based on hitherto unused sources, see L. T. Gibson, *Luther Rice's Contribution to Baptist History*, an unpublished doctoral dissertation (Temple University School of Theology, Philadelphia, 1944) in the Eastern Baptist Theological Seminary's library, Philadelphia, Pa., 148-53.

it was centrally located. In addition, there is some indication that while the leading spirit in this plan for national organization was Boston, deference was paid to Philadelphia as the center of the oldest Baptist Association. Indeed, seventeen of the thirty-three delegates present were members of the Philadelphia Association. Several of these were active on committees, and six or seven were elected eventually to the Board of the new society, which was named "The General Missionary Convention of the Baptist Denomination in the United States for Foreign Missions." Soon it came to be known as the Triennial Convention, because its meetings were held every three years.

The constitution provided that not more than two delegates should be sent from each of the local and state mission societies and from other religious bodies of the denomination that contributed at least one hundred dollars a year to the missionary fund of the convention. Its managing board was to consist of twenty-one members, who were to be elected by the Convention; it was to be known as "The Baptist Board of Foreign Missions for the United States."[56] It is significant that the basis for representation was determined by voluntary support of the missionary enterprise, rather than by ecclesiastical connection between the churches and the Convention.

Dr. Richard Furman, the outstanding pulpit orator of the denomination and pastor of the First Baptist Church of Charleston, South Carolina, was elected president of the Convention. Dr. Baldwin of Boston was selected to be secretary. Thus did the South and North share in the administration of the new national body.

At the first meeting of the Board, on May 24, Baldwin was elected its president and Dr. Staughton of Philadelphia, its corresponding secretary. The next day, Luther Rice reported concerning his fund-raising efforts since his return from India. He was appointed as the first missionary of the Board, but was requested to continue temporarily his promotional work in the states, a task which prevented his return to the field in the years ahead. The Judsons were appointed also and authorized to begin such work in Burma as they judged best. Philadelphia was chosen as the headquarters for the Board. It was most fitting that at the birthplace of the

[56] For full details, see Vail, *op. cit.*, 393-400, and Edmund F. Merriam, *A History of American Baptist Missions* (Philadelphia, 1900), 14-7.

national government, Baptists should have attained an organic unity which at the same time protected the autonomy of the local churches. Yet, it was a continuance of the society method which was adopted, rather than the plan of denominational organization which had been advocated by the Philadelphia Association in 1770.

The reception of the new venture throughout the country was favorable. The following year, Rice reported that practically all of the one hundred and fifteen associations of the denomination supported the enterprise. At the second meeting of the Convention, in 1817, its constitution was amended so as to allow home as well as foreign mission work. John Mason Peck and James E. Welch were sent to Missouri as home mission workers.[57]

From 1820 to 1835 the Protestant missionary movement was characterized by the formation of national societies, a movement in general conformity to the nationalism of the times. Politically, the United States had purchased the Louisiana Territory in 1803 and had acquired Florida in 1819. The War of 1812 had suffused the nation with a flush of national pride. Henry Clay's American System, Calhoun's proposal that the Federal Government build roads and canals, John Marshall's decisions in favor of national authority, and the Monroe Doctrine gave additional evidence that men were living in an era of nationalism. This spirit was expressing itself also in religious circles. The American Education Society (1815), the American Bible Society (1816), the Sunday School Union (1824), the American Tract Society (1825), the American Society for Promoting Temperance (1826), the American Home Missionary Society (1826) and the American Peace Society (1828) were all of national scope and emphasis, and all represented interdenominational co-operation.

The various Protestant denominations also had been organizing along national lines; the Methodist Episcopal Church in 1784; the Protestant Episcopal Church in 1789; the Presbyterian General Assembly in the same year; the American Dutch Reformed Church created a General Synod in 1793; and so did the Lutheran Church in 1820. The first Roman Catholic Synod was formed by Bishop Carroll in 1791 in Baltimore. With such a national consciousness, it is not surprising that the Baptists should have constituted their

[57] Elsbree, *The Rise of the Missionary Spirit in America*, 105-18.

missionary work along similar lines. In fact, Baptists, in their long and strenuous struggle for religious liberty, had developed a national spirit, a national Baptist tradition, and even a national Baptist college in Rhode Island (organized in 1764).[58]

In 1820 the Baptists' Triennial Convention instructed John Mason Peck, its principal missionary, to cease his work among the white settlers of Missouri and move to an Indian post at Fort Wayne. He refused, and continued in Missouri independently. Four years later the Massachusetts Baptist Missionary Society commissioned him as its representative. This assignment he accepted, working in the West with their support until the American Baptist Home Mission Society was founded in 1832, when he became one of its foremost missionaries.

The unwillingness of the Triennial Convention to continue its direction of home missions is an indication of the tensions rising out of the two views of Baptist polity: the one, which might be called denominational connectionalism, which sought expression through a convention which would assume leadership in all phases of denominational life and activities, and the other, which has been termed the society method. The purpose of the latter alternative was, as we have seen, to prevent the development of a centralized polity which might endanger the autonomy of the local churches. That some desired to convert the Triennial Convention from a foreign mission agency or society into a convention responsible for guiding all denominational activities is evident from a study of developments between 1814, the year of its organization, and 1820. In that time, men like Luther Rice and President Francis Wayland of Brown University—men who saw strength in unity of action—encouraged the development of home missions and educational activities within the Triennial Convention. But it was the society method which triumphed in the Triennial Convention, a decision which undoubtedly was greatly influenced by New England Baptists who had long opposed centralization.[59] The triumph of the society over the convention motif was also due to the philosophy of individualism so strong

[58] Edward F. Humphrey, *Nationalism and Religion in America: 1774-1789* (Boston, 1924), 320.

[59] It is significant that President Wayland reversed his view before 1832. Thereafter he rejected the concept of a denominational organization based upon the churches in favor of the society method in which those were members who actually contributed to the work of the societies. See Baker, *op. cit.*, 15-17. See also chapter 10 on p. 266.

at the time, to the prevailing influence of revivalistic pietism, and to the mushrooming of voluntary societies as workable agencies in many areas of American social and religious life.

By this time Baptists were spreading rapidly into almost every state of the Union. This is obvious from a report made in 1836 by a deputation from the Baptist Union in England to the United States and Canada. Here the statement was made and confirmed by statistics that the deputation was "not aware that, excepting the Congregationalists in New England, any but the Baptists adhere to the divisions of the states, and no other denomination is diffused so generally throughout the Union.[60]

To summarize, it may be said that Baptist work in this formative period of organization and expansion was characterized by (1) a great missionary zeal; (2) a limited leadership, chiefly from such urban centers as Charleston, Philadelphia, New York, and Boston; (3) a strong appeal to the plain people of the agrarian areas through the zealous ministry of preachers and evangelists of limited training; (4) a missionary enthusiasm which led to local, state, and national organizations; (5) a dual interest in home and foreign missions; (6) a preference for denominational work, although they were not averse to interdenominational co-operation; (7) an increasing concern for education;[61] and (8) a vision of winning the West for Protestantism.

Through the combination of these factors, Baptists achieved an unprecedented growth. By 1844 the total membership was 720,046 with 9,385 churches and 6,364 ministers. This represented an increase of 360 per cent in thirty years, whereas the population of the United States had increased only 140 per cent in that period of time.[62]

[60] F. A. Cox and J. D. Hoby, *The Baptists in America* (New York, 1836), 471.

[61] See chap. 11.

[62] A. H. Newman, *A History of the Baptist Churches in the United States,* (revised edition, 1898), 442.

CHAPTER NINE

SMALLER BAPTIST BODIES

T HE majority of Baptists in the early nineteenth century shared a common tradition; they were Anglo-Saxon, Calvinistic, and united in a Triennial Convention which had been organized to support a new world mission outreach in Burma. Like other Protestants they had been influenced by the Great Awakening, and more than some they had grown in numbers and evangelistic zeal under its spell. Yet the very emphasis upon personal religious experience which characterized the revival enthusiasm led, as we have seen, to a division of Baptists into Old Lights and New Lights, or Regulars and Separates. The distinction rested largely upon a difference of opinion concerning the validity of an evangelistic appeal to the individual.

Since the main leaders of the Awakening, with the exception of Wesley, were Calvinists, the success of that movement gave an evangelistic zeal to many who adhered to Reformed doctrine. At the same time, the publication of a Calvinistic Confession of Faith by the Philadelphia Baptist Association in 1742 and by the Charleston Association in 1767 gave to Regular Baptists a theological tradition which was in accord with the best thought of Edwards and Whitefield. As the influence of these associations developed, their point of view provided guidance to the growing number of churches which were the product of the revivals. We have observed how the Separate Baptists united with Regular Baptists, and how the General Baptists, as in North Carolina, were transformed into Particular Baptists, until by 1800, Calvinism was the prevalent theology among them.

Yet, in spite of the general crystallization of Baptist thought, there were minority groups who deviated from the traditional pattern in one or more particulars. Those who held Arminian or hyper-Calvinistic doctrines represented a departure from the theological norm. Other variations were in the category of polity or mores. Some observed the seventh day for worship instead of the first day

254

of the week, or administered the local church by a plurality of elders instead of a single pastor, or followed a church government which was strongly centralized under a Conference. Those whose background was German or Dutch brought with them to the New World the European traits of extreme pietism practiced particularly by the Mennonite sects.

While these were but minorities as contrasted with the main body of Baptists, their existence was dramatic evidence of influences playing upon Baptists to alter their understanding of the church. The repeated waves of revival which had produced rapid growth and expansion of Baptists in this early formative period of American history were also a disruptive influence upon older church patterns. The strict Calvinism of Baptists was being weakened by the evangelical trend which stressed a personal response of the individual leading to a conversion experience. This individualism of the revivals weakened the early connectionalism which had bound Baptists together in associations during the seventeenth and eighteenth centuries. The idea of the universal church and of the interdependence of congregations began to drop out of common use in favor of a local church view. This was evident to some extent in the position of Isaac Backus of Massachusetts, and to a greater extent in that of John Leland of Virginia. They typified the Separate or revivalistic Baptists' stress upon the religion of the heart and the immediacy of the Holy Spirit in personal experience and in the life of the local congregation. The emphasis upon personal experience led to a disregard for theological understanding. As a result some Baptists lost sight of the importance of their confession of faith with its stress upon the community of faith which sustains equally both the individual believer and the local congregation.

With the abandonment of a connectional view of the church, these Baptists not only denied that local churches can be represented in a larger body, but they accepted their viewpoint as traditional. This, of course, was a distortion of the Philadelphia Baptist tradition, yet it was reinforced by exaggerated emphasis of the Jacksonian era in American politics upon local and state rights. Thus, many Baptists were in danger of a similarly exaggerated individualism at a time of rapid expansion because they were either disregarding or rejecting the restraining influence of authoritative confessions and statements of church order which their forebears had relied upon to maintain a balance between freedom and authority.[1]

In this chapter we shall identify the smaller Baptist bodies, gathering them for convenience under the categories of Arminian, extremely Calvinistic, and miscellaneous. Their story should be seen against the fact that they constituted minorities in contrast to that main body of Baptists who achieved an appreciable degree of unity and a continuing denominational growth. The next chapter will be devoted to a consideration of issues which produced dissension and strife among the main body of Baptists in the troubled era of American history which culminated in civil war in 1861. These issues are illustrations of the way in which a rapidly growing denomination was affected by social, economic, and other environmental influences.

Early Arminian Baptist Bodies

Arminian Baptists were among the earliest in America, although later they were replaced in prominence by the Calvinists. The first to appear were the General Six-Principle Baptists, who were organized in Rhode Island in 1670. Like their counterparts in England, they based their confession of faith upon Hebrews 6:1-2, from which they drew the teachings of repentance from dead works, faith toward God, baptism, the laying on of hands, the resurrection of the dead, and eternal judgment. At the beginning of the twentieth century, they had less than one thousand members in three states, Pennsylvania, Rhode Island, and Massachusetts. Since that time their number has decreased to less than three hundred.[2] It appears that they represent the slow extinction of a point of view which was never widely held.

A second group was organized in 1729 in Virginia and North Carolina. They called themselves the Original Freewill Baptists, thereby identifying themselves with Helwys' congregation of seventeenth-century England. Their peculiar emphases were foot washing, anointing the sick with oil, plural eldership, and the regulation that only male members could hold church office. They had a conference

---

[1] For amplification, see Winthrop S. Hudson, "Stumbling into Disorder," and Robert G. Torbet, "Baptist Thought About the Church," *Foundations,* Vol. 1, No. 2 (April, 1958).

[2] The sources of statistics in this chapter are H. K. Carroll, *The Religious Forces of the United States,* (revised for 1910) and E. E. Irvine, ed., *The World Almanac and Book of Facts for 1946.*

type of organization, which had authority to "silence" preachers and to settle difficulties between churches. Although limited in resources, they maintained their identity fairly well, for in 1890 the Conference was composed of one hundred and sixty-seven churches with nearly twelve thousand members. Their property valuation was not over fifty-seven thousand dollars. By the close of the century, they were to be found only in North and South Carolina. In 1940, they numbered about one hundred and eighteen thousand. While others have sometimes adopted their name, they represent the earliest effort to trace American Baptist lineage to seventeenth-century England.

The Separate Baptists or New Lights have been mentioned several times. They arose, it will be recalled, out of the revivals of the Great Awakening in New England, but were absorbed after a period of remarkable activity and growth by the Regular Baptists. Few maintained a distinct existence. By 1910 there were in Indiana twenty-four churches with a combined property value of but little more than nine thousand dollars. In 1945 there were still approximately sixty-five hundred on their membership rolls in Indiana, Kentucky, Tennessee, Maryland, and Illinois.

By far the most prominent group were the Freewill Baptists, who arose in New England in 1780 and spread throughout the country, finally uniting with the Northern Baptist Convention in 1911. Their founder and first leader was Benjamin Randall, son of a ship captain of New Castle, New Hampshire. After a few years as a youth at sea, he became a tailor, by which means he earned his livelihood even after his ordination.

His conversion was prompted by the shock which he suffered on hearing the news of the death of George Whitefield on September 30, 1770. At the time, Randall was in Portsmouth, New Hampshire, under great conviction because of the indifference which had caused him to fail to attend the great man's meetings. Soon afterward, he yielded to the call of Christ and in the winter of 1771 united with the Congregational Church in New Castle. He soon became distressed, however, by the laxity of life which he noted on the part of most of its members. Gathering a few of the more devout together, he held, with the permission of the pastor, cottage meetings for prayer and fellowship. Later, his continued dissatisfaction caused him to withdraw from membership in the church.

It was following his service in the Continental Army (1775-1776) that he became convinced by a study of the New Testament of the validity of believer's baptism. On October 14, 1776, he and three friends were baptized by a Baptist minister, William Hooper, at Berwick, Maine, where he united with the Baptist church. Almost at once he began to preach with marked results. While on a tour of eastern New Hampshire in 1777, he was called to the pastorate of the Congregational church at New Durham. This he accepted on the condition that he be set free to carry on his evangelistic tours and that he not be paid out of the town treasury.

Supporting himself by his trade and his farm, he found time to travel extensively through New Hampshire, Vermont, and Maine. In 1779 he found himself under the critical scrutiny of many Baptists in New Hampshire and Maine, where an extreme Calvinism prevailed, although his views did not differ greatly from those of the General Baptists of England or of many in Rhode Island and Connecticut. The intolerance of his critics wounded him deeply and caused him severe soul-searching. In March he removed his membership from Berwick, Maine, and united with the newly organized Arminian Crown Point Church in Strafford, New Hampshire. He was ordained in April at New Durham by two Arminian Baptist churches. On June 30, he organized at New Durham a Free Baptist church. Sometime in July, 1780, while meditating in a cornfield on his views which were causing such criticism, he enjoyed a mystical experience which resolved his troubled thoughts into harmony within the framework of what he called "the universal love of God to men, the universal atonement in the work of redemption by Jesus Christ . . . the universal appearance of Grace to all men, and . . . the universal call of the Gospel."[3]

With New Durham as a center, he set forth upon a series of evangelistic tours between 1781 and 1792, which resulted in the planting of approximately fifteen additional churches. Randall was an able organizer, wisely gathering the Free Baptist churches into Quarterly Meetings and a Yearly Meeting, the latter having been organized in 1792 to exercise "a general supervision over the whole denomination." In October, 1827, the General Conference of Free-

---

[3] C. Raymond Chappell, "Benjamin Randall—'Frail but Unafraid,'" *The Chronicle,* Vol. IV, No. 3 (July, 1941), 104.

will Baptists, composed of delegates from the Yearly Meetings, was established with authority to discipline Yearly Meetings and Associations, but not empowered to reverse or change the decisions of the churches, Quarterly, or Yearly Meetings. This represented a compromise between the traditional Baptist associational relationship to the churches, which was purely advisory, and the presbyterial concept of legislative authority. Actually, the General Conference had moral authority over its members without ruling them.[4] The Quarterly and Yearly Meetings were attended by thousands of people and became occasions for evangelism. "There was a deep soul hunger among the great middle class of New England, and the Free Baptists, as no other body of Christians at that time, made an appeal to them."[5]

When Randall succumbed to pulmonary disease in 1808, broken in health by the strain and exposure of his long journeys, there were 130 churches with a combined membership of about six thousand and a leadership of 110 ministers. The denomination had gained a foothold in Maine, New Hampshire, and Vermont, with scattered beginnings of congregations in New York, Ohio, and Canada.[6] To the credit of Randall, it must be said that his revolt against the rigid theological formulas held by the Calvinistic Baptists, although ahead of his times, provided a corrective which has influenced Baptists favorably by causing them to combine with their traditional point of view a warm evangelism. His principles of free grace, free salvation, free will, and free communion have become increasingly acceptable to numerous Baptists, particularly in the Northern States.

Upon Randall's death a period of twenty years ensued in which confusion reigned. Some leaders sought to unite the Freewill Baptists with the Christian denomination or Disciples. However, John Buzzell of Maine, who had been converted under Randall's preaching, and John Colby of New Hampshire stemmed the tide. Colby planted churches in New York, Pennsylvania, Indiana, and Ohio. He organized the first Freewill Baptist church in Rhode Island. In 1827 the General Conference, in one of its first sessions, decided to ordain Negroes to the ministry, a significant forecast of the strong position which it was to take against slavery in later years. In time

---

[4] *Ibid.*, 105-6; J. M. Brewster *et al*, *The Centennial Record of Freewill Baptists: 1780-1880* (Dover, N. H., 1881), 61-2.

[5] Chappell, *op cit.*, 107.

[6] Brewster, *op. cit.*, 16.

a further indication of its liberality became clear, for it ordained women ministers without opposition. Religious periodicals were established in Maine and New Hampshire.

The period from 1830 to 1845 was one of rapid growth. At its close there were sixty thousand members and the denomination had spread as far west as Illinois. Revivals, which had continued quite steadily from 1790, culminated about the time that the Millerite movement was drawing to its unhappy close. This movement, to be described more fully in the next chapter, was the product of the preaching of William Miller, a Baptist minister of Low Hampton, New York. His predictions of the imminent return of the Lord and the consummation of the world drew a large following from various denominations in New England, New York, and Pennsylvania. Its failure contributed to the decline of the revivals because of the distaste for religion which followed as a result of his dogmatic teachings.

Yet in spite of Miller's failure, a core of the group remained intact and grew. Its members were immersionists; they ordained their ministers by the laying on of hands, and practiced a congregational polity, except in the Seventh Day branch, which had a presbyterial character. At the opening of the twentieth century, there were six different bodies of Adventists, totaling well over sixty thousand members in more than seventeen hundred churches. Their property valuation was over one and a quarter million dollars. They are spread at the present time throughout forty-five states of the Union.

The years from 1845 to the War between the States represented an uneasy time of transition for the Freewill Baptists. Some of the more reactionary leaders sought to block a general interest in developing an educated ministry. They were opposed also to Sunday schools, and to temperance and missionary societies. A schism occurred in 1845, which removed nearly eight thousand from the membership rolls, leaving the majority free to further plans for establishing schools in New England, New York, and Michigan. The home mission enterprise begun in 1834 was continued in the rural areas. By 1870 the loss of membership suffered as a result of the split was recovered through gains made during the revivals of 1857-1858 and the steady progress that followed the war. Foreign missionaries were being sent to India, and a service was rendered to

Freedmen at Storer College, which was established by the Home Mission Society at Harper's Ferry. By 1880 there were more than seventy-seven thousand members in over one thousand four hundred churches with an equal number of ministers.[7]

In 1910 the Freewill Baptists had fifty-one associations which were composed of 1,586 churches, having a property value of more than three million dollars. Its approximately ninety thousand members were scattered through thirty-three states, with the greatest strength in New England, especially in Maine. The merger in 1911 with the Northern Baptist Convention, the leading body of Baptists in the North, indicated the increasing tolerance of the Freewill emphasis on the part of Baptists of the Calvinistic tradition.

Still in existence are remnants of the United Baptists, the product of the union of Separate and Regular Baptists in Virginia and Kentucky. While most of them relinquished the name in later years, some twenty-seven thousand in twelve associations scattered throughout Kentucky, Tennessee, Alabama, Arkansas, and Missouri still maintain a separate existence. They regularly observe the practice of foot-washing in their churches.

Similarly, a remnant of General Baptists has staunchly kept its identity in the tradition of the earliest Baptists of England; their brethren, meanwhile, either became Regular Baptists or Freewill Baptists. In 1870 these General Baptists formed a General Association in which all of their associations were represented. Increase in membership was steady, from eight thousand in 1870 to over twelve thousand in 1880. Since 1890 the number has swelled to more than twenty-one thousand, scattered throughout Illinois, Kentucky, Tennessee, Missouri, Arkansas, and Nebraska. Their three hundred and ninety-nine churches were united in twenty-two associations, and their property valuation was over two hundred and one thousand dollars. In 1945 they were more than maintaining their strength with thirty-nine thousand six hundred adherents.

Hyper-Calvinistic Baptist Bodies

In general the hyper-Calvinists among Baptists were opposed to missionary societies, Bible societies, temperance societies, Sunday schools—all of which they regarded as man-made efforts to

[7] *Ibid.*, 39-44.

evangelize, and as unscriptural and contrary to their extreme emphasis upon predestination. Because conversion, from their point of view, was entirely an act of God, emotionalism was to be avoided. While they usually demanded a fairly well trained ministry, they often opposed a paid ministry. It is quite possible that their biblicism was not alone in influencing their thinking. Being a frontier people, they undoubtedly shared the quite general suspicion of the East, which so many regarded as controlling the finances of the nation.

The earliest of such groups seems to have been the Baptist Church of Christ, which was organized in 1808 in Tennessee, but which has become extinct. A more interesting example of the hyper-Calvinists may be found in the old Two-Seed-in-the-Spirit Predestinarian Baptists. This strange group was organized by Elder Daniel Parker of Virginia in the 1820's. Parker had been ordained in Tennessee in 1806, and labored there until 1817. Thereafter, he ministered in Illinois until 1836, where he edited a periodical known as the *Church Advocate*. The latter years of his ministry were spent in Texas. While in Illinois, he had published in 1826 and 1829 two pamphlets setting forth his peculiar theory of the two seeds in Eve, imparted by God and Satan respectively. This was his explanation of the doctrine that some are predetermined to be saved and some to be lost. According to his teaching, Christ can reach sinners without the aid of ministers or organizations of any kind. He and his followers, however, believed in a ministry invested with "legal authority" through the laying on of hands by the presbytery acting for a gospel church. Many were opposed, nevertheless, to a paid clergy. Like Arminian Baptists, they followed the practice of footwashing, regarding it as an ordinance. While their number was not larger than thirteen thousand members at the close of the nineteenth century, they were to be found in twenty-four states, though most numerous in Arkansas, Kentucky, Mississippi, Tennessee, and Texas. Their four hundred and seventy-three churches, with a property value of more than one hundred and seventy-two thousand dollars, were organized in fifty associations. The decline of extreme forms of Calvinism among Baptists is nowhere more clearly apparent than in the diminishing membership of this group which numbered a mere two hundred in 1945.

The Primitive, Old School, or Anti-mission Baptists trace their origin back to 1835 when the Chemung Association, which covered territory on both sides in the New York-Pennsylvania boundary, urged a disunion with those associations which had begun missionary societies on a monied basis. In 1836 the Baltimore Association in Maryland agreed with them that such organizations had no precedent in the New Testament church. While they were hyper-Calvinists, they did not share the extreme views of the Two-Seed-in-the-Spirit-Predestinarian Baptists. For example, they were careful not to attribute to God responsibility for evil, thereby nullifying human accountability. Moreover, they were not opposed to evangelistic preaching of a sort, so long as organized efforts such as Bible societies, Sunday schools, state conventions, or theological seminaries were banned. They also regarded foot-washing as an ordinance. Their growth at first was rapid; they increased from over sixteen hundred churches with sixty-one thousand members in 184 associations in 1844 to well over one hundred twenty-one thousand members in nearly three thousand churches with a property value of more than a million and a half dollars in 1890. At the opening of the twentieth century, Primitive Baptists were scattered in twenty-eight states and Washington, D. C. They were strongest in Alabama, Georgia, North Carolina, Kentucky, and Tennessee; in the North, they had little strength except in Illinois and Indiana. Today their number, decreased by nearly half, is about sixty-nine thousand.

It is noteworthy that the extreme Calvinistic Baptist sects mentioned have been strongest in the Southern States. This phenomena may be explained on the basis of the strong Scotch-Irish and Presbyterian influx into the South during the latter part of the eighteenth century. The natural conservatism of the southern people may also explain the continuance of these groups. This same reluctance to change may account for the maintenance by hyper-Calvinists of anti-organizational and anti-missionary attitudes in the face of the strongly organized and missionary-minded Southern Baptist Convention. In the North, Baptists have become increasingly less Calvinistic.

Miscellaneous Bodies

Of those Baptists who do not fall into either of the previously mentioned classifications, the earliest to be organized were the Seventh Day Baptists. In 1671 an English Sabbatarian Baptist named Stephen Mumford organized a church in Newport, Rhode Island. A German Seventh Day Baptist church was formed in Germantown, Pennsylvania, in 1728. Early in the nineteenth century there were enough churches to organize a General Conference which met triennially down to 1846; since then, annually. In 1842 a Missionary Society, a Tract Society, and a Publishing House were established. There have been two colleges under their auspices, one at Milton, Wisconsin, and the other at Alfred Center, New York. They differ from other Baptists only with respect to their observance of the seventh day as the Sabbath. At the end of the century, they had a membership of over nine thousand in 106 churches with property valued at approximately two hundred sixty-five thousand dollars. By 1945 their numbers had diminished to 6,581.

Several small groups of immersionists, which were of German origin and actually Mennonite associations, may be mentioned briefly lest they be confused with regular German Baptists. Among these were the Conservative Dunkers, long known as German Baptist Brethren and later as the Church of the Brethren. They arrived in Germantown, Pennsylvania, in 1719. Their origin in 1708 in Germany had been in some respects parallel to the founding of the English Baptists a century earlier. Both had sought to restore a pure church by restricting baptism to believers. But the German Baptist Brethren followed the Mennonite tradition of strict pietism, being conservative in attire, opposed to oath-taking, and in being pacifists. They were called Dunkers because they practiced trine immersion. In every way possible they sought to retain their German language and customs even to the extent of opposing public schools which would have provided their children a relatively free education. Fearful lest learning rob their ministry of spirituality, they were hostile to theological institutions. They also opposed a paid ministry. Along with Quakers, they raised their voices very early against slavery, and shared with them their opposition to the use of force during periods of war.[8] During the nineteenth century, divisions occurred as the result of tensions between the conservative and progressive elements.

In 1751 a small group of Christians settled in Lancaster County,

[8] Robert G. Torbet, *A Social History of the Philadelphia Baptist Association: 1707-1940*, 49, 92-3.

Pennsylvania. They became known as River Brethren and likely were also of Mennonite origin. About 1820 they effected an organization under the name Brethren in Christ. They have comprised a small sect which is marked by its pacifism and strict nonconformity to the practices of the world. Trine immersion and foot-washing have been observed consistently in their churches. They, too, have been divided into smaller groups during the years.

A third group which might be identified to some extent with Baptist practice arose in the early nineteenth century under the leadership of a German Reformed communicant of Philadelphia, who led a revival in 1817 which extended into the rural areas of Pennsylvania and Maryland. His converts organized their own Conference in 1831 and sent out itinerant preachers. They came to be known as Winebrennerians, although they preferred to be called the Church of God. It was their conviction that believers in any one community should truly constitute one body, the Church of God, undivided by creedal distinctions. For that reason they refrained from using confessions of faith. While they were noncreedal in their outlook in this respect, they were Baptist in their insistence upon immersion. Foot-washing they also observed as an ordinance. While their numerical strength has been chiefly in Pennsylvania, Ohio, and Indiana, they have spread also to several other states. Between 1900 and 1910 they reported 479 churches with 22,500 members. Listed in 1952 as The Church of God in North America (General Eldership), its membership totaled more than 35,000. The group maintains a publishing house in Harrisburg, Pennsylvania, and a college in Findlay, Ohio.

CHAPTER TEN

DISSENSION AND STRIFE

THE period of organization and initial growth revealed among the Baptists those problems that naturally arise in a young denomination. There were new leaders who did not always "fit in" well. Baptist unity was disrupted frequently by sensitive reactions to changes in the social scene, as was evident in the anti-Masonry and slavery issues. It was, more or less, a testing time for Baptists. The stability of the majority underwent a severe probationary period out of which was revealed both the strength and the weakness of a decentralized polity.

The chief sources of controversy were theology and missionary interest. It will be recalled that the theological differences between General and Particular Baptists with reference to Arminianism and Calvinism respectively had their antecedents among European Baptists almost from the beginning of the latter's history. We have seen how Arminianism was predominant among New England Baptists even after the First Baptist Church of Providence had accepted a Calvinistic confession of faith. Yet, the influence of the Particular Baptists of the Philadelphia Association was felt there as well as in the South. The commitment of the Charleston Association to Calvinism prepared the way for southern Arminianism to yield to the reformed doctrine, though in a moderate form, following the White-field revival.[1] Certainly in Virginia, the Philadelphia Confession was a dominant influence.

It has been observed also that differences over methods of evangelism were occasioned by the Great Awakening, which resulted in the distinction being made between the emotional and somewhat mystical Separate or New Light Baptists and the more moderate and conservative Regular Baptists. To the former has been ascribed the chief credit for the phenomenal growth of Baptists in the South and

[1] B. F. Riley, *Baptists in the Southern States East of the Mississippi* (Philadelphia, 1898), 166.

West, where their informal and heart-warming methods had a strong appeal to those upon the frontier. In Virginia, however, where the division had been sharply marked, a union of both groups occurred in 1787. In Kentucky a similar result took place following a period of revivals.

In the later years of the eighteenth century, two forms of heresy began to plague Baptists in some areas. One of these was Unitarianism, which presented a threat to New England Baptists in particular. At a time when Congregationalists and Episcopalians were feeling its strong impact after the influence of the Edwards-Whitefield revival had declined, Baptists stood firmly against this teaching which threatened the doctrine of the deity of Christ. A high tribute is paid to their stability by one historian who says that "in 1800, two out of six orthodox churches left in Boston were Baptist, while eight Congregational churches and one Episcopal church had gone over bodily to Unitarianism." [2]

An interesting incident of the outcropping of the heresy outside of New England occurred in Kentucky where James Garrard, a Baptist prominent in political life, and his pastor became involved. Garrard was a Virginian who had moved to Kentucky and joined the Cowpers Run Baptist Church. In time he became active in the politics of his state; he assisted in the forming of Kentucky's constitution and served two terms as its governor. During his occupancy of office he appointed as his Secretary of State a scholarly Englishman by the name of Harry Toulmin, who was a Unitarian preacher. Before the close of the governor's second term, he had been converted to Unitarianism. Indeed, his pastor, Mr. Eastin, also became enamored of Unitarian doctrine. Accordingly, the Elkhorn Association, to which the Cowpers Run church belonged, in 1803 found it necessary to exclude the church from membership. [3]

That Baptists did not succumb to Unitarianism was probably due to their emphasis upon believer's baptism and the literal fulfillment of Scriptural teaching. This emphasis kept them close to the power of the Holy Spirit working through a regenerate church membership. It was due also to the moderately Calvinistic theology adhered to by most of their associations—a theology which provided

[2] Henry C. Vedder, *A Short History of Baptists*, 335.
[3] J. H. Spencer, *A History of Kentucky Baptists from 1769 to 1885*, 133-4.

a steadying influence. Then, too, most Baptists were of the common people who had enjoyed but little of the formal training of those to whom Unitarianism made its strongest appeal.

Another heresy which troubled Baptists about this time was Universalism or Universal Restoration, a teaching that all the wicked would go to hell, there to suffer the penalty for the sins committed in the flesh, but that ultimately they would be redeemed from their torments and received into heaven. It appeared as early as 1781 in Philadelphia where Elhanan Winchester, a prominent Baptist minister, became a Universalist, and organized there a society which was given the name "Universal Baptists." In New Jersey several Baptist ministers and their congregations accepted his teaching. Indeed, the influence of Universalism extended into New England, for in 1803 the issue confronted the New Hampshire Association and the York Association in Maine. As late as 1826 the church at Lewiston, Maine, was obliged to dismiss a Universalist minister who had pretended to be a Baptist in order to secure a call to the pastorate. The young churches in Kentucky were annoyed by the doctrine from about 1790 until 1800. There the two most intellectual and eloquent preachers among the Separates, John Bailey and William Bledsoe, were its main exponents, for which they were excluded from the Baptist ministry.[4] It was the general watchfulness which the associations maintained over the doctrine of the local churches that saved Baptists from more serious inroads of this heresy.

The Anti-Mission Controversy

The first controversy which actually split the ranks of the Baptists, particularly in the South and West, occurred during the first quarter of the nineteenth century. It arose over the missionary venture of the denomination. Actually, it was due partly to theological differences and partly to the development of the organizations which had been brought into existence to carry on the work. The anti-mission forces in the churches (the "anti-effort" forces, as they were called) were opposed to centralization of authority, to an educated and paid ministry, and to such man-made organizations as Sunday schools, missionary societies, and theological seminaries. The hyper-

---

[4] Henry S. Burrage, *A History of Baptists in Maine*, 134; J. Millett, *A History of Baptists in Maine*, 77, 127; Spencer, *op. cit.*, 452-3, 483-4.

Calvinism, which so often characterized the theological frame of mind of this group, was frequently used to bolster and justify their other arguments against exerting any effort to evangelize the lost.

In addition to these general contributing factors, there were in all probability certain specific causes for hostility to missions, especially in the West.[5] The universal hostility to the Indians along the frontier, where white settlers at times had been subjected to cruel treatment at their hands, intensified any antimissionary spirit that might have arisen from theological reasoning. This was particularly true on the part of many Christians who were unfriendly to the work of Isaac McCoy among the Indians of the Wabash Valley in Indiana. Then again, many western Baptists feared that those of the East might get financial and political control of their church polity by administering the missionary funds. Many accused Luther Rice (falsely, to be sure) of financial peculation when some of his too visionary projects failed. The chief argument presented by such leaders as John Taylor of Kentucky and Daniel Parker of Illinois against missionary organizations was that the cities benefited from funds collected and sent East. They frequently charged that the money was consumed by overhead expenses. Alexander Campbell, the prominent anti-mission spokesman along the Ohio Valley, expressed the fear that missionary societies, which he regarded as unscriptural, would dominate the churches, thus impairing local autonomy. Many western ministers, who were themselves without education, manifested a somewhat jealous attitude toward the better trained clergy of the East who from time to time were sent into the outlying regions by the home mission agencies. Indeed, they were genuinely suspicious of any of their own young men who attached much importance to formal learning. Undoubtedly, the apathetic attitude and low state of vitality in many churches abetted the opposition to the missionary enthusiasm of the Triennial Convention.

There were at least four prominent leaders of the movement, one of whom was Daniel Parker, the responsible leader of the Two-Seed-in-the-Spirit Predestinarian Baptists. Always stern and dogmatic, Parker taught constantly through the *Church Advocate*, his periodical in Illinois, that missionary organizations were human

[5] John F. Cady, *The Origin and Development of the Missionary Baptist Church in Indiana* (Berne, Indiana, 1942), 36-46.

agencies for which there was no scriptural justification and which, therefore, should be mistrusted. In Kentucky there were two leaders, Wilson Thompson and John Taylor. Thompson, when a young man, had heard the call to missionary service without yielding to it. As if to rationalize his decision, he spent his ministry in Indiana, Ohio, and Kentucky in the anti-mission movement. Taylor had moved from Virginia to Kentucky early in the nineteenth century. He was always a highly respected and an earnest man. His two general charges against missions were that such societies were interested in getting money, and that the entire missionary scheme was unbaptistic because it threatened Baptist democracy.

The fourth and most renowned was Alexander Campbell, of Scotch Presbyterian background.[6] He was the son of Thomas Campbell, pastor of a Seceder Presbyterian Church in Ireland until he moved to America for reasons of health about 1807. Here he became pastor of a Seceder church in Washington County, Pennsylvania, but eventually withdrew from the Anti-Burgher Synod, to which it belonged, and established in 1809 "The Christian Association of Washington," because he desired a more ecumenical church union upon the basis of the Bible rather than creeds, which he felt were divisive. In the midst of these events, his son Alexander arrived from a year of study at the University of Glasgow where he had come in contact with the Haldanes' evangelistic efforts. He found himself in complete accord with his father. To prevent their new Association becoming just another sect in opposition to sectarianism, they sought union with the Presbyterian Synod of Pittsburgh in October, 1810, but were refused on the ground that their principles would be destructive to the peace of the church. Thereupon the Christian Association organized a regular church in May, 1811, at Brush Run. Thomas Campbell was appointed elder; Alexander was licensed to preach, and four deacons were chosen.

On January 1, 1812, Alexander Campbell was ordained to the ministry by the laying on of hands, a ceremony which he regarded merely as a public testimony that he possessed the necessary authority to preach the gospel and administer the ordinances. When his first

[6] An excellent account of Campbell and his movement may be found in Errett Gates, *The Early Relation and Separation of Baptists and Disciples* (Chicago, 1904); see also Winfred E. Garrison and Alfred T. De Groot, *The Disciples of Christ: A History* (St. Louis, 1948).

child was born, he was obliged to face the question of baptism. Becoming convinced of the scriptural validity of believer's baptism, he, his wife who was a Presbyterian, and his father with his family, seven in all, were immersed by a Baptist preacher near Washington. Soon most of the members of the Brush Run church were immersed; the others withdrew. That this congregation became Baptist is of special interest, for the Campbells had felt an antipathy to the Baptists as a comparatively uneducated people. In time, however, they came to appreciate the laymen in particular, although they did not change essentially their view that the ministers were small men for their task.[7]

In the fall of 1813 the Brush Run church applied for membership in the Redstone Baptist Association of Pennsylvania. Campbell's independence and unwillingness to subscribe to the Philadelphia Confession which had been adopted by the Association, and his hostility to the ministers prompted much debate and a protest from a minority of ministers. However, the church rather than individuals was being received, and the differences of view on some other matters did not become apparent at that time. In spite of the objections which had been raised by Campbell's critics, the church was received into fellowship.

At this period the main disparities between Campbell's views and those held by Baptists had to do basically with the meaning of the ordinances. He taught that baptism was "the first formal and comprehensive act of obedience of faith"; therefore nothing more than a confession of faith in Jesus Christ at the time of baptism was necessary. Baptists required an examination of the candidate's experience of regeneration before baptism. The Brush Run church, in the interest of conforming to the practice of the early church, celebrated the Lord's Supper each Sunday, whereas Baptist churches observed it monthly or quarterly. Campbell's view that Christians were not under the old covenant of law in any sense, but under the new covenant of grace was not acceptable to Calvinists. The chief point of conflict was his doctrine of faith in its relation to regeneration; in 1812 Alexander Campbell denied that a man must be regenerated prior to the first act of faith "for if regeneration be the communication of spiritual and eternal life, and if this be previous

[7] *Millennial Harbinger* (1848), 344; *Memoirs*, I, 438; cited in Gates, *op. cit.*, 19.

to faith, then a man may live and die and enjoy eternal life without faith." [8]

Early in the 1820's, he began to debate the subject of baptism with Presbyterian ministers who were critical of the Baptist view. However, instead of his defending the traditional Baptist doctrine of baptism as an ordinance bearing witness to an experience of spiritual regeneration previously received, it became increasingly apparent to many Baptist ministers in particular, that he was developing the teaching of baptismal regeneration. His chief debate was held in October, 1823, at Washington, Kentucky, before which time he had transferred his membership from the Redstone Association in Pennsylvania to the Mahoning Association in the Western Reserve, where his friends were numerous and his influence greatest. In his debate with Maccalla, a Presbyterian minister of Kentucky, he said, "The water of baptism, then, formally washes away our sins. The blood of Christ really washes away our sins. Paul's sins were really pardoned when he believed. Yet he had no solemn pledge of the fact, no formal acquittal, no formal purgation of his sins until he washed them away in the water of baptism." [9]

Impressed by the power of the press to publicize his debates on baptism, he undertook in August, 1823, publication of the *Christian Baptist*, a periodical which became the voice of his reform efforts. It seems clear that he was using the name "Baptist" in the title of his paper as an expedient, for they, more than any other group, tolerated his views. The primary word was "Christian," by which he intended to indicate the reform purpose which he had for all churches, including Baptists. In his paper, he exposed what he called "the pride, worldliness and paganism" of the churches. He caricatured in successive numbers missionary societies, ordination of the clergy, ministerial calls, the pew rent system, salaried clergy, Bible societies, and church associations. He enjoyed being called "the Reformer," for he was convinced that a complete return to New Testament Christianity with a minimum of organization and a maximum of the working of the Holy Spirit was needed. His iconoclasm left little in organized Christianity unscathed. The clergy he called "hireling

---

[8] *Memoirs*, I, 416; cited in Gates, *The Early Relation and Separation of Baptists and Disciples*, 24.

[9] *Debate with Maccalla*, 144; cited in Gates, *op. cit.*, 36.

priests;" seminaries he termed "priest factories;" church associations he accused of being tyrannous over the churches. He opposed human creeds as tests of membership. In 1829 he terminated the *Christian Baptist,* replacing it by the *Millennial Harbinger,* which was devoted to the same theme.

As he toured the western states, his influence grew. In Kentucky where he swayed Baptists more than in any other state,[10] ministers were divided as to the soundness of his doctrine. Some, like Silas Noel, William Vaughan, George and Edmund Waller, and John Taylor, opposed him from the first. Others, like Jeremiah Vardeman hesitated in uncertainty, but Jacob Creath resolutely espoused him as a reformer. The effect of Campbell's teaching was to reduce still more the pittance which ministers received from their churches for their support. Efforts to establish educational institutions were discouraged; Baptist missionary societies were dwarfed. Several associations were disbanded and reorganized as yearly meetings for counsel and fellowship. An increasing number of "Reformed Baptist churches" either withdrew from their respective associations or were excluded from fellowship.

Between 1825 and 1830 the greatest defection occurred from Baptist churches to the ranks of the Reformers, largely because the "reform" preachers were being received in many Baptist churches without any suspicion of their menace to Baptist usages. But after 1830, they were better known and more generally avoided by Baptists. Campbell's teaching nevertheless permeated Kentucky, western Pennsylvania, Ohio, Tennessee, and Virginia. Even in Indiana, Illinois, and Missouri, some churches adopted his views. Entire associations came under the influence of his teachings, the first of which was the Mahoning of Ohio, which dissolved in 1830, the Baptists having lost it. In Kentucky the three largest associations were controlled by the Reformers, largely through the influence of the preaching of John Smith. In varying degrees all the denominations contributed to the swelling of the ranks—Methodists, Universalists, Presbyterians, even one Episcopal and one Lutheran minister joined them.[11] Those who had been under the revival influence of

[10] Spencer, *History of Kentucky Baptists,* chaps. 32, 33.
[11] Gates, *Early Relation and Separation of Baptists and Disciples,* 67-9.

"New Lights" or Separates were especially fertile soil for Campbell's doctrines.

About March, 1826, Spencer Clack and George Waller in Kentucky had begun to oppose Campbell with a periodical first known as the *Baptist Register*, then the *Baptist Recorder*, published at Bloomfield. The *Pittsburg Recorder, The Western Luminary,* and the *Columbian Star and Christian Index* of Philadelphia also were enlisted in the war on "Campbellism," as his teachings were known to Baptists. By means of the pulpit and through resolutions passed by associations, efforts were made to refute his doctrine and to undermine Campbell's influence. The personal element was not omitted; his character was attacked by charges as varied as being a Unitarian, a Deist, and even an immoral man.

In the eventual separation of the "Reform" element from the Baptist ranks, the latter were the aggressors. It was they who initiated action to exclude the followers of Campbell. When the excluded body was the larger, the Baptists handled it by withdrawing fellowship from them, as in the case of the North District Association in Kentucky in 1829. The first association to take formal action against the Reformers was the Redstone of Pennsylvania in 1825-1826. In 1830 "the Franklin, the North District, the Boone's Creek, the Tate's Creek, the Elkhorn, the Bracken, the Union, and the Campbell County Associations of Kentucky, the Appomattox and the Dover Associations of Virginia excluded or anathematized the Reformers and made their fellowship with Baptist churches thereafter impossible." [12] Farther west, a disrupted situation troubled the churches in the thirties. In Indiana, in particular, Baptist work was impaired by the withdrawal of "reformer" groups or the exclusion of them by disturbed associations and churches which refused to accept Campbell's doctrines. A similar story could be told of Baptists in Ohio and Illinois.

From the year 1830, the separate existence of Campbell's followers may be traced. They preferred to be known as "Disciples of Christ," although they were called at times "The Christian Church," a term used by Barton W. Stone and his adherents who had withdrawn from the Presbyterian Church in Kentucky. Campbell objected to the name "Christian," because he felt that Stone's followers had

[12] *Ibid.,* 91, 101.

sectarianized it. The Mahoning and Stillwater Associations of Ohio, formed on the basis of the old Baptist Associations bearing the same names, represent the earliest distinct organization of the Reformers or Disciples. They did not preserve features characteristic of Baptist associational bodies, but held in their place a "yearly meeting" for worship and instruction. The pattern thus set by churches on the Western Reserve provided an example for all such meetings throughout the country.[13]

Although Campbell continuously had sought to avoid denominationalism, avowing that his movement was nonsectarian, the Disciples Church was established in 1832, thereby opening its founder to further criticism from the Baptists. What had come to be virtually a new denomination increased in size, particularly west of the Alleghenies. Its strong appeal for a vital, simple, biblical gospel was felt everywhere and was especially successful in areas where confessionalism and theological preaching had resulted in sectarian rivalries and an unhealthy authoritarianism. In a way, it was an attempt to restore a concept of the unity of the church and the significance of the ordinances in frontier churches where there had developed an extremely individualized expression of Christianity during the era of revivalism.

Its effect upon Baptist churches of the West and Southwest, in particular, had been divisive, adding to the problems created by the hyper-Calvinistic antimissionary exponents. When the new denomination of Disciples was formed, Baptists declared it heretical and separated themselves from it at great cost. In Kentucky where the controversy took the greatest toll among Baptists, about 9,580 members were lost between 1829 and 1831. In Indiana disruption over Campbell's teachings spread throughout the southern half of the state, producing a general decline among Baptists.[14]

Along the Atlantic seaboard, hyper-Calvinism was to a great extent responsible for the anti-mission sentiment. In Delaware, after 1825, opposition to missionary, Bible, and tract societies, and to Sunday schools produced a marked decline from which the churches never recovered. By 1836, one entire association in Maryland had

[13] *Ibid.*, 102-3.
[14] Spencer, *History of Kentucky Baptists,* 643; John F. Cady, *The Baptist Church in Indiana,* 70-5.

become outspokenly antimissionary and the other largely so, having been influenced by similar sentiment of an earlier date in Kentucky. Open pronouncements against missions were being made by churches and associations in Virginia and North Carolina from 1827 to 1838. The first official declaration by an association came from the Kehukee Association of North Carolina in 1827. In 1832 and 1833 the missionary-minded Sandy Creek Association's messengers of correspondence were rejected by Abbott's Creek Union Association and the Country Line Association, both of which were antimissionary.[15]

The controversy was very costly. Not only was the missionary enterprise hindered, but the accompanying opposition of so many to an educated ministry delayed the development of stronger leadership at a time when it was needed greatly. Moreover, the attacks upon the clergy and the bitterness of debate cost the churches much influence and prestige.

The Anti-Masonry Controversy

The anti-Masonry struggle which for a time had national prominence in American politics threatened the peace of the Baptist churches in the Middle States and the West between 1826 and 1840. It added to the strife produced by the anti-mission forces. The fraternity of Masons had played an important role in the early days of American settlement, and often had served as a strong influence for peace and harmony in communities which had not yet learned respect for law and order. However, to many Christians who were not members of the Order, the secrecy of its ritual and meetings was an undesirable feature which violated the kind of freedom which they believed the New Testament intended among God-fearing men.

When the Order was incorporated in South Carolina in 1791, the question of membership of Baptists in Masonic lodges troubled all of the churches in the Charleston Association. In 1798 the Association found only one fault with the Order which would militate against "serious Christians" joining it, and that was the vow of secrecy; yet it advised that the matter be left with the judgment of the individual. Not all churches adopted so tolerant a view, for there were cases in

[15] Richard B. Cook, *The Early and Later Delaware Baptists* (Philadelphia, 1880), 78-80, 90-6; Maring, *History of Maryland Baptists, 1742-1882*, 65-90; Purefoy, *History of Sandy Creek Baptist Association*, 51-9, 152-6; Paschal, *History of North Carolina Baptists, 1663-1805*, 505-11.

other parts of the state, especially in 1793 and 1801, where membership in the lodge brought church discipline. About the same time, the Shaftsbury Association in Vermont took a position similar to that adopted by the Charleston Baptists.[16]

In the 1820's the problem attracted unusual attention when an exposé of Masonry was made by a former member, William Morgan of New York State. Excitement mounted rapidly when Morgan disappeared in 1826, simultaneously with the discovery of a body in a New York river. The juxtaposition of events aroused rumors that Morgan had been murdered as the Masons' revenge. Public interest was sufficiently high to warrant the Whig political leaders, who were very much in need of a popular issue to catch votes from church people outside of their own party, to make the most of the incident as evidence of un-American and un-Christian practices in American life. When the matter assumed almost nation-wide significance, many churches of various denominations experienced division of opinion; some of their members were loyal Masons, while others opposed secret fraternities as being unscriptural and undemocratic.

Between 1822 and 1840 the issue was sufficiently significant both in politics and in the churches to threaten the peace of all the Baptist associations. The churches of the Shaftsbury Association, for example, repeatedly opposed membership of Baptists in Masonic lodges, a position which led some churches between 1822 and 1831 to withdraw from membership in that body. The Sandy Creek Association in North Carolina in 1827 agreed to exclude Masons from fellowship, an action which apparently was not adhered to in later years. A similar policy was followed by many churches in Indiana.[17] Actually, there was no unanimity of action among Baptist churches. In congregations where the majority of members shared anti-Masonic views, the issue was in some cases made a test of membership, and Masons accordingly were deprived of membership. However, since the matter did not involve morals or doctrine, the majority of Baptists took a lesson from the crisis. When after 1840 the excitement died down, they no longer interfered with those

[16] Townsend, *History of South Carolina Baptists, 1670-1805*, 114, 133-4, 208.

[17] Wright, *History of Shaftsbury Baptist Association*, 170, 186-7, 195, 198-200, 228; Purefoy, *op. cit.*, 138; Cady, *The Baptist Church in Indiana*, 45-6.

members who desired to belong to secret societies, although a difference of opinion on the matter continued to exist.

The Bible Society Controversy

Among the national organizations established in the Philadelphia area during the early years of the nineteenth century, and which were supported either entirely or in part by Baptists, was the American Bible Society. It had been founded in 1816 by representatives of seven Protestant denominations for the dissemination of the Scriptures. It was the American counterpart of the British and Foreign Bible Society, founded in England twelve years earlier. Inasmuch as Baptists in the New World were from the first active contributors to the British Society, of which Rev. Joseph Hughes, a London Baptist, was secretary, it is not surprising that they supported strongly a similar agency in the United States.

In these two Bible Societies (the British and the American) the denominations had co-operated without conflict. But when the Baptists expressed a desire to publish a version of the Scriptures in which the word *baptizo* would be translated "immerse" or "dip," instead of being transliterated (as the custom was) to avoid any debate over the mode of baptism, controversy began. Simultaneously in England and America, the issue produced much discussion, and, as we shall see, led eventually to the withdrawal of the Baptists.

In August, 1835, the American Baptists presented to the American Bible Society an application for money to aid in the printing of a Bengali version of the Scriptures, prepared by William Yates, a Baptist missionary in Calcutta, on the principle of the Burmese version which had been prepared earlier by Adoniram Judson, in which the word *baptizo* had been translated "immerse." After months of discussion, the Board voted on March 17, 1836, to appropriate $5,000 to the Baptist Board of Foreign Missions subject to the restrictions adopted in a resolution on March 25, 1836, that only such versions should be encouraged "as conform in the principles of their translation to the common English version, at least so far as that all the religious denominations represented in this Society can consistently use and circulate said versions in their several schools and communities." At an annual meeting in May of that year, the Society approved the action of the Board. The Baptist Foreign Mission Board declined the funds proferred on such conditions and adopted resolutions to augment their own funds for the printing and distribution of the version.[18]

Resenting what they regarded as an unreasonable decision and determined to gain their end in another way, a convention of three hundred and ninety delegates from Baptist churches in twenty-three states met in Philadelphia in April, 1837, to organize their own agency for printing and distributing the Scriptures. It was called the American and Foreign Bible Society. Dr. Spencer H. Cone, a New York minister, was elected president; Dr. Charles G. Sommers, also of New York, was the first corresponding secretary; and William Colgate, a prominent manufacturer, was the first treasurer. After much discussion the new Society decided in May, 1850, to circulate only the standard version in English. It did not think it necessary to issue a new version in English which would translate *baptizo* by the word "immerse," to substantiate the Baptist interpretation. But not all were in agreement, and those who desired to print a Baptist version in English formed in June of that year a rival society, the American Bible Union. Thereafter, neither society made out well financially.

This unfortunate controversy was finally settled when a Bible Convention was held in Saratoga, New York, in May, 1883. There it was decided that Bible work at home was to be carried on by the American Baptist Publication Society, while that for foreign distribution was to be carried on by the American Baptist Missionary Union. Thus the agency for distributing versions in foreign dialects was separated from that which handled the English versions for home use, leaving each free to carry out its own policy.

Millerism

As has already been pointed out, another disturbing influence was Millerism. In 1833, William Miller, a member of the Baptist church in Low Hampton, New York, was licensed to preach by that body. It then was not difficult for him to find ready access to the churches of his denomination. Although a man of limited education, his familiarity with the Scriptures, the earnestness and eloquence

[18] The Baptist Missionary Magazine (Boston), Vol. XVI (1836), pp. 122-3.

with which he set forth his views, and the uniqueness of his peculiar doctrines concerning the near approach of the end of the world attracted large audiences not only of Baptists, but also of other evangelical denominations. Through certain computations connected with the seventy weeks in Daniel 9:24, he calculated that the Lord's coming to establish His millennial rule was due in 1843, which date he later changed to October 22, 1844. While he was in Maine in 1842, a revival spirit was manifested in his meetings, and large numbers of converts became ardent Adventists or Millerites, as they were called. He met with a similar response elsewhere in New England, New York State, and parts of Pennsylvania and New Jersey. As far west as Indiana, Old School or Calvinistic Baptists were finding in the Millerite conjectures and predictions a rationale for their declining fortunes. The financial panic of 1839, with its concomitant circumstances of depression, undoubtedly also encouraged a ready response to Miller's prophetic teachings. It will be recalled that the adventism taught by Alexander Campbell had played an important part in attracting followers to him at about this same period.[19]

When, however, the advent of Christ did not materialize on the date set, the greater number of Miller's followers lost confidence in his views. But unfortunately, their disillusionment in many cases extended to their attitude toward religion in general. Consequently, the churches suffered not only from the loss of many to the new movement, but also from the aftermath of spiritual lethargy which followed its collapse. During the years immediately after 1844, there was a noticeable decline in conversions, and the period of revivals came almost to an abrupt end. It seems not unlikely, therefore, that the Millerite movement was in part responsible.

On January 29, 1845, an associational council voted to sever relations with Miller and his following in the Baptist church at Low Hampton, New York. The minority, who had not shared his views, were left to constitute the Baptist church in Low Hampton.[20] In its effect, Millerism proved to be divisive, for many of his followers had left the fellowship of their own churches to becomes his disciples, and when disillusioned, they did not return to their churches.

[19] Cady, *The Baptist Church in Indiana*, 54-5, 153-5.
[20] Burrage, *History of the Baptists in Maine*, 197-201.

Old Landmarkism

In the South another teaching caused much discussion and some controversy. It was set forth by two prominent clergymen, Dr. James R. Graves of Memphis, Tennessee, and Dr. J. M. Pendleton of Bowling Green, Kentucky. It was the purpose of Graves, who became editor of *The Tennessee Baptist* in 1846, to restore to the churches the practices of the early church, many of which he felt were being neglected by Baptists in his day. He assumed that the apostolic Christians were Baptists, hence everyone who was not a Baptist could not rightly be considered Christian. By the same line of reasoning, he refused to consider paedobaptist preachers as gospel ministers. In 1854 Pendleton wrote a pamphlet in which he expressed a similar view.

Their emphasis was shared by many able writers and preachers of the South and West. It has come to be called "Old Landmarkism," because of the concern of its advocates to restore the pristine purity of the early church by keeping a faithful Baptist membership and ministry. Its proponents have opposed "alien immersion"; that is, they have refused to recognize as valid for membership in a Baptist church immersion administered by a non-Baptist. They also have opposed the practice of "pulpit affiliation" (that is, the friendly exchange of pulpits by Baptists and non-Baptists) on the ground that the latter are not true ministers of the gospel. Indeed, they have denied consistently that paedobaptist congregations are churches in the correct sense of the word. Finally, they have not admitted members of different Baptist churches to share together in the observance of the Lord's Supper, for they have held that the ordinance is only for the members of the local church. In these ways they have sought to preserve what they regard as the "old landmarks" of New Testament Christianity.

The effects of this movement were felt strongly in the Southern Baptist Convention as early as the 1850's. The Landmarkists' protest against "organized" work beyond the local churches militated against the Convention in several ways. Their objection to the financial basis of representation in the Convention, which had been inherited from the society method of conducting missions, threatened the very life of the Convention. The issue came to a head in 1859 when a proposal to substitute a church basis for representation was defeated. Thus was avoided the change of the Convention into a "church-centered denominational organization." The Landmarkists' dislike for supervision of missions by boards of the Convention precipitated what came to be called the "Gospel Mission" controversy. The Land-markists established their own missions under the direction of the local churches in opposition to Board Missions. While the Con-vention did not submit to their leadership, "the emphases and methods of Landmarkism impressed themselves upon the Convention in such a paradoxical manner that they encouraged the rise of denomina-tionalism," [21] a trend which will be noted in later chapters.

The Slavery Issue and the Civil War

Although Mennonites, Quakers, German pietists in Pennsylvania, and Congregationalists in New England had gone on record as opposing slavery in the late eighteenth and early nineteenth centuries, Baptists seem to have been absorbed too greatly in their own struggle for religious liberty to have occupied themselves much with this issue which was still in its infancy. Then, too, it should be remembered that they had committed themselves to a policy of noninterference in civil affairs which precluded preoccupation with what many re-garded as a nonreligious issue. The Great Awakening, however, had aroused humanitarian concern, a concern which grew during the colonies' struggle for independence. Presbyterians, Methodists, and Baptists alike had made a strong appeal to the Negroes, and had received them into membership in their churches.

By the close of the American Revolution, in the full flush of victory for a free republic, Baptists were beginning to question the validity of slavery as a practice among Christians. In Virginia, for example, the Ketockton Association in 1787 "determined that heredi-tary slavery was a breach of the divine law." Accordingly, a com-mittee was appointed "to bring in a plan of gradual emancipation." When this was done, the churches were so greatly disturbed that the Association deemed it the part of wisdom to drop the matter. Never-theless, John Leland presented a resolution to the Baptist General Committee in 1789, which was adopted; it called upon the Legislative

[21] Robert A. Baker, *Relations between Northern and Southern Baptists*, 163.

Assembly of the state to abolish slavery gradually and to free the slaves in a manner "consistent with the principles of good policy." The action of the Roanoke Association with respect to the resolution is typical of the general Baptist approach to the problem. The next year that association professed a lack of clarity as to the wisdom of the resolution and so left the issue to the individual conscience; they advised slave-owners, however, to suppress cruelty to the slaves. The Strawberry Association in 1792 went so far as to advise the General Committee not to interfere with slavery. By 1793, therefore, the committee had decided to dismiss the subject.[22]

In Philadelphia likewise a cautious policy was followed. This was evident in 1789 when the Association was urged by the First Baptist Church of Baltimore to make an effort to form abolition societies in the Philadelphia area. It responded by expressing its approbation of the several societies already in existence in the United States and Europe, and recommended that the churches of its constituency form similar societies.[23] The Salem Association in Kentucky, however, refused to be drawn into the discussion when asked by a local church in 1789 whether slave-holding was lawful for a Christian.

When the Elkhorn Association in the same state appointed a committee in August, 1791, to memorialize the constitutional convention to include a guarantee of abolition of slavery along with religious liberty, so much agitation was aroused among the member churches who were divided on the issue, that the plan was dropped the following year. For the next several years, the associations were not inclined to express themselves on the issue. But in the churches, emancipation parties were formed and abolitionist preachers were loud in support of the cause. In 1805 the Elkhorn Association urged the ministers to refrain from meddling with slavery or any other political subject, but to little avail, for two years later there was organized an Abolition Society of Baptist churches and ministers, called the "Friends of Humanity Association." For thirty years this abolitionist feeling caused schism among Kentucky Baptists.[24]

In South Carolina, where approximately one-third of the Baptist laymen and two-fifths of the ministers were slave-holders, there was

[22] Gewehr, *The Great Awakening in Virginia*, 235-41.

[23] *Philadelphia Baptist Association Minutes: 1707-1807*, 247.

[24] William W. Sweet, *Religion on the American Frontier: the Baptists, 1783-1830* (New York, 1931), 79; Spencer, *History of Kentucky Baptists*, I, 183-5.

an equal hesitancy on the part of associations to make pronouncements on the question of slavery. In 1799, for example, the Bethel
Association suppressed an inquiry from the Cedar Spring Church
concerning the right of a Christian to own slaves. Yet, the churches
of the state generally included Negroes in their membership and
imposed upon their slave-holding members a strict code to regulate
the religious care and treatment of the slaves. A similar policy was
followed in other southern states including North Carolina and Maryland. It appears that the Negro members were provided with a
certain space in the meeting-house for worship, but were not permitted to vote in business sessions, although they might be heard in
cases related to their own race. Among Maryland Baptists the
slavery issue was a disturbing factor to the churches until about
1830 when the matter was dropped in the interest of harmony. The
Sandy Creek Association in North Carolina, as late as 1835, took a
stand against the "selling and buying of slaves," although they were
not unitedly opposed to slave-holding.[25]

In general, it may be said that the majority of Baptists were
cautious about the issue for three reasons: (1) their preference for
unity wherever possible; (2) their hesitancy to violate the principle
of noninterference of the church in civil affairs; (3) the presence
of slave-holding members in their churches. Yet the issue in time
became increasingly troublesome. The events surrounding the admission of Missouri and Maine to the Union intensified it. The ensuing controversy ended in the unsatisfactory Compromise of 1820,
which maintained the balance of power between free and slave states
in the Senate by admitting Missouri as a slave state and Maine as
a free state, but it pleased no one. The minority group of abolitionists
was growing ever more insistent that action be taken, for the growth
of the frontier to the West and Southwest kept alive the fear that
new territories would be admitted to statehood as slave states.

The influential Philadelphia Association adopted a policy of
conciliation when confronted in 1820 with a query from the Vincent
Baptist Church at Chester Springs, Pennsylvania, concerning the
advisability of the Association's calling a national meeting to plan

[25] Townsend, *History of South Carolina Baptists, 1670-1805*, 242, 255, 259, 280-1;
John S. Bassett, *Slavery in the State of North Carolina* (Baltimore, 1899), 47-52, 61;
Maring, *History of Maryland Baptists, 1742-1882*, pp. 31-3, 46-9; Purefoy, *History of
Sandy Creek Baptist Association*, 163-4.

for the emancipation of slaves among the Baptists. After some hesitancy and deliberation, the answer was that it was "inexpedient to enter on such business at this time." [26] When the church asked, in the following year, if it were wise for the Association to fellowship with slave-holding Baptists, the answer was the same. Obviously, the Baptists of the Philadelphia area were seeking to keep the slavery issue in the background in order to maintain unity. It is also possible that they reflected the general attitude of Philadelphians, which was gauged so as not to disrupt their profitable trade with the South.

In other sections of the country, the attitudes were quite different. Southern Baptists grew irritated by the propaganda of northern abolitionists, and shifted from their earlier willingness to forsake slavery to a readiness to defend the institution. In 1822 and again in 1835, the Charleston Association in South Carolina defended the practice before the state legislature. The clergy of Richmond, Virginia, among whom were many Baptists, passed a resolution in 1835, disapproving of abolitionist interference from other states. At the same time, the Tyger River Baptist Association in the same state went so far as to give warning against abolitionists who might come into the community under the garb of "strange" ministers. In the North, on the other hand, a small but vigorous group of anti-slavery Baptists, in the 1830's, gained control of some churches and associations, particularly in Maine. In 1836 the Hancock Association urged immediate emancipation, while the Washington Association, also in Maine, forbade its members to have fellowship with slave-holders.[27] The Freewill Baptist periodical, *The Morning Star*, became so vocal against slavery that the printing establishment, between 1835 and 1846, was twice refused the privilege of incorporation at Dover, New Hampshire. In 1839 the Freewill Baptist General Conference, meeting at Conneaut, Ohio, broke fellowship with some five thousand free-communion Baptists in North and South Carolina over slavery. In 1843 the Freewill Baptist Anti-Slavery Society was organized at the New Hampshire Yearly Meeting as a means of keeping the issue alive before the denomination.[28]

[26] *Philadelphia Baptist Association Minutes* for 1820, 7-9.

[27] Putnam, *The Baptists and Slavery: 1840-1845*, 13-6.

[28] J. M. Brewster, *et al*, *The Centennial Record of Freewill Baptists, 1780-1880* (Dover, N. H., 1881), 192-200.

Kentucky continued to be a center of anti-slavery agitation, although this agitation did not split the denomination. In Illinois, Elder James Lemen, a friend and admirer of Thomas Jefferson, led Baptist anti-slavery forces. Many Baptists, however, regarded the Illinois Friends to Humanity Association, with which he was connected, as a schismatic movement.[29] In Indiana, minority groups of Baptists were active in anti-slavery agitation and in supporting the secret plan for transporting slaves to freedom in Canada, a plan which was known as the "Underground Railway." The majority of Baptist Associations there, however, followed a consistent policy of conciliation.[30]

Despite these abolitionist developments, Baptist leaders generally sought, during the twenties and thirties, to keep peace by pursuing a policy of moderation. The peace, however, proved to be only the lull before the storm, for there were numerous influences at work to arouse anti-slavery feeling in the North. Abolitionist societies supported by ardent orators and a vocal press were taking advantage of every opportunity to arouse public opinion. Runaway slaves provided test cases in northern states. Arguments used by southern statesmen and clergymen were publicized widely in satirical replies by incensed emancipationists.

In the 1830's a subtle change was taking place in the relationship of the churches to the abolitionist cause. William Lloyd Garrison, chief advocate of emancipation in New England, was losing the support of large sections of the northern church people by his fierce denunciation of the moderates as black-hearted traitors. Meanwhile, a new anti-slavery movement was taking shape in the central states, centering in Ohio. The leader was Theodore Dwight Weld, one of Charles G. Finney's converts. When Lane Theological Seminary opened in 1832 under the presidency of Lyman Beecher, Weld was one of the students and a leader of abolitionist sentiment. Lewis Tappan, a New York importer, supported the seminary financially and encouraged Weld in his zeal for abolitionism. When criticism arose over the students' fraternization with the colored population, the majority of abolitionists moved to Oberlin College on condition that Finney become professor of theology. Thus the anti-slavery cause was

[29] Sweet, *op. cit.*, 81-101.

[30] Cady, *The Baptist Church in Indiana*, 196-200.

made a necessary part of the Christian witness and Finney's revivalistic methods were used to win new supporters to the movement. As the influence of Oberlin students spread eastward, church support increased especially among Methodists, Baptists, and New School Presbyterians. The success of the new movement was due to the fact that Weld and his associates worked with and through the churches.[31]

On the other hand, forces seeking to stem the rising tide of conflict were numerous. Statesmen, realizing the danger of civil war, were feverishly searching for some measure of compromise. Merchants, anxious to retain normalcy in business, nervously opposed the excesses of the abolitionists. Many clergymen, hoping to maintain unity in their respective denominations, worked for understanding and conciliation, and sought to offset the fanaticism of those who had become apostles of abolition.

However, open controversy in the denomination could not be prevented much longer. The focal point for national disagreement was in the missionary enterprise. Since its organization in 1814, the Triennial Convention had carried on the missionary activities of both northern and southern Baptists, but not without some discontent on the part of Baptists from Philadelphia to Atlanta. It will be recalled that by 1826 the New Englander's point of view of decentralization had triumphed in the Convention. Instead of a denominational organization exercising a general direction of missionary, educational, and publication enterprises, the Convention became primarily a foreign mission society, while home mission work was placed in the hands of the American Baptist Home Mission Society, organized in 1832, and education and publication were put in the hands of societies established for those purposes. From several southern states, complaints were raised against the American Baptist Home Mission Society for devoting its major attention to the West, to which emigrants had gone chiefly from New England and the Middle States, while Florida, Louisiana, Arkansas, and other southern states were being neglected.

As early as 1835, a call for a southern convention to meet the needs in the South and Southwest was issued by Robert T. Daniel,

[31] Gilbert H. Barnes, *The Anti-Slavery Impulse, 1830-1844* (New York, 1933); cit. William Warren Sweet, *The Story of Religion in America* (New York, revised edition, 1950), 296-97.

a North Carolinian who had gone west, had preached in Tennessee and northern Mississippi, and had seen the great need. Leaders in Kentucky and Tennessee, however, considered the move to be premature. Nevertheless, in 1839 a Southern Baptist Home Mission Society was organized in Columbus, Mississippi, under Daniel's leadership, but it lapsed after his death three years later. Plans for a general convention of western Baptists were also explored in Louisville in 1840 in the home of Dr. W. C. Buck of Kentucky.

Thus it becomes apparent that division was already in the air prior to the actual schism of 1845. Without doubt, the sectional tensions over slavery which became acute by 1840 hastened the cleavage.[32]

The issue of slavery had been suppressed successfully until the American Baptist Anti-Slavery Convention met in New York City in April, 1840. This gathering was the product of radical feeling against slavery among some northern Baptists, and among certain Baptist missionaries in Burma who had severed their connection with the Triennial Convention and had formed a Foreign Provisional Missionary Committee under whose direction they might work without association with slave-holders.

In November, the Alabama Baptist Convention forwarded a resolution to withhold funds from the Board of Foreign Missions and from the American and Foreign Bible Society until Alabama Baptists were assured that those agencies had no connection with abolitionism, and if the reply were unsatisfactory, to form a Southern Board through which Alabama Baptist funds might be transmitted directly.

Facing pressure from missionaries, ministers, and laymen who wished an outspoken expression of the Convention on the slavery issue, the Convention's Board of Managers made a statement on November 2, 1840, that members of the Board as individuals might act as they wished, but that as officials of the Triennial Convention, they had no right to do or say anything with respect to slavery.[33] Neither the abolitionists nor the slave-holders were entirely satisfied with this position. Nevertheless, the Alabama Convention's fears

[32] William W. Barnes, "Why the Southern Baptist Convention Was Formed," *The Review and Expositor*, Vol. XLI, No. 1 (Jan., 1944), 3-17.

[33] *The Baptist Missionary Magazine* (Boston), Vol. XXIII, (1843), 167-9.

were allayed for the time being. Meanwhile the abolitionists' strength in the denomination was increasing. On January 19, 1841, the Baptist Anti-Slavery Convention meeting in Maine reported that more than one hundred and eighty of the two hundred and fourteen ministers in that state were decided abolitionists.

When the Triennial Convention met at Baltimore in 1841, both sides were prepared for battle. Some effort was made, however, to avoid the issue again; for in a secret caucus of northern conservatives and southerners, a compromise article "discouraging innovation and 'new tests' and disclaiming participation in the doings of the abolition Baptists was signed by seventy-four persons. The understanding was that slavery was a subject with which the Convention had no right to interfere."[34] In the same year, the Board of the American Baptist Home Mission Society also issued a declaration of neutrality.

All this was not agreeable to many northern men, who criticized the "Baltimore Compromise." The Provisional Foreign Mission Committee of the American Baptist Anti-Slavery Convention sent a circular letter to one or more of the missionaries of the Foreign Board of the Triennial Convention, presumably inviting them to receive their support from the Anti-Slavery Convention. This seems clear from the reply written on November 15, 1842, by Solomon Peck, the secretary of the Foreign Board. He insisted that the Board members had not "yielded their *personal* neutrality," as they were accused, but that they refused to be subservient to either the South or the North. He admitted, however, that they were no apologists for slavery.[35] The number of abolitionists was increasing among the common people, and the anti-slavery movement was taking on a definitely religious tone as the churches were being enlisted in its support. Many wished to send their missionary funds through some channel other than a Convention which condoned slavery. Consequently, the American and Foreign Free Baptist Board of Foreign Missions was formed in Boston in 1843, but the Baptist Board of Foreign Missions, which administered the missionary funds of the Convention, ruled against the existence of such an organization.

When the Triennial Convention met in Philadelphia in 1844,

[34] Mary B. Putnam, *The Baptists and Slavery, 1840-1845* (Ann Arbor, Mich., 1913), 27, 29-30.

[35] *The Baptist Missionary Magazine,* Vol. XXIII, (1843), pp. 169-70.

there were four hundred and sixty delegates present, eighty of whom were from states below the Mason and Dixon's line. The proportion of Southerners was small because of distance. In addition, there were delegates of other societies of the denomination who were holding their annual meetings at the same time. This swelled the number of visiting Baptists to six or seven hundred. At the time, there were about seven hundred thousand Baptists in the country, so the proportion of members represented at the Convention was fairly good especially since it was on a voluntary basis. Massachusetts sent the largest delegation, having 103 representatives of the state's 31,843 Baptists, whereas, Virginia with 82,732 Baptists had only forty-three delegates present.[36] The Massachusetts abolitionists were evidently ready for a struggle. Pennsylvania had forty-six delegates to represent the 28,044 Baptists in the state. This percentage of representation was not large for the state in which the Convention was being held.

Dr. W. B. Johnson, the retiring president of the Convention and a Southerner, declined re-election for reasons of health. Since the Convention had been led by a Southerner for twenty-one out of thirty years, and possibly to appease the Northerners, Dr. Francis Wayland of Rhode Island, a moderate on the abolition question, was chosen as president. A Virginian, Dr. J. B. Taylor, became secretary.

On Thursday evening, April 25, Dr. Richard Fuller, a Baptist minister of South Carolina, presented a resolution calling upon the Convention to restrict itself solely to its missionary enterprise. Dr. Fuller, being a slave-owner, quite naturally argued in this manner. Dr. Spencer H. Cone, a prominent minister of New York City, favored this attempt to isolate the issue of slavery from the Convention's policies. But Dr. Nathaniel Colver, pastor of Tremont Temple, Boston, rose to speak against the resolution as being simply an avoidance of the issue at hand. After much debate, the resolution was withdrawn and a new one was introduced by Dr. George B. Ide, who then was pastor of the First Baptist Church in Philadelphia. The new resolution was a second attempt to maintain unity by a noncommittal policy on the institution of slavery. Dr. Ide urged that the members of the Convention continue to co-operate

[36] Putnam, *op. cit.*, 35-6. The author based the membership of Baptists per state on figures in the *Baptist Register* for 1845.

in the work of foreign missions, disclaiming "all sanction either expressed or implied, whether of slavery or of anti-slavery," but as individuals, being free to express and promote whatever views they held. The concession that individuals might speak their views evidently appealed to the delegates, for the resolution was passed unanimously without discussion. Thus the whole matter was again laid on the table in this Convention. The Home Mission Society again declared its neutrality by a vote of 123 to 61, but appointed a committee to consider amicable dissolution of the Society.[37]

This action renewed the fears of southern Baptists. As a test case, therefore, the Georgia Baptist Convention, just a few days after the Triennial Convention had adjourned, instructed its executive committee to recommend to the Board of the Home Mission Society James E. Reeves of Georgia for appointment as a missionary to the Cherokee Indians, his support to be guaranteed by the Triennial Convention. In proper manner, the Board was informed that he was a slave-holder and that this was to be a test case. The Board reached a decision in October, after having held five meetings of three hours each. The vote was seven to five against appointing Mr. Reeves.

This response led the Alabama Convention to present to the Foreign Mission Board, not a specific case, but a hypothetical question. Certain southern men claimed that just subsequent to the Philadelphia Convention in 1844, the Board had caused the retirement from its service of the Reverend John Bushyhead, a highly respected Indian preacher, because he owned slaves. Accordingly, the Alabama Baptist Convention in November, 1844, sent a letter embodying what is known as the Alabama Resolutions to the Board of Managers of the Triennial Convention, insisting that the Foreign Mission agency which they supported give slave-holders and non-slave-holders the same privileges. In December, the Board gave a reply which in reality was a departure from the principle laid down by the Convention at its annual meeting. Their decision was as follows: "If any one should offer himself as a missionary, having slaves, and should insist on retaining them as his property, we could not appoint him. One thing is certain, we can never be a party to any arrangement which would imply approbation of slavery."

[37] *Ibid.*, 37-8; Barnes, "Why the Southern Baptist Convention Was Formed," *The Review and Expositor*, Vol. XLI, No. 1 (Jan., 1944), 16.

This decision of the Board appears to have been a clear violation of the Convention's instructions, although the Board insisted that its statement was not an impairment of its position of neutrality with respect to the slavery issue in the denomination. Solomon Peck, the Board's secretary, explained in a letter that he had given his vote in favor of the decision with reluctance and with a full consciousness that "it verges closely, at best, on the limits of our constitutional power, and it is wise to avoid in the eyes of all members of the Convention the least approach to a violation of constitutional rights." Moreover, he felt that such action "threatens to be virtually an act of division of the Convention," the responsibility for which "should be devolved on the members of Convention, who are the principals and would act for themselves." He justified his approval of the Board's reply to the Alabama Convention principally on the ground that a division between the North and South would be less harmful to their missionary undertakings than the withdrawal of support in the North, which would leave "an ever-diminishing minority at the North to co-operate with the South."[38]

From the decisions of these two mission boards, it appears that abolitionist sympathizers were gaining more influence than the advocates of union in the national bodies. This is not to be wondered at, because the major societies of the denomination had originated in the North, principally in Philadelphia, New York, and Boston. The policies, therefore, were influenced, if not actually formulated, chiefly by ministers and laymen of these centers. This is all the more remarkable since there were more Baptists in the Southern States than in the North and West combined.[39] But the distance from the urban centers of Baptist work in all probability prevented the southern states from enjoying a full representation at the meetings of the societies.

Naturally enough, when the decision of the Foreign Mission Board became known, debate concerning the action began almost at once. The southerners did not attempt to defend the evils in the

[38] *The Baptist Missionary Magazine* (Boston), Vol. XXV (1845), pp. 220-3; Solomon Peck's letter is included in a typescript copy of the Board's Records for February 27, 1843, to May 3, 1847, which is in possession of The American Baptist Foreign Mission Society, New York City (see pp. 75-7).

[39] Wm. Cathcart, *The Baptist Encyclopedia*, II, 1324. The statistics for 1840 show that there were approximately 322,985 Baptists in the states below the Mason and Dixon's line to 248,306 in the states above it.

slavery system, but described the institution as an inherited disease to be cured slowly; many justified its continuance on biblical grounds, pointing out that the Negroes' contacts with white masters brought them in touch with the gospel. Northern abolitionists also argued from the Scriptures, holding that they taught the inherent dignity and worth of every individual in the sight of God and the moral wrong of the enslavement of men by their fellows. At the same time, others were seeking to bring about conciliation between the two groups.[40]

Despite all efforts for appeasement, the tension within the denomination finally reached the breaking point. The long-threatened schism came. The American Baptist Home Mission Society decided, at a meeting in April, 1845, that it would be more expedient if its members should thereafter carry on their work in separate organizations in the South and in the North. Consequently, the Virginia Foreign Mission Society issued a call for a convention to be held in May. Three hundred and twenty-eight delegates from the churches of the South met at Augusta, Georgia, to organize the Southern Baptist Convention. It proved to be a new type of Baptist organization, being a firmly centralized denominational body functioning through various boards. Thus it was unlike the Triennial Convention, which in reality had been principally a foreign mission society, which it continued to be even after the division when it changed its name to the American Baptist Missionary Union. The newly constituted Convention was of a type of organization that "had the denominational emphasis of the Associational method which had been rejected by the Northern leaders after 1820." After 1860 the Landmark movement unwittingly was to give further denominational direction to the new Convention by pressing for a church basis of representation. "The completely different character of this method of conducting missions from the society method laid the foundation for an ideological conflict between Northern and Southern Baptists" in the years to come.[41]

About the same time, the Methodist Episcopal Church suffered

[40] For summaries of debates between Dr. Francis Wayland and Dr. Richard Fuller of the North and South respectively, see James O. Murray, *Francis Wayland* (New York, 1891), 263-4; also *The Baptist Record*, (Philadelphia weekly) Nov. 20, 1844.

[41] Baker, *Relations Between Northern and Southern Baptists*, footnote 4 on p. 280 and p. 90. For evidence of the conflict, see later chapters on home missions and recent trends.

a cleavage over the same issue. The Presbyterians of the New School General Assembly split in 1857 when the pro-slavery supporters formed the United Synod of the South. The Old School Presbyterians experienced a like schism in 1861. Of the denominational bodies working in both the North and South, only the Episcopal Church was successful in avoiding a break.

Not only had the long expected schism actually occurred, which has lasted to the present time, but it became increasingly difficult for the moderationists to maintain their policy in the face of the rising temper of anti-slavery sentiment which followed the enactment by Congress of the Fugitive Slave Law in 1850, and the repeal of the Missouri Compromise in 1854, which threatened to extend slavery over hitherto free territory. When war came, however, northern Baptists, having cast the die earlier, were in a position to support the Union cause wholeheartedly. To them, the issues involved included much more than opposition to slavery and the extension of slavery into free territory; they involved the defense of democracy, of a government which guaranteed those religious and political liberties which were of paramount significance to them. In their view, the nation's existence was at stake, threatened by the secession of certain southern states.[42]

It is possible to gain some idea of the reaction of Baptists throughout the country to the war by sampling the character of their attitudes and actions in widely separated areas. Among New England Baptists, as might be expected, there was universal and enthusiastic acclaim of the issues involved. In Maine, Baptists were prominent in the war effort. The Maine Baptist Convention in June, 1861, pledged its full co-operation and sympathy. Ministers participated freely in the public gatherings which were held everywhere. Members of the churches enlisted in the Union Army, while those at home carried on relief work for the sick and the wounded. Freewill Baptists were equally ardent, fifty-eight of their ministers entering the Army. Scarcely was the war over, when the Baptists of Maine planned to assist Freedmen in developing schools and churches.[43]

[42] For the story of Philadelphia Baptists who were typical of the moderationists, see Torbet, *A Social History of the Philadelphia Baptist Association: 1707-1940*, 104-11.

[43] Burrage, *History of Baptists in Maine*, 203, 325-7; *Proceedings of the Maine Baptist Convention* for 1861, 6-7, for 1862, 10; for 1866, 8; Brewster; *The Centennial Record of Freewill Baptists, 1780-1880*, 42-4.

Philadelphia Baptists devoted themselves loyally to the war effort. Young men from nearly every church went into the Army. The clergy and their congregations gave moral support to the struggle through their constant spirit of co-operation. This co-operation was manifested in sermons and in the service rendered by men and women alike in fund raising enterprises, in canteen work, and in nursing care during the dark days of the Battle of Gettysburg in the summer of 1863. The ministers provided a leadership which was welcomed by the city authorities, and by the soldiers at the front to whom they ministered frequently as chaplains. The Association wholeheartedly supported President Lincoln's Emancipation Proclamation and busied itself in raising funds to aid the Negro population of the South through the agency of the American Baptist Home Mission Society.

Lincoln's assassination was regarded by the Philadelphia Association as a great crime against humanity. At the close of hostilities, they adopted an attitude of tolerance toward the South. In their opinion, the majority of Southerners were not responsible for the rebellion. They considered the reunion of northern and southern Baptists to be desirable, but not probable. Their leaders insisted and preached that the greatest concern of the nation should be to guarantee the freedom of the Negro, not to seek revenge. To help the Negro to adjust himself to his new liberty was the task which lay before them. They saw a partial answer in the support of training schools for Negroes who might become the teachers and preachers of their race in the United States, as well as in the West Indies and Africa. Further service was to be rendered to the Negro population of the city through the efforts of the denomination's City Mission Society in the years that followed.

Among Indiana Baptists there was a shift in attitude from the Christian view of moderation, the view that all had sinned and therefore should share the blame, to what was perhaps a less Christian outlook—that the war was a special manifestation of Divine Providence. Through it, they saw Christians being united around the principle of human freedom. Among those who preached and drafted resolutions, the evil effects of the conflict for the most part were overlooked in a patriotic denunciation of the rebellious South. The vindictive spirit did not lessen the harmful effects of the war upon the churches. Disorders were engendered in many congregations, while worldliness and lack of faith emerged in the associational life. With many churches pastorless, missionary activities ceased. Consequently, there was little spiritual vitality left to combat the postwar moral letdown. Indeed, the public seemed too fagged emotionally to respond to a religious repeal. To add to the problem facing not only Indiana Baptists, but the churches generally, there emerged the complexities of rapid urban development and increased European immigration.[44]

Baptists in the border states were divided in their sentiments. This was true in Maryland, where the Maryland Baptist Union Association was never ardently in favor of slavery, although it had approved the formation of the Southern Baptist Convention in 1845. Most of their leaders subordinated personal preferences in the broader interest of unity.[45] Kentucky was not so peaceful, for during the war, "almost without exception, every Baptist church in the state was divided on the question of secession. Some of the churches had a majority of unionists, and others a majority of secessionists. . . . Comparatively few people attended religious worship, and a large proportion of those who did, felt little or no interest in it. The jealousy of the political parties in the churches prevented the exercise of discipline, and on this account, the worshipers became further demoralized. . . ."[46] Many ministers were forced to resign because they were not in agreement with the view of the dominant element in their congregations. During the war, the Baptists of the state suffered a loss of forty thousand members, including the colored, because of migration and casualties of the conflict.

Among Baptists in the states further south, there was naturally a loyalty to the Confederacy. It was next to impossible for them to carry on a full program because of lack of funds and because of the difficulty of keeping communications open to mission fields during the conflict. Through the terrible years of reconstruction which followed, comparatively little could be done. A devastated economy left the churches with little or no resources to carry on the missionary and educational enterprises which had been interrupted by prolonged

[44] Cady, *The Baptist Church in Indiana*, 203-9.

[45] Maring, *History of Maryland Baptists, 1742-1882*, 152-61, 163-9.

[46] Spencer, *History of Kentucky Baptists*, I, 741-2.

warfare. While the Northern Societies continued to carry on their work in the South during the postwar era, the leaders of the Convention led the churches to a decision in 1879 to remain separate from the organization of Northern Baptists while maintaining cordial relations with them. Undoubtedly, the decision was the product of several factors: a sectionalism which had been accentuated by the wounds of bitter controversy and war; a difference of polity which prompted Baptists in the South to cherish a stronger denominationalism than was desired in the North; and a feeling that the Northern Societies were not meeting the needs of vast territories in the South and Southwest.[47] While there emerged from the schism two strong bodies to carry on Baptist work in America (the northern Societies, which ultimately were to unite in the Northern Baptist Convention in 1908, and the Southern Baptist Convention), and while each has been determined to maintain friendly relations with the other, the tensions that have arisen through the years reflect the continuance, if not the deepening, of sectional differences which might have been overcome with patience and understanding, had they not been perpetuated by the development of separate organizations.

[47] For an account of the relations between the Northern Societies and the Southern Baptist Convention, see Baker, *Relations between Northern and Southern Baptists,* chap. 11. For a good study of the problems faced during the War and the Reconstruction Era, see B. F. Riley, *History of the Baptists of Alabama, 1808-1894* (Birmingham, 1895), chaps. 21-4.

CHAPTER ELEVEN

EVANGELISM AND EDUCATION

O NE of the unique features in the development of American Christianity as it adapted itself to the frontier environment was the phenomenon of revivalism which characterized the evangelical denominations in particular.[1] In essence, this revivalism was the product of an evangelistic zeal and a yearning for a deepened spirituality in the church. Neither of these factors was peculiar to the American scene, but both of them expressed themselves in the manner which was most suited to the simplicity of pioneer life.

It will be recalled that when the first wave of revivalism engulfed the thirteen colonies about 1740, a great emotionalism and conviction of sin gripped men, women, and children alike with such effective results that the period has been known since as the Great Awakening. A spiritual declension followed in its wake, during which the cold blasts of rationalism, revolution, and materialism chilled the glowing embers. But about 1795 another wave of revivals began, which was destined to continue until about 1842 when an era of well-being and national prosperity again engulfed the deeper interests of religion. One of the chief differences between this period of revivals and the Great Awakening, apart from its longer duration, was its general character. Almost universally the scattered sparks of revival fire were fanned into flame by prayer. In the East there were few signs of unusual emotionalism, such as had characterized the earlier era, but in the West excesses frequently accompanied the numerous "camp meetings."[2] This change in the East affords an illustration of the tempering influence of civilization upon what were once frontier communities. Education and sophistication were the principal forces which tended to restrain the emotional element in religious experience.[3]

[1] William W. Sweet, *Revivalism in America* (New York, 1944).
[2] Arthur B. Strickland, *The Great American Revival* (Cincinnati, Ohio, 1934), 56-7; cf., 104.
[3] This thesis is set forth by W. W. Sweet, *op. cit.*

298

It is worthy of note that among Baptists there were far-sighted leaders in America, as in England, who saw the importance of combining with the evangelistic zeal of a developing sect a persistent emphasis upon a trained ministry. While this insight was not characteristic of the rank and file of Baptists in their early development, it became increasingly significant to them during the nineteenth century, as is made evident by the multiplication of schools established by 1900. A review of their remarkable achievements in both evangelism and education will indicate the close interrelationship between the two interests.

Achievements in Evangelism to 1900

The outstanding revivalistic churches in the growing nation were those of the Baptists, Congregationalists, Methodists, and Presbyterians. It is not surprising then that in 1795, two prominent Baptists, Stephen Gano of Providence, Rhode Island, and Isaac Backus of Middleboro, Massachusetts, joined with twenty-one other New England ministers in issuing a "Circular Letter," calling upon all ministers and churches to pray for a revival. Their proposal for a nation-wide "Concert of Prayer" met with enthusiastic approval from church and college leaders throughout the country. The Moravian and Reformed Synods, the Methodist Districts, the Presbyteries, and the Baptist and Congregational Associations led the churches in a great intercessory movement which developed into a widespread revival of evangelical Christianity.[4]

The revival currents ran deep and without unusual display through the church life of the East. For example, the First Baptist Church of Boston, which had opposed Whitefield's revivalism in 1740, experienced in 1803 a remarkable spiritual awakening. In two years, one hundred and thirty-five were baptized. In the Second Church of Boston a still larger number were converted, and this at a time when Unitarianism had claimed all but one of the Congregational churches in that city.[5] This was typical of many Baptist churches in New England and the Middle States. In the South, even greater gains were being made.[6]

[4] Strickland, *op. cit.,* 44-9.
[5] N. E. Wood, *The History of the First Baptist Church of Boston,* (Philadelphia, 1899), pp. 294-6.
[6] See Chapter Eight.

Practically all of the colleges, which in the main were church schools, enjoyed revivals. In fact, in these institutions we see the commingling of evangelism and education. College presidents in their annual reports to their boards of trustees expressed their great concern for the spiritual welfare of their students. In western schools in particular, evangelistic services were common, and in many cases they were integral parts of the school's yearly schedule.[7] Out of a Christian group of students at Williams College, in Massachusetts, came the famous Haystack Prayer Meeting of 1808, which resulted in a great missionary enthusiasm among students. Indeed, it was a contributing factor to the organization of the foreign missionary societies, for out of such a revivalistic atmosphere came Adoniram Judson and Luther Rice, whose conversion from Congregational to Baptist principles prompted the Baptists to undertake a national missionary organization just six years later.

In the West, the center of the revivals was Kentucky into which state there flowed at the turn of the century, waves of immigrants from Virginia and North Carolina, most of whom were Baptists or Presbyterians. These two denominations, with the Methodists, comprised the major church groups in the western territories. In 1786, Baptists and Presbyterians each had sixteen churches in the state. Whereas the Presbyterian ministers usually were well trained, most of the Baptist ministers were poorly trained, and frequently they were hostile to classical education. Coming out of a background of New Light Baptist development and of the accompanying persecution by the Established Church of Virginia, the Baptists were opposed to anything that suggested an established clergy. Nevertheless, there was spiritual warmth in their "Covenant Meetings," held on the Saturday evening preceding the monthly Communion Sunday. Out of these stimulating times of soul-searching came periods of spiritual refreshing. Likewise, local revivals developed quite naturally out of the pre-communion preparatory services of the Presbyterians and out of the class-meeting experiences of Methodists. Under the leadership of James McGready and Barton W. Stone, both of whom were Presbyterians, and with the assistance of Methodist preachers, who frequently were laymen with a gift of exhorting, there developed the

[7] Strickland, *The Great American Revival,* chap. 5; and Peter G. Mode, *The Frontier Spirit in American Christianity* (New York, 1923), chap. 4.

"camp meetings" to which hundreds of people came for the inspiration of preaching and fellowship.

It is notable that Baptists in Kentucky did not experience the physical excitements which were so prominent among Presbyterians and Methodists. Except in the upper Green River country and eastern Tennessee, where the Separate Baptists were most numerous, their revivals continued in an orderly manner.[8] The effects of these revivals were felt widely in the local churches and associations. The South Elkhorn Baptist Church, with a membership of 127 in 1800, baptized 318 during the revival period. The Great Crossing Church, which had been organized in 1785, twelve years after Daniel Boone had come to Kentucky, had never been strong; indeed, only six members had been added through experience and baptism from 1795 to 1800. Then came the revival, and 175 were added; in 1801, 186 additional converts were added. In time, three new churches grew out of the mother church. The Elkhorn Association, whose twenty-nine churches reported in 1799 only twenty-nine conversions, was able to announce in 1801 the reception of over three thousand members by baptism and experience and nine new churches. A year later, it had grown to forty-eight churches and 5,300 members.

Such records were typical of the remarkable growth among Baptists not only in Kentucky, but also in western Pennsylvania and adjoining territories. In New York State, Baptists increased from four thousand in 1790 to twelve thousand in 1800, to sixty thousand in 1832, and to more than ninety-seven thousand in 1843. The number of their churches had grown from ninety-four in 1800 to 803 in 1843. Between 1800 and 1830 the Baptists ranked third in general increase in membership. By 1850 they were second only to the Methodists.[9]

The "camp meeting" variety of evangelism was not universally acceptable to Baptists. Along the seaboard from New England to Georgia, Baptists viewed with disfavor the emotional excesses attendant upon it. When some Baptists in Alabama resorted to camp

[8] William H. Spencer, *A History of Kentucky Baptists from 1769 to 1885.* 2 vols. (Cincinnati, 1885), I, 535.

[9] Strickland, *The Great American Revival*, 92-103, 188-9. From 1800 to 1830, Methodists increased sevenfold (64,000 to 476,153); Presbyterians fourfold (40,000 to 173,329); Baptists threefold (100,000 to 313,138); Congregationalists, in spite of Unitarian inroads, twofold (75,000 to 140,000). By 1850 the Methodists had grown to 1,323,631; Baptists to 815,212; Presbyterians to 487,691; Congregationalists to 197,197.

meetings about 1831 and in Georgia in the 1840's, the experiment did not meet with unanimous favor. John Mason Peck, the intrepid evangelist in the West and co-founder of the American Baptist Home Mission Society in 1832, was critical, although not unfriendly to any good which might come of the camp meetings. Generally speaking, Baptist revivals were experienced in the local churches and associational gatherings during the course of regular meetings or in periods of several days or weeks, known as "protracted meetings." [10]

During this era of revival impetus, the Baptists not only organized the Triennial Convention for foreign missions and the American Baptist Home Mission Society, but established several schools. In addition, there emerged such religious periodicals as *The Watchman*, in 1819, and the *Morning Star*, a Free Will Baptist publication, in 1826; these especially were products of the revival era. The Baptist General Tract Society was organized in 1824, later to be called the American Baptist Publication Society. Similar developments were occurring in the other evangelical denominations. Without a doubt, the Great Revival of the early nineteenth century provided the dynamic for growth and spiritual vigor among Protestants generally.

In the years following the War of 1812, the focal point of revivals shifted from Kentucky to central and western New York. The revival influence was felt also in New England. During a revival in Vermont in 1816, nearly two thousand were added to Baptist churches. The Berkshire Association in Massachusetts almost doubled its baptisms, increasing their number from 138 to 263. In New York State, the Hudson River Association, in the same year, increased from 988 members to 1,267 members; while the Saratoga Association reported four new churches and 450 baptisms in one year.[11]

In the thirties and forties, Charles G. Finney, a lawyer of Adams, New York, who was converted at twenty-nine years of age, was the outstanding revivalist. Among other revivalists contemporary with him was a fellow Presbyterian, Jedidiah Burchard; and four prominent Baptists, Thomas Sheardown, Jabez Swan, Elder Jacob Knapp, and Emerson Andrews. Swan conducted evangelistic meet-

[10] B. F. Riley, *History of the Baptists of Alabama, 1808-1894*, 53, 78, 188-90; B. D. Ragsdale, *Story of Georgia Baptists*, III, 391-4; Rufus Babcock, *Memoir of John Mason Peck, D.D.*, 200-1.

[11] Strickland, *The Great American Revival*, 113-4.

ings with great success in New York and Connecticut baptizing during his ministry ten thousand converts. Knapp, a graduate of Hamilton Literary and Theological Institute, the Baptist school in New York State, was not only a successful evangelist, but also was largely responsible for the impetus to converted drunkards to organize in 1840 the famous temperance fellowship known as the Washington Society. Andrews was Massachusetts-born, but devoted his ministry to New York as well as New England. He was a convert of Asahel Nettleton, the Congregational evangelist, but became a Baptist while at college. In thirty-five years he held three hundred protracted meetings.

In the fifth decade of the century, there was a marked decline in the revivals, a trend which continued until the Panic of 1857. In all probability, two factors were responsible for this declension. The Millerite Movement, as we have seen, reached its height in 1844, only to lose prestige when the Lord did not return on the date which Miller had set. The New York Baptist Missionary Convention, for example, reported in 1844 only 274 baptisms as the result of missionary labor, in contrast to 1,857 during the preceding year. The total number of baptisms in the established churches of the state suffered a proportionate drop from 15,794 in 1843 to 4,028 in 1844. The second contributing factor was a reaction to the methods employed by evangelists of the more professional type.[12] In addition, the period of prosperity which preceded the great depression of 1857 was not conducive to serious concern for spiritual welfare.

The panic which followed upon an era of careless speculation and overexpansion brought many to grips with poverty and to an awareness of their spiritual need. In a little room on the third floor of the "Consistory" of the old Dutch Reformed Church on Fulton Street, New York City, a handful of people began to gather at noonday for prayer. In a comparatively short time, their number had outgrown their quarters. Not only was the place of meeting moved to the more spacious John Street Methodist Church, but similar prayer services began in other parts of the city, and soon were being held in Philadelphia, Boston, and eventually across the country. Newspapers reported the meetings, and a great revival swept the

[12] *Ibid.*, 132; Charles W. Brooks, *A Century of Missions in the Empire State* (Philadelphia, 1909, revised edition), 137-8.

nation and moved even across the Atlantic to Great Britain. It has been estimated that through this medium, which came to be known as the "Prayer-meeting Revival," one million persons were converted. In a way, America was thus prepared for the strain of five years of civil conflict. During that period the revivals were continued in the military camps and in the churches.

Following the war, an era of professional evangelists brought to the limelight Dwight L. Moody, B. Fay Mills, M. B. Williams, J. Wilbur Chapman, William E. Biederwolf, Billy Sunday, Reuben A. Torrey, Gipsy Smith, and a host of others who represented an inter-denominational and often highly organized appeal for converts to Protestantism. In general, all of the evangelical churches benefited greatly from their efforts. While the frontier was passing away, the frontier type of evangelism had been, for the time being at least, successfully supported by mass choirs, fine song leaders, and careful preparation, lending it strong appeal even to the city populace. It is apparent from the continuous growth of Baptists throughout the country to the close of the century that they were rewarded by their participation in the constant program of evangelism which character-ized that period in American church life.

Baptists shared in the development of the evangelistic methods which emerged out of the early preaching services and shaped them to meet the peculiar needs of the times.[18] The camp meetings were devised for the benefit of the many scattered frontier families. Some families traveled great distances to hear the preaching of the gospel for a period of three or four days and then returned to their isolated homes. In time the Presbyterians and Baptists dropped this method, but the Methodists continued it. During Nettleton's ministry, the meetings for inquirers, which followed the preaching service, became popular with many, including Baptists; for such meetings prevented the embarrassment which individuals experienced when they were pressed to make a public display of their need for guidance and in-struction in the Christian life. Out of the Saturday Covenant Meet-ings of Baptists and the pre-communion three-day preparation services of Presbyterians came the protracted revival meetings, which soon became an integral part of the church year in most of the evangelical denominations. Such meetings, in turn, gave rise to the

---

[18] For a good presentation of evangelistic methods, see Strickland, *op. cit.*, chap. 10.

professional revivalist or evangelist who devoted his entire time to an itinerant ministry of a week or two in each church or community.

Some evangelists were well trained and earnest; others were poorly prepared for their task, though sincere; and not a few were charlatans who played upon the emotions of the people in an unworthy manner, often for selfish purposes. It was the latter type who caused a reaction in many quarters to revival meetings. Finney's innovations—prolonged invitations, praying for the unconverted by name, encouraging women to speak and pray in public meetings, and the practice of inviting sinners to come forward to the "anxious seat" as a method of helping them reach a decision—although criticized by some, were adopted by many. Among Baptists, itinerant evangelists were employed by the Home Mission Society and by state conventions to conduct revival meetings. Associational gatherings also afforded some opportunity for evangelistic preaching. And always, the Baptist academies and colleges were looked upon as effective agencies for the evangelizing as well as the educating of youth. Likewise, the Sunday schools, which were developed in the nineteenth century, provided fertile soil for evangelism.

The Formative Period of Education to 1850

While Baptists traditionally have not placed education foremost in the requirement of their ministers, insisting first of all upon personal piety and the leading of the Spirit in preaching, they have not disregarded education and many have devoted themselves diligently to its promotion. While the majority have regarded it sufficient for laymen to know how to read the Bible for themselves, many have realized the importance of a trained minstry. Hence, Baptists were participants in the academy movement that began in the Colonies in the eighteenth century. This was an effort to establish secondary schools to prepare young men for a theological seminary training. Since that time there has been a steady increase in interest in higher education on the part of Baptist leaders. In this respect they have been influenced greatly by the superior standards of the Presbyterians and Episcopalians, as well as by the generally advancing standards of American education. The story of their interest in education reflects the gradual rise of their cultural level through the past two and a half centuries.

Colonial education was primarily religious in character and was controlled more or less by the religious "meeting" of the Congregational Church in New England, by the Quakers of Pennsylvania, and by the Established Church in Virginia. Thus, the training of youth for the most part, was in the hands of the clergy, several of whom established in their own homes informal schools for the education in particular of candidates for the ministry. There were, of course, elementary schools of a sort, especially in New England and Pennsylvania. In the latter colony, German pietistic sects insisted upon a parochial training for their children which would guarantee the continuance of their own customs and ideals.

Although the records are scanty and incomplete concerning Baptist church schools on the elementary level, it is reported that there was a schoolhouse connected with the Lower Dublin Baptist Church, Philadelphia, in the early eighteenth century. It is said also that schools were conducted in connection with the Southampton and Great Valley churches near Philadelphia. Along the frontier, Baptist settlers in Somerset and Cambria Counties (about seventy miles southeast and east respectively of Pittsburgh) used their churches as schoolhouses from the first.[14]

In addition to these elementary church schools, there were secondary schools or academies which provided a classical training for the purpose of preparing boys of suitable qualifications to pursue advanced studies for the ministry. The Baptists were among the first to project plans for such schools. As early as 1722 the Philadelphia Association asked the churches for recruits who might be sent to such a school at the expense of a liberal Baptist contributor of London, Thomas Hollis, 2d, a merchant who had given generously to Harvard College. A similar request to encourage likely boys to enter the ministry was made in 1731.[15]

In 1756 the Reverend Isaac Eaton founded an academy or Latin grammar school at Hopewell, New Jersey, where he was pastor. In that year and the two ensuing, the Philadelphia Association engaged in its first attempt to raise money among its member churches

---

[14] James P. Wickersham, *A History of Education in Pennsylvania*, 101.

[15] *Philadelphia Baptist Association Minutes: 1707-1807*, 27, 32. On Hollis' benefactions, see Reuben A. Guild, *Life, Times, and Correspondence of James Manning and the Early History of Brown University*, 121 (footnote); David A. MacQueen, "Thomas Hollis: Early Baptist Benefactor," *The Chronicle*, Vol. VI, No. 2 (April, 1943), 75-82.

for the support of education. It not only contributed to the support of the new institution, but also appointed a committee for regular inspection, thereby bringing the school under its oversight. During the eleven years of the Academy's existence, the Philadelphia Baptists contributed £400 toward its support. When the school ceased to exist, the invested monies were placed in a general educational fund of the Association.[16]

The Association, not satisfied with only a preparatory school for its ministerial students, made plans for the erection of a college in Rhode Island, where sectarian tests were not required to secure a charter.[17] To the Reverend James Manning, who had been a pupil of Eaton at Hopewell Academy, and who had graduated from the College of New Jersey (now Princeton University) in 1762, was delegated the task of presenting the proposition to a company of New England Baptists at Newport, Rhode Island, in July, 1763. With the aid of such Philadelphia clergymen as Morgan Edwards and Samuel Jones, a charter was secured in February, 1764, from the General Assembly of that state. Thereupon, Manning moved to Warren, a town about ten miles from Providence, where he established an academy or Latin school to prepare students for the college, and where he became pastor of a newly organized church. In 1765 he was elected president of the college which was opened in Warren. The institution became a nucleus for Baptist activities in New England, for in 1767, the Warren Association was organized, largely under the influence of its president. As the Association grew, it gave material support to the young school. In 1770 the college was moved to Providence where a building was erected.[18]

The charter placed chief control of the new Rhode Island College in Baptist hands, but assured that it should never become narrowly sectarian by permitting men of other denominations to serve as trustees and teachers. In the first Corporation of twenty-four men there were one Congregationalist, two Episcopalians, of whom one was Governor Joseph Wanton, and four Quakers, of whom the Honorable Stephen Hopkins was selected to be Chancellor. The remaining seventeen members were Baptists. It was carefully specified

---

[16] Morgan Edwards, *Materials towards a History of Baptists in America,* II, 48-50.

[17] Isaac Backus, *History of the Baptists in New England,* II, 137.

[18] Today this college is Brown University. For a detailed account, see Reuben A. Guild, *Manning and Brown University.*

that no religious tests of any kind should ever be introduced; that youths of any religious denomination should share alike the advantages, emoluments, and honors of the institution; and that sectarian differences might be studied and explained, but never made a part of the public instruction.[19] Baptists had suffered too many educational restrictions at the hands of state churches to inflict the same kind of treatment upon others.

The Philadelphia Association continued to manifest interest in its protégé, contributing financial and moral support through the years. In 1774 it endorsed a plan which had been adopted by the Charleston (South Carolina) and Warren Associations requesting every Baptist to pay sixpence annually for three successive years for the support of the college. Thus were the poorer members encouraged to support this educational enterprise in order to supplement the larger gifts of the wealthy.[20] While the Association's interest in Rhode Island College overshadowed its other educational interests, there were several private academies under the tutelage of Baptist ministers in the vicinity of the Association. Besides Eaton's Latin Grammar School at Hopewell, New Jersey, which remained in existence until 1767, there was an academy at Lower Dublin, a suburb of Philadelphia, which was conducted by the pastor of the Lower Dublin Baptist Church, Dr. Samuel Jones, from 1765 to 1795. It was a boarding school where classical and theological subjects were taught.

In the South also there were evidences of a growing interest in a trained ministry.[21] While Episcopalians and Presbyterians had given the initial impetus to both ministerial and secular education in Virginia, the Baptists of that state undertook in 1788 to establish a seminary, a project which did not actually materialize until the next century (1832). Prior to this time, their social attitude and antipathy to the Anglican clergy, under whose intolerance they had suffered, caused them to be slow to sponsor education. This picture changed, however, when they had won their struggle for religious freedom.

[19] R. A. Guild, *Manning and Brown University,* Chap. 1.

[20] *Philadelphia Baptist Association Minutes: 1707-1807,* 109, 135; Henry C. Vedder, *History of Baptists in the Middle States* (Philadelphia, 1898), 210.

[21] Wesley M. Gewehr, *The Great Awakening in Virginia, 1740-1790* (Durham, N. C., 1930), 219, 234; Wood Furman, *A History of the Charleston Association of Baptist Churches in the State of North Carolina* (Charleston, S. C., 1811), 14-15, 21, 51.

The Charleston Association, which had been organized in 1751 by the Baptists of Charleston, South Carolina, and vicinity, assisted, as we have seen, in raising funds for Rhode Island College. In 1789 it established a plan for an education fund to assist pious young candidates for the ministry. Between 1791 and 1810 a total of $8,480 was received from churches, individuals, and accumulated interest on invested monies. During that period nearly $3,400 was expended in the purchase of a library and in the education of students. The outstanding leader in this enterprise was Dr. Richard Furman of Charleston, whose vision and effort was to arouse Baptists to their need for trained leadership in the years ahead.

The Philadelphia Association, which from the beginning of the movement to establish Baptist schools had been the motivating center, was to play an even more important role in this period than in the period of expansion and consolidation which followed. It set the pattern for Baptists throughout the country by establishing in July, 1812, the Baptist Education Society of the Middle States. Though nominally for the Middle States, it really was local to the city and was called also "The Baptist Education Society of Philadelphia." The Society appointed Dr. William Staughton, former pastor of the First Baptist Church, as tutor to carry out its purpose in educating ministerial students. He took such boys into his own home for instruction; from that beginning was to develop a theological seminary.

Following the example set by Philadelphia, Baptists of Massachusetts, Rhode Island, New York, South Carolina, Georgia, and Maine, in the next seven years, organized state education societies. When the Triennial Convention was formed in 1814, its first president, Dr. Richard Furman of Charleston, South Carolina, worked toward the eventual appointing of a committee to establish a theological institution of the Baptist General Convention. A house was rented in Philadelphia, and this work was carried on from 1818 until 1821 under the direction of Dr. Staughton and the Reverend Ira Chase, his associate.

In 1821, a plot of ground in Washington, D. C., was presented to the Convention for the location, in the nation's capital, of a great Baptist institution. This enterprise was the dream and hope of Luther Rice, agent for the Triennial Convention, with responsibility not only to promote missions but also to advance the cause of ministerial education. Since his return to America from Burma in 1813, he had persistently visited the churches in the interest of the foreign mission enterprise in which his colaborer, Adoniram Judson, was engaged. His experience had taught him that the ultimate success of foreign missions was dependent upon a trained ministry, and it was his awareness of this fact that impelled him to call upon his fellow Baptists throughout the nation to establish colleges to train missionaries.

The full scope of Rice's vision was embodied, therefore, in the charter obtained from Congress in February, 1821, incorporating "the Columbian College in the District of Columbia" with full powers to establish faculties in ordinary classical instruction, law, divinity, and medicine. Dr. Staughton was elected president. Consequently the little school in Philadelphia was moved to Washington, D. C., to be merged with Columbian College as the theological department under the direction of Ira Chase. The merger, however, was not permanent; many did not favor the trend to broaden the functions of the Triennial Convention. Financial difficulties engulfed the struggling institution, and the Convention gave up the project. In 1825 Professor Chase was invited to Newton Centre, Massachusetts, to form a course of study for a newly organized Baptist school to be known as Newton Theological Institution. Columbian College in Washington, D. C., was reorganized within a few years and enlarged into a university. Columbian University was never strong; yet it has continued in existence to the present day, and is now known as George Washington University, a coeducational and nonsectarian school under private auspices.

Perhaps the attempt to establish a national Baptist college was premature, for state lines were still sharply drawn in the minds of Americans. This was particularly true in the older states along the eastern seaboard. Yet, the impulse which the launching of Columbian College had given to Baptist education in America was felt widely. Indeed, it had been antedated in New England by the chartering in 1813 of The Maine Literary and Theological Institution. That school, however, did not begin operations until 1818, when a site was selected in Waterville. Dr. Jeremiah Chaplin, of Danvers, Massachusetts, was secured to direct the school. In 1820, the school was incorporated as Waterville College, and it possessed a theological department. Five years later, however, when the Newton Theological Institution was established near Boston, the latter instruction was discontinued. The school at Waterville then developed into what came to be called Colby University in 1867 (later, Colby College). It was named in honor of its chief benefactor, Gardner Colby, a wealthy Boston merchant whose mother had been befriended by Dr. Chaplin.

The Newton Theological Institution was founded in 1825 under the direction of the Massachusetts Baptist Education Society. The Reverend Ira Chase was invited to bring the theological department from Columbian College in Washington, D. C. He was the first professor of the new seminary, and to it he devoted sacrificial service for twenty years. By the close of the century, endowment funds had been secured, and more than eight hundred students had been graduated. This was the first American Baptist educational institution to be devoted exclusively to a three-year theological curriculum for college graduates.

Throughout New England several academies were established, some by state education societies, some by associations, and some by individuals. Among these were three in Maine: Hebron Academy (1804), Coburn Classical Institute (1829), and Houlton Academy (1847), all of which were affiliated with Colby University in 1877. The Connecticut Literary Institution in Suffield was founded in 1833 by the Baptist Education Society of that state. In Vermont and New Hampshire, six academies came into existence within thirty-seven years: Brandon (1832), Black River Academy at Ludlow (1834), Leland and Gray (1835), Derby (1840), New Hampton (1853), and Vermont (1869), which was coeducational.

In New York State an Education Society had been organized at Hamilton in 1817. This organization became the nucleus for the development of a university and a theological seminary at Hamilton, and later, of two institutions at Rochester. The Hamilton Literary and Theological Institution, which opened in 1820, was restricted until 1839 to its original purpose of educating students for the ministry. After that date a limited number of young men who did not have the ministry in view were admitted. By 1846 the collegiate department was chartered as Madison University, the theological department being kept as a separate corporation so as not to become subject to the supervision of the state.

The following year there began a heated controversy over a proposal to remove the two schools to Rochester, which had the advantages of a growing urban center. About the same time, the Baptists in the western part of the state were anticipating the establishment of a theological seminary at Rochester. While court litigation was in process, an educational convention of Baptists met in Albany on October 9, 1849, to work out a compromise whereby Hamilton agreed to the proposed removal of the university to Rochester and Rochester abandoned the project of a theological school. The New York Supreme Court, however, ruled against removal of the two institutions from Hamilton. In the years that followed, the friends of the schools at Hamilton increased, the chief donor being James B. Colgate, banker, and son of the soap manufacturer, in whose honor Madison University was renamed Colgate University; its preparatory school likewise was named Colgate Academy. In 1893 the seminary was placed under the administration of the University, although the Education Society still maintained influence in the election of the theological faculty and assisted students who were preparing for the ministry.

When the litigation concerning the removal of Madison University and its seminary to Rochester was ended, the Baptists in the western part of the state organized the University of Rochester in 1850 and obtained a permanent charter a year later. It was to be a denominational college without being narrowly sectarian, with control vested in twenty Baptists of the corporation, the remaining four members of the corporation representing various denominations. Rochester Theological Seminary was established simultaneously by The New York Baptist Union for Ministerial Education, which had been organized for the purpose. The relations between the two schools were not without friction, owing to failure in arranging a compact between the Board of the University and the Educational Union, as had been done at Hamilton. In 1854, a German department of the Seminary was organized to provide leadership for the increasing number of German Baptists in the country. Both institutions had attained great prominence by the close of the century.

In western Pennsylvania, Baptists undertook as early as 1846 to establish an educational center where their children might be trained under denominational influence. The Northumberland Baptist Association in that year founded an academy, first located in the basement of the Baptist church at Lewisburg, a town centrally situated in the Association. Within three years the plan had enlarged so as to expand the school into "The University of Lewisburg." The object of the institution was to provide broader educational facilities for men and women who were not necessarily preparing for the ministry. A "University Female Institute" was added within a year of the opening of the college, with which it was merged later, thereby representing an early venture in American coeducation. The founding of the school was significant, because it indicated the interest of rural Pennsylvania Baptists in providing education for young people who were not preparing for the ministry and who were not financially able to secure the usually expensive college training. It also was an indication of a liberal attitude toward the education of girls at a time when it was not popular to provide for them on a coeducational basis. Among the staunch supporters of the school was William Bucknell, a wealthy Philadelphia broker, whose large gifts to erect new buildings and to establish an endowment were recognized, after his death, by giving his name to the institution. Thus the University of Lewisburg has been known since as Bucknell University.

The pattern of the formation of schools in the western states was much the same as that already reviewed in the East. Education societies were established in the West, although not so strictly along state lines, for Baptists were not numerous or strong enough in some areas to support agencies for each state. The leading spirit in behalf of education as well as missionary expansion in the West was John Mason Peck. Out of his practical experience since 1817 in the pioneer territory of Missouri and Illinois, he realized the need for a seminary which would provide, as he put it:

A practical English education [in contrast to the typical classical theological training of his day] . . . open to all on very economical principles, and where teachers of common schools could receive better instruction than many of them had enjoyed, but especially . . . where ministers of the gospel, whether young, or farther advanced in years, could come and spend more or less time, according to their several circumstances and exigencies, in learning those things in which their deficiencies were the most painfully felt. . . .[22]

On January 1, 1827, such a school was organized in Peck's home at Rock Spring, Illinois, with the co-operation of Baptists in

[22] Babcock, *Memoir of John Mason Peck, D.D.*, 225.

Missouri and Illinois. The new institution was opened on the following November 1, in spite of the opposition of anti-mission advocates, who were opposed to seminaries. It was known as the Rock Spring Seminary until 1832, when it was moved to Upper Alton, a site agreed upon by Peck and his friend, Dr. Jonathan Going of Massachusetts, during the latter's visit to the West the preceding year.

It was through the joint planning of these two men and the enthusiastic report of Dr. Going to the Massachusetts Baptist Missionary Society that The Western Baptist Educational Association was founded in 1832 for the purpose of promoting good schools and education in the Mississippi Valley. A sum of two thousand dollars was raised for the special training of teachers for the West. This Society was one of three organized within a period of five years; the other two being The Western Baptist Education Society, established in Cincinnati, Ohio, in 1833, and the Pennsylvania Baptist Education Society a few years later. It is significant that the agency for advancing ministerial training in the West came into existence in the same year and through the efforts of the same men of vision, Peck and Going, whose planning was responsible for the organization of the American Baptist Home Mission Society. It serves as a further illustration of the interrelationship between education and evangelism among Baptists.

By 1835 Peck's school at Upper Alton, Illinois, had obtained a charter as a college and been renamed Shurtleff College in recognition of a gift of ten thousand dollars made by Dr. Benjamin Shurtleff, a wealthy Baptist of Boston. Other Baptists of the East subscribed an equal sum toward the creation of an endowment for the institution.

Another center of educational development among western Baptists was Granville, Ohio, where a manual-labor school was established in 1832 under the name of The Granville Literary and Theological Institution. In 1845 it became a college, and in 1856 was renamed and expanded into Denison University in honor of its chief benefactor. Typical of the practice of the time, a Ladies' Institute also was organized at Granville in 1832. Because of the added expense entailed in the maintenance of separate schools for young men and young women, Baptists later in the century began to abandon the plan in favor of coeducational institutions.

In the Michigan Territory there appeared as early as 1829 a young man by the name of Thomas W. Merrill, who had been trained at Colby College in Maine and at Newton Theological Institution in Massachusetts. In 1833 he became the founder of the Michigan and Huron Institute at Kalamazoo, with financial assistance from the Baptist Missionary Convention of New York State. In 1849 the Kalamazoo Theological Seminary was opened in the same place under the management of the Baptist Convention of the state of Michigan. Six years later the Institute was reincorporated as Kalamazoo College. In 1837 Indiana Baptists, through an Education Society which they had organized in 1834, founded a Manual-Labor Institute at Franklin, which in 1844 became Franklin College.

In the South the leadership of Dr. Richard Furman was felt strongly, for as president of the Triennial Convention and also of the Convention of South Carolina, his own state, he was able to guide educational policies. It was at his request that the second Triennial Convention, meeting in Philadelphia in 1817, undertook plans to establish a national Baptist school at Washington, D. C. He was chairman of the Committee on Education which recommended to the Convention a plan to form associated educational societies throughout the country.[23] A school bearing his name, the Furman Academy and Theological Institute, was organized in 1826 under the auspices of the Charleston Association. After many struggles to gain financial and academic stability, it developed in 1851 into Furman University.

Alabama Baptists manifested an early interest in education. At the first meeting of their state convention in 1823, a generous financial contribution was made to Columbian College at Washington, D. C. In 1835 a brave attempt was made to establish a manual-labor institute on home soil in the founding of the Alabama Institute of Literature and Industry at Greensboro. It was forced to close, however, in 1837 for lack of funds and students. Through the efforts of individual Baptists, three schools for girls were organized in the state between 1836 and 1839. The second project of the Convention was not undertaken until 1841, when the foundation of Howard College was laid in a high school for boys. The college opened at Marion in

[23] *Proceedings of the Baptist Convention for Missionary Purposes, 1814-1826*, 140, 194, 298-307.

1842. A fire which destroyed the building the following year did not defeat the enterprise, for within four years, college work was begun. By 1854 education was the foremost interest of Alabama Baptists, and Associations vied with one another to establish local schools of high grade.[24]

In Georgia the leading advocate of education was Dr. Jesse Mercer, a prominent preacher and editor from 1833 to 1840 of the *Christian Index*. He aroused interest in providing an educated ministry by keeping the academic needs of the denomination before his fellow Baptists. In 1833 Mercer University was organized. At the same time, Georgia Baptists were carrying on educational work for their colored Baptist population. In North Carolina a manual-labor school was brought into existence in 1834 under the name Wake Forest Institute. Five years later it became a college, and like others of its type, it afforded an opportunity for poor boys to secure training by making it possible for them to work for their expenses.

The Virginia Baptist Education Society had been organized as early as 1830. It manifested special interest in the newly established Columbian College. Two years later, a manual-labor school was founded at Richmond under the direction of a prominent Baptist, Robert Ryland. In 1840 it became a college which developed into the University of Richmond. It did not receive active support from the Maryland Baptists, for their proximity to Columbian College in Washington, D. C., caused them to devote to that institution such interest as they had in education.

From the foregoing survey, it becomes apparent that the conviction among Baptists of the necessity for an educated ministry had spread rapidly, finding its chief expression in institutions within the several states. But with the exception of a few farsighted men like James Manning, Morgan Edwards, Richard Furman, Luther Rice, Jonathan Going, and John Mason Peck, there had been few who had seen the need for co-ordination and conservation of effort in the educational enterprise. All too frequently, rivalry between associations, educational societies, and conventions, while stimulating achievement, unfortunately depleted resources which were all too meagre to begin with.

[24] B. F. Riley, *History of the Baptists of Alabama, 1808-1894* (Birmingham, 1895), 40, 87-91, 124-37, 193, 215.

Baptists generally were not yet ready for a closely knit denominationalism. When Luther Rice sought support for Columbian College, which he envisioned as the national school to train Baptist leaders, he soon met with criticism and suspicion that he was diverting funds from local needs. When the Northern Baptist Education Society was organized in 1829 to replace the Massachusetts Baptist Education Society and to widen its usefulness by having branches in all of the New England States, the Maine Baptist Education Society did not agree to become an auxiliary. Twenty years passed before Maine Baptists consented to enter into such a relationship, and then it was maintained only until 1858. The reason for the separation at that time was that the Society in Maine was losing income, a plight which they attributed to the general appeals which were being made by the Northern Baptist Education Society for institutions outside of the state.[25] While the case in point should not be construed as typical of all areas, it is indicative of a provincial feeling which militated against strong denominational solidarity.

In the West, state patriotism and local pride had not as yet become a hindrance to the development of a theological school that transcended state lines.[26] In November, 1833, a General Meeting of Baptists was held in Cincinnati, Ohio, to consider the advisability of providing theological training for western Baptists. As a consequence, a Western Baptist Education Society was organized the following year; and in 1840 a valuable property was secured at Covington, Kentucky, on the Ohio River. It was not until five years later, however, that the Western Baptist Theological Institute was fully organized and put in operation. The president, Dr. R. E. Pattison of Massachusetts, and the faculty were all northern men of anti-slavery sentiments. Embroiled as the Baptists were in the controversy which brought the Southern Baptist Convention into existence, the Institute with its pronounced stand against slavery could not hope to survive. The president was forced to sever his connection with the school when it became known that he had been seeking privately to remove

[25] *Proceedings of Maine Baptist Convention* for 1849, p. 25, and for 1858, p. 32.

[26] The following account is based primarily upon a presentation of theological education among Southern Baptists in two articles in *The Review and Expositor* (Louisville), Vol. XLIV, No. 2 (April, 1947) and Vol. XLIII, No. 2 (April, 1946) respectively: William W. Barnes, "The Theological Curriculum of Tomorrow in the Light of the Past"; W. O. Carver, "The Southern Baptist Theological Seminary in the Growing of the Denomination."

the institution to the northern side of the Ohio River, thereby assuring its control by anti-slavery Baptists. A successor was chosen in the person of Dr. S. W. Lynd, but the increasing friction necessitated sale of the property in 1855 with an equal division of the proceeds between the claimants.[27]

At that time Kentucky's Georgetown College, which had been founded in 1829, had no theological department. The portion, therefore, which fell to the South, was appropriated to the maintenance of a professor of theology in Georgetown College. Strong sentiment prevailed, however, among Southern Baptists in favor of a southern seminary which should give to the South and Southwest a center of unity for the newly organized Southern Baptist Convention. After a preliminary education conference at Nashville, held in conjunction with the sessions of The American Baptist Indian Mission Association on October 28, 1847, the question of establishing a southern school was left to the Southern Baptist Convention in its next triennial session to be held in May, 1849. Owing to various circumstances, however, the subject did not reach the Convention proper, but was considered at a special conference on the day following adjournment of the Convention. A committee of twenty was appointed to place the subject before Southern Baptists. Of this committee Dr. A. M. Poindexter of Virginia was chairman.

Up to this time leadership of the movement had been in the hands of the vice-president of the Convention, Dr. R. B. C. Howell of Nashville, Tennessee. But his removal to Richmond in 1850 left Baptists in the West without a leader. Moreover, Landmarkism was producing factionalism there; it was being led by J. R. Graves of Tennessee, who opposed a south-wide seminary. Consequently, the establishing of the projected institution was in the hands of Baptists of the seaboard states. The guiding spirit in the founding of the new school was James P. Boyce who, after completing his training at Princeton Seminary in the North, had recently become pastor at Columbia, South Carolina.

In 1859 the Southern Baptist Theological Seminary was established at Greenville, South Carolina, with a faculty of four professors, of which Dr. Boyce was chairman, and twenty-six students. Its suc-

[27] J. H. Spencer, *A History of Kentucky Baptists, 1769-1885,* 2 vols. (Cincinnati, 1886), I, 685-6.

cessful launching was indicative of the triumph of a denominational solidarity over state loyalties. It gave to the Southern Baptist Convention a strength which was invaluable, for it shaped the doctrinal and ecclesiastical viewpoint of the ministerial leadership throughout the Southern States.

The War between the States placed a great strain upon the financial resources of the young seminary. During the course of the conflict, the institution was obliged to suspend operation under the provisions of the Conscript Act of the Confederacy, which called young men into the army. On October 1, 1865, however, the seminary was reopened with a full faculty, but only eight students. Gradually the student body increased and likewise the financial needs. In 1866 the Southern Baptist Convention subscribed over ten thousand dollars to its support. The school was moved to new quarters in Louisville, Kentucky, with the Convention's approval, in 1873, when the Baptists of that state pledged three hundred thousand dollars for its support.[28] A financial crash prevented the pledge from being fulfilled completely, and economic difficulties harassed the institution. These were relieved from time to time by generous gifts. In spite of discouragements, the seminary grew until it took first place among southern theological schools.

By the time the country had emerged from the disruptions of war, great progress had been made in the educational phase of Baptist work. Several academies and colleges had been founded which gave evidence of a general interest in secondary and higher education. Theological training enjoyed continued emphasis as new seminaries arose in various parts of the country. While the standard of academic achievement was not high when contrasted with the present level, it compared quite favorably with like schools of other denominations, with the possible exception of the older Episcopalian and Presbyterian institutions. This was the more significant since Baptists generally were people of limited economic and cultural privileges.

The Strengthening Period of Education since 1850

By 1850 the "manifest destiny of America" had become more than a slogan; for already the flag had been borne in triumph to the Pacific coastline on the west and to the Rio Grande on the southwest.

[28] *Southern Baptist Convention Proceedings* for 1866, p. 16; for 1873, pp. 17-9.

Prosperity had characterized this era of railroad building, stock expansion, increased production, and growing international trade. To be sure, the general sense of well-being was interrupted by the brief, though severe, depression of 1857; and by the years of war between 1861 and 1865, which hampered the work of most educational institutions by depleting financial resources and personnel. This was particularly true in the Southern States. But the expansion of industry in the postwar era developed new riches, some of which found their way into the endowment funds of schools and educational societies. As Baptists grew in numbers from one in every thirty-two persons in the population in 1850, to one in every eighteen in 1900, so did the number of their institutions of learning increase. Between 1850 and 1860, twenty-three colleges were established, and still more came into being in the years that followed.

Among these was William Jewell College, which was incorporated at Liberty, Missouri, in 1849, as the cherished dream of Dr. William Jewell of Columbia, Missouri, who contributed sixteen thousand dollars to it. Instruction began on January 1, 1850. Later, because of the war, its doors were closed and did not reopen until 1868. The college was fostered by the General Association of Missouri Baptists. Stephens College, which was incorporated in 1856 as The Baptist Female College of Columbia, Missouri, was turned over to the General Association in 1870, when that body wanted a college for young women. James L. Stephens, a businessman of Columbia, provided the sum of twenty thousand dollars as endowment for the institution. While there were other schools established by Baptists in the state, these were the only two colleges adopted by the General Association. Indeed, between 1870 and 1880, resentment was rife in that body when other colleges than William Jewell laid claims upon it for support, so intense was its sense of loyalty to its chosen institution.[29]

In 1851 an educational convention met at Beloit, Wisconsin, to organize the Northwestern Baptist Education Society, which was to include Baptists in Wisconsin, Illinois, and Minnesota. Its purpose was to provide an educational institution which would be adequate to serve the states mentioned and perhaps Iowa and Michigan also. There was no agreement, however, as to its location, for Michigan

[29] R. S. Douglass, *History of Missouri Baptists* (Kansas City, Mo., 1934), 275-89.

Baptists favored Kalamazoo, while Wisconsin and Illinois Baptists desired it to be located in their respective states. A second convention met in 1860 in Chicago, where another step was taken; namely, the organization of a corporate body, to be known as the Baptist Theological Union for the Northwest, with authority to establish a seminary at Chicago. Its charter was not obtained until 1865, so it was not until 1867 that the desired institution came into existence under the name of The Baptist Union Theological Seminary. Ten years later it was removed from Chicago to Morgan Park. It then came under the able leadership of Dr. Thomas Wakefield Goodspeed, pastor of the Morgan Park church. He accepted the secretaryship of both the Theological Union and the Seminary in 1876.

Another school to be established in Chicago was the old University of Chicago, whose origin was due largely to the initiative of Baptist leaders in the city and of Dr. John C. Burroughs, who resigned the pastorate of the First Baptist Church of Chicago to become its first president. A gift of land was made by the Honorable Stephen A. Douglas, then United States Senator, whose late wife had been a Baptist. Buildings were erected between 1857 and 1866, but financial reverses suffered in the years that followed brought the institution to an untimely end in 1887.

It was succeeded in 1890 by the new University of Chicago, to which John D. Rockefeller contributed an initial gift of six hundred thousand dollars; this gift was followed by even larger sums, totaling several millions. Wealthy donors of Chicago made handsome contributions, and the members of the First Baptist Church subscribed eighty thousand dollars. Two-thirds of the trustees and the president of the University were to be Baptists, thus assuring its denominational affiliation without requiring it to be narrowly sectarian. The choice of the first president was a fortunate one—Dr. William R. Harper, who for several years had been professor of Hebrew and Old Testament Interpretation in the Baptist Union Theological Seminary at Morgan Park. He was the real creator of the institution. Through his sagacity, an illustrious faculty was gathered from all parts of the country, thereby assuring competent instruction in all departments, including post-graduate instruction. In 1892 the seminary at Morgan Park was transferred to Chicago, where it became the divinity school of the new university. A third school in Chicago was the Baptist Missionary Training School, founded in 1881 under the auspices of the Baptist women of the city.

The Wisconsin Baptists created an Education Society in 1854 with a view to establishing an institution of learning in that state. But they made the same error that so many other Baptists of the nineteenth century had made in carrying the cost of two separate schools for young men and young women. The one for boys was Wayland University at Beaver Dam; the one for girls was known as the Baptist Female College at Fox Lake. The result was financial distress and the closing of Wayland for eighteen months between 1859 and 1861, reopening it as a coeducational school, while the Fox Lake school in 1862 was turned over to the Congregationalists.

It was not until 1876, however, that Wayland was on a secure basis, and then, not as a university, but as an academy. For Wisconsin at the time was "academy" conscious, and many Baptists saw in the denominational preparatory schools the chief means for combating the secularism that was infiltrating state college campuses.[30]

In 1868, a theological seminary was organized in Pennsylvania. The Normal Institute at Upland, on the outskirts of Chester, had been built by John P. Crozer. His son, Samuel A. Crozer, upon his father's death, gave the property to the Baptists. After conferences between the Philadelphia Baptist Ministers' Conference and the University of Lewisburg, it was arranged to transfer the latter's theological department to Upland. The new seminary came to be known as the Crozer Theological Seminary for Baptists. As was the case with many other educational institutions, its existence had been made possible by the benefactions of a Christian businessman.

In 1886 Dr. Russell H. Conwell, pastor of the Grace Baptist Church, a great institutional church in Philadelphia, founded Temple College, a school for poor boys who could not afford the customary cost of a higher education. The college met for several years in the church; then buildings were secured for it by its untiring founder and president. While this school has been nonsectarian from its inception, it has had the support of Baptists and bears the impress of its founder, who was a truly great Baptist leader. It is a notable contribution of a church of working men and women who, without

    [30] A. E. Wichman "The Story of Baptist Education in Wisconsin," *The Chronicle*, Vol. XI, No. 2 (April, 1948), 66-76.

the aid of large gifts, responded nobly to their pastor's challenge to make higher education available to those of their own class.[31]

Among other institutions which came into existence, not hitherto mentioned, was Ottawa University. It was organized by the Kansas Baptist Convention at its initial meeting in 1860; however, it did not function as a college until 1869. In 1901 Kansas City Seminary (now known as Central Baptist Theological Seminary) was founded to provide ministerial leadership for Kansas and adjoining states. It includes The Woman's Training School as an integral part of its work. Sioux Falls College in South Dakota came into existence first as the Dakota Collegiate Institute in 1883, then as Sioux Falls University in 1885. Free Baptists also built schools in this era: a college at Spring Arbor, Michigan, in 1844, which was moved to Hillsdale in 1855; and a second in Maine in 1857, which became Bates College in 1863.

There was some attempt to provide denominational oversight of the Baptist schools in the North as early as 1868, when the American Baptist Educational Commission was brought into being in New York City. It was intended to serve as a medium of communication between prospective donors and needy institutions and as a source of counsel for schools and colleges, particularly in the newer states. It functioned through advisory committees and conventions held in larger cities. Although the Educational Commission did not become permanent, its general function was taken over later by the American Baptist Education Society, which was created in 1888 upon the recommendation of Dr. Henry L. Morehouse, secretary of the American Baptist Home Mission Society. Its purpose was to assist in formulating wiser plans in the founding of new schools and in the erection of buildings for new institutions of learning. Counsel was given through the corresponding secretary of the Society, the Reverend F. T. Gates of Minneapolis. The new agency also proved to be a helpful liaison office between generous donors and the Baptist schools and colleges which they chose to assist. The latter years of the century witnessed an appreciable increase in endowments by nearly all of the Baptist institutions whose rise has been mentioned in this survey.

[31] Agnes Rush Burr, *Russell H. Conwell and His Work* (Philadelphia, 1926), chaps. 27-9.

In the Southern States, most of the schools were under the supervision of associations, state conventions, or the Southern Baptist Convention. As church membership increased, the need for new schools became more pressing. This was especially true in the vast state of Texas, the population of which increased 404.57 per cent between 1860 and 1900, whereas the number of Baptists in the state during the same period increased by 1,643.48 per cent.[32] In 1841, when there were only four or five small churches in the state, Baptists had formed the Texas Baptist Education Society, which in turn had established the first Baylor University at Independence four years later. The primary purpose was to train ministers for the churches. Baylor Female College, which was included in the University for the first five years of its existence, was separated from it in 1851, although it had the same board of trustees and president. In 1866 it was entirely detached.

In 1856 Waco University had its humble beginnings as a male high school under the auspices of the Trinity River Association. Instruction was given in the First Baptist Church of Waco. In 1860 the Waco Association was organized and took over the school the year following as a University and Classical School. Not until 1866 does there appear to have been a theological department. Twenty years later the old Baylor institutions and Waco University were consolidated as the new Baylor University at Waco and the new Baylor College for Women at Belton. In 1894 a Department of Bible Teaching was established at Baylor University, with Dr. B. H. Carroll serving as principal. In 1905 this department became Baylor Theological Seminary. Within three years it was separated from the University, thereby becoming the Southwestern Baptist Theological Seminary (1908).

In the nineties, approximately fifteen Baptist colleges were formed in Texas under various auspices. None of them, however, was launched by the State Convention as Baylor University had been. All of them soon were suffering from indebtedness to the point that an Education Commission was set up by the Convention in 1897 to place them on a more secure financial basis. Dr. B. H. Carroll led the campaign to raise half a million dollars for this purpose.

<hr/>

[32] William W. Barnes, "The Theological Curriculum of Tomorrow in the Light of the Past," *The Review and Expositor*, Vol. XLIV, No. 2, 149.

Many other schools and benefactors might be mentioned, for the latter half of the nineteenth century was characterized by generous philanthropy and the establishment of church schools as well as state-supported institutions of learning. By the turn of the century the progress of Baptists in the field of denominational education was marked throughout the country. An over-all picture may be gained from a report made in 1902 to the Philadelphia Association. There were then in the United States thirty-six Baptist colleges and universities, with twelve thousand students; seven theological seminaries, with over one thousand students; twenty-nine colleges for women, of which Vassar at Poughkeepsie, New York, was the greatest, with a combined student body of four thousand; thirty-three institutions of learning for Negroes and Indians, with five thousand students; sixty-four preparatory schools and academies with twelve thousand students; a grand total of one hundred sixty-nine educational institutions with more than fifty-four thousand students, and with endowments, property, and invested funds amounting to not less than thirty million dollars.[83]

Sunday Schools and Publications

There is no better evidence of the interrelation of evangelism and education among Baptists than in their development of Sunday schools and periodical literature. Although a few such schools had been conducted prior to 1791, that date usually has been given for the beginning of permanent Sunday school work in America, for about that time schools "were organized almost simultaneously in Philadelphia, in Providence, Rhode Island, and in Passaic Falls, New Jersey." The instruction was largely secular, and was given by teachers who were paid.

It is believed that the first Sunday school for exclusively religious instruction was organized by the Second Baptist Church of Baltimore, in 1804. In September, 1815, a Presbyterian school was established in Philadelphia, and a week later three women of the First Baptist Church organized another. Baptists may therefore very properly claim to have been among the foremost in recognizing the importance of this work, and to have had no inconsiderable share in giving to it the form that it finally assumed.[84]

[83] *Philadelphia Baptist Association Minutes* for 1902, 24.

[84] Henry C. Vedder, *A History of the Baptists in the Middle States* (Philadelphia, 1898), 256. The following account is based primarily upon this source.

The movement gained popularity quickly and by 1825 had extended to most of the large cities and to many small towns. With the organization of the American Sunday School Union in 1824, it may be said that the new institution had become permanently established in Protestant churches. In many places the rapid growth of the Sunday schools led to the organization of new churches. This was particularly true in the West, where as new towns were built up, the Sunday schools preceded and later made possible the building of churches. Baptists everywhere utilized the Sunday school, for it became to them a vehicle of evangelism as well as of instruction.

The need for a distinctive Sunday school literature was supplied almost at once by the organization of a Baptist General Tract Society in Washington, D. C., on February 25, 1824. The Reverend Noah Davis, of Maryland, having picked up a tract on a street in Brooklyn in 1823 or earlier, laid hold upon the idea that Baptists should use the printed word as a means of evangelism. It was through his suggestion, therefore, that the Tract Society, forerunner of the American Baptist Publication Society, was founded. The first president was Dr. Obadiah B. Brown; the treasurer was the Reverend Luther Rice; and the general secretary, then called "agent," was George Wood. Over the vigorous protest of Luther Rice, who desired to centralize all national Baptist agencies in Washington, D. C., the Society voted on November 14, 1826, to move to Philadelphia where printing facilities were more easily accessible.

There, on Front Street, in a second story room, fifteen feet square, the first periodical, *The Baptist Tract Magazine,* was issued in July, 1827. In 1832 the Society began to publish tracts for foreign missionary service. Soon appeals for printed materials were coming from John Mason Peck in the West. About the same time, the new general secretary, the Reverend Ira M. Allen, urged the Society to undertake publication of Sunday school lessons. In this early period of Protestant Sunday school organization, he felt that the Baptist witness could best be maintained by preparation of denominational materials for use in Baptist churches. By 1840 the Baptist General Tract Society became the general publication agency of the denomination under the new name, The American Baptist Publication and Sunday School Society. To the original emphasis upon tract publication was added the preparation and distribution of Sunday school supplies and books. The first editor of Sunday school materials was Dr. John Newton Brown, appointed in 1849.

Between 1840 and 1856 the Society developed a plan of employing traveling missionaries, known as colporters because they carried Bible and denominational tracts and books. These missionaries preached in pastorless churches, visited Sunday schools, and touched families that lived lonely lives in the sparsely settled sections of the country. By 1867 it had become obvious that missionaries were needed also to plan new Sunday schools and to strengthen those already in existence. With the extension of the railroads, chapel cars were added to the colporters' equipment. These specially designed railroad cars made it possible to hold meetings in unchurched communities; they also served as homes for the itinerant missionaries. The first chapel car was put in service in 1891.

Beginning with the regime of Dr. Benjamin Griffith, who served as general secretary from 1857 until his death in 1893, the Society placed special emphasis upon the strengthening of the Sunday school movement in America. This was accomplished, not only through the colportage work already described, but also through the increase of Sunday school periodicals, such as *The Young Reaper,* begun in 1856, the *Baptist Teacher,* first issued in 1870, and *Our Little Ones,* a story paper first published in 1872. Much credit for this phase of the Society's work is due Dr. Christopher R. Blackall, who served from 1867 to 1916, being editor-in-chief of Sunday school publications for the last thirty-four years of that period. He began most of the thirty-three periodicals that were being published in 1916.

In 1871 a plan to make uniform the Sunday school lessons in all denominations was agreed upon in New York City by publishers representing twenty-six periodicals. B. F. Jacobs, a Baptist Sunday school superintendent of Chicago, who had been writing the helps for Sunday school teachers appearing in the *Baptist Standard,* had long been advocating such a system and had an important part in securing the adoption of the plan by the National Sunday School Convention of 1872. In due time, the National Series of Sunday school lessons (commonly spoken of as the Uniform Lessons) became International. Graded lessons were introduced in 1909. Since that time there has been an amazing growth in the number and variety of the curricular materials provided for use in the churches.

During these years the Society received generous financial support from the churches and from such Baptist laymen as William Bucknell, chairman of the Board of Managers from 1867 to 1890, and John P. Crozer and his sons, Samuel, George, and Robert. Eventually, more adequate buildings were acquired, including a modern printing plant.

The state conventions were not slow to share in the Sunday school movement. Most of them organized Sunday school conventions or committees to supervise instruction in Sunday schools and to assist in establishing new ones. Not infrequently, those in the North were auxiliary to the American Baptist Publication Society.

The Sunday school interest in southern states did not assume commanding proportions until about 1840, although local schools had been in existence in Baltimore since 1804 and in Charleston since 1816. After 1820 they were more numerous, especially in the upper tier of the Southern States. Such schools in the rural churches were rarely heard of before 1825. The American Sunday School Union stimulated the development of the movement by wisely appointing Baptist leaders in each of the older states of the South to serve as its agents among Baptists. Thus it was that the state conventions of North Carolina, Mississippi, Alabama, and Kentucky undertook Sunday school work after 1830.[35]

However, when Kentucky Baptists, in 1854, complained of the undenominational character of the Union's literature, interest was aroused in developing a denominational press. A Southern Baptist Publication Society without denominational affiliation was organized in 1854. Then, in November, 1858, the Southern Sunday School Union was established at Memphis, Tennessee. This brought the need for denominational supervision to the attention of the Southern Baptist Convention. Accordingly, in 1863, a Sunday School Board was created by the Convention and located at Greenville, South Carolina. With it was merged the Southern Baptist Publication Society, the resulting organization being called the Sunday School and Publication Board.

During the trying years of war, the Sunday schools made pressing demands upon the Sunday School and Publication Board.

---

[35] B. F. Riley, *A History of the Baptists in the Southern States East of the Mississippi* (Philadelphia, 1898), chap. 11.

Owing to the fact that the secular schools were closed during much of the period of hostilities, people were largely dependent upon the Sunday schools for the training of their children. Baptists had been almost alone in the promotion of this type of work in the South, and their schools, therefore, were eagerly patronized by persons of all denominations. As an added responsibility, Sunday school work was conducted among the Negroes. Thus, the great need for literature prompted the Board to buy up what books it could secure from the American Sunday School Union, the American Baptist Publication Society, the American Tract Society, and other publishers. In 1868 the Sunday School Board was consolidated with the Southern Baptist Sunday School Union and transferred from Greenville, South Carolina, to Memphis, Tennessee. Financial distress and internal friction during the reconstruction years, however, led to the merger of the Board in 1873 with the Domestic Mission Board, which continued the publication of Sunday school papers. Being without southwide supervision, some of the Southern States organized Sunday school Boards which secured their supplies from the American Baptist Publication Society. The importance of the work of that Society during the years that followed is evident from the tribute paid to it by a Baptist historian of the South:

Without the timely aid of the Publication Society, Sunday school and colportage work in the South would have been most seriously retarded, if not effectually blocked. It was destined for almost a score of years to sustain the struggling Sunday school interests of the South, both of the whites and of the blacks.[36]

By 1891 the Southern Baptist Convention was in a position to establish a new Sunday School Board, with headquarters at Nashville, Tennessee. Thereafter, Southern Baptists produced their own literature in increasing volume and variety.

To evangelize and educate, American Baptists have utilized the printed page consistently since 1801 when Henry Holcombe, of Georgia, established *The Analytical Repository*. The second venture of Baptist journalism was *The Massachusetts Baptist Missionary Magazine*, which appeared in 1803. Luther Rice was not slow to realize the value of the press in arousing missionary interest. In 1816 he published *The Latter Day Luminary* in Washington, D. C., first

[36] *Ibid.*, 284.

as a quarterly, then as a monthly. Its life was short because of insufficient funds. This was followed in 1821 by *The Columbian Star*, also developed under Rice's influence. In 1828 this paper was moved to Philadelphia and Dr. W. T. Brantly, of Georgia, pastor in Philadelphia at the time, became its editor. Its name was changed to *The Columbian Star and Christian Index;* then in 1832 it became known simply as *The Christian Index*. The year following, it was moved to Washington, Georgia, where it became a powerful influence in the hands of Dr. Jesse Mercer in arousing interest in missions and education. In 1840 he presented it to the Georgia Baptist State Convention.

Other Baptist periodicals did not differ greatly in manner of development. Nearly every state had at least one Baptist publication. They served by providing wholesome reading at a time when newspapers and magazines were not so plentiful as today. But more important, they developed a denominational consciousness, aroused enthusiasm for missionary and educational enterprises, and shaped Baptists' thinking on the social and theological issues of the day.

Thus, through a combination of agencies—evangelists, colporters, educators, and editors—Baptists within two centuries produced in America a zealous and intelligent witness, the influence of which extended through Baptist mission fields around the world. From a small minority sect, despised and persecuted in colonial days, Baptists, by 1900, had grown with the nation to one of the leading denominations of the country.

CHAPTER TWELVE

BURMA AND BEYOND

I T will be recalled that the earliest missionary interests of American Baptists stemmed from their natural evangelistic zeal to minister to the spiritual needs of the unchurched white frontiersmen and the unconverted Indians. The channels through which this concern flowed were the only available ones then in existence, namely, the local churches and the associations. Near the close of the eighteenth century, however, more specific agencies were developed in the form of state missionary societies. Through these extra-associational organizations, those who were missionary-minded sought to avoid the criticism of some who were fearful that the growing activities of the associations might threaten the democracy of the local church. To supplement the work of these societies, similar organizations of women and youth were formed in various places, and these served as collecting agencies and centers of missionary education. In time the women's work became fully as important as that carried on by the general societies, yet it never detracted from the missionary income of the latter. To the contrary, it increased the enthusiasm and generosity of Baptists in the support of missions.[1]

The organization of the Triennial Convention in 1814 was a triumph of the principle of national co-operation in the foreign missionary enterprise. While some Baptists were unwilling to support the effort on the ground that it was undemocratic procedure to place power in agencies other than the local churches, the work of the Convention moved ahead under the leadership of such men as Furman, Staughton, and Rice. In many respects Luther Rice was a fortunate choice as promotional agent of the Board, for he combined vision, untiring energy, and a knowledge of the foreign field. He, therefore, was instrumental in developing financial support.[2]

---

[1] Albert L. Vail, *The Morning Hour of American Baptist Missions*, chaps. 1-4. See also Chapter Eight above for details of organization.

[2] See Chapter Eight.

Foreign Missions to 1845

The beginnings of Adoniram Judson's work in Burma, into which country he had gone in 1813 with Carey's approval, provided a source of constant inspiration to American Baptists. His letters, which related the need for Christ in that land of heathenism, were published in the missionary periodicals. They aroused wide interest and enlisted financial support. When, in 1816, Judson sent a request for a printer and a press to be sent to Burma for the printing of the Gospel of Matthew and some tracts which he had translated into Burmese, the Reverend George H. Hough and his wife, natives of New Hampshire, were commissioned by the Convention to sail in the autumn. They arrived on October fifteenth as the first reinforcements. Carey's Serampore Mission supplied the printing press, and thus, in a short time, the spread of the gospel in the Burmese tongue began.

When the Convention met in 1817, important decisions were made, as we have seen. *The American Baptist Magazine* was adopted as the Convention's official organ. A seminary was authorized for the training of ministers, resulting in the founding of Columbian College in Washington, D. C. The work of the Convention was extended to include home missions among white settlers and Indians. In addition, the churches were urged to observe the first Monday in every month as a day of prayer for missions. Thus were combined four important factors for Baptist growth: interest in foreign missions, home mission concern, education, and prayer.

Guided by the continuous promptings of Judson to broaden their missionary enterprise to include Siam, Indo-China, China, and Japan, the Board sent out four new missionaries, the Rev. James Colman and the Rev. Edward W. Wheelock, of Boston, with their wives. They arrived in Rangoon in September, 1818. For their use, Judson wrote his Burmese grammar. News of the conversion of three Buddhists and the consequent forming of a church in Rangoon in 1819 was hailed by American Baptists as the first fruits of their foreign missionary harvest. The next year, the first effort to evangelize India was undertaken when the Colmans opened a station at Chittagong. Thus Baptists entered upon their second foreign field. That station, however, was closed upon the death of Colman in 1822.

In 1819 the Triennial Convention's Board contributed funds to assist the Negro "African Baptist Mission Society," founded in Richmond in 1814, to send two of their own Baptist preachers to open a mission station in what came to be Liberia. It is significant that their first undertaking to convert Africans was a co-operative enterprise of white and colored Baptists.

In August, 1821, Mrs. Judson was forced to return to America for the benefit of her health, leaving her husband alone in Burma until the arrival in December of Dr. Jonathan Price, the first medical missionary to be sent out by the Convention. Mrs. Judson's presence in America stirred an increasing interest in the growth of the Burmese mission. Meanwhile, in Burma, the King of Ava had heard of the skill of Dr. Price and had invited him and Judson to the capital of Burma. Seeing an opportunity for a new station, they went. In 1823 Mrs. Judson returned to Burma, together with a new missionary family, the Rev. Jonathan Wade and his wife. By that time Judson had completed his translation of the entire New Testament into Burmese. Including the missionaries, there were eighteen members in the Rangoon church.

During the next two years, however, the little mission endured a period of severe testing, for the first Burman War with the British brought the fall of Rangoon. Wade and Hough fled to India, where they printed Judson's Burmese dictionary and the Gospel of Matthew at Carey's Serampore Press. Meanwhile, Judson and Price were imprisoned at Ava. The Burmese New Testament manuscript and a part of the Old Testament were saved from the suspicious officials by being sewed up in a pillow which, in turn, was transported out of their reach by a native convert. Through the heroic intercession of Mrs. Judson and her sacrificial efforts in securing for them food and medicine, their lives were saved; and they were released from prison in 1826. A short time later, Ann Judson died, leaving a lonely man to carry on. At the close of the war, Judson and the Wades settled at Amherst, the new British headquarters in Burma; Price and Hough resigned, but stayed on in the country in the service of the government.

The first white missionary to be sent by the Board to Africa was Calvin Holton, a graduate of Waterville College, Maine. He joined the Negro missionaries who had been sent out earlier to

Monrovia, the capital of Liberia. In this colony established by the American Colonization Society as a means of caring for the "Negro problem" in the United States, Holton opened a school and organized a church in 1824, his first year on the field. His work reflects the continued good relations between the Negro Baptist Mission and white Baptists, as well as a deepening interest in the Christianizing of Africa.

In 1826 the Triennial Convention took steps to extricate itself from involvement in home mission work and Columbian College, which was heavily in debt. In the opinion of its leaders, only then could it give full attention to foreign missions, which it regarded as its primary purpose. Moreover, the unfortunate financial management of the college at Washington, D. C., had become a source of embarrassment to the Convention. Not only were many accusing Rice of negligence and even of dishonesty (these charges were proved to be unfounded), but also the anti-mission forces in the South and West were citing the large expenditure of funds in such enterprises as evidence of the dangers inherent in centralization and organized agencies outside of the local church. The result was a loss of financial support from some quarters. The Convention, therefore, voted to sever its relations with the college and with home mission enterprises, restricting its operations wholly to foreign missionary extension. The headquarters of the Board were moved from Philadelphia to Boston in the hope of gaining greater financial support from New England Baptists, whose missionary zeal had been great from the first. In addition, Boston offered better facilities for missionaries leaving for foreign fields. Dr. Lucius Bolles, who had served the First Baptist Church of Salem, Massachusetts, for twenty-one years, was elected corresponding secretary.

The years that followed comprised a notable period of expansion in the history of American Baptist missions. Additional missionaries were sent out to an increasing number of foreign fields, and the American Baptist Home Mission Society was established in 1832, just eight years after the organization of the Baptist General Tract Society (1824), which in 1840 became known as the American Baptist Publication and Sunday School Society. It is safe to say that these two additional national agencies of Baptist work were by-products of foreign missionary enthusiasm.

Following the Burmese War, Baptist work expanded in that country. In December, 1825, the Reverend George Dana Boardman, Sr., first foreign missionary from Maine, arrived in Calcutta with his wife. In March they visited Amherst where Judson was, then proceeded to Moulmein, a new mission station in eastern Burma. In 1827 Cephas Bennett, a printer, arrived with a press and began work. Within a year, twenty-one converts had been baptized and a church organized. In April of 1828 the Boardmans moved to Tavoy, a Buddhist stronghold of some nine thousand inhabitants. From this center, Boardman, with the assistance of a converted Karen, Ko Tha Byu, whose freedom he had purchased, began a very successful work among these hill people. When a Chinese was converted in Tavoy, it was proposed that a missionary be sent there to learn Chinese in preparation for entering China. In 1831 Boardman died, but the work continued to grow. One year later, the Reverend John Taylor Jones, a missionary at Moulmein, opened a new center of evangelism in Siam among the Siamese, Chinese, and Burmese. No foreign government was more friendly; yet the results continued to be small.

The year 1832 was a significant one for American Baptist missions. Interest in the Convention was keen in view of the progress of foreign missions and in anticipation of the organization of a home mission society. One hundred and twenty-two delegates were in attendance, which was a marked increase over the previous high number of seventy-two. There were fourteen missionaries in Burma, five new ones ready to sail, and another five then in school awaiting appointment. During a recess of the Convention, the American Baptist Home Mission Society was organized "to aid in the spreading of the kingdom of Christ in North America," an enterprise which had the full blessing of the Convention. Only work among the American Indians was retained by the Convention when it withdrew from other phases of the home mission enterprise. This it was not to relinquish until 1865, when such work was turned over to the Home Mission Society. At its meeting in 1832, the Convention adopted a resolution to consider the feasibility of undertaking mission stations in France, Germany, and Greece.[8]

[8] *American Baptist Magazine*, Vol. XII, April, 1832, pp. 12-3; June, 1832, pp. 169 ff.; Henry C. Vedder, *A History of Baptist Missions*, p. 459.

In the years prior to the next Triennial Convention in 1835, the expansion of foreign missions to Europe was the significant achievement. As a result of the visit of a deputation of American Baptists to Europe from the Mission Board, France was opened for missionary service in 1833. In Germany a small group of Baptists gathered around a leader of remarkable talents, Johann G. Oncken. German Baptists then, in turn, became missionaries to Denmark, Sweden, Norway, and Russia. In 1835 work was begun on the island of Corfu, off Greece.[4] *Due to influence and work of Oncken. work was begun in Norway, Sweden, and Russia.*

When the Convention met in Richmond, Virginia, in 1835, enthusiasm ran high, for it was reported that the entire Bible had been translated into Burmese, that a native missionary society had been formed there in 1833 which had sent out two workers, and that the Board had appointed its first single woman missionary, Miss Sarah Cummings, to begin work in Burma. Including the Arakan field in northwest Burma, which had been reopened in 1835, there were twenty-five missionaries in Burma, twenty-one native workers, and nearly six hundred church members. It was announced also that a number of new missionaries were ready to sail.

This spirit of progress extended to other fields. Four missionaries and one Chinese assistant were at work in Siam. A mission station had been opened in Haiti with a Negro in charge. Three missionaries were at work in France. The total report for all fields included twenty-five mission stations, seventy-two missionaries, forty native workers, eighteen churches, and thirteen hundred and fifty members. While the expenditures had exceeded the income, contributions were increasing steadily. The delegates were in a suitable frame of mind to lay plans for expansion in the year ahead. These plans called for raising one hundred thousand dollars, sending out new missionaries, and establishing "new missions in every unoccupied place where there may be a reasonable prospect of success. . . ."[5]

In the following year, the Board opened the South India Mission for the Telugus and began a work among the Shans in Assam.

[4] For details, see Chapter Six.

[5] Edmund F. Merriam, *A History of American Baptist Missions*, 43; cf., *Proceedings of the Baptist General Convention* for 1835, pp. 8-10. The proposal was made by the Youth's Missionary Society of the Second Baptist Church, Richmond, Va. For statistics on mission fields, see Board's report, p. 51.

Financial receipts increased, particularly from the South, and grants of nine thousand dollars from the General Tract Society and ten thousand five hundred dollars from the newly organized American and Foreign Bible Society aided the cause of missions materially. Gains in the membership of the Convention and of the local and state societies, as well as increased interest in the missionary periodicals and educational institutions of the denomination, marked this period. Indeed, as the successes of home missionary efforts and of foreign enterprises became generally recognized, even the spirit of anti-missions declined.

By 1838 the number of mission stations had increased to sixty-nine, the number of missionaries to ninety-eight, and the number of native workers to seventy; there were thirty-eight native churches, of which twenty had been established since the previous Convention of 1835. Fifty schools and five printing establishments had been set up, while books had been prepared in fifteen foreign languages. During the three-year period, there had been eleven hundred baptisms.[6] Such results were achieved in spite of a controversy between the Baptists of the American Bible Society and those of other denominational affiliations—a controversy which led to the creation of a Baptist Society, which required further expenditure of funds.[7]

A more serious threat to peace within the denomination was the slavery controversy, which was involving the feelings of Baptists of the North and South alike. By 1840 the issue had reached such national proportions that schism was threatened within the Convention. Nevertheless, missionary interest did not diminish, and in the three-year period between 1838 and 1841, thirty-one additional missionaries were employed, and thirteen million pages of Scripture and tracts were printed on mission presses in 1840 alone. The income for the three years did not meet the expenditures, however, being only $238,000 as over against an outlay of $261,000. To help meet this amount, the American and Foreign Bible Society contributed $50,000 in the three-year period.[8]

The story of the abolitionist controversy and the ensuing schism which occurred in 1845 has been related in an earlier chapter.[9] Let

[6] The *American Baptist Magazine*, Vol. XVIII (June, 1838), 121-65.
[7] For detailed account, see Chapter Ten.
[8] *American Baptist Magazine*, Vol. XXI (June, 1841), 137-212.
[9] See Chapter Ten.

it suffice to say here that while the separation of southern Baptists from the Triennial Convention to form the Southern Baptist Convention seems to have produced a permanent division among Baptists in America, it did not retard the cause of foreign missions. Both the American Baptist Missionary Union, which grew out of the old Convention after the split, and the Southern Baptist Convention were motivated by a devotion to the missionary task. Their efforts were stimulated undoubtedly by a determination to offset any possible decline in their enterprise which might result from a divided effort. Baptist missions after 1845, although carried on separately by Northerners and Southerners, were conducted with good feeling and mutual consideration.

Foreign Missions of Northern Baptists after 1845

At a special meeting in New York on November 20, 1845, the Triennial Convention drew up a new constitution and made arrangements to secure from the Legislature of Pennsylvania permission to change its name to "The American Baptist Missionary Union," and also to obtain incorporation in the State of Massachusetts under the same title. Dr. Edward Bright was elected the corresponding secretary, a position which he retained until 1855. During that time, he was, to a great extent, responsible for the successful handling of the receipts of the new body. Realizing the added responsibility of northern Baptists to carry on alone the work once undertaken by southerners as well, he set about to systematize the giving of local churches and state missionary conventions. Accordingly, the funds advanced from over $82,000 in 1845 to more than $100,000 in 1846. Thereafter, they continued to average approximately $15,000 in excess of the last years of united action until in 1851 they reached the amount of $120,826. In the years that followed, the receipts never fell below $100,000, except in 1858, following the financial panic of 1857 and during the first two years of the War Between the States.[10]

In the first year of the Union's existence (1846), it had 99 missionaries and assistants, 155 native workers, and 82 churches under its support and supervision. The total membership of native converts was 5,300. In their 50 schools there were 2,000 pupils. Mission stations were located in Burma, Siam, China, Assam, India,

[10] Merriam, *A History of American Baptist Missions*, 72-3.

Africa, France, Germany, Denmark, and Greece. By 1900 new fields had been added to Baptist responsibility in Japan, the Congo Free State, Sweden, Russia, Finland, and Spain.[11]

The progress of the American Baptist Missionary Union was not entirely unaffected by internal dissension. It stemmed from the almost ever-present fear on the part of some Baptists of denominational organization. It appeared as early as 1843, when a group of Baptists who were strongly abolitionist, anti-Masonic, and opposed to centralization and oath-taking, organized "The American and Foreign Missionary Society" on the ground that the Managing Board of the Triennial Convention had not taken a sufficiently definite attitude on those matters. Later the name was changed to The American Baptist Free Mission Society, at which time another principle was added to its platform, that "Christian missionaries are the servants of Christ and not of man"; by which they meant that no board should stand between the missionary and the churches or individuals who supported him. This move had been prompted by dissatisfaction on the part of some of the missionaries with policies worked out at a convention of workers called by the American Baptist Missionary Union and held at Moulmein, Burma, in 1853. They were opposed especially to certain restrictions placed upon the establishment and conduct of the school work. The result was that they withdrew from connection with the Missionary Union, and found some support from sympathetic friends in the homeland.

This division continued for seventeen years in the case of the Rangoon Sgaw-Karen Mission and for thirteen years in the Bassein Sgaw-Karen Mission. During this period the dissenting missionaries were supported by the natives and by independent contributions sent from America through the American Baptist Free Mission Society. In 1859 the Missionary Union adopted a new missionary policy which dispensed with organized missions in respective countries and placed each missionary under the direction of the Board's Executive Committee. Missionaries on the field were to be free to form their own associations for mutual consultation and encouragement. Wives of missionaries were no longer to be regarded as assistants and hence were not to be held responsible for missionary service. Mission

[11] American Baptist Missionary Union, *Annual Reports* for 1846, p. 48; A. H. Newman, ed., *A Century of Baptist Achievement* (Philadelphia, 1901), 185.

presses were to be dispensed with except where necessary, leaving the missionaries free to print what they thought best for their purposes on the field.[12]

The Society maintained work for a few years in Haiti, in Africa, in Japan, and in Burma. In 1872, when all causes for difference had passed away, the work of the organization was transferred to the American Baptist Missionary Union. In this shift, the Union took over the first mission work which Baptists had ever undertaken in Japan.

In the second half of the nineteenth century, Northern Baptists experienced four remarkable successes on their foreign fields. The first great ingathering occurred on their oldest mission field, Burma. In that land, Baptists have enjoyed such progress in developing an indigenous church that other denominations have taken it almost for granted that Burma is a Baptist field. In 1850 a Karen Home Mission Society was formed in Bassein. Four years later a similar society was organized at Rangoon. On May 16, 1878, fifty years after the conversion of the first Karen, Ko Tha Byu, the Bassein Karens dedicated the Ko Tha Byu Memorial Hall for the use of the Sgaw-Karen Normal and Industrial Institute, a building which cost $22,000 to erect. Then they raised $31,000 to cover its cost and for its endowment. The Rangoon Karens, with the assistance of English and American friends, erected a chapel which furnished accommodations for their school and religious worship on the mission compound at Rangoon. From a theological school which was established at Insein in 1838 by Dr. Edward A. Stevens and from the Karen Literary and Theological Institution which was organized in 1846 at Moulmein, there developed a worthy educational program among these people. By 1872 the Rangoon Baptist College was founded to provide higher education for youths of all races in Burma.

In 1855 there were nine Baptist mission stations in Burma, five of which had been opened since the Convention of 1853 at Moulmein. In 1876 two more stations were opened. By 1900 forty-seven tribes in that country had benefited from Baptist missionary endeavors. In that year the total church membership of all races approached fifty thousand, thirty-five thousand being Karens and thirty-five hundred

[12] Merriam, *op. cit.*, 91-4; for the full report of the committee appointed by the American Baptist Missionary Union to study the relations of the Union and its missionaries, see A.B.M.U., *Annual Reports* for 1855, pp. 27-46; also for 1859, pp. 15-9.

being Burmans. Of the 685 churches in Burma, 482 were self-supporting. Thus within eighty-seven years from the arrival of the Judsons, a strategic center for Christianity had been established in southeastern Asia.[13]

The second area of remarkable expansion for the gospel was Assam, the most northeastern province of British India, with a population in the nineteenth century of five and a half million people representing a variety of races. Baptist missionary success there has been greatest among the animistic population in the hills and among the immigrants who have entered the country to work in the tea gardens. The Garos were the first tribe to receive the gospel, in the southwestern portion of Assam. In 1878 a station was established by the Reverend Marcus C. Mason and the Reverend E. G. Phillips at Tura in the Garo Hills. By 1900 there were more than four thousand church members, with their own associational organization on the plan of Baptist associations in America. Another work of marked success was begun by the Reverend E. W. Clark and his wife in 1875 at Molung, a spot far in advance of the British outposts. The presumably savage people received the missionaries with cordiality, and in time the entire village was converted. In this way the gospel was extended to the Nagas, who also were animists of the hill country. By the close of the century, two other stations had been opened among them.

Third, The most dramatic occurrence of mass conversions ever to have been witnessed by nineteenth-century Baptists took place among the Telugus at Ongole, India. Contact with these people came about through the visit to America of the Reverend Amos Sutton, a missionary of the English Baptist mission in Orissa, and his wife, the widow of the Reverend James Colman who had been an American Baptist missionary until his death in Arakan, Burma. At the Triennial Convention meeting in Richmond, Virginia, in 1835, Sutton told of the needs of the Telugu people to the south of Orissa. Immediately, the burden was laid on the hearts of the delegates, and they determined to send help. The next year the Reverend Samuel S. Day sailed for India, where he founded the American Baptist mission among the Telugus. Eventually, he made his headquarters at

[13] Merriam, *op. cit.*, 102-21; cf., A.B.M.U., *Annual Reports* for 1901, statistical table opposite p. 226.

Nellore; there he was joined in 1848 by Dr. Lyman Jewett. So discouraging was the response that the Convention in 1853 actually considered closing the station there, but the delegates were dissuaded by Dr. Edward Bright, home secretary of the Missionary Union, who "declared that he would never write the letter calling for the blotting out of the 'Lone Star' on the map of India." Again in 1862 the Union considered abandoning the field, but were dissuaded this time by the urging of Dr. Jewett, who had just returned home.[14]

Two years later, a young Iowan, John E. Clough, who had some knowledge of engineering, determined to go to India as a missionary. He applied to the American Baptist Missionary Union for appointment, and was accepted for work in the Ongole District. In 1876 famine overtook India in its all too frequent cycle. To avert mass starvation, the British Government undertook the building of the Buckingham Canal from Madras to a point near Ongole. As his contribution to the employment of the starving people of his district, Clough contracted for the construction of four miles of the canal. He appointed his native preachers as overseers. When the natives were not at work, the preachers read the Bible to them and taught them the gospel. Then, when these people returned to their homes, they passed on the Good News. The consequence was that the seed was sown so widely that on Christmas morning, 1877, no less than 2,300 persons presented themselves for baptism.

Dr. Clough, thinking that they hoped for more material relief, put them off until such aid was no longer forthcoming. In June, 1878, he began examinations for baptism. To his amazement and joy, the applicants came by the hundreds. So, early in July, when the period of examination had been completed, six ordained native preachers, taking turns by twos, immersed 2,222 persons in a single day. July 3 was the memorable day. By the close of the year, nine thousand had been added to the church; most of them, by reason of being leather workers, were outcastes. By 1879, the total number of converts had reached 10,500.[15] Truly, by the measurement of the early church, it was another Pentecost. Its effect was not only to cause the revival to spread to the Deccan and to Hyderabad, but to

---

[14] Merriam, *A History of American Baptist Missions*, 134; cf., A.B.M.U., *Annual Reports* for 1853, pp. 27-30; for 1862, pp. 20-1.

[15] *Ibid.*, 137-44; cf., A.B.M.U., *Annual Reports* for 1879, p. vii, xv-xvi.

revolutionize missionary methods in India. Direct evangelism came to be the foremost approach, in place of education, which had been the earlier method.

The fourth outpouring of God's Spirit came in Africa. It has been called the "Pentecost of the Congo." A Baptist work had been begun there following contacts which Dr. H. Grattan Guiness, a wealthy Christian leader of England, had made with American Baptists. In 1884 he turned over to the American Baptist Missionary Union the mission which he had supported for several years at the mouth of the Congo River. The Reverend Henry Richards took up the work there at Banza Manteke. In the brief span of six months, news arrived in America of a revival akin to that among the Karens of Burma and the Telugus of India. More than a thousand natives had placed their idols at the feet of Richards, and had professed faith in Jesus Christ as their Savior. By 1900 there were fifteen hundred church members among them, with fifty-seven native preachers and teachers, gathered in three large churches.[16] Despite the obstacles of distance and poor communications, this wave of conversions spread to other fields in the Congo Mission.

The American Baptist Missionary Union, taking advantage of a treaty made in 1844 by the United States and China which allowed the erection of chapels and hospitals in five open ports, placed missionaries in strategic spots—William Ashmore at Swatow (South China) in 1863; Josiah Goddard at Ningpo (East China) in 1846 —and assumed support of William Upcraft and George Warner at Suichaufu (West China) about 1889. By 1900 a self-supporting work had been established at Swatow. In spite of severe persecution, the Chekiang Baptist Association was formed in East China in 1872. The West China Mission had established four centers for evangelism: Yachow, Chengtu, Kiating, and Suifu. The Scriptures were translated into the Swatow and Ningpo colloquials respectively by Dr. Ashmore and his son, William Ashmore, Jr., and Dr. Goddard and his son, J. R. Goddard. Medical missionaries like Dr. Francis Wayland Goddard, Dr. James Grant, and Dr. M. D. Eubank developed hospitals which became centers of healing and evangelizing.

During the period just reviewed, the American Baptist Missionary Union had developed two significant policies with respect to its

[16] *Ibid.*, 182-7.

work in foreign lands.[17] It put the preaching of the gospel ahead of its mission schools as a means of securing conversions. Evangelism was placed in the forefront, yet Christian education was not neglected; for by 1894 the American Baptist Missionary Union had nine boarding schools for girls—two in India, two in Burma, one in China, four in Japan; three schools to train Bible women, located in Burma, China, and Japan; a school for Eurasian girls in Moulmein, Burma; and two mission colleges—one of twenty years' existence at Rangoon, Burma, and another recently opened at Ongole, India.

When criticism was raised concerning the value of schools and higher education to missionary operations, a committee was appointed to report to the Union in that year; this committee vindicated the Board's policy, but cautioned its members on two points. First, it was unwise for the Baptist schools in India, Assam, and Burma to receive "grants-in-aid" from the British Government. Second, it recommended that such changes should be made in the educational work as to increase its efficiency in promoting evangelism. The report was adopted with a directive that state aid to Baptist schools should be discontinued. In the year 1897-1898, a little more than one-thirteenth of the entire appropriation of the Union was used for the schools. They were regarded as an important support to evangelization and the training of leaders to produce indigenous churches. In the Telugu Mission, where abject poverty and a caste system were prevalent, industrial training was advocated as a means of alleviating economic suffering among Christians.

The second policy, that of developing self-supporting and indigenous churches, was therefore closely allied to the educational program. In 1895 it was reported that the number of self-supporting Baptist churches in non-Christian lands had increased within a year from 377 to 458, and of self-supporting mission schools from 247 to 369. This was a trend which was destined to produce, within the next fifty years, churches sufficiently strong to survive two world wars.

In 1900, the American Baptist Missionary Union reported four hundred and seventy-four missionaries, nearly forty-seven hundred native helpers, almost two thousand churches with nearly two hundred and seven thousand members, and eleven hundred and forty-

[17] A.B.M.U., *Annual Reports* for 1845, p. 18; Newman, *A Century of Baptist Achievement*, p. 185.

five schools serving over thirty-seven thousand pupils. Contributions to the support of this work had increased from $82,000 in 1845 to more than $543,000 in 1900. This increase was due partly to the able and zealous efforts of the Union's corresponding secretary for foreign work from 1863 to 1893, Dr. John N. Murdock.[18]

Of themselves, the statistics are cold and meaningless, but when translated into their significance for the progress of Christianity and men's welfare, they mean much. The missionary enterprise of Northern Baptists meant the spread of the gospel into other languages than English through the preaching and translation of the Scriptures. It resulted in the building of schools abroad. Moreover, it set up a bulwark against the efforts of traders to introduce rum into Africa. It likewise served as a check on the low standards of commerce and government in various lands. The work also encouraged an international interest and sense of social responsibility in the homeland.

Foreign Missions of Southern Baptists after 1845

On May 8, 1845, in the meeting-house of the First Baptist Church, Augusta, Georgia, two hundred and ninety-three men from Maryland, Virginia, North Carolina, South Carolina, Georgia, Alabama, Louisiana, Kentucky, and the District of Columbia, met to organize the Southern Baptist Convention. Its constitution, as adopted, differed in one important respect from that of the Triennial Convention under which Southerners and Northerners had worked together for thirty-one years. It provided that home and foreign missions should be conducted by two co-ordinate boards of the Convention. This was in marked contrast to the Northern agencies which were independent mission societies. The Foreign Mission Board was located in Richmond, Virginia. Its first president was a Richmond pastor of note, Dr. Jeremiah B. Jeter, and its first corresponding secretary was Dr. James Barnett Taylor, also of Richmond. He served in that capacity until December, 1871, shortly before his death. Dr. Henry Allen Tupper of Georgia, his successor, held that office until 1893 when he was succeeded by Dr. R. J. Willingham. The Home or Domestic Mission Board, as it was called at first, was established at Marion, Alabama. Its early history was one of discouragement through lack of popular support. In 1855 it

18 A.B.M.U., *Annual Reports* for 1894, 12-23; for 1895, 245; for 1898, 19-20.

became known as the Domestic and Indian Mission Board, which name it held until 1874. In 1882 it was removed to Atlanta, Georgia, where a new era of popularity and expansion began under the executive leadership of Dr. Isaac T. Tichenor, who came from the presidency of the Agricultural and Mechanical College of Alabama at Auburn.

The Foreign Mission Board began its work in South China. The interest of the Southern Convention in that field had been aroused by the vision and enthusiasm of the Reverend J. Lewis Shuck, who toured the South upon his return to America in 1846. Shuck and his wife, both Virginians, had been sent out to China in 1835 by the Triennial Convention, as the vanguard of the American Baptist missionaries to China. Mrs. Shuck had died in 1844 in Hong Kong, where they had organized a Baptist church. Now that the break had come in the Triennial Convention, Shuck devoted himself to the new work of Southern Baptists. He was instrumental in raising five thousand dollars for a chapel to be built in Shanghai. In the meantime, two young men, Samuel C. Clopton and George Pearcy, had been sent to Canton. Clopton died in a short time and Pearcy's health began to fail. But others took up their work in the years that followed. In 1849 Mr. and Mrs. B. W. Whilden landed in Canton; in 1854 Mr. and Mrs. C. W. Gaillard arrived, and in 1856 the Reverend Roswell P. Graves of Baltimore, who had been turned to China by the appeal of Shuck. By 1864, through deaths and illness, Graves was left alone with a work at Canton and one at Shiu Hing to care for. Through the skillful training of native preachers and teachers he was able to carry on and even to expand the work to other stations when new missionaries arrived from time to time. In spite of hardships, persecution, and the hatreds engendered by a Chinese-French War in 1885, a Chinese Association was organized in February of that year. The following year found four schools for boys and eleven schools for girls under the mission's care. In 1891 the native Christians opened a school of their own with forty pupils. In 1899 a Chinese Baptist Publication Society was organized. On its Board of Directors were missionaries of the Southern Baptist Convention and of the American Baptist Missionary Union. Dr. Graves was elected its president. The Chinese themselves contributed four thousand dollars to its work. In the same year there were over five hundred baptisms in the Canton Mission, but a few months later the work was retarded temporarily by the Boxer Rebellion which forced most of the missionaries to flee for their lives.[19]

As the shadow of Dr. Graves fell across the South China Mission, so that of Matthew T. Yates fell across forty years of the early history of the Central China Mission which had its beginnings in Shanghai when he and his wife arrived in that city on September 12, 1847. Though suffering from poor eyesight, Yates became most proficient in the use of spoken Chinese and in translation work. From the Christian witness of Mr. and Mrs. T. W. Tobey, the Shucks, and a medical missionary, Dr. J. Sexton James, an influence was extended eventually throughout Shanghai. In 1849 the first converts were baptized; thereafter growth was steady, despite the damage to mission property occasioned by the Tai Ping rebellion of peasants and mountaineers against the Empire in 1850. During the war years in America, the missionaries supported themselves with some aid from friends in Maryland and Kentucky. By 1867, twenty years after the arrival of Yates, the entire countryside around Shanghai was open to the gospel, and the Scriptures had been widely distributed in the Chinese language with the assistance of the British Foreign Bible Society. The First Baptist Church of Shanghai had become strong enough to contribute in 1874 more than eight hundred dollars to the Southern Baptist Convention.[20]

In January, 1882, after twenty-three years of lonely service, reinforcements came to Yates in the person of W. S. Walker, of Georgia. As the years passed, other workers were added. On June 1, 1883, the Baptist church in Soochow was dedicated. Nine years later the missionaries met in that building to organize the Central China Baptist Missionary Conference. In 1896, seven schools were under the care of the Mission.

Southern Baptist work in North China began in 1860 upon the arrival of Mr. and Mrs. J. L. Holmes at Chefoo, which they hoped to use as a base for work in the great city of Tungchow. Within two years' time, the North Street Baptist Church was organized in Tung-

[19] Mary E. Wright, *The Missionary Work of the Southern Baptist Convention*, 59-75. Other sources for material in this section are H. A. Tupper, *The Foreign Missions of the Southern Baptist Convention* and The Southern Baptist Convention, *Proceedings*.

[20] *Ibid.*, 98; cf., Southern Baptist Convention, *Proceedings* for 1868, p. 47; for 1874, p. 36.

chow with eight members, including Mrs. Holmes and the Hartwells, who also were missionaries. Mr. Holmes had been brutally murdered by rebel bandits in the autumn of 1861. In August, 1863, Dr. and Mrs. T. P. Crawford came to take charge of the mission, while Hartwell relieved Yates at Shanghai. Within a period of two years, Hartwell returned to Tungchow, and Crawford opened an independent mission in another part of the city. There were frequent conversions in spite of constant threats upon the missionaries' lives by the Chinese. In 1870, the first native minister, Woo Tswun Chau, was ordained in Shantung Province. During the same year, Mrs. Holmes opened a school for girls in Tungchow. As the years passed, several new workers arrived from the United States. By 1891 the churches of the North China field were organized into the Tung Lai Association.

The progress of the Mission was hindered somewhat in the eighteen-nineties because of repercussions of the Landmarkist controversy in the Convention at home. Under the influence of Dr. Crawford, who held to Landmarkist principles, several missionaries withdrew from the North China Mission to form what they called the "Gospel Mission," which took up work in a new station farther west. Dr. Crawford's dissatisfaction stemmed from the Foreign Board's refusal to adopt his proposal that the missionaries be supported by individual churches or groups of churches, entirely independent of the Board. According to his policy, the Board was to have no control over the missionaries in the carrying on of their work, nor was it to have anything to do with the funds collected.[21] A second deterring factor to the progress of the Mission was the increasing tensions in China which finally issued in the Boxer Rebellion of 1900, during which time the mission was attacked, property damaged, and several native workers carried away and abused.

In the face of great obstacles, Southern Baptists by 1900 had organized in their three Chinese fields twenty-four churches and thirty-six outstations. There were forty-seven missionaries and fifty-five helpers. The total membership was nearly twenty-three hundred, and there were nine hundred and forty pupils in thirty-four schools under the Mission's care.[22]

Work in Africa began with the transfer of the Baptist mission

[21] *Ibid.*, 131-3.
[22] S.B.C., *Proceedings* for 1900, 120.

in Liberia to the Southern Convention in 1856 by the American Baptist Missionary Union, at the former's request. Between 1861 and 1865 all help was withdrawn because of war in the United States; and the native churches were thrown upon their own resources to support the mission.[23] The missionaries all stayed at their posts, and the mission passed through the crisis without serious loss. In 1871, however, the Convention resumed aid to the African enterprise, realizing that in return for the expenditure involved the conversions there had been more numerous than on the Chinese fields. In addition, southern Negroes were contributing funds for the support of the Liberian work. The mission was faced with another crisis in the next few years when illness due to climatic conditions made it impossible for white men to stay there. So, in 1875, the missionaries transferred their efforts to Yoruba along the Niger River on the west coast of Africa, leaving the Liberian work to the Negroes. Since the middle of the century, missionaries had been seeking to win converts among the Yorubas; the results were steady though not spectacular. By 1900 there were three stations, at Lagos, Abbeokuta, and Ogbomoshaw, with a total church membership of nearly two hundred and fifty.[24]

The challenge of Roman Catholic Italy presented itself to Southern Baptists as early as 1850, but it was not until 1870 that the Convention actually decided to open European mission work. In that year, Dr. William N. Cote, a medical man who up to that time had served in France as secretary of the Young Men's Christian Association, was appointed by the Board. He went at once to Rome and was the first Protestant missionary to enter the city after religious toleration had been granted by Victor Emmanuel II, the new ruler. By January, 1871, a church of eight members was organized. From this center, evangelistic efforts were extended northward to the Waldensian valleys in the north of Italy. The work was hindered for a time by dissension, but the replacement of Dr. Cote by Dr. George B. Taylor, a pastor from Staunton, Virginia, ushered in an era of new achievements. Under his careful leadership, a journal, *Il Seminatore* (The Sower), was undertaken in 1876, and a mission station

[23] H. A. Tupper, *The Foreign Missions of the Southern Baptist Convention*, 358.

[24] Wright, *The Missionary Work of the Southern Baptist Convention*, 173; for reports on Liberia during the war years, cf., S.B.C., *Proceedings* for 1863, 30-1 and for 1866, 65-7.

In 1878

was opened in Venice. Two years later, [a permanent property for headquarters in Rome was purchased at a cost of ten thousand dollars, a sum which Northern Baptists joined in raising. In April, 1884, the pastors and evangelists of nearly all the Baptist churches in Italy met with the representatives of the Baptist Mission Boards in the Apostolic Baptist Union to plan for the future. That the plans adopted had a measure of fulfillment is indicated by the report of progress made in 1900: There were then in Italy twenty-four churches, twenty outstations, six hundred and twenty-four members, with one missionary and twenty native helpers.[25]

When Mr. T. J. Bowen asked the Foreign Mission Board to transfer him from the Yoruba Mission in West Africa to a mission in Brazil in 1859, hoping to find a more suitable climate for his health, Southern Baptists agreed, for they had been entertaining plans for taking up a work in Central and South America. The endeavor did not last beyond 1861, however, owing to Bowen's poor health. Nevertheless, in 1873 a small congregation of Americans who had settled in Santa Barbara, in the province of Sao Paulo, asked the Convention to make Brazil a mission field. After careful deliberation, the Convention agreed to do so. In 1880 the Convention sent Mr. and Mrs. W. B. Bagby to work under the Board's direction with the Reverend E. H. Quillin, pastor of the Santa Barbara church. In 1882 Mr. and Mrs. Z. C. Taylor from Texas arrived. The missionaries surveyed the field and decided to change the base of operations to Bahia, a coast city seven hundred miles northeast of Sao Paulo. As the second largest city of the Brazilian Empire, it had strategic value. The work there at first met with persecution from Roman Catholics, but in a year or two the people became more friendly, for they observed that the missionaries did not seek money for the salvation offered. In 1884 a station was opened in Rio de Janeiro; the staff was enlarged by three new arrivals in 1885.

Although in 1890 a republican form of government was inaugurated in Brazil, with a new constitution which provided for religious liberty, the Roman Catholics continued the persecution, even doing bodily harm to some of the converts and molesting the missionaries. Nevertheless, progress was steady. By 1892 the several missions in Brazil were united in a convention. A press was

[25] *Ibid.*, chap. 9; Newman, *op. cit.*, 199.

established at Bahia for the printing of Scripture and tracts. Two years later the churches in South Brazil met in Rio de Janeiro to organize the first Baptist association in that country. Another mission was undertaken at Pernambuco; it prospered in like manner. By 1900 Brazil had become "the most fruitful field under the auspices of the Southern Baptist Convention," having twenty-seven churches, forty-five outstations, nineteen missionaries, a like number of native assistants, and over nineteen hundred members.[26]

When the Southern Baptist Convention decided to open a mission in Mexico, in 1880, it was possible to build upon efforts of Texas Baptists to convert the Mexicans. As early as 1864 such attempts had been made, chiefly with private or state convention support. The first missionaries to be sent out by the Foreign Mission Board were the Reverend W. D. Powell and Mrs. Powell's sister, Miss Anna J. Mayberry. In the fall of 1882, they took up their work in Saltillo, a city of twenty-five thousand. Within two years they had organized a church with some fifty members. Through the generosity of Governor Madero, of Coahuila, a school was established, known as the Madero Institute at Saltillo. The governor had offered to Powell, whom he liked, several pieces of valuable property for schools in Saltillo, Parras, and Patos, cities of Coahuila. After the arrangements had been worked out so as not to violate Baptist principles of religious liberty and separation of church and state, a building on the property in Saltillo was renovated. A donation of a thousand dollars was received for books from William Bucknell, of Philadelphia, and new workers were added. An unfinished cathedral was purchased by the Foreign Mission Board and reconstructed into a church house to serve as a nucleus for missionary activities. With an ever-increasing number of missionary appointees arriving in the late eighties, the work moved ahead in spite of persecution, until by the end of the century there were thirty-two churches, thirty-nine outstations, twelve missionaries assisted by twelve native workers, and close to two thousand members.[27]

The last mission field to be opened by Southern Baptists in the nineteenth century was Japan, a country which had challenged them

[26] Wright, *The Missionary Work of the Southern Baptist Convention*, 245; S.B.C., *Proceedings* for 1900, p. 120.
[27] Wright, *op. cit.*, chap. 11; S.B.C., *Proceedings* for 1900, p. 120.

ever since Commodore Perry in 1854 had forced it into the sphere of world commerce. It was not until 1860 that the first missionaries were appointed for the islands. Unfortunately, however, they never arrived, for two were lost at sea and the others were prevented from sailing by the lack of funds. When times became better, the Convention of 1888 appointed four missionaries, Mr. and Mrs. J. A. Brunson and Mr. and Mrs. J. W. McCollum, who arrived at Kobe in 1889, where the American Baptist Missionary Union had a station. Relations between the two groups of Baptists were cordial and co-operative, the latter turning over their station in Osaka to the Southern Baptists, while they retained Kobe. By 1891 Mr. McCollum had organized a church of fifteen members in Osaka, in addition to a mission school. The task, however, became so discouraging to the missionaries because of the teeming population and their unfamiliarity with the language and customs that they turned the mission over to the American Baptist Missionary Union. They opened, however, a new field on the island of Kiushiu, where transportation was sufficiently good to make it possible for one missionary to carry on effective work if necessary. Since the Northern Baptists were willing to turn over that island to the Southern Baptists, it is clear that the best of feelings existed between them, even to the extent of mutual aid. By 1896 stations had been opened at Fukoka and Nagasaki, although the Japanese attitude was hostile due to the hesitancy of the American Government to permit Japanese immigrants into the United States. When an agreement as to this was finally reached, the Japanese Government became more friendly to the spread of Christianity. This continued until the war with China, which caused Japan to become indifferent to religious interests. During the eleven years of work prior to 1900, eight missionaries and seven native assistants were engaged in evangelistic and educational work. The fruitage was represented by seventy-five members in Japanese Baptist churches.[28]

That the schism between Northern and Southern Baptists had not deterred the carrying on of the American Baptist missionary enterprise is evident from the accomplishments of both groups. It is the more remarkable that the Southern Baptist Convention should have achieved within fifty-five years the labors of at least ninety

[28] Wright, *op. cit.*, chap. 12; S.B.C., *Proceedings,* 1900, p. 120.

missionaries in six fields on four continents. Though there were the difficulties of war and reconstruction, their total contributions from 1845 to 1900 were nearly three million dollars, a large sum to be expended in addition to the support and extension of churches in the homeland.[29] In such a spirit of world-wide evangelism, Southern Baptists grew in numbers from nearly three hundred thousand in 1845 to more than one and a half million at the close of the century.[30]

Negro Baptist Missions

The first Baptist preacher to carry the gospel to a foreign land, preceding William Carey by at least fifteen years, was a Negro slave, George Lisle. Prior to the American Revolution, he was emancipated by his owner, a Baptist deacon named Sharp, for the purpose of preaching. During the war, Lisle preached in Georgia as the first ordained Baptist Negro in America. He established the first Negro Baptist church in or near Savannah about 1778 or earlier. When his former owner died, he borrowed funds to take him to Jamaica in 1783 in order to escape re-enslavement by Sharp's children. He repaid the sum by serving as an indentured servant. In Jamaica, he conducted preaching services, and within eight years baptized five hundred Negroes. In 1789 he was instrumental in the erection of a chapel at Kingston. He directed urgent appeals to the British Baptists to send missionaries to the island.[31]

Another prominent Negro to win his freedom and become a foreign missionary was Lott Cary, born near Richmond, Virginia. His youth was that of a vicious young slave who labored in a tobacco warehouse in Richmond. In 1807 he was converted and became a member of the First Baptist Church (white) of that city, for there were no organized colored churches in the South at that time. It was from the galleries of that church that his heart was set aglow with a zeal to preach to his people. Through the efforts of a young white man, he learned to read the New Testament, and it was not long before he was licensed to preach.

For several years, he was allowed to gather up the bits of

[29] Newman, *A Century of Baptist Achievement,* 203. The exact amount was $2,984,295.
[30] Joseph T. Watts, *One Hundred Years of Southern Baptist History,* 1. In 1845 there were 811,935 Baptists in the U.S., 352,950 being in the South, including colored but exclusive of nearly 150,000 irregular groups. In 1900 there were 1,657,966 southern white Baptists.
[31] Lewis G. Jordan, *Negro Baptist History, U.S.A., 1750-1930* (Nashville, 1930), 46-7.

tobacco which he found lying about the warehouse floor. From the sale of his hoardings and the tips he received from merchants for whom he did errands. Cary finally accumulated the sum of eight hundred and fifty dollars. With this sum he secured in 1813 his freedom and that of his children. His wife had already died. Obtaining work in the city, he made a good livelihood, but always the need of his people was upon his heart. In 1815 he helped to found the African Missionary Society of Richmond, one of the first established in America.[32]

When the American Colonization Society was organized in 1816 for Negro deportation to Liberia, Baptists shared in the enthusiasm engendered by this plan to solve the country's freed-Negro problem. They contributed funds to send Negro missionaries to the new colony in Liberia, among whom was Lott Cary, who sailed with another colored preacher, Collin Teague, on January 16, 1821. Cary established the First Baptist Church in Monrovia, capital of Liberia. Later, white missionaries undertook work in the territory, but as we have seen they found the fevers too rigorous for their health.

The missionary motive was strong in the development of denominational unity among the colored Baptists. Their first independent organization of churches in America was the Providence Missionary Baptist District Association of Ohio, founded in 1836. Three years later, the Wood River Baptist Association of Illinois was established. Both bodies were composed of churches made up of fugitives from slavery. In 1840 the American Baptist Missionary Convention was organized as a foreign mission agency for New England and the Atlantic seaboard states. It was merged in 1865 with the Conventions already in existence in the Northwest and South to form the Consolidated American Baptist Convention. This body which met triennially represented nearly one hundred thousand members of colored Baptist churches; its Executive Board met annually and was responsible for the administration of the organization. By 1877 its membership had increased to six hundred thousand Baptists in twenty states.[33]

The Reverend W. W. Colley, a native of Virginia and a Negro missionary to Africa under the foreign Mission Board of the Southern

[32] B. F. Riley, *A History of the Baptists in the Southern States East of the Mississippi*, 315-7.
[33] Jordan, *op. cit.*, 89-90.

Baptist Convention, was mainly instrumental in the organization of the Baptist Foreign Missionary Convention at Montgomery, Alabama, in November, 1880. Colley was its first corresponding secretary, a position which he occupied until 1893 when he returned to Africa with five other missionaries sent out by the new Convention. In an effort to unite all Negro Baptists for missions, the American National Baptist Convention was organized by six hundred delegates representing seventeen states, meeting in the city of St. Louis on August 25, 1886. The Reverend W. J. Simmons, of Louisville, Kentucky, was elected the first president. The forming of this body, however, did not solve the problem created by the multiplicity of missionary agencies among colored Baptists. In 1893 another was organized in Washington, D. C., under the name of the Baptist National Educational Convention. By 1895 it was possible to unite Negro Baptists in one body, the National Baptist Convention of America, organized at Atlanta, Ga. It was to function through a Foreign Mission Board, a Board of Education, and a Board of Missions. In 1915 the Convention was divided over a dispute concerning control of property and publications. The larger segment was incorporated as the National Baptist Convention of the U.S.A., Inc. The smaller segment retained the original name by court action. Both organizations represent today a combined membership of approximately seven millions, and exert a much greater influence in American life than becomes evident to the casual reader of Baptist history. Their story is yet to be told adequately.

While some efforts were put forth to establish mission stations in the West Indies and South America, the main mission field of the National Baptist Convention has been Africa. The three principal stations in Liberia have been the Suehn Industrial Missions, the Bible Industrial Mission at Grand Bassa, and the Bendoo Mission at Cape Mount. In addition, the Carrie V. Dyer Memorial Hospital was built in Monrovia, the capital of Liberia. In Nigeria was established the Pilgrim Baptist Mission, and in Nyasaland on the east coast, the Providence Industrial Mission. At Johannesburg, South Africa, the W. W. Brown Mission operated through twenty substations. Since 1900, new work has been opened in British Guiana and the West Indies.[84]

[84] C. C. Adams and M. A. Talley, *Negro Baptists and Foreign Missions* (Philadelphia, 1944), 50.

CHAPTER THIRTEEN

"NORTH AMERICA FOR CHRIST"

THE success of Baptist home missionary endeavors was due to the persistence and zeal with which their leaders accompanied the streams of migrants down the Mohawk Valley from New England, and out from the mid-Atlantic seaboard through southern Pennsylvania and Maryland, as well as through the Valley of Virginia and the Blue Ridge passes into Kentucky and Tennessee. Early Baptists were hardy people, woodsmen, hunters, pioneer stock with a will to work and the courage to face the unknown with God. Their ministers were of the same calibre, plain-spoken men with a heart-warming message told in the homespun language of the frontier. In some cases they went right along with their migrant congregations; in other cases they were missionaries who spent a winter or two along the edge of civilization, establishing little churches, then returning to their homes. Such were Thomas Tinsley who preached in the vicinity of Harrodsburg, Kentucky, in 1776; John Taylor from Virginia, who spent the winter of 1779 in Kentucky preaching the gospel; and Joseph Redding also from Virginia, who replaced Taylor in the spring of 1780. The first permanent preacher in Kentucky was William Marshall, whose earlier work had been in Virginia. The first Baptist church to be organized west of the Thirteen Colonies was the Severns Valley church in Kentucky, established on June 18, 1781.[1]

New streams of immigrants moved out from the economically depressed East following the Revolution; these were made up principally of the lower middle class. Many came from Virginia and North Carolina. Some congregations, like that of the Gilbert's Creek church in Kentucky, were "traveling churches," holding services on the road as the members journeyed from its place of origin in Upper Spotsylvania, Virginia.

[1] See Chapter Eight above; also W. W. Sweet, *The Story of Religion in America* (New York, 1939), chaps. 14-5; Sweet, *Religion on the American Frontier*. Vol. I, *The Baptists* (New York, 1931), chap. 2.

Associations were organized rapidly, as we have seen. Inter-denominational work among Presbyterians, Methodists, and Baptists was common. As revival fires spread across the frontier country, the number of associations increased in Kentucky alone to twenty-five. These were composed of nearly five hundred churches and over thirty-one thousand members.[2] In Tennessee a similar growth occurred during the last half of the eighteenth century. By 1809 there were four associations in the state. Near the close of the last decade of the eighteenth century, Baptist settlers entered the Little Miami territory in Ohio, coming from Connecticut, New York, and New Jersey. At the same time, Indiana and Illinois were being settled. When Missouri was ceded to the United States, Kentucky Baptists began to move into that territory. The first Baptist church there was formed in 1804 in Cape Girardeau County. As settlers came in from Virginia, North Carolina, Kentucky, and Tennessee, John Mason Peck and James E. Welch were sent to St. Louis in 1817 by the Triennial Convention as missionaries. They organized the first Baptist church in St. Louis in 1818. This was followed by an elementary school and a Sunday school for Negro slaves. By 1830 Missouri had seven associations; four years later, the Missouri Baptist General Association was organized for the extension of the missionary movement which had brought it into existence. When settlers from South Carolina and Georgia moved into Mississippi and Louisiana, the Protestants among them were persecuted by Catholics. Baptist growth, therefore, was not rapid in those territories; but by 1806, the first association in Mississippi had been organized with a constituency of six churches. Thus, there was an infiltration of Baptists into the western territories, where a struggle was to ensue, in some quarters at least, between Protestant and Roman Catholic Christianity for dominance. In the vanguard had been Baptists along with Methodists and Presbyterians.

The frontier Baptists were strongly individualistic, poorly educated, hard-working farmers and artisans. In these respects, their preachers and churches were a reflection of themselves. Very frequently, a likely speaker within the congregation would be called upon by the members to become their pastor. After a simple service of licensing, he went about in the community exhorting. If he im-

[2] Sweet, *The Baptists*, 24-6.

pressed his brethren, he was ordained. Ordination in the beginning seems to have been a local church matter only; indeed, the preacher was usually ordained for each new charge. But in time, the local church ordained after having sought the general approval of the sister churches of the association. Church discipline was strongly administered to maintain order and decency, and to oversee slaves who were held by members. Theology usually was mildly Calvinistic, the local church generally determining its own particular doctrinal statement. The church buildings were plain and often crude in construction; some congregations met in the homes of members. Churches were named after creeks, valleys, runs, and rivers. Associational organization was developed, as we have seen, after the pattern of the Philadelphia, Charleston, and Warren Associations. These frontier Baptists were careful to preserve the authority of the local church, and they sought to maintain confessional purity largely by moral and spiritual suasion and indoctrination.[3]

With the exception of the anti-mission Baptists, the frontier churches were eager to evangelize. Indeed, state societies for home mission work were established as early as 1802 in Massachusetts, and every two or three years thereafter. By 1830 such bodies existed in fourteen states. These, which were the precursors of the state conventions, united their efforts in co-operation with the American Baptist Home Mission Society, which was formed in 1832 in order to consolidate their forces for the purpose of winning the continent for Christ.

The American Baptist Home Mission Society[4]

In the minds and hearts of two great men of God was born the American Baptist Home Mission Society. One was John Mason Peck; the other, Jonathan Going. Peck's early life was spent in Connecticut, where he was converted at the age of eighteen. In 1813, when he was twenty-four, he was ordained by the church of which he was pastor in Catskill, New York. It was then that he gave evidence of a deep missionary concern. A meeting with Luther Rice

[3] *Ibid.*, chap. 3.

[4] The material in this section is based largely on the records of the Society and on Charles L. White, *A Century of Faith* (Philadelphia, 1932), a centenary history of the Society.

in June, 1815, directed his new interest to the Missouri Territory. Leaving New York State a year later, he attended Dr. Staughton's seminary in Philadelphia, preaching frequently and making valuable acquaintances for the great work that lay ahead. Although not robust in health, his intrepid spirit took him westward to St. Louis in 1817. He was then a young man of twenty-eight, with a wife and three small children—the newly appointed agent of the Triennial Convention. After one hundred and twenty-eight days of rough and uncertain travel through the wilderness in a small one-horse wagon, the little family arrived. It was not long before Peck was organizing a church in the frontier town. His presence was a source of encouragement and inspiration to the small group of Baptists in the area. In 1819, at the second meeting of the Missouri Association (renamed St. Louis Association in 1853), he presented his dream and plan for "The United Society for the Spread of the Gospel," which was to have separate funds for education, missions, and Indian work. In a few weeks both the Illinois and the Missouri Associations approved it. Under the indefatigable promotion of Peck, the Society established fifty public schools in remote settlements, planned for itinerant missionary work, collected funds through "mite" societies, envisioned a college, and helped to support Isaac McCoy, a missionary to the Indians in the Wabash region.

It was not long, however, before the anti-mission spokesmen raised their voices in loud opposition to organizations which collected funds and imported into their territory missionaries who were better trained than many of the native preachers. The Triennial Convention, which had supported Peck's work since his arrival, suddenly in 1820 withdrew its appropriation to the western work, leaving him stranded without support. Three reasons for the momentous decision are recorded in the minutes of the Western Mission under date of July 9, 1820, by Peck, who was its secretary:

1. The want of ample funds for its vigorous prosecution.

2. A supposition on the part of the Board that this region would be soon supplied by the immigration into it of preachers from the Middle and Eastern States.

3. The opposition in the West was also urged as a reason for its being abolished. . . .[5]

[5] Rufus Babcock, *Memoir of John Mason Peck, D.D.* (Philadelphia, 1864), 166.

Welch was requested by the Board to continue his labors in St. Louis as a private minister, not as a missionary. Peck was directed to remove to Fort Wayne, Indiana, to assist McCoy in his Indian Mission. Being strongly aware of the strategic territory in which the Western Mission had been begun, Peck replied that he would not leave his post. It should be said that the relationship of Welsh and Peck to the Board of the Convention remained friendly in spite of its decision. The Convention's withdrawal from the task of home missions involved no criticism of its agents, but represented a return to its original purpose of foreign missions. Those who had sought to broaden its scope to include all phases of denominational activities had failed. Baptists preferred, as we have seen in an earlier chapter, to rely upon the society method rather than the convention principle as a safeguard against ecclesiasticism.

For two years, Peck struggled along at his own support; at the end of that time, the Massachusetts Baptist Missionary Society voted to allot him a salary of five dollars a week. His labors for the Society can never be measured in money. In one year he was absent from his home as much as fifty-three days. He traveled widely, in one year journeying on horseback nine hundred and twenty-six miles, preaching thirty-one sermons, and delivering numerous speeches, lectures, and addresses. He established seven new Bible societies, strengthened two weak ones, arranged for the founding of four more, and established several Sunday schools.[6] Through such means he laid the foundation of a permanent church life in the West.

In 1826 Peck's promotional work brought him east, where he met Jonathan Going, pastor of the First Baptist Church at Worcester, Massachusetts. In this fellow minister he found a deeply interested friend, whose missionary vision was so much akin to his own that he visited the Mississippi Valley in the spring of 1831. There, Going saw for himself the possibilities of the expansion of Protestantism, if the Baptists were united. Upon his return, he recommended to the Massachusetts Baptist Missionary Society in Boston that a general home mission society should be formed after the pattern of Peck's dream. The Board not only agreed, but appointed Dr. Going as its chief promotional agent. Going thereupon resigned his pastorate in Worcester, and threw himself into the work of promoting the or-

[6] White, *A Century of Faith*, 33.

ganization of the first national home mission society for Baptists in the United States.

On April 27, 1832, in the Oliver Street Baptist meeting-house in New York City, the Triennial Convention, which was then in session, adjourned to permit the delegates to attend a conference on home missions in the Mulberry Street Church. There, on motion of Dr. Spencer H. Cone, pastor of the Oliver Street Church, the American Baptist Home Mission Society was brought into existence. When the organization was completed, the extension of its field of work had been determined as North America, its motto being "North America for Christ." Its officers included the Honorable Heman Lincoln, of the Massachusetts legislature, as president; William Colgate, the soap manufacturer of New York, as treasurer; and Jonathan Going as corresponding secretary. The headquarters were established in New York City and in 1962 were moved to Valley Forge, Pa.

The first ten years of the Society's history were characterized by remarkable vision and courageous action. During the first year, eighty-nine appointments were made, some for a temporary term of service and some for permanent work. Fifty missionaries actually agreed to accept the assignments which were distributed in ten states, two territories, and Lower Canada. The baptisms for the year were four hundred. The next year, eighty missionaries accepted appointment, and new work was added in Louisiana, Michigan, and Upper Canada. In spite of anti-mission sentiment, disease, and other obstacles, sixteen hundred baptisms were reported, forty churches were constituted, fifty Sunday schools organized, ten Bible classes formed, forty temperance and twelve mission societies created, and three Baptist Associations constituted. As each year passed, new achievements were reported until the decade closed with nearly eleven thousand baptisms, the organization of four hundred churches, the ordination of one hundred and forty-two ministers, and the creation of benevolent societies, Sunday schools, and Bible classes— a notable achievement for the Home Mission Society in its first ten years of service.[7] Truly, it laid in those early years the foundation of Baptist work along the frontiers of America and implanted in the churches an aggressive spirit of evangelism which has been the secret of Baptist growth.

[7] White, *op. cit.*, 49-54.

The missionary's task was one of ceaseless travel, often as many as forty-five hundred miles in a single year. By horse, on foot, and frequently by swimming rivers which could not be forded—these heroic ambassadors of the cross made their way into the scattered communities and humble cottages of settlers whose loneliness and spiritual longings found a lasting satisfaction in the gospel of Christ. In those formative years, their sacrificial labors benefited the new country culturally as well as religiously; they lifted the level of life everywhere they went.

Then came the railroads, spanning a continent within two decades. New frontiers opened as General Fremont's explorations beyond the Rocky Mountains brought Oregon to the attention of the Society in 1843. Five years later, the first Baptist church on the Pacific Coast was built by Hezekiah Johnson at Oregon City. For some time, however, the settlement of the Northwest was deterred by the gold rush to California. In the meantime, the annexation of Texas in 1845 opened another large field, to which was added a few years later the Southwest Territory acquired from Mexico after the Mexican War. By the mid-century, missionaries were being sent to California. Simultaneously the Society was pushing into Minnesota in 1849, expanding the work in Indiana, Wisconsin, Illinois, and Iowa, and entering such new fields as Kansas in 1854, Nebraska in 1856, Colorado, Dakota, Wyoming, and Idaho in 1864, and the Washington Territory in 1870.

In the Southern States, the Society had curtailed its work between 1846 and the outbreak of war in 1861 to avoid further tension over the slavery issue which had been a contributory factor to schism in 1845. The war quite naturally widened the breach between the Home Mission Society and the Southern Baptist Convention. Yet, in 1862, the Society again began missionary operations in the older Southern States, becoming concerned chiefly with the evangelization and education of the freedmen and also with the erection of church edifices for white as well as colored congregations. Indeed, by 1869, one-third of all its missionary force was at work in the South. The intricate relations and tensions which developed between the Society and the Home Mission Board of the Southern Convention will be related in the next section of this chapter. By the fiftieth anniversary of the organization, there were five hundred and thirteen missionaries under appointment in every western state and territory, laboring among peoples of four races and nine languages.[8]

From 1882 on, new problems emerged to be dealt with by the Home Mission Society. Some parishes were not sufficiently populous to support churches of several denominations; hence the question quite naturally arose as to what comity arrangements might be worked out. In some smaller towns, with new modes of transportation, it was possible to work out a union or federated type of church which represented the merging of local congregations of denominational groups. Up to 1907 the missionaries followed the railroads, along which Scandinavians, Germans, and representatives of other nationalities in lesser numbers had settled. By that date western Baptists were in a financial position to support their own work, with the possible exception of those in the irrigation belt of the Far West where Baptists needed missionary assistance for a few years more.

The operation of the American Baptist Home Mission Society during the nineteenth century was varied and exceedingly important to the growth of the denomination. Evangelization of the frontier peoples was its foremost task. By 1850 it had become necessary to make plans for assisting feeble churches in building meeting-houses. To this end, the Church Edifice Department of the Society was created; it made loans and administered gifts to needy congregations. Several hundred churches owe their buildings as well as their existence to the ministry of this agency; yet, the Congregationalists, Presbyterians, and Methodists far outstripped the Baptists in church edifice work.[9] Another phase of the Society's missionary enterprise was the evangelization of foreign-speaking groups in rural and urban centers. Aid was given also to the Negro in his emergence from bondage. The American Indian received much encouragement and defense at the hands of kindly missionaries, whose attitude was in sharp contrast to that of the exploiter and the indifferent American public. A further contribution of the Society was represented in the challenge which its work presented to the advance of Roman Cath-

---

[8] For an excellent account of the work of the Home Mission Society in Southern States, see Robert A. Baker, *Relations between Northern and Southern Baptists* (Fort Worth, 1948), chaps. 6-9; for statistics at the 50th Anniversary, see White, *A Century of Faith*, 61.

[9] *Ibid.*, 220.

olicism in the cities of the United States and in Mexico, Puerto Rico, and Cuba.

In carrying on this large work, the Home Mission Society had the services of a number of remarkably capable corresponding secretaries. Their executive ability and spiritual vision inspired Baptists to give to this work more than ten and a half million dollars in contributions and legacies in the seventy-year period from 1832 to 1902.[10] The first was Jonathan Going who served the Society for five years. He resigned in 1837 to accept the presidency of Granville Literary and Theological Institution, now Denison University. From 1838 until his death in 1839, Luther Crawford served as secretary. For the next twenty-two years, Benjamin Hill, a native of Rhode Island, steered the Society through the difficult slavery controversy, through the panic of 1857, and through the opening years of the war. From 1862 to 1874 Jay S. Backus, of New York City, headed the organization. He was succeeded by Nathan Bishop, who served more or less as acting secretary after Backus' health had broken. In 1876 Sewall S. Cutting, editor of several Baptist periodicals and professor at Rochester University for thirteen years, took up the task in a difficult period when his talents were greatly needed. The Society was in debt for improvements in two of its Negro schools in the South, and the women's home mission work, which they had begun to develop in 1873, needed to be integrated into the over-all enterprise. When Cutting declined re-election in 1879, Henry L. Morehouse, of New York State, was selected. This able leader served the Society for a total period of thirty-eight years. From 1893 until 1902 he occupied the new post of field secretary while General Thomas J. Morgan undertook the duties of the office. From 1903 to 1917 Morehouse again served as corresponding secretary. During his terms of service, he conceived the plan and inaugurated the Church Edifice Gift Fund, from which grants were made to two thousand churches throughout the country. He worked closely with Southern Baptists in missionary enterprises. He was thoroughly familiar with the Indian missions and was very co-operative with Negro Baptist bodies.

The Society has maintained good relationships with the state conventions, preventing them from becoming so preoccupied with their own immediate rural and city problems as to lose the missionary

[10] White, *A Century of Faith*, 269-70.

passion, and often assisting them in the support of home missionaries within their own territory. When the Society was organized in
1832, a plan was developed to integrate the work of other home mission bodies by enrolling them as auxiliaries to the national society.
These fell into three general types: those who carried on their own
mission activities, but gave no financial assistance to the Society,
merely reporting whatever work was accomplished; those who contributed to the Society in addition to doing work locally; and those
who paid all of their funds for home missions into the treasury of
the Society and had the privilege of designating the field of labor in
which their funds were to be used. The latter class was the more
desirable from the point of view of the Society. This auxiliary system was entirely voluntary; hence some state conventions were spas-
modic in their relations to the Society. During the first decade of
the Society's life, the system was utilized with some success. Nearly
all of the southern conventions were at one time or another in some
form of auxiliary relationship. A few of the conventions in the East
voted to become auxiliaries. The strongest support seems to have
come from the Baptist Missionary Convention of New York, which
represented numerically one-sixth of the Baptists of the country.

The conventions were not consistently co-operative throughout
the years. Older states were usually sufficiently strong to carry on
their own home mission program. The major assistance given to
state conventions by the Society went to those in the West and
Southwest where pioneer work was being done. Complaints were
voiced frequently by Baptists of the South that the Society neglected
such needy areas as Florida, Mississippi, Arkansas, Tennessee, and
Louisiana. That their criticisms had some justification is evident from
the regret expressed by the leaders of the Society that there were
not so many volunteers for work in the South as in the North. The
reason undoubtedly was to be found in the fact that the volunteers
would rather labor among their own people and in a climate to which
they were accustomed.[11] This grievance was a factor leading to the
organization of the Southern Baptist Convention in 1845.

Women's organizations which were established first in Massachusetts, Ohio, Illinois, Connecticut, and Michigan, in the years after
1865 sent annual contributions to the Home Mission Society. In the

[11] Baker, *Relations between Northern and Southern Baptists*, chap. 2.

years from 1882 to 1896 these contributions amounted to as much as one hundred and ninety-six thousand dollars.[12] When these women's organizations in 1877 brought into being the Women's Baptist Home Mission Societies, they made their gifts apply directly to the support of their own missionaries. The relations between these and the Home Mission Society have been most cordial. This has also been true of the contacts between the Home Mission Society and the Foreign Mission Society. The closer co-operative relations of the American Baptist Home Mission Society to interdenominational comity and religious educational enterprises did not develop to any extent until the twentieth century.

The Home Mission Board of the Southern Baptist Convention

Unlike Northern Baptists, the Baptists of the South have no separate home mission society; instead, they have a home mission board which is a closely integrated unit of the Southern Baptist Convention. It originally was known as the Board of Domestic Missions and was located at Marion, Alabama. From the first, it was a department of the Convention and therefore under the jurisdiction of that body. In keeping with this relationship, the first missionaries to be commissioned for home service were given their credentials by the Southern Baptist Convention at its second session, held in Richmond, Virginia, in June, 1846. They were the Reverend J. W. D. Creath and his wife. They had come to assist James Huckins, who was Texas' first Baptist missionary, sent there by the American Baptist Home Mission Society in 1839 in response to a request from the first missionary Baptist church in the state, a church which had been organized in Washington County in 1837.

The objectives of home missionary endeavors had been clearly outlined by the Convention in 1845 when it had set up the Board of Domestic Missions. They included work among the Indians, the Negroes, and the populace of New Orleans, which city was located strategically at the gateway of the Mississippi River Valley. At that time the slave population of the South numbered around two and a half millions; there were, in addition, almost a third of a million free blacks. The total Negro membership in white churches was over one

---

[12] White, *A Century of Faith*, 245.

hundred thousand. It was quite evident from these figures that insufficient work was being carried on among the Negroes; those who were converted were baptized by white preachers and given membership in white churches, a special section being assigned to them in the building for worship. Frequently, the colored folk held Sunday afternoon services of their own in which the white pastor often participated. The only organized work which had been conducted among the slaves prior to 1845 appears to have been under the direction of district associations which engaged white missionaries to visit the plantations. Occasionally an association would purchase a gifted Christian slave and set him free to labor among his people. The Board, however, from its inception until the outbreak of War in 1861, had appointed only two missionaries for full-time service among the Negroes. Both of these were stationed in Georgia. From Board reports, it appears that direct work with slaves on the plantations was possible only to the extent that owners became alert to their spiritual needs and were willing to pay the expenses of the missionaries. Certainly, interest was not lacking on the part of the Southern Baptist Convention, for a mission was carried on in 1853 among the colored population of Washington and Baltimore, in cooperation with the Maryland Union Baptist Association.[18]

Since the Indian work in those early years of the Board's existence was under an organization independent of the Convention and known as the American Indian Mission Association, located in Louisville, Kentucky, little more than the making of financial contributions to that agency was accomplished by the Home Mission Board. During the next four years Southern Baptists contributed over sixty-one thousand dollars for the evangelizing of the Indians.

Attention was directed also to the winning of New Orleans to Protestantism. The strategy of that move was obvious to all Baptists, north and south, for the defeat or victory of Roman Catholicism in the Mississippi Valley would be determined quite largely by the influence of that key city. The American Baptist Home Mission Society had begun a mission there earlier, when the Reverend Russell Holman, who became the first corresponding secretary of the Southern

---

[18] Joe W. Burton, *Epochs of Home Missions: Southern Baptist Convention, 1845-1945* (Atlanta, Ga., 1945), 16-7. B. F. Riley, *A History of the Baptists in the Southern States East of the Mississippi* (Philadelphia, 1898), 318. S.B.C., *Proceedings* for 1851, 35; for 1853, 17, 57.

Board of Domestic Missions, organized a church there in 1843. Ten years later, the Southern Baptist Convention planned to appoint four missionaries to supplement the work of the Baptist pastor in the city, and an agent was appointed to raise fifteen thousand dollars. Eventually an effective city mission enterprise was established with the assistance of local churches and surrounding associations, which were desirous of strengthening the Protestant witness in that Catholic city.

The basic function, however, of the Home Mission Board in those early years was to send the gospel to the destitute areas of the South. The need was very great, for entire sections were untouched by the ministry of the church. One-sixth of the inhabitants of western North Carolina had no knowledge of the Bible. Colporters in Alabama reported that many adults in that state had never heard a sermon. In several counties of Maryland, there was no Baptist church. Arkansas was almost entirely destitute of preaching and Christian instruction. Yet in spite of the great need, the obstacles to mission work were not entirely external. Anti-mission forces, which had harassed the workers of the American Baptist Home Mission Society, were equally troublesome in the South. Nevertheless, the work of planting churches continued in practically every state of the Southern Convention. Funds were gathered by the agents of the Board, but only after miles of arduous travel. Many found the strain of the work too great, and succumbed to disease. But others arose to take their places until the number of missionaries and agents commissioned by the Home Mission Board in fifteen years had reached the nine hundred mark. Within that period, over thirteen thousand converts had been won and one hundred and seventy-nine churches established. In that work the missionaries had traveled more than nine hundred thousand miles. Since 1855 the Board had been undertaking the Indian work which the American Indian Mission Association had turned over to it because of its own financial inability to carry on the task. The Board was supporting thirty-five missionaries among the Choctaws, Cherokees, Creeks, and Pottawotomies. During the next four years, Southern Baptists contributed more than sixty-one thousand dollars toward this new obligation. In addition, a Chinese mission was established in San Francisco under the care of the Reverend J. Lewis Shuck, a former missionary to China. To finance this program, Southern Baptists contributed an average of nineteen thousand dollars a year, making a total of over two hundred and sixty-six thousand by 1860.[14]

Between 1861 and 1865, the war produced a period of spiritual decline and of economic and political distress which played havoc with the missionary enterprise of the Convention. Effects of inflation and a steadily rising cost of living were felt severely by missionaries to whom support was not forthcoming. Many had to flee for their lives from the border states as hatreds increased. California was dropped from the Board's responsibility in 1861. The Indian missions were cut off from supplies and contacts with headquarters by the Union armies, once the Mississippi had been captured. City mission work was sadly curtailed owing to the lack of leaders free to engage in such activities. Yet, the spirit of missions did not die; instead, it found a new outlet in service to the Confederate armies in which chaplains were all too few. To help the situation, preaching missions were conducted by ministers who visited the camps or the front lines while on leave of absence from their churches.

The man to face the almost insurmountable difficulties of war and reconstruction was M. T. Sumner, corresponding secretary of the Home Mission Board from 1862 to 1875. To finance the major task of rehabilitation, Sumner responded to an invitation from Kentucky Baptists to present the needs in that state, where money had not yet lost its value. In six weeks he collected from them the sum of ten thousand dollars. Missouri and Baltimore, Maryland, also gave liberally. Before long, the total collections amounted to nearly twenty-three thousand dollars, making possible the employment of fifty-three missionaries in twelve states of the South, five of whom were assigned to work among Negroes. One hundred and twenty-four workers were engaged in 1866, four of whom were in Indian Territory.[15]

The impoverished condition of the southern states and the willingness of northern agencies, such as the American Baptist Home Mission Society, the American Baptist Publication Society, and the American and Foreign Bible Society, to assist the Baptists of the South in carrying on their missionary work, seemed to the southern leaders to be a serious threat to the future of the Southern Baptist Convention. While the receipts of the American Baptist Home Mis-

14 *Ibid.*, 34, 37; cf., S.B.C., *Proceedings* for 1859, p. 66.
15 Burton, *Epochs of Home Missions*, 54-6.

sion Society in the North in 1870 comprised one hundred and forty-four thousand dollars, those of the Board of Domestic Missions amounted to only twenty-one thousand. Yet the membership in the two bodies was about the same, six hundred thousand in each.[16] What was happening was that the northern agencies were lending money to churches or state conventions in the South on the condition, of course, that a generous part of it be replaced by the recipients. The result of such well-meant assistance was to cause contributions to be drained off into northern instead of southern channels. More and more Baptists of the southern states were becoming thereby affiliated with northern societies.

Discussion was bound to center about the question of realigning with the Northern Baptists, especially when the American Baptist Home Mission Society sent a committee to the meeting of the Southern Baptist Convention in Baltimore in 1868 with an invitation for fraternal relations and a proffer of assistance. A resolution to accept the proposal was presented to the Convention by Dr. J. B. Jeter of Virginia in 1869 at Macon, Georgia; but it was rejected. In 1870 Dr. John A. Broadus, a member of the faculty of the Southern Baptist Theological Seminary at Louisville, submitted a substitute resolution which was adopted. He stated that any attempt to secure organic connection between the Boards, North and South, would "tend rather to keep up strife among the brethren." His resolution called for each section to do its own work while maintaining cordial and co-operative relations. The decision was influenced by the Sunday School Board, which had objected to the willingness of the American Baptist Publication Society to engage some Negro editors to prepare materials for the Negro churches which looked to it for literature. The southerners were of the opinion that perfect equality could not be attained between the whites and the blacks.

In 1879 the Southern Convention, at Atlanta, Georgia, faced the issue once again when Dr. Isaac T. Tichenor, president of the Agricultural and Mechanical College at Auburn, Alabama, presented resolutions calling for a burial of the past and the holding of a meeting of representatives from all states in the Convention to devise plans of co-operation between that body and other Baptist organizations in the United States. The report of the committee, of which

[16] *Ibid.,* 62.

Tichenor was chairman, was a recommendation to continue fraternal relations, but "preserve our separate organizations." [17]

Southerners were desirous of the assistance of the American Baptist Home Mission Society in the task of evangelizing the freedmen, provided it were given through the Southern Convention. This the Society refused to do, for it would not recognize the territorial limitation which the Convention sought to impose upon the Society's work. Accordingly, the tension increased as the Society continued its services to various state conventions in the South which had requested aid, and as it developed its educational program for the freedmen, always in the hope that unity might ultimately be achieved between itself and the Southern Convention. The hope was not without some foundation, for when the Society celebrated its fiftieth anniversary in 1882, representatives attended from all of the southern states and two were enrolled as representing the Southern Baptist Convention. There had been many voices speaking in terms of union, but "the reports of the Southern Baptist Convention continued to show a definite territorial consciousness." [18] In other words, while there were in the South many Baptists who welcomed co-operative activity with the Home Mission Society, the official leadership of the Convention was desirous of maintaining and strengthening its own Home Mission Board. The Southern Baptist Convention, whose constitution set for itself no territorial limits in the United States, was actually developing a sectionalism which was proving embarrassing to the American Baptist Home Mission Society, whose motto was "North America for Christ."

The die was cast in 1882, when the Convention determined to inject new life into its Home Mission Board by removing its headquarters from Marion, Alabama, to the active urban center of Atlanta, Georgia. With a new personnel, and with Dr. Tichenor as its corresponding secretary, it was hoped that the loyalty of Southern Baptists to their own missionary agency might be assured. The new Board was instructed to be in actuality the sole channel for the missionary co-operation of all southern bodies, thus ending the existing reliance of some southern associations and state conventions upon northern agencies.

[17] S.B.C., *Proceedings* for 1869, 21; for 1870, 13, 19, 21-2; 35; for 1879, 14, 26.
[18] Baker, *Relations Between Northern and Southern Baptists*, 117; see also chap. 11.

This that had been voted was difficult to accomplish, owing to the fear of centralization which many Baptists felt. Then, too, the Board of Domestic Missions conducted work only in Arkansas, Florida, Louisiana, Texas, California, and the Indian Territory, for Maryland, North and South Carolina, Georgia, and Virginia with the exception of one missionary, carried on their own home mission work.[19] In some of the states mentioned, the American Baptist Home Mission Society had been serving by request in a co-operative capacity, a relationship which constituted a further hindrance to a complete loyalty to southern agencies. Tichenor faced unflinchingly what he called "a great defeat and a lost cause." In the words of a Southern Baptist historian:

He surveyed the area west of the Mississippi, and judged that the entire territory had passed out of the hands of the Southern Board. East of the river the outlook was not much brighter. Mississippi was allied with the Publication Society of the North, Georgia was co-operating with the Home Mission Society in freedman missions, while Florida was seriously considering an official alignment with the Home Mission Society. Tennessee Baptists also were studying the possibility of Northern alignment. Indian Territory and Louisiana were the only areas that offered the possibility of alignment with the Southern Convention, and in the former the Home Mission Society was pressing an aggressive campaign.[20]

The president of the Home Mission Board, E. T. Winkler, wrote an article in August, 1882, in which he challenged the right of the Home Mission Society to operate in the South. He pointed out that:

Every one of the border States of the South is occupied by the Home Mission Society; and most of our older States are in co-operative alliance with the American Baptist Publication Society in colportage and Sunday School work. . . . The number of missionaries employed in the South by the Home Mission Society is 120—just three times the number of those under commission of our own Home Mission Board. . . .[21]

[19] S.B.C., *Proceedings* for 1881, 25.

[20] Baker, *Relations Between Northern and Southern Baptists*, 173-4.

[21] Reprinted in *Home Mission Monthly* (New York, organ of A.B.H.M.S.), IV, 274-5; cited in Baker, *op. cit.*, 175.

The uncompromising reply of H. L. Morehouse, corresponding secretary of the Home Mission Society, was that the Society was in the South to stay. Such was the situation when Tichenor took up the duties of his office.

The Southern Baptist Convention was not disappointed in the leadership of Dr. Tichenor. He gave statesmanlike service to the cause of Southern Baptist missions from 1882 until 1899. His program called for an annual expenditure of one hundred thousand dollars. By 1883 the receipts totaled more than forty-five thousand dollars; in five years, the number of missionaries had increased from 41 to 251; baptisms had been multiplied more than thirty times.

So energetic was Dr. Tichenor's policy of aggressive home mission work through the Board of the Southern Convention that "in five years [after he took office in 1882] there was not a missionary to the white people of the South who did not bear a commission from either the Home Mission Board of the Southern Baptist Convention, or one of our State Boards in alliance with it." [22] This change is not to be explained by any lessening of activity in the South by the Home Mission Society, nor simply by any increase of contributions to the Southern Board, but rather by the development of a denominational consciousness which was fostered by a *convention* type of polity. "Unlike the meetings of the Northern Baptist Societies, which did not represent the churches and associations, and whose organizational form were specifically designed to avoid connectionalism or denominationalism, gatherings of the Southern Baptist Convention spoke with a denominational accent." [23] The aggressive promotion of home missions by Dr. Tichenor had won the respect and co-operation of the various state conventions in the South which had not heretofore supported the Board.

As the Home Mission Society and the Southern Board pursued their respective work in western territories, conflicts arose which demanded a compromise solution. This was true in Missouri and Indian Territory in particular, where the Southern Convention's insistence upon territorial alignment met with objection from the Home Mission Society's interest there. In 1894 the Convention initiated

[22] S.B.C., *Proceedings* for 1892, p. xi of Appendix A; cited in Baker, *op. cit.*, 180.

[23] Baker, *op. cit.*, 182. For a detailed analysis of the Fortress Monroe Conference discussed below, see chap. 11 of Baker's study.

a conference which was held at Fortress Monroe, Virginia, on September 12-13, for the purpose of working out a formula to permit Southern Baptists a larger role in the work among the freedmen of the South.

After an amicable discussion, the Conference arrived at three agreements: (1) the Convention should appoint local advisory committees at points where the American Baptist Home Mission Society had schools for freedmen for the purpose of recommending to the Society any changes thought desirable in the schools; (2) the Society and the Convention should co-operate in work among the colored people by the joint appointment of missionaries after consultation between the white and colored state conventions, and that there should be held ministers' and deacons' training institutes to help strengthen colored Baptist leadership; (3) that favorable consideration should be given to a comity agreement between the Society and the Convention in order to avoid antagonism; the proposition being that antagonism be avoided in work already begun on contiguous fields or on the same field, and that no new work be opened by one agency in a territory where the other is already at work. This third item was unanimously adopted, after special study, subsequent to the Conference.

The Fortress Monroe Conference was significant for several reasons: (1) It promised much greater financial co-operation by the South in missions conducted by the Society for the colored. (2) It represented the first formal recognition by the Society of the territorial limits desired by the Southern Baptist Convention. (3) It undoubtedly served as a warning to the Society that it was overreaching its strength in aggressive activity in the territory of the Southern Baptist Convention. (4) Some hope for a future attainment of organic union was offered by the compromise reached in the Conference.[24] Hence, from 1894 on, the Home Mission Society's extensive operations in the South were curtailed by a new relationship of co-operation on the basis of comity agreements. It was the beginning of a recognition by Northern Baptists of a geographical boundary between them and the Southern Baptist Convention.

After 1894 there was a rapid growth in the South of denominational consciousness and also of home mission expansion. By the

[24] *Ibid.*, 192.

close of Dr. Tichenor's administration in 1899, the number of missionaries had tripled that of 1887; baptisms amounted to 6,552, or nearly twice as many as in 1887; and the number of churches and mission stations had grown from over 100 in 1882 to 2,580. The receipts amounted to nearly $66,000 plus $50,000 used for the erection of church buildings.[25] His remarkable leadership had virtually saved the Southern Baptist Convention; he had developed a definite plan of co-operative support of home mission work through regular giving; had established a church building department in 1884, much like the Church Edifice Department of the American Baptist Home Mission Society in the North; had fostered and built a Sunday school work until it was ready to go ahead on its own power under the present Sunday School Board organized in 1891; and he had made the South a base for world missions which began in the city missions in the states and continued out to the far-flung foreign missions which were so vitally related to his own task of home missions. He inaugurated work in Cuba, broadened the program for Negro education, established a chain of mountain mission schools for the underprivileged, and encouraged the Indian missions.[26]

When Dr. Tichenor reached the age of retirement, not only had a new century dawned, but an era of expansion had been ushered in by his untiring leadership. The missionary program for which the Southern Baptist Convention had come into existence was being carried on not only by the Home and Foreign Mission Boards, but by the Woman's Missionary Union, which had been created in 1888, and by the Sunday School Board established at Nashville, Tennessee, in 1891. By a combination of evangelism, Christian education, and missionary emphasis, the Southern Baptists were ready to meet the challenging problems of the twentieth century.

Baptist Work Among the Indians

Prior to 1861 the Triennial Convention and its successor, the American Baptist Missionary Union (north) carried on work among various Indian tribes: the Indians of Indiana; the Cherokees in

[25] S.B.C., *Proceedings* for 1882, 48-50; for 1887, p. xxxi of Board's report; for 1899, pp. lxxv, lxxxviii of Board's report.

[26] Burton, *Epochs of Home Missions*, 77-84.

North Carolina and in the Indian Territory, to which they were removed after 1838; the Creeks, until their removal to the Indian
Territory in 1838; several tribes in New York from 1824 to 1850;
the Ottawas in Michigan until 1854; the Ojibwas in the same state
until 1854; the Choctaws in the Southwest from 1826 to 1844, after
their removal to the Indian Territory; and several tribes along the
Mississippi between 1833 and 1865. Up to the outbreak of the War
between the States sixty missionaries had been commissioned to
serve among the Indians. They reported two thousand baptisms
among the Indian converts.[27]

The war, however, seriously affected the missions in both the
North and the South. When the American Baptist Home Mission
Society took over the Indian missions in 1865 from the American
Baptist Missionary Union, there were but two active missions remaining; these were among the Cherokees and the Shawanos and
Delawares in the Indian Territory. Among Southern Baptists, the
work had been brought to a virtual standstill. In 1867, there were
only two white and two Indian missionaries in the employ of the
Home Mission Board, all of whom were at work among the Choctaws. At the same time the Creeks and Cherokees were requesting
missionaries. Within the next few years funds were made available
by local associations in Georgia to support workers who should be
under the Board's direction. Georgia Baptists bore most of the
expense for Indian missions in the postwar period.[28]

In 1876 the Northern Baptists determined, through their Home
Mission Society, to build a school for the Indians. The moving spirit
in this enterprise was Almon C. Bacone, a graduate of Rochester
University, who went to Indian Territory in 1878 to teach in the
Cherokee Male Seminary, a tribal school at Tahlequah. In 1880 he
opened a school to serve the five tribes of the Territory; it came to
be known as the Indian Normal and Theological School at Tahlequah.
Desiring a more central location for the school, Bacone secured a
grant of one hundred and sixty acres from the Creek Council, on a
site three miles from Muskogee. The erection of buildings was made
possible through the gifts of John D. Rockefeller, Sr., and the Euclid

[27] White, *A Century of Faith*, 81-3.

[28] Wright, *Missionary Work of the Southern Baptist Convention*, 349-50.

Avenue Baptist Church of Cleveland, Ohio, of which he was a member. At the time of President Bacone's death, in 1896, the college had one hundred and twenty-five students.[29]

The Southern Baptists opened the Levering Mission Manual Labor School for the Creek Indians at a suitable site in their Territory on September 5, 1881. It was so named in memory of a wealthy Baltimore Baptist merchant who had died in 1870, leaving a large legacy for missionary use. The Reverend J. A. Trenchard, a graduate of the University of Georgia, was made its superintendent. The institution proved to be a success, especially as the means of converting several and arousing a missionary interest among the Indians themselves. In 1891 the school was transferred to the control of the Creek nation.

The work of the American Baptist Home Mission Society among the civilized tribes of Oklahoma produced a group of Indian churches which had become self-supporting to a large extent by 1914, at which time the total membership was over three thousand. The tensions which had been created by the presence of the Society and the Southern Convention at work in the Territory was settled when the Oklahoma Baptist Convention aligned itself with the Southern Baptist Convention, whereupon the Home Mission Society withdrew from the field. In 1887 work was begun among the so-called Blanket Tribes. Stations were opened among the Gaddoes and Wichitas in the same year, among the Kiowas in 1892, the Comanches in 1893, the Cheyennes in 1895, and the Arapahoes in 1898. After 1900, work was undertaken among the Navahos in New Mexico and among the Crow Indians in Montana. Quite obviously, the attention of Baptists to these first Americans had expanded greatly within half a century. In evangelizing them, Baptists had been most successful, for the majority of Indian converts were Baptists; but in providing educational facilities, other denominations far outstripped the Baptists. Undoubtedly, the lack of financial resources was chiefly responsible for this fact.[30]

But most certainly the Baptists, in their Indian missions, were true to their genius of ministering to the disinherited peoples of society.

[29] White, *op. cit.*, 84-6.

[30] Based upon a report made to the Southern Baptist Convention in 1876 by the chairman of the Committee on Indian Tribes. See S.B.C., *Proceedings* for 1876, p. 18.

Baptist Work Among the Negroes

While the American Baptist Home Mission Society conducted no work among the Negroes between 1832 and 1862 because of the slavery issue, which had become tense throughout the country, there was a general sense of obligation to do something for them.[31] As emancipation of the slaves drew near, the Society took steps to provide Christian instruction, through missionaries and teachers, for freedmen in the District of Columbia and elsewhere as changing conditions permitted. In 1863 the Society established a Freedmen's Fund; most of the support of the project came from New England Baptists where abolition sentiment had long been strong. By 1865 five thousand dollars had been received, and sixty-eight missionaries were at work in twelve southern states. Four years later the Home Mission Society became the sole agency for Northern Baptists in carrying on Negro work, for at that time the National Theological Institute, which had been organized in Washington, D. C., in 1864 for a similar purpose, turned its task over to the Society. Accordingly, by 1870, Northern Baptists were operating schools for freedmen in the nation's capital; at Nashville, Tennessee; Raleigh, North Carolina; New Orleans, Louisiana; Richmond, Virginia; St. Helena, South Carolina; and Augusta, Georgia. These schools offered normal and theological courses. Within the next few years, Baptists contributed in special gifts a total of $368,875 for the erection of buildings and equipment for nearly twenty schools for Negroes of both sexes. This amount was supplemented by contributions from the Government's Freedmen's Bureau.[32]

Southern Baptists responded also to the need for providing missionaries for freedmen. In 1868 six hundred and eleven baptisms were reported by workers of the Home Mission Board.[33] As the colored people became increasingly aware of their new-found freedom, they began to resent white preachers, preferring workers of their own race. The Board, therefore, began to employ Negro missionaries. Its chief method of helping the freedmen was to hold institutes in various sections where preachers might receive training to carry on

[31] White, *A Century of Faith,* 102.

[32] *Ibid.,* 105-6.

[33] Wright, *Missionary Work of the Southern Baptist Convention,* 316.

their leadership more adequately. In 1878 both Southern and Northern Baptists entered into a co-operative effort to maintain such institutes throughout the South. The Home Mission Society appointed a superintendent of missions to conduct them with the aid of the Southern Board, but without the latter's incurring any expense in the enterprise. The state boards of Georgia, Florida, Alabama, Louisiana, Texas, and Maryland were among those local agencies which gave material assistance to the Home Mission Board of the Southern Convention in employing colored missionaries for the training of the Negroes. Again in 1894-95, in accordance with the agreement of the Fortress Monroe Conference, the Northern and Southern Baptists joined in a common plan of training deacons and ministers of Negro churches. By joint action of the Home Mission Society, the Home Mission Board, and the state conventions in the South, both white and colored, general missionaries were appointed to supervise the work in various states. In addition, ministers' and deacons' institutes were held. By 1897 fourteen missionaries were "in the joint employ of these Boards, three in Alabama, three in South Carolina, four in North Carolina, and four in Virginia." [34] The plan received general support on the part of white and colored Baptists. The Baptist women of the South were encouraged to carry on a training work among Negro women and children, the slight expense involved being borne by the Home Mission Board.

Baptist Work Among the Immigrants

In 1845, the year of the schism in the Triennial Convention, the Nativist Party, which was strongly opposed to immigration and radically anti-Roman Catholic, held its first national convention. Its existence reflected the growing hostility to the influx of Irish immigrants, in particular, who were Roman Catholic. The Nativists were composed largely of Americans of the old Protestant stock of northern Europe. During the decade, 1840 to 1850, they had become increasingly alarmed as more than 1,713,000 immigrants crowded the shores of the United States in contrast to only 600,000 in the previous ten-year period. From 1820 to 1890, over four and a half million Irish, chiefly Roman Catholic, arrived in America.[35] The fertile farm

[34] S.B.C., *Proceedings* for 1897, p. lxxii of Board report.
[35] Carl Wittke, *We Who Built America: the Saga of the Immigrant*, xvi, 129.

A HISTORY OF THE BAPTISTS

[handwritten annotation in top margin: The immigrants settled on the eastern sea Board and in the midwest along the Mississippi River. They came in waves— first, the Germans; second the Irish; Third the Italians. The Irish and Italians con to come to the US after 1900's began.]

lands of the Mississippi River Valley provided a strong attraction to seemingly innumerable German, Irish, and Scandinavian newcomers who saw in the United States the promised land of freedom and prosperity. As the century drew to a close, all the better unclaimed land was taken up, and the foreign population began to congest in the urban centers along the eastern seaboard, thereby creating new social and economic problems.

The opportunity for a foreign mission outreach within the nation's boundaries was not lost upon the American Baptist Home Mission Society. As early as 1836, work among the Welsh began. A decade later, the Society's interest was extended to the Germans, a people more generally distributed over the United States than any other foreign group. While they represented only seven per cent of the population in the South, they have been more numerous than any other foreign element there. The majority of them settled in the Midwest. In 1839 the first converts were won to the Baptist fellowship by Konrad A. Fleischmann, who had come to America as a missionary. He organized a church in Philadelphia in 1843. Eight years later another church was formed in New York City. As German Baptists migrated west, they established eight churches by 1851. In the same year a German conference was formed in Philadelphia. By 1859 the growth of German Baptist work had spread to such an extent that it was possible to organize the General Conference of German Baptist Churches in America.

The American Baptist Home Mission Society, when assisting in the establishing of many of the German churches, found in Dr. Augustus Rauschenbusch, professor in the German Department of the Rochester Theological Seminary, a valuable counselor. In cooperation with regional conferences of German Baptists, the Home Mission Society was instrumental in the expansion of the work into New England and the western states. The work in Virginia, Tennessee, and Texas was chiefly the product of the missionaries of the Home Mission Board of the Southern Baptist Convention. As early as 1857 they had opened missions among the German population of St. Louis, Missouri, and Louisville, Kentucky. By 1882 the German Baptist churches throughout the country numbered 137, with a membership of 10,334.[36] The German Baptists were a group which was

[36] White, *A Century of Faith*, 133.

destined to develop within the following century an independently supported work of large proportions.

A large and effective mission work among the Scandinavians was begun in 1848 when the first Norwegian Baptist Church was organized at Indian Creek, Illinois, with Hans Valder, an appointee of the Home Mission Society, as pastor. By 1882 there were thirty Danish-Norwegian churches, which eventually became larger and self-supporting in the following century. The Swedish work began with the founding of a Baptist church at Rock Island, Illinois, in 1852. Its pastor, Gustaf Palmquist, was appointed a missionary of the Society in 1853; he served in several states. The second Swedish Baptist church was established at Houston, Minnesota, in 1853 by a group of immigrants led by F. O. Nilsson, who had suffered persecution as a pastor in Sweden and Denmark. He was the leading pioneer in founding Swedish Baptist churches in Minnesota. A third Swedish leader in America was Anders Wiberg. After his baptism in Copenhagen, he came to the United States where he served as a pioneer missionary and organizer of churches. By 1882 there were one hundred and four churches in more than seven states in the Midwest, having a combined membership of nearly five thousand. The Swedish Conference likewise became self-supporting and independent in the twentieth century.[37]

Work among the Mexicans and French Canadians was undertaken by the Society in 1849. Mexicans and Indians in Texas and New Mexico received the services of two or three missionaries until 1868, when work was halted there until 1880, at which time a worker again was sent to New Mexico. When the Canadian Baptists found it financially impossible to carry on a Christian school at Grand Ligne, Quebec, the Home Mission Society assumed the responsibility until 1860. From 1853 on, workers were sent into areas of the United States to which French immigrants had come: Illinois, Michigan, Ohio, and New England. Their converts became members of English-speaking churches.

The Southern Baptists were represented among the Chinese of California by the Reverend J. L. Shuck, who had returned from Shanghai in 1854. Northern Baptists had undertaken work there five years before, but had experienced little success in finding a suit-

[37] *Ibid.*, 137-8.

able worker to place there. Finally, in 1870, John Francis was appointed with a Chinese assistant to establish a mission in the basement of the First Baptist Church at San Francisco, the scene of Shuck's labors. The difficulties of work among the Chinese was aggravated by the anti-foreign feeling of the Californians. In 1884 the Home Mission Society took over the Chinese Mission in the city, which had been relinquished by the Home Mission Board of the Southern Convention. Anti-Chinese feeling continued to harass the work in spite of the friendly attitude of the California Baptist Convention. During the nineties similar missions were opened in Chicago, New York, and Butte City, Montana.

In 1888 the Home Mission Society began work among the Poles in Detroit, Michigan; the work spread to Milwaukee, Pittsburgh, Chicago, Newark, Philadelphia, Chicopee (Massachusetts), and other eastern cities. At the same time the Portuguese were being given attention in Alameda County, California, and in New Bedford, Massachusetts. In 1891 a missionary was appointed to work among the Finns in Massachusetts. The first Italian mission was established in Buffalo, New York, in 1894; it was operated by the Baptists of the city. Two years later similar missions were opened in Stamford and New Haven, Connecticut, and still later in Newark, New Jersey. In the years that followed, Baptists worked among Italians in New York and Philadelphia with much success. The Home Mission Society extended its services to the Jews in 1896, to the Japanese in 1898, to the Lettish and Hollanders in 1898, and to the Syrians in 1899. With the turn of the century other groups were reached by its missionaries.

It is to be noted that the major immigrant work has been carried on by the American Baptist Home Mission Society, and quite understandably so, for the greatest numbers of foreign-speaking peoples have settled in the northern and western states. In most cases the Society has received hearty co-operation from state conventions, city mission societies, and the local churches of the denomination. The influence of the work cannot be overestimated, for it has produced several strong organizations among national groups, known usually as "conferences"; more often it has been an assimilating force among foreign-speaking elements; and in many cases, it has resulted in the conversion of Roman Catholics to Protestantism.

Baptist Work in Central America

The first Protestant mission work in Mexico was undertaken by a Scotch Baptist, James Thompson, who served there as a colporter of the British and Foreign Bible Society from 1827 to 1830. The first Protestant church there was established by an Irish Baptist minister from Texas, James Hickey, who was converted from Roman Catholicism in his youth. He served as a colporter of the American Bible Society; upon his death in 1866, Thomas Westrup was appointed in his place. In 1870 he became the agent of the American Baptist Home Mission Society. Ten years later the Southern Baptist Convention selected his brother, John Westrup, to open a station in the country. When he was assassinated shortly thereafter, the Foreign Mission Board sent out two replacements and set up a station at Saltillo.

In 1883 the Northern Baptists opened work in Mexico City, and that city became the center for the spread of the gospel to other areas of the country. Within the Mexican Baptist Convention, which has been organized since 1900, there are churches which belong to both the Northern and the Southern Baptist missions. They have worked together in carrying on pioneer work among the Indians in the mountains.

Northern Baptists did not undertake missionary work in Puerto Rico or Cuba until after the Spanish-American War; for this reason the story belongs in the next chapter. However, we may note that the Southern Baptists began supporting missionaries there as early as 1884, when the Florida Convention employed a young Cuban girl, Adella Fales, who had been converted in Key West, as a teacher and interpreter for the Baptist pastor of that town, the Reverend W. F. Wood. The same Convention one year later employed a second Cuban, Alberto J. Diaz, a physician trained in Havana University and converted in New York City where he pursued graduate study. Diaz's work in Havana is the story of a hero of the faith. He endured severe persecution from the Roman Catholic Church. In 1886 he became a missionary under the Home Mission Board of the Southern Baptist Convention.

Dr. Tichenor, the corresponding secretary of the Board, was instrumental in the Board's purchase near the center of the city of a theater building which it converted into a church. Day schools were opened on the island; these were followed by the building of a high school. Thus by evangelistic preaching and education, the Christian influence was extended among the people. By 1900 there were five churches in Cuba. Of the twenty-five missionaries, the great majority were teachers.[38] After the Spanish-American War, a church was organized in Santiago by the Reverend J. R. O'Halloran, a missionary of the Board. A short time later, the provinces of Oriente and Camaguey were turned over to the American Baptist Home Mission Society by agreement with the Home Mission Board. In 1900 the Southern Board increased its staff of workers by appointing two women missionaries.

The opening of new missions in El Salvador, Nicaragua, Honduras, and Haiti belongs to the story of Baptist missions since 1900. The latter half of the nineteenth century had been one of noble beginnings in Central America that promised well for the future.

[38] S.B.C., *Proceedings* for 1888, p. vi of Board's report; for 1889, p. xlvii of Board's report; for 1900, p. cxxii of Board's report.

Here, he emphasized the differences between the approach to missions of the northern Baptists and the southern Baptists.

Baptists have emphasized:
1) going to the population centers
2) not doing institutional work
3) starting local, self-supporting congregations.

CHAPTER FOURTEEN

MISSIONS UNDER FIRE

A NEW world of change, of breath-taking progress, and dreadful tensions dawned with the advent of the twentieth century. Scientific advancements followed one upon another in unparalleled rapidity. The automobile and the airplane gave wheels and wings to the age of oil, steel, and aluminum. Radio and television provided ears and eyes of uncanny perception to draw the world into one great whispering gallery. Discoveries in medicine and surgery promised generations to come an increased and happier longevity. Yet out of the maelstrom of laboratory techniques and inventions issued new and more fearsome weapons of warfare culminating in the dread atom bomb first used on Hiroshima and Nagasaki in 1945.

In the midst of such amazing physical developments, education was viewed as the salvation of civilization. As popular education dissipated the clouds of illiteracy, so the growing interest in college training sharpened the intellectual acuteness of a larger section of the American public. Leaders of religion and statesmen alike relied generally upon education to build character and a better world. To implement the spiritual objectives of such a program, Christians undertook a lively interest in religious education.

Yet withal, the religious forces of American life were faced with the severe competition of a growing secularism. The higher living standards of the new century had led many to place the premium of necessity upon luxuries. The materialistic philosophy of pragmatism gave to a large sector of the intelligentsia a *rationale* to justify their indifference to religion. Furthermore, in a world of vast commercial interdependence, economic thought was given the primacy belonging to religion in an earlier age. As men and nations grappled with the complex forces of supply and demand, the rightists experimented with fascistic totalitarianism, a regulated capitalism under dictatorship, while the leftists set forth the communist ideal, an economic dictatorship of the Marxian variety. Ever being squeezed between these two extremes was democracy. Its destiny was held in the balance in the thirties, only to be revived in the caldron of world conflict in the forties. In the United States, an avowedly Christian nation, the traditional adherence to the principle of the separation of church and state had resulted in an almost complete secularizing of education and moral philosophy.

Such interplay of economic forces and opposing ideologies against a backdrop of heightened nationalism and imperialism was destined to issue in two major world conflicts within a brief period of years. Both wars have produced thus far only armed truces among the nations who are competing desperately for national self-sufficiency and prosperity.

The tragic years of World War II made it increasingly clear that the basic ill of civilization is spiritual maladjustment of men to God and society. To grapple with the problem, two channels of activity have been created without much reference to each other. The one is the United Nations, a noble effort of nearly fifty states to stabilize international relations by arbitration. The other is the World Council of Churches, an equally inspiring effort of 147 communions (charter members) in 44 countries to stabilize international relations by spiritual rejuvenation. While diplomats and military and political leaders are admitting the gravity of the situation, they show little evidence of conceding that the church actually has the solution to the extent that they will come to her for help. The church instead must go to them; hence its missionary program assumes significance as good statesmanship.

Some pronouncedly divergent tendencies have characterized the efforts of the Christian church to cope with the world situation. Among many, there has come a growing realization of the social emphasis of the gospel and the need for an ecumenical witness to the world. This we may call the leftist tendency. With equal force, a strong reactionism has arisen within a segment of Protestantism known as Fundamentalists, who prefer to emphasize primarily the individual expression of the gospel and the need for a nondenominational, fundamentalist witness to the world. This we may term the rightist tendency. A less vocal but none-the-less significant middle group who represent the old-line denominational alignment of Protestantism prefer to combine the emphases of the two extremes in an effort to save the world through the impact of the organized agencies of the churches for evangelism, missions, education, and social action. A fourth tendency is evident in an alert Roman Catholicism which is making its adjustments to the demands of science and social theory without sacrificing any of its doctrines or traditions of polity, theology, or ritual. Accordingly, it is renewing its world missionary emphasis.

In such a *milieu*, Baptists, who represent more than eighteen million of the world's approximately one hundred and thirty-eight million Protestants, have been carrying on missionary work through their several agencies.[1] In general, Baptist missions have been characterized by (1) a steady growth up to the postwar era of the twenties, (2) a period of retrenchment at the close of that decade and in the early thirties during world-wide economic depression and internal theological conflict, and (3) an era of advance in the face of the losses of World War II and the challenge of the new postwar period.

Modern Baptist missions are being administered and supported chiefly by Baptists of America, by British and European brethren, and by indigenous churches in Africa, Asia, and the islands of the sea. Here it will suffice to survey briefly the work being done by Baptists of the United States, for the story of British and European Baptist missionary endeavors was given in an earlier chapter.

Northern Baptist Foreign Missions

In the period prior to the outbreak of World War I, the foreign mission enterprise was characterized by steady growth. The general outlook represented in the annual reports of the American Baptist Missionary Union in the opening years of the century was one of optimism and vision. The fast-moving events which brought the United States into the orbit of world imperialism inspired most Christian leaders to regard the newly acquired American possessions in the Pacific and Caribbean as fields for missionary expansion. Accordingly Baptist work was undertaken in the Philippines in 1901 on the Island of Panay by the Reverend Eric Lund, once a missionary in Spain, and by Señor Braulio Manikan, a convert from Roman Catholicism in Barcelona.

[1] See Appendix B.

Elsewhere the older mission fields were enjoying unusual expansion. By 1905 several indications of progress had become evident.[2] In East China and Japan, Northern and Southern Baptists effected a union of their educational work. Baptisms in Asian and African fields totaled ten thousand five hundred, a number in excess of the converts enrolled in those missions during the previous forty years. Great ingatherings were experienced among the Telugus of South India and the Muhsos at Kengtung in northern Burma—revivals which bordered on a new Pentecost. As India, China, and Japan assumed a larger role in world affairs, and as Christians gained an enlarged vision of what was called "the new Orient," Northern Baptists began to plan for larger Christian schools which should prepare a well-trained indigenous leadership. In two other areas of endeavor, medical and Christian education work, a gradual expansion was reported. Increased commerce in the Far East and the impact of the Russo-Japanese War (1904-1905) were arousing keen public interest in the Orient, a fact of which Baptists were taking advantage. Army hospitals and the movement of troops through China gave the missionaries opportunities for a far-reaching evangelistic ministry.

The influence of Christian missions upon eastern civilization did not go unnoticed. It was reported to the Missionary Union, meeting at St. Louis in 1905, that:

> Missionary effort is molding the civilization of the East. The new school system of China is modeled after missionary schools and is dependent upon them for its force of instructors; while in Japan there is scarcely a school higher than the primary grade which is without teachers trained through the agency of Christian missions.[3]

Thus, while American big business was seeking to mold the Orient to western ways, the Christian Church was creating its own type of influence, which stemmed from a different motive.

During the years that followed, the expenditure of Baptist lives and money in missionary service continued apace with good results. In the interest of closer co-ordination of efforts to raise the funds necessary for the maintenance of the work of the various societies in the North, the Northern Baptist Convention was organized in 1907.

This is a pivotal date for Northern Baptists.

[2] A.B.M.U., *Annual Report*, 1904-5, pp. 42, 44, 46, 356.

[3] *Ibid.*, 48.

The move came after several conferences held by representatives of the major societies. The plan which resulted represented a compromise between the traditional *society* method in use in the North and the *convention* method utilized by Southern Baptists since 1845. The respective societies were to retain autonomy, but were to function co-operatively in the planning and raising of the budget each year. The annual meetings of the societies were to be held during the convention sessions, a procedure which was not a serious departure from the current practice of holding simultaneously the anniversary meetings in the month of May. The avowed purpose of the newly organized convention was to unify appeals for funds by the various denominational societies and to secure a larger co-operation in their activities in the interest of greater efficiency.

An important by-product of the move was the eventual development of a denominational connectionalism which gave rise to serious tensions when advocates of the older society method opposed the trend. This tendency will be discussed in the next chapter. Suffice it to say here that the existing societies were to continue their work as agencies of the new convention. Accordingly, the American Baptist Missionary Union continued as an autonomous agency, though altering its name in 1910 to the American Baptist Foreign Mission Society. In 1911 the Free Baptists, hitherto an independent denomination, merged with the Northern Baptist Convention, thereby strengthening the missionary enterprise by the addition of their fields, workers, and properties. Two years later the women's work of the denomination was consolidated by the merging of the general Woman's Baptist Foreign Missionary Society, which had headquarters in the East, and the Woman's Baptist Foreign Missionary Society of the West, which had headquarters at Chicago, into the Woman's American Baptist Foreign Mission Society with headquarters in New York City.[4]

In 1912 the Northern Baptist Convention, meeting at Des Moines, Iowa, reached a significant decision. Confronted by reports of an increasing number of converts in the Kengtung area of northern Burma and in South India and Belgian Congo, placing increasingly heavy burdens upon the limited staff of workers in the respective fields, the recommendation was made that the Society, for the present, should undertake an intensive work, rather than open new fields. It

[4] For a brief account, see *A Century of Service by Baptist Women* (New York, 1933).

A HISTORY OF THE BAPTISTS

was made clear that such a policy was not to be construed as retrenchment, but a progressive step in the direction of establishing lasting, self-supporting, and self-perpetuating churches on Baptist fields.

In view of this decision, the Board of Managers of the Foreign Society in 1913 undertook an intensive development of stations which were then in existence and inadequately supplied. It was also decided that at strategic points, strong Christian communities should be established as permanent forces of evangelization. Through this means were to be developed strong, indigenous churches which would in time carry on their own missionary program. To implement this program, educational facilities of such stations were to be given primary consideration. It was agreed also that interdenominational co-operation in the realm of providing higher education would be necessary and feasible. In the execution of such a policy, the relatively new work in Japan and the Philippine Islands was narrowed to certain areas where a concentrated effort could be effected.[5]

Reflecting the enthusiasm of the times, the Convention authorized larger expenditures in those early years of the century than were warranted by the actual receipts collected; consequently, the Foreign Society, like the Home Mission Society, experienced a discouraging deficit. By 1914 it became obvious that some curtailment was necessary; whereupon reduction were made in outlay at home and abroad. Moreover, a withdrawal from Central China was planned with a view to strengthening the work in the southern and eastern territories of that country. A policy of interdenominational co-operation in the administration and support of medical colleges and other types of higher education was undertaken in China and Japan, where Baptists and Presbyterians were laboring together. The principle of intensive development was also apparent in the solidifying of native missionary work, especially in Assam and Burma where native Baptist conventions were organized in 1914.[6]

The outbreak of war in Europe in August of that year was a disturbing factor to Americans generally and equally so to the mission boards. With the uncertainty of economic life, a slight depression with its attendant unemployment occurred the following year. Yet, the benevolences and interest in foreign missions increased rather

[5] N.B.C., *Annual,* 1913, pp. 229-44.

[6] *Ibid.,* 1914, pp. 295-328.

than decreased. The Society attributed the increased giving to a revived spiritual interest and willingness to sacrifice because of world
conditions. It was not long, however, before the effects of war were
felt, for the transmission of funds and the transportation of missionaries became ever more difficult. Mission property in northern France
and Belgium was destroyed, while mission workers were drafted into
the armies. In British India the Society found it necessary to assume
responsibility for the care of missionaries of other missions, whose
funds had been cut off. The increased cost of living was felt in the
most remote mission stations. To add to the problems faced by the
Society, it became impractical to send out a sufficient number of
missionary replacements, owing to the accumulated deficits due to the
overexpansion in the preceding years. To counteract the serious effect
of such curtailment and to carry forward the intensive policy, greater
attention was given to the development of schools to train native
workers.[7]

In 1916, however, the Society closed the year with no deficit for
the first time in six years. Several legacies, an economy in home
expenditures, and increased giving during a period of higher incomes
were largely responsible. Yet on the mission fields, the war had
produced conditions which were deleterious to native support. In
Burma and the Belgian Congo, a business depression and poor crops
reduced contributions. In Europe conditions grew steadily worse;
in some countries churches were demolished and congregations scattered, and in other countries, their brethren were being harassed due
to efforts of the state church to enforce conformity. Baptists contributed a large portion of America's relief money for Europe, given
without reference to the religious beliefs of those helped.[8]

As the war progressed, Americans became increasingly world-
conscious; and Wilsonian idealism caught the imagination of the
people. Like many other Christians, Baptists caught the spirit and
reaffirmed their Society's policy of co-operating with evangelicals of
all denominations "whenever and wherever such co-operation can be
undertaken without any sacrifice of principles." [9] This policy became apparent in many areas—on the fields in joint operations in

[7] N.B.C., *Annual,* 1915, pp. 339-40, 364-71.

[8] *Ibid.,* 1916, pp. 441-9, 521, 595, 606-12; for 1917, pp. 822-8.

[9] *Ibid.,* 1918, p. 448.

medical and educational work; at home, in the representation of the Society on committees of the Foreign Missions Conference, on the Board of Managers of the Missionary Education Movement, and on the committee of twenty-eight which outlined mission study themes and policies. Contacts were maintained also with the Laymen's Missionary Movement, the International Missionary Council, the Student Volunteer Movement, the Federal Council of Churches of Christ in America, and other interdenominational organizations.

The war years made Baptists conscious of several major needs. The necessity of making Christian principles basic to all international relationships spurred interest in the missionary cause. As nationalism revived in the postwar era, it became increasingly evident that the development of a strong indigenous leadership in India, China, Japan, and elsewhere was imperative.

The years immediately following the cessation of hostilities in November, 1918, were characterized by an enthusiastic and optimistic expansion program. Actively engaged in this enterprise were the Baptist laymen whose prominence in the Northern Baptist Convention had increased during the War. As early as May, 1918, the Convention had requested the National Committee of Northern Baptist Laymen to study, from the layman's point of view, the need for a more efficient co-operation in raising funds for the various Societies. In 1919 the Convention met in Denver, Colorado. It there launched, on the basis of their report, what came to be called the New World Movement. It was essentially an over-all effort of the Convention to raise a single budget to be divided among its various agencies through a General Board of Promotion and its Administrative Committee, which was to be representative of all national, state, and city mission societies. After careful study of the needs of each agency, a general budget was to be adopted and raised through the efforts of the Board of Promotion, thereby leaving the societies free of fund-raising burdens.[10]

In 1920 more than three thousand Northern Baptist churches heard "minute men and women" present the purpose and significance of the movement in four-minute addresses, a method which was reminiscent of the wartime techniques of the Liberty Loan Drives. The goal was to raise one hundred million dollars before April 30,

[10] For details of organization, see Chapter Fifteen.

1924. In spite of the depression of 1921 to 1922, the generous sum of more than twelve and a half million dollars was received in the fiscal year, 1920-1921, through this co-operative effort. But disappointment was felt when it became known that only a little more than 50 per cent of the one hundred million had been subscribed by 86 per cent of the churches up to the time of the Convention's meeting in 1922.[11]

Effects of the enthusiasm at home were felt among the native Christians on the foreign fields. The churches of the Sgaw Karen Mission in Burma, for example, undertook the raising of three hundred thousand rupees for a new school building. Burmese Christians also planned to establish two mission stations across the Chinese border from their own country. In 1920 it was reported that nearly three thousand Karens had been baptized during the previous year.[12] The theological seminary at Ramapatnam in South India was enlarged and strengthened. About the same time three new churches were organized in Japan.

The five-year New World Movement came to an end in 1924. The financial objectives had not been attained; only half of the goal had been raised. Yet other benefits of the co-operative effort became evident in the elevation of the general level of missionary giving in the churches and in an increased interest in mission study classes among laymen. In addition, there had been created in the Board of Promotion an agency for the encouragement of stewardship as a denominational ideal. Its effectiveness in raising the total contributions of Baptists to the support of their local churches as well as to the missionary enterprise was evident; gifts to the former had increased 34.5 per cent, and to the latter 117.5 per cent. Baptist schools had been brought, for the first time, into the comprehensive missionary program of denominational support. Many of the smaller schools were actually saved from extinction by funds collected in the New World Movement.[13]

[11] N.B.C., *Annual,* 1920, pp. 70-1; 1921, pp. 66, 148, 562-3; 1922, pp. 67, 73.

[12] *Ibid.,* 1920, pp. 618-35.

[13] N.B.C., *Annual,* 1923, pp. 160-1; 1924, pp. 61, 73, 118, 133 (total receipts for the New World Movement Fund from 1920-4 amounted to $45,009,378.04). Mission study classes increased from 4,439 in 1920-1 to 7,856 in 1923-4, with a commensurate increase in the sale of mission study books from 20,179 in 1920-1 to 26,533 in 1923-4. For chart studies of co-operative financing results, see *Annual* for 1924, pp. 154-98.

Significant trends also were apparent on the foreign fields. The intellectual awakening and national self-consciousness which was sweeping over the Orient during the postwar years had aroused in the Christians of Burma, Assam, South India, and Bengal-Orissa a determination to accept an increasing measure of independence and initiative, and a desire to secure and train their own leaders. In 1923 nearly fifty Baptist Oriental students were in America for advanced study through financial assistance from the Foreign Board. A greater responsiveness to Christianity in India and Burma was also evident. In China a native Baptist Council was created in 1923 to bring together representatives of the three major missions in that country. In areas of the Belgian Congo where Baptist converts met persecution at the hands of Jesuit priests, growth was remarkable.[14]

Once the sustained effort of the New World Movement was past, a decline in financial support again made retrenchment a necessity. The contributions to the united budget dropped from $9,818,813.74 in 1920-1921 to $4,389,612.68 in 1926-1927. The Foreign Society's share in these contributions declined from $1,371,-636.84 to $832,955.14 in the same period.[15] In the face of such a shrinking income, the number of missionary units (i.e. a family or single person) under appointment by the General Society dropped from its peak of 313 in 1923 to 265 in 1929, to 240 in 1934, to 179 in 1939, a decline amounting to 42.9 per cent in sixteen years. Between 1928 and 1938, the staff of the Woman's Society dropped from 204 to 153, a loss of 25 per cent.[16]

Such retrenchments represented a serious retreat in the face of ever-widening opportunities for missionary expansion. In the South India mission nearly six thousand converts were baptized in 1925, the largest number for any one year in the mission's history since the revival of 1878. Filipino leaders were coming forward to help the missionaries. Only in the Orient was there a serious obstacle; between 1925 and 1930, an anti-Christian feeling was aroused by those anti-foreign propagandists among the Chinese intellectuals who saw in the missionary enterprise a "western" movement. Nevertheless,

[14] *Ibid.*, 1923, pp. 606-26.

[15] *Ibid.*, 1927, p. 325.

[16] P. H. J. Lerrigo and D. M. Amidon, eds., *All Kindreds and Tongues*, 4th issue (New York, 1940), p. 97.

the year 1927 witnessed a total of 20,482 baptisms in the ten fields of
Northern Baptists—and that with a reduced staff of missionaries.[17]

Included among the probable causes for this period of decline,
which continued until the mid-thirties, were the world-wide economic
depression which reached its peak in 1933, the theological controversy
which prompted some loss of contributions,[18] and the tendency of the
Society to overexpand when funds were plentiful, without setting
aside sufficient available reserves.

Illustrative of the theological dissension within the Northern
Baptist Convention and of the opposition to the modification of the
society method was the creation of a new missionary agency in 1928,
known as "The Association of Baptists for World Evangelism, Inc."
It was organized, with headquarters in Philadelphia, when three
missionaries of the American Baptist Foreign Mission Society withdrew from that Society over doctrinal differences and disagreement
with what they regarded as liberal policies in the Northern Baptist
Convention. They opened a new work in Manila early in that year.
Within the next twenty years, mission stations were opened in other
parts of the Philippine Islands, in Ceylon, in South America in
the upper Amazon region, and in South China; there were plans also
for expansion into Tibet and New Guinea. Strongly fundamentalist
in point of view, the Association has required of its missionaries and
board members the signing of a doctrinal platform and has discouraged fraternization with members of the Northern Baptist Convention. It has regarded itself as a "faith mission." In accordance
with this position, its financial policy forbids working on an anticipated
income or relying upon financial campaigns to raise funds. In 1948
the Association reported eighty-six missionaries and appointees in
service. Baptist support has come from approximately four hundred
churches comprising the General Association of Regular Baptist
Churches, North, which was organized in 1933 for reasons described
in the next chapter.

Actual appropriations to meet the budget of the American Baptist
Foreign Mission Society for 1931-1932 were fifty thousand dollars
less than the total appropriation for 1930-1931. This was but the
beginning of sharp reductions in the budget. In 1932 the General

[17] N.B.C., *Annual*, 1925, p. 415, 424, 430-3; 1927, p. 275-7; 1930, pp. 396-7.
[18] See Chapter Fifteen.

Objectors to the Northern Baptist "Convention"
The general Association of Regular Baptist (GARB)
The Conservative Baptist Convention. They objected
1) to the end of the Society method
2) to the theological liberalism which they
   accused The Convention leaders of.

Other Baptist churches did not join another or other Baptist groups when they left—they merely became independent Baptist churches. The northern Baptist Convention.

Society sent out only nine new missionaries, the smallest group since 1885, except in the war year of 1915 when a similar number sailed. The budget for 1933-1934 represented a decrease of almost one-third in three years' time. It provided for only one new missionary family. By 1934 the trend of benevolence giving had begun a very slow upturn. The depth of the depression had been reached,[19] but the hills ahead were steep and treacherous to surmount.

In the midst of the depression years, an interdenominational committee of eight laymen, of which five were Baptists, had undertaken an inquiry concerning missions, to determine how wisely and economically this enterprise had been administered during its one hundred years of existence. The laymen's committee had been created by Baptists who had heard Dr. John R. Mott, chairman of the International Missionary Council, report in 1930 on his recent world tour of the mission fields. The findings and conclusions of the committee's survey, known popularly as *Rethinking Missions*, pronounced the aim of Christian missions to be the presenting of the Christian way of living and thinking. The report recommended that education, medicine, and similar allied pursuits of missionaries should be freed from the direct motivation of evangelism. Missionaries were criticized for having a "limited outlook and capacity" and for seeking to establish western-type churches in a sectarian manner. The committee advocated that missionaries refrain from attacking non-Christian systems of religion. The basic point of view set forth in this study was challenged by most Baptists.

From the spirited discussion provoked by the Inquiry, laymen were aroused to a new interest in the work of the missionary, and were made more aware of certain weaknesses in missionary methods and administration which already were well known to many workers on the foreign fields. Baptists generally preferred a basically evangelistic motive for all of their varied missionary enterprises. As they surveyed the character of their work, they were able to point to more than four thousand schools, thirty hospitals, sixty-one dispensaries, leper asylums, orphanages, agricultural stations in China, Burma, and India, and to large indigenous churches among the Karens and Kachins of Burma, the Garos and Nagas of Assam, the Telugus of South India, the Bantus of Congo, and the Chinese. They

[19] N.B.C., *Annual*, 1932, p. 596; 1933, pp. 367, 400, 415; 1934, pp. 402, 447.

were able also to point to their social influence in the anti-opium efforts in the Orient, against foot-binding in China and child marriage in India, and in behalf of public health and literacy. In 1931, 63 per cent of the three thousand Baptist churches in non-Christian lands had been reported as self-supporting.[20]

The sixth year of financial depression and economic uncertainty (1935) brought the work of the Foreign Society to a very critical situation. Donations from churches and individuals were still below normal, although the decrease was lower than in any previous year. From 1930 to 1935, receipts from this source had dropped from $807,822.51 to $438,936.47. To raise the missionary quotas of the churches, the Council on Finance and Promotion inaugurated in 1935 a denomination-wide movement to obtain from individuals "One More Dollar" as a gift over and above regular pledges.[21]

For the next two years the Convention undertook the raising of a Forward Movement Fund, which it was hoped might enable the mission societies to hold their own financially. Actually the contemplated budget provided for no new missionary appointees. In 1936 a slight increase in contributions was announced for the first time in seven years. By 1937 it was possible to send two new families to the foreign field. It appeared to many that the industrial depression was in the background, yet any permanent increase in contributions was not in evidence.[22]

To add to the problems of missionary administration, there was the growing threat of world conflict as the Fascist Axis in Europe laid claim, first, to Ethiopia, then to Austria, Czechoslovakia, and ultimately Poland on September 1, 1939. Not until then did the democracies gird themselves to stop the advance of totalitarianism. The flames of burning villages and bomb devastated cities swept swiftly over Europe, first to engulf the Lowlands and France, then to threaten Britain's very existence, and finally to destroy thousands of Russian towns as the Nazi juggernaut in 1942 moved relentlessly

[20] P. H. J. Lerrigo, compiler and ed., *Northern Baptists Rethink Missions: A Study of the Report of the Laymen's Foreign Missions Inquiry,* New York, 1933, pp. 24, 47-60, 69, 100.

[21] N.B.C., *Annual,* 1935, pp. 405, 426. The decrease in donation receipts in 1931-32 was 15 per cent; in 1932-33, 20 per cent plus; in 1933-34, 12 per cent plus; in 1934-35, 7 per cent plus.

[22] *Ibid.,* 1936, pp. 390-6; 1937, pp. 381, 424, 427; 1938, pp. 386-7, 409.

toward Stalingrad. In the meantime Japan's surprise attack upon Pearl Harbor on December 7, 1941, brought the United States into the war. This only increased the already serious hindrances to mission work in the Orient.

As early as 1937, China's millions had known the bitter experience of war and invasion. By November, 1940, only one church building remained intact in Chungking, the inland capital of the Chinese National Government. Japanese bombs had laid desolate Protestant and Catholic churches and hospitals alike. The Baptist work in South China suffered from frequent air raids. In East China, mission property in at least one-third of the area, including the University of Shanghai, fell into Japanese hands. West China became the rallying point for the hopes of China's future. At Chengtu, Northern Baptists co-operated with other Protestant denominations in the West China Union University which served as host to the refugee schools of invaded areas.[23]

In 1940 Baptists in Japan were united in a single convention which was required to register with the Government. On June 24, 1941, forty-one denominational groups, including the Baptists, united in the Protestant Church in Japan, independent of foreign funds and official direction from missionaries. The only major bodies which did not join were the Episcopalians and the Seventh Day Adventists. Baptists had a degree of autonomy in the organization. When the war began, Japanese Christians assumed full leadership as missionaries were removed.[24] To many, this was portentous of a new basis for future missionary service in Japan, one which might probably be directly under the United Church.

Burma and Assam, being in the path of moving armies, first of the invading Japanese and then of the Allied Forces, suffered grievously in property damages and loss of lives, but not in Christian courage. In Burma and to a degree in Assam, as elsewhere in war-torn areas, the Baptist policy of having developed a strong native leadership paid rich dividends when all of the missionaries were compelled to evacuate by 1943. The invasion of the Philippines

[23] *Toward the Mark: Baptist World Advance, 1940-1944*, p. 20; Lerrigo and Amidon, *All Kindreds and Tongues*, 1940, 198, 205, 210-8; N.B.C., *Year Book*, 1942, p. 291; 1943, p. 206.

[24] *Toward the Mark*, pp. 23-4; N.B.C., *Year Book*, 1942, pp. 288-9.

issued not only in the almost total destruction of Baptist property at Manila, Iloilo, and elsewhere, but in the loss of eleven missionaries and a thirteen-year-old boy who were arrested in their hide-out on Panay Island and put to death by the Japanese military on December 20, 1943.[25]

At home, the budget was raised in full during the year, 1942-1943. Accordingly, the Convention, meeting at Wichita, Kansas, in 1943, adopted an undiminished budget and at the same time authorized the raising of an additional $600,000 as a World Emergency Fund for wartime needs. The goal was reached and a new goal of two million was set for the year 1944-1945. At the same time, missionaries were returning to their posts; others were already back. In spite of the hazards and complications of wartime travel, one hundred and fifty-seven, new and old, had sailed for foreign fields between the outbreak of war in 1939 and the spring of 1944.[26]

By 1943 a long smoldering dissatisfaction on the part of the Fundamentalists with the so-called "inclusive" policy of the Foreign Society, and with the development of denominational connectionalism in the Convention, came to a head. The critics of the Foreign Mission Society declared that its Board was willing to send out missionaries who were unorthodox as well as those who satisfied the traditional doctrinal position of Baptists. The Society's reply was that it did not have an inclusive policy in the sense indicated by the critics, but rather an evangelical policy, by which it meant that its board was willing to commission missionaries who were within the limits of the "Anderson statement," an interpretation set forth in 1924 by Dr. Frederick L. Anderson, then chairman of the Board of Managers of that body. At that time, Dr. Anderson had crystallized the working policy of the Board as follows:

With these things in mind your Board has sought to find the common ground on which we all or nearly all stand. Guided by the facts that Baptists have always been known as evangelicals, and that the gospel is the most important message of the Scriptures, we have demanded that all our officers and missionaries be loyal to the gospel. We will appoint only suitable evan-

[25] N.B.C., *Year Book*, 1943, p. 202; 1944, pp. 303, 310. For the story of the heroic martyrs, see pamphlet, *Through Shining Archway*, published by the American Baptist Foreign Mission Society and the Woman's American Baptist Foreign Mission Society. New York, 1945.

[26] N.B.C., *Year Book*, 1944, p. 313.

gelical men and women; we will appoint evangelicals, and we will not appoint non-evangelicals. And by the gospel we mean the good news of the free forgiveness of sin and eternal life (beginning now and going on forever) through a vital union with the crucified and risen Christ, which brings men into union and fellowship with God. This salvation is graciously offered on the sole condition of repentance and faith in Christ and has in it the divine power of regeneration and sanctification through the Spirit. The only reason we have for accepting this gospel is our belief in the deity of Christ in whom we see the Father, a faith founded on the trustworthiness of the Scriptures, and the fact that we have experienced this salvation in our own hearts.[27]

Many Fundamentalists felt that the statement did not sufficiently guarantee that all missionaries subscribing to it should believe unequivocally in the deity of Christ. They, therefore, desired that acceptance of the doctrine of the virgin birth of the Savior should be made the test question put to candidates. When this was refused, dissatisfaction mounted, issuing ultimately in the creation of a new Foreign Mission agency.

The new society, called the Conservative Baptist Foreign Mission Society, was organized in Chicago on December 15, 1943, when a board of eighteen members was chosen, six each from the western, central, and eastern sections of the Northern Baptist territory. As its name implies, its purpose was to foster Baptist missions upon a theological basis, the orthodoxy of which should be safeguarded by the annual subscription to a doctrinal statement on the part of all its officers and missionaries. National headquarters were established in Chicago.

In May, 1945, the General Council of the Northern Baptist Convention, acting for that body in the absence of a convention meeting, adopted at its meeting in Chicago the majority report of a Committee on Conference and Co-operative Unity. This committee had been created two years before to study the relationship of the new Society to the Convention and to restore as large a measure of co-operative unity as possible. In substance, the report refused to recognize the new organization as "another society within the framework of the Northern Baptist Convention." Instead, it recommended that the name "conservative" be dropped and that the Society become simply "a fellowship to encourage churches to contribute to the sup-

[27] Frederick L. Anderson, *Rich Harvests and Ominous Clouds*. An address. New York: The Board of Missionary Co-operation of the Northern Baptist Convention, 1924.

port of Convention missionaries whom it approves." A minority report, presented by Dr. W. Theodore Taylor, president of the Conservative Baptist Foreign Mission Society, requesting recognition as "an independent foreign mission society, supported by Northern Baptist churches and members of Northern Baptist Convention churches" was rejected.[28] This action arose from the view of many that the newly organized society constituted a rebellious element in the Convention, that it had been organized without consulting that body, and that it was unwilling to subject itself to the rules governing the activities of the co-operating agencies of the Convention.

The Conservative Baptist Foreign Mission Society accordingly continued its work without Convention recognition. Within five years, more than one hundred missionaries were sent to thirty new stations in India, West China, Japan, the Philippine Islands, Argentina, Brazil, French West Africa, Belgian Congo, and five European countries.[29] Support has been derived chiefly from two sources: non-Convention Baptist churches which previously had supported non-denominational "faith" missions and from individuals within the Convention who had become dissatisfied with the policies of the Foreign Society and of the Convention in general. To many the unified budget within which the missionary agencies operated represented a sad departure from the society method which had been in vogue prior to 1907.

In 1945 the General Council of the Northern Baptist Convention approved plans for a World Mission Crusade to be conducted under the direction of the Council on Finance and Promotion for two fiscal years (1945-1947) to raise fourteen million dollars, of which sum ten million should be used to meet the non-recurring needs of rehabilitation created by war, and four million for recurring needs over and above those covered in the unified budget. This effort was coupled with a Christian Life Crusade designed to strengthen the local churches through emphasis on evangelism and stewardship. It was planned that nearly 63 per cent of the goal of fourteen million dollars be used for foreign and home mission projects.[30] At the Northern Baptist Convention meeting at Atlantic City, New Jersey,

[28] N.B.C., *Year Book*, 1945, pp. 51-2.

[29] *News and Views, Bulletin of the Conservative Baptist Foreign Mission Society*, Vol. V, No. 4 (Sept., 1948), p. 1; Vincent Brushwyler, *The Story of the Conservative Baptist Mission Society* (Chicago, 1945), a pamphlet by the Society's General Director.

[30] *Ibid.*, 1945, pp. 86-8, 114-8. See also *Crusader*, No. 6 (May, 1946).

in May, 1947, it was announced that the amount had been over-subscribed by more than two million dollars. Northern Baptists were facing the postwar era with realistic courage.

Southern Baptist Foreign Missions

At the opening of the twentieth century, Southern Baptists, challenged by much the same vision as their Northern brethren, undertook new stations in old fields and opened new fields of missionary labor.[31] In 1900 a native Brazilian, the Reverend F. F. Soren, who had been trained in America, returned to his homeland to become pastor in Rio de Janeiro. At the same time Mrs. W. B. Bagby undertook the instruction of girls in Sao Paulo, from which effort developed the Anna Bagby College with an annual enrollment of some five hundred students. A similar work was begun simultaneously in Pernambuco, resulting in a Baptist college and seminary which provides evangelists for northern Brazil. Also in 1900 a mission station was opened in Beirut, under the able leadership of S. M. Jureidini, a native worker of marked ability. A year later the Southern Baptist Convention sent Dr. Dexter G. Whittinghill to found a theological school at Rome, Italy. His wife was instrumental in the formation of the Italian Woman's Missionary Union, and together they devoted thirty-eight years to work in that city. It is significant that the earliest undertakings of the new century should have been the establishing of schools to train native Christian leaders.

The first new mission field to be opened after 1900 was Argentina. The decision was made by the Foreign Mission Board at the behest of the Convention in 1903. A total of four young men and their wives were located within two years' time in Buenos Aires and Rosario de Santa Fe, the two largest cities of the Republic. In 1904 a Baptist Publishing House was established at El Paso, Mexico. After six years of joint effort to establish a college and seminary at Shanghai, Southern and Northern Baptists purchased ground, selected a Southerner, Dr. R. T. Bryan, as president of the seminary, Dr. Frank J. White to represent Northern Baptists, and Dr. J. T. Proctor of the North to be president of the college. The seminary was moved to the campus in 1907, and the college was opened in 1908. By 1911,

[31] A good popular survey of Southern Baptist missions by countries may be found in Eugene C. Routh, *The Word Overcoming the World* (Nashville, 1941).

the two divisions were united as the University of Shanghai under the presidency of Dr. White. About the same time, the Foreign Board opened a station at Chengchow, in Honan Province, whose thirty-five million people had only two missions—the China Inland Mission, which was non-sectarian, and the Free Methodist Mission. Southern Baptists added a station at Kaifeng, capital of the Province in 1906.

In that same year and again in 1909, the first medical missionaries were sent to Africa when Dr. George Green and Dr. B. L. Lockett and their wives sailed for Nigeria. (*Unusually successful*)

Like the Northern Baptists, the Southern Board sought to develop self-supporting churches. The results of their efforts were manifest before the close of the first decade of the twentieth century. On June 23, 1907, the Brazilian National Baptist Convention was organized at Bahia with its own Home and Foreign Mission Boards established at Rio de Janeiro. Brazilian Baptists carried the gospel far into the interior of that vast country and on into Chile and Portugal. The Baptist women of Brazil assisted materially in this missionary undertaking through the Woman's Missionary Union. A similar pattern was followed in the republic to the south when the Argentina Baptist Convention was organized in December, 1908, composed of one hundred and fifty-three members in five churches. At once, the new body began to raise money to support mission work in Chile. In 1911 a Baptist seminary was opened in Buenos Aires to train leaders. By 1915 the Nigerian Baptists of North Africa became strong enough to organize the Nigerian Baptist Convention; they also opened a school at Lagos, which has grown to be the largest Baptist educational institution in Nigeria with an enrollment in 1940 of eight hundred and fifty-six.[32]

When government changes were adopted in Mexico in 1917, depriving all churches of the right to hold property and taking from their ministers the right to perform religious duties in the country, native leadership was relied upon for the most part to carry on the work. To train Mexican leaders, Southern and Northern Baptists in 1917 united in establishing the National Baptist Theological Seminary in Saltillo.

Likewise, the Foreign Mission Board of the Southern Baptist Convention further expanded its work by sending two missionaries

[32] Routh, *op. cit.*, 79.

to Chile in the fall of 1917. This decision brought relief and assistance to the Argentine Baptists who had been carrying the sole responsibility there.

American participation in the First World War created for Southern Baptist missions much the same kind of problems that it had produced for Northern Baptist missions. Europe and the Near East were the regions affected most directly by the conflict. As the war drew to a close, there was at home a general upsurge of optimism and enthusiasm for future expansion. Under the leadership of the Laymen's Missionary Movement, which had been organized in 1908, a survey of denominational fields and institutions at home and abroad was undertaken in 1919. An appeal was then made for the sum of seventy-five million dollars to be paid in five annual installments of fifteen million each. With unbounding zeal, the churches pledged ninety-two million, well exceeding their goal.[33]

Meanwhile, the Baptists gathered from various countries of the world for a five-day conference in London, in July, 1920, to consider a missionary program for the war-stricken countries. Southern Baptists gave their enthusiastic support on the strength of the success of their campaign. The Southern Convention opened new mission stations, erected new buildings, sent out additional missionaries, and assumed large obligations. In Tokyo, capital of Japan, a new work for students had been started in the preceding year. At Hiroshima and Nagasaki, Southern Baptist missionaries were laboring in comparatively new centers. In 1920 fifty-four Japanese women organized a Woman's Missionary Union of Japan to help support the missionary enterprise in their country. In particular response to the London Conference, the Southern Baptist Convention arranged to send missionaries to Palestine and Syria, where Baptists of Illinois had been carrying on a small work heroically against great difficulties. On March 6, 1923, four missionaries landed at Jaffa; two had to return because of ill health, but the others brought needed reinforcements to the work.

The European work was expanded as another outgrowth of the London Conference. Southern Baptists moved into Yugoslavia, Hungary, Rumania, and the Ukraine, in addition to increasing their earlier operations in Italy. In 1921 the Foreign Mission Board agreed

[33] S.B.C., *Annual*, 1919, pp. 73-4; 82, 108.

to take over responsibility for a mission in Spain which the Swedish Baptists had been carrying on for the past forty years.[34]

The period of development reached its peak in 1921, when foreign mission receipts exceeded three and a half million dollars, while the total income for home missions soared to an all-time high of nearly two million dollars.[35] An unhappy turn of events occurred, however, shortly after the first installment of the seventy-five million goal had been received. Cotton prices dropped from forty cents to twenty-five, then to fifteen, and finally to ten. The effects of this economic slump in 1921-22 were felt through the remaining years of the decade. Consequently, only fifty-eight and a half million dollars of the ninety-two million dollars pledged were collected in the five years that followed. Each year thereafter, Southern Baptist Convention and state convention finances showed deficits as spending exceeded receipts in an over-expanded program at home and abroad. In face of the difficult task of contracting rapidly the programs already in operation, the Convention accumulated by December 31, 1926, a debt approximating six and a half million dollars.[36]

Yet, despite the burden of indebtedness, the Foreign Board had opened a mission station two years previously at Harbin, Manchuria, with the assistance of Chinese Baptist churches and four missionaries, Mr. and Mrs. C. A. Leonard and Dr. and Mrs. C. E. James, who were transferred from China proper. The European work was maintained also with some enlargement of facilities in both Rumania and Italy.[37]

In the late twenties, however, one agency after another of the Convention defaulted on monies borrowed by bond issues, bank loans, or individual loans. Loans had to be renewed without payment on principal with interest rates between 5½ and 7 per cent. To aggravate the situation, the treasurer of the Home Mission Board defaulted in the amount of $909,461, a fact which was discovered in September, 1928. As creditors were clamoring for payment of loans, some even

[34] For the story of European Baptists, see Chapter Six.

[35] S.B.C., *Annual*, 1921, pp. 392, 474; Joe W. Burton, *Epochs of Home Missions: Southern Baptist Convention, 1845-1945*, 93. Figures in annual reports include *all* sources of income such as legacies, investments, etc.

[36] See historical summary of Southern Baptist indebtedness up to 1945 in S.B.C., *Annual*, 1942, pp. 64-5.

[37] Routh, *The Word Overcoming the World*, 195, 201-4, 211.

threatening legal proceedings to collect or throw the Convention and its agencies into bankruptcy, the morale of the people and workers was severely tested. It is a tribute to their courage and their faith in the Kingdom that they did not hesitate or turn aside, but accepted full responsibility for the deficit. By unflinching sacrifice, the churches saved the Convention from disaster.

In 1928 the Convention, meeting at Chattanooga, Tennessee, enlarged the powers of its Executive Committee to help plan and guide the work of its several agencies, thereby giving greater stability and unification to their undertakings. A co-operative plan of maintaining a unified budget from which all agencies should receive funds was placed also under the direction of the Executive Committee. Facing the lowest appropriation in ten years and a debt of over a million dollars, the Foreign Board began to sell several of its properties. In the Orient their troubles were of a different nature, for the nationalists in China were suspicious of foreigners and were planning to create a Chinese public school system. The Baptists hastened to make clear that their purpose in having schools in China was solely for evangelism and not for the Americanizing of the Chinese.[38]

A survey of foreign mission growth between 1919 and 1930 revealed that in the ten fields in Africa, Asia, Europe, and Latin America, the number of churches had increased from 505 to 1,407, of which 643 were self-supporting in 1930 as compared with 143 in 1919. The membership had jumped from 49,695 to 161,059, with native contributions increasing from $173,372 in 1919 to $472,820 in 1930. The personnel of the Board included 423 missionaries and 2,045 native workers. On the foreign fields were thirteen theological seminaries, having no endowments, but serving one-third as many students as in the three Convention seminaries at home. The nine hospitals abroad treated nearly seventy-four thousand patients in a year as over against more than eighty-five thousand patients being cared for by twenty-four hospitals at home.[39]

As the nation became involved in a world-wide depression, contributions declined in spite of debt-clearing efforts set in motion by the Convention in 1932. The bank holiday in March, 1933, made it

[38] S.B.C., *Annual*, 1929, pp. 57-9, 148-52.

[39] *Ibid.*, 1930, pp. 152; 1931, pp. 167-8.

difficult to gather in such monies as had been pledged. Consequently, on April 12 and 13, the Executive Committee met in day and night sessions with south-wide executives of denominational agencies to consider the plight of the denomination. Out of the meetings came a plan suggested by the Reverend Frank Tripp of St. Joseph, Missouri, known as the Baptist Hundred Thousand Club. As adopted by the Convention in Washington, D. C., on May 20, it provided for membership in the Club of all persons who would pay one dollar per month over and above their regular church subscriptions. The accumulated funds were to be allocated to pay the debts of the various agencies on a percentage basis of their total indebtedness. The Baptist Sunday School Board undertook to pay all expenses of the movement so that all money raised could be applied to the principal. The chief problem faced was the lack of debt-consciousness on the part of Southern Baptists generally. Of the twenty-four thousand churches in the Convention, one-third made no contribution at all in 1933 and a large percentage of the nearly four million members was equally irresponsible.[40] But the new effort was successful in arousing concern for the Convention's dilemma as is evident from the figures released in April, 1937, which indicated that $662,490.32 had been raised to date. When the creditors heard that all funds so raised were to be applied on principal, they became willing to enter into debt adjustment agreements. In 1938 the Convention was able, therefore, to consolidate its debts in one bond issue of $565,000 at 5 per cent, a saving of 1 per cent. It later refinanced the obligations of the Home Mission Board and of the Southern Baptist Theological Seminary.[41]

It soon became apparent that the period of retrenchment was drawing slowly to a close, for not only was the indebtedness gradually being liquidated, but several achievements were to be observed on the foreign fields. Two new schools came into existence in China in 1938, the product of Southern Baptist efforts. They were the China Baptist Theological Seminary and the Women's Training School in Kaifeng.[42] These, when added to other Christian schools such as the Graves Theological Seminary at Canton, the Eliza Yates Girls' School

[40] S.B.C., *Annual,* 1933, pp. 65, 145-6; 1934, p. 52; 1935, p. 55.

[41] *Ibid.,* 1933, 1934, 1935 (same pages as above); 1937, p. 34; 1942, pp. 64-5.

[42] Routh, *The Word Overcoming the World,* p. 31.

at Shanghai, the North China Baptist Theological Seminary at Hwenghsien, and the University of Shanghai operated jointly by the Northern and Southern Conventions, represented a sizable achievement in educational leadership in the face of internal dissension within the Chinese Republic. At Kweilin the provincial authorities confiscated Baptist property; elsewhere, mission equipment and buildings were falling into the hands of the Japanese who, since 1937, had been moving into the country by force. In Shanghai, Southern Baptists alone lost a quarter of a million dollars. At Canton a church and school buildings were demolished. Then, late in the year, 1938, Dr. Herman C. E. Liu, the Chinese Christian president of the University of Shanghai, was assassinated.

War had come to China, and once again the Mission Board was faced with crisis. One hundred and seventy-eight missionaries and eighty-four children had to be evacuated from the country. To do this, the Board borrowed one hundred thousand dollars. By 1939 its losses in China had reached a total of six hundred thousand dollars. To handle the problems entailed, a China Emergency Fund was set up by the Convention to transport missionaries and reimburse them for losses of personal possessions. A China Relief Fund was established also to help Chinese nationals. In spite of wartime losses, spiritual advances were evident as seven thousand persons were baptized in 1939 and fifteen thousand pupils were enrolled in two hundred and twenty-eight Sunday schools. A new Chinese Baptist seminary was located at Kaifeng in the same year. An all-China evangelization movement was undertaken during the following year. Day schools were reopened with the aid of the Woman's Missionary Union in America.[43]

The war conditions prompted Northern and Southern Baptists to unite their efforts in Japan in 1940. At that time the United Baptist Convention of the country established a seminary in Tokyo. Only this institution and a boys' school at Fukuoka remained in the Board's control by 1941, when the Board was obliged to discontinue financial and missionary support in order to recognize the Christian Federation forced upon Protestant groups in Japan by the Government.

[43] S.B.C., *Annual,* 1937, pp. 158-9; 1938, pp. 36, 178-83; 1939, pp. 29, 192-7; 1940, pp. 164-5.

Fortunately, the income of the Foreign Mission Board had been increasing steadily as the debt was being reduced; for, in 1940, the Baptist Missionary Society in England sought aid in carrying on its mission stations. Southern and Northern Baptists united in this relief measure, the Southern Baptists contributing nearly two hundred thousand dollars to the support of British Baptist stations, mainly in India, Ceylon, China, and Africa.[44]

When the Japanese attacked Pearl Harbor on December 7, 1941, nearly one hundred and five missionaries of the Southern Board were in China, Japan, and the Philippines. Many of the eighty or more in occupied China and the ten in Manila were interned, including Dr. M. T. Rankin, Secretary for the Orient, who, upon his release, became Executive Secretary of the Foreign Board.[45]

At San Antonio, Texas, the Convention, in 1942, appointed a committee of nineteen on postwar planning. It recommended a broad and varied program of southwide evangelism, promotion of denominational papers, a debt-free Convention by January 1, 1944, and missionary expansion. The committee also indicated the importance of turning over leadership on foreign fields to Christian nationals. In 1943, the Foreign Board made the last payment of $114,500 on a ten-year indebtedness of $1,110,000 which had been owed to four banks in Richmond. In addition, Southern Baptists contributed $500,000 to a World Emergency Relief Fund between January 1, 1942, and June, 1943. By 1944 the gifts to missions totaled more than seventeen million dollars, an increase of nearly four million over 1943. The Baptist Hundred Thousand Club had been a great success, having produced a debt-free Convention in 1944 with a balance of nearly $49,000 which was applied as a reserve fund of the Old Annuity Plan.[46]

The war had dealt severely with Southern Baptists. In 1945 the Foreign Board reported that it had lost one million dollars worth of mission property in China and one-half that amount in Europe. It was estimated that two million dollars would be necessary for rehabilitation and enlargement with a staff of five hundred and four missionaries already under appointment for nineteen separate na-

[44] *Ibid.*, 1940, p. 102, 163; 1941, p. 100.

[45] *Ibid.*, 1942, p. 171.

[46] *Ibid.*, 1942, pp. 57-60, 106-7; 1943, pp. 134, 215-9; 1945, pp. 30-1.

tional areas throughout the world. Accordingly, a budget of two and one-half million dollars was set for 1945. This was a long step from the modest figure of six hundred and five thousand dollars adopted twenty-two years before.[47] But this was not all, for in the spring of 1948 the Foreign Mission Board "adopted a program for a goal of 1,750 missionaries and an annual budget of $10,000,000." This represented an anticipated increase of approximately 150 per cent; for there were at the time 663 active missionaries in the employ of the Board with a budget of four million dollars.[48] Such optimistic planning was characteristic of the era following the Second World War.

Northern Baptist Home Missions

Under the leadership of Dr. Henry L. Morehouse, field secretary of the American Baptist Home Mission Society from 1893 to 1917, the keynote of emphasis was expansion and interdenominational co-operation. Two thousand churches were assisted in the erection of houses of worship by a plan known as the Church Edifice Gift Fund. The American Baptist Education Society had been organized in 1888 under his guidance. With the financial assistance of John D. Rockefeller, Sr., the Education Society had been instrumental in the founding of the University of Chicago four years later. Since that time it has disbursed over a million dollars to thirty Baptist schools.[49] A plan of co-operation with Southern Baptists was effected, as has been noted, for training Negro pastors. Educational facilities for the Negroes in the South were improved greatly by the creation of an interdenominational General Education Board for the purpose of co-ordinating the efforts of Presbyterians, Methodists, Episcopalians, and Baptists. Between 1908 and 1928, that Board gave to the American Baptist Home Mission Society for use in its Negro schools the sum of nearly two and a half million dollars. The contributions made by the young people who have been trained in these schools indicates that the Society has had a large influence upon Negro life in America. Out of 100,000 Negro pupils who have attended Baptist schools, "10,677 are academic graduates, 2,436 college graduates, 860 theological graduates, 4,015 ministers, 422 professors and college

[47] S.B.C., *Annual*, 1945, pp. 141-4.
[48] *The Watchman-Examiner*, Vol. 36, No. 23 (June 3, 1948), 567.
[49] White, *A Century of Faith*, 234-5.

presidents, 20,135 teachers, 197 dentists, 212 lawyers, 914 physicians, 255 pharmacists, 74 editors, and 26 authors, as well as a growing band of Christian workers in Northern and Southern communities" where there is a combined Negro Baptist church membership of three million in thousands of churches.[50]

When the Baptists of the North reorganized in 1907 and established a Convention with a sectional name (Northern Baptist Convention), the earlier policy of the Home Mission Society to recognize no territorial limitations was apparently reversed. It will be recalled that since the Fortress Monroe Conference, the relationship between the Society and the Southern Baptist Convention had been governed by comity agreements. A consideration of the relationship between the newly created Northern Baptist Convention and the Southern Baptist Convention became a matter of paramount concern soon after 1907. To face the issues involved, a conference was held by representatives of the Home Mission Society and the Southern Baptist Convention in Washington, D. C., on April 15, 1909. The occasion for the meeting was a division among the Baptist churches of New Mexico, resulting from the activity which the Southern Convention had undertaken in co-operation with some of the churches there. This activity was regarded by the Northern Convention as a violation of the Fortress Monroe agreement. It was generally agreed by both parties that the stipulations of that agreement were no longer binding. It was also decided that the Home Mission Society should withdraw from New Mexico in favor of the Southern Board. The problem of territorial adjustment was to be considered settled for at least five years. When, however, the Southern Convention insisted that nothing in their agreements should be construed to limit the freedom of any Baptist church, association, or convention in choosing its alignment, Northern Baptist leaders refused to approve the compromise settlement drawn up. In order to adjust the unhappy situation, the Northern Convention requested a joint conference, which met at Old Point Comfort, Virginia, on September 27-28, 1911.

The joint committee which met on the appointed date sought to work out a new basis for comity. After a second meeting on January 24-25, 1912, at Hot Springs, Arkansas, the principles of comity were adopted which have provided the foundation for Northern-

[50] *Ibid.*, 108, 111-2.

Southern Baptist relationships to the present. They were under-girded by three fundamental principles: (1) a recognition of the autonomy of the local Baptist church; (2) a recognition of the "moral interdependence and co-operation of Baptist churches"; and (3) a recognition of the "advisory nature of all denominational organizations." The following general principles of comity were then formulated around the premise that "the voluntary principle should be primary in all general organizations" of Baptists. It was recognized that financial aid by a denominational body should not impinge upon the freedom of the local church. It was conceded that denominational organizations should regard the rights and liberties of other bodies in the interest of harmony. Finally, it was agreed that Baptist bodies should adjust their work in any area so as not to compete unfavorably with any other Baptist group; in all cases the right of the state bodies to terminate co-operation without interference from outside was to be recognized. It was urged that the churches should have one state organization if at all possible, and that "allocation of funds should be left to the administrative agencies and not be a matter of division among the churches." [51]

By 1919 tensions in southern Illinois, New Mexico, Oklahoma, and Missouri had been relieved in accordance with the principles recognized by the Northern and Southern Baptist Conventions in 1912. In Illinois sectional differences had existed from the time of its settlement. The southern area had been pro-slavery and naturally aligned with the South. In 1907 the churches of that section organized the Illinois Baptist State Association in protest against liberalism and the practice of open communion among Baptists in the Illinois Baptist General Association in which the northern and southern areas of the state had been united since 1845. In 1910 the new Association became affiliated with the Southern Convention. The decision of Baptists in the other states mentioned to affiliate with the Southern Baptist Convention was dictated by a strong affinity for the interests and emphases of fellow Southerners.

The areas of tension since 1919 have involved Baptists in Arizona, California, Washington, Oregon, Alaska, and Kansas. But since the occasion for controversy has been prompted by theological

---

[51] Baker, *Relations between Northern and Southern Baptists.* The aforegoing quotations are from pp. 200-2. The writer is greatly indebted to Dr. Baker for this account of relations between Baptists, North and South. See particularly his chapters 13 and 14.

differences and the migration of Southern Baptists into northern territory, their story will be related in the next chapter. It only remains to emphasize here that in 1925, as a result of tension in Arizona, and again in 1942, as a consequence of Southern Baptist activity in California and Illinois in alleged violation of the comity principle of 1912, adherence to these principles was affirmed by both the Northern and Southern Conventions.[52]

From the foregoing survey of the relations between Northern and Southern Baptists in their home mission work, it becomes evident that the work of the American Baptist Home Mission Society was complicated by its relationship to other Baptist bodies. On the whole, however, its operations have been facilitated in areas of conflicting interests by the sincere desire on the part of Baptist leaders of both the North and the South to win men to Christ. This was evident in all phases of the work. Northern and Southern Baptists co-operated in Indian mission enterprises in New Mexico and Oklahoma, where the Baptist Convention in each territory was free, by mutual consent, to affiliate with the home mission agency of either group. Northern Baptists opened new work among the Crow Indians in Montana in 1903, among the Hopi and Navaho tribes in Arizona in 1910, and in Nevada in 1920. By 1926 the Home Mission Society had twenty missionaries in its Indian stations and as many teachers in the six government schools. Fifteen additional workers were supported by the Woman's Home Mission Society and two by the Northern California Convention. Up to that time, the total number of converts was 4,688 in thirty-one organized churches.[53]

During the incumbency of Dr. Charles L. White as executive secretary of the American Baptist Home Mission Society from 1917 to 1929, another phase of work gained in importance; it was the endeavor, chiefly in the cities, to win foreign-speaking peoples to Protestant Christianity. The difficulties of the task were accentuated by language and cultural differences, by the Roman or Greek Catholic background of many of the foreign-speaking groups, and by the tensions of the First World War, when the national sympathies of those of Central European background were divided. Dr. Charles A. Brooks supervised this work ably between 1914 and 1924. During that time

[52] *Ibid.*, 202.
[53] White, *A Century of Faith*, 96.

an important Italian work was developed along the Atlantic sea-board. In 1907 an Italian Department of the Colgate Divinity School was established in Brooklyn, New York, to train workers under the leadership of Dr. Antonio Mangano, a native of Italy, who was the Society's evangelist and general missionary in that city. In 1913 a mission was founded in Cleveland, Ohio, followed in 1915 by one in Racine, Wisconsin. By 1920 there were 3,265 members in Italian missions and churches.[54]

Bilingual churches were established at the same time among the Mexicans in California, Arizona, Colorado, Kansas, Idaho, and Missouri as thousands of these immigrants streamed into the country during the war years when labor was scarce. By 1920 there were seventeen churches composed of 712 Finnish Baptists scattered throughout the midwest and along the East coast. Russian work, which had been begun in North Dakota in 1901, had increased to fourteen churches of 668 members within thirty years. During this same period, there were more than 1,500 Polish Baptists, nearly an equal number of Hungarian Baptists, 816 Czechoslovakian Baptists, and 522 Rumanian Baptists in the country.[55]

Among the Orientals, Baptists were able to establish a few missions, one in Seattle for the Japanese; one in Berkeley, California, for Hindu students; and three for the Chinese, two in California, a work in San Francisco turned over to them by the Southern Baptists in 1884 and one in Berkeley, and a third in New York City known as the Morning Star Mission. The Baptists on the west coast have exerted a helpful influence in modifying legislation unfriendly to the Orientals.[56]

To facilitate this important task of interpreting the gospel to the foreign groups of American cities, the Home Mission Society "encouraged the organization of Baptist City Mission Societies, and the joint appointment of missionaries supervised by their secretaries. This co-operative effort was required because experience had shown that the churches in the cities were retreating before the foreign invasion and were preoccupied in ministering to the increasing number of persons entering them from rural communities.[57] As large foreign-

[54] White, *A Century of Faith*, 145.
[55] *Ibid.*, 145-56.
[56] *Ibid.*, 162.
[57] *Ibid.*, 168.

speaking populations settled down in the industrial centers which families of old American stock had deserted for the suburbs, it became necessary to establish another type of agency to substitute a Christian environment for the evil one which was developing so rapidly. These were known as Christian Centers. Such Christian Centers as Emmanuel House, Brooklyn, and Rankin Center, Pittsburgh, were founded by the Home Mission Society with the aid of special gifts and contributions from the Woman's Home Mission Society, state conventions, and city mission societies. By 1945 there were fifty-one such Centers in the industrial cities of twenty-one states and Puerto Rico and Alaska, providing instruction in the gospel and in wholesome living for underprivileged families.[58]

The urban situation was made more complex by the influx of Negroes from the South into the North and West during and immediately after the First World War. Between 1910 and 1920 there was an increase in the Negro population in the North of 43.3 per cent and of 55.1 per cent in the West as compared with the 1.9 per cent in the South. New York City developed the largest Negro center in the world. The colored population "of St. Louis increased 60 per cent, Omaha 133 per cent, Chicago 150 per cent, Youngstown 244 per cent, Cleveland 300 per cent, Tulsa 333 per cent, Detroit 600 per cent, Pittsburgh 50 per cent, Philadelphia 60 per cent, and Gary 1,300 per cent." [59] To meet the problems of adjustment to this shift in population, the Home Mission Boards of the major Protestant denominations co-operated in making surveys, setting up social agencies, establishing new Christian Centers and assisting in the founding of churches.

The home mission enterprise of Northern Baptists consistently has reached out beyond the borders of the United States to Central America. There, as within this country, it has followed the policy of interdenominational co-operation in reaching comity agreements to prevent a multiplicity of denominational stations in any one area. This policy was adopted at the beginning of the century when such agencies as the Federal Council of Churches of Christ in America and the Home Missions Council came into existence. In Mexico, where the government's constitution of 1926 permits only a native

[58] *Home Mission Digest,* No. II (New York, 1945), 67.

[59] White, *A Century of Faith,* 165.

religious ministry, the Mexican Baptist Convention, which includes churches established by both Northern and Southern Baptists, has been maintaining its own missionaries to the neglected Indians of the mountain regions. American teachers and physicians, however, are permitted in the country; for that reason, outside help was directed for many years to educational centers at Saltillo and Puebla.

In Puerto Rico, after the Spanish-American War, the Home Mission Society joined with several missionary bodies in a comity agreement by which they divided responsibilities. In 1919 a single theological seminary was established out of the Baptists' Grace Conaway Institute at Coamo, in which enterprise six denominations jointly engaged. Non-doctrinal courses were to be taken by all of the students, while instruction in denominational doctrines and polity was given to each group separately. Similar intersociety co-operation was undertaken in Cuba where Northern and Southern Baptists have shared in evangelizing the island. In 1920 a Cuban Home Mission Society was formed to which the American Baptist Home Mission Society and the American Baptist Publication Society gave financial assistance.

New fields were opened by comity arrangements in El Salvador in 1911, in Nicaragua in 1916, in Honduras in 1918, in Haiti in 1919, and in Jamaica in 1921. To the latter two fields, which had been developed earlier by the American Baptist Free Mission Society of anti-slavery days and by English and Jamaican Baptists, the Northern Baptists of America gave welcome support.

The economic depression of 1929 produced a series of circumstances which created new problems and demands that could be met best only by further interdenominational co-operation. Important fields of foreign groups were conserved by placing two adjacent churches of the same race or nationality under a single missionary or by federating with groups of another denomination. Reduced appropriations were working a distinct injury to Negro Baptist schools in the South; their academic rating was being affected by low salary scales and inadequate facilities. In 1934 the home mission boards of the Presbyterian, Methodist Episcopal, Congregational, Reformed and Northern Baptist churches met to discuss instances of duplication and overlapping in an effort to redistribute missionaries and mission churches for greater economy and efficiency. Baptists also found it helpful to work in close relationship with such agencies as the Interdenominational Council on Spanish-speaking work, the Town and Country Committee of the Home Missions Council, and the Interdenominational Committee on the Christian Approach to the Jews. Religious directors working in Indian Government Schools were appointed customarily by the Home Missions Council and supported by the united contributions of the denominations co-operating. Not only was there advantage in such procedure, but it was coming to be required by the various governments. In Central America the Home Mission Society continued to work as a constituent member of the Committee on Co-operation in Latin America, in which all the denominations having work in Spanish and Portuguese-speaking lands united for certain common tasks.[60]

As the depression years intensified the migratory movement of the unemployed, city churches faced the problem of dwindling membership as many moved back to the country, while their surrounding neighborhoods were changing rapidly to include a majority of Roman Catholics, Jews, or Negroes. The growing imperative of ministering to these groups was felt by ministers and laymen alike. To counterbalance the fast emptying city church edifices there were opportunities for establishing new churches in the mushrooming suburban communities. Alert city mission societies saw the need, but often they were handicapped in their efforts to build new churches in growing population centers by a lack of financial resources and at times by an absence of foresight on the part of established churches.

In rural areas thousands of churches were ceasing to exist. All too many others were operating on a basis too meager to render the service which their communities needed. The weakness of rural work was due to several factors. Farms were transferred from owners to tenants, with the result that the absentee landlords ceased to support the churches, while the renters and farmhands proved to be a transient, unstable type of constituency. A second factor was the decline in income, which cause a decreased budget and inadequate facilities.[61]

In the forties the Second World War accentuated the problems already facing Baptist home missions. The town and country churches

[60] N.B.C., *Annual,* 1934, pp. 691-5, 711; 1936, p. 727; 1937, p. 613.
[61] *Ibid.,* 1937, pp. 630, 646.

began to experience the loss of young men to defense industries and then to the armed forces. In addition to the loss of lay workers, the number of ministers decreased, for many potential theological students entered military service, and many experienced pastors heeded the persistent call for chaplains. To meet the emergency existing in many areas, the colporter-missionary work which the American Baptist Publication Society and the American Baptist Home Mission Society had been carrying on for many years was depended on increasingly. From their auto-trailers, faithful workers distributed tracts, Bibles and New Testaments, held preaching services, and organized Sunday schools. As the war progressed, uprooting nearly thirty-five million Americans and transplanting them to new government projects and war industrial plants, this type of service was extended to new towns and developments.[62]

Since 1942 Baptists have co-operated with the Home Missions Council's program for the share-croppers and tenant farmers in the Southwest. The program includes holding institutes for pastors and for home builders, and the maintaining of loan libraries. The "Lord's Acre Plan" of stewardship of farm production has been promoted as a means of financing Christian work.[63]

During the war the Home Mission Society, the state conventions, and the city mission societies gave help to members of the armed forces by various forms of canteen service and evangelistic effort. In addition, they rendered assistance to the Japanese of the West Coast who in 1942 were moved to relocation centers far inland. A third group which needed assistance because of war conditions was the one hundred and seventy-three Northern Baptist young men whose stand against war led them to choose "work of national importance under civilian direction" rather than service in the armed forces, and twelve who, for conscientious reasons, refused to obey the enacted legislation, and who in consequence received federal prison terms. Between 1941 and 1945 the Home Mission Society, through designated contributions of interested individuals, turned over $31,867 to the pacifist denominations who bore the major cost of the support of these men in Civilian Public Service Camps. The Society also co-operated with the National Service Board in behalf of these Civilian

[62] *Home Mission Digest*, No. I (New York, 1944), pp. 3-4, 6-9; No. II (1945), p. 42.
[63] *Home Mission Digest*, No. II (1945), pp. 10-1.

Camp assignees when they were to be demobilized and returned to their communities and churches.[64]

Work on the mission fields in Central America was continued in spite of the duress of war. By 1945 there were 205 churches, 432 outstations, with 25,446 members in the six different republics where Baptist work was carried on. The leadership was largely in native hands, as is evident from the fact that there were 236 national missionaries, as compared with 16 American missionaries. There were thirty-nine schools and a total mission property in all six fields of nearly a million dollars.[65]

Southern Baptist Home Missions

The twentieth century opened for Southern Baptists with a new era of prosperity and good feeling. The effects of the War between the States had been dissipated at last. The home mission work had been reorganized and the notable Dr. I. T. Tichenor, who had retired in 1899, was succeeded, after the brief administrations of Dr. F. H. Kerfoot and Dr. F. C. McConnell, by Dr. B. D. Gray in 1903. The popular support of the Home Board had reached a new peak as is evident from a 23 per cent increase in receipts over the preceding year. By reason of the Convention's approval in 1901 of a plan for establishing a system of mountain schools, the Board appropriated in 1904 over six thousand dollars for the support of thirteen such schools. In the same year it supported, in whole or in part, 616 missionaries who supplied 2,244 churches and stations. The results of their work were gratifying, for in one year they baptized 7,526 converts, organized 157 churches, and built or improved 179 houses of worship.[66]

The strength of Southern Baptist work was in the rural areas; only in Atlanta, Richmond, and Louisville were urban Baptists notably strong. The new secretary accordingly urged the Convention to permit the Board to spend twenty-five thousand dollars annually for ten years lest the Baptists lose the country as well as the cities by failing to seize their opportunities in those areas. With this in view, the Board pressed forward its frontier work in Texas, Arkansas,

[64] *Ibid.*, pp. 17-9.
[65] *Ibid.*, p. 105.
[66] Joe W. Burton, *Epochs of Home Missions*, 85-7.

Louisiana, Missouri, and Oklahoma. In Missouri a German evangelist was appointed to labor amongst German immigrants. In Oklahoma, support of the work was shared with Northern Baptists. At Baltimore, Maryland, aid was given the state Baptist Board in a mission enterprise carried on at the immigrant piers. A similar joint effort with the Virginia State Board made possible the employment of five white and four Negro missionaries. The destitute mill population of the Carolinas challenged Baptist missionary interests in like manner. To meet the universal need for winning men to Christ, the Home Mission Board created a department of evangelism in 1907, which was unique among Protestant denominations. By 1913 its staff totaled twenty-five workers.

There were nearly eight thousand congregations within the Southern Baptist Convention which had no meeting-houses or were obliged to conduct services in dilapidated church buildings. This condition prompted the launching of a Million Dollar Church Building Loan Fund in 1913. At the same time, the increase in church membership continued. The Home Mission Board crowned the next year with a glowing report: 30,861 baptisms; 1,447 missionaries, most of them in co-operative work with state boards; 3,349 churches and stations; and receipts totaling $397,589. The gains were indicative of the general trend which had characterized the past ten years, during which time receipts had increased 300 per cent, baptisms 270 per cent, and the number of members by as much as 340 per cent.[67]

Indeed, all of the varied undertakings of the Home Board were thoroughly imbued with the spirit of evangelism. Its work extended to the seaports and mining centers into which came annually more than a half million immigrants who were mostly Roman Catholics. Thirty missionaries served in those areas. Work among the Negroes was conducted co-operatively with the National Baptist Convention (colored), while the Board's department of evangelism employed a number of Negro evangelists on its staff.

Another area of home mission service was Cuba and Panama. By 1906 twenty-five missionaries were serving in Cuba where the churches had organized their own convention. Three missionaries were stationed in Panama.

[67] *Ibid.*, 90.

During World War I, Southern Baptists faced much the same need for adjustment to the problems created by population shifts, war work, and servicemen as did Baptists in the North. Similarly also, their horizons were broadened by the world conflict. Even as they expanded their work abroad, they saw the need for the enlargement of home missions. In the first flush of optimism following the postwar campaign to raise seventy-five million dollars, Southern Baptists spent $331,463 in excess of receipts in 1921, a year in which home mission receipts reached an all-time high of $1,634,449. The decline of cotton prices added to the setback which continued for the next seven years, until the receipts had dropped to 59 per cent of the 1921 amount. Retrenchment became necessary, so that "by 1928 the number of missionaries had decreased from 1,656 to 765, a 54 per cent decline; churches and mission stations went from 8,952 to 951, an 89 per cent loss; baptisms fell from 56,164 to 17,649, a 69 per cent drop; churches constituted dropped from 305 to 105, a 65 per cent decrease." [68]

The unheeded trend of spending beyond income was aggravated by the discovery in September, 1928, of the defalcation of the Board's treasurer in the amount of $909,461, thereby increasing its total indebtedness to the staggering sum of approximately two and a half million dollars.[69] After a careful investigation, the treasurer was prosecuted and the Board reorganized, although the only criticism raised against its members was misjudgment of the character of an employee and error in delegating to him too much power.

The executive committee of the Convention, led by Dr. George W. Truett of Texas, the Convention's president, undertook the task of repaying the indebtedness in full. Southern Baptists responded in an initial collection of nearly four hundred thousand dollars on November 11, 1928, known as Honor Day. The new executive secretary-treasurer selected the following year was Dr. J. B. Lawrence, general superintendent of the executive board of the General Association of Baptists in Missouri. He outlined a program of debt liquidation and maintenance of the mission work under a plan which called for rigid economy and consolidation of the gains already made. Under

[68] Burton, *Epochs of Home Missions*, 93-4, 98.

[69] S.B.C., *Annual*, 1930, gives the figure for total indebtedness on May 1, 1929, as $1,970,981.10 (p. 254). Burton places the figure at $2,527,453.44 which appears to be his estimate of the total indebtedness, including the amount of defalcation (*op. cit.*, 100).

his direction, the Board's co-operative support of state missionaries was dropped as a measure of economy. As a result of these stringent measures, only one hundred and fifty missionaries were left on its staff in 1928. The heroic struggle of Southern Baptists to clear the Convention of debt during the years of economic depression through the Hundred Thousand Club has been related in the story of Southern Baptist foreign missions.

In 1931 the Board began adding each year a few more missionaries to its staff. As the nation began to emerge from the economic depression, a reappraisal of the Board's task was undertaken in 1934. Its plans for evangelism included the winning of the wealthy members of society as well as the underprivileged in the industrial areas. Greater attention was paid to the social origins of the moral and spiritual problems of the times. As economic conditions improved, receipts for home missions showed an upturn in 1936. By 1938 there were three hundred and thirty-two missionaries being employed on home mission fields in southern states, in Cuba, and Panama.[70]

Advances were made in all phases of the home missionary enterprise. Educational missionaries were placed in nearly a score of Negro colleges to teach biblical subjects. Additional workers and newly acquired properties resulted in an expanded field in Cuba. The local churches were encouraged and guided by a reinstituted department of evangelism to win Jews and foreign immigrant groups to Christ. The city mission program was extended to more than forty cities, while a rural program for the rehabilitation of the country churches was undertaken.[71]

With the expansion of the armed services during World War II, the Convention, in 1941, designated the Home Mission Board to be the agency to promote religious work in army camps and contiguous communities and to certify ministers for the chaplaincy. Up to 1945, 1,042 Southern Baptist ministers had served as chaplains in the army and navy. Throughout the war years, as the Board enjoyed the increased receipts of more prosperous days, the number of employed missionaries reached, by 1945, the total of 654, including 71 student missionaries for summer assignments. This represented

[70] S.B.C., *Annual*, 1935, p. 253; 1936, p. 254; 1938, p. 267.
[71] Burton, *Epochs of Home Missions*, pp. 113-6.

an increase of 494 over the year 1928, when the Board was re-organized.[72]

Baptist missions since 1900 had been under fire—harassed by two world conflicts, a major economic depression, and internal frictions in the North. Yet they had emerged without serious damage. In some respects, they were the stronger for having been subjected to the cross-currents of a world in confusion. The keynote of the Christian message among most denominations following World War II was evangelism. This promised a bright future for missions.

[72] S.B.C., *Annual*, 1942, p. 254; 1945, pp. 242, 290.

CHAPTER FIFTEEN

FACING A REVOLUTIONARY CENTURY

Iₙ 1850 there were approximately 700,000 Baptists in the United States, or one out of every thirty-two persons in the population. Fifty years later the number had reached 4,181,686, or one Baptist out of every eighteen or nineteen in the population. Commensurate with growth in membership was the evident increase of educational facilities from twenty-one collegiate institutions to sixty, and from two seminaries to five during the same period. The establishing of these new schools indicated that Baptists were sharing in the generous philanthropy and the growing appreciation of the role of education in American life which were characteristic of the times. While internal dissensions had not entirely disappeared from the main Baptist bodies, there was a deeper sense of unity, and Baptist relations with other communions were greatly improved. Mutual respect, comity, and co-operation were significant words by 1900.

Baptists were still maintaining basic accord in doctrine and practical teaching, although the last decades of the century had evinced on the part of some in the denomination a more liberal attitude toward the Scriptures. At the same time, there was a noticeable decline in the discipline maintained among Baptist churches. The simple practice of "dropping" a name from the roll of membership was being resorted to, instead of the traditional method of exclusion with its attendant stigma. As the frontier character of Americans gave way to the increasing sophistication of an urban culture, particularly in New England and the Middle Atlantic region, the frequency of revivals also declined. The majority of converts received into the churches did not come directly from the pagan community, but through the Sunday school and the young people's society. The conversion of adults was becoming increasingly rare.

Another trend was the developing strength of the denominational Societies in their control over the missionary and educational enterprises of the churches. Too often, as able and earnest men

424

executed the affairs of the Societies with wisdom and integrity, the result was an estrangement of the churches from the Societies and the actual work in the field which they represented.[1] The method, if not the spirit, of big business was being felt in the denomination as men struggled to meet the overwhelming demands of a changing age in a manner which would be effective and efficient. At the same time, unrest was being aroused by the spread of theological liberalism, and by the preaching of those who were seeking the salvation of society through the "Social Gospel," which had sprung into prominence through the writings of Walter Rauschenbusch, church historian and professor at Rochester Theological Seminary.

Changing Emphases in Theology

At the organization meeting of the Baptist World Alliance in London in 1905, Professor E. Y. Mullins, of the Southern Baptist Theological Seminary at Louisville, Kentucky, outlined the axioms for a new Baptist apologetic. His basic theological principle was that the holy and loving God has a right to be sovereign over His creatures. Dr. Mullins followed this with an ecclesiastical axiom that "all believers have equal privileges in the church." This was implemented by an emphasis upon the accessibility of God to all men and the free responsibility of each individual before God, hence a free church in a free state.[2] It was evident that the traditional Calvinistic theology of many Baptists had been modified appreciably by the influence of democratic thought. Indicative of this trend was the merger in 1911 of the Free Baptists, an Arminian group, with the Northern Baptist Convention.

But even as the Baptist World Alliance was sending forth to the world its expression of doctrinal belief, divergent forces were at work among Baptists, producing almost imperceptible changes in the meaning of time-worn phraseology and relegating some theological expressions to the limbo of outmoded traditionalism. From European universities came a rationalism which challenged the adequacy of faith as a way of knowing God's revelation to men. From England came Charles Darwin's theory of biological evolution,

[1] H. C. Vedder, "Fifty Years of Baptist History," *The Chronicle*, Vol. IX, No. 4 (Oct., 1946), pp. 163-70.

[2] Baptist World Congress, *Proceedings*, 1905, p. 152.

with its emphasis upon the "survival of the fittest," the impact of which was felt in religious circles. Man's position as the special creation of God, endowed with full mental and spiritual capacity from his beginning, was challenged. In its place was developed a concept of man as the product of natural evolution from lower animal forms, whose capacities have been increased gradually through a slow process of adaptation to his environment. This developmental theory inspired the more optimistic to accept the idealist's philosophy that man's ultimate salvation lies in the acquisition of knowledge. They viewed man's religious experience as an evolution from a very primitive outreach for God through fear to a mature worship through love. The Bible no longer was looked upon as a direct revelation from God, but as a historical record of the religious development of a people. The principles of historical and literary criticism were applied, often by non-Christian scholars, to the Scriptures to determine the authenticity of the manuscripts and hence of the validity of their message.

Under the impact of these ideas, the traditional views of man as a lost sinner apart from the atonement of Christ, of eternal punishment and eternal blessedness, of justification by faith, of predestination and the perseverance of the saints, and of sanctification, began to lose their significance for many seminary-trained men. Even the Bible, which had been the final authority of Baptists for matters of faith and life, seemed about to be overthrown by the findings of science. In a desperate effort to retain their hold upon Christianity without forsaking the new learning about them, some sought refuge in a liberal theology which taught that sin is the product of ignorance, that man has an innate goodness within him which merely needs unfolding, that the miracles recorded in the Bible are expressions of the manner of describing natural processes in an unscientific age, that the resurrection may be interpreted as the continuance of the teachings and exemplary life of Jesus in His disciples, and that the main task of the church is to reform society and so make the kingdom of God an actuality here on earth. Among the earlier Baptist exponents of the new liberalism were Dr. Shailer Mathews of the Divinity School of the University of Chicago, Dr. Walter Rauschenbusch of the Rochester Theological Seminary in Rochester, and Dr. Harry Emerson Fosdick, pastor of the Riverside Church in New

[handwritten margin notes top: "Different phases or aspects of the modernist/liberal movement" | "Social Gospel" Gladden, Rauschenbusch / "EVOLUTION" / "German Rationalism" Baur, Ritchl, Schleiermacher and Wellhausen / Unitarianism]

York City. They made a genuine attempt at mediation between an uncritical evangelicalism and "scientific modernism," which fundamentally drew its authority from science and scholarship and not from the faith. In this respect they represented what might be called "evangelical liberalism." *[handwritten: Wm. Channing, the early leading proponent]*

With equal earnestness, the theological traditionalists sprang to the defense of orthodoxy, finding ready response among kindred spirits of other denominations who were facing a like challenge in their churches and schools. Known as Fundamentalists, from a series of apologetic volumes produced by them in 1910-1915 under the title, *The Fundamentals,* they emphasized the inerrancy of the Sacred Scriptures, the deity of Jesus Christ, His virgin birth, the substitutionary nature of His atoning death, His bodily resurrection, and the imminent and personal return of Christ to establish His Kingdom on earth.[3] *[handwritten margin: Doctrines]* The leading Baptist exponents of this position were such men as J. C. Massee of Tremont Temple in Boston; William B. Riley, pastor of the First Baptist Church and president of the Northwestern Bible School in Minneapolis; I. M. Haldeman and John Roach Straton, pastors respectively of the First Baptist Church and the Calvary Baptist Church in New York City; and T. T. Shields, president of the then existing Des Moines University.

Although most Baptists accepted the theological views set forth by the Fundamentalists, they did not agree with the Fundamentalists' insistence that the orthodox doctrinal position should be safeguarded by uniform conformity to a creedal statement. *[handwritten margin: creeds / q.r. 429]* At the second Baptist World Congress held in Philadelphia, in 1911, Rev. J. Moffat Logan of Accrington, England, reflected the general Baptist position in an address on "An Authoritative Creed," in which he made the statement that:

> The desire for an authoritative creed is surely a departure from the standpoint of our Baptist sires. It is an endeavor to escape from spiritual risks by artificial aids and so is scarcely honoring to one another nor to Him who is supposed to be our chosen Guide. Let us insist on spirituality and loyalty and having these be well content to pay the price of liberty. A Baptist is a man who, through his baptism, declares not only that he is, through Christ, in vital connection with the Father, but also that the words of Christ

[3] For a detailed but somewhat biased account of the fundamentalist movement, see Stewart G. Cole, *The History of Fundamentalism* (New York, 1931), chaps. 5 and 13 in particular.

[handwritten bottom: Reactions to Modernism/Liberalism / Neo-orthodoxy / "Fundamentalism"]

historically interpreted are now his laws, and such a man is surely worthy to be trusted in the realm of religion, anywhere. For three hundred years the Baptists in both hemispheres have stood for loyalty to Christ and liberty amongst each other and the principle which has sufficed to make us powerful will suffice to keep us true.[4]

Yet the desire to offset the impact of rationalism became stronger. The Baptist University of Chicago, with its Divinity School, had been established in 1890 that it might be such a bulwark, but that institution was becoming a leading center of academic secularism and theological liberalism.

In 1906 theological controversy was aroused in the Chicago Baptist Association over the publication of Professor George B. Foster's book, *The Finality of the Christian Religion*. Foster, who was a member of the faculty of the Divinity School of the University of Chicago, was ejected from the Chicago Baptist Ministers' Conference because of his radical views. To allay further criticism and yet to avoid giving the impression that his academic freedom was being violated, the University authorities transferred him from the Divinity School to its Department of Comparative Religion. But the bitter controversy continued to be waged between liberal and conservative Baptists at ministers' meetings, associational gatherings, and state conventions.

In 1910 the Illinois Baptist State Association, which three years before had been organized at Pinckneyville, Perry County, in southern Illinois, as a protest against the inclusion of theological liberals in the state convention, became affiliated with the Southern Baptist Convention. The issue was not exclusively theological, for the majority of Illinois Baptists held conservative views, but were unwilling to disfellowship the liberal element and so endanger harmony in the state. They did, however, provide a training school for a conservative ministry, the Northern Baptist Theological Seminary, which was founded in Chicago in 1913. Its curriculum was also adapted to the needs of those who were not academically qualified for admittance to standard seminary courses. The members of the Second Baptist Church of Chicago took a leading part in the establishment of this institution.[5]

[4] B.W.C., *Proceedings*, 1911, p. 120.

[5] Perry J. Stackhouse, *Chicago and the Baptists* (Chicago, 1933), 167-70, 187-90.

During the First World War and in the years immediately following, the forces of liberalism and fundamentalism became more strongly entrenched within the denomination, thereby creating a tension which exists to the present. The strength of the Liberals lay primarily in the older seminaries and in the urban churches of the North. In the South, their influence was negligible. The Fundamentalists took varying courses of action. Many cast in their lot with an interdenominational organization called the World's Christian Fundamentals Association, founded in Philadelphia in 1919. Of these, the more denominationally minded, like J. C. Massee, W. B. Riley, John Roach Straton, and Curtis Lee Laws, editor of the Baptist weekly, *The Watchman-Examiner,* led in the organization of the Fundamental Fellowship of the Northern Baptist Convention in 1920. The action had resulted from a Pre-convention Conference on the Fundamentals of the Baptist Faith held at the Delaware Avenue Baptist Church in Buffalo on June 21 at the call of one hundred and fifty ministers and laymen. This was the first of a series of annual pre-convention meetings held by Fundamentalists within the Northern Baptist Convention prior to the sessions of that body.

The Fundamental Fellowship denounced the Interchurch World Movement, which was born prematurely of the postwar sentiment in behalf of church unity. It also called upon the Northern Baptist Convention to make a thorough investigation of Baptist schools, many of which were suspected of harboring modernism. The request was granted by the Convention at Buffalo that year, and a report of the survey was made at the next meeting in Des Moines, Iowa, in 1921, giving the schools a general approval.

The Fundamentalists sought to safeguard orthodoxy by committing the Convention to a uniform confession of faith, thereby raising the question, "Shall Baptists adopt a creed?" At the annual meeting in 1922 at Indianapolis, Indiana, Dr. William B. Riley, of Minneapolis, presented a resolution that the New Hampshire Confession of Faith be recommended by the Convention to all such local Baptist churches within its bounds "as felt the need of a clear and competent confession, and stand ready to announce their faith both to the believing and unbelieving world." Dr. Cornelius Woelfkin, a New York minister and former president of the American Baptist Foreign Mission Society, was spokesman for those who opposed the use of creeds to attain doctrinal uniformity. He offered a substitute motion to the effect that "the Northern Baptist Convention affirms that the New Testament is the all-sufficient ground of our faith and practice, and we need no other statement." By a vote of 1,264 to 637, Woelfkin's motion was carried.[6]

At the same Convention, Professor Frederick L. Anderson of the Newton Theological Institution and chairman of the Board of Managers of the American Baptist Foreign Mission Society, replied to charges of laxness in examining missionary candidates on doctrine with a lengthy explanation of the procedure followed. His statement was prompted also by the fact that the Society had been offered a sizable gift of money on the condition that it should maintain an orthodox creedal position. The Society's reply was that such gifts were difficult to administer and therefore the donors should be advised by the Convention to trust their Societies and Boards who were endeavoring to be loyal to fundamental Baptist doctrines.[7] Thus the matter rested at the close of the Convention meeting, with a profession of doctrinal soundness without commitment to a specific doctrinal statement. Needless to say, the Fundamentalists were disappointed, for they feared the intrusion of liberal ideas into the interpretation of the New Testament by responsible Baptist leaders.

Although the Southern Baptist Convention suffered from no such theological division, it was troubled by the encroachments of rationalism and the teaching of biological evolution in the schools which its youth attended. In the face of strong demands from many quarters that the Convention go on record against what was being taught in some schools on scientific subjects, President E. Y. Mullins met the challenge in his opening address at the Convention in 1922. Under the heading of "Science and Religion," he protested, not against valid scientific investigation, but against "the imposition of this theory (i.e., evolution) upon the minds of our children in denominational or public schools as if it were a definite and established truth of science." He then outlined a doctrinal statement as follows:

We record again our unwavering adherence to the supernatural elements in the Christian religion. The Bible is God's revelation of Himself through men moved by the Holy Spirit, and is our sufficient, certain, and authorita-

[6] N.B.C., *Annual*, 1922, pp. 130, 133-4.
[7] *Ibid*, pp. 87, 561-3.

tive guide in religion. Jesus Christ was born of the Virgin Mary through the power of the Holy Spirit. He was the Divine and eternal Son of God. He wrought miracles, healing the sick, casting out demons, raising the dead. He died as the vicarious atoning Savior of the world and was buried. He arose again from the dead. The tomb was emptied of its contents. In His risen body he appeared many times to His disciples. He ascended to the right hand of the Father. He will come again in person, the same Jesus who ascended from the Mount of Olives.[8]

Loyalty to such a statement of faith, he felt, was necessary to qualify any school or teacher to receive the support of the Convention. In accordance with his position, that body authorized the printing of his full statement in the Minutes. This action was significant, for the seminaries of the South were under the direct control of the Convention, and the colleges and academies were the object of the immediate interest of the state conventions, a situation which did not obtain in the North.

In 1925 the Southern Convention actually authorized publication of the New Hampshire Confession of Faith with ten additional sections concerning the resurrection, the return of the Lord, religious liberty, peace and war, education, social service, co-operation, evangelism and missions, stewardship, and the kingdom of God. It was intended to be expressive of the faith generally held by Southern Baptists, rather than to be authoritative and binding upon them.[9] Thus, while they refrained from using a creed to enforce uniformity, they went beyond their Northern brethren in willingness to adopt a general confession of faith, a step which was made easier by the almost total absence of theological conflict among them.

Meanwhile the rumblings of discontent were growing louder in the Northern Convention as the Foreign Society came again under attack. At Milwaukee, in 1924, Dr. J. C. Massee, of Boston, presented a resolution calling for a commission of seven persons to be named by the president of the Convention to investigate and report as to the conduct, policies, and practices of the Board of Managers and Secretaries of that Society in the selection of new missionaries and in the doctrinal stand of older appointees. The resolution was adopted with an allotment of twenty-five thousand dollars for expenses.[10] The

8 S.B.C., *Annual*, 1923, pp. 19-20.
9 *Ibid.*, 1925, pp. 71-6.
10 N.B.C., *Annual*, 1924, pp. 51-2.

Society, in turn, presented to the Convention a statement prepared by the chairman of its Board of Managers, Professor F. L. Anderson, describing its "evangelical policy," and defining the gospel as "the good news of the free forgiveness of sin and eternal life (beginning now and going on forever) through a vital union with the crucified and risen Christ, which brings men into union and fellowship with God. . . ." [11]

At the Convention meeting in Seattle, Washington, in the following year, the Commission of seven presented its testimony and material in four volumes and offered a summary report as follows: (1) They did not find that the Secretaries and the Board of Managers knowingly had appointed liberals because they were liberals; but they did find evidence that there had been a tendency to underestimate the value of thoroughly sound, evangelical Christian views in a missionary. (2) They found that the Board followed what they termed an "inclusive" policy, i.e., "it would appoint and retain missionaries of varying theological beliefs provided they came within certain limits which the Board regarded as 'the limits of the gospel.' " (3) They found some evidence of wrong teaching among missionaries. (4) They noted that in the last ten years more emphasis had been placed upon education than evangelism, but that the reason was practical, not theological. These trends, so it appeared, had been due to the Board's eagerness to train an adequate number of capable native leaders for the indigenous churches. [12]

The Board received the report in good spirit and set up a committee to carry out the adoption of the constructive criticisms made. Not satisfied with this, the Reverend W. B. Hinson, of Oregon, presented a series of resolutions to the effect that men and women who were out of harmony with the evangelical faith, as he defined it in detail, be removed from their appointments. After much discussion, the Reverend R. V. Meigs of Illinois proposed amendments which eliminated the doctrinal statement, simply referring to the Indianapolis decision of 1922 to use the New Testament only, and leaving the action to be taken, in the light of the facts discovered, to

[11] *Ibid.*, pp. 529-38; for full statement of Professor Anderson, see above, p. 399.

[12] N.B.C., *Annual*, 1925, pp. 79-94. The committee members were A. W. Beaven, chair., Mrs. H. F. Compton, Judson A. Crane, John F. Herget, J. C. Massee, Mrs. John Nuveen, H. F. Remington, secretary.

the Board. The amendments were adopted by a vote of 742 to 574, indicating a wide divergence of opinion on this issue.[13]

At this same Convention, an amendment to its by-laws was presented to safeguard the preservation of the Baptist witness in the face of a tendency to open membership among some Baptist churches. It defined a Baptist church as "one accepting the New Testament as its guide and composed only of baptized believers, baptism being by immersion." At the next meeting, in 1926, at Washington, D. C., the Convention adopted a substitute amendment which defined its constituency in the same vein. It read as follows:

> The Northern Baptist Convention recognizes its constituency as consisting solely of those Baptist churches in which the immersion of believers is recognized and practiced as the only Scriptural baptism; and the Convention hereby declares that only immersed members will be recognized as delegates to the Convention.[14]

It was quite obviously a period of restiveness among Northern Baptists, who were becoming defined slowly in three rather distinct categories theologically: the Liberals, the rather large middle group of Conservatives, and the Fundamentalists. From a small group of the latter two divisions, there emerged, in 1925, support for a new seminary in Philadelphia known as The Eastern Baptist Theological Seminary, established to provide an avowedly conservative leadership for the denomination. To ensure a preservation of its orthodox witness, its trustees and faculty were required to subscribe annually to a doctrinal statement.

The reasons for dissension within the Convention were numerous, and at times indicative of sectional characteristics. For example, the Arizona Baptist Convention as early as 1920 had refused to cooperate with the Interchurch World Movement, and in 1924 had expressed serious dissatisfaction with the alignment between the Northern Convention and the Federal Council of Churches of Christ in America. Among Baptists of the state who sympathized with Landmarkist views, there was strong opposition to open communion, alien immersion, and interdenominational comity agreements. By 1928 this group, which was composed principally of Baptists from the South, withdrew from the state convention and organized the

[13] *Ibid.*, pp. 94-6, 174-5.
[14] N.B.C., *Annual*, 1926, pp. 80-1.

Many northern Baptist Churches joined The Independent Fundamental Churches of America (IFCA)

Baptist General Convention of Arizona, which in the following year became auxiliary to the Southern Baptist Convention.

The presence of two conventions within the state created some tension between the Northern and Southern Conventions, which was lessened in 1932 when the Executive Committee of the Southern Convention notified the leaders of the Northern Convention that "the organization of another convention in Arizona did not result from the activities of any Southern Baptist Convention agency, and that the two Arizona conventions alone had the responsibility of adjusting matters of difference." [15]

Landmark sentiment which had been strong in Oregon in the latter years of the nineteenth century kept alive dissatisfaction with the doctrinal views of the Northern Convention relative to open communion, alien immersion, comity agreements, and the "inclusive policy." Churches sharing this sentiment affiliated with the Middle Oregon Baptist Association, which had parted company with the Northern Convention in 1925 over the policy of the Foreign Society. Churches with similar views arose in California in the thirties. These churches were composed chiefly of immigrants to the state from Southern Baptist territory. These independent churches in 1940 organized the Southern Baptist General Convention of California.

Dissatisfaction with denominational connectionalism and with the presence of theological liberalism in the Northern Baptist Convention crystallized in 1933 in the withdrawal of nearly fifty churches from that body to organize the General Association of Regular Baptist Churches (North). It was intended to be a fellowship with a minimum of organization, rather than a convention. Essentially it represented a protest against liberalism in the Convention and its policy of affiliation with the Federal Council of Churches of Christ in America, which appeared to the schismatics as a "mixed multitude" to be shunned.

The new organization adopted the New Hampshire Confession of Faith, with a premillenial interpretation of the last article. While it has had no organic union with any mission agency, preferring to designate funds to "approved" missions, the chief channels for its foreign work have been the General Council of Co-operating Baptist Missions (known also as Mid-Missions), organized in 1921 with head-

[15] Robert A. Baker, *Relations between Northern and Southern Baptists*, 221-2.

quarters in Cleveland, Ohio; the Association of Baptists for Evangelism of the Orient (now the Association of Baptists for World Evangelism), established in 1925 with headquarters in Philadelphia; and the African Christian Mission, another independent Baptist Board with headquarters in Paterson, New Jersey. It has supported six independent Baptist home mission agencies. Its main educational institutions are the Baptist Bible Seminary in Johnson City, New York, established in 1932; the Los Angeles Baptist Theological Seminary in California, founded in 1927; the Baptist Bible Institute and School of Theology in Grand Rapids, Michigan; and the Phoenix Baptist Bible Institute in Phoenix, Arizona. The constituency of the General Association has grown to approximately four hundred churches in twenty-six states, being strongest in Michigan, New York, Indiana, Illinois, Iowa, Ohio, and California.[16]

Within the Northern Baptist Convention, dissatisfaction with the "inclusive" policy of the Foreign Board continued. By 1933 it became necessary for the Society to reaffirm the statement of its "evangelical" policy issued in 1924. However, discontent continued, and it was charged that missionary candidates were being appointed who denied the virgin birth of Christ, and that the Board's statement of policy did not require a specific affirmation of that doctrine. How that issue merged with a persistent criticism of the organizational pattern of the Convention to eventuate, in the early forties, in demands for a more specific statement of doctrinal policy and the elimination of the Council on Finance and Promotion has been related.[17] It will be recalled, therefore, that in 1943 the Foreign Mission Society, when confronted with a doctrinal statement prepared by the Fundamental Fellowship as a more specific interpretation of that policy, reaffirmed its former "evangelical" position on the grounds that the Convention in 1922 had refused to make normative any creedal statements, preferring to abide solely by the New Testament. It will be recalled, further, how the Conservative Baptist Foreign Mission Society came into being late in 1943 as an agency for those who opposed the policy followed by the American Baptist Foreign Mission Society; and how at Grand Rapids, Michigan, in 1946, the

16 For a brief history, see *The Baptist Bulletin*, Vol. IX, No. 12 (May, 1944); also Vol. XII, No. 3 (August, 1946), The Year Book Number.

17 See Chapter Fourteen for further details on Convention organization; see also the following section on polity in this chapter. See pages 399-401 for reference to formation of new foreign mission society.

Convention again refused to adopt a confession of faith, preferring to subscribe only to the New Testament as the norm of faith and practice.

At the annual pre-convention meeting in May, 1947, at Atlantic City, New Jersey, the Conservative Baptist Fellowship of Northern Baptists (formerly the Fundamental Fellowship of the Northern Baptist Convention) organized The Conservative Baptist Association of America, to be "composed of autonomous Baptist churches without regard to other affiliations." During the following year a constitution was adopted which allowed membership to all Baptists who subscribed to its doctrinal platform and who refrained from fellowship or support of agencies which, in the opinion of the Association, followed the "inclusive" policy. Plans were projected for the establishing of societies for home mission and publication purposes, which would be in conformity to the policy already followed by the Conservative Baptist Foreign Mission Society, with which it was in accord.[18] In 1948 there was organized the Conservative Baptist Home Mission Society, with headquarters in Chicago.

Changing Emphases in Church Polity

The creation of more efficient organization so characteristic of big business at the close of the nineteenth century had a marked influence upon the development of polity in American churches. Its modifying effect upon the structure of Baptist enterprises was especially noticeable because of the simple autonomy of the local church. Yet, as we have seen, the organization of associations, state and national conventions, and national societies was a natural product of Baptist practice of interchurch co-operation in missionary and educational enterprises throughout their history. The changes which have marked the past fifty years have been concerned with a shift of organizational emphasis from the local church and association to state and national agencies. The churches thereby have become more dependent for leadership upon the state conventions than upon the local associations. There has also been among many Baptists a gradual growth of an ecclesiastical view of the church; that is to say, the local churches are conceived as constituting one corporate body. This trend has been particularly prevalent among many Northern

[18] *News Letter*, Vol. III, No. 4 (May, 1947) and ensuing issues.

Baptists who tend to conceive of the denomination as a Church within which the local churches operate.[19]

It is significant that at the dawn of the twentieth century, three important organizations came into being, two of them Baptist, the third interdenominational: the Baptist World Alliance (1905), the Northern Baptist Convention (1907), and the Federal Council of Churches of Christ in America (1908). The strengthening of denominational effectiveness and the development of a united Protestant witness were aims which to many Christians did not appear to be incongruous. Among Baptists there was more divergence of opinion than among other less radically Protestant communions. The continuance of that variance as Baptists react to the molding influence of the times—some seeking to comply, others to resist— provides the theme of this section.

As early as 1896 the American Baptist Missionary Union adopted a resolution, endorsed by the American Baptist Publication Society and the American Baptist Home Mission Society, calling for the appointment of a Commisssion on Systematic Beneficence to eliminate duplication of financial appeals by the various Societies to the churches. A Commission on Co-ordination was appointed representing the general societies and women's organizations. In 1901, at the May meeting of Northern Baptists at Springfield, Massachusetts, this Committee recommended: (1) that the same delegates be seated at meetings of all societies; (2) that a mid-year meeting of executive officers of the societies be called to co-ordinate their activities; (3) that the societies agree to make a joint appeal to the churches; (4) that a committee of nine be appointed to make further study and report in 1902.[20] The plan was carried out during the year, and at the May meeting in 1902, a committee of fifteen was named to make further study. In 1903 the committee advised against any merger of the societies.

After some delay a call was issued in 1906 for a general meeting of all the societies to be held in connection with the May meeting in 1907 at Washington, D. C. Accordingly, in the Nation's capital, the three general societies previously named met on May 16-17 at the

[19] S. L. Morgan, "Baptists Fifty Years Ago and Now," *The Chronicle*, Vol. IX, No. 4 (Oct., 1946), pp. 176-7.

[20] *The Watchman*, Vol. 82, No. 22 (May 30, 1901), pp. 10-7.

Calvary Baptist Church. Dr. W. C. Bitting of St. Louis, Missouri, who was to serve as Corresponding Secretary of the new organization for a period of twenty years, proposed that a committee of fifteen draft a plan of organization which would preserve the independence of the local church and yet provide co-ordination of denominational work. The product was not to be a legislative body.[21] The committee was appointed and undertook a task which was completed three years later.

At Chicago, in 1910, the Northern Baptist Convention was incorporated legally under the Laws of the State of New York. Charles Evans Hughes, Chief Justice of the United States Supreme Court, was its first president. The new organization, as stated in its declaration of purpose, was to provide a means of giving "expression to the opinions of its constituency upon moral, religious and denominational matters, and to promote denominational unity and efficiency in efforts for the evangelization of the world." [22]

The by-laws set forth several important provisions: (1) Delegates were to be appointed by the churches and co-operating organizations—not as, heretofore, on the basis of who contributed money, but of membership representation—with the voting privilege extended by each Society to all delegates seated in the Convention. (2) The Executive Committee was to be composed of officers, former presidents, and thirty others, fifteen of whom were to be laymen. The term of office was to be a maximum of six years. This Committee was to act for the Convention between sessions. (3) No salaried worker of the Convention was to have the right to vote on the Nominating Committee, although one member of the Executive Committee could be on it without vote. (4) The legal independence of each co-operating organization was guaranteed. Such co-operating societies were required to agree "to regulate expenditures in accordance with the budget to be annually approved by the Convention"; and "to solicit funds only on the approval of the Finance Committee given between the Annual Meetings of the Convention." [23] (5) The books of the co-operating agencies were to be subject to annual inspection by the Finance Committee. (6) The relationship between a

[21] W. C. Bitting, A *Manual of the Northern Baptist Convention, 1908-1918*, 9.

[22] *Ibid.*, 11.

[23] *Ibid.*, 12-4.

Society and the Convention could end on one year's notice from either party.

In 1919 the Convention's structure was altered at Denver, Colorado (May 21-27), upon recommendation of a Committee of five laymen which had been appointed at the preceding annual meeting at Atlantic City to plan a more effective and democratic organization. By 1920 a Board of General Promotion was created for the purpose of reviewing in the fall of each year the work of the Convention, of its Boards and Societies, and to make plans and prepare a budget for the ensuing year. Its purpose was to provide a representative, yet small enough planning agency for the Convention, since that body was deemed too large for deliberative planning sessions. In its membership were the Convention president, four members of the Executive Committee selected by that Committee, an administrative officer, and three members from the boards of managers of each co-operating organization of the Convention, one officer and one representative (either layman or clergyman) from each affiliated organization, one representative from each City Mission Society, and thirty-six members-at-large elected by the Convention. In the Board of Promotion a smaller Committee of Administration, composed of officials and six members-at-large from the churches, was projected.

This new agency was charged with the task of policy-making and promoting the five-year New World Movement which followed the First World War (1919-1924). In 1924 the name of the agency was changed to "The Board of Missionary Co-operation." For ten more years it carried on the promotional work of the Convention. Inasmuch as the Convention had come into existence at a time when theological controversy was developing between the advocates of liberalism and fundamentalism, it is not surprising that the usual fear of centralization, so characteristic of Baptists, should be accentuated. Almost from its inception voices were raised in warning that the new organization was a revolutionary step for Baptists to take.[24] For Northern Baptists, who had been accustomed for nearly a century to the society method of conducting their denominational enterprises, it was, indeed, a departure from traditional procedure. Some saw in the change a plan on the part of the theologically liberal

---

[24] *The Watchman-Examiner*, Vol. 7, No. 17 (April 24, 1919), p. 509.

element to gain control of the societies. Others saw the autonomy of the local churches threatened by the Board of Promotion, which they felt was in a position to impose a unified budget upon congregations that had little to say about its adoption. For these reasons, many refused to support the Board of Promotion in its task of raising funds for the societies.

In the midst of the lean years of the Depression, faced with criticism and a steadily declining income, the Convention, meeting at Washington, D. C., in 1933, appointed a Commission of Fifteen to restudy its organization in the light of historic Baptist democracy and to find an equitable basis of representation for co-operation without centralization. In presenting its report in 1934, the Commission said: "We have steadily sought to achieve simplicity, economy, and democracy of representation. We have, at the same time, tried to avoid the evils caused by the centralization of authority. We have believed that functions rather than the preservation of existing societies should determine the form of our denominational organization." [25]

The Commission recommended, in the interests of simpler organization, that the Board of Missionary Co-operation be abolished and its promotional work undertaken by a Council on Finance and Promotion, which should be representative of all Boards and Societies in the Convention. It also recommended that the Executive Committee be replaced by a General Council which should be an administrative agency for the Convention and to which the various committees of the Convention should be responsible. The General Council was to be composed of thirty members representing the East, West, and Central areas of the Convention, none of whom should be a salaried officer of any Board or Council of the Convention, plus the officers of the Convention. Between convention sessions, it was "to have all the powers vested in the Northern Baptist Convention and which the Convention has not expressly reserved to itself." [26] It was given wide powers, covering arrangements for meetings of the Convention; adoption of regulations, not in conflict with the constitution; appointment of subcommittees; nomination of members to the Ministers and Missionaries Benefit Board and to the

[25] Wm. R. McNutt, *Polity and Practice in Baptist Churches* (Philadelphia, 1935), 167-8.
[26] N.B.C., *Annual*, 1934, 125-52.

Board of Education; the right of one member to sit without a vote with the Convention's Nominating Committee; management and rent of all properties of the Convention; the right to borrow money in the name of the Convention; the authority to approve all special financial campaigns to be conducted by any organization participating in the Convention's Unified Budget.[27]

This new plan met with criticism similar to that raised against the old. Five years after these changes were placed in operation, Shailer Mathews, a long-time supporter of the Convention and one who had helped to draft its original constitution, warned Baptists against establishing unwittingly a presbyterial polity. Also symptomatic of a growing discontent, not unmixed with theological tensions, was the proposal made in 1945 by the executive committee of the Conservative Fellowship of Northern Baptists (formerly known as the Fundamental Fellowship), that the powers of the General Council be limited to those of a clearing committee of the Convention.[28]

Southern Baptists, in 1927, followed a similar course. They placed all of their Convention's fiscal and other affairs, not assigned to other agencies, in the hands of an Executive Committee, with headquarters in Nashville, Tennessee. This administrative unit of the Convention fulfilled functions which, in the Northern Baptist Convention, were held separately by the General Council and the Council on Finance and Promotion. In some respects, the Co-operative Program which the Southern Baptists adopted was not unlike the Unified Budget Plan of the Northern Baptist Convention. State Mission Boards had the responsibility of raising benevolent funds, a proportion of which was sent to the treasurer of the Southern Baptist Convention. Six states divided the Co-operative Program receipts equally between state and southwide work; in the others, the funds were divided in different ratios according to agreements made by each state convention or association. According to some Southern leaders, this disproportionate sharing of funds raised in the Co-operative Program has been a serious handicap to Convention activities, but it has been offset in some measure by large contribu-

---

[27] See Article IV of the Convention's By-Laws.

[28] Shailer Mathews, "Shall We Have a General Assembly?" *The Watchman-Examiner*, Vol. 34, p. 478; editorial, "What the Fundamental Fellowship Proposes," *News Letter*, Vol. I, No. 6 (June, 1945).

tions to Convention objects specially designated by interested individuals.[29] While there was considerable disturbance over the relation of the Southern Convention to the state conventions in the Co-operative Program, the situation was not complicated by theological tensions. The Southern Baptists had been accustomed to a single Convention organization with a direct control of its various Boards and agencies since 1845, and they were, therefore, less prone to chafe at the further development of a unified leadership centered in the national body.

There also appears to have emerged among the Baptists of the South, who were more than four times as numerous as Northern Baptists, a stronger sense of oneness and of loyalty to their Convention than has manifested itself in the North. A Baptist historian of the South notes what he calls a developing "ecclesiology" in the Southern Baptist Convention which he attributes to a combination of factors: (1) an early union of Baptist forces to protect themselves against persecution; (2) a General Baptist background with its more centralized polity; (3) a developing centralization in state conventions quite early in the nineteenth century; (4) a typically American criticism of the financial basis of representation which is inherent in the older co-operative society system; (5) pressure of the Landmarkists to substitute a *church* basis for the financial. Landmarkism appears to be the main source of this trend among Southern Baptists. This is not due so much to an adoption of their views by the Convention as to an almost unconscious absorption of their emphasis.

When the Convention declined to adopt a purely church basis of representation and was unwilling to accept certain other of their views, the Landmarkists of the Southwest began to withdraw. In March, 1902, they organized at Texarkana a General Association of Baptist Churches, composed of fifty-two churches. This was the beginning of a separation throughout the South over a difference in methods of conducting missionary operations and over church relations. It is related to the Gospel Mission controversy already mentioned; it is also related to a strong ecclesiasticism which traces the local Baptist church through a long succession back to primitive

[29] S.B.C., *Annual,* 1927, 64-72; Joseph T. Watts, *One Hundred Years of Southern Baptist History* (a pamphlet, Baltimore, 1945), 11-2.

Christian times, and which, therefore, rejects alien immersion, open communion, and non-Baptist ordination.

The emphasis upon the central idea of Landmarkism—the local church—has influenced Baptist thinking in many respects. "They make the church a member of the association, forgetting that the association was originally not an organization as we know it today, but a group of churches *associating* together for mutual help. They would make the convention composed of churches, regardless of the interest that the churches may have in the work of the convention. Beginning with a plea for due recognition of the churches, their ecclesiology results in the church being lost in the larger organization." [30] This influence, buttressed by the effect of the ideals and methods of modern commercial life upon the churches and by the growing habit of Baptists to look to their Convention leaders to speak for them on issues of faith, polity, and morals, has done much to develop what some regard as a tendency to ecclesiasticism within the Southern Baptist Convention.

While there are some evidences of the effect of similar factors upon Northern Baptists, the trend has not been so strongly in the direction of centralization as in the South. This has been due, in all probability, to the comparatively recent origin of the Northern Baptist Convention, to the maintenance of autonomous societies, affiliated with but not incorporated within the Convention, and to the ever-present tensions which have accompanied social, cultural, and educational developments among Northern Baptists.

Complexity, which is characteristic of the modern era, has invaded the churches. Indeed, the intricate pattern of Convention organization is but the counterpart of a similar trend in the local churches, where the minister's task as an administrator has become overtaxing because of the multiplicity of organizations and committees. The programs provided by Baptist "headquarters" for the guidance of ministers and churches have afforded a much-needed assistance to many with limited vision and ability; moreover, they have aided the development of a consciousness of fellowship and oneness. But in producing this uniformity it is possible that they have

[30] William W. Barnes, *The Southern Baptist Convention: A Study in the Development of Ecclesiology* (Fort Worth, Texas, 1934), 50. This excellent study is the basis for the foregoing discussion of the ecclesiastical trend in the Southern Baptist Convention.

weakened individual initiative and responsibility. What is most to be avoided is any trend toward institutionalism and ecclesiasticism by which the spiritual nature of the Baptist witness might be lessened or obscured.

Baptist polity has been affected by another development of the present century; that is, by the movement towards greater interdenominational co-operation. This is not to say that Baptists were unwilling to participate in interdenominational evangelistic and reform efforts in the nineteenth century, but rather that the degree of acceptance of comity agreements and united programs has increased. Receiving an impetus from the common needs of missionary boards, Baptists of the North and, to a lesser degree, those of the South co-operated with other denominations in the Home Missions Council, organized in 1908. Both Baptist groups participated in the Foreign Missions Conference of North America, established in 1893. They agreed to territorial delimitation of mission fields, as in the Philippines where Baptists, Congregationalists, Methodists, Presbyterians, and United Brethren were developing distinct fields under a comity agreement so as to present a united Christian front, and as in China where they were united with other denominations in the maintenance of collegiate institutions.

The Northern (called "American" since 1950) Baptist Convention has been a member of the Federal (called "National" since 1950) Council of Churches of Christ in America since the organization of that body in 1908. Southern Baptists have refrained from taking such a step because they feel that membership would impair the autonomy of the local church. Moreover, they regard the Council as being under the influence of theological liberals who "have magnified the implications of the gospel to the disparagement of the gospel itself." They also criticize the Council for the social emphasis of its program, holding that it promotes "class consciousness instead of social consciousness," and for its policy of pacifism with reference to war. Perhaps their most important argument against identifying themselves with this interdenominational agency is that it impairs the cause of religious liberty by reason of the number of denominations within it which maintain an incomplete conception of religious liberty, and whose parent bodies in Europe still enjoy the privileges of state churches.[31]

[31] W. R. White, *Baptist Distinctives* (Nashville, 1946), 81-4.

It is not surprising, therefore, that the Southern Baptist Convention declined an invitation to membership in the World Council of Churches on the grounds that such "a great over-all world ecclesiasticism would depend more on political pressure than upon spiritual power" and that "a close compact union of all non-Catholics would intensify the conflicts of Christendom" by arousing the Roman Catholics to an unprecedented rivalry. In addition, they claimed that membership in the World Council would threaten the autonomy of free churches and might jeopardize the witness of Baptists to believer's baptism and a regenerate church.[32] On this issue the Baptist World Alliance maintained a neutral position, holding that its member Unions and Conventions must make their own decision.[33] The Northern Baptist Convention, however, sent delegates to the first assembly of the World Council of Churches, meeting in Amsterdam, Holland, in the summer of 1948.

Generally speaking, Baptists have been less receptive to the interdenominational co-operation than many other communions.[34] This has been due largely to their unique anti-paedobaptist emphasis and to their fear of any encroachment upon the freedom of the local churches. Yet, such factors as the radio, the intermarriage of Baptists with those of other communions, the impact of the Second World War, the influence of education in behalf of ecumenicity, and the experience of Baptists in interdenominational missionary and religious education enterprises have contributed to the development of a stronger interdenominational feeling among them.

Trends in Education

The first half of the present century will be remembered among Baptists as a period of marked advance in educational emphasis, particularly observable in the development of a religious education program and in the strengthening of their schools of learning. In 1911 the Northern Baptist Convention established a Board of Education to provide co-ordination and promotion of the numerous academies, colleges, and seminaries within its sphere. Its executive secretary was Dr. Frank W. Padelford, who served in that capacity for twenty-nine

[32] *Ibid.*, 84-5; S.B.C., *Annual*, 1940, p. 99.

[33] B.W.C., *Proceedings*, 1939, pp. 132-4.

[34] Archer B. Bass, *Protestantism in the United States* (New York, 1929), 150 ff., 165.

years. Since 1900 seven new theological seminaries were established within the area of the Northern Baptist Convention, and in addition a number of Bible training schools. The seminaries include: Central Baptist Theological Seminary in Kansas City, Kansas, (1901); Berkeley Baptist Divinity School in Berkeley, California, (1904); Northern Baptist Theological Seminary in Chicago, Illinois, (1913); Norwegian Baptist Theological Seminary in Chicago, Illinois, (1913); the Spanish-American Training School in Los Angeles, California, (1921); the Eastern Baptist Theological Seminary in Philadelphia, Pennsylvania, (1925); and the California Baptist Theological Seminary in Los Angeles, California (1944). An additional seminary, not listed in the Northern Baptist Convention Yearbook, is the Western Baptist Theological Seminary in Portland, Oregon, (1927). The University of Redlands was founded at Redlands, California, in 1909; and two junior colleges were established: Bethel (now a four-year college) at St. Paul, Minnesota, in 1931, and Bucknell at Wilkes-Barre, Pennsylvania, in 1933.

Under the direction of the American Baptist Publication Society, there was developed an ever-widening program of religious instruction for children, youth, and adults through Sunday schools, vacation church schools, and week-day religious instruction.

This was accomplished through the Department of Religious Education, organized in 1909 by Dr. William E. Chalmers. It is significant that Baptists were the forerunners in both daily vacation Bible school work and week-day religious education on public-school released time. The former was started by Mrs. W. A. Hawes in July, 1898, in connection with the Epiphany Baptist Church of New York City. The latter originated in 1910 when the Reverend D. D. Forward, pastor of the First Baptist Church, Greeley, Colorado, was instrumental in securing adoption by the State Teachers' College, located there, of a plan to give credit to pupils who had done prescribed work in their church Bible classes. Roman Catholics joined Protestants in the plan, which spread to other states.[35]

Due largely to the efforts of Dr. Benjamin Griffith, general secretary of the American Baptist Publication Society, and the support given by that society, the Baptist Young People's Union of America was organized in Chicago in July, 1891. It was an organi-

[35] Lemuel C. Barnes, *et al.*, *Pioneers of Light*. (Philadelphia), 167-70.

zation *of* Baptist youth *for* Baptist youth. Under the direction of Edwin Phelps, its secretary, local and state unions were organized throughout the territory of the Northern Baptist Convention.

In the fall of 1895, the Baptist Young People's Union Auxiliary to the Southern Baptist Convention was launched in Atlanta, Georgia. Its first twenty-five years in the South were devoted exclusively to youth work; the second twenty-five years, to the development of the modern graded all-church membership training program known as the Baptist Training Union. The original B. Y. P. U. is still a department of the Baptist Training Union, which came into existence in 1934 and now includes also the Baptist Adult Union.

In the North, the B. Y. P. U. began in 1931 to plan for the ultimate unification of all youth-serving departments of all denominational agencies. At the Denison Youth Conference held in December, 1939, a plan to achieve this goal was envisioned. It came to be known as the Baptist Youth Fellowship. Through a "Discipleship Program" this organization is leading Baptist youth to a deeper understanding of the Christian life.

In the interests of greater efficiency and of a co-ordination of all the interrelated functions of Christian education, there was effected in 1944 a merger of the Board of Education of the Northern Baptist Convention and the Board of Managers of the American Baptist Publication Society. The new agency became known as the Board of Education and Publication of the Northern Baptist Convention, and its administration was assigned to Dr. Luther Wesley Smith, who served concurrently as executive secretary of the Publication Society and of the Board of Education. Young people's work, which first had been promoted by the Baptist Young People's Union of America, and then was made a function of the Council on Christian Education of the Northern Baptist Convention, was related administratively to this newly created denominational Board.

In February, 1944, another significant move was made when the Northern Baptist Assembly was established at Green Lake, Wisconsin, on a beautifully spacious estate purchased by the Convention upon the recommendation of the executive secretary of the Board of Education and Publication, and with the co-operation of all the national agencies of the Convention. The purpose of the new enterprise was to provide a national training and conference center for Northern Baptist leadership. Now known as the American Baptist Assembly, its Board of Managers is representative of the various co-operating agencies of the Convention.

Under the leadership of the Board of Education and Publication, a survey of theological training in the Northern Convention was undertaken between 1943 and 1945 under the professional direction of Dr. Hugh Hartshorne assisted by Dr. Milton C. Froyd. It was revealed that of the pastoral leadership in Convention churches, "31.9 per cent of the ministers have had no college training whatever, 9.8 per cent have had no more than high school and 22.1 per cent have had only theological training; and that 19.1 per cent of the ministers who are in the pastorate have had no theological training of any kind, either seminary or Bible institute." [36] Of the 68.1 per cent of ministers who have had some college training, one year or more, 19.8 per cent received it in Baptist colleges, 36.1 per cent in other colleges, and 12.3 per cent in theological colleges which are departments of the newer seminaries established since 1900. Schools of this latter type have made a significant contribution to the lifting of the educational preparation of ministers. "The number entering the ministry without college training has been cut from 38.6 per cent before 1920 to 23.2 per cent since 1935." Since 1935 "they have contributed 19.8 per cent of the college training of the entire ministry in the Baptist denomination." Because of their large enrollment, these schools have increased appreciably "the over-all output of the Baptist seminaries." [37]

The report further revealed that the percentage of university trained men had increased "from 12.8 per cent for the entrants previous to 1920, to 15.5 per cent for the entrants since 1935." Even the state university contribution had risen "during the same period from 5.6 per cent to 10.8 per cent." [38] While there has been an apparent gradual rise in the cultural and theological training of Baptist ministers, the total proportion of those having a standard college and seminary training has not increased appreciably beyond 36 per cent in a quarter of a century. At the same time, the number of

---

[36] Hugh Hartshorne and Milton C. Froyd, *Theological Education in the Northern Baptist Convention* (Philadelphia, 1945), 99-100.

[37] *Ibid.*, 102-3.

[38] *Ibid.*, 102.

ministers without training in *Baptist* schools approximates at least 53 per cent, a factor which represents a serious threat to the maintenance of a strong denominational emphasis.[39]

In the South, the picture is not any brighter, although a slowly rising educational standard for the ministry is evident. The strength of Southern Baptists lies chiefly in a virile Sunday school and youth-adult training program, which is under the direction of the Sunday School Board at Nashville, Tennessee. In 1944, under the guidance of Dr. T. L. Holcomb, the present Secretary, the receipts from its publications totaled more than four million dollars.[40] These earnings are used in the promotion of Sunday schools, Training Unions, and other denominational activities. Through an active program of promotion, the membership of Southern Baptist Sunday schools has increased from 492,292 in 1891 to 3,380,630 in 1944. During the next ten years, there was a gain of 250,000.[41] This provided an important field for evangelism, which has been contributory to Baptist growth in the South. The Sunday School Board was entrusted by the Convention, in 1944, with administration of the Southern Baptist Assembly at Ridgecrest, North Carolina, which is to Southern Baptists what Green Lake, Wisconsin, is to Baptists of the north.

In 1919 the Convention established at Birmingham, Alabama, the headquarters for a newly organized Education Board. The first years were characterized by ambitious undertakings which resulted in a large indebtedness, due to the failure of many churches to meet in full their subscriptions to the postwar Campaign for Seventy-five Million Dollars. Possibly not being ready for a permanent educational program, the Convention abolished the Board in 1928, appointing in its stead an Educational Commission without salaried officers or funds. The debts of the Board were transferred to the Executive Committee of the Convention and were paid in full. The Commission has continued to the present in a similar capacity to that of the Northern Convention's Board of Education. It published after 1936 a monthly periodical, *The Southern Baptist College News and Views,* which had a counterpart in the North after 1946 under several dif-

[39] Milton C. Froyd, "Are We Heading Toward Denominational Disintegration?" *Missions,* Vol. 37, No. 8 (Oct., 1946), p. 488.

[40] S.B.C., *Annual,* 1945, p. 315.

[41] Watts, *One Hundred Years of Southern Baptist History,* 7.

ferent names. The Commission also interests itself in guiding revival meetings held annually in the colleges.

From 1900 to 1950 five theological schools were established in the South: the Woman's Missionary Union Training School at Louisville, Kentucky (1907); Southwestern Baptist Theological Seminary at Fort Worth, Texas (1908); the Baptist Bible Institute, now New Orleans Baptist Theological Seminary at New Orleans, Louisiana (1917); the American Baptist Theological Seminary for colored students at Nashville, Tennessee (1924); and Southeastern Baptist Theological Seminary at Chattanooga, Tennessee (1948). At least two more colleges and five junior colleges came into existence in the same period. The aggregate endowment and property value of the eight academies, twenty-three junior colleges, thirty senior colleges and universities, and four theological institutions of the Southern Convention amounts to nearly seventy-three and one-half million dollars. By comparison, the Baptist educational institutions in the Northern Convention, comprising ten academies, eight junior colleges, ten schools for Negroes, twenty colleges and universities, three training schools, and twelve seminaries (including four ministering to specific national groups), have an aggregate endowment and property value of more than two hundred forty-one and a half million dollars.[42] The superior financial resources of Northern Baptists, who have less than one-fourth the membership of Southern Baptists, may be attributed to their higher income and their earlier interest in higher education.

In general, it may be concluded that interest in education among American Baptists has been heightened in recent decades in response to the challenge of a better trained public. However, the progress has been gradual owing to limited financial resources, to the fact that the churches have been dependent to so large a degree upon ministers whose own limited and inadequate training has made them unenthusiastic about education, and to the longtime and widespread suspicion among Baptists that education and spirituality are incompatible. Yet, the advance of recent years gives hope that in the matter of higher education they will attain a higher standing among the denominations than they now occupy.

[42] S.B.C., *Annual*, 1948, pp. 330-3; N.B.C., *Year Book*, 1948, pp. 528-31. The exact amounts are $73,432,192.62 and $241,691,049.42 respectively.

Other Changing Trends

In addition to the major shifts in emphasis just described, there are others which have become evident among American Baptists within the past half century. They touch a variety of interests which concern their social views, their anti-Catholic reaction, and their missionary emphasis—all of which have undergone some change in response to the modifying influence of an environment which has been in continuous flux. Since these topics are treated in some detail in other chapters, it will suffice here to interpret them in a summary fashion.[43]

Traditionally, Baptists in the United States have followed a Puritan pattern of conduct which they have required of faithful church members. In this respect, they have reflected the attitudes which Puritans in New England and Dissenters in Pennsylvania had brought to America. Church discipline, until the present century, was fairly consistent in maintaining a strict code of behavior. This code prohibited drunkenness, profanity, gambling, dancing, covetousness, negligence in church attendance, adultery, and a score of other sins. It was quite natural for them early in the nineteenth century to attempt to extend their code to the public generally in an effort to curb such evils as the liquor traffic, Sabbath desecration, legalized gambling, indecent standards of conduct in amusements, and unethical behavior in politics and business. As the impact of urbanization and industrialization was felt in American social life, Christian churches generally became increasingly active in reform efforts; in this, Baptists shared to an appreciable extent.

However, while the public conscience became more alert to social evils, other influences were at work which brought about a general lapse of church discipline. An almost universal reaction against the severity of Puritan standards combined with a modern interest in the psychology of human behavior to soften public opinion with respect to the subject of sin. Churches became loath to exclude members for minor misdemeanors which were not recognized by all Christians as sins. Protestants had doffed the cloak of strict Puritan righteousness without having found a suitable substitute. Indeed, many willingly kept the cloak without drawing it too tightly about them. With the

[43] See Chapters Fourteen and Seventeen in particular.

declining emphasis upon sin, the standard of conduct for church members in many cases dropped to the level of worldly respectability.

Accordingly, it may be observed that Baptist discipline of wayward members has become rare, except in cases of flagrant immoral conduct. As a substitute for the practice of exclusion, churches have preferred to "drop" names from the membership roll, a course of action which attaches to the delinquent no stigma of inquiry, charges and trial.[44] This practice may be viewed also as a tacit admission of the indifference to which the church is subjected by its nominal adherents.

It should be said, however, that a survey of the resolutions adopted by Northern and Southern Baptists in their national and state conventions and associational gatherings indicates a continued stand against intemperance, Sabbath desecration, gambling, and indecency in the motion picture industry. Toward family life, they have cast anxious eyes, seeking to encourage higher Christian standards without, however, taking a sharp stand against divorce. Indeed, there is evidence of a more liberal attitude toward divorce on the part of many church members and of some ministers. Similar trends are noticeable in the expressions of the Third Congress of the Baptist World Alliance.[45] Thus it may be concluded that Baptists still remain within the Puritan tradition, although their standards have been influenced by the changing mores of recent times.

With respect to problems arising from industrialism and the labor movement, Baptists, being chiefly of the working classes, have manifested a sympathetic attitude toward labor, while disavowing any radicalism. Undoubtedly the writings of Walter Rauschenbusch, the leading advocate of the "social gospel" at the turn of the century, inspired many to undertake an application of the teachings of Jesus to the problems in this area. The Baptist World Alliance has maintained a steady influence in behalf of the laboring man, while at the same time warning its constituency against socialism as a threat to the freedom of the individual. However, it has generally been true

[44] H. C. Vedder, "Fifty Years of Baptist History," and S. L. Morgan, "Baptists Fifty Years Ago and Now," *The Chronicle*, Vol. IX, No. 4 (Oct. 1946), 168-9, 173-4.

[45] Based on a sampling of records; see also B.W.C., *Proceedings,* 1923, pp. 218, 227, 237; for 1928, p. 36; for 1934, pp. 42-9, 50-6; for 1939, pp. 233-4. See also Torbet, *A Social History of the Philadelphia Baptist Association: 1707-1940,* chap. 11.

of Baptists that they have subordinated their social interest to their evangelistic concern.[46]

In their own ranks, however, there has been a growing sense of responsibility on the part of the churches for the care of aged ministers and missionaries. In evidence of this, one may point to the Ministers and Missionaries Benefit Board, which was organized by the Northern Baptist Convention in 1911, with headquarters in New York City; and to the Relief and Annuity Board of the Southern Baptist Convention, which has been in existence since 1918, with headquarters in Dallas, Texas.

The racial, national, and international tensions of the twentieth century have prompted expressions on the part of Baptists in behalf of peace and better interracial relations. In 1939 the Sixth Baptist World Congress interceded in behalf of persecuted Jews in totalitarian states. In 1941 the Social Service Commission of the Southern Baptist Convention reported a more generous and just attitude manifested toward Negroes by Education Boards in the various states. About the same time there was organized the Baptist Fellowship Center in Louisville, Kentucky, to encourage wholesome Christian contacts with the Negro race.[47]

Baptists have consistently opposed resort to war as a means of settling international disputes, but they have almost as consistently supported their country in the two world conflicts of the present century. During the period between the wars, the cause of pacifism received much encouragement; accordingly, when the Second World War broke, both Baptist Conventions were faced with the presence of conscientious objectors in their midst. Both bodies recognized the right of a conscientious objector to abide by his conscience, but neither appropriated funds for his support in labor camps. There were only one hundred and twenty-five so registered from nineteen states of the South. In the Northern Convention there were one hundred and seventy-three who chose to work in camps under civilian direction as provided by the Selective Training and Service Act of 1940. Indicative of the clergy's support of the war effort was the presence of

[46] *Proceedings of the First European Baptist Congress*, 1908, p. 232; see also B.W.C., *Proceedings*, 1905, pp. 265-8; for 1911, pp. 64-9, 365, 374-6; for 1923, pp. 64-6, 119; for 1928, pp. 36, 40-3, 237-9, 262-5.

[47] B.W.C., *Proceedings*, 1939, p. 38; S.B.C., *Annual*, 1941, pp. 126-7.

1,064 Southern Baptist chaplains and 547 Northern Baptist chaplains in the armed forces.[48] The quota of chaplains assigned to each Convention was filled without difficulty.

After both wars, Baptists shared in the public approval of plans for international co-operation. In 1919, through resolutions from local churches, associations, and conventions, and through Baptist periodicals, they backed President Woodrow Wilson's efforts to secure membership of the United States in the League of Nations. When his attempt was defeated by the triumph of isolationism, they expressed general chagrin and disappointment; but in the years that followed, the issue was lost sight of, for other interests emerged to demand attention.[49] As the Second World War drew to a close, American Baptists again gave expression to an international point of view by supporting the proposed United Nations. In 1944 the Southern Convention appointed a Committee on World Peace to express, mobilize, and register, where possible, the sentiments of its five and a half million members in behalf of lasting peace, a democratic world, Christian race relations, equal economic opportunity, and religious liberty. Dr. J. M. Dawson, chairman of the Committee, attended the Dumbarton Oaks Economic Conference in 1944 and the San Francisco Conference in 1945 to organize the United Nations. In the North, a similar position was taken.[50]

Large sums were raised for the purposes of world relief, aid to European Baptists, and the rehabilitation of demolished mission stations. To this end, Northern Baptists raised over sixteen million dollars in their World Mission Crusade, while the Southern Baptists contributed for world relief the amount of three and a half millions. Their combined contributions represented the Baptist portion of the one hundred and twenty-five millions raised by all Protestant denominations in America for relief and reconstruction needs.

In order to implement the chief political concern of Baptists, the preservation of religious liberty and the separation of church and state, the Southern Baptist Convention in 1936 extended the duties of its Committee on Chaplains of Army and Navy to include "all

[48] S.B.C., *Annual,* 1941, pp. 38-9; 1945, p. 27; *Home Mission Digest* No. II, (1945), p. 17; N.B.C., *Year Book,* 1945, p. 124.

[49] Ira D. Hudgins, "The Attitude of the Baptists of the United States Toward the League of Nations," *The Chronicle,* Vol. VI, No. 2 (April, 1943), 64-74.

[50] S.B.C., *Annual,* 1943, pp. 103-9; 1945, p. 61; N.B.C., *Year Book,* 1945, pp. 129-30.

matters involving the relations of our organized work to our own and other governments." The name of the committee was changed to that of the Committee on Public Relations. Dr. Rufus Weaver, a prominent pastor in Washington, D. C., until his death in 1947, was made its chairman. In 1937 the Northern Baptist Convention set up a similar type of committee with Dr. Gove G. Johnson, also of Washington, D. C., as its chairman. The following year, the two committees joined forces as a Joint Conference on Public Relations, to which were added representatives of the National Baptist Convention, U. S. A., Inc., and the National Baptist Convention of America (both Negro). The Conference represented a constituency of more than fourteen and a half million Baptists in the four conventions. Under the chairmanship of Dr. J. M. Dawson, the committee established offices in the nation's capital. These are strategically located when there is need for Baptists to defend religious liberty by raising their voices against encroachments of the state upon the church, and against what Baptists regard as Roman Catholic aggression in behalf of sectarianism in education and political favor.

The rising role of Roman Catholicism in the United States has stirred Baptists to fresh expression of anti-Catholic feeling. Two issues are of current interest. One has to do with the efforts of the Catholics to gain state support for the transportation of their children to parochial schools. The other was created by the appointment of Myron C. Taylor by the late President Roosevelt as his special envoy to the Vatican.[51] Basically it is a fear of their intolerance and political pretensions which underlies the universal attitude of Baptists toward Catholics.

In spite of the changing times, a vital concern for evangelism and the missionary enterprise still characterizes American Baptists. Always close to the common people, their message is set forth, for the most part, by men of simple background with plain and straightforward speech. The methods of evangelism are changing gradually from the older forms of revivalism to the more recent devices of visitation, radio broadcasting, and varied adaptations of mass evangelism, with an emphasis upon youth response. Among Southern Baptists, the perennial revivals held in the churches constitute an important source of new members. In 1944 the Southern Convention launched a Cen-

[51] For details, see Chapter Seventeen.

tennial Evangelistic Crusade under the leadership of Dr. M. E. Dodd of Shreveport, Louisiana. The plan called for the holding of an evangelistic crusade in every church in the Convention. In 1947 the Northern Baptists engaged in a Crusade for Christ through Evangelism under the leadership of Dr. Sidney W. Powell, pastor of Tremont Temple Baptist Church, Boston, Massachusetts. Thus Baptists in the postwar years sought to revitalize their spiritual life.

CHAPTER SIXTEEN

DEVELOPMENTS SINCE MID-CENTURY

THE face of the world had changed for most people by the middle of the twentieth century. Science had unveiled such new wonders concerning the universe that its very nature seemed to have changed. Space and time took on more meaning, and outer-space became a familiar term. The potentialities of these new sources of physical power for good or evil brought hitherto irreligious men to consider more closely the nature of man and his apparent incapacity to avoid self-destruction. The main achievements of the time were technological. Yet, religion, while growing in popularity among a fearful populace, lacked depth of insight and strength of conviction and purpose.

Society was changing also under the impact of rapid technological progress. From a predominantly family-centered people, Americans, at least, had been transformed into a highly organized mass-man without individuality or the zest to be different. Great urban expanses were changing the face of the countryside. Life was becoming more mechanized and standardized. Automation was rapidly replacing direct personal contact in the production of the good things of life. Impersonalized organization and collective action had all but displaced face-to-face relationships.

A greatly accelerated population growth had become a worldwide problem. Underprivileged nations faced the threats of an increasing scarcity of food and the breakdown of their outmoded and inadequate forms of government. More affluent countries, like the United States, had problems too. The concentration of humanity in great metropolitan areas increased diversity in race and culture; it sharpened the distinction between the "haves" and the "less-favored," between the suburbanites and the inner-city dwellers. Meanwhile the mobility of the population, accelerated during the war years, continued at a high rate, with close to a fifth of the families in the United States relocating each year.

457

Within a generation general education had arisen to a new level in American life, creating profound need for a professionally educated ministry in the churches. The accelerated growth of church membership and support which had been mounting since the war had begun to level off by the early 1960's, and there were signs of impatience with the irrelevancy of church programs and the platitudes of innocuous clergymen. At the same time, there was cause for social concern; crime, delinquency, and low ethical standards in business, professional and public life were increasingly prevalent. Moreover, in social welfare and racial integration, the role of the state, in public schools and other areas of public life, was in many instances greater than that of the church. Where the church did speak out, as in the case of the National Council of the Churches of Christ in the United States of America, loud protests against it were raised by a strongly reactionary segment of American Protestantism.

To the careful observer of American church life, there was little doubt that Protestantism was undergoing critical changes. It was losing much of its essential unity and cohesiveness in spite of the progress of ecumenical organizations like the National Council of Churches or the National Association of Evangelicals. This loss was caused partly, at least, by several factors: First, Protestants were becoming uneasily aware that they were no longer in a majority position in American society. Many were dismayed and perplexed to discover that they now lived in a religiously pluralistic society. Second, a Protestantism which basked in the achievements of the nineteenth century was ill-prepared for the rapid changes of the twentieth century. Third, sectarianism, which had harassed Protestants during the nineteenth century, had intensified denominational distinctions. These factors were aggravated further by such successful expansion in membership and resources that even those churches open to participation within the ecumenical movement were not likely to sacrifice their vested interests, even for so lofty an ideal as Christian unity. Fourth, Protestantism was unprepared theologically for the new era. Having become something of a culture-religion in American life, Protestantism had accommodated itself to such an extent to the mores and values of the social order that it had forgotten its faith and mission.

Indeed the character of Protestantism was changing.[1] The "growing edge" lay outside of what might be called "co-operative Protestantism," as found in the National Council of Churches. The Southern Baptist Convention, largest of Baptist bodies (which had grown from 4,949,174 members in 1940 to 9,731,591 in 1960), and the Missouri-Synod Lutheran Church, which had enjoyed a similar rate of increase, stood firmly apart from the ecumenical movement. An analysis of Protestant church statistics for 1960 showed two facts: One, that the fastest growing communions were among the non-co-operative bodies; two, that a third force was emerging within Protestantism composed of three sizeable new groups which differed in temper and spirit from the older major denominations. These new groups were the Fundamentalists, the Holiness groups, and the Adventist bodies. Their combined membership totaled some thirty million as compared with slightly more than the forty million in the thirty-four member bodies of the National Council of Churches. Because this third force was vocal and aggressive in its conservatism, it was identified by the unchurched public with American Protestantism in general.

As a result of the complex situation in which a changing Protestantism found itself, the churches were faced with a number of major problems. First was the need to recover a sense of identity and mission within a pluralistic society. A second problem, closely related to the first, was the need of each denomination to determine its relationship to co-operative Protestantism and to overcome divisive influences within its midst. A third problem was what Professor Robert T. Handy has called the danger that the churches will get tied down to defending the rapidly disappearing nineteenth-century synthesis of Protestantism with American culture (which was predominantly middle-class and "small town" in mentality) instead of making its understanding of the Christian faith relevant to people who live in a radically changed society. A fourth problem that confronted the churches was how to overcome the fragmentation and compartmentalization of modern life, as a result of which their members committed only a part of themselves to the life of the church. This all called for a serious challenge to the basic dichotomy in Western culture which had separated reason from faith, science from religion,

[1] Winthrop S. Hudson, *American Protestantism* (Chicago, 1961), chap. 3. This presents an excellent analysis of Protestantism in what Hudson calls "post-Protestant America."

theory from practice, and proclamation of the Word from action.[2]

That many Protestants were seriously engaged in confronting such problems cannot be denied, but that others were either indifferent to them or distracted from their solution must be regretfully admitted. Nonetheless, it is within this setting that Baptists were at work and that their achievements were to be measured.

Changing Currents Among Baptists

To many, diversity seems to be the main characteristic of Baptists. It stems in part from their origins and development, which were open to many influences as we have seen. While the main influence in the Baptist tradition has been the Reformed faith, with such emphases as the sovereignty of God, the Lordship of Christ, the centrality of the Bible, the primacy of faith, and the nature of the Christian life, other currents have also played upon it. Among these have been the Anabaptist-Mennonite spirit of the seventeenth century, the pietist and enlightenment movements of the eighteenth century, and the revivalist and later liberal currents of the nineteenth century. The very diversity of these influences and the openness of Baptists to them has led to a blurring of what really has distinguished Baptists throughout their history.

Their heterogeneity was intensified during the twentieth century by at least two internal factors; one relating to theology, the other to polity. The relative indifference of Baptists to theology made it possible for the various currents flowing in modern religious life—pietism, revivalism, conservatism, liberalism, fundamentalism, and neo-orthodoxy—to have a heavy and fragmenting impact upon their church life. They lacked a strong unitive theological frame of reference, like the Calvinism of earlier years, to serve as a norm and a balance. Their polity also contributed to their heterogeneity. The earlier balance between the congregational and associational principles had given way during the nineteenth century to an exaggerated emphasis upon congregational autonomy, minimizing or neglecting the interdependence of the churches in associations. This trend led to needless and harmful diversifications.

In addition to these internal influences, there have been environ-

[2] From an address delivered by Professor Handy of Union Theological Seminary, New York City, to the American Baptist Education Association in Minneapolis, June 15, 1962.

mental factors to which Baptist churches have been vulnerable and which have intensified their heterogeneity. Among these have been the influences upon the churches of the class, sectional, and racial contexts in which they were located.[3] These markings have contributed to the social, cultural, and racial stratification of the churches to the extent that such factors are more responsible for Baptist heterogeneity than are theological differences.

Still another influence contributing to diversity among Baptists has been the rising spirit of conservative reactionism in American life in the 1950's. This was an expression of popular fear in the face of a series of communist victories in Cuba and Laos, and in the Soviet Union's successful launching of the first man into outer space. It was also a reaction against unrelieved taxation and social welfare developments in government. A focal point of attack was the National Council of Churches, which, since its organization in 1950, had inherited the liberal reputation of one of the organizations it had absorbed, the Federal Council of Churches. When it expressed, through various study commissions and departments of its work, viewpoints on social issues which favored a liberal policy with respect to integration, economic injustice, or foreign policy, it was charged with encouraging socialism or even communism. Well known church leaders were accused of communist sympathies on the basis of association at one time or another with organizations which were thought to have been fronts for communist activities. Since Russia had been an ally of the United States during the Second World War, there were a number of these organizations and agencies which were then very respectable, but fell out of favor when public opinion changed towards Russia during the post-war period.

In 1960 a list of 660 Baptist clergymen was released by Circuit Riders, Inc., condemning them for having been affiliated with organizations "soft" on communism.[4] This was part of a growing rightist attack upon member denominations of the National Council of Churches for so-called pro-communist sympathies.

When the American Baptist Convention met in Rochester in June, 1960, the issue of continued membership in the National Coun-

[3] Walter G. Muelder, "Institutionalism in Relation to Unity and Disunity," Paul S. Minear, ed., *The Nature of the Unity We Seek* (St. Louis, 1958), 90-102.
[4] *A Compilation of Public Records—660 Baptist Clergymen* (Cincinnati, 1960).

cil of Churches was raised by representatives of the First Baptist Church of Wichita, Kansas. Charging that the National Council was communistic, a demand was made that the Convention withdraw from membership. The General Council of the Convention presented a resolution reaffirming its continued participation in the National Council of Churches and reaffirming the right of any local church to express dissent and withhold its financial support from the National Council and to be so listed in the official Yearbook. After an orderly debate, by a ratio of ten to one the Convention approved the resolution of the General Council, thereby settling the issue of continued participation in co-operative Christianity.[5]

Unhappy over the decision, a majority of 739 members of the Wichita Church later that summer voted to withdraw from the American Baptist Convention, the Kansas Baptist Convention, and the Wichita Association of Baptist Churches to protest the denomination's affiliation with the National Council of Churches. The voting minority of 294 members sought a court injunction to prevent the church property from passing into the hands of the majority. This precipitated a two-year court action which resulted in a decision of the Kansas Supreme Court in May, 1962, that the First Baptist Church of Wichita might not be withdrawn from the American Baptist Convention even though a majority of the congregation voted for such an action. In reversing a decision of a state district court, the Supreme Court declared that "not even in an autonomous Baptist church may the denomination of the church be changed by a mere majority vote."[6] The minority was sustained on the grounds that it, rather than the majority, continued to perpetuate the principles of the parent body, and so was entitled to retain the property as the traditional First Baptist Church of Wichita.

Sensing the injustice of attacks made upon the Convention and some of its leaders, including Dr. Edwin T. Dahlberg, then president of the National Council of Churches, the General Council of the American Baptist Convention, at its mid-year meeting in Chicago, November 1-2, 1961, adopted a resolution addressed to the Congress of the United States. It expressed a concern and an affirmation—deploring:

[5] *Missions,* Vol. 158, No. 6 (June, 1960), 24.
[6] *Christianity Today,* Vol. 6, No. 18 (June 8, 1962).

. . . the release by congressmen, for general distribution, of unproved and unevaluated material secured from the House Committee on Un-American Activities. This material gives the false impression that certain of our outstanding American religious leaders are associated with communism. . . .

We reaffirm our opposition to communism and protest guilt by association and the un-American practice of holding a man guilty until proved innocent.[7]

Southern Baptists were being troubled by other stresses affecting the South during this same period. Although they continued to enjoy in the 1950's a large degree of homogeneity culturally and theologically, there were signs of an encroaching diversity within the Southern Baptist Convention. The racial integration issue, heightened by a decision of the United States Supreme Court in 1954 which declared segregated public schools unconstitutional, created an uneasy tension throughout the South. In 1954 and again in 1959 and 1961, the Southern Baptist Convention voted resolutions urging acceptance of the decision by the churches and calling upon Negro and white Baptist leaders to engage in mutual planning to assist racial reconciliation. Reports of the Christian Life Commission annually included recommendations to lessen racial tensions, but implementation was slow.[8]

An equally controversial issue faced Southern Baptists when biblical literalists began to attack the seminaries of their Convention for harboring professors who they believed challenged the historical accuracy and infallibility of the Bible. The main centers of attack were Southern Baptist Theological Seminary at Louisville, Kentucky, the oldest and most venerable of Southern Baptist schools for training ministers, and Midwestern Baptist Theological Seminary, the newest institution, founded in Kansas City, Missouri, in 1958. This story, which is told later in this chapter, is indicative of tensions rising within the Southern Baptist Convention as a consequence of conflicting cultural levels in leadership. Unfortunately, these tensions were intensified by the higher educational standards which were coming into existence.

As Baptists sought to relate themselves to this complex period of

[7] *Crusader,* Vol. 16, No. 11 (Dec., 1961), 3.
[8] For resolutions see the Southern Baptist Convention *Annual* for 1954, p. 56; for 1959, p. 78; for 1961, p. 84. For "Reports of the Christian Life Commission," see consecutive issues of the *Annual* from 1954 to 1960.

change, they were confronted by the need to identify themselves within the movement toward co-operative Christianity, which emerged in the twentieth century. In their quest, they became painfully aware of the harmful effects of an exaggerated individualism in their common life. But their reactions differed. Some engaged in rigorous self-criticism in an effort to re-evaluate their tradition and relate themselves meaningfully to other communions. Others intensified their self-consciousness and thereby deepened the sectarianism which had developed in the nineteenth century, most notably in the Landmark movement.[9] The former group became impatient with the misguided devotion to religious freedom which they saw in the insistence of many Baptists that every church member had the right to think as he liked about the Christian faith, "with no specific relationship either to the Scriptures or to the fellowship of the faithful, and yet remain in full standing." There was a growing sentiment in favor of the proposition that "Baptist-congregational-associational polity is one which calls for free but responsible cooperation in every level of the church's life, with a proper balance of freedom and order at each level."[10]

American Baptists sought to penetrate the ever-widening urban centers of American society by several means. One was a re-evaluation of the mission of the church in urban areas which took place in two significant urban convocations held in 1958 in Indianapolis, Indiana, and in 1961 in Minneapolis, Minnesota. The second was a search for a new approach to evangelism during the years of the Baptist Jubilee Advance (1959-64), a joint effort of the major Baptist bodies in North America looking toward the sesquicentennial celebration of the beginning of nationally organized Baptist work. Through vocational evangelism, an emphasis upon the Christian's daily witness through his work, and through a deepening understanding of the mission of the church to social frontiers, an effort was being made to reach the unchurched and to broaden Baptists' understanding of the true role of the laity. A third means of penetrating the urban centers was to encourage the interracial integration of church membership. In 1957 the American Baptist Convention voted to oppose segregation and

[9] See pp. 281 ff. for an account of Landmarkism.

[10] Drawn from an analysis of Baptist church life in *Theological Education in the American Baptist Convention: A Report of the Committee of Seventeen* (Valley Forge, Pa., 1962). Mimeographed.

called upon its member churches to determine membership on merit, "without regard to race or national origin."[11]

A fourth means was the development of a more adequate ministerial leadership. To the present, American Baptists have made more progress in this respect than have Southern Baptists, whose predominantly rural milieu has changed more slowly. Both groups show hopeful signs of developing a leadership more adequate for the changing times. Since 1950 American Baptists have been engaged in theological studies through regional and national conferences held under the supervision of a Theological Advisory Board related to the Board of Education and Publication of the Convention. During the same period a study of theological education has been conducted, culminating in a Report of the Committee of Seventeen. This committee was appointed by the Convention in 1960 and made its report to the Convention in 1962. Southern Baptists have added to their list three new seminaries since 1950: Golden Gate Theological Seminary in the San Francisco Bay area, Southeastern Baptist Theological Seminary at Wake Forest, North Carolina, and Midwestern Baptist Theological Seminary in Kansas City, Missouri. If seminaries constitute the intellectual centers of church life, both conventions' concern was well placed.

American Baptists Come of Age

Already we have noted that the American Baptist Convention, which had been basically a rural denomination, was by mid-century fast becoming urban. Their problem, therefore, was to discover how to adjust their nineteenth-century pattern of church life and thought to the needs of the emerging metropolitan society. The traditional residential base of Christian witness, with its center of activities within the organizational church structure, had rapidly been left on the fringe of the new center of modern urban society where the power structures were anchored in the planning commissions of metropolitan areas. The average church member's life was no longer centered in the residential community which he called home; he worked in one community, often shopped in another, and at times attended a church in still another. Moreover, the vital centers of direction for the complex social relationships of the emerging metropolis were not in

[11] *Crusader,* Vol. 12, No. 6 (June, 1957), 2-11; *The Watchman-Examiner,* Vol. 45, No. 26 (June 27, 1957), 583-98.

the residential community where suburban churches might be located. For this reason, the professional clergy found themselves removed from the areas of strategic influence. The problem of how the church might still fulfill its role of interpreting the will of God to the social order called for a new understanding of the function of the laity.

Within the ecumenical movement, especially since the war, European Christians had been rediscovering the meaning of the lay apostolate, the whole people of God called to witness to their faith in the world. Increasingly it became clear, on the grounds of the biblical meaning of the church, that the Christian vocation (or calling) was not to be restricted to a class of professional clergymen. This insight was reinforced by the changing structures of modern urban society, where the real centers of influence were in the economic, social, and political areas of life. If the Christian witness was to be felt, it must be exerted by dedicated laymen and laywomen in these areas of their daily life and work.

Such were the issues being faced by the first urban convocation of American Baptists held in Indianapolis in 1958.[12] When a second convocation, on the general mission of the church, was held in Minneapolis in January, 1961, delegates were surprised to discover that there had been a steady shift in the Convention from town-country to urban churches. Although three-fifths of the congregations were still classified as town-country (in communities of less than ten thousand population), about two-thirds of the total membership within the Convention were in urban churches serving communities of more than ten thousand population. This trend was especially noticeable on the West Coast, where sixty-one per cent of the churches were in urban communities. There American Baptists were experiencing their greatest growth, and the trend was toward larger churches, with multiple staffs and programs designed to adjust to social and cultural changes. In the northeastern part of the nation, which had one half of the churches, the majority of congregations were relatively small and in smaller communities. Although the Convention had lost some churches and others had been consolidated, a total of 719 new churches had been established since 1950, while the total membership had been increasing by about 11,500 members per year since 1955.[13]

[12] Paul O. Madsen, "No Easy Answers to the Problems of the Urban Church," *Missions,* Vol. 156, No. 1 (Jan., 1958), 21-23.

[13] James A. Scott, *The 1960 American Baptist Census* (New York, 1960), 23-26.

The approach to penetrating the American metropolis was calling for more than new methods and strategy. It was calling for an understanding of a conformist, highly organized society in which the familial-residential community life was becoming increasingly separated from the social order where the basic decisions of American economic and political life were being made. It was calling also for a re-evaluation of the purpose of the church and a review of its nature. Concurrent with the sociological analysis of the complexion of American Baptist churches and the society in which they found themselves was the development of a broader and deeper concept of evangelism under the leadership of Dr. Jitsuo Morikawa, director of evangelism for the American Baptist Home Mission Societies. His stress upon the lay apostolate witnessing through their vocations had an important effect upon the understanding of the ministry within the Convention. In this, Baptists were reflecting the new insights drawn from the biblical and theological renaissance in Protestantism. The role of the minister as a *pastoral-ruler* was being challenged in favor of a *pastoral-director* or teacher of the church preparing the laity to fulfill its vocation of Christian witness within the various structures of the social order.[14] The new emphases were revolutionary to Baptists steeped in the pietistic individualism of traditional American Protestantism which defined the role of the minister as the authority figure leading his congregation in a program of church-centered activities, often quite aloof from the world in which the members spent most of their time.

The overseas mission of American Baptists was likewise undergoing transition. At mid-century, fully two-thirds of all churches related to the missionary enterprise were self-supporting. There were 3,706 schools, enrolling more than 188,000 students. Medical service was an established part of all mission undertakings except in Japan and Bengal-Orissa. The number of missionaries in 1951 was one-half the peak figure of 800 in 1923-24. The decline was due largely to higher costs involved in sending and maintaining missionaries abroad in a period of inflation. It was also because of the enlarged role of the nationals in their own leadership and administration of their church life.[15] This process of transfer of leadership extended in some

[14] H. Richard Niebuhr, *The Purpose of the Church and Its Ministry: Reflections on the Aims of Theological Education* (New York, 1956), 82-83.

[15] *Missions*, Vol. 149, No. 1 (Jan., 1951), 21-25.

areas to the actual transfer of property ownership and control of mission funds, as in the case of the Burma Baptist Convention. By the 1960's the American Baptist Foreign Mission Societies were engaged in planning consultations with overseas leaders participating as equals. Even in the new Congo Republic (1960) the churches maintained a significant degree of stability in the face of civil strife and confusion in the transition from colonial supervision.

The American Baptist Home Mission Societies were wrestling with the changing character of a very mobile and complex American society. Through a variety of means the ministry of the gospel was being brought to bear upon human need. Among these projects were the Christian Americanization program conducted for first-generation immigrants, an expansion of Christian Centers for underprivileged people within the inner city of metropolitan areas, a program of juvenile protection to offset the rising delinquency of the post-war period, a continuance of the relocation of displaced persons from Europe begun during the war, the continued development of a trained ministry for the town-country churches which still constituted sixty per cent of the total in the Convention, a program of co-operation with chaplains in the armed services, a broadening of the concept of evangelism through the Department of Evangelism begun in 1919, and the study of the problems of the inner city in the great metropolitan areas.[16] This variety of ministries was indicative of the complexities of modern society and the creative efforts being made to meet the changing needs.

A further indication of American Baptists' efforts to adjust to the enlarging dimensions of their task was the intensified program of reorganization which occupied the attention of the Convention from 1950 to 1962. The Convention in 1950 created the office of general secretary, established a denominational journal called *Crusader,* and called upon the four national mission societies (home and foreign) to amalgamate.[17] In 1952 the General Council of the Convention began a series of studies, analyzing the problems confronting American Baptists and recommending a closer co-ordination of the work of the national societies and state conventions and city mission societies.[18]

[16] *Ibid.*, 26-31.
[17] *The Watchman-Examiner,* Vol. 38, No. 24 (June 15, 1950), 591-614.
[18] *Crusader,* Vol. 6, No. 9 (Feb., 1952), 6.

In 1953 the Convention, meeting at Denver, Colorado, approved a survey to be made of its business operation and structure by the American Institute of Management, and voted to launch a Church Extension Campaign to establish new churches.[19] While the two actions were not related in the minds of the delegates, they did reveal the concern of the Convention with growth and efficiency of operation.

In 1955 the General Council, fresh from its study of the American Institute of Management Report, called for a realignment of all convention agencies in the interest of consolidation within a single headquarters building. The first steps in this direction were taken when the Convention approved the Council's proposal and voted for the amalgamation of the boards of the two home and two foreign mission societies respectively. The location of a site for headquarters precipitated a prolonged debate within the Convention between the advocates of the newly projected Inter-Church Center to be built in New York City and those who favored a mid-west location. The issue was complicated by a consideration of sectional interests within the Convention and by opposition from a vocal segment to locating in the Inter-Church Center, which was to them a symbol of deepening involvement of the Convention in the ecumenical movement.[20] Many felt that New York City represented a psychological disadvantage as the site for headquarters, an attitude which reflected the general antipathy of traditional American Protestantism to the emerging metropolitan culture of the nation's life.

In 1956 at Seattle, Washington, the Convention adopted a plan for the reorganization of its general structure which created a widely representative staff committee on program co-ordination, enlarged the membership of the General Council from thirty to thirty-six, and entrusted to that body responsibility for administering the work of the Convention. A Commission on Evaluation and Recommendation, composed of nine members, was appointed to review the progress of organizational changes and to report to the Convention in 1958.[21] A year later American Baptists meeting at Philadelphia voted to launch a campaign to raise 7.5 million dollars to strengthen the support of its colleges, seminaries, and campus ministry to students. At the same

[19] *The Watchman-Examiner*, Vol. 41, No. 24 (June 11, 1953), 573-602.

[20] *Crusader*, Vol. 10, No. 2 (June, 1955), 1-10.

[21] *Missions*, Vol. 154, No. 6 (June, 1956), 20-27; American Baptist Convention, *Year Book* for 1956, 64-70.

time the Convention approved participation with other Baptist bodies in a five-year program of evangelism to be known as the Baptist Jubilee Advance (1959-64).[22]

When the American Baptist Convention met at Cincinnati in 1958, a prolonged debate on the location of headquarters underscored an uncertainty about such a move to centralize and a resistance from the Mid-West to a location in the Inter-Church Center in New York City. In opposition to the recommendation of its duly appointed study commission, the Convention rejected the New York site, failed to marshal enough votes for Chicago, and settled on a compromise site at Valley Forge, Pennsylvania. In the light of these developments, the editor of *Crusader* called this meeting "the People's Convention."[23]

A year later a more placid and agreeable Convention met at Des Moines, Iowa. Dr. Edwin T. Tuller was elected as its second general secretary to succeed Dr. Reuben E. Nelson, whose failing health had prompted his premature retirement. Dr. Nelson died in the following January, 1960, bringing to an untimely close a rich and useful life as a Christian statesman of unusual stature and breadth of ecumenical vision.

In May of that year the Convention at Rochester, New York, showed new signs of maturity and responsible leadership in handling difficult issues. The question of headquarters was settled by a decision to approve the erection of a building at Valley Forge at a cost of eight million dollars. The Convention's response to a minority proposal to discontinue participation in the National Council of Churches, described earlier in this chapter, indicated a strong conviction that involvement in co-operative Christianity was not inconsistent with a Baptist witness. The Convention received assurance of the success of the Campaign for Christian Higher Education. The delegates demonstrated an unusually deep concern for the crucial issues calling for Christian answers—the threat of nuclear war, racial tensions, religious intolerance, the economic needs of under-developed countries, and the spread of communism.[24]

At the fifty-fourth annual meeting of American Baptists in Port-

[22] *Missions,* Vol. 155, No. 6 (June, 1957), 20-25.

[23] *Crusader,* Vol. 13, No. 4 (April, 1958), 2-6; *The Watchman-Examiner,* Vol. 46, No. 28 (July 10, 1958).

[24] *Missions,* Vol. 158, No. 7 (Sept., 1960), 15; *Crusader,* Vol. 15, No. 7 (July-Aug., 1960), 4.

land, Oregon, in June, 1961, the long-developing plan of reorganization was completed. The General Council was to include thirty-six
voting members elected by the Convention and fifty non-voting members from the incorporated boards, the co-operating societies, and the
affiliated organizations. The chief executives of the Foreign and
Home Mission Societies, of the Board of Education and Publication,
and of the Ministers and Missionaries Benefit Board were to become
associate general secretaries of the Convention. The general secretary
was to be assisted by the traditional associate general secretary and
two newly created associate general secretaries for program and research respectively. The reorganization was interpreted as a development of the Convention from a loosely united confederacy in 1907 to
a true federation or union in 1961.[25] A year later, at Philadelphia,
the Convention delegates made a pilgrimage on May 26 from Independence Hall, where they reaffirmed their principle of religious
liberty, to Valley Forge to dedicate the headquarters building which,
in its circular design, symbolized the organizational unity which had
been achieved.

Still unresolved for American Baptists was the problem of disunity among Baptist bodies within the United States, the degree to
which they should become more involved in the deepening ecumenical
developments within Protestantism, and the quest for self-identity and
a discovery of the true meaning of the church and ministry in a
rapidly changing culture. In some respects American Baptists had
come of age; in other respects they stood with uncertainty upon the
threshold of a new age.

Southern Baptists in an Era of Growth

Southern Baptists at mid-century were engaged in unprecedented
expansion. In 1950 there were 27,788 churches with 7,079,889 members. Their Sunday church school enrollment had passed the five
million mark. Nearly one and a half million were enrolled in Sunday
evening training unions. The Sunday School Board reported net
sales for 1949 amounting to $9,377,237. Through thirty-four book
stores, fifty-five million pieces of its own literature were distributed
in addition to a general book trade. More than ninety per cent of

[25] *Missions,* Vol. 159, No. 6 (June, 1961), 22.

Southern Baptist churches were using the literature prepared by the Sunday School Board. Church property was valued at more than $645 million. The budget for 1950 Convention enterprises exceeded $10.5 million, one-third of which was spent for overseas missions. The Foreign Mission Board supported 803 missionaries; the Home Mission Board, 779. There was little doubt that Southern Baptists had entered upon an era of growth and big business.[26]

Within fifty years, church membership had increased 300 per cent; Sunday church school enrollment, 542 per cent; training union enrollment, 1,600 per cent; baptisms had mounted from 80,000 in 1900 to 334,864 in 1949; gifts from $2,500,000 to $178,000,000. The Convention supported 22 orphanages, 25 hospitals, 5 theological seminaries, 28 senior colleges, 24 junior colleges, and 8 academies. The Home Mission Board reported to the Convention meeting in Chicago in May, 1950, a total of 1,030 missionaries, including 251 student workers, and 167 new churches and 517 missions spread throughout the nation. He promised that the Board would expand its ministry wherever there were unchristianized areas throughout the land.[27] The old geographic limits of Southern Baptist work were a thing of the past. Indeed the holding of the Convention in a northern city for the first time symbolized the new era.

Accompanying this burst of expansionist enthusiasm was an intensification of denominational self-consciousness. A Committee on Common Problems of the Southern Baptist Convention reported to the Chicago Convention through its chairman, Dr. T. C. Gardner, pastor in Dallas, Texas, that Baptists who do not have distinctive doctrinal convictions have no reason for existence. He affirmed that membership of Baptists in the World Council of Churches would weaken their "age-long struggle for separation of church and state" and would open them to theological liberalism. Comity agreements, he insisted, would violate cherished Baptist doctrines such as believer's baptism, a regenerate church membership, soul competency, and salvation by grace.[28]

The phenomenal growth of Southern Baptists within less than a

[26] "Southern Baptists: Big Business for the Lord," *Crusader*, Vol. 5, No. 10 (March, 1951).

[27] *The Watchman-Examiner*, Vol. 38, No. 21 (May 25, 1950), 513.

[28] T. C. Gardner, "Four Common Problems of American Baptists," *The Watchman-Examiner*, Vol. 38, No. 22 (June 1, 1950), 538.

generation (a gain of four million members) was attributed by a leading Protestant weekly in 1951 to the following reasons: (1) The movement of southerners west and north had scattered intensely evangelistic Southern Baptists who, in turn, multiplied themselves. (2) In urban areas and small towns of the South, Baptist churches had become identified with the dominant middle class which controlled the prevailing cultural patterns. (3) Southern Baptists held the allegiance of rural people. Indeed, their ability to recruit rural Baptists who moved to town gave their churches a numerical lead over other denominations. (4) The Southern Baptists' emphasis upon local church independence had made it possible to retain the allegiance of churches of widely diverse attitudes in rural areas. (5) The stress upon fellowship and sociability had given a sense of identity to the individual and allowed room for lay leadership in church life. (6) A rising social consciousness among Southern Baptists had resulted in their exerting some influence against racial demagoguery and bitterness. (7) Their stress upon the plain reading of the Bible, devoid of theological complexity, held a strong appeal for the uneducated.[29]

In 1957 Southern Baptists returned to Chicago for their annual convention, claiming to be America's fastest growing denomination. They reported a rise in the number of churches from 27,788 in 1950 to 30,834 in 1957, and an increase in membership from 7,079,889 to 8,703,823 during the same period. The value of church property had doubled since 1951, exceeding $1.5 billion. Indicative of expanding needs for new leadership, the Convention voted to establish a new seminary in Kansas City, Missouri, to be known as Midwestern Baptist Theological Seminary. Although the preponderance of Southern Baptist churches were in rural and small town areas, the Home Mission Board was engaged in a *Cities for Christ* emphasis. The number of urban churches had risen to nearly one-fourth of the total.[30]

The spiraling denominational statistics continued. By 1959, church membership surpassed nine million and total contributions reached nearly $420 million. Yet, a Stewardship Commission was established by the Convention to raise additional funds. The Foreign Mission Board maintained an overseas staff of 1,283 missionaries—

[29] Charles G. Hamilton, "What Makes Southern Baptists Tick?" *The Christian Century*, Vol. 68, No. 4 (Oct. 3, 1951), 1125-26.
[30] *The Watchman-Examiner*, Vol. 45, No. 25 (June 20, 1957), 559, 568; *Word and Way* (Missouri Baptist Journal), Vol. 95, No. 10 (March 6, 1958), 5.

387 in Africa, Europe, and the Near East; 465 in the Orient; and 431 in Latin America. New work was begun in 1959 in six additional countries: Vietnam, Nyasaland, Northern Rhodesia, Guinea, France, and Okinawa, bringing the total to forty-four. Seventy-three per cent of the 3,269 churches on Southern Baptist mission fields were self-supporting.[31]

By 1961 the total Southern Baptist membership reached nearly the ten million mark; the churches, which numbered 32,598, were to be found in every state of the Union. Contributions to all causes surpassed $501 million. Yet there were signs that all was not well. Since 1959 baptisms had declined by about 30 per cent. Enrollment in the six theological seminaries had dropped from 4,004 in 1957 to 3,406 in 1959.[32] Some observers believed that Southern Baptists were feeling the general decline in religious enthusiasm in American life. Others saw signs of reaction against a stereotype of church life which reflected a rural American pietism that no longer challenged thoughtful youth.

When the Convention met in San Francisco in June, 1962, a smoldering dissatisfaction with the teaching in the theological seminaries (referred to earlier in this chapter) burst into open controversy. The advocates of a literal interpretation of the Bible had for some time been critical of scholars in the seminaries who had been moving cautiously "toward the biblical criticism accepted by most other Protestant denominations, which suggests that parts of Holy Scripture are symbolically valid but literally impossible."[33] The most notable case in point was a book published in 1960 by the denominationally-owned Broadman Press, *The Message of Genesis,* written by Dr. Ralph Elliott, professor of Old Testament and Hebrew at Midwestern Baptist Theological Seminary. He reflected the more moderate judgments of Protestant biblical scholarship by positing that more than one person might have had a hand in writing Genesis, by suggesting that certain of its stories might be considered in the same category as the parables of Jesus, and by regarding the name of Adam as a symbolic term for all mankind, and the Flood as regional in extent rather than universal. He was accused of denying the historicity of the first

[31] *The Watchman-Examiner,* Vol. 47, No. 24 (June 11, 1959), 495, 503-5; *The Baptist World,* Vol. 7, No. 5 (May, 1960), 13-14.

[32] *Newsweek* (New York), March 12, 1962; *The Tie* (Southern Baptist Seminary monthly), Vol. 29, No. 8 (Oct., 1960), 2.

[33] *Time* (New York), Vol. 79, No. 24 (June 15, 1962), 69.

eleven chapters of Genesis and challenging the inerrancy of the Bible.

The Convention's Executive Committee, hoping to avoid open controversy, recommended the creation of a special committee to study the possibility of rewriting the statement of faith and purpose adopted by the Convention in 1925 (a modified and extended version of the New Hampshire Confession). Although the recommendation was adopted, the attack upon the seminaries could not be side-stepped. The issue broke into heated controversy, led principally by leaders from Texas, Oklahoma, Missouri, and California. They presented a series of resolutions designed to rid the Convention of heresy. By an overwhelming standing vote, the delegates reaffirmed "their faith in the entire Bible as the authoritative, authentic, infallible Word of God." This was followed by adoption of a resolution which expressed the Convention's objection to any theological views presented in the seminaries which threaten to undermine "the historical accuracy and doctrinal integrity of the Bible," and requested the trustees and administrative officers of the schools to remedy such situations at once.[34] A third resolution to ban Professor Elliott's book was rejected under pressure from the moderates within the Convention, who supported the denominational publishers' assertion of their freedom to publish any book which was "in keeping with the historic Baptist principle of the freedom of the individual to interpret the Bible for himself."[35]

Observers reported that the Southern Baptist Convention had, for the time being at least, averted a crisis. Schism had been avoided, but at the price of an uneasy truce with the forces of traditional conservatism within the Convention. Southern Baptists, who had remained virtually unaffected by the modernist-fundamentalist controversy of the 1920's, were feeling the first effects of the biblical and theological renaissance. This renaissance had displaced the modernism of the earlier period with a neo-reformation theology which allowed room for a broader view of biblical inspiration and interpretation.

Other Baptist Bodies

Among the bilingual Baptist church groups affiliated with the American Baptist Convention at mid-century were two whose rela-

[34] *Ibid.* Also cf. *Christianity Today,* Vol. 6, No. 19 (June 22, 1962), 25, and *The Christian Century,* Vol. 29, No. 26 (June 27, 1962), 818, 825.

[35] *The Christian Century,* Vol. 29, No. 12 (March 21, 1962), 350.

tionship to the Convention underwent change. The first was the Norwegian Baptist Conference of America, whose work had become so closely integrated within the structures and unified budget of the American Baptist Convention as to render continuance of a separate organization unnecessary. Accordingly, the Conference was dissolved in 1956 and the assets were distributed to support the work of the American Baptist Convention.[36]

The second was the Baptist General Conference of America, composed traditionally of Swedish Baptist churches who had maintained a close relationship with the American Baptist Home Mission Society and the American Baptist Publication Society even before there was an American Baptist Convention. But unlike its Norwegian counterpart, the Baptist General Conference loosened its ties with the Convention after 1944. This divergence was partly due to the same dissatisfaction with the so-called "inclusive" policy of the American Baptist Foreign Mission Society which had resulted in the withdrawal of the Conservative Baptists from the Convention in 1944. Another reason resulted from a plan for reorganization of the Conference into a self-sufficient denomination with its own boards and agencies for home and foreign missions, education, and publication work. When reorganization occurred in 1945, there were within the General Conference thirteen district conferences in the United States and two in Canada, embracing a total of 320 churches which reported 40,224 members.[37]

Conservative in theological outlook, the Baptist General Conference oriented itself, in its wider contacts, toward the National Association of Evangelicals, rather than the National Council of Churches. With a strong evangelistic impulse, its foreign mission outreach extended by 1960 into six fields—Burma, Assam, Japan, the Philippines, Ethiopia, and Brazil. The total number of missionaries had increased from eight in 1945 to 117 in 1960. Meanwhile, at home, the number of churches in the Conference had multiplied sixty per

[36] Peder Stiansen, "Contribution of the Norwegian Baptist Conference of America," *The Chronicle,* Vol. 20, No. 1 (Jan., 1957), 44-48.

[37] David Guston and Martin Erikson, eds., *Fifteen Eventful Years; A Survey of the Baptist General Conference, 1945-1960* (Chicago, 1961), 10-17.

cent in the same period, reaching a total of 536 with more than 72,000 members.[38] The Conference supported Bethel College and Seminary in St. Paul, Minnesota, and maintained a national headquarters center in Chicago, Illinois.

The Conservative Baptist Association of America, formed in 1947 by a group of churches dissatisfied with the refusal of the American Baptist Convention to require a creedal test of membership, had grown by 1961 to 1300 churches. It was described by its leaders as "a back-to-the-Bible fellowship of autonomous churches, dedicated to soul-winning, missions, church planting and the defense of the faith and is opposed to modernism, all forms of theological inclusivism and ecumenicalism."[39] It supported four theological institutions, three colleges, and two Bible institutes. Its world mission outreach was conducted, through a staff of 390 missionaries sent out by the Conservative Baptist Foreign Mission Society, to the Congo, Europe, Israel, South America, India, French West Africa, Formosa, Japan, and the Philippines. The Conservative Baptist Home Mission Society worked through 94 missionaries in Alaska, Mexico, and unchurched areas in the United States.[40]

Negro Baptists continued to function at mid-century through two major conventions, the National Baptist Convention U.S.A., Inc., and the National Baptist Convention of America, which had a combined membership of nearly eight million. Both bodies were participants in the National Council of Churches and the World Council of Churches. In 1961 a third convention was formed when delegates from fourteen states met in Cincinnati on November 15 to withdraw from the National Baptist Convention U.S.A., Inc., and organize the Progressive Baptist Convention of America. The new convention was in effect a protest against the failure of the National Baptist Convention to limit the tenure of its officers at its meeting in Kansas City, Missouri, in the preceding September.[41] It also reflected, as its name suggested, a desire for a more orderly church life and higher standards of ministerial leadership.

[38] *Ibid.*, 17, 73-130.

[39] *A News Release* of the Conservative Baptist Association of America, announcing the eleventh annual meeting, June 25-July 1, 1958. See also Bruce L. Shelley, *Conservative Baptists: A Story of Twentieth-Century Dissent* (Denver, 1960), 33 ff.

[40] *Christianity Today,* Vol. 5, No. 19 (June 19, 1961), 29-30.

[41] *The Baptist Herald* (Richmond, Va.), Vol. 18, No. 8 (Oct., 1960), 2, 6; *The Christian Century,* Vol. 78, No. 51 (Dec. 20, 1961).

Reactions to Ecumenical Trends

Although Baptists were divided in their attitude toward the growing ecumenical movement, they were united, with few exceptions, in acceptance of the Baptist World Alliance as a broadly denominational expression of Christian fellowship. When the Eighth Congress of the Alliance met in Cleveland, Ohio, in July, 1950, delegates were present from twenty-two countries. They found a common platform in a "Mid-Century Call to Religious Freedom" and were united in a program of world relief for their fellow Baptists in war-torn countries. They had contributed more than nine million dollars and relocated hundreds of displaced persons in new homes in the United States, Britain, Australia, Brazil, Argentina, and Israel. When some American Baptist delegates sought to pressure the Congress toward ecumenicity, their efforts "were received good-naturedly and were soon submerged by the greater enthusiasm for Baptist tenets and principles, and particularly the ideal of the New Testament church."[42]

Ten years later, thirty thousand Baptists from sixty-eight countries on six continents assembled in Rio de Janeiro, Brazil, on June 26, 1960, for the opening of the Tenth Congress of the Baptist World Alliance. They represented upwards of twenty-three million Baptists in more than one hundred countries. Voting delegates numbered 12,800. This was the first Congress outside of the United States, Canada, or Europe (the Congress of 1955 was held in London).

The Congress of Rio de Janeiro reflected the rising importance of the smaller Baptist groups, including many from the newly emerging nations of Asia, Africa, and Latin America. They were moving into the center of the Alliance to share the leadership previously assumed by Baptists of the United States and Europe. Symbolic of the new leadership in the Alliance was the election of a Brazilian to the presidency. He was Dr. John F. Soren, pastor of the First Baptist Church in Rio de Janeiro. Nine vice presidents were selected from six continents. Dr. Arnold T. Ohrn, general secretary of the Alliance since 1947, entered retirement and was succeeded by Dr. Josef Nordenhaug, president of the Baptist Theological Seminary at Ruschlikon, Switzerland.[43]

[42] John W. Bradbury, "Report of the Eighth Congress of the Baptist World Alliance," *The Watchman-Examiner*, Vol. 38, No. 3 (Aug. 17, 1950), 811; Vol. 38, No. 34 (Aug. 24, 1950), 825.

[43] *Missions*, Vol. 158, No. 7 (Sept., 1960), 20-25; *Crusader*, Vol. 15, No. 7 (July-Aug., 1960), 8-9; *The Baptist World*, Vol. 8, No. 1 (Jan., 1961), 3.

The one effort of Baptists in the United States to merge with another communion was conducted unsuccessfully between American Baptists and the Disciples of Christ. In 1908 conferences had been held between Free Will Baptists, Northern Baptists (renamed American Baptists in 1950), and the Disciples. Although Free Will Baptists merged successfully with the Northern Baptist Convention in 1911, the separation between the Disciples and Baptists continued. In 1928 overtures were resumed as a result of an address by Edgar DeWitt Jones, a Disciples minister from Detroit, at the Northern Baptist Convention. The proposal was opposed in 1929 by Professor Frederick L. Anderson, of the Newton Theological School, on doctrinal grounds. Between 1930 and 1947 efforts were again made to develop union. Among the advocates of the merger was Hillyer H. Straton, American Baptist minister in Detroit from 1939 to 1945. In 1944 both conventions appointed members to a Joint Commission. Conversations continued and in 1949 the Joint Commission established a time-table for the merger to be completed by 1955. When American Baptists met in convention at Chicago in 1952, the plan was already defeated, although a joint communion service was held with the Disciples of Christ. The conversations broke down because of opposition from Baptists in the Mid-West and the West on the grounds that the Disciples taught baptismal regeneration. The effects of the Campbellite controversy of the nineteenth century had not been entirely forgotten. While this was no doubt an issue, many felt that the main factors were institutional rather than theological—a fear that merger would result in defection of those who opposed it from the American Baptist Convention to the Southern Baptist Convention.[44]

Eleven Baptist bodies were among the 197 communions holding membership in the World Council of Churches in 1962. They were the American Baptist Convention, the Burma Baptist Convention, the Union of Baptist Churches of Cameroon (admitted in 1961), the Baptist Union of Denmark, the Baptist Union of Great Britain and Ireland, the Baptist Church of Hungary, the National Baptist Convention of America, the National Baptist Convention U.S.A., Inc., Baptist Congregations in the Netherlands, the Baptist Union of New Zealand, and the Seventh Day Baptist General Conference. These

[44] Franklin E. Rector, "Behind the Breakdown of Baptist-Disciple Conversations on Unity," *Foundations*, Vol. 4, No. 2 (April, 1961).

constituted approximately forty per cent of the total Baptist world membership of twenty-four million. Dr. Ernest A. Payne, general secretary of the Baptist Union of Great Britain and Ireland, was elected vice-chairman of the Council's Central Committee at its Second Assembly at Evanston, Illinois, in 1954, and re-elected for a second term at the Third Assembly in 1961 at New Delhi, India. Four other Baptists shared seats with him in 1961 on the Central Committee of one hundred: U S'Aye, president of the Burma Baptist Convention, Joseph H. Jackson, president of the National Baptist Convention U.S.A., Inc., Paul Mbende, president of the Cameroon Baptist Union, and Edwin H. Tuller, general secretary of the American Baptist Convention.[45]

Summary

From this survey of developments among Baptists in the period, 1950-62, we may make certain generalizations. First, Baptists in the United States have become increasingly identified with the dominant culture patterns of modern society, a trend which has contributed in part to their growth and rise in economic status and in part to their preoccupation with organization and program activities calculated to produce growth and denominational prestige. Second, Baptists around the world are divided in their understanding of their role in world-wide Christianity. The majority prefer to stand within their own tradition, bearing their witness through the Baptist World Alliance. A growing minority see their role in relationship to other communions within the ecumenical movement, bearing a witness to their free church tradition, but also learning and being enriched by association with other Christian traditions.

Third, Baptists have yet to re-evaluate fully their mission. Once a despised sect bearing their witness at a fearful cost, they have become numerically a leading communion within Protestantism. Once a rural people, they are rapidly becoming urbanized and sophisticated. Once a people of simple faith in the Christian verities of a Calvinistic theology, they are becoming better educated but less knowledgeable in how to interpret the Christian faith to a generation conditioned by technology and materialism. They must determine how to preserve

[45] *The Baptist World*, Vol. 9, No. 1 (Jan., 1962), 7; Vol. 9, No. 2 (Feb., 1962), 4.

what is valid and of permanent worth in their tradition and relate it meaningfully to the total Christian witness in a world which longs for the healing of its divisions and for the miracle of wholeness and peace.

CHAPTER SEVENTEEN

BAPTIST CONTRIBUTIONS TO PROTESTANTISM

WHILE the principles held by Baptists may be traced back to the primitive Christian church, the historical beginnings of Baptists as a distinct group, as was shown in earlier chapters, may be dated from that era in the development of Christianity in which evangelical Protestantism took its rise as a reform movement. The Protestant leaders generally raised their voices in protest against the medieval axiom that traditionalism shared equal authority with the Sacred Scriptures in matters of faith and polity. They also stood diametrically opposed to the practice of hierarchical control vested in a priesthood which was regarded as superior in character and sacred office to the lay believers. In the third place, they represented an equally strong protest against that system of sacramentalism whereby the grace of God was understood to be administered by material means and through an ordained priesthood. On a closely related point, they found fault with the doctrine of merit according to which good works are deemed efficacious for salvation.

With respect to these basic tenets of Protestantism's revolt against medieval Catholicism, the Baptists who represented a left wing position in the reform movement, made the most far reaching contribution by carrying each principle to its consistent end, thereby strengthening the Protestant position. To some, this view may come as a surprise, inasmuch as the Anabaptist teachings of the sixteenth century have been all but forgotten by many students of the Reformation. Their teachings have been ignored by many because they represented a thorough-going consistency which Luther, Zwingli, and Calvin would not allow; that is to say, the Anabaptists, in their insistence upon going all the way in conformity to the Scriptures, repudiated the practice of infant baptism and the principle of religious intolerance. As we survey the survival and modification of their teachings as set forth by their spiritual descendants, the modern Baptists, we note in them a remarkable contribution to the Protestant cause.

482

Doctrinal Contributions

In the first place, it may be observed that Baptists, to a greater degree than any other group, have strengthened the protest of evangelical Protestantism against traditionalism. This they have done by their constant witness to the supremacy of the Scriptures as the all-sufficient and sole norm for faith and practice in the Christian life. All through the history of the Christian church, there have been minority groups who have sought to restrict the basis for church doctrine and polity to biblical teaching. Accordingly, such spiritual forebears of Baptists as Peter Waldo, John Wyclif, and John Huss, challenged the extra-biblical practices of celebrating the sacrifice of the mass for the dead, of granting indulgences for sins yet to be committed, of encouraging sacred pilgrimages, worship of the saints, and an excessive emphasis upon ritualism. For their pains, they were persecuted severely by a church which accepted the principle that tradition occupies a position of equal authority with the Scriptures.

It was Balthasar Hubmaier, that stalwart Anabaptist, who dared to challenge Zwingli on this very point. He insisted, in a conference with the Swiss reformer, that "in all disputes concerning faith and religion, the Scripture alone, proceeding from the mouth of God, ought to be our level and rule."[1] Baptists have maintained this consistent stand through all the centuries that have followed Hubmaier's day, even at the expense of their personal safety. An examination of the earliest confessions of English Baptists reveals reliance upon Holy Scripture alone. The articles of faith proposed by John Smyth, the English Separatist refugee who was converted to the Anabaptist position in Amsterdam in the early seventeenth century, set the pattern for all later Baptist confessions of faith by providing Scripture references for every statement.

But even more significant is an article in the "Declaration of Faith" drawn up by Thomas Helwys in 1611 just before his little group, which had broken with Smyth, returned to England to give that country a Baptist witness in the face of persecution. In Article 23, he wrote:

That the scriptures off the Old and New Testament are written for our instruction, 2. Tim. 3.16 and that wee ought to search them for they testifie off

[1] Henry C. Vedder, *Balthasar Hübmaier, the Leader of the Anabaptists.* (New York, 1905), 59.

CHRIST, Io. 5:39. And therefore to bee used withall reverence, as conteyning the Holie Word off God, which onelie is our direction in al things whatsoever.[2]

Still more specific is the statement in the famous London Confession drawn up in March, 1660, by the General Assembly of some twenty thousand General or Arminian Baptists for presentation to King Charles II. Article 23 reads as follows:

That the holy Scriptures is the rule whereby Saints both in matters of Faith, and conversation are to be regulated, they being able to make men wise unto salvation, through Faith in Christ Jesus, profitable for Doctrine, for reproof, for instruction in righteousness, that the man of God may be perfect, throughly furnished unto all good works, 2 Tim. 3. 15, 16, 17. John 20.31. Isa. 8:20.[3]

Likewise, did seven churches of Calvinistic or Particular Baptists in London set forth the same view in their Confession of 1644 when they wrote in Article 7:

The rule of this Knowledge, Faith, and Obedience, concerning the worship and service of God, and all other Christian duties, is not man's inventions, opinions, devices, lawes, constitutions, or traditions unwritten whatsoever, but onely the word of God contained in the Canonical Scriptures.[4]

The same use of Scriptures became prevalent among American Baptists, for in 1742 the Philadelphia Association published as its Declaration of Faith another Calvinistic Confession which had been drawn up by London Baptists in 1689. This, in turn, became the pattern for most Baptist associations organized in the late eighteenth and early nineteenth centuries. That the principle of the supremacy of the Scriptures had not been lost sight of is evident from the very influential New Hampshire Confession of Faith, which was drawn up in 1830 to offset Arminian teaching in New England. In it there is a more specific statement concerning the Scriptures than is to be found in any earlier confessions. Moreover, its importance in the minds of its authors is evident from the fact that they made it Article 1:

We believe (that) the Holy Bible was written by men divinely inspired, and is a perfect treasure of heavenly instruction; that it has God for its author,

[2] W. J. McGlothlin, *Baptist Confessions of Faith,* (Philadelphia, 1911), 91.
[3] *Ibid.,* 119.
[4] *Ibid.,* 176.

salvation for its end, and truth, without any mixture of error, for its matter; that it reveals the principles by which God will judge us; and therefore is, and shall remain to the end of the world, the true centre of Christian union, and the supreme standard by which all human conduct, creeds, and opinions should be tried.[5]

Indeed, it may be conjectured that American Baptists, cut off from European traditionalism to a greater extent than was true of their overseas cousins, laid even more stress than the latter upon this principle. It may be said without hesitancy that Baptists generally have quite universally placed their uncompromising faith in the authenticity of the Sacred Writings through divine inspiration of the writers by the Holy Spirit, and have stressed the necessity of Bible reading by every Christian for himself. Moreover, while they have frequently followed the practice of voluntarily accepting and adhering to a confession of faith as an expression of their understanding of the teachings of Scripture, they have refrained from elevating such man-made statements to the position of uniform authority given to ecclesiastical creeds.

In another respect, it may be observed that Baptists have made a doctrinal contribution by strengthening and making more consistent the protest of evangelical Protestantism against the Roman Catholic system of sacramentalism and meritorious work. While Luther and Zwingli virtually admitted that there was no justification in the Scriptures for a mixed membership, that is to say, of both regenerate and unregenerate members, both leaders failed to apply the principle of the authority of the Scriptures consistently. By retaining the practice of paedobaptism and the union of church and state, they continued an ecclesiastical system which inadvertently perpetuated the evils of an unregenerate church membership. It was for Anabaptists like Hubmaier and Denck to withstand Zwingli on this point at the peril of their lives. Concerning baptism, Hubmaier wrote as follows:

But the right of baptism of Christ, which is preceded by teaching and oral confession of faith, I teach, and say that infant baptism is a robbery of the right baptism of Christ, and a misuse of the high name of God, Father and Son and Holy Spirit, altogether opposed to the institution of Christ and to the customs of the apostles.[6]

[5] McGlothlin, *Baptist Confessions of Faith*, 301-2.
[6] Balthasar Hübmaier, *Short Apology*, cited by Vedder, *Balthasar Hübmaier*, 204.

Like their spiritual forebears, Baptists of later generations have embraced a concept of the church as a body or fellowship of the regenerated, in contrast to the concept of the church as an organization embracing all who are born within its geographic confines and who have received its sacraments from birth to death. Their view has cost the lives of numerous men and women who refused to lend support to a state church composed of both regenerate and unregenerate. It was this conviction, rather than any debate over the *mode* of baptism, which caused Anabaptists and Baptists to lay down their lives rather than to present their infants for baptism into a state church of mixed membership. They defended their stand by pointing to the absence in the New Testament of any teaching to substantiate either infant baptism or baptismal regeneration.

Stress was not laid on the manner of baptizing, for it appears that the earliest Anabaptists did not practice immersion, resorting instead to affusion. At least, this was true of Hubmaier. However, Grebel and some of the later Anabaptists did practice immersion, although many continued affusion—but in every case it was *believer's baptism*. As the full significance of believer's baptism became uppermost in their minds, English Baptists, as we have seen, practiced immersion exclusively. The first Baptist church to specify that mode was Spilsbury's Particular Baptist Church in London, in 1638. Six years later, seven such churches drew up a document known as the London Confession, which defined the mode of baptism as immersion. Since then, there has been among Baptists general agreement on that subject.

Baptists generally have regarded the Lord's ordinances as expressions of spirit and life, rather than of matter and form. They have held that, to the regenerate heart, Christ's finished work on Calvary precludes any dependence on meritorious works as a means of salvation. Baptism and the Lord's Supper, therefore, have been viewed as symbols of a deed already completed, not as fragments of a divine grace continuously being expended for believers.

Two further contributions to Protestantism in this respect possibly may be attributed to Baptists. The first is that their anti-paedobaptist teaching very likely has influenced such paedobaptist denominations as Presbyterians, Congregationalists, and Methodists to give to infant baptism a status very much akin to a dedicatory ceremony.[7] The second contribution is one which will be considered in more detail later in this chapter, namely the fact that the Baptist emphasis upon conversion as a requisite to church membership has caused them to be strongly evangelistic. Suffice it to say here that this has been a strong factor in the development of the Protestant foreign missionary movement and in the progress of Protestantism in the United States.

Contributions in Polity

Baptists have strengthened and gone beyond evangelical Protestantism's protest against hierarchical control. In this respect, they have made a contribution to the development of polity in Christendom. The Protestant Reformation was essentially an attack upon the worldliness and authoritarianism of the papal court at Rome. Luther and Zwingli both taught the priesthood of believers in opposition to the Roman Church's priesthood of an ordained hierarchy. In this, the Reformers were right, but in the application of their principle, they fell short; for they did not give to the congregations, particularly in Germany, the right to interpret the Scriptures and to control their churches.

In order to guarantee the Scriptural teaching that all believers are their own priests before God, having free access at any time to God the Father for spiritual comfort and forgiveness of sins through the one and only High Priest, Jesus Christ our Savior, Baptists consistently have opposed the making of any distinction between clergy and laity that savors of sacerdotalism. Moreover, for the same reason, they have refrained from excessive ritualism and the use of priestly garments.

This democratic principle is at the heart of Baptist polity and largely explains the tremendous popularity and appeal of the denomination in the development of the religious life of the United States. The Baptist pattern of congregational polity, which was the logical expression of the teaching of the priesthood of believers, was widely received by frontier people who desired in their religious life the same freedom which they expected in the political and social life. In states where Baptists were notably numerous, such as Kentucky, Indiana,

[7] Shailer Mathews, "The Social Influence of the Baptists," an article in I. Boone, *Elements in Baptist Development*, (Boston, 1913), 153.

and Illinois, the democratic quality of their state constitutions, as they entered the Union, undoubtedly reflected Baptist thinking, and in turn influenced the older seaboard states appreciably toward a more liberal form of government.

Needless to say, the Baptist emphasis attracted the rank and file of men and women—so much so that historians frequently refer to Baptists as "the church of the common people." In addition, their congregational polity enabled them to withstand schisms and other crises more successfully than did many religious bodies which were hampered by a greater degree of centralized church government. Moreover, the emphasis upon local autonomy has been an important factor in preserving the precious spirit of democracy. In fact, the churches and the associational and convention bodies have afforded an opportunity for experience in self-government. The Baptist emphasis upon the worth of the individual has given recognition to the truth that the foundation of democracy is spiritual rather than material.

An important corollary of their teaching concerning a regenerate church membership has been an insistence upon holy living. This has had the effect of spreading widely a sanely pietistic emphasis in the religious life of America, an emphasis which otherwise might have been restricted to such small, localized sects as the German Brethren and the Mennonites. Thus there has been a wholesome moral influence exercised by this denomination whose members are numerous and close to the pulsating heart of America.

Baptists have made a unique contribution to Protestantism, for which the world is their debtor, in their consistent witness to the principle of religious liberty. Belief in this principle has been founded upon the Scriptural truth that the individual is responsible solely to God for his eternal destiny. While the germ of this tenet lay dormant in Luther's teaching concerning the right of private interpretation of the Bible, Luther lacked the courage to permit such freedom lest it destroy his state-church connection. It was left, therefore, to Anabaptists and Baptists to maintain consistently, and at times to defend with their lives, the right of individuals and groups to worship God in their own way and to believe or disbelieve.

This principle was set forth clearly in the writings of John Smyth in the early seventeenth century. In Article 84 of his long

Confession of one hundred articles of faith prepared in 1612 by the little English congregation at Amsterdam, Smyth wrote these strikingly memorable words which comprise one of the earliest statements in behalf of religious liberty:

> That the magistrate is not by virtue of his office to meddle with religion, or matters of conscience, to force or compel men to this or that form of religion, or doctrine: but to leave Christian religion free, to every man's conscience, and to handle only civil transgressions (Rom. 13), injuries and wrongs of man against man, in murder, adultery, theft, etc., for Christ only is the king, and lawgiver of the church and conscience (James 4:12).[8]

Thomas Helwys, at about the same time, expanded Smyth's plea for liberty of conscience in a book entitled, *A Short Declaration of the Mistery of Iniquity*. His was the first claim for freedom of worship published in England where a state church insisted upon religious conformity. It read, in part, as follows:

> Let the King judge, is it not most equal that men should choose their religion themselves, seeing they only must stand themselves before the judgment seat of God to answer for themselves . . . [We] profess and teach that in all earthly things the king's power is to be submitted unto; and in heavenly or spiritual things, if the king or any in authority under him shall exercise their power against any they are not to resist by any way or means, although it were in their power, but rather to submit their lives as Christ and his disciples did, and yet keep their consciences to God.[9]

An even stronger word in the inscription to this book, written about 1613, brought him imprisonment in Newgate Prison by order of King James I; it read:

> The King is a mortall man and not God, therefore hath no power over y immortall soules of his subjects to make lawes and ordinances for them and to set spirituall Lords over them.[10]

This same principle was maintained in the various confessions of faith which were drawn up in the years that followed. In England men of Baptist views like John Bunyan and John Milton upheld the right of every man to religious liberty. Moreover, it was made crystal clear in the American Colonies in the teachings and work of Dr. John

[8] McGlothlin, *Baptist Confessions of Faith*, 82.
[9] W. T. Whitley, *A History of British Baptists*, (London, 1923), 33.
[10] *Ibid.*, 34.

Clarke, Roger Williams, Isaac Backus, and John Leland. The story of their persecution is so well known that a bare mention of it here suffices to recall to us today the everlasting debt we owe to them and to others who with them courageously denied the right of a civil magistrate to interfere in matters of conscience and religion. Democratic America should be eternally grateful to the Baptists of colonial New England and Virginia, for it was, in part at least, their struggle for religious liberty which culminated victoriously in the omission of any religious tests or restrictions when the Constitution of the United States was being framed.

The logical corollary of the doctrine of religious liberty is the principle of the separation of church and state. As minority groups in the sixteenth, seventeenth, and eighteenth centuries, Anabaptists and Baptists had learned the serious restrictions upon religious liberty which a state church may place upon an individual or a congregation. It has been to safeguard their beliefs in the priesthood of believers and in religious freedom that Baptists have insisted upon the complete separation of church and state. By this, they have meant that the state has no right to interfere with the religious beliefs and practices of individuals or congregations; and that the church on its part, has no claim upon the state for financial support. Thus a new principle of voluntary church support was introduced into Christian polity. That principle has now become universal in the United States, and widespread among dissenter churches in the British Isles and in Europe.

It should be pointed out also that Baptists generally have maintained an anti-Catholic attitude in order to safeguard these great principles of religious liberty and the separation of church and state. In this respect, they have not been inconsistent, for they have been, on occasions, the first to defend the right of Roman Catholics to worship according to the dictates of their conscience. However, they have refused to admit the validity of the avowed Catholic principle of intolerance. Thus, they have opposed such pretension as was expressed by Pope Leo XIII in his Encyclical of November 1, 1885, *Immortale Dei*, when he declared that "the State must not only 'have care for religion, but recognize the *true* religion.'" Two eminent Catholic political scientists, in commenting on this statement, interpreted "the true religion" as meaning "the form of religion professed by the Catholic Church," a position which they called "thoroughly logical."[11]

Baptists in the United States, in particular, have protested repeatedly against Catholic demands for state support of parochial schools, while at the same time they have refused equally to admit the right of Protestants to similar favors from the state. In the late nineteenth and early twentieth centuries, great urban centers like New York, Philadelphia, and Boston were often scenes of bitter conflicts over the issue.[12] In recent years, the issue has grown even more acute, for the Catholics have won privileges in several states. By 1947 there were laws in sixteen states and in the District of Columbia which permitted the use of public funds to transport children to Roman Catholic parochial schools. On February tenth of that year, the United States Supreme Court, on a five to four decision, supported such a law in the State of New Jersey on the grounds that it might be classified as social or public benefit legislation from whose provisions no person should be excluded by reason of his religion. The Baptists, however, favored the minority opinion of the Court to the effect that "such use of tax money contravenes the prohibition of the First Amendment to the Constitution against taxation of a citizen for support of beliefs to which he is opposed." They saw in parochial education the forefront of Roman Catholic advance and accordingly identified any school aid as encouragement to the spread of Catholicism.[13]

During the course of the Second World War, it was the Baptists, chiefly through the voice of Dr. Louie D. Newton of Atlanta, Georgia, then president of the Southern Baptist Convention, supported by denominational editors and an interdenominational weekly, *The Christian Century,* who took the lead in opposing American representation at the Vatican by a presidential appointee of diplomatic prestige. Between 1945 and 1946 the protest gained the backing of the Federal Council of Churches of Christ in America, whose representatives obtained from President Harry S. Truman a promise to

[11] John A. Ryan and F. J. Boland, *Catholic Principles of Politics* (New York, 1940), 313-4.

[12] Robert G. Torbet, *A Social History of the Philadelphia Baptist Association: 1707-1940,* 120-7.

[13] *The Watchman-Examiner,* Vol. 35, No. 8 (Feb. 20, 1947), p. 176.

terminate such a relationship with the Vatican as soon as the emergency which warranted it had ended.[14]

From a brief survey of the facts available, it is evident that the anti-Catholic attitude of the Baptists, which has been strong enough to arouse an effective public protest in many quarters against sectarianism in public education and Catholic political influence, has not gone unchallenged. Yet, it is equally clear that their attitude reflects a fear of the increasing political prestige of the Roman Catholic Church in many areas of American life, brought about, in considerable measure, by the efforts of the National Catholic Welfare Conference in Washington, D. C.

Contributions to Protestant Expansion

The evangelizing zeal of Baptists, arising out of their emphasis upon regeneration through Christ and the need of a conversion experience as a requisite to church membership, has been a leading factor in the development of Protestant foreign missions. In reality, it provided the original impetus to that movement. The English cobbler and school teacher of Northamptonshire, William Carey, stirred his fellow Baptists to organize at Kettering on October 2, 1792, the Particular Baptist Society for the propagation of the Gospel amongst the Heathen, later known as the Baptist Missionary Society. Carey then went himself as a missionary to India. Though a small beginning, other denominations were inspired by it to organize missionary societies. In 1804 the British and Foreign Bible Society, an interdenominational agency, was created with a Baptist secretary, the Reverend Joseph Hughes, to publish translations of the Bible for missionary distribution. This British missionary activity fired the imagination of American evangelical Protestants, and they gave support to the American Board of Commissioners for Foreign Missions, which had been organized by Congregationalists in 1812. Then, when two of its appointees, Adoniram Judson and Luther Rice, were converted to Baptist views *en route* to India, the Baptists, as we have seen, were awakened to establish in 1814 the General Missionary Convention of the Baptist Denomination in the United States for Foreign Missions.

[14] For a detailed account, see Clyde K. Nelson, Baptist Reactions to United States-Vatican Relations: 1939-1945, an unpublished Th.M. dissertation, The Eastern Baptist Theological Seminary, Philadelphia, Pa.

Likewise, through the various associations and state missionary societies, the ever westward-moving frontier was evangelized. By 1832, largely through the efforts of John Mason Peck and Jonathan Going, the American Baptist Home Mission Society came into being. In 1845 the Southern Baptist Convention was established. It organized at once its own evangelizing agencies known as the Board of Domestic Missions and the Board of Foreign Missions. So, across the three thousand miles of the American continent and north to Alaska and south to the Isthmus of Panama, the task of evangelism has been carried on, resulting in the nineteenth and twentieth centuries in the establishing of churches, Sunday schools, and academic institutions throughout the United States, Alaska and Central America.

Baptist work on the American frontier was largely influential in the development of the Protestant witness in the United States. It contributed greatly to the winning of the Middle West and Far West to Protestantism. Furthermore, the Baptist foreign mission enterprise has borne fruit in the existence today of self-supporting churches, notably in Burma, South India, the Belgian Congo, China, and Brazil. The attendant benefits of the missionary's labors have not gone unnoticed. Hospitals, schools, and evangelistic stations have provided an indirect deterrent to inhuman pagan practices and to the exploitation of western traders. Wherever Baptist churches have been established, they have left the example of democracy.

Within three and one half centuries of Baptist history—that is to say, since that time when, in 1612, a small congregation of religious refugees dared to return to England under the intrepid Thomas Helwys, willing to endure persecution in order to give to England and the world a Baptist witness—Baptists have grown to a communion of nearly twenty-four million.[15] This remarkable growth has been due in large measure to the energetic evangelism and the strong popular appeal of the democratic polity that have been characteristic of these free evangelical churches which represent today one of the largest and most virile Protestant communions.

[15] Based on the statistical information given in the *Yearbook of American Churches, 1962,* and *The Baptist Handbook, 1961.* According to these figures, the world total Baptist membership is 23,998,495, of which 21,176,041 are in the United States. See the statistical summary and footnote 4 in the following Appendix B, page 515.

Social Contributions

Since the Baptist ministry has been directed chiefly to the humble people, often to the socially, economically, and politically disinherited of society, it is quite natural that social reforms should be numbered among its contributions to Protestantism and to the life of those countries in which Baptists have worked. Their social interests have arisen out of their concern for the people to whose ranks they largely belong. Almost entirely, these interests have been associated with their evangelistic zeal. However, while Baptists have made their contribution to social reform, their role has been less spectacular in this respect than that of such other denominations as the Episcopalians, Presbyterians, and Methodists.

There are several reasons for this, the first of which is that the evangelism of the individual has been and still is the primary concern of Baptists. Second, the Baptist principle of separation of church and state has precluded any serious legislative efforts on their part, except where moral or religious issues have been involved. Third, the decentralized character of Baptist polity has made for a scattered social impact, rather than for a strongly united one. Indeed, the very nature of Baptist organization has made it difficult to interpret to what degree their resolutions have been effective in arousing concerted action or to what extent individuals have behaved socially as Baptists and to what extent they have been motivated by other than religious considerations. A fourth explanation may be found in a fear, on the part of many Baptists, especially in America, of the so-called "social gospel," because of what they deem to be its theologically liberal implications. For these reasons they often have fallen short of emphasizing the need for united action in carrying out in social practice all that Christ has taught; namely, to be peacemakers, to love one's enemies, to feed and clothe the needy, to modify the structure of human society so as to make it less unchristian, to face race relations, and to integrate with Christian faith the best fruits of scholarship. Yet, despite these limitations upon social action, the rank and file of Baptists have produced a significant impact upon society.

Because English Baptists did not share with the Dutch Anabaptists or Mennonites their religious antipathy to civil service, many of them were not unwilling to participate in producing legislative reforms which would benefit the masses. This was particularly true, as we have seen, during the nineteenth century when vital religious and moral issues were at stake.[16] A few examples may be cited.

Early in the nineteenth century, when parliamentary reform was in the air, the Baptists of Yorkshire, a northern county that had not been well represented in Parliament, reflected grave concern for a better distribution of voting privileges and of seats in that body, so as to strengthen the efforts of Lord John Russell and the Whig Party to achieve repeal of the Test and Corporation Acts which placed religious disabilities upon Dissenters. Between 1815 and 1830, such leading Baptist clergymen as Robert Hall, Joseph Ivimey, and Francis Cox were active among the Dissenters who had entered into an alliance with the Whigs in the struggle to reform Parliament.[17] In the years that followed, the Baptists showed marked sympathies with the Chartists and Trade Unionists who represented organized attempts of the working classes to win universal suffrage, the secret ballot, the removal of property qualifications for membership in the House of Commons, and the abolition of tariffs on cereals so as to lower the price of bread. Such Baptist leaders as Cooper, O'Neil, and Vince actually espoused their cause and sent delegates to their conventions.[18]

An issue of equal importance to reformers in that same period was the abolition of the slave trade. In this struggle Baptists took a lively interest, for they saw that an important moral issue was involved. In the late eighteenth century the Western and Midland Associations and the General Assembly of General Baptists expressed their sympathy with the abolitionist cause, proffered financial aid to the interdenominationally supported Anti-Slavery Society, and through petitions pressed Parliament for action. Joseph Ivimey, a prominent Baptist clergyman who served on the Agency Committee or inner circle of the Anti-Slavery Society, and William Knibb, a Baptist missionary to Jamaica, who in the summer of 1832 aroused public opinion against the horrors of slavery on the plantations, share

[16] For details, see Chapter Four.

[17] C. E. Shipley, ed., *The Baptists of Yorkshire* (London, 1912). 300-1; Raymond G. Cowherd, *Protestant Dissenters in English Politics: 1815-1834* (Philadelphia, 1942), 61-9, 87.

[18] Austen K. deBlois, "Social Rights and Baptist History," *The Christian Review* (Philadelphia), June, 1936. See the entire article in March and June issues.

with William Wilberforce, the great evangelical who engineered emancipation through Parliament, the credit for achieving an end to the traffic by 1838.[19]

In other areas of reform, Baptist leaders also were prominent. John Howard's report to Parliament, in 1774, on prison conditions in England as compared with those on the Continent, contributed to the passage of two Acts which improved England's prison facilities considerably.[20] In the field of education, the chief accomplishments of English Baptists have been in connection with the training of ministers, Sunday school work, and the safeguarding of the public schools against sectarian control and instruction. Since 1770 ten colleges have been established in the British Isles for the training of Christian workers, one of which was for women.[21] Only nine remain today.

To William Fox, a Baptist deacon of London, is due the credit for adapting Robert Raikes' Sunday-school movement to strictly biblical instruction with voluntary teachers. Through his efforts a Sunday School Society to sponsor such schools was organized in the Prescott Street Baptist Church in London on September 7, 1785. In 1803 the interdenominational Sunday School Union was organized by another Baptist layman, William Brodie Gurney, who served as stenographer in the House of Lords.

When the Government encouraged the establishment of public schools, Baptists, like other Dissenters, did not respond well to the opportunity to establish their own denominational schools. Instead, they followed the policy of opposing any possibility of Anglican domination of those schools. Their chief spokesman was Dr. John Clifford, who led the Evangelical Free Churches in a passive resistance movement against paying a tax to support schools in which religious instruction was to be given according to the Education Bill of 1902. While parents might withdraw their children during the religious instruction period if they so desired, all schools—Anglican, Catholic, and Dissenter—were to be supported by public funds. Such an ar-

[19] Joseph Ivimey, *History of English Baptists: 1760-1820* (London, 1830), 63; W. T. Whitley, ed., *Minutes of General Assembly of the General Baptist Churches in England: 1654-1728, 1731-1811*, 2 vols. (London, 1909-1910), II, 194, 196; Cowherd, *op. cit.*, 74; John H. Hinton, *Memoir of William Knibb, Missionary to Jamaica* (London, 1849), chaps. 10-12.

[20] See John Stoughton, *Howard the Philanthropist* (London, 1884) and William E. H. Lecky, *History of England in the Eighteenth Century* (London, 1913), 7 vols., Vols. 3, 7.

[21] Based on listings in *The Baptist Handbook for 1939* (London, 1939), 326-30.

rangement, Dr. Clifford felt, would give the Anglicans undue control over the educational system and might possibly increase the number of Catholic schools inasmuch as they became eligible thereby for state support. Under his leadership as President of the National Council of Evangelical Free Churches in England, enough support was secured to enable the Liberals to win the election of 1906. A new bill then was passed. It provided that schools supported by public taxes should be managed by the state and could maintain no religious tests for teachers.[22]

Running all through the interest of English Baptists in reform was the typically Baptist issue of liberty. They supported the Dissenters' political alignment with the popular Whig Party, because they saw in it the only means whereby the cause of religious and civil liberty could be implemented in English political life. They gave sympathetic backing to social reforms because of an appreciation of the individual as a free person before God. This was inherent in their understanding of New Testament teaching.

The influence of Baptists on American life has been more widespread than the influence of their brethren in Europe on the life of that continent, because of their greater numbers and also because they have become to so large an extent an integral and accepted part of the United States. Their insistence upon the separation of church and state won for this country a guarantee of religious liberty in the Federal Constitution. To the Baptists is due also much credit for the disestablishment of the state church in Virginia (1787) and in Massachusetts (1833).

It has been observed already that their democratic polity undoubtedly influenced the trend in government and political thought, especially on the frontier. Baptists of the eighteenth and early nineteenth centuries were considered radicals in this respect by the Federalists. Indeed, they were loyal supporters of Jefferson and Madison in Virginia and also along the frontier where rural interests were predominant. As new states came into the Union, especially such states as Kentucky, Indiana, and Illinois, in which Baptists were numerous, the effect of their thinking was plainly felt. It is not too much to claim that the emphasis which Baptists placed upon the in-

[22] W. T. Whitley, *History of British Baptists* (London, 1923), 260-3, 324-5; Charles T. Bateman, *John Clifford: Free Church Leader and Preacher* (London, 1904), 252, 284-5.

dividual gave the naturalistic "contract" basis of democratic thought a spiritual foundation which has prompted, in part at least, the continued association between democracy and Christian principles to the present day.

Their large membership among the common people has caused their pattern of thought and life to be felt in American society. Until recent years historians have tended to neglect the influence of religious groups upon social life. This is still true with respect to Baptists. Because of their decentralized organization, historians have let them go virtually unnoticed, despite their great numbers. Yet their interest in the Indians, the Negroes, and other minority groups has been significant.

Very early in the history of the country, concern for the American Indians was shown by Roger Williams in New England. Various associations and state mission societies sent missionaries among them. It was a Baptist representative of the Triennial Convention, Isaac McCoy, who in 1817 set out for Indiana to minister to the Indians. In 1821 he succeeded in getting educational measures incorporated in the treaties with the Potawatomi, Miami, and Ottawa tribes. Under his direction, missions were established for their evangelization and instruction. In 1823 he conceived a plan for the colonization of all Indian tribes in one general area lying west of Illinois, Missouri, and the Territory of Arkansas, which should be divided into counties for individual tribes, with a county seat in each. The Indian's right to hold the land was to be guaranteed. A territorial government was to be set up which should license traders and prohibit the introduction of intoxicating liquors. Funds for education, for agricultural and industrial improvement, and for missionary establishments where desired were to be made available. All officers of the territorial government were to be paid by the United States, and there was to be a delegate in Washington, D. C., during sessions of Congress.

From 1823 to 1839 this plan went through a period of evolution as parts of it were put into effect by Congress. By 1830 McCoy was appointed agent of Indian affairs for the Government, which position he occupied until 1842. By 1839 largely through his constant agitation, twenty-two Indian tribes were settled in the Indian Territory. Owing to such possible causes as opposition from some Indian chiefs, from Indian agents who feared a decrease in their number as the plan went into effect, from some traders, and from the Roman Catholic Church, the plan of organization failed in 1838 to pass the House of Representatives, after having passed the Senate. Thus came to a futile end fifteen years of effort to promote it. From 1842 until his death in 1846, McCoy was agent and correspondent of the American Indian Mission Association which he had helped to organize in Louisville, Kentucky.[23]

The spirit and work of Isaac McCoy has been carried on in spite of difficulties and limitations, by the American Baptist Home Mission Society in the North and by the Home Mission Board of the Southern Baptist Convention.[24] After the War between the States, Baptists joined in the general protest against the government's unjust treatment of the American Indians.[25]

At a comparatively early date the condition of the Negroes became a matter of concern. In the latter part of the eighteenth century, Baptists generally opposed slavery, even in the South. With the invention of the cotton gin, the marketing of cotton became more profitable and the economic importance of slaves increased. In the early years of the nineteenth century a division of sentiment concerning slavery appeared between the Baptists of the North and of the South. Many Baptists sought to follow a policy of moderation. They continued their efforts to achieve a peaceful solution of the problems until open hostilities began. The effects of this conflict and the partisanship aroused by it remain to some extent to the present day.

Since 1865, Baptists of the North and South have worked, often jointly, in support of training schools for Negroes. There are ten such institutions of higher learning in the South. At the present time, the Baptists of this race number nearly eight million and largely direct their own program through two major conventions, the National Baptist Convention, U. S. A., Inc., and the National Baptist Convention of America.[26] While race tensions have not yet been fully resolved in America, the growing appreciation on the part of Baptists of their bond in Christ and the efforts of both American and

[23] Emory J. Lyons, "Isaac McCoy and His Plan for Indian Colonization," *The Chronicle*, Vol. X, No. 1 (January, 1947), 17-23.

[24] See Chapters Thirteen and Fourteen.

[25] Torbet, *A Social History of the Philadelphia Baptist Association*, 178-80.

[26] *Ibid.*, 180-4; N.B.C., *Year Book*, 1947, 676.

Southern Conventions to face the issue are contributing to the ultimate solution of this major social problem.

The traditional Puritan pattern of morals characteristic of Baptists has influenced the social scene by reason of their large numbers, their evangelistic zeal, and their crusading instinct. Baptists have urged legislation for Sunday observance, prohibition of gambling, and temperance. Churches, associations, and conventions have sent petitions to legislatures. In recent years the churches in the American Baptist Convention have frequently taken a joint stand on reform issues through the National Council of the Churches of Christ in the U.S.A., of which body the American Baptist Convention is a member. Southern Baptists speak unitedly through the Social Service Commission of their Convention. And still more recently, a Joint Conference Committee on Public Relations has been set up in Washington, D. C. Of this Committee Dr. J. M. Dawson of Texas is executive secretary. It represents the combined interests of the American Baptist Convention, the Southern Baptist Convention, and the two national conventions of Negro Baptists. While its function is primarily to safeguard the separation of church and state, it keeps a watchful eye upon the trend of other great moral and spiritual issues.

A survey of the moral subjects covered by Baptists, North and South, reveals a wide concern over gambling, the use of alcoholic beverages and narcotics, moral delinquency among youth, the sanctity of the home and family relations, the immoral influence of many motion pictures, the moral evil of war, and the violation of the sanctity of the Sabbath. In the case of Sabbath observance, their efforts to impose their religious views upon the entire citizenry has been viewed by some as inconsistent with their principles of religious freedom.

With respect to war, it may be noted that Baptists generally have agreed that it is an unsatisfactory and immoral method of settling disputes, but they have, by and large, refused to adopt a pacifist attitude, preferring to be free to support their country when the issues at stake seem to justify such extreme measures as a state of hostilities requires. That this policy has been a consistent one is indicated by a review of their support of such wars as the Civil Wars in England during the seventeenth century, the American Revolution, the American struggle between the states, the Spanish-American War, and the two World Wars.

With respect to economic reform, one may generalize quite safely by saying that their strong emphasis upon individualism has caused Baptists to shy away from radical theories; at the same time, it has made them willing to support the capitalistic system of individual enterprise. Herein may be noticed the interaction of the environment upon Baptists. Whereas their spiritual ancestors, the European Anabaptists, often held economic views bordering on socialism, Baptists in England and America, with a few notable exceptions, have fitted into the capitalistic system, which, in all probability also reflects their strong emphasis upon individualism. British and American Baptists are perhaps still more definitely associated with the working class in society than with the middle class into whose ranks only a segment of their membership has emerged. For this reason, Baptists in both countries and in Europe have entertained a liberal and sympathetic attitude toward labor.[27] Generally speaking, relatively few wealthy men have arisen among Baptists to dominate their church life; hence they have remained, for the most part, a denomination of the common people. In spirit, then, they have remained democratic, although not radical in social theory.

Like other revivalistic churches in America, Baptists very early encouraged the establishing of academies, colleges, and theological seminaries for the training of ministers and laymen. The first of their institutions of higher learning was Rhode Island College, now Brown University at Providence, chartered in 1764 with a specification that there should be no creedal barriers to student admission. This general policy has been followed by Baptist schools since, and is another indication of their contribution to religious liberty. One of the earliest co-educational schools in the country had its beginnings at Lewisburg, Pennsylvania, in 1846, when out of an academy and a girls' school, organized by members of the Northumberland Baptist Association, the University of Lewisburg developed, later to be called Bucknell University after its chief donor. The founding, in 1896, of Temple University by Dr. Russell H. Conwell and his church, the Grace Baptist Temple of Philadelphia, represented an unusual contribution to the encouragement of popular higher education for city youth of

---

[27] See Torbet, *op. cit.*, chap. 14; also *Proceedings of the Baptist Congress for the Discussion of Current Questions* (1882-1912); reports of resolutions in *Annals* of the N.B.C. and S.B.C. respectively.

limited financial resources. The school was chartered as a nonsectarian institution, which status it still retains.

By 1962, Northern and Southern Baptists combined were supporting eighteen seminaries, fifty-eight colleges and universities, twenty-three junior colleges, thirteen academies, and six other training schools.[28] While Baptists lag behind some other denominations in educational standards, these schools represent the investment of men and women, mostly of modest incomes, in the training of youth in a Christian environment. Baptists, therefore, are not opposed to education. On the contrary, they have been willing supporters of non-sectarian public education. For example, in Pennsylvania, Baptists joined with Presbyterians and Methodists in supporting passage of the School Act of 1834 which established a public school system in the state, while German Protestants, Catholics, Episcopalians and most of the Quakers opposed it on grounds of cultural solidarity or on the ground that they already had their own parochial schools. Perhaps more than any other group, Baptists have opposed sectarianism in public schools. In so doing they have sought to preserve religious liberty and to maintain the separation of church and state.

In conclusion, it may be said that in the Baptist witness the vital principles of the Protestant Reformation have come to full fruition. Baptist work among the immigrants, who are chiefly Catholic, has helped to maintain a Protestant influence in the great American cities where the Roman Catholic Church and the Orthodox Churches have made their greatest advance. In Europe, Baptists have kept alive a small, but effective Protestant witness in behalf of a regenerate church and in defense of religious liberty in Catholic countries. In Asia, Africa, North and South America, and the islands of the sea, they represent a leading force in the missionary expansion of Christianity.

Baptists have appealed most strongly to the common people, whether in Europe, Great Britain, or in the United States, and they have ministered chiefly to the working classes, both white and colored. This has been true also on mission fields where the greatest ingatherings have been from the depressed classes. This universal distinctive of Baptists may be explained in several ways. They have presented consistently a warm evangel of personalized religion. The simple

[28] A.B.C., *Year Book*, 1962-63, pp. 400-2; S.B.C., *Annual*, 1962, pp. 227-30.

democracy of their church life has made a strong appeal to the disinherited of society. The encouragement of the individual to read the Bible for himself has had its own special attraction to those who feel that God has a message of salvation and security for all who will but read and take heed. To produce such a heritage of spiritual freedom and equality, Baptists have labored and many have even given their lives. By their sacrifice, they have enriched the ages and earned the acclaim of free men everywhere.

APPENDICES

APPENDIX A

A Chronological Table

1525 Swiss Anabaptists broke with Zwingli.

1525 Baptism of Hubmaier.

1525 Peasants, Revolt led by Thomas Münzer.

1535 Anabaptists in Zurich were suppressed.

1535 The Münster Rebellion.

1537 Menno Simons became leader of Dutch Anabaptists.

1538 Efforts made to expel Anabaptists from England.

1609 First English General Baptist church formed in Holland under John Smyth.

1611 Organization of first General Baptist church in England by Helwys and Murton.

1638 The first Particular Baptist church organized by Spilsbury.

1638-1639 Organization of the first Baptist church in America; at Providence, R. I., by Roger Williams, or in Newport, R. I., by John Clarke.

1641 Baptism by immersion emphasized by John Spilsbury.

1644 London Confession of 1644: Calvinistic, it emphasized religious liberty and baptism by immersion.

1644 Organization of Association of London Particular Baptists.

1650 Welsh Association formed of three churches.

1651 Midland Association of thirty General Baptist churches formed.

1660 Organization of General Assembly of all Associations of General Baptists in London.

1670 Organization of General Six-Principle Baptists in Rhode Island.

1677 Confession of 1677, a revision of the Westminster Confession.

1689 General Assembly of General Baptists threatened by Arian teachings of Matthew Caffyn.

1689 London Confession of Particular Baptists.

1689 General Assembly of Particular Baptists organized in London.

1707 Organization of Philadelphia Association, the first in America.

1727 Organization of Original Freewill Baptists in Virginia and North Carolina.

1728 Organization of the first Seventh Day Baptist church in America at Germantown, Pennsylvania.

1739 (*circa*) Division of American Baptists into Regular and Separate Baptists as a result of differences over the Great Awakening.

1742 London Confession of Particular Baptists (1689) adopted by the Philadelphia Association.

1750 (*circa*) Organization of the River Brethren in Eastern Pennsylvania.

1764 Founding of the College of Rhode Island, now known as Brown University.

1770 "New Connection" Free Grace General Baptist Assembly organized in England.

1780 Organization of Freewill Baptists in New Hampshire.

1787 The General Assembly of General Baptists in England sent a petition to Parliament in behalf of abolition of slavery.

1792 Organization of the English Baptist Missionary Society at Kettering, at the instigation of William Carey.

1797 Formation of English Baptist Home Mission Society.

1799 Formation of Baptist Union of Wales.

1802 Organization of Massachusetts Baptist Missionary Society, the first state convention to be organized in America.

1808 Organization of the Baptist Church of Christ in Tennessee.

1813 Organization of General Union of Baptist Ministers and Churches in England, forerunner of Baptist Union of Great Britain and Ireland.

1813 Conversion of Adoniram Judson to Baptist principles.

1814 Formation of the Triennial Convention in Philadelphia.

1814 Organization of the Irish Missionary Society.

1817 Organization of the Church of God by John Winebrenner in Philadelphia.

1817 Peck and Welch sent out as home missionaries to the Middle West by the Triennial Convention.

1818 Founding of Hamilton Literary and Theological Institution in New York.

1819 Organization of the first Baptist church in France.

1824 Organization in Washington, D. C., of the Baptist General Tract Society, now known as the American Baptist Publication Society.

1825 Founding of Newton Theological Institution near Boston.

1826 (*circa*) Origin of Old Two-Seed-in-the-Spirit Predestinarian Baptists.

1831 Organization of Adventists by William Miller.

1832 Organization of the American Baptist Home Mission Society in New York City.

1832-33 William Knibb's agitation against the slave traffic in the British Colonial Empire.

1833 New Hampshire Confession written to combat the Arminianism of Free-will Baptists.

1834 Organization of the first Australian Baptist church in Sydney.

1835 Organization of the Primitive Baptists in New York and Pennsylvania.

1835 Appointment of Oncken as an agent for the Triennial Convention in Germany.

1837 Organization of the American and Foreign Bible Society in Philadelphia by Baptists.

1839 Organization of the first Danish Baptist church.

1840 Formation of the Bible Translation Society in England.

1841	Organization of the first Lithuanian Baptist church under Oncken's guidance.
1843	American and Foreign Free Baptist Missionary Society organized by abolitionists in Boston.
1845	Organization of the Southern Baptist Convention at Augusta, Georgia.
1845	The Triennial Convention renamed American Baptist Missionary Union.
1848	Establishment of the first Baptist church in Sweden.
1849	Beginning of Baptist work in Hungary.
1850	Organization of the American Bible Union.
1851	Organization of the first New Zealand Baptist church.
1860	Organization of the first Baptist church in Norway.
1861	First baptism on Latvian soil.
1865	Fusion of the Bible Translation Society and the Irish Missionary Society into the British and Irish Baptist Home Mission Society.
1868	American Indian work transferred to the American Baptist Home Mission Society by the American Baptist Missionary Union.
1869	Formation of the Baptist Union of Scotland.
1869	Organization of the first Baptist church in Finland.
1870	Southern Baptists undertake work in Italy.
1877	Organization of the Women's Baptist Home Mission Society of the East; also organization of the Women's Baptist Home Mission Society of the West.
1879	Important decision of the Southern Baptist Convention to maintain its organization apart from the American Baptist Missionary Union.
1879	Beginning of first permanent mission work in Spain.
1882	Organization of the Baptist Union of New Zealand.
1883	Bible controversy settled in the Bible Convention at Saratoga, N. Y.
1884	Immersion of first Baptists in Estonia.
1888	Organization of the American Baptist Education Society at Washington, D. C.
1889	Southern Baptist work in Japan actually begun.
1891	Formation of the Baptist Union for Great Britain and Ireland; a merger of the Particular Baptists and the New Connexion of General Baptists.
1891	Organization of the Baptist Young People's Union of America.
1893	Participation of Baptists in the National Free Church Council in England.
1895	Organization of the National Baptist Convention of America. Owing to a division of this body in 1915, the larger segment incorporated in that year as the National Baptist Convention of the U.S.A., Inc.
1901	Missionary work undertaken in the Philippines.
1905	Organization of the Baptist World Alliance in London.
1906	Union of Freewill and Particular Baptists in the United Baptist Convention of Canada.
1907	Establishment of the Northern Baptist Convention at Washington, D. C.
1908	The first Congress of European Baptists, meeting at Berlin.
1909	Union of the two Women's Home Mission Societies into the Woman's American Baptist Home Mission Society.
1911	Merger of the Free Baptists with the Northern Baptist Convention.
1911	Second Congress of Baptist World Alliance at Philadelphia.

1913   Creation of a Department of Evangelism by the Southern Baptist Convention.

1919   A five-year New World Movement undertaken by Northern Baptist Convention.

1923   Third Congress of Baptist World Alliance at Stockholm.

1928   Fourth Congress of Baptist World Alliance at Toronto, Canada.

1934   Fifth Congress of Baptist World Alliance at Berlin, Germany.

1935   Organization of the Baptist Hundred Thousand Club by Southern Baptist Convention.

1939   Sixth Congress of the Baptist World Alliance at Atlanta, Georgia.

1941   Formation of the Baptist Youth Fellowship of the Northern Baptist Convention.

1943   Formation of the Conservative Baptist Foreign Mission Society.

1944   Southern Baptists liquidate their indebtedness.

1944   Founding of the Northern Baptist Assembly, Green Lake, Wisconsin.

1945   Inauguration of the World Mission Crusade by Northern Baptist Convention and of a similar effort by the Southern Convention.

1947   Seventh Congress of the Baptist World Alliance at Copenhagen, Denmark.

1947   Formation of the Conservative Baptist Association of America.

1948   Formation of the Conservative Baptist Home Mission Society.

1948   The Northern Baptist Convention sends representatives to the organization meeting of the World Council of Churches in Amsterdam, Holland.

1948   Formation of the European Baptist Union on the pattern of the Baptist World Alliance, yet independent of it.

1948   Proposals made for the organization of a Baptist Union of North America.

1949   Organization, in Zurich, Switzerland, of the European Baptist Federation.

1950   The Northern Baptist Convention, in session in Boston, voted to change its name to the American Baptist Convention. The office of general secretary of the Convention was created, and the Council on Finance and Promotion was renamed Council on Missionary Cooperation.

1950   Eighth Congress of the Baptist World Alliance at Cleveland, Ohio.

1950   Conservative Baptist Theological Seminary founded by the Conservative Baptist Association in Denver, Colorado.

1950   The Southern Baptist Convention held in Chicago its first meeting in the North, symbolic of a new policy of nation-wide expansion.

1951   Organization of the National Council of American Baptist Women.

1952   Centennial of the Baptist General Conference of America (Swedish) observed June 26-29 in St. Paul, Minnesota.

1954   Baptist delegates from various parts of the world participated in the Second Assembly of the World Council of Churches at Evanston, Illinois.

1955   Ninth Congress of the Baptist World Alliance at London, England.

1955   Integration achieved between the American Baptist Foreign Mission Society and the Woman's American Baptist Foreign Mission Society,

510

and between the American Baptist Home Mission Society and the Woman's American Baptist Home Mission Society.

1955 The American Baptist Convention authorized the General Council to re-organize its administrative structure and co-ordinate its work in a single headquarters building.

1957 The American Baptist Convention voted to oppose segregation and to urge its member churches to determine membership on merit regardless of race or national origin. Approval given to a Christian Higher Education Campaign to raise $7.5 million dollars.

1958 The American Baptist Convention decided on Valley Forge, Pennsylvania, as site for national headquarters.

1958 First urban convocation held in Indianapolis by American Baptists, marking a new emphasis in a Convention hitherto predominantly rural.

1959 A five-year Baptist Jubilee Advance through evangelism launched by major Baptist bodies in the United States, to culminate in 1964 with the observance of the sesquicentennial celebration of the national organization of American Baptists to support their first world mission outreach in Burma.

1959 The Foreign Mission Board of the Southern Baptist Convention expanded service to six additional countries, bringing the total to forty-four.

1960 Tenth Congress of the Baptist World Alliance at Rio de Janeiro, Brazil.

1960 The American Baptist Convention reaffirmed its participation in the ecumenical movement, and authorized financing of a headquarters building at Valley Forge, Pennsylvania.

1961 A plan of reorganization adopted by the American Baptist Convention to make the General Council the central agency for the coordination of its work, with the chief executives of national agencies becoming associate general secretaries of the Convention.

1961 A new Negro Baptist national convention—the Progressive Baptist Convention of America—organized on November 15 in Cincinnati by former churches of the National Baptist Convention, U. S. A., Inc.

1961 Baptist delegates from many parts of the world participated in the Third Assembly of the World Council of Churches in New Delhi, India.

1962 Puerto Rico Baptist Convention received as an affiliated state convention of the American Baptist Convention; the first instance of a receiving church being granted full status with the sending churches.

1962 Headquarters of the American Baptist Convention at Valley Forge, Pennsylvania, dedicated on May 26.

APPENDIX B

Table of Baptist Bodies

NAME	DATE OF ORGANIZA-TION[1]	NUMBER OF CHURCHES	MEMBER-SHIP, 1960[2]
Larger Bodies in the U. S. (above 100,000)			
American Baptist Association (Successor to the General Association of Baptist Churches, organized in 1905; independent missionary churches in the Southwest)	1925	3,091	648,000
American (Northern) Baptist Convention	1907	6,262	1,543,198
Conservative Baptist Association of America	1947	1,350	300,000
General Association of Regular Baptist Churches (North)	1933	934	136,292
National Association of Freewill Baptists (Arminian Baptists originating in North Carolina and Virginia, and in New England in 1787. Now in South and Middle West)	1727	2,232	191,448
National Baptist Convention of America (unincorporated)	1895	11,398	2,668,799
National Baptist Convention, U. S. A., Inc. (incorporated in year 1915)	1895	26,000	5,000,000
North American Baptist Association	1950	1,980	330,265
Southern Baptist Convention	1845	32,251	9,731,591
The United Free Will Baptist Church (In the South)	1870	836	100,000
Smaller Bodies in the U. S. (under 100,000)			
Bethel Baptist Assembly, Inc.	1934	27	6,925
Christian Unity Baptist Association (In Tennessee and Virginia)	1934	12	643
Duck River (and kindred) Associations of Baptists (No general organization; in Tennessee, Alabama, Georgia, and Mississippi)	....	28	3,139

NAME	DATE OF ORGANIZA-TION[1]	NUMBER OF CHURCHES	MEMBER-SHIP, 1960[2]
Evangelical Baptist Church, Inc. (Free-will Baptists in No. Carolina)	1935	31	2,200
General Baptists (Arminian Baptists from England, transplanted to Virginia in 1714 and found today in the Middle West) ...	1611	792	58,530
General Six-Principle Baptists (Mainly in Rhode Island)	1653	2	58
Independent Baptist Church of America (Swedish Free Baptists in Middle West and South)	1893	2	30
National Baptist Evangelical Life and Soul Saving Assembly of U. S. A. (Organized by A. A. Banks, Sr., as a charitable, educational, and evangelical body. In Middle West)	1921	264	57,674
National Primitive Baptist Convention of the U. S. A. (Formerly Colored Primitive Baptists. Opposed to church organization; in Florida)	....	1,100	80,983
Primitive Baptists (Mainly in South; opposed to centralization; antimissionary)	ca.1830	1,000	72,000
Regular Baptists (In the South; about 22 associations; no general organization)	....	266	17,186
Separate Baptists in Christ (Originated in North Carolina. Now found in Indiana, Kentucky, Tennessee, Maryland, Illinois)	1758	85	7,358
Seventh Day Baptist General Conference. (Originated in Rhode Island; now in New York and Middle West).	1671	61	5,849
Seventh Day Baptists (German) (Refugees from Palatinate, Germany, arriving in Philadelphia in 1720)....	1728	3	150
Two-Seed-in-the-Spirit Predestinarian Baptists (Organized by Elder Daniel Parker of Virginia. In the South)	ca.1826	16	201
United Baptists (in Kentucky)	1838	586	63,641

Foreign-speaking Baptist Bodies in the U. S.

Baptist General Conference of America (Swedish)	1879	536	72,056
*Czechoslovak Baptist Convention in America	1912	31	2,843
*Danish Baptist General Conference ...	1910	28	4,025

NAME	DATE OF ORGANIZA- TION [1]	NUMBER OF CHURCHES	MEMBER- SHIP 1960 [2]
*Finnish Baptist Missions Union of America	1901	15	1,050
*French-speaking Baptist Conference of New England	1895	7	405
*Hungarian Baptist Union of America..	1908	31	2,216
*Italian Baptist Association of America	1898	44	4,566
*(Mexican Baptists)[3]			
Arizona Mexican Baptist Churches..	....	6	200
California (Northern) Mexican Baptist Convention	1934	8	300
California (Southern) Mexican Baptist Convention	1924	33	1,100
New Mexico Mexican Baptist Churches	....	6	200
The Texas Mexican Baptist Convention	1918	220	4,000
North American Baptist General Convention (German)	1865	300	50,646
*Polish Baptist Conference in U. S. A. ...	1912	11	1,000
*Portuguese Baptist Convention	1903	13	990
*Romanian Baptist Association of America	1913	11	1,125
*Russian-Ukrainian Baptist Union	1919	35	1,759
*Spanish-American Baptist Convention (Predominantly Mexican)	1928	32	1,400
English-speaking Baptist Bodies Outside of U. S.			
Baptists of England	....	2,101	198,597
Baptists of Wales and Monmouthshire .	....	952	93,114
Baptists of Scotland	....	155	20,067
Baptists of Ireland	....	70	5,582
Baptists of Channel Islands	....	6	275
Baptists of Isle of Man	....	1	47
Baptist Federation of Canada (Co-ordinating agency for Baptist Convention of Ontario and Quebec, Baptist Union of Western Canada, United Baptist Convention of the Maritime Provinces. Does not include the Union of Regular Baptist Churches of Ontario and Quebec) ..	1944	1,542	167,005
Baptist Union of Australia (Federation of Six Unions)	1926	570	37,283
Baptist Union of New Zealand	1882	135	14,000
Baptist Union of South Africa	1877	156	40,700

514

NAME	DATE OF ORGANIZA-TION[1]	NUMBER OF CHURCHES	MEMBER-SHIP, 1960[2]
Foreign-speaking Bodies Outside of U. S.			
Baptists of Europe (Does not include Baptists of Great Britain and Ireland)	....	7,561	778,509
Baptists of Asia	....	7,314	788,507
Baptists of Africa (Exclusive of the Baptist Union of South Africa)	....	3,609	354,456
Baptists of Central America and West Indies	....	1,137	125,844
Baptists of South America	....	1,945	198,468
* * * * *			
TOTALS			
Baptists in the U. S.		91,445	21,176,041
English-speaking Baptists outside the U. S.		5,688	576,670
Foreign-speaking Baptists outside the U. S.		21,566	2,245,784
GRAND TOTALS		118,699	23,998,495 [4]

[1] From *Yearbook of American Churches,* 1962 edition.

[2] Membership statistics for Baptist Bodies in the United States are based upon the *Yearbook of American Churches,* 1962, 249-50. Figures for some small Baptist bodies in the U. S. and for some foreign-speaking Baptists (marked by an asterisk*) are not up to date, but are the latest available. Statistics for Baptists outside of the United States are based upon *The Baptist Handbook,* 1961 (British), 215-20.

[3] Mexican Baptists are not as yet united in one body, hence they are listed separately. Statistics on the number of churches also include missions, and are only approximate.

[4] Statistics in *The Baptist World,* Vol. 9, No. 6 (June, 1962) show a grand total of 24,309,538 Baptists in the world residing in more than 100 countries. Since the number of churches in each country is not given and since there are variations with the figures cited above, only the totals for major regions are listed here as follows: Africa, 373,549; Asia, 810,613; Central America, 121,447; Europe (including Great Britain and Ireland), 1,142,508; Middle East, 556; South America, 212,029; Southwest Pacific, 82,753; North America (Canada, 174,000; Mexico, 17,551; United States, 21,374,532), 21,566,083.

APPENDIX C

Table of Baptist Schools and Colleges in the United States, 1961

AMERICAN BAPTIST[1]

NAME	LOCATION	FOUNDED

Theological Seminaries

Andover Newton Theological School	Newton Centre, Mass.	1807
Berkeley Baptist Divinity School	Berkeley, Calif.	1904
California Baptist Theological Seminary	Covina, Calif.	1944
Central Baptist Theological Seminary	Kansas City, Kans.	1901
Colgate Rochester Divinity School	Rochester, N. Y.	1819
Crozer Theological Seminary	Chester, Pa.	1868
Divinity School, University of Chicago	Chicago, Ill.	1891
Eastern Baptist Theological Seminary	Philadelphia, Pa.	1925
Northern Baptist Theological Seminary	Chicago, Ill.	1913
Spanish-American Baptist Seminary	Los Angeles, Calif.	1921

Training Schools for Religious Workers

Baptist Institute for Christian Workers	Philadelphia, Pa.	1892
Baptist Missionary Training School, affiliated with Colgate Rochester Divinity School since 1961	Rochester, N. Y.	1877

Academies

Higgins Classical Institute	Charleston, Maine	1836
Mather School	Beaufort, S. C.	1867
Peddie School, The	Hightstown, N. J.	1864
Ricker Classical Institute	Houlton, Maine	1848
Suffield Academy	Suffield, Conn.	1833
Wayland Academy	Beaver Dam, Wis.	1855

Junior Colleges

Bacone College	Bacone, Okla.	1880
Colby Junior College	New London, N. H.	1837
Colorado Women's College	Denver, Colo.	1888
Keystone College	La Plume, Pa.	1868
Stephens College	Columbia, Mo.	1833

516

Universities and Colleges

Alderson-Broaddus College	Philippi, W. Va.	1871
Bates College	Lewiston, Maine	1864
Benedict College	Columbia, S. C.	1870
Bishop College	Dallas, Texas	1881
Bucknell University	Lewisburg, Pa.	1846
Carleton College	Northfield, Minn.	1866
Chicago, University of	Chicago, Ill.	1891
Colby College	Waterville, Maine	1813
Denison University	Granville, Ohio	1831
Eastern Baptist College	St. Davids, Pa.	1932
Florida Normal and Industrial College	St. Augustine, Fla.	1892
Franklin College	Franklin, Ind.	1834
Hillsdale College	Hillsdale, Mich.	1844
Kalamazoo College	Kalamazoo, Mich.	1833
Keuka College	Keuka Park, N. Y.	1890
Linfield College	McMinnville, Ore.	1857
Morehouse College	Atlanta, Ga.	1867
Ottawa University	Ottawa, Kans.	1865
Redlands, University of	Redlands, Calif.	1907
Ricker College	Houlton, Me.	1926
Shaw University	Raleigh, N. C.	1865
Sioux Falls College	Sioux Falls, S. Dak.	1883
Spelman College	Atlanta, Ga.	1881
Virginia Union University	Richmond, Va.	1899
William Jewell College	Liberty, Mo.	1849

Schools of Nursing Education

Mounds-Midway School of Nursing	St. Paul, Minn.	1907

SOUTHERN BAPTIST[2]

Theological Seminaries

American Baptist Theological Seminary	Nashville, Tenn.	
Carver School of Missions	Louisville, Ky.	
Golden Gate Baptist Theological Seminary	Berkeley, Calif.	1957
Midwestern Baptist Theological Seminary	Kansas City, Mo.	1950
New Orleans Baptist Theological Seminary	New Orleans, La.	1918
Southeastern Baptist Theological Seminary	Wake Forest, N. C.	1951
Southern Baptist Theological Seminary	Louisville, Ky.	1859
Southwestern Baptist Theological Seminary	Ft. Worth, Texas	1908

Academies

Acadia Baptist Academy	Eunice, La.	
Fork Union Military Academy	Fork Union, Va.	1897
Hargrave Military Academy	Chatham, Va.	1909
Harrison-Chilhowee Baptist Academy	Seymour, Tenn.	
Oak Hill Baptist Academy	Mouth of Wilson, Va.	
Oneida Baptist Institute	Oneida, Ky.	
San Marcos Baptist Academy	San Marcos, Texas	1906

NAME	LOCATION	FOUNDED

Junior Colleges

Anderson College	Anderson, S. C.	1911
Averett College	Danville, Va.	1859
Bethel College	Hopkinsville, Ky.	
Bluefield College	Bluefield, Va.	1922
Brewton-Parker College	Mount Vernon, Ga.	1922
Campbell College	Buie's Creek, N. C.	1887
Chowan College	Murfreesboro, N. C.	1848
Clarke Memorial College	Newton, Miss.	1908
Cumberland College	Williamsburg, Ky.	1889
Decatur Baptist College	Decatur, Texas	1891
Gardner-Webb College	Boiling Springs, N. C.	1928
Hannibal-LaGrange College	Hannibal, Mo.	1858
Mars Hill College	Mars Hill, N. C.	1856
Norman College	Norman Park, Ga.	1900
North Greenville Junior College	Tigerville, S. C.	1934
Southern Baptist College	Walnut Ridge, Ark.	1941
Southwest Baptist College	Bolivar, Mo.	1878
Truett-McConnell College	Cleveland, Ga.	
Virginia Intermont College	Bristol, Va.	1884
Wingate Junior College	Wingate, N. C.	1896

Universities and Senior Colleges

Baylor University	Waco, Texas	1846
Belmont College	Nashville, Tenn.	
Blue Mountain College	Blue Mountain, Miss.	1873
California Baptist College	Riverside, Calif.	
Campbellsville College	Campbellsville, Ky.	1906
Carson-Newman College	Jefferson City, Tenn.	1851
Corpus Christi, University of	Corpus Christi, Texas	
East Texas Baptist College	Marshall, Texas	
Furman University	Greenville, S. C.	1827
Georgetown College	Georgetown, Ky.	1829
Grand Canyon College	Phoenix, Ariz.	
Hardin-Simmons University	Abilene, Texas	1892
Howard College	Birmingham, Ala.	1842
Howard Payne College	Brownwood, Texas	1890
Judson College	Marion, Ala.	1839
Louisiana College	Pineville, La.	1906
Mary Hardin-Baylor College	Belton, Texas	1845
Mercer University	Macon, Ga.	1833
Meredith College	Raleigh, N. C.	1899
Mississippi College	Clinton, Miss.	1826
Oklahoma Baptist University	Shawnee, Okla.	1911
Ouachita Baptist College	Arkadelphia, Ark.	1886
Richmond, University of	Richmond, Va.	1832
Shorter College	Rome, Ga.	1873
Stetson University	DeLand, Fla.	1883
Tift College	Forsyth, Ga.	1847

518

NAME	LOCATION	FOUNDED
Union University	Jackson, Tenn.	1834
Wake Forest College	Wake Forest, N. C.	1834
Wayland Baptist College	Plainview, Texas	1909
William Carey College	Hattiesburg, Miss.	
William Jewell College	Liberty, Mo.	1849

Bible Schools

Baptist Bible Institute	Graceville, Fla.	
Clear Creek Baptist School	Pineville, Ky.	
Fruitland Baptist Bible Institute	Hendersonville, N. C.	
Mexican Baptist Bible Institute	San Antonio, Texas	
Southern Illinois College of the Bible	Carbondale, Ill.	

[1] Source of information is American Baptist Convention, *Year Book*, 1961, pp. 369-71.

[2] Statistics, except dates for founding, are based on Southern Baptist Convention, *Annual*, 1961, pp. 245-55. Dates for founding (in some cases the date is for the transition of an institution's status from an earlier one to its present one) are based on the following: Jesse P. Bogue, editor, *American Junior Colleges*, Second Edition, Washington, D. C.: American Council on Education, 1948. ix, 537 pp. A. J. Brumbaugh and Mary Irwin, editors, *American Universities and Colleges*, Fifth Edition. Washington, D. C.: American Council on Education, 1948. xiii, 1054 pp. Homer L. Patterson, editor, *Patterson's American Education Directory*, Vo. XLIII. Chicago: American Educational Company, 1946. 1024 pp. Gould Wickey and Ruth E. Anderson, editors, *Christian Higher Education, A Handbook for 1940*. Fourth Edition of the *Christian Education Handbook*. Washington, D. C.: Council of Church Boards of Education, 1940. 342 pp.

APPENDIX D
MISSION SOCIETIES AND THEIR WORK [1]

ESTAB-LISHED	AGENCY	FIELDS OF WORK	MISSION-ARIES	NATIONAL WORKERS	MISSION CHURCHES	CHURCH MEMBERSHIP	SCHOOLS	COLLEGES	BIBLE SCHOOLS, SEMINARIES	HOSPITALS, CLINICS
1792	Baptist Missionary Society (Britain)	10	369	3,000	2,519	125,868	1,074	4	10	28
1814	American Baptist Foreign Mission Societies	9	334	10,026	5,268	645,451	2,043	14	32	80
1842	Seventh Day Baptist Missionary Society (USA)	4	13	61	65	3,556	3	..	..	1
1845	Foreign Mission Board, Southern Baptist Convention (USA)	51	1,563	3,396	3,399	452,975	785	26	37	90
1861	Strict Baptist Mission (Britain)	2	27	27	91	2,250	2	..	..	4
1872	Scandinavian Independent Baptist Union (Sweden)	4	29	22	..	4,546	21	..	..	4
1873	Canadian Baptist Foreign Mission Board	5	136	460	221	42,117	58	..	5	13
1878	The North American Baptist General Missionary Society	5	82	125	317	34,800	75	3	1	22
1880	Foreign Mission Board, National Baptist Conv., Inc. (USA)	11	590	197	87	200,000	21	1	2	11
1880	Foreign Mission Board, National Baptist Conv. of America	3	..	..	..	..	..	..	..	..
1885	New Zealand Baptist Foreign Missionary Society	2	31	155	90	4,000	93	..	1	4
1889	Baptist Union of Sweden	7	57	345	8	15,927	27	..	2	6
1892	Oerebro Missionary Society (Sweden)	7	150	335	75	21,000	35	..	7	16
1892	South African Baptist Missionary Society	2	50	130	271	25,360	..	..	2	3

Year	Organization									
1897	Lott Carey Baptist Foreign Mission Convention	4	105	15	..	13,383	..	..	..	..
1913	Australian Baptist Missionary Society	4	109	87	181	..	153	..	2	12
1915	Norwegian Baptist Union Congo Mission	1	21	264	193	13,413	..	..	2	3
1921	Baptist Mid-Missions (USA)	28	700	250	2,000	200,000	20	..	12	23
1923	Danish Baptist Mission	1	21	118	3	3,113	35	..	2	4
1923	Irish Baptist Foreign Mission	1	14	5	18	230	..	..	..	..
1927	Association of Baptists for World Evangelism (USA)	8	266	..	250	..	..	..	6	2
1933	Portuguese Baptist Convention	2	6	5	10	361	2	1	1	1
1935	Free Will Baptist Foreign Mission Board (USA)	8	43	43	35	3,250	2	..	1	1
1943	Conservative Baptist Foreign Mission Society (USA)	17	389	..	227	21,593	30	..	8	6
1944	Baptist General Conference, Board of Foreign Missions (USA)	6	125	..	215	8,000	3	..	3	12
1947	Missionary Commission of the Netherlands Baptist Union	1	8	..	..	..	..	..	..	..
1950	North American Baptist Association	8	35	11	85	..	2	..	5	..
1954	European Baptist Foreign Missionary Society	1	25	2	2	20	2	..	..	..
1959	Polish Evangelical Missionary Association (USA)	1	1	..	..	..	..	..	..	..
	TOTALS	213	5,299	16,080	15,630	1,841,213	4,486	49	141	346

[1]Dr. John Allen Moore, *The Baptist World*, Vol. 9, No. 6, (June, 1962).

BIBLIOGRAPHY

NOTE: This is not intended to be an exhaustive bibliography, but rather a list of materials referred to in the course of this history. In addition, there are several titles which have been valuable for general background. A few entries marked by an asterisk (*) are included for reference although they were not used extensively in this research. They are obscure sources, chiefly for the history of the Anabaptists, which, unless otherwise indicated, are to be found in the Library of the Andover Newton Theological School.

Abell, Aaron I., *The Urban Impact on American Protestantism, 1865-1900.* Cambridge: Harvard University Press, 1943, x, 275 pp. Valuable.

Adams, C. C. and Marshall A. Talley, *Negro Baptists and Foreign Missions.* Philadelphia: The Foreign Mission Board of the National Baptist Convention, U. S. A., Inc., 1944. 84 pp. Inadequate.

Adlam, Samuel, *Historical Facts versus Historical Fictions.* Edited by J. R. Graves. Memphis, Tenn.: Southern Baptist Book House, J. R. Graves & Son, 1890. 200 pp. Part I. "The first Baptist church in America not founded or pastored by Roger Williams. . . ." Part II. "A brief history of Roger Williams, Dr. John Clarke, and Obadiah Holmes. . . ."

Albaugh, Dana M., *Between Two Centuries; A Study of Four Mission Fields, Assam, South India, Bengal-Orissa, and South China.* Philadelphia: The Judson Press, 1935. 245 pp.

——————, *Who Shall Separate Us?* Valley Forge, Pa.: The Judson Press, 1962. 128 pp. The story of American Baptists' participation in world relief and refugee programs.

Allen, Alexander V. G., *Christian Institutions.* New York: Charles Scribner's Sons, 1897. xxi, 577 pp. Provides an excellent survey of the development of the organization, doctrine, and worship of the church.

Allison, Wm. Henry, *Baptist Councils in America: A Historical Study of Their Origin and the Principles of Their Development.* Chicago: University of Chicago Press, 1906. 112 pp. A doctoral dissertation bound with other pamphlets on the Baptists, in the New York Public Library. Valuable.

American Baptist Missionary Union, *Annual Reports, 1826-1906.* 20 volumes. Contains proceedings of the Baptist General Convention, the annual reports of the American Baptist Board of Foreign Missions, and proceedings of its successor after 1845, the A.B.M.U. In the Library of the American Baptist Foreign Mission Society in Valley Forge, Pa.

Anderson, Frederick L., *Rich Harvests and Ominous Clouds.* New York: the Board of Missionary Co-operation of the Northern Baptist Convention, 1924. An address published in pamphlet form.

Ante-Nicene Christian Library, The. Translations of the Writings of the Fathers down to A.D. 325. 23 volumes. Edited by the Rev. Alexander Roberts, D.D., and James Donaldson, LL.D. Edinburgh: T. & T. Clark, 1867-1880.

Armitage, Thos., *A History of the Baptists; Traced by their Vital Principles and Practices, from the Time of Our Lord and Saviour Jesus Christ to the year 1889.* New York: Bryan Taylor & Co., 1889. xviii, 990 pp. Interesting style and broad knowledge, but should be used with care.

Ayer, Joseph C., *A Source Book for Ancient Church History*. New York: Scribner's Sons, 1913. xxi, 707 pp. Covers the period from *circa* A.D. 100 to 800.

Babcock, Rufus, *Memoir of John Mason Peck, D.D., Edited from His Journals and Correspondence*. Philadelphia: American Baptist Publication Society, 1864. 360 pp. Important.

Backus, Isaac, *A History of New England with Particular Reference to the Denomination of Christians Called Baptists*. 2 volumes. Newton, Mass.: Backus Historical Society, 1871. Second edition with notes by David Weston, Vol. I written in 1777, Vol. II in 1784, Vol. III in 1796. A work of prime importance; fair-minded and abundant documentary material.

———————————, *The Journals and Records of Isaac Backus*. Microfilm copy in Library of Central Baptist Theological Seminary, Kansas City, Kan.

Baker, Robert A., *Relations Between Northern and Southern Baptists*. Fort Worth, Texas: Seminary Hill Press, 1948. 295 pp. A scholarly analysis.

Banes, Charles H., ed., *Benjamin Griffith, Biographical Sketches*. Philadelphia: American Baptist Publication Society, n.d. 296 pp. Griffith was general secy. of the American Baptist Publication Society from 1857-93.

Baptist Annual Register, The. London, 1790-1802. Edited by John Rippon, D.D. A half-yearly magazine published from 1790-1802, with many extras. When publication ceased, the remainders were bound in four volumes, with the extras after the fourth. A nearly complete file in Library of Eastern Baptist Theological Seminary. Complete in Library of American Baptist Historical Society, Rochester, N. Y.

Baptist Bulletin, The. Grand Rapids, Mich.; Butler, Ind., 1935 to date. Monthly publication of the General Association of Regular Baptist Churches, North. Complete file in Library of American Baptist Historical Society, Chester, Pa.

Baptist Commonwealth, The. Philadelphia, 1908-1914. Deposited in the editorial offices of the *Watchman-Examiner*, New York, N. Y.

Baptist Congress for the Discussion of Current Questions, *Proceedings*, 1882-1912. 30 vols. in 8. New York, etc., 1883-1913. File in Library of the Eastern Baptist Theological Seminary.

Baptist Freedom, Galesburg, Ill., 1944 to date. Monthly publication of the Roger Williams Fellowship of the American Baptist Convention. Presents a more liberal point of view than the Conservative Baptist Fellowship.

Baptist General Convention for Foreign Missionary Purposes, *Proceedings*, 1814-1828. One unbound volume in Library of the American Baptist Foreign Mission Society in Valley Forge, Pa.

Baptist Handbook, The. Edited and published under the direction of the Council of the Baptist Union of Great Britain and Ireland. London: The Baptist Union Publication Department. Published annually.

Baptist Historical Society Transactions. Vols. 1-7 (1908-1921). Superseded by *The Baptist Quarterly*, London. In New York Public Library.

Baptist Home Missions in North America: Including a Full Report of the Proceedings and Addresses of the Jubilee Meeting, and a Historical Sketch of The American Baptist Home Mission Society, Historical Tables, etc., 1832-1882. New York: American Baptist Home Mission Society, 1883. 619 pp. Historical sketch was written by Henry L. Morehouse, corresponding secretary of the Society, pp. 291-544.

Baptist Magazine, The. London, 1809-1882. 75 vols. in the Library of the Eastern Baptist Theological Seminary, Philadelphia, Pa. The volume for 1867 includes a "History of the Baptist Missionary Society, 1792-1867."

Baptist Missionary Magazine, Boston. 93 vols. under various titles: *Massachusetts Baptist Missionary Magazine* (1803-1816), *The American Baptist Magazine and Missionary Intelligencer* (1817-1824), *The American Baptist Magazine* (published by the Baptist Missionary Society of Massachusetts from 1825-1826 and by the Board of Managers of the Baptist General Convention from 1827-1845), *The Baptist Missionary Magazine* (published by the Executive Committee of the American Baptist Missionary Union from 1846-1909). A complete file is in the Library of the American Baptist Foreign Mission Society in Valley Forge, Pa.

Baptist Missionary Society, *Ter-Jubilee Celebrations, 1942-4, Programmes of Meetings and Services, etc.* London: Baptist Missionary Society, 1945.

Baptist Record, The. Philadelphia, 1838-1845. Incomplete file (vols. 3-10) in the Library of American Baptist Historical Society, Rochester, N. Y.

Baptist World, The. Washington, D. C. A monthly publication of the Baptist World Alliance since 1954.

Baptist World Congress, *Proceedings,* 1905, 1911, 1923, 1928, 1939, 1947, 1950, 1955, 1960.

Barnes, Gilbert H., *The Anti-Slavery Impulse (1830-1844).* New York: Appleton-Century-Crofts, Inc., 1933. ix, 298 pp. Based upon careful research.

Barnes, Lemuel C., *et al., Pioneers of Light: The First Century of the American Baptist Publication Society, 1824-1924.* Philadelphia: American Baptist Publication Society, n.d. 454 pp.

Barnes, William W., *The Southern Baptist Convention: A Study in the Development of Ecclesiology.* Seminary Hill, Texas, 1934. 80 pp. Shows keen insight.

Bass, Archer B., *Protestantism in the United States.* New York: Thomas Y. Crowell Company, 1929. xii, 364 pp.

Bassett, John Spencer, *Slavery in the State of North Carolina.* Johns Hopkins University Studies in Historical and Political Science, Ser. 17, nos. 7-8. Baltimore: The Johns Hopkins Press, 1899.

Bateman, Charles T., *John Clifford: Free Church Leader and Preacher.* London: National Council of the Evangelical Free Churches, 1904. xvi, 346 pp.

Batiffol, Pierre, *Primitive Catholicism.* Translated by Henri L. Brianceau. London: Longmans, Green & Co., 1911. xxvii, 424 pp.

Bax, E. Belfort, *Rise and Fall of the Anabaptists.* London: Swan Sonnenschein & Co., 1903. 407 pp.

Belcher, Joseph, Andrew G. Fuller, *et al., The Baptist Irish Society; its Origin, History, and Prospects: with an outline of the Ecclesiastical History of Ireland, and a Lecture, enforcing its claims on the Sympathy and Efforts of Christians in England.* London: Printed for the Baptist Irish Society, 1845. The first three chapters of the history of the Irish Society were written by the Rev. Joseph Belcher, D.D., and the remaining by the Rev. Andrew G. Fuller. The Lecture is by the Rev. J. W. Massie, D.D. The Outline of Ecclesiastical History of Ireland is by the Rev. George Gould of Dublin.

Bender, Harold S., *Conrad Grebel, the Founder of the Swiss Brethren.* Goshen, Ind.: Mennonite Historical Society, 1950. 326 pp. Excellent.

Benedict, David, *A General History of the Baptist Denomination in America and Other Parts of the World.* New York: Lewis Colby & Co., 1848. viii, 970 pp. Originally published in Boston, 1813, in 2 vols. Chapters 7-29 are devoted to Baptist developments in America. An important early source on American Baptists.

Bill, Ingram E., *Fifty Years with the Baptist Ministers and Churches of the Maritime Provinces of Canada*. St. John, New Brunswick: Barnes & Co., 1880. xii, 778 pp.

Bitting, William C., ed., *A Manual of the Northern Baptist Convention, 1908-1918*. Philadelphia: American Baptist Publication Society, 1918. viii, 135 pp.

Blair, Adam, *History of the Waldenses* . . . , 2 vols. Edinburgh: Adam Black, etc., 1832-33.

Bolshakoff, Serge, *Russian Nonconformity: The Story of "Unofficial" Religion in Russia*. Philadelphia: The Westminster Press, 192 pp. Contains valuable chapter on the Baptists.

Boone, Ilsley, ed., *Elements in Baptist Development: a Study of Denominational Contributions to National Life*. . . . Boston: The Backus Historical Society, 1913. xiii, 250 pp. Lacking in historical balance.

Boyd, Jesse L., *A Popular History of the Baptists in Mississippi*. Jackson, Miss.: The Baptist Press, 1930. 331 pp.

Boyd, William K., *The Ecclesiastical Edicts of the Theodosian Code*. Columbia University studies in history, economics, and public law, vol. 24, no. 2. New York: Columbia University Press, 1905.

Brewster, J. M., *et al.*, *The Centennial Record of Freewill Baptists: 1780-1880*. Dover, N. H.: The Printing Establishment, 1881.

Brooks, Charles Wesley, *A Century of Missions in the Empire State, as exhibited by the Work and Growth of the Baptist Missionary Convention of the State of New York*. Revised edition. Philadelphia: American Baptist Publication Society, 1909. xvi, 380 pp. Based upon the personal knowledge of the author, who was district missionary from 1869-1909.

Bronson, Walter C., *The History of Brown University, 1764-1914*. Providence: Brown University, 1914.

Brown, Hugh D., *The Past and Future of Baptists in Ireland*. Dublin: Alex. Thom & Co., Ltd., 1914. 44 pp. Pamphlet. Presidential address at centenary meeting of the Irish Baptist Home Mission held in Dublin, May 27, 1914.

——————, *Prospect and Retrospect*. Belfast: Printed by Wm. W. Cleland, Ltd., 1900. A pamphlet. Presidential address delivered at the Baptist Union of Ireland Meetings held in Dublin, May, 1900.

Brown, J. Newton, *History of the American Baptist Publication Society, from its Origin in 1824 to 1856*. Philadelphia: American Baptist Publication Society, n.d. 275 pp.

Brown, Louise F., *The Political Activities of the Baptists and Fifth Monarchy Men in England during the Interregnum*. Washington, D. C.: American Historical Association, 1912. xi, 258 pp.

Brushwyler, Vincent, *The Story of the Conservative Baptist Foreign Mission Society*. Chicago: C.B.F.M.S., 1945. A pamphlet by the general director of the Society.

*Bullinger, H., *Adversus Anabaptistas*. Libri VI, Nunc Primume. Froschouerum, 1560.

Burgess, G. A. and J. T. Ward, editors, *Free Baptist Cyclopaedia, Historical and Biographical*. Boston: Free Baptist Cyclopaedia Co., 1889. 724 pp.

Burkitt, Lemuel and Jesse Reed, *A Concise History of the Kehukee Baptist Association*. 1803. Important for early North Carolina Baptists.

Burr, Agnes Rush, *Russell H. Conwell and His Work*. Philadelphia: The John C. Winston Co., 1926. 438 pp.

Burrage, Champlin, *The Early English Dissenters in the Light of Recent Research 1550-1641*. 2 vols. Cambridge: University Press, 1912. Volume I contains history and criticisms; volume II, illustrative documents. Very valuable.

Burrage, Henry S., *A History of the Anabaptists in Switzerland*. Philadelphia: American Baptist Publication Society, 1881. xvi, 231 pp.

———————————, *History of the Baptists in Maine*. Portland, Me.: Marks Printing House, 1904. viii, 497 pp. Abundant references to associational and convention minutes. Not always accurate in details.

———————————, *A History of the Baptists in New England*. Philadelphia: American Baptist Publication Society, 1894. 319 pp. A helpful but brief survey.

Burton, Joe W., *Epochs of Home Missions: Southern Baptist Convention, 1845-1945*. Atlanta, Georgia: Home Mission Board, Southern Baptist Convention, 1945. 127 pp. A good summary for laymen.

Cady, John F., *The Origin and Development of the Missionary Baptist Church in Indiana*. Berne, Ind.: The Berne Witness Co., 1942. 354 pp. Scholarly.

Carey, Samuel P., *William Carey*. Philadelphia: The Judson Press, 1923. xvi, 428 pp. Good.

Carlberg, Robert L., *The Development of Centralizing Tendencies in the Northern Baptist Convention*. An unpublished dissertation for the Master of Theology degree, The Eastern Baptist Theological Seminary, 1947. 88 pp.

Carroll, Henry K., *The Religious Forces of the United States Enumerated, Classified, and Described. Returns for 1900 and 1910 Compared with the Government Census of 1890*. New York: Charles Scribner's Sons, 1912. lxxxvii, 488 pp.

Carroll, J. M., *A History of Texas Baptists*. Edited by J. B. Cranfill. Dallas: Baptist Standard Publishing Co., 1923. xv, 1030 pp. The book is interesting chiefly for the numerous documents transcribed in it.

Carter, Paul A., *The Decline and Revival of the Social Gospel: Social and Political Liberalism in American Protestant Churches, 1920-1940*. Ithaca: Cornell University Press, 1956. 265 pp.

Case, S. J., ed., *A Bibliographical Guide to the History of Christianity*. Chicago: University of Chicago Press, 1931. viii, 265 pp.

Catalogue of the Books and Manuscripts in the Library of the American Baptist Historical Society. Philadelphia, 1874.

Cathcart, William, *The Baptists and the American Revolution*. 2nd ed. Philadelphia: S. A. George & Co., 1876. 118 pp.

———————————, ed., *The Baptist Encyclopedia*. 2 vols. Philadelphia: Louis H. Everts, 1881.

A Century of Service by Baptist Women. New York: The Woman's American Baptist Foreign Mission Society, 1933. A pamphlet.

Chaplin, Jeremiah, *Life of Henry Dunster: First President of Harvard College*. Boston: James R. Osgood & Co., 1872. xix, 315 pp.

Chesterman, A. de M., *Axholme Baptists, Heralds of Christian Freedom*. Crowle, Lincolnshire, England: Isle of Axholme Printing Co., Ltd., 1949. 24 pp. An examination of early records of the General Baptists of Lincolnshire.

Christian, John T., *A History of the Baptists*. 2 vols. Nashville, Tenn.: Sunday School Board of Southern Baptist Convention, 1922. Useful chiefly for transcription of sources.

Christian Chronicle, The. Philadelphia, 1846-1865. Vols. 1-4 of this Baptist weekly are in the Library of the American Baptist Historical Society, Rochester, N. Y., and only scattered numbers of vols. 6-18 for 1851-63.

Christian Index, The. Philadelphia, January 1, 1831-June 29, 1833. Only vols. 4-8 of this Baptist weekly are in the Library of A. B. H. S.

Christian Review, The. Philadelphia, 1932-1941. A quarterly magazine published by The Eastern Baptist Theological Seminary until January, 1941.

Christian Watchman, The. Boston, 1819-1848. A Baptist weekly. File in the Library of A. B. H. S.

Chronicle, The. Chester, Pa., 1938 to 1957. A quarterly published by the American Baptist Historical Society.

Clark, Henry W., *History of English Nonconformity from Wiclif to the Close of the Nineteenth Century.* 2 vols. London: Chapman & Hall, 1911, 1913. A valuable study.

Clarke, John, *Ill Newes from New-England: or A Narative [sic] of New-Englands Persecution.* London, 1652. Vol. II of *Collections of the Massachusetts Historical Society.* Boston, 1854.

Cobern, Camden M., *The New Archaeological Discoveries and Their Bearing upon the New Testament and upon the Life and Times of the Primitive Church.* 3rd ed., New York: Funk & Wagnalls Co., 1918. xxxiv, 698 pp.

Cole, Stewart G., *History of Fundamentalism.* New York: Richard R. Smith, Inc., 1931. 360 pp. Somewhat biased against Fundamentalism, but valuable.

Columbian Star, The. Philadelphia, 1828. This Baptist weekly was merged with *The Christian Index,* of Washington, D. C., in 1829. File in the Library of the American Baptist Historical Society, Rochester, N. Y.

Columbian Star and Christian Index, The. Philadelphia, 1829-1830. In 1830 this Baptist weekly became *The Christian Index,* the other part of the name being taken over by a Georgia publisher. File in the Library of the American Baptist Historical Society.

Cook, Henry, *What Baptists Stand For.* London: The Kingsgate Press, 1947. 188 pp. Fine exposition of Baptist principles.

Cook, Richard B., *The Early and Later Delaware Baptists.* Philadelphia: American Baptist Publication Society, 1880. 156 pp. Good.

——————————, *The Story of the Baptists in All Ages and Countries.* Baltimore: Rev. W. M. Wharton, 1884. 416 pp. Of little value.

*Cornelius, C. A., *Berichte der Augenzeugen über das Münsterische Wiedertaüferreich.* Münster, 1853.

*——————————, *Geschichte des Münsterischen Aufruhr in drei Buchern.* Vol. I, *Die Reformation.* Leipzig, 1855.

Cote, Wolfred N., *The Archaeology of Baptism.* London: Yates & Alexander, 1876. xix, 336 pp.

Cowherd, Raymond G., *Protestant Dissenters in English Politics: 1815-1834.* Philadelphia, 1942. 142 pp. A doctoral dissertation, University of Pennsylvania. Excellent study.

Cox, F. A. and J. Hoby, *The Baptists in America: A Narrative of the Deputation from the Baptist Union in England to the United States and Canada.* New York: Leavitt, Lord & Co., 1836. 516 pp.

Cramp, J. M., *Baptist History: from the Foundation of the Christian Church to the Close of the Eighteenth Century.* Philadelphia: American Baptist Publication Society, n.d. 598 pp. Originally published in 1856-58; revised in 1868. Attempts to cover too much ground.

Crocker, Henry, *History of the Baptists in Vermont.* Bellows Falls, Vt.: The P. H. Gobie Press, 1913. 700 pp. This book contains histories of associations, churches, and the state convention drawn from primary sources. Not well integrated.

Crosby, Thomas, *The History of the English Baptists from the Reformation to the Beginning of the Reign of King George I*. 4 vols. London, 1738-1740. Lacking in organization of material and often uncritical. Valuable for his citation of original materials before they became generally known. The reader may be confused by the author's failure to distinguish between General and Particular Baptists.

Crusader, Philadelphia, 1945 to date. This is the American Baptist Newsmagazine.

Dargan, Edwin C., *Ecclesiology: A Study of the Churches*. Louisville, Ky.: Chas. T. Dearing, 1897. 585 pp. Good.

Davies, Horton, *Worship and Theology in England from Watts and Wesley to Maurice, 1690-1850*. Princeton: Princeton University Press, 1961. xiv, 355 pp.

———————————, *Worship and Theology in England; from Newman to Martineau, 1850-1900*. Princeton: Princeton University Press, 1962. xiv, 390 pp.

Davis, J., *History of the Welsh Baptists,* A.D. *63-1770*. Pittsburgh: D. M. Hogan, 1835. iv, 204 pp. Informative, but should be used with care. Only one chapter is devoted to pre-Reformation times.

Dawson, Joseph M., *A Century with Texas Baptists*. Nashville, Tenn.: Broadman Press, 1947. 161 pp. Popular presentation.

deBlois, Austen K., *Fighters for Freedom: Heroes of the Baptist Challenge*. Philadelphia: The Judson Press, 1929. 437 pp.

———————————, *The Pioneer School; a History of Shurtleff College, the Oldest Educational Institution in the West*. New York: Fleming H. Revell Co., 1900. 356 pp.

Dexter, Henry M., *The True Story of John Smyth, the Se-Baptist, as told by Himself and His Contemporaries*. Boston: Lee & Shepard, 1881. viii, 106 pp. The "ancient records" on which 1599 is assigned as the date of the foundation of the Baptist church at Crowle, Lincs., are proven fraudulent.

The Dictionary of National Biography. Edited by Sir Leslie Stephen and Sir Sidney Lee. 25 vols. Oxford University Press, London: Humphrey Milford, 1917-1937.

Donat, Rudolf, *Wie das Werk Begann: Entstehung der deutschen Baptistengemeinden*. Kassel: J. G. Oncken Verlag, 1958. 478 pp. The story of German Baptist work to 1850. Not documented.

Dosker, Henry E., *The Dutch Anabaptists*. Philadelphia: The Judson Press, 1921. 310 pp. Very good; utilizes Dutch sources.

Douglas, David, *History of the Baptist Churches in the North of England from 1648 to 1845*. London: Houlston & Stoneman, 1846. xxvii, 308 pp.

Douglass, Robert S., *History of Missouri Baptists*. Kansas City, Mo.: Western Baptist Publishing Co., 1934. xxii, 545 pp.

Dunkerley, Roderic, ed., *The Ministry and the Sacraments: Report of the Theological Commission Appointed by the Continuation Committee of the Faith and Order Movement under the Chairmanship of the Right Reverend Arthur Cayley Headlam, Bishop of Gloucester*. London: Student Christian Movement Press, 1937. ix, 560 pp. Includes papers on Baptist views, pp. 219-29.

Eaton, W. H., *Historical Sketch of the Massachusetts Baptist Missionary Society and Convention, 1802-1902*. Boston: Massachusetts Baptist Convention, 1903. vii, 240 pp. Helpful.

Edwards, Morgan, *Customs of Primitive Churches.* Philadelphia, c. 1774. 110 pp. Useful for early Baptist polity.

————————, *Materials Towards a History of the American Baptists.* Philadelphia, 1770-1792. Of the twelve-volume work projected, only four have been published: Pennsylvania, New Jersey, Delaware, and Rhode Island. Copies of these are in the New York Public Library and the Library of the American Baptist Historical Society, Rochester, N. Y. Brief manuscript volumes, dealing with Delaware, Virginia, North Carolina, South Carolina, and Georgia are also at Rochester. A manuscript history of Maryland Baptists is in possession of Mr. Alester G. Furman, Greenville, S. C. An important source of early information.

Elsbree, Oliver W., *The Rise of the Missionary Spirit in America, 1790-1815.* Williamsport, Pa.: Williamsport Printing Co., 1928. 187 pp. Very good.

European Baptist Congress, *Proceedings,* 1908. London: Baptist Union Publication Department, 1908.

Evans, B., *The Early English Baptists.* 2 vols. London: J. Heaton & Son, 1862-1864. Material arranged by the reign of monarchs, from Henry VIII through Charles II.

Evans, Philip S., *History of Connecticut Baptist State Convention: 1823-1907.* Hartford: Smith-Linsley Co., 1909. 297 pp. Useful.

*Fighen, Benedict, *Historia Fanaticorum Oder eine vollkomne Relation und Wissenschafft von den Alten Anabaptisten und Newen Quäkern. . . .* Danzig, 1664.

Foundations. Rochester: American Baptist Historical Society. A quarterly of Baptist history and theology published since 1958 as successor to *The Chronicle.*

Furman, Wood, *A History of the Charleston Association of Baptist Churches in the State of South Carolina.* Charleston, S. C.: Press of J. Hoff, 1811. Copy in Library of Andover-Newton Theological School, Newton Centre, Mass.

Gardiner, Samuel R., *History of the Great Civil War, 1642-1649.* 3 vols. London: Longmans, Green & Co., 1886-1891.

Garrison, Winfred E. and Alfred T. De Groot, *The Disciples of Christ: A History.* St. Louis, Mo.: Christian Board of Publication, 1948. 592 pp. The best general history of this denomination to date.

Gates, Errett, *The Early Relation and Separation of Baptists and Disciples.* Chicago: R. R. Donnelly & Sons, 1904. 124 pp.

Gaustad, Edwin S., *The Great Awakening in New England.* New York: Harper and Brothers, 1957. 173 pp.

Gewehr, Wesley M., *The Great Awakening in Virginia, 1740-1790.* Durham, N. C.: Duke University Press, 1930. x, 292 pp. A good study.

Gibson, L. Tucker, *Luther Rice's Contribution to Baptist History.* Unpublished dissertation, Temple University School of Theology, Philadelphia, Pa., 1944. xiv, 158 pp. Based on previously unused materials.

Gillette, A. D., ed., *Century Minutes of the Philadelphia Baptist Association: 1707-1807.* Philadelphia: American Baptist Publication Society, 1851. 468 pp.

Goen, C. C., "Revivalism and Separatism in New England, 1740-1800; Strict Congregationalists and Separate Baptists in the Great Awakening." Doctoral dissertation, Yale University, 1960.

Goodykoontz, Colin B., *Home Missions on the American Frontier.* Caldwell, Idaho: Caxton Printers, 1939. 460 pp. Valuable.

Griffiths, Thomas S., *A History of Baptists in New Jersey*. Hightstown, N. J.: Barr Press Publishing Co., 1904. xiv, 542 pp. Useful.

Guild, Reuben A., *Life, Times, and Correspondence of James Manning, and the Early History of Brown University*. Boston: Gould and Lincoln, 1864. xxii, 523 pp. Very useful.

Guston, David and Martin Erikson, eds., *Fifteen Eventful Years, A Survey of the Baptist General Conference, 1945-1960*. Chicago: Harvest Press, 1961. 231 pp.

*Haft, J., *Geschichte der Wiedertäufer von ihrem Entstehen zu Zwickau in Sachsen bis auf ihren Sturz zu Münster in Westfallen*. Münster, 1836.

Haight, E. F., "The Beginning of the Baptist Denomination in New Orleans," *Bulletin of Furman University*, XXIX (May, 1946), 21-30.

——————————, "An Account of the Baptists of New Orleans, 1850-1900," *Bulletin of Furman University*, XXX (May, 1947), 5-15.

Haldane, Alexander, *Memoirs of the Lives of Robert Haldane of Airthrey, and of His Brother, James Alexander Haldane*. London: Hamilton, Adams & Co., 1852. xvi, 676 pp.

Hall, Thomas C., *The Religious Background of American Culture*. Boston: Little, Brown & Co., 1930. xiv, 348 pp. Valuable for interpretation.

Hank, Arthur, *et al.*, compilers, *Baptist General Association of West Virginia: Jubilee Volume, 1865-1915*. n. d. 358 pp. The book is a collection of reports and papers read at the 50th Anniversary of the B. G. A.

Hanserd Knollys Society Publications of Early English and Other Baptist Writers. Edited by Edward Bean Underhill:

Confessions of Faith and other Public Documents Illustrative of the History of the Baptist Churches of England in the Seventeenth Century. London, 1854. 360 pp.

A Martyrology of the Churches of Christ Commonly Called Baptists During the Era of the Reformation. 2 vols. London. Vol. I (1524-1660), 1850. 447 pp.; Vol. II (1552-1568), 1853. 450 pp.

The Records of a Church of Christ meeting in Broadmead, Bristol, 1640-1687. London, 1847. 522 pp.

Records of the Churches of Christ gathered at Fenstanton, Warboys, and Hexham, 1644-1720. London, 1854. 426 pp.

Tracts on Liberty of Conscience and Persecution, 1614-1661. London, 1846. 392 pp.

Harkness, R. E. E., "Social Origins of the Millerite Movement." A doctoral dissertation in manuscript, University of Chicago, 1927.

Harnack, Adolf von, *Bible Reading in the Early Church*. Translated from German. London: Williams & Norgate, 1912. x, 159 pp.

——————————, *The Constitution and Law of the Church in the First Two Centuries*. New York: G. P. Putnam Sons, 1910. xiv, 349 pp.

——————————, *History of Dogma*. Translated from 3rd German edition. 7 vols. Boston: Little, Brown & Co., 1895-1900.

Harrison, Paul M., *Authority and Power in the Free Church Tradition: A Social Case Study of the American Baptist Convention*. Princeton: Princeton University Press, 1959. 248 pp. A provocative study.

Hartshorne, Hugh and Milton C. Froyd, *Theological Education in the Northern Baptist Convention; A Survey, 1944-1945*. Philadelphia: The Judson Press, 1945. 242 pp.

Hayne, Coe, compiler, *Baptist Trail-Makers of Michigan*. Philadelphia: The Judson Press, 1936. 180 pp. Biographical.

Helwys, Thomas, *A Short Declaration of the Mistery of Iniquity*. London: Kingsgate Press, 1935. Copy in New York Public Library. Reproduced by replica process from copy presented by Helwys to King James, which is now in the Bodleian Library. An introduction by the late Dr. H. Wheeler Robinson, president of the (British) Baptist Historical Society.

Herrick, Everett Carleton, *Turns Again Home: Andover Newton Theological School and Reminiscences from an Unkept Journal*. Boston: The Pilgrim Press, 1949. 202 pp. A delightful account by the first president of the federated faculty.

Hinton, Isaac T., *A History of Baptism, both from the Inspired and Uninspired Writings*. Philadelphia: American Baptist Publication and Sunday School Society, 1840. xvi, 372 pp. A revised edition was prepared by John Howard Hinton in 1864 and published in The Bunyan Library, Vol. XII.

Hinton, John H., *Memoir of William Knibb, Missionary in Jamaica*. 2nd ed. London: Houlston & Stoneman, 1849. xii, 522 pp.

Hiscox, Edward T., *The New Directory for Baptist Churches*. Philadelphia: American Baptist Publication Society, 1894. 608 pp. A standard church manual for the nineteenth century.

Home Mission Digest, Valley Forge, Pa., 1944 to date. An occasional periodical published jointly by the Woman's American Baptist Home Mission Society and the American Baptist Home Mission Society. The first issue appeared in 1944.

Hoop Scheffer, and Jacob de Gijsbert, *History of the Free Churchmen called the Brownists, Pilgrim Fathers, and Baptists in the Dutch Republic, 1578-1701*. Edited by William E. Guffis. Ithaca, N. Y.: Andrus & Church, 1922. In the New York Public Library.

Hopkins, Charles H., *The Rise of the Social Gospel in American Protestantism, 1865-1915*. New Haven: Yale University Press, 1940. xii, 352 pp. Valuable.

Hovey, Alvah, *A Memoir of the Life and Times of the Reverend Isaac Backus*. Boston: Gould & Lincoln, 1859. xvi, 369 pp. Useful.

Hovey, George R., *Alvah Hovey, His Life and Letters*. Philadelphia: The Judson Press, 1928. 267 pp. Important for the life of Hovey and for the history of Newton Theological Institution, of which he was president from 1868 to 1898.

Howell, Robert Boyle C., *The Early Baptists of Virginia*. Philadelphia: Bible and Publication Society, 1857. "Reliable" (Mode).

Hudson, Winthrop S., *American Protestantism*. Chicago: The University of Chicago Press, 1961. vii, 198 pp. Valuable for an understanding of the American environment of Baptist church life.

——————————, ed., *Baptist Concepts of the Church*. Philadelphia: The Judson Press, 1959. 236 pp. A valuable collection of historical essays on varying strands of the Baptist tradition.

Hughes, H. Estcourt, *Our First Hundred Years: The Baptist Church of South Australia*. Adelaide, Australia: South Australian Baptist Union, 1937. Good interpretation.

Humphrey, Edward F., *Nationalism and Religion in America: 1774-1789*. Boston: Chipman Law Publishing Co., 1924. viii, 536 pp. Very helpful for background.

Hunter, C. Earl, "American Baptist Foreign Missions, 1814-1845." A typescript study made in 1945, The Eastern Baptist Theological Seminary. 47 pp.

Irvine, E. Eastman, ed., *The World Almanac and Book of Facts for 1946*. New York: The New York World Telegram, 1946.

Ivimey, Joseph, *A History of the English Baptists*. 4 vols. London: 1811-1830. Traces the history of English Baptists to approximately 1820.

The Life of Mr. William Kiffin, upwards of Sixty Years pastor of the Baptist Church, Devonshire Square, London. From 1639 to 1701. . . . London, 1833. 192 pp.

James, Charles F., *Documentary History of the Struggle for Religious Liberty in Virginia*. Lynchburg, Va.: J. P. Bell Co., 1900.

Jenkins, Daniel T., *Congregationalism: A Restatement*. New York: Harper and Brothers, 1954. 152 pp.

Jones, Samuel, *A Treatise of Church Discipline and a Directory*. Philadelphia: S. C. Ustick, 1798. Bound with other Baptist pamphlets in Bucknell Library of Crozer Theological Seminary, Chester. Pa.

Jordan, Lewis G., *Negro Baptist History, U. S. A., 1750-1930*. Nashville, Tenn.: The Sunday School Publishing Board, National Baptist Convention, 1930. 394 pp. Copy in Library of Harvard Divinity School. Poorly organized. Little interpretation.

Keen, William W., ed., *The Bi-Centennial Celebration of the Founding of the First Baptist Church of the City of Philadelphia, 1698-1898*. Philadelphia: American Baptist Publication Society, 1899. 511 pp. Includes an extensive history of the church by Dr. Keen, biographical sketches of the pastors, and miscellaneous sketches and documents.

Kehukee Baptist Association; Minutes of, with letter of Joel Battle Fort and introduction and notes by Kemp Plummer Battle. Chapel Hill, N. C.: The University Press, 1904. Copy in Widener Library, Harvard University.

Keller, Charles R., *The Second Great Awakening in Connecticut*. New Haven: Yale University Press, 1942. ix, 275 pp. A careful study.

*Keller, Ludwig, *Geschichte der Wiedertäufer und ihres Reichs zu Münster*. Münster, 1880.

King, Henry M., *Rev. John Myles and the Founding of the First Baptist Church in Massachusetts*. Providence, R. I.: Preston & Rounds, 1905. An historical address delivered at the dedication of a monument in Barrington, Rhode Island (formerly Swansea, Mass.), June 17, 1905.

Klaiber, Ashley J., *The Story of the Suffolk Baptists*. London: The Kingsgate Press, 1931. 226 pp. Well done. Based on local church and association records.

Knight, Allan R., "Basic Factors Underlying Inter-church Relations of Period to A.D. 140." A doctoral dissertation in microfilm, The Eastern Baptist Theological Seminary, Philadelphia, Pa., 1946.

Knight, Richard, *History of the General and Six-principle Baptists in England and America*. Providence, R. I.: Smith and Parmenter, 1827. 370 pp. A copy is in the Library of the American Baptist Historical Society, Rochester, N. Y.

Knowles, James D., *Memoir of Roger Williams*. Boston, 1834.

Kraus, C. Norman, *Dispensationalism in America: Its Rise and Development*. Richmond: John Knox Press, 1958. 156 pp.

*Kripp, Johann von, *Achtes Programm des Kaisers Königs*. Staats-Gymnasium zu Innsbruck, veröffentlicht am Schlusse des Schuljahres, 1857. Contains original documents of value pertaining to the expulsion of the Anabaptists from Tyrol and Saltzburg, and especially statements made at the trials of Anabaptists.

*Krohn, Barthold N., *Geschichte der Fanatischen und Enthusiastischen Wiedertäufer vornehmlich in Niederdeutschland. Melchior Hofmann und die Secte der Hofmannianer*. Leipzig, 1758.

532

Kurzawa, Alfred W., "The Baptist Movement in Poland." An unpublished Master's dissertation, Andover Newton Theological School. Newton Centre, Mass., 1945.

Lake, Kirsopp, *The Apostolic Fathers with an English Translation.* 2 vols. London: William Heinemann; New York: G. P. Putnam's Sons, 1930.

Lappin, Maitland M., *Baptists in the Protestant Tradition.* Toronto: The Ryerson Press, 1947. xiv, 112 pp. A popular interpretation.

Latch, Ollie, *History of the General Baptists.* Poplar Bluff, Mo.: The General Baptist Press, 1954. xvi, 428 pp.

Latourette, Kenneth Scott, *A History of the Expansion of Christianity.* 7 vols. New York: Harper, 1937-1944. Unexcelled for erudite scholarship and brilliant interpretation.

Lea, Henry Charles, *A History of the Inquisition of the Middle Ages.* 3 vols. New York: Macmillan, 1922. Best treatise on the subject.

Lecky, William E. H., *A History of England in the Eighteenth Century.* 8 vols. London: Longmans, Green & Co., 1878-90.

Lerrigo, P. H. J. and Doris M. Amidon, editors, *All Kindreds and Tongues: An Illustrated Survey of the Foreign Mission Enterprise of Northern Baptists.* (Fourth issue.) New York: American Baptist Foreign Mission Society and Woman's American Baptist Foreign Mission Society, 1940. 298 pp.

Lerrigo, Peter Hughes James, compiler and editor, *Northern Baptists Rethink Missions: A Study of the Report of the Layman's Foreign Missions Inquiry.* New York: Baptist Board of Education, Department of Missionary Education, 1933. 128 pp.

Levy, George E., *The Baptists of the Maritime Provinces, 1753-1946.* St. John, New Brunswick: Barnes-Hopkins, Ltd., 1946. xii, 336 pp. A careful use of sources. Good interpretation.

*Linden, Friedrich Otto Zur, *Melchior Hofmann, ein Prophet der Wiedertäufer.* Haarlem: De Erven F. Bohn, 1885.

Littell, Franklin H., *The Free Church.* Boston: Beacon Press, Inc., 1957. xiii, 171 pp. Throws new light on Anabaptist-Mennonite sources and their relevancy to other communions.

Little, Lewis Peyton, *Imprisoned Preachers and Religious Liberty in Virginia; A Narrative Drawn Largely from the Official Records of Virginia Counties, Unpublished Manuscripts, Letters, and Other Original Sources.* Lynchburg, Va.: J. P. Bell Co., 1938. xix, 534 pp. Valuable.

Lofton, George A., *English Baptist Reformation; from A.D. 1609 to 1641.* Louisville, Ky.: C. T. Dearing, 1899. viii, 280 pp. A study of Baptist origins to disprove the *visible succession* theory.

Lord, F. Townley, *Achievement: A Short History of the Baptist Missionary Society, 1792-1942.* London: The Carey Press, 1942. 150 pp. Good survey.

*Loserth, Johann, *Doctor Balthasar Hübmaier und die Anfange der Wiedertäufe in Mähren.* Schoeniche dei Berlin Friedrianshagen, 1923.

Lumpkin, William L., ed., *Baptist Confessions of Faith.* Philadelphia: The Judson Press, 1959. 430 pp. A new and enlarged edition of McGlothlin's volume by the same title.

————————, *Baptist Foundations in the South.* Nashville: Broadman Press, 1961. vii, 166 pp. An admirable study of the rise of Separate Baptists and their spread in the South.

Lützow, the Count, *The Life and Times of Master John Hus.* London: J. M. Dent & Co.; New York: E. P. Dutton & Co., 1909. ix, 398 pp.

Lynd, S. W., ed., *Memoir of the Rev. William Staughton, D.D.* Boston, 1834.

Magruder, Edith C., *A Historical Study of the Educational Agencies of the Southern Baptist Convention, 1845-1945*. New York: Teachers College, Columbia University, 1951. xi, 161 pp.

Maring, Norman H., and Winthrop S. Hudson, *A Baptist Manual of Polity and Practice*. Valley Forge: The Judson Press, 1963. Valuable for historical insights.

McCall, Duke K., ed., *What Is the Church? A Symposium of Baptist Thought*. Nashville: Broadman Press, 1958. viii, 189 pp. Valuable.

McDaniel, George W., *The Churches of the New Testament*. New York: George H. Doran Co., 1921. ix, 299 pp. A study from the Baptist point of view.

McGlothlin, W. J., *Baptist Confessions of Faith*, Philadelphia: American Baptist Publication Society, 1911. xii, 368 pp.

——————————, *A Guide to the Study of Church History*. Revised edition. New York: George H. Doran Co., 1914. 359 pp.

McNutt, William R., *Polity and Practice in Baptist Churches*. Philadelphia: The Judson Press, revised edition, 1959. 266 pp. Very useful.

Maine Baptist Missionary Convention, *Proceedings* for 1824-1914. In possession of the State House Library of Augusta, Me.

Maring, Norman H., "History of Maryland Baptists, 1742-1882." An unpublished doctoral dissertation in manuscript, University of Maryland, 1948. 228 pp.

Marshall, Edward P., *A Treatise upon Baptist Church Jurisprudence*. . . . Washington, D. C.: The Columbian Publishing Co., 1898. 557 pp.

May, Henry F., *Protestant Churches and Industrial America*. New York: Harper & Brothers, 1949. x, 297 pp. An excellent history of the rise of the "social gospel" and a social consciousness among Protestant denominations.

Mead, Frank S., *Handbook of Denominations in the United States*. Second revised edition. New York: Abingdon Press, 1961. 272 pp. Useful.

Merriam, Edmund F., *A History of American Baptist Missions*. Philadelphia: American Baptist Publication Society, 1900. xii, 261 pp.

Mesquita de, Antonio N., *Historia dos Batistas do Brasil de 1907 até 1935*. Casa Publicadora Batista, 1940. Two volumes.

*Migne, J. P., *Patrologiae Cursus Completus*. Paris: First Series, 1844-55; Second Series, 1857-66.

Miller, Perry G. E., *Roger Williams: His Contribution to the American Tradition*. Indianapolis: Bobbs Merrill Co., 1953. 273 pp. Valuable insights.

Millet, Joshua, *A History of the Baptists in Maine*. Portland: printed by Charles Day & Co., 1845. viii, 472 pp. Chiefly devoted to accounts of local churches and ministers.

Milman, Henry Hart, *History of Latin Christianity including that of the Popes to the Pontificate of Nicolas V*. 6 vols. London: John Murray, 1857.

Missions, Valley Forge, Pa., 1910 to date. This periodical was formed by the union of various Baptist missionary journals. It is successor to the *Baptist Missionary Magazine* (Boston). Complete file in Library of American Baptist Historical Society, Rochester, N. Y.

Mode, Peter G., *The Frontier Spirit in American Christianity*. New York: Macmillan, 1923. x, 196 pp. Good.

——————————, *Source Book and Bibliographical Guide for American Church History*. Menasha, Wis.; George Banta Publishing Co., 1921. xxvi, 735 pp.

Moody, Robert E., ed., *Province and Court Records of Maine*, Vol. III, *Province of Maine Records, 1680-1692*. Portland: Maine Historical Society,

534

1947. lvii, 330 pp. Valuable for important section on William Screven, xxxiv-xxxix.

Moore, George C., *The Life of Alexander Carson, LL.D.* New York: Edward H. Fletcher, 1851. xii, 156 pp.

Mosteller, James D., *A History of the Kiokee Baptist Church in Georgia.* Ann Arbor, Mich.: Edwards Brothers, Inc., 1952. xv, 275 pp. Useful.

Mullins, Edgar Y., *The Axioms of Religion: A New Interpretation of the Baptist Faith.* Philadelphia: The Griffith and Rowland Press, 1908. 316 pp.

————————, *Freedom and Authority in Religion.* Philadelphia: The Griffith and Rowland Press, 1913. 410 pp.

Murray, James O., *Francis Wayland.* Boston and New York: Houghton, Mifflin & Co., 1891. vii, 293 pp. In "American Religious Leaders Series."

National Baptist, The. Philadelphia, 1865-1894. A complete file in the Library of American Baptist Historical Society, Rochester, N. Y.

National Monthly, Philadelphia, 1836-1838. This organ of the Baptist General Tract Society in Philadelphia became *The Baptist Record* in 1838.

Neal, Daniel, *The History of the Puritans, or Protestant Nonconformists.* 4 vols. London: Richard Hett, 1732-1738.

Neander, Augustus, *General History of the Christian Religion and Church.* Translated from German by Joseph Torrey. 7th American edition. 5 vols. Boston: Crocker & Brewster, 1859.

Nelson, Clyde K., "Baptist Reactions to United States-Vatican Relations, 1939-1946." Unpublished Th. M. dissertation, The Eastern Baptist Theological Seminary, Philadelphia, Pa., 1945. 104 pp.

Newman, Albert H., ed., *A Century of Baptist Achievement.* Philadelphia: American Baptist Publication Society, 1901. xix, 460 pp. Useful.

————————, *History of Antipedobaptism; from the Rise of Pedobaptism to* A.D. *1609.* Philadelphia: American Baptist Publication Society, 1897. xi, 414 pp. Good bibliographies at end of chapters and on pages 395-406.

————————, *A History of the Baptist Churches in the United States.* Philadelphia: American Baptist Publication Society, 1898. v-xv, 513 pp.

News and Views. Chicago, 1944 to date. Monthly publication of the Conservative Baptist Foreign Mission Society since 1944.

News Letter, Chicago, 1945 to date. Monthly publication of the Conservative Baptist Fellowship of Northern Baptists.

Niebuhr, H. Richard, and others, *The Purpose of the Church and Its Ministry: Reflections on the Aims of Theological Education.* New York: Harper and Brothers, 1956. xvi, 134 pp. Vol. 1 of three-volume Survey of Theological Education in the United States and Canada, 1954-56.

Northern Baptist Convention, *Annual* (or *Yearbook*), 1907-1948. Complete file in Library of The Eastern Baptist Theological Seminary, Philadelphia, Pa.

Northern Baptist Education Society, *Annual Reports of the Directors.* 2 vols. (1829-44 and 1845-67). Boston and Cambridge, 1867. In the Library of Andover Newton Theological School. Valuable chiefly for New England.

Norwood, John Nelson, *The Schism in the Methodist Episcopal Church, 1844: A Study of Slavery and Ecclesiastical Politics.* Alfred, N. Y.: Alfred University Press, 1923. 225 pp. Useful for comparison.

Nutter, Stephen Bernard, *The Story of the Cambridge Baptists and the Struggle for Religious Liberty.* Cambridge, Eng.: W. Heffer & Sons Ltd., 1912. xi, 173 pp. A popular presentation.

535

Olson, Adolf, *A Centenary History as Related to the Baptist General Conference of America.* Chicago: Baptist Conference Press, 1952. xiii, 635 pp. Most recent history of Swedish Baptists in America.

Orchard, G. H., *A Concise History of Foreign Baptists . . .* 12th edition. Nashville: Graves, Marks & Co., 1855. xxiv, 382 pp. Attempts to trace Baptist history from A.D. 33 to 1800.

Owens, Wayne Leonard, "A Brief History of the American Baptist Student Movement." A B.D. thesis, Northern Baptist Theological Seminary, Chicago, 1960. Typescript. 135 pp. Useful.

Paschal, George Washington, *History of North Carolina Baptists, 1663-1805.* Vol. I of a projected series. Raleigh: The General Board, North Carolina Baptist State Convention, 1930. 572 pp. Scholarly.

Patterson, T. A., "The Theology of J. R. Graves and Its Influence on Southern Baptist Life." Unpublished Th.D. dissertation, Southwestern Baptist Theological Seminary, Fort Worth, Texas, 1944. 293 pp.

————, "A Critique of the Successionist Concept in Baptist Historiography." An unpublished Th.D. dissertation, New Orleans Baptist Theological Seminary, 1956. A typescript, vi, 126 pp. Valuable.

Payne, Ernest A., *The Anabaptists of the 16th Century.* London: The Carey Kingsgate Press, 1949. 23 pp.

————, *The Baptist Movement in the Reformation and Onwards.* London: The Carey Kingsgate Press, 1947. 24 pp.

————, *The Baptist Union: A Short History.* London: The Carey Kingsgate Press, c. 1958 by author. First published 1959. x, 317 pp. Valuable.

————,*The Fellowship of Believers: Baptist Thought and Practice Yesterday and Today.* Enlarged edition, 1952. London: The Carey Kingsgate Press. 168 pp. Very good.

————, *The Free Church Tradition in the Life of England.* London: Student Christian Movement Press, Ltd., 1944. 3rd ed., 1951. 192 pp. Valuable for roots of early Baptist life.

————, *Henry Wheeler Robinson: Scholar, Teacher, Principal; A Memoir.* London: Nisbet & Co., Ltd., 1946. 212 pp. Provides a good picture of a Baptist scholar and educator and of Rawdon College and Regent's Park College, with which he was associated.

Pelt, Owen D., and Ralph Lee Smith, *The Story of the National Baptists.* New York: Vantage Press, 1960. 272 pp. Relies upon secondary materials. Limited usefulness.

Pendleton, J. M., *Distinctive Principles of Baptists.* Philadelphia: American Baptist Publication Society, 1882. 239 pp.

Pike, E. C., *The Story of the Anabaptists.* London: National Council of Evangelical Free Churches, 1904. xi, 128 pp. Popular presentation.

Posey, Walter Brownlow, *The Baptist Church in the Lower Mississippi Valley, 1776-1845.* Lexington: University of Kentucky Press, 1957. viii, 166 pp. Valuable.

Purefoy, George W., *A History of the Sandy Creek Baptist Association, 1758-1858.* New York: Sheldon & Co., 1859. 329 pp. Very useful.

Putnam, Mary B., *The Baptists and Slavery: 1840-1845.* Ann Arbor, Mich.: G. Wahr, 1913. 96 pp. Scholarly.

Ragsdale, B. D., *Story of Georgia Baptists.* 3 vols. Vol. III, *The Convention, Its Principles and Policies, Its Allies and Its Agencies, Its Aims and Its Achievements.* Atlanta: Foote & Davies Co., 1938. viii, 427 pp. Interesting material; not well organized. Volumes I and II tell the story of Mercer University (pub. in 1932 and 1935).

Randolph, Corliss F., *Seventh Day Baptists in Europe and America*. 2 volumes. Plainfield, N. J.

The Review and Expositor, Louisville, Ky. A Baptist Theological Quarterly edited by the Faculty of the Southern Baptist Theological Seminary since 1906.

Riley, Benjamin F., *History of the Baptists of Alabama . . . 1808-1894*. Birmingham: Roberts & Son, 1895. 481 pp. Good.

——————, *A History of the Baptists in the Southern States of the Mississippi*. Philadelphia: American Baptist Publication Society, 1898. Good.

——————, *History of the Baptists of Texas*. Dallas: Published for the author, 1907. 509 pp. Carries the story to 1906. Well organized.

Robinson, H. Wheeler, *Baptist Principles*. London: The Kingsgate Press, 1945. 80 pp. Originally published in 1925. A good summary.

——————, *The Life and Faith of the Baptists*. Revised edition. London: The Kingsgate Press, 1946. ix, 158 pp. Very good.

Rosser, John L., *A History of Florida Baptists*. Nashville: Broadman Press, 1949.

Routh, Eugene C., *The Word Overcoming the World*. Nashville: Broadman Press, 1941. 230 pp. A survey of mission fields under the Foreign Board of the Southern Baptist Convention.

Rushbrooke, J. H., *The Baptist Movement in the Continent of Europe*. London: The Kingsgate Press, 1915. viii, 207 pp. A revised edition appeared in 1923.

——————, *Some Chapters of European Baptist History*. London: The Kingsgate Press, 1929. 131 pp.

Russell, C. Allyn, "A History of the Regular Baptists in Rhode Island, 1825-1931." An unpublished doctoral dissertation, Boston University, 1959. Typescript. 383 pp. Valuable.

Ryan, John A. and Francis J. Boland, *Catholic Principles of Politics*. New York: Macmillan, 1940. viii, 366 pp. Presents the Roman Catholic view.

Schaff, Philip, *History of the Christian Church*. 7 vols. in 8. New York: Charles Scribner's Sons, 1892-1926. Thoroughly acquainted with sources; like Neander, he interprets the history of the church as evidence of the divine power of the gospel.

Scharf, John T. and Thompson Wescott, *History of Philadelphia: 1609-1884*. 3 vols. Philadelphia: L. H. Everts and Company, 1884.

Semple, Robert B., *A History of the Rise and Progress of the Baptists in Virginia*. Revised and extended by G. W. Beale, Philadelphia: American Baptist Publication Society. 1894. ix, 536 pp. Originally written in 1810, this work still holds a recognized place because of its accuracy.

Shakespeare, John H., *Baptist and Congregational Pioneers*. London: The Kingsgate Press, 1906. x, 196 pp. Very good.

Shanafelt, T. M., *The Baptist History of South Dakota*. Sioux Falls: South Dakota Baptist Convention, 1899. 273 pp. Chapters 1-5 provide a general account. Other chapters are devoted to biographies and association histories.

Sharp, W. A. Seward, *History of Kansas Baptists*. Kansas City: The Kansas City Seminary Press, 1940. 259 pp. Not well organized.

Shelley, Bruce L., *Conservative Baptists: A Story of Twentieth-Century Dissent*. Denver: Conservative Baptist Theological Seminary, 1960. 164 pp. Useful.

Shipley, C. E., ed., *The Baptists of Yorkshire, being the Centenary Memorial Volume of the Yorkshire Baptist Association.* London: The Kingsgate Press, 1912. 328 pp. Chapters by various authors; useful.

————————, *Baptists in Yorkshire, Lancashire, Cheshire, and Cumberland.* London, 1913. Useful.

Shortt, Adam and Sir Arthur G. Doughty, editors, *Canada and its Provinces.* 23 vols. Toronto: Glasgow, Brook & Co., 1914. Vol. XI. A notable history contributed to by recognized authorities on Canadian history, biography, and economics. See pp. 345-76 of Vol. XI for story of Canadian Baptists as told by J. L. Gilmour.

Simpson, E. P. Y., "A History of the New Zealand Baptist Missionary Society, 1885-1947." An M.A. dissertation, University of New Zealand, 1948. Typescript in possession of author. xvi, 176 pp.

Smith, Herbert Maynard, *Pre-Reformation England.* London: Macmillan, 1938. xv, 556 pp.

Smith, H. Shelton, Robert T. Handy, and Lefferts A. Loetscher, *American Christianity, 1607-1820.* Volume I of 2 volume series. New York: Charles Scribner's Sons, 1960. xv, 615 pp.

Smith, Justin A., *A History of the Baptists in the Western States East of the Mississippi.* Philadelphia: American Baptist Publication Society, 1896. 420 pp. Good.

Smithson, Robert J., *The Anabaptists: Their Contribution to Our Protestant Heritage.* London: James Clarke & Co., 1935. 228 pp.

Southern Baptist Convention, *Annals* (or *Proceedings*), 1845-1948. A complete file in the Library of the American Baptist Historical Society, Rochester, N. Y.

Spencer, David, *The Early Baptists of Philadelphia.* Philadelphia: William Syckelmoore, 1877. 203 pp.

Spencer, J. H., *A History of Kentucky Baptists, from 1769 to 1885 Including More than 800 Biographical Sketches.* 2 vols. Cincinnati: T. R. Baumes, 1885. Useful.

Sprague, William B., *Annals of the American Pulpit.* 9 vols. New York: Robert Carter & Bros., 1857-69.

Stackhouse, Perry James, *Chicago and the Baptists: A Century of Progress.* Chicago: The University of Chicago Press, 1933. xvii, 250 pp. An excellent study.

Starr, Edward C., ed., *A Baptist Bibliography: Being a register of printed material by and about Baptists; including works written against the Baptists.* Sections A-Giordano. Philadephia: The Judson Press, 1947. 240 pp. Published for the Samuel Colgate Baptist Historical Collection, Colgate-Rochester Divinity School. The first eight volumes in a projected Master Catalogue of Baptist Historical Materials.

Stealey, Sydnor L., ed., *A Baptist Treasury.* New York: Thomas Y. Crowell Co., 1958. 323 pp.

Stevens, Daniel Gurden, *The First Hundred Years of the American Baptist Publication Society.* Philadelphia: American Baptist Publication Society, 1925. 120 pp.

Stiansen, Peder, *History of the Baptists in Norway.* Chicago: The Blessing Press, 1933. xi, 176 pp. Very useful.

Stoughton, John, *Howard the Philanthropist and His Friends.* London: Hodder and Stoughton, 1884. vii, 379 pp.

Straton, Hillyer H., *Baptists: Their Message and Mission.* Philadelphia: The Judson Press, 1941. 179 pp. A popular presentation.

Streeter, Burnett, H., *The Primitive Church, Studied with Special References to the Origins of the Christian Ministry.* New York: Macmillan, 1929. xiii, 323 pp.

Strickland, Arthur B., *The Great American Revival; a case study in historical evangelism, with implications for today.* Cincinnati, Ohio: Standard Press, 1934. 235 pp.

Strong, Augustus H., *Miscellanies.* 2 vols. Volume I. Philadelphia: The Griffith and Rowland Press, 1912. xi, 493 pp. Contains addresses and lectures of an historical nature.

Sweet, William Warren, *Religion in Colonial America.* New York: Charles Scribner's Sons, 1942. xiii, 367 pp.

—————————, ed., *Religion on the American Frontier.* 4 vols. Vol. I, *The Baptists, 1783-1830.* New York: Henry Holt & Co., 1931. ix, 652 pp. A valuable collection of source materials, prefaced by several interpretive chapters.

—————————, *Revivalism in America: its origin, growth, and decline.* New York: Charles Scribner's Sons, 1944. xv, 192 pp.

—————————, *The Story of Religion in America.* Revised edition. New York: Harper and Brothers, 1950. vi, 656 pp.

Taylor, Adam, *The History of the English General Baptists.* 2 vols. London, 1818. Written for the New Connexion General Baptists. It is based on local and associational records; organized chronologically by churches and areas. Better organized than Crosby or Ivimey.

Taylor, George B., *Southern Baptists in Sunny Italy.* New York: Walter Neale, Publisher, 1929. 295 pp. Free use of missionary correspondence. Limited worth.

Thom, William T., *The Struggle for Religious Freedom in Virginia; the Baptists.* Baltimore: The Johns Hopkins University Press, 1900. 105 pp. Important.

*Thomas, Joseph, *Le Mouvement baptiste en Palestine et Syria (150 av. J.C.— 300 ap. J.C.).* Gembloux (Belgique), Duculot, 1935. In Andover-Harvard Divinity School Library.

Thomas, Joshua, *A History of the Baptist Association in Wales from the Year 1650 to the Year 1790. . . .* London, 1795. viii, 88 pp. In the Library of Andover Newton Theological School. Usually appended to Rippon's *Register,* IV. Useful.

Thompson, Donald N., "The History of Baptist Confessions of Faith: 1610-1800." An unpublished B. D. dissertation, Eastern Baptist Theological Seminary, Philadelphia, Pa., 1945. 56 pp.

Thorning, Joseph F., *Religious Liberty in Transition.* 1st series: *New England.* New York: Benziger Bros., 1931. vi, 252 pp. Written by a Jesuit priest.

Through Shining Archway. New York, 1945. A pamphlet published jointly by the American Baptist Foreign Mission Society and the Woman's American Baptist Foreign Mission Society to memorialize the martyrdom of Baptist missionaries in the Philippines during the Second World War.

Tobias, a Fellow Elder with H. N. in the Household of Love, *Mirabilia Opera Dei: Certaine wonderfull Works of God which hapned to H. N. even from his youth: and how the God of Heaven hath united himself with him, and raised up his gracious Word in him, and how he hath chosen and sent him to be a Minister of his gracious Word.* Translated out of Base Almain. n. d. Possibly translated by C. Viret in London, 1550. (See p. 1499 of *Catalogue of Books in the Library of the British Museum printed to the*

539

year 1640. Vol. III. London, 1884.) There is a copy in the Houghton Library, Harvard University.

Torbet, Robert G., *The Baptist Ministry: Then and Now.* Philadelphia: The Judson Press, 1953. 134 pp.

—————————, *A Social History of the Philadelphia Baptist Association 1707-1940.* Philadelphia: Westbrook Publishing Co., 1944. 247 pp.

—————————, *Venture of Faith: The Story of the American Baptist Foreign Mission Society and the Woman's American Baptist Foreign Mission Society, 1814-1954.* Philadelphia: The Judson Press, 1955. xiv, 634 pp.

Torbet, Robert G., and Henry R. Bowler, *Reuben E. Nelson: Free Churchman,* Philadelphia: The Judson Press, 1961.

Toward the Mark: Baptist World Advance, 1940-1944. New York: Council on Finance and Promotion, Northern Baptist Convention, 1944. 56 pp.

Townsend, Leah, *South Carolina Baptists, 1670-1805.* Florence, S. C.: Florence Printing Co., 1935. 391 pp. Scholarly.

Trowbridge, M. E. D., *et al., History of Baptists in Michigan.* Published under the auspices of the Michigan Baptist State Convention, 1909. x, 338 pp. Mediocre.

Tumbelston, Robert T., *History of "Old Pennepack."* A printed account incorporated in the 250th Anniversary Program Booklet of the Old Pennepack Baptist Church, 1938. A copy is in the Library of the American Baptist Historical Society, Rochester, N. Y.

Tupper, H. A., *The Foreign Missions of the Southern Baptist Convention.* Philadelphia: American Baptist Publication Society, 1880. xv, 512 pp. A collection of biographical sketches of missionaries with narrative interspersed. All major missions are treated.

Tustin, Josiah P., *A Discourse Delivered at the Dedication of the New Church Edifice of the Baptist Church and Society in Warren, R. I., May 8, 1845.* Providence: H. H. Brown, 1845. viii, 125 pp.

Underhill, Edward Bean, ed., *Tracts on Liberty of Conscience and Persecution, 1614-1661.* London: printed for the Hanserd Knollys Society by J. Haddon, 1846.

Underwood, A. C., *A History of the English Baptists.* London: The Baptist Union Publication Dept. (Kingsgate Press), 1947. 286 pp. Excellent account.

Vail, Albert L., *The Morning Hour of American Baptist Missions.* Philadelphia: American Baptist Publication Society, 1907. 477 pp. An excellent account.

Vedder, Henry C., *Balthasar Hübmaier: the Leader of the Anabaptists.* New York and London: G. P. Putnam's Sons, 1905. xxiv, 333 pp. Excellent.

—————————, *A History of the Baptists in the Middle States.* Philadelphia: American Baptist Publication Society, 1898. 355 pp. Very good.

—————————, *A Short History of Baptist Missions.* Philadelphia: The Judson Press, 1927. 559 pp. Good.

—————————, *A Short History of the Baptists.* New and illust. ed. Philadelphia: American Baptist Publication Society, 1907. xvi, 431 pp.

Wallace, O. C. S., *What Baptists Believe: The New Hampshire Confession, An Exposition.* Nashville, Tenn.: Sunday School Board of Southern Baptist Convention, 1913. 208 pp.

Walton, Robert C., *The Gathered Community.* London: The Carey Kingsgate Press, 1944. Helpful on Baptist beginnings in England.

Warren, Frederick E., *The Liturgy and Ritual of the Ante-Nicene Church*

London: Society for Promoting Christian Knowledge, 1897. xvi, 343 pp.

Watchman, The, Boston, 1883-1912. A complete file is in the American Baptist Historical Society, Rochester, N. Y.

Watchman-Examiner, The, New York City, 1914-1948. A national Baptist weekly; a complete file is in the editorial offices, New York, N. Y.

Watts, Joseph T., One Hundred Years of Southern Baptist History. Baltimore, 1945. A pamphlet. 13 pp.

Wayland, Francis, A Memoir of the Life and Labors of the Rev. Adoniram Judson, D.D. 2 vols. Boston: Phillips, Sampson & Co., 1853. Based on an extensive use of correspondence.

——————, The Principles and Practices of Baptist Churches. Edited by John Howard Hinton, Vol. I of The John Bunyan Library. London: J. Heaton & Son, 1861. xl, 306 pp. Indicates the viewpoint of an important Baptist of the North during the eighteen-forties and fifties.

Weeks, Stephen B., Church and State in North Carolina. 11th series. "Johns Hopkins University Studies in Historical and Political Science." Baltimore: Johns Hopkins Press, 1893. 65 pp.

Weis, Frederick L., The Colonial Churches and the Colonial Clergy of the Middle and Southern Colonies, 1607-1776. Lancaster, Mass.: Society of the Descendants of the Colonial Clergy, 1938. 140 pp.

——————, The Colonial Clergy and Colonial Churches of New England. Lancaster, Mass.: Society of the Descendants of the Colonial Clergy, 1936. 280 pp.

Wenger, John C., Glimpses of Mennonite History and Doctrine. 2nd ed. revised and enlarged. Scottdale, Pa.: Herald Press, 1947. 258 pp. Well written and based upon most recent research.

Wertenbaker, Thomas J., The Planters of Colonial Virginia. Princeton: Princeton University Press, 1922.

White, Charles L., A Century of Faith, Centenary Volume of The American Baptist Home Mission Society. Philadelphia: The Judson Press, 1932. 320 pp.

White, W. R., Baptist Distinctives. Nashville: The Sunday School Board of the Southern Baptist Convention, 1946. 122 pp. Expresses the viewpoint of Southern Baptists.

Whiting, C. E., Studies in English Puritanism from the Restoration to the Revolution, 1660-1688. New York: Macmillan Co., 1931. 584 pp. Chapter 3 valuable on Baptists.

Whitley, William T., A Baptist Bibliography; being a Register of the Chief Materials for Baptist History, whether in Manuscript or in Print, Preserved in Great Britain, Ireland, and the Colonies. 2 vols. London: The Kingsgate Press, 1916-1922. Vol. I covers period 1526-1776; Vol. II, 1777-1837, and addenda from 1613. A third volume is in preparation.

——————, The Baptists of London: 1612-1928, their Fellowship, their Expansion, with Notes on their 850 Churches. London: The Kingsgate Press, n. d. 331 pp.

——————, Baptists of North-West England, 1649-1913. London: The Kingsgate Press, 1913. 365 pp. Very useful.

——————, Calvinism and Evangelism in England, especially among Baptists. London: The Kingsgate Press, n. d. 46 pp. A careful study.

——————, ed., The Church Books of Ford or Cuddington and Amersham in the County of Bucks. London: The Baptist Historical Society, 1912. xvi, 263 pp.

—————————————, *A History of British Baptists*. London: Chas. Griffin & Co., 1923. xii, 381 pp. A second edition appeared in 1932. Very good.

—————————————, ed., *Minutes of the General Assembly of the General Baptist Churches in England, with Kindred Records*. 2 vols. (1654-1728, 1731-1811). London: The Kingsgate Press, 1909-1910.

—————————————, *The Witness of History to Baptist Principles*. London: Alexander & Shepheard, 1897. v, 99 pp. Good.

—————————————, *The Works of John Smyth*. 2 vols. Cambridge: The University Press, 1915. Very valuable.

Whitsitt, William H., *A Question in Baptist History: Whether the Anabaptists in England Practiced Immersion before the Year 1641?* Louisville, Ky.: Chas. T. Dearing, 1896. 164 pp. Includes an appendix on the baptism of Roger Williams in 1639.

Wickersham, James P., *A History of Education in Pennsylvania, Private and Public, Elementary and Higher*. Lancaster, Pa.: Inquirer Publishing Co., 1886. xxiii, 683 pp.

Wilkin, F. J., *Baptists in Victoria: Our First Century, 1838-1938*. East Melbourne: The Baptist Union of Victoria, 1939. xiv, 211 pp. Useful in the story of Australian Baptists.

Winslow, Ola E., *Master Roger Williams*. New York: Macmillan Co., 1957. 328 pp. Careful research in Williams' English background.

Wittke, Carl F., *We Who Built America: The Saga of the Immigrant*. New York: Prentice-Hall, 1939. xviii, 547 pp.

Wood, Nathan E., *The History of the First Baptist Church of Boston, 1665-1899*. Philadelphia: American Baptist Publication Society, 1899. x, 378 pp. Based upon church records.

Woodhouse, Arthur S. P., ed., *Puritanism and Liberty: Being the Army Debates (1647-9) from the Clarke Manuscripts with Supplementary Documents*. London: J. M. Dent and Sons, 1950. 506 pp. Very valuable for Baptist involvement in the Cromwell era.

Woodson, Carter G., *The History of the Negro Church*. 2nd ed. Washington, D. C.: The Associated Publishers, 1921. 330 pp. A readable general history of Negro Protestants.

Wright, Mary Emily, *The Missionary Work of the Southern Baptist Convention*. Philadelphia: American Baptist Publication Society, 1902. Helpful.

Wright, Stephen, *History of the Shaftsbury Baptist Association from 1781 to 1853*. Troy, N. Y.: A. G. Johnson, 1853. xii, 464 pp. Includes also accounts of associations formed from the Shaftsbury Association, and biographical sketches and statistics.

Yearbook of American Churches, 1962; Information on All Faiths in the U. S. A., edition for 1962. Edited by Benson Y. Landis. New York: National Council of the Churches of Christ in the U.S.A., 1961. 314 pp.

Young, Robert H., "A History of Baptist Hymnody in England, 1612-1800." An unpublished doctoral dissertation, University of Southern California, 1955.

Yuille, George, ed., *History of the Baptists in Scotland from Pre-Reformation Times*. Glasgow: Baptist Union Publications' Committee, 1926. 312 pp. Informative, but rather disorganized.

Chaplains, 422, 454f.
Chaplains of Army and Navy, Committee on, 454
Chaplin, Jeremiah, 310
Charleston Association, 230, 285, 308f.
Chartists, 495
Chase, Ira, 310 f.
Chemung Association, 263
Chicago, Divinity School of the University of, 428
Chicago, University of, 321, 410, 426, 428
China Baptist Theological Seminary, 407
China Inland Mission, 403
Chinese Baptist Publication Society, 346
Christian Baptist, 272
Christian Centers, 415, 468
Christian Century, The, 491
Christian Higher Education Campaign, 470
Christian Life Crusade, 401
Church Building Department of Southern Baptist Convention, 375
Church Edifice Department of the American Baptist Home Mission Society, 363, 375
Church Edifice Gift Fund, 410
Church Extension Campaign, 469
Church of the Brethren, 264 f.
Clark, E. W., 341
Clarke, John, 203 f., 489 f.
Clifford, John, 88, 107, 114, 116 f., 125, 496
Clopton, Samuel C., 346
Clough, John E., 342 f.
Colby College, 311
Colby, Gardner, 311
Colby, John, 259
Colgate, James B., 312
Colgate Divinity School, 414
Colgate University, 312
Colley, W. W., 354
Colman, James, 332
Colporters, 327, 368, 383, 418
Columbian College, 310 f., 315 ff., 332, 334
Colver, Nathanial, 290
Comity agreements between Northern and Southern Baptists, 411 ff.
Commission on Co-ordination of Northern Baptist Societies, 437
Committee of fifteen of Northern Baptist Convention, 437 ff.
Committee on Co-operation in Latin America, 417
Cone, Spencer H., 279, 290, 361

Confessions of faith, early English, 45; early usage, 46; of London Particular Baptists (1644), 484; of London General Baptists (1660), 484; of Philadelphia Baptist Association (1742), 213, 484; New Hampshire Confession (1830), 429, 431, 434, 484
Conscientious objectors, 418, 453
Conservative Baptist Association of America, 436, 477
Conservative Baptist Foreign Mission Society, 400 f., 435 f.
Conservative Baptist Home Mission Society, 436
Conservative Dunkers, 264
Conservative Fellowship of Northern Baptists, 436, 441
Consolidated American Baptist Convention, 354
Convention of Regular Baptists of British Columbia, 159
Conwell, Russell H., 322, 501
Cook, Henry, 195
Co-operative Program of Southern Baptist Convention, 441
Cote, William N., 349
Council on Christian Education, 447
Council on Finance and Promotion, 397, 401, 435, 440
Cox, Francis, 495
Cramp, J. M., 141, 150
Crawford, Luther, 364
Crawford, T. P., 348
Crawley, E. A., 140 f., 144
Creath, J. W. D., 366
Creed, Baptist attitude toward, 427, 429 ff.
Cromwell, Oliver, 46 ff.
Crozer, John P., 322, 328
Crozer, Samuel A., 322, 328
Crozer Theological Seminary for Baptists, 322
Crusader, 468
Cuban Home Mission Society, 416
Cummings, Sarah, 336
Cutting, Sewall S., 364

Dahlberg, Edwin T., 462
Daily vacation Bible school, 446
Daniel, Robert T., 287
Danish Baptists, 179
Darwin, Charles, theory of evolution, 425 f.
Davis, Noah, 326
Dawson, J. M., 454 f., 500
Day, Samuel S., 341
Denck, John, 485
Denison University, 314

548

Mathews, Shailer, 426, 441
Matthys, Jan, 23
Mayberry, Anna J., 351
Mbende, Paul, 480
Meigs, R. V., 432
Mennonites, 24 ff., 238, 488, 494; in England, 25 ff.; Waterlanders, 35; Rhynsburgers or Collegiants, 42; in Russia, 180 f.
Mercer, Jesse, 316, 330
Mercer University, 316
Merrill, Thomas W., 315
Mexican Baptist Convention, 383, 416
Millennial Harbinger, 273
Miller, William, 260, 279 f.
Millerism, 279 f.; effect on revivals, 303
Million Dollar Church Building Loan Fund of Southern Baptists, 420
Milton, John, 489
Ministers and Missionaries Benefit Board, 440, 453
Missionary Education Movement, 392
Missouri, General Association of Baptists in, 357, 421
Moral standards of Baptists since 1900, 451 ff.
Morehouse, Henry L., 323, 364, 373, 410
Morgan, Thomas J., 364
Morikawa, Jitsuo, 467
Mott, John R., 396
Moulton College, 153
Moulton, Ebenezer, 136 ff.
Mullins, E. Y., 425, 430
Münster Rebellion, 23
Münzer, Thomas, 23
Murdock, John N., 345
Murton, John, 36, 39 f.
Myles, John, 204

National Association of Evangelicals, 476
National Baptist Convention of America, 355, 455, 477, 499
National Baptist Convention, U.S.A., Inc., 355, 420, 455, 477, 499
National Baptist Theological Seminary in Saltillo, 403
National Catholic Welfare Conference, 492
National Council of the Churches of Christ in the U.S.A., 458 f., 476, 500
National Council of Evangelical Free Churches in England, 116 f., 129 f., 497
National Sunday School Convention (1872), 327
Negro Baptist schools, 410 f., 450
Negro Baptist missions, 353 ff.

Negro missions of American Baptist Home Mission Society, 378; of Southern Baptists, 378 f.
Nelson, Reuben, 470
Nettleton, Asahel, 303 f.
New Brunswick Baptist Association, 140, 146
New Connection General Baptists, 76 f., 87, 111
New Hampshire Confession of Faith (1830), 429, 431, 434, 484
New Light Baptists, American, 216, 224, 227, 237, 239, 257, 300; Canadian, 136 f.
New Orleans Baptist Theological Seminary, 450
New World Movement, 392 f., 439
New York Baptist Education Society, 311
New York Baptist Missionary Convention, 303, 365
Newton, Louie D., 491
Newton Theological Institution, 310 f.
Nicholas, Henry, 27
Nigerian Baptist Convention, 403
Nilsson, F. O., 381
North China Baptist Theological Seminary, 408
Northern Baptist Assembly (Green Lake, Wis.), 447
Northern Baptist Convention, 187, 297, 388 ff., 392, 395, 399 ff., 437; organization and development of, 438 ff.
Northern Baptist Education Society, 317
Northern Baptist Foreign Missions since 1900, 387 ff.
Northern Baptist Home Missions since 1900, 410 ff.
Northern Baptist Laymen, National Committee of, 392
Northern Baptist Theological Seminary, 428, 446
Northern California Baptist Convention, 413
Northumberland Baptist Association, 501
Northwestern Baptist Education Society, 320
Norwegian Baptist Conference of America, 476
Norwegian Baptist Theological Seminary, Christiana, 178; Chicago, 446
Norwegian Baptist Union, 179
Nova Scotia Baptist Association, 138 ff.
Nova Scotia Baptist Education Society, 140

Oberlin College, 286
O'Halloran, J. R., 384

Öie, O. J., 178
Oklahoma Baptist Convention, 377
Old Point Comfort Conference, 411 f.
Olney, Thomas, 202
Oncken, Johann Gerhard, 171 ff., 191, 196, 336
Ontario and Quebec Baptist Convention, 154, 156
Open membership, 134; action of Northern Baptist Convention on, 433; in England, 129
Original Freewill Baptists, 256
Ottawa Baptist Association, 150
Ottawa University, 323

Pacifism, 453
Padelford, Frank W., 445
Palmer, Paul, 218 ff.
Palmquist, Gustaf, 381
Parker, Daniel, 262, 269
Particular Baptist Society for the Propagation of the Gospel Among the Heathen (Baptist Missionary Society of London), 82, 98 ff., 131, 194, 492
Particular Baptists, defined, 22; connections with Anabaptists, 40 ff.; beginnings of, 40 ff.; persecution of, 46 ff.; theological trends, 63; trends in polity, 67 ff.; estimated numbers in 18th century, 71; reasons for religious decline, 72; influence of Wesleyan Movement, 77; Carey's influence, 80 ff.; theological tensions, 110 f.; confession of 1644, 484.
Passive Resistance Movement, led by Clifford, 125, 496
Patterson, W. Morgan, 19
Payne, Ernest A., 22, 134
Pearcy, George, 346
Peck, John Mason, 251 f., 302, 313, 316, 326, 357 ff., 493
Peck, Solomon, 289, 292
Pendleton, J. M., 281
Pennepack Church, 210 ff.
Pennsylvania Baptist Education Society, 314
Periodicals, Baptist, 274, 302, 326 f., 329 f.; of English Baptists, 106
Phelps, Edwin, 447
Philadelphia Baptist Association, 211 ff., 232, 246 ff., 284 f., 295, 308 f., 484
Philadelphia, First Baptist Church of, 211 ff.
Phillips, E. G., 341
Phoenix Baptist Bible Institute, 435
Piggott, John, 69
Polish Baptists, 188
Polity, changing emphases of, 436 ff.; contributions of Baptists in, 487 ff.

Powell, Sidney W., 456
Powell, Vavasor, 48, 90
Powell, W. D., 351
Prairie Regular Baptist Fellowship, 159
Prayer-meeting Revival, 304 f.
Price, Jonathan, 333
Progressive Baptist Convention of America, 477
Protestant expansion, Baptist contributions to, 492 ff.
Public Relations, Committee on, 455; Joint Conference on, 455; Joint Conference Committee on, 500

Quakers, English, 56, 184, 211
Quillin, E. H., 350

Racial integration, 463
Raikes, Robert, 122, 496
Ramapatnam Theological Seminary, 393
Randall, Benjamin, 257 ff.
Rangoon Baptist College, 340
Rankin, M. T., 409
Rauschenbusch, Augustus, 380
Rauschenbusch, Walter, 158, 425, 426, 452
Redlands, University of, 446
Redstone Baptist Association, 233, 271 f.
Regular Baptist Missionary Convention of Canada West (Ontario), 151, 153
Regular Baptists, 223 ff., 227, 229, 254
Regulator movement, 242 f.
Relations between Northern and Southern Baptists, 370 ff.
Relief and Annuity Board of the Southern Baptist Convention, 453
Religious Education, Department of the American Baptist Publication Society, 446
Religious liberty, 488 ff.; early struggle for in England, 46 ff.; in the 19th century in England, 84, 99, 108 f., 127; struggle for in America, 234 ff.
Religious Tract Society, 105
Rethinking Missions, 396
Revivals, 221 ff., 299 ff.
Rhode Island College, 126, 202, 235, 252, 307, 501
Rice, Luther, 248 ff., 269, 300, 309 f., 316 f., 326, 329, 331, 334, 358, 492
Richards, Henry, 343
Richmond, University of, 316
Riley, William B., 427, 429
Rippon, John, 105
River Brethren, 265
Robinson, John, 25
Rochester Theological Seminary, 158, 312, 425 f., 443
Rock Spring Seminary, 314

553